Microeconomics and decision models of the firm

The Harbrace Series in Business and Economics

Thomas H. Naylor
Duke University

John M. Vernon
Duke University

MICROECONOMICS

and decision models of the firm

Harcourt, Brace & World, Inc.
New York / Chicago / San Francisco / Atlanta

to our wives,

Judy and Jerry

Library of Congress Catalog Card Number: 75-79283

Printed in the United States of America

Preface

In this book we outline a general economic theory of the firm which includes four major elements—goals, production processes, information, and decisions. Within this general framework we develop a collection of economic decision-making models of the firm. We begin with conventional marginal analysis models of the firm, then formulate and analyze mathematical programming models, dynamic models, risk and uncertainty models, computer simulation models, investment models, game theoretic models, and behavioral models. We have made a serious attempt to synthesize as well as to compare and contrast these somewhat diverse approaches to the theory of the firm.

Our presentation of the general economic theory of the firm differs from existing books on microeconomics and managerial economics in at least two important ways. First, we take the position that the economic theory of the firm is, in fact, a collection of theories of the firm rather than a single unified theory. Second, our presentation is decision oriented. That is, we are concerned with the derivation of optimal decisions and the process by which decisions are made by the firm.

Whereas some economists consider conventional marginal analysis to be almost synonymous with microeconomics and the economic theory of the firm, our view of marginalism is that it is simply one of many important approaches to the theory of the firm.

The book is aimed toward advanced undergraduate and beginning graduate students in courses on microeconomics and managerial economics; it may also serve as a reference book for students of management science, operations research, and business administration. A course in calculus is assumed, and some knowledge of mathematical statistics is desirable. Two mathematical appendices are included—one on multivariable constrained and unconstrained optimization (chapter 2) and the other on linear algebra and simultaneous linear equations (chapter 7). Detailed bibliographies are included at the end of each chapter.

Part 1, "Introduction to the theory of the firm" (chapter 1), is sufficiently general to accommodate a number of different models of the firm.

Part 2, "Marginal analysis models of the firm" (chapters 2 through 5), is a survey of the material usually covered in traditional courses on microeconomics: the development of theories of demand, production, and cost, followed by the formulation of several marginal analysis models of the firm as a whole. A mathematical model of a multiproduct, multifactor firm concludes this part, along with a critical appraisal of marginal analysis.

Part 3, "Mathematical programming models of the firm" (chapters 6 through 10), introduces the Kuhn-Tucker theorem as well as a transitional model of the firm that possesses some characteristics of both marginal analysis and mathematical programming models. Linear programming is introduced and applied. A detailed comparison of marginal analysis and linear programming models is followed by a discussion of nonlinear programming and integer programming. In each case, solution techniques are described and example models are analyzed.

Part 4, "Dynamic and probabilistic models of the firm" (chapters 11 and 12), introduces the variable "time" for analysis purposes. The calculus of variations and Pontryagin's maximum principle are used to formulate and solve dynamic models. Models of the firm under risk and uncertainty are discussed; a summary of decision criteria under risk and uncertainty is included.

Part 5, "Computer simulation" (chapters 13 and 14), outlines a six-step procedure for designing computer simulation experiments on models of the firm. This procedure is applied to a single-product, multiprocess firm. A computer program and sample results are given.

Part 6, "Investment models of the firm" (chapters 15 and 16), considers cases of complete certainty and also treats cases of risk and uncertainty.

Part 7, "Other models of the firm" (chapters 17 and 18), concludes with game theoretic models and behavioral models.

It is impossible for us to acknowledge all the assistance we have received in writing this book; however, the contributions of a few are mentioned: Eugene T. Byrne, Jr., Southern Methodist University, for the contribution of chapter 12, "Models of the firm under risk and uncertainty," and chapter 16, "Investment models of the firm: risk and uncertainty"; the editors of the *Southern Economic Journal, Management Science, Communications of the ACM,* and *Journal of the American Statistical Association* for permission to use previously published material; the National Science Foundation for support to the Econometric System Simulation Program, Duke University; and the Duke University Research Council for its support.

We especially thank David Kendrick, Harvard University, and David D. Martin, Indiana University, for reviewing early drafts; James Boughton and W. Earl Sasser for particularly helpful comments and criticisms; Stephanie Goldsberry, with sincere appreciation, for typing the manuscript; and the other staff members of the Econometric System Simulation Program, Duke University, for their direct assistance and inspiration.

THOMAS H. NAYLOR
JOHN M. VERNON

Contents

PART 1

Introduction

1

Introduction to the theory of the firm

INTRODUCTION

For our purposes a firm is defined as a conceptual unit of analysis assumed to be capable of transforming a set of inputs, consisting of raw materials, labor, capital, and information about markets and technology into a set of outputs that take the form of goods or services to be consumed either by other firms or individuals and groups of individuals within the society in which the firm exists. What is designated in economics as "the economic theory of the firm" is a collection of theories about the behavior of firms operating under a very special set of environmental conditions known in the aggregate as a market economy.

Although some of its historical underpinnings can be traced back to the classical economics of Adam Smith and David Ricardo, for the most part contemporary versions of the economic theory of the firm stem from the work of Augustin Cournot in 1838 [9].[1] In a book which has been practically unequaled for sheer originality in the history of economic thought, Cournot was the first economist to define and draw a downward-sloping demand function (but without the underpinnings of utility theory). He treated the profit-maximizing monopolistic firm as the pure case and defined a demand function $D = f(P)$, a total revenue function $R = P \cdot D$, and a cost function $C = \Phi(P)$. Total profit was defined as $\pi = R - C$. Differential calculus was used to derive a set of necessary and sufficient conditions for profit maximization for the firm, resulting in a decision rule for the firm analogous to the well-known rule of equating marginal revenue and marginal cost.

Surprisingly enough, Cournot's conception of the theory of the firm and what was later to become known as marginal analysis had relatively little impact on the economic thought of his own day. The first exposition in England of an approximation to the modern theory of the firm was Lardner's *Railway Economy* in

[1] Numbers in brackets refer to bibliography at end of chapter.

1850. Lardner showed that profits are maximized at a level of output at which tangents to the firm's total cost and total revenue functions are parallel. However, Jevons, who borrowed extensively from Lardner and Cournot, apparently failed to see the significance of their equimarginal profit maximization condition, for he never referred to it. Although both Jevons (1871) and Marshall (1890) drew heavily upon Cournot's earlier analysis, neither of them developed an integrated theory of the firm using marginal analysis. Jevons showed no apparent awareness for the need of such a theory, and Marshall limited his treatment of the problem of the profit-maximizing monopolistic firm to a discussion of total revenue and total cost rather than marginal revenue and marginal cost. The concept of marginal revenue had to be rediscovered in the late 1920's when economists turned their attention to imperfect competition and the downward-sloping demand curve.

Equally important as Cournot's profit maximization conditions was von Thunen's work on marginal productivity theory. His statement of the equimarginal principle that the total product is maximized only when resources are allocated equimarginally was of no small consequence. However, it was not until the 1930's that marginal analysis and the theory of the firm were fully and explicitly developed by Chamberlin [6], Harrod [15], Hicks [17], Kaldor [19], Joan Robinson [30], Stackelberg [35], and others.

Among the first mathematical statements of the theory of the multifactor, multiproduct firm was that of J. R. Hicks in *Value and Capital* [17]. The Hicksian model is essentially an adaptation of Walrasian general equilibrium analysis to the individual firm. Prior to 1950 the Hicksian model was considered by many economists to be *the* economic theory of the firm. Hence, in this book we will use the Hicksian marginal analysis model as the point of departure for discussing a number of alternative models of the firm. Although the economic theory of the firm has undergone substantial changes since 1950, Hicks' definition of the problem of the firm does encompass most of the elements found in the more recent theories and, hence, is worthy of quotation. Hicks defines the problem of the firm (which he equates with the problem of the entrepreneur) as follows:

> It will usually be characteristic of an entrepreneur that he acquires some services (factors of production), not because he has any desire for them, but because he needs them for the full exploitation of his productive opportunities. The amount of these factors he employs may be taken to depend entirely upon the production which they make possible; consequently, the enterprise (the conversion of factors into products) may be regarded as a separate economic unit, detached from the private account of the entrepreneur. It acquires factors, and sells products; its aim is to maximize the difference between their value [17, pp. 78–79].

THE ECONOMIC THEORY OF THE FIRM

Before going any further in our discussion it seems appropriate to place some boundaries on the domain of the definition of the *economic* theory of the firm so as to avoid confusion with several related theories of the firm such as organization theory, conflict theories, and environmental theories. We, therefore, propose to outline a general conceptual framework for an economic theory of the firm which is sufficiently broad to include marginal analysis models, mathematical programming models, dynamic models, probabilistic models, computer models, investment models, game theoretic models, and behavioral models. For our purposes the economic theory of the firm is assumed to consist of four loosely defined elements [28]:

1. Goals
2. Production transformation process
3. Information
4. Decisions

Goals

Although few economists would disagree with the inclusion of "goals" as a basic element of the economic theory of the firm, there would be little agreement in answering the question, "Whose goals should the economic theory of the firm concern itself with?" Alternatively, "Whose problem should a theory of the firm attempt to solve?" Clearly there is no straightforward answer to these two questions, for arguments may be presented to the effect that individuals in any one of the following groups may be suitable subjects for the formulation of a theory of the firm.

1. Consumers
2. Employees
3. Managers
4. Society
5. Stockholders

For the most part, neoclassical price theory [13] with its holistic view of the firm treats the firm as a collective economic unit which pursues one or more goals in a completely "rational" manner. If the firm pursues more than one goal, it is assumed to assign "weights" or "priorities" to its different goals. This view assumes that the firm, its stockholders, and its managers are one and the same, and that they share a common goal—profit maximization or utility maximization.

On the other hand, if the firm is assigned goals which are most consistent with those of the consumer, then one of these goals might be the minimization of the cost of producing a particular set of goods and services. Alternatively, the consumer might be interested in increasing the firm's output of a given product, while holding production costs constant.

In a socialist economy the goal of the firm is likely to be "production for use" rather than "production for profit." The goal of the firm in the eyes of a socialist is to provide consumers with specified amounts of goods and services in accordance with an initial plan. Every other possible goal of the firm is subservient to this single objective.

An official of a labor union is likely to view the firm from yet a different perspective. To the unionist, the problem of the firm may be defined in terms of job opportunities, wage increases, fringe benefits, and improved working conditions.

To the extent that the interests of social workers, religious leaders, educators, public officials (in a democratic society), and the like are representative of the interests of society as a whole, we are likely to find that their definition of the problem of the firm differs considerably from that of the aforementioned groups. Even though their views on the problem of the firm are usually not as sharply defined as those of consumers and labor unions, this factor alone does not justify the omission of social goals from a list of the possible goals of business firms.

Of the various groups of individuals who have some "ax to grind" concerning the behavior of business firms in a capitalistic system, stockholders are probably somewhat less difficult to analyze than other special-interest groups. In the case of large corporations in which there is a clear dichotomy between owners (stockholders) and management, one can argue that more often than not stockholders are interested in making money. To be sure, the individual businessman may be more interested in maximizing the time he has available for fishing or playing golf (subject to the condition that his income does not fall below some minimum level) rather than maximizing total profit. Or the stockholders of a closed, family-owned corporation may simply wish to provide future employment for their children and grandchildren. In spite of these possible exceptions to the rule and the arguments of some economists to the contrary, it does not appear to be at all unrealistic to assume that the principal goal of stockholders is monetary, be it over the short or long run.

Having presented a number of alternative views on the problem of the firm as defined by some of the different interest groups, we must emphasize that it is not our purpose in this book to endorse any one of these particular viewpoints. In other words, this is not a book on the subject, "What should be the goals of the firm?" The answer to this question cannot be derived from economic theory or by purely deductive reasoning, for it rests primarily on metaphysical and theological grounds. Although we are in full accordance with Joan Robinson's statement in *Economic Philosophy* that "Any economic system requires a set of rules, an ideology to justify them, and a conscience in the individual which makes him strive to carry them out" [31, p. 13], we shall not concern ourselves here with the relative merits of alternative goals of the firm or with the reasons why a particular individual prefers one goal to another.

Instead, this book is oriented toward the goals of a particular group of individuals, namely the managers of business firms. The decision to concentrate on the concept of the firm as viewed by managers is completely arbitrary. We shall make no attempt to justify this approach on the basis of *laissez faire* ideology or any other economic or metaphysical position which claims that in the long run the interests of managers coincide with those of consumers, employees, stockholders, and society as a whole. According to J. M. Keynes,

> The world is not so governed from above that private and social interests always coincide. It is not so managed here below that in practice they coincide. It is not correct deduction from the Principles of Economics that enlightened self-interest always operates in the public interest. Nor is it true that self-interest generally is enlightened; more often individuals acting separately to promote their own ends are too ignorant or too weak to attain even these [20, pp. 312–313].

Recognizing that in our economic environment managerial goals may indeed be in conflict with those of other individuals, we now turn our attention to the means by which the goals of managers are achieved.

Throughout this book the problem of the firm will be defined in terms of a decision problem for the managers of the firm. We shall be interested in how managers *should* make decisions (normative economics) in order to achieve particular goals. To the extent that these normative models correspond to the real world behavior of firms, we shall be attempting to explain how managers of firms *actually* make economic decisions (positive economics). Hence, in each model of the firm that we describe the goals of the firm's decision makers will be taken as given.

Although we have reduced the scope of our discussion considerably by restricting ourselves to the goals of managers, we will find that managers themselves have a multiplicity of complex goals. We do not wish to belabor our treatment of the subject of goals; however, some discussion of possible alternative goals of managers does seem appropriate.

For taxonomic purposes we shall classify the goals of managers as (1) profit maximization, (2) functional goals, and (3) personal goals. Although the profit-maximization goal could certainly be considered to be both a functional and a personal goal of managers, its long-standing position as by far the most popular goal of the firm in the eyes of economists at least partially justifies treating it separately.

The goal of profit maximization rests primarily on the assumption that managers either voluntarily or of necessity behave in a manner consistent with the interests of the stockholders of the firm (assuming, of course, that the owners of the firm want to make a profit). To the extent that managers are motivated to relate their behavior to the goals of the stockholders, profit maximization can be considered an operational goal of the firm.

The assumption of profit maximization as a goal of managers has been widely criticized by economists, businessmen, and other social scientists. For example, Adam Smith suggested that monopolistic power merely enables a "company to support the negligence, profusion, and malversation of their own servants, whose disorderly conduct seldom allows the company to exceed the ordinary rate of profit in trades which are altogether free" [33, p. 712].

Berle and Means have argued that management and stockholders may have conflicting interests when there is a separation of ownership and management in a firm.

> . . . Have we any justification for assuming that those in control of a modern corporation will also choose to operate it in the interests of the stockholders? The answer to this question will depend on the degree to which the self-interest of those in control may run parallel to the interests of ownership and, insofar as they differ on the checks or the use of power which may be established by political, economic, or social conditions [4, p. 121].

Berle and Means have further observed that, with separation of ownership and management, "control may be held by the directors or titular managers who employ the proxy machinery to become a self-perpetuating body, even though as a group they own but a small fraction of the stock outstanding" [4, p. 5].

In spite of widespread discontent with the profit maximization assumption,[2] it still plays a leading role in most of the leading textbooks on the theory of the firm [3,5,7,13,16,34].

The distinguishing characteristic of functional goals is that they usually deal with some subsystem of the firm rather than the firm as a whole. They are, however, by no means independent of the profit-maximization goal or the personal goals of managers. Functional goals may either be consistent with or in complete opposition to profit maximization and personal goals of managers of the firm. Cyert and March [10] have suggested four possible functional goals of management in addition to profit maximization:

1. Production goal
2. Inventory goal
3. Sales goal
4. Market-share goal

Production goals are for the most part the goals of the individuals responsible for the production operations of the firm. Some possible goals of a production manager are to:

1. Complete all orders on time.
2. Minimize the sum of capital investment expenditures, operating costs, and in-process inventory charges.
3. Achieve an even distribution of workloads among all production facilities and a smooth (as opposed to fluctuating) production rate.

These goals are not necessarily consistent with the goal of profit maximization. (This will become obvious when we formulate models of the firm as a whole in later chapters.)

[2] Comprehensive surveys of the literature criticizing the profit-maximization assumption may be found in Chap. 1 of Williamson's *The Economics of Discretionary Behavior: Management Objectives in a Theory of the Firm* [38] and Chap. 1 of Cyert and March's *Behavioral Theory of the Firm* [10].

The goal of managers who are responsible for inventory levels of finished goods, goods in process, and raw materials usually takes the following form. How much should the firm produce (or order) and how often should the firm produce (or reorder) to minimize total carrying costs, setup (or reorder) costs, and shortage costs? A vast collection of mathematical tools exists for solving problems of this type, as well as the aforementioned production problems. These mathematical tools are usually labeled inventory models and production-scheduling models, respectively, and represent subsets of the even larger collection of mathematical and statistical tools known as "operations research" or "management science" techniques.

Baumol has suggested that the objective of most corporate executives is sales maximization rather than profit maximization [2]. He contends that firms often seek to maximize their total revenue subject to the constraint that their profits do not fall below some minimum level.

> That is, so long as profits are at a satisfactory level, management will devote the bulk of its energy and resources to the expansion of sales. Such a goal may perhaps be explained by the businessman's desire to maintain his competitive position, which is partly dependent on the sheer size of his enterprise, or it may be a matter of the interests of management (as distinguished from shareholders), since management's salaries may be related more closely to the size of the firm's operations than to its profits, or it may be simply a matter of prestige [3, p. 296].

An empirical study by McGuire and others has shown "that there is a valid relationship between sales and executives incomes as Baumol assumed, but not between profits and executive incomes" [23].

The market-share goal was proposed by Cyert and March [10] and others as follows:

> The market-share goal is an alternative to the sales goal insofar as the concern is for a measure of sales effectiveness. Either or both may be used, depending on the past experience of the firm and the traditions of the industry. In addition, the market-share goal is linked to the demands of those parts of the organization that are primarily interested in comparative success (e.g., top management, especially top sales management) and to the demands for growth [10, p. 42].

A discussion of the goals of managers would be incomplete without at least some reference to their personal goals. Although a manager may very well pursue one of the aforementioned operational goals (including profit maximization), in a free society he will do so only if the pursuit of a given functional goal is compatible with his own personal goals.

> . . . The behavior of people in organizations is purposive in two senses. First, behavior must be minimally oriented to a common organizational purpose, or it would not be meaningful to speak of an organization. Secondly, behavior within organizations is oriented toward personal goals [36, p. 81]. The theory of the firm has traditionally recognized only the first of these—or, to the extent that the importance of personal goals has been acknowledged, these have seldom been made to have an explicit influence on analysis [38, p. 28].

Some of the personal goals of managers considered by Williamson [38] and others[3] are

1. Salary
2. Security
3. Status
4. Power
5. Prestige
6. Social service
7. Professional excellence
8. Utility

Williamson has proposed an economic model of the firm in which the decision makers (managers) of the firm seek to maximize their utility, which is assumed to depend on (1) the salaries they receive from the firm, (2) the size and quality of the staff reporting to them, (3) the extent to which they (the decision makers) are able to direct the investment of the firm's resources, and (4) the type and amount of emoluments that they receive from the firm over and above the amount required for the firm's operations.[4]

One final consideration which must be mentioned with regard to managerial goals is the degree of rationality with which managers pursue their given goals. Cohen and Cyert [7, p. 308] have defined three different types of rational behavior: objectively rational, subjectively rational, and nonrational.

> Either of the first two [types of behavior] assumes that the economic agent chooses that course of action from the discovered alternatives which maximizes the value of his pay-off function. If the set of discovered alternatives from which the best action is chosen is the set of all possible behavior alternatives, then [behavior] is objectively rational. If the set of discovered alternatives from which this "best" action is chosen is a subset of all possible behavior alternatives, then [behavior] is subjectively rational. In contrast, the agent's behavior will be called nonrational if he selects an action from among the discovered alternatives which does not maximize his pay-off function [7, p. 308].

Throughout this book (with the exception of Chapter 18) we shall treat only the case in which decision makers are assumed to be objectively rational.

Production transformation process

The second element which one usually finds in an economic theory of the firm is the notion of a production transformation process. The firm is assumed to possess one or more production transformation processes which enable it to convert some finite number of inputs (factors of production) into a finite number of different outputs (products). The literature abounds with alternative theories on the exact nature of production processes.

[3] For a detailed treatment of these topics see Chapter 3 of Williamson's *The Economics of Discretionary Behavior: Managerial Objectives in a Theory of the Firm* [38], as well as the works of Barnard [1], Cole [8], Gordon [14], Simon [32], and Thompson [36].

[4] See Cohen and Cyert [7], p. 355.

Economists have obtained a great deal of information about the behavior of firms in a market economy by using the so-called production function to determine technologically feasible product possibilities. The production function is said to be a function of the fixed and variable factors in the firm's production process. We will introduce the notion of the production function by considering the assumptions underlying three different types of production functions. First, we will outline the assumptions underlying a typical neoclassical marginal analysis production function. Second, we will formulate a production function within the framework of linear programming. Third, we will consider the production function of a firm under dynamic conditions, where output is a random variable.

Before turning to a discussion of the production function we must tentatively define the terms "marginal analysis" and "linear programming." (We will elaborate on these definitions in later chapters of the book.) Marginal analysis is primarily concerned with the process of making choices between alternative factor-product combinations considering infinitesimal changes in factor-product combinations. In order to apply marginal analysis to the economic theory of the firm it is necessary to reduce the problem of the firm to one of finding the optimal values of some objective function subject to a set of production constraints. The objective function and the constraints must be continuous and of the proper shape with nonzero first- and second-order partial derivatives. On the other hand, linear programming is concerned with problems involving the optimization of a *linear* objective function subject to a set of *linear* production constraints (which may be inequalities) imposed on the variables of the objective function [27].

In the marginal analysis concept of the production function for any given factor quantities, the dependent variable is usually defined as the maximum quantity of the particular product that can be produced, at a given state of technology, from the specified factor quantities. In the case of the multiproduct, multifactor firm, all products and factors are considered to be independent variables of the production function. The dependent variable is then defined as the maximum quantity of output of some arbitrarily selected product, attainable from the specified factor quantities along with the other specified product quantities. In other words, the production function is the result of the previous solution of an entire set of technical suboptimization problems [21].

Probably the best known formulation of a production function under the assumptions of neoclassical marginal analysis is the one in Hicks' model of the multiproduct, multifactor firm [17]. The Hicksian production function rests on the following assumptions [25,27,28]:

1. The firm possesses a production process capable of transforming a maximum of m variable factors of production into p products. (There are no limitations on the availability of the factors.)

2. The production function is continuous (with nonzero first- and second-order partial derivatives) and relates the set of independent factor variables to the set of independent product variables.
3. The exact nature of the production function is predetermined by a set of technical decisions made by the firm's engineers and technicians.
4. The firm's production function is characterized by: a decreasing marginal rate of technical substitution between any two factors; a decreasing marginal product for all factor-product combinations; and an increasing marginal rate of product transformation between any two products.
5. All of the firm's factors and products are perfectly divisible.
6. The parameters which determine the firm's production function will not change over the time period considered.
7. The parameters of the production function are not permitted to be random variables.

Linear programming provides another possible analytical framework for the formulation of a production function under conditions of static equilibrium. The assumptions underlying a production function formulated in accordance with the premises of linear programming are summarized below [27]:

1. The firm has p independent processes or activities available, where an activity is defined as a particular way of combining a maximum of m variable factors with a maximum of n fixed factors for the production of a unit of output. (A unit of output is analogous to a unit of product.)
2. Each activity is characterized by a set of ratios of the quantities of the factors to the levels of each of the outputs. These ratios are constant and independent of the extent of each activity. (The firm's production functions are homogeneous of degree one, i.e., constant returns to scale are assumed.) [11]
3. The firm is constrained in its selection of activity levels by its fixed endowments of certain resources (fixed factors) required to support the p activities.
4. Two or more activities can be used simultaneously, subject to the limitations of the fixed factors available to the firm, and if this is done the quantities of the outputs and inputs will be the arithmetic sums of the quantities which would result if the activities were used separately [11].
5. The exact nature of the firm's activities is predetermined by a set of technical decisions by the firm's engineers and technicians.
6. All of the firm's factors and products are perfectly divisible.
7. Neither the factor and product prices, nor the coefficients which determine the firm's activities (input-output coefficients) will change over the time period considered. (This is a static model.)

As an example of a production function based on conditions other than the static equilibrium conditions of marginal analysis and linear programming, consider a production function based on the following assumptions:

1. The firm possesses an n-stage production process capable of producing a single product. Each unit of final output must pass through all n of these stages or processes in a particular order.
2. Each process has its own separate production function which is independent of the production functions of the other $n - 1$ processes.
3. The production function for the jth process states that the rate of output $Q_j(t)$ of the jth process during planning period t is a function of the rate of input of factors of production at the jth process during planning period t and a random variable $u_j(t)$ (with a known probability distribution, expected value and variance), but independent of the rate of output of process $j - 1$.
4. Although the Hicksian production function was designed to measure $Q_j(t)$, the quantity of output per unit time at time t, it is more convenient to use the reciprocal relationship, $ST_j = 1/Q_j(t)$, where ST_j denotes the time required to produce one unit of output or one production order in the jth process ($j = 1, 2, \ldots, n$). The probability density function for ST_j and its parameters are completely determined by the level of factor inputs for process j and the probability density function, expected value, and variance of u_j. But the firm is assumed to know $f(u_j)$, EU, and VU, the probability density function, expected value, and variance respectively of u_j. Therefore each process ST_j may be treated as a random variable with a known probability density function $f_j(ST_j)$, expected value ET_j, and variance VT_j. In other words, the firm cannot completely control the value of ST_j, but it can affect ET_j or VT_j, or even $f_j(ST_j)$ by altering the rate of factor inputs for process j. Hence, for specified rates of factor input at the jth process, ST_j is a random variable which is not subject to further control by the firm [28].

To illustrate the concept of the production function, we have considered briefly three alternative formulations. In the remainder of the book we will explore each of these forms of the production function (and others) in considerably greater detail.

Information

The decision makers of the firm are assumed to have access to three different types of information—product-demand information, factor-supply information, and production-technology information.

Under the assumptions of neoclassical marginal analysis, product-demand information usually takes one of two possible forms. Either the firm knows the prices of each of its products (and these prices are assumed to be constant) or it knows its total revenue function. In the case of perfect competition, the prices of the firm's products are assumed to be fixed and known and independent of product output levels. Alternatively, the firm may be assumed to know its total revenue function, i.e., the relationship between total revenue and the output of its various products. The theory of demand is concerned with the relationship between the quantity which will be bought and the price of a given product. In Chapter 2 we will consider three alternative theories of demand:

1. The utility theory of demand
2. The indifference-curve theory of demand
3. The revealed-preference theory of demand

However, product-demand information may also be available in forms other than product prices and revenue functions. For example, the amount that a firm can sell of a particular product at a given price may be dependent on the variable time, or it may be a random variable with a known probability distribution and known parameters. We will examine a number of different forms which product-demand information may take.

The firm is also assumed to know its present state of technology. That is, the firm's decision makers are assumed to know the exact nature of the firm's production function. In Chapter 3 the neoclassical marginal analysis production function will be analyzed in detail. Chapter 8 treats the production function under the assumptions of linear programming, while Chapters 11 and 12 consider dynamic and probabilistic production models, respectively.

Finally, the firm is assumed to have access to factor-supply information. That is, either factor prices are known or something is known about the nature of factor-supply functions. Several alternative forms of factor-supply information will be discussed in Chapter 4.

Decisions

On the basis of a given set of goals and given product-demand, factor-supply, and production-technology information, the firm makes two different types of decisions—input decisions and output decisions. The input decisions are concerned with "Which factors of production to buy?" and "In what quantities should these factors be purchased?" The output decisions are concerned with "Which products to produce?" and "In what quantities should these products be produced?" A flow chart (Figure 1-1) provides a convenient graphical device for depicting the decision process of the firm. The broken lines represent information flows and the solid lines denote flows of factors of production and final products.

A special class of input decisions that are of particular interest concern the acquisition and use of "durable" factors of production, such as machinery, equipment, plant, etc. These decisions are called investment decisions. Chapters 15 and 16 will be devoted exclusively to investment decisions of the firm.

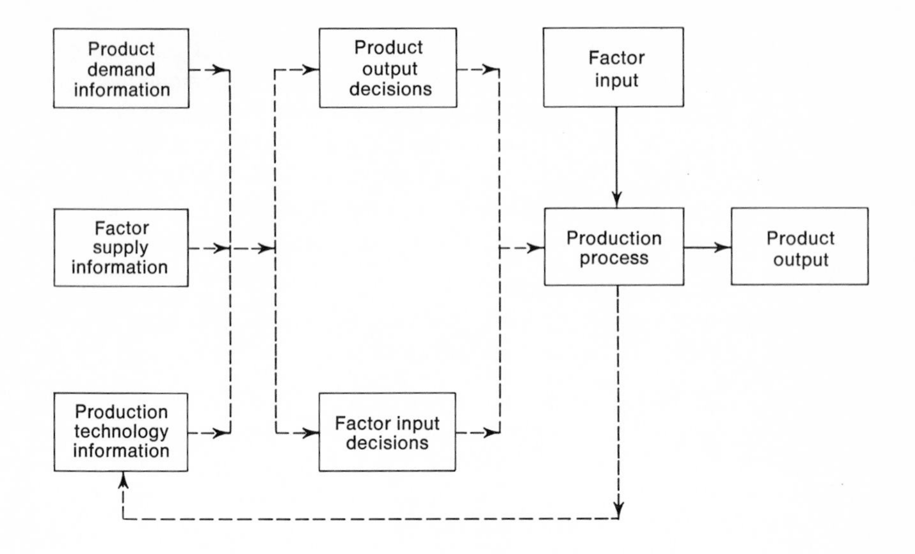

FIGURE **1-1**

A flow chart of the decision process of a firm [28]

CLASSIFICATION OF ECONOMIC MODELS OF THE FIRM

Cohen and Cyert [7, p. 308] have suggested that three dimensions be used to classify economic models of the firm—time, state-of-information, and degree-of-rationality. We have discussed the "degree of rationality dimension" of economic models in an earlier section of this chapter, pointing out that in all models in this book (with the exception of those in Chapter 18) we will assume objective rationality on the part of the firm's decision makers.

As for the time dimension, economic models of the firm may either be described as *static* or *dynamic*. Static models are those that do not explicitly take the variable time into account, while models which deal with time-varying interactions are said to be dynamic models. Hicks has expressed the distinction between static and dynamic models in the following way:

> I call Economic Statics those parts of economic theory where we do not trouble about dating; Economic Dynamics those parts where every quantity must be dated. For example, in economic statics we think of an entrepreneur employing such-and-such quantities of factors and producing by their aid such-and-such quantities of products; but we do not ask when the factors are employed and when the products come to be ready. In economic dynamics we do ask such questions: and we even pay special attention to the way changes in these dates affect the relations between factors and products [17, p. 115].

For a more recent interpretation of the distinction between static and dynamic models we might consider the version proposed by Cohen and Cyert:

> If the alternative courses of action among which the economic agent must choose and the possible future states of affairs which might result all pertain to a single time period, and if the pay-off function which defines the agent's preference ordering on the set of outcomes depends only upon events of this same time period, then the decision model is static. In contrast, if both the alternative courses of action and the possible resulting outcomes involve considerations pertaining to more than one time period, then the decision model is dynamic [7, p. 307].

Chapters 2 through 10 of this book utilize such techniques as differential calculus, linear programming, and nonlinear programming to analyze static models of the firm. Chapter 11 contains a collection of dynamic models which require the use of such mathematical tools as differential equations and calculus of variations. The model presented in Chapter 14 is dynamic in nature.

The state of information available to the decision makers of the firm may take on one of three forms—*certainty*, *risk*, or *uncertainty*.

> In a certainty model it is assumed that the economic agent possesses complete information which relates a unique outcome to an alternative course of action.
>
> In the absence of certainty, multiple outcomes may result from at least some actions the decision makers can take. If the agent is able on an objective basis to compute the probability that a particular outcome will result if any given action is taken, then the decision model is an objective risk model. When the economic agent has no objective basis for determining these probabilities but nevertheless feels that he knows them, then the decision model is a subjective risk model. Finally if the economic agent is unwilling or unable to formulate, either on objective or subjective grounds, the probabilities that specific outcomes will correspond to particular actions, but instead is able only to indicate the range of outcomes which might follow from any action, then the decision model is an uncertainty model [7, pp. 307–308].

Chapters 2 through 11 of this book deal exclusively with models of the firm under conditions of complete certainty. The models presented in Chapters 12 and 14 are formulated on the assumptions of risk and uncertainty. Chapters 15 and 16 include models of certainty, objective risk, subjective risk, and uncertainty.

OTHER THEORIES OF THE FIRM

Although this book is primarily concerned with economic theories of the firm, there are many other theories of the firm which are worthy of consideration. These include game theory, decision theory, cybernetics, behavioral theories, organization theory, personality theory, learning theory, and theories of culture, to mention only a few [22]. Game theory is treated in Chapter 17. Statistical decision theory is discussed in Chapters 12 and 16. Behavioral theories of the firm (including organization theories) are surveyed in Chapter 18.

BIBLIOGRAPHY

[1] BARNARD, C. I. *The Functions of the Executive.* New York: Cambridge University Press, 1962.

[2] BAUMOL, WILLIAM J. *Business Behavior, Value and Growth.* New York: Macmillan and Co., 1959.

[3] BAUMOL, WILLIAM J. *Economic Theory and Operations Analysis.* Englewood Cliffs, N. J.: Prentice-Hall, Inc., 1965.

[4] BERLE, A. A., and G. C. MEANS. *The Modern Corporation and Private Property.* New York: Harcourt, Brace, & World, Inc., 1968.

[5] BOULDING, KENNETH E., and W. ALLEN SPIVEY (Eds). *Linear Programming and the Theory of the Firm.* New York: The Macmillan Co., 1960.

[6] CHAMBERLIN, E. H. *The Theory of Monopolistic Competition.* Cambridge: Harvard University Press, 1933.

[7] COHEN, KALMEN J., and RICHARD M. CYERT. *Theory of the Firm: Resource Allocation in a Market Economy.* Englewood Cliffs, N. J.: Prentice-Hall, Inc., 1965.

[8] COLE, A. H. *Business Enterprise in its Social Setting.* Cambridge: Harvard University Press, 1959.

[9] COURNOT, AUGUSTIN (trans. by N. T. Bacon). *Récherches sur les Principes Mathematiques de la Théorie des Richesses.* New York: Macmillan and Co., 1897.

[10] CYERT, RICHARD M., and JAMES G. MARCH. *A Behavioral Theory of the Firm.* Englewood Cliffs, N. J.: Prentice-Hall, Inc., 1963.

[11] DORFMAN, ROBERT. *Application of Linear Programming to the Theory of the Firm.* Berkeley: University of California Press, 1951.

[12] DORFMAN, ROBERT, PAUL A. SAMUELSON, and ROBERT M. SOLOW. *Linear Programming and Economic Analysis.* New York: McGraw-Hill, 1958.

[13] FRIEDMAN, MILTON. *Price Theory.* Chicago: Aldine Publishing Co., 1962.

[14] GORDON, R. A. *Business Leadership in the Large Corporation.* Berkeley: University of California Press, 1961.

[15] HARROD, R. F. "Doctrines of Imperfect Competition," *Quarterly Journal of Economics* (May, 1934), 442–470.

[16] HENDERSON, JAMES M., and RICHARD E. QUANDT. *Microeconomic Theory.* New York: McGraw-Hill Book Co., 1958.

[17] HICKS, J. R. *Value and Capital.* Oxford: Clarendon Press, 1939.

[18] JEVONS, WILLIAM STANLEY. *The Theory of Political Economy.* New York: D. Appleton, 1871.

[19] KALDOR, NICHOLAS. "The Equilibrium of the Firm," *Economic Journal,* **XLIV** (March, 1934), 60–76.

[20] KEYNES, JOHN MAYNARD. *Essays in Persuasion.* London: Macmillan and Co., 1931.

[21] KOOPMANS, TJALLING C. *Three Essays on the State of Economic Science.* New York: McGraw-Hill Book Co., 1957.

[22] MCGUIRE, JOSEPH W. *Theories of Business Behavior.* Englewood Cliffs, N. J.: Prentice-Hall, Inc., 1964.

[23] MCGUIRE, JOSEPH M., JOHN S. Y. CHIU, and ALVAR O. ELBING. "Executive

Incomes, Sales, and Profits," *American Economic Review*, **LII** (September, 1962), 753–761.

[24] MARSHALL, ALFRED. *Principles of Economics*. London: Macmillan and Co., 1890.

[25] MAUER, WILLIAM A., and THOMAS H. NAYLOR. "Monopolistic-Monopsonistic Competition: The Multi-Product, Multi-Factor Firm," *Southern Economic Journal*, **XXXI** (July, 1964), 38–43.

[26] NAYLOR, THOMAS H. "Some Theoretical Models of the Firm," Unpublished Ph.D. dissertation, Department of Economics, Tulane University, New Orleans, Louisiana, 1964.

[27] NAYLOR, THOMAS H. "The Theory of the Firm: A Comparison of Marginal Analysis and Linear Programming," *Southern Economic Journal*, **XXXII** (January, 1966), 263–274.

[28] NAYLOR, THOMAS H. "The Economic Theory of the Firm: Three Tools of Analysis," *Quarterly Review of Economics and Business* (1966), 33–49.

[29] NAYLOR, THOMAS H., JOSEPH L. BALINTFY, DONALD S. BURDICK, and KONG CHU. *Computer Simulation Techniques*. New York: John Wiley and Sons, 1966.

[30] ROBINSON, JOAN. *The Economics of Imperfect Competition*. London: Macmillan and Co., 1933.

[31] ROBINSON, JOAN. *Economic Philosophy*. Chicago: Aldine Publishing Co., 1963.

[32] SIMON H. A. *Administrative Behavior*. New York: The Macmillan Co., 1961.

[33] SMITH, ADAM. *The Wealth of Nations*. Modern Library ed. New York: Modern Library Inc., 1937.

[34] SPENCER, MILTON H., and LOUIS SIEGELMAN. *Managerial Economics*. Homewood, Ill.: Richard D. Irwin, 1964.

[35] STACKELBERG, H. V. "Grundlagen einer reiner Kostentheorie," *Zeitschrift für National-Oekonomie* (May, 1932).

[36] THOMPSON, V. A. *Modern Organization*. New York: Alfred A. Knopf, Inc., 1961.

[37] VICKREY, WILLIAM S. *Microstatics*. New York: Harcourt, Brace & World, Inc., 1964.

[38] WILLIAMSON, OLIVER E. *The Economics of Discretionary Behavior: Managerial Objectives in a Theory of the Firm*. Englewood Cliffs, N. J.: Prentice-Hall, Inc., 1964.

PART 2

Marginal analysis models of the firm

2

Theory of demand

INTRODUCTION

In Chapter 1 we outlined an economic theory of the firm which assumed that three different types of information are available to the decision makers of the firm: product-demand information, production-technology information, and factor-supply information. In this chapter we illustrate product demand by analyzing several models and their underlying assumptions. Chapters 3 and 4, respectively, treat models of production and models of cost and supply.

Basic to all the models described in this book is the assumption that the firm's total revenue function and demand function are known to its decision makers. That is, the firm is assumed to know the relationship between its total revenue and the quantity of output it sells or alternatively the relationship between the amount of output consumers will purchase and the price of the firm's products. In this chapter we analyze three alternative models of individual consumer behavior within the general framework of static equilibrium: a utility model of demand, an indifference-curve model of demand, and a revealed-preference model of demand. Given these models of individual behavior, we then consider the aggregate behavior of consumers as reflected in the market-demand function. Market-demand functions are classified according to the type of market in which the firm operates: perfect competition, monopoly, monopolistic competition, duopoly, or oligopoly. Finally, four other types of demand models are described briefly at the end of the chapter: multivariate models, dynamic models, probabilistic models, and behavioral models.

The reader who is not familiar with multivariable constrained and unconstrained optimization techniques would be well advised to read through the mathematical appendix at the end of this chapter before continuing.

A UTILITY MODEL OF DEMAND

Definitions

Utility is a measure of the subjective benefit or satisfaction which a consumer receives from the possession of various amounts of different commodities. Utility is a purely hypothetical construct which serves as a common denominator to be used by an individual consumer in making comparisons among alternative commodities. If we let $X_1, X_2, X_3, \ldots, X_n$ denote the quantities of various commodities, "then the notion that these commodities have some element in common and that the magnitude of this common element, utility, depends on the amounts of the various commodities can be expressed" [35, p. 38] by writing utility U as a function of $X_1, X_2, X_3, \ldots, X_n$,

$$U = U(X_1, X_2, \ldots, X_n) \qquad \text{(2-1)}$$

This function yields *total utility*. Another useful concept is that of *marginal utility*. Marginal utility is defined as the rate of change in total utility per unit change in the consumption of a given commodity while the quantity of other commodities is held constant. Mathematically, the marginal utility of the ith commodity is denoted by

$$MU_i = \frac{\partial U}{\partial X_i} \qquad i = 1, 2, \ldots, n \qquad \text{(2-2)}$$

Assumptions

Our utility model of demand is based on the following assumptions:

1. The consumer is confronted with a finite number of commodities whose prices are fixed and known.
2. The consumer is limited in his purchases of the various commodities by a fixed income.
3. The consumer has a continuous *cardinal*[1] utility function which relates his total utility to his consumption of the set of different commodities.
4. The exact nature of the consumer's utility function is known to the consumer.
5. The consumer's utility function is characterized by diminishing marginal utility with respect to all of the various commodities available to the consumer. (The law of diminishing marginal utility is assumed to hold.)
6. The objective of the individual consumer is to maximize total utility subject to the constraint imposed by his limited income.

[1] The adjective *cardinal* simply means that if total utility is 80 for one group of commodities and 40 for another, then the first group can be regarded as providing twice as much satisfaction as the second. In contrast, if the same values were derived from an *ordinal* utility function, then the only inference that can be drawn is that the first group is preferred to the second.

7. The consumer's utility function is independent of the utility functions of other consumers.
8. All of the commodities available to the consumer are perfectly divisible.
9. Neither the commodity prices, the consumer's income, nor the parameters which determine the consumer's utility function will change over the time period considered. (This is a static model.)
10. Neither the commodity prices, the consumer's income, nor the parameters which determine the consumer's utility function are permitted to be random variables. (Complete certainty is assumed.)

Utility maximization

Consider a consumer who possesses a continuous cardinal utility function which relates his total utility to his consumption of a set of n different commodities. The consumer's utility function is given by

$$U = U(X_1, X_2, \ldots, X_i, \ldots, X_n) \tag{2-3}$$

where U is the total utility and $X_i \geq 0$ $(i = 1, 2, \ldots, n)$ is the quantity of the ith commodity consumed by the individual consumer.

The prices of $X_1, X_2, \ldots, X_n$ are respectively $P_1, P_2, \ldots, P_n$. These prices are fixed and known. The consumer's income is given by Y, which implies that his income or budget constraint may be expressed as

$$Y = P_1X_1 + P_2X_2 + \cdots + P_nX_n \tag{2-4}$$

The individual must decide how much of each of the n commodities to consume so as to maximize his total satisfaction (2-3) subject to his budget constraint (2-4). This problem can be solved in a straightforward manner by the Lagrangian multiplier method, which is described in the mathematical appendix at the end of this chapter. We simply define a Lagrangian function L as

$$L = U(X_1, X_2, \ldots, X_n) + \lambda\left(Y - \sum_{i=1}^{n} P_iX_i\right) \tag{2-5}$$

where λ is a Lagrangian multiplier. If we let U_i denote $\partial U/\partial X_i$, then the necessary or first-order condition for constrained utility maximization requires that the following conditions be satisfied:

$$\frac{\partial L}{\partial X_i} = U_i - \lambda P_i = 0 \qquad (i = 1, 2, \ldots, n) \tag{2-6}$$

$$\frac{\partial L}{\partial \lambda} = Y - \sum_{i=1}^{n} P_iX_i = 0 \tag{2-7}$$

By solving these $n + 1$ equations for $X_1, X_2, \ldots, X_n$, and λ we can determine the quantity of each commodity which the consumer should consume in order to maximize his total utility subject to his budget constraint.

We shall pause here to consider the second-order condition for a utility maximum, subject to the income constraint. For ease of exposition, consider the two-good case. Then, depending on whether the sign of the bordered Hessian determinant is positive or negative, we have a maximum or minimum (refer to the appendix for details). Hence if

$$\begin{vmatrix} U_{11} & U_{12} & -P_1 \\ U_{21} & U_{22} & -P_2 \\ -P_1 & -P_2 & 0 \end{vmatrix} > 0 \tag{2-8}$$

for a particular combination of X_1 and X_2 for which (2-6) and (2-7) hold, utility is maximized. Note that U_{ij} is the second-order partial derivative of U, with respect to X_j and then X_i. The subscripts on the P_i refer to the commodity and do *not* indicate differentiation.

Next we consider the economic interpretation of U_{ij}. It is simply a measure of the rate of change of the marginal utility of the jth good due to a change in the quantity of the ith good. By assumption 5 (p. 21), we have restricted U_{11} and U_{22} to be negative. This is the assumption of *diminishing marginal utility*. If U_{12} $(= U_{21})$ happened to be zero (or negative and small), that assumption would be equivalent to the second-order condition for a maximum. To see this, the determinant (2-8) can be evaluated as

$$2P_1P_2U_{12} - P_2^2U_{11} - P_1^2U_{22} > 0$$

Clearly, (2-8) will *always* be positive, given that U_{11} and U_{22} are less than zero, if U_{12} $(= U_{21})$ is zero. However, if U_{12} is large in magnitude and negative, our assumption is *not* sufficient to ensure that utility is maximized. For example, if an increase in the quantity of Scotch whisky greatly reduced the marginal utility of beer, then U_{ij} would be large and negative.

Returning to the economic interpretation of the first-order condition, we see that (2-6) can be rewritten in the following form:

$$\frac{U_1}{P_1} = \frac{U_2}{P_2} = \cdots = \frac{U_n}{P_n} = \lambda \tag{2-9}$$

The economic interpretation of this expression is that the marginal utility per dollar's worth of commodity 1 must equal that of commodities 2, 3, . . . , n as well as the marginal utility per dollar of income, λ. See the appendix for a discussion of the interpretation of λ as the marginal utility of income.

For any two commodities X_i and X_j $(i \neq j)$ it follows logically from the assumption of utility maximization and the assumption of diminishing marginal utility that

$$\frac{U_i}{P_i} = \frac{U_j}{P_j} \qquad (i, j = 1, \ldots, n) \quad (i \neq j) \tag{2-10}$$

The marginal utility obtained per dollar of X_i cannot be greater than the marginal utility obtained per dollar of X_j; otherwise the consumer could increase his utility without increasing his total expenditures by spending one dollar more for X_i and one dollar less for X_j.

Alternatively, (2-10) may be expressed as

$$\frac{U_i}{U_j} = \frac{P_i}{P_j} \qquad (i, j = 1, 2, \ldots, n) \quad (i \neq j) \tag{2-11}$$

But by the implicit function rule of differential calculus (defined in the appendix)

$$\frac{U_i}{U_j} = -\frac{\partial X_j}{\partial X_i} \qquad (i, j = 1, 2, \ldots, n) \quad (i \neq j) \tag{2-12}$$

Therefore, we can rewrite (2-10) as

$$-\frac{\partial X_j}{\partial X_i} = \frac{P_i}{P_j} \qquad (i, j = 1, 2, \ldots, n) \qquad (i \neq j) \tag{2-13}$$

which states that the *marginal rate of substitution* of commodity i for commodity j must equal the price ratio P_i/P_j. The marginal rate of substitution of commodity i for commodity j is a measure of the quantity of j that must be sacrificed per unit of i to leave the utility level unchanged.

As an illustration of our discussion so far, consider the following specific utility function

$$U = 2X_1 + 4X_2 + X_1X_2 + 8 \tag{2-14}$$

Assume that the market prices of X_1 and X_2 are 5 and 10 respectively and that the consumer's income is 50. Then the Lagrangian function is

$$L = 2X_1 + 4X_2 + X_1X_2 + 8 + \lambda(50 - 5X_1 - 10X_2) \tag{2-15}$$

Setting the partial derivatives of L equal to zero, we get

$$\begin{aligned} \frac{\partial L}{\partial X_1} &= 2 + X_2 - 5\lambda = 0 \\ \frac{\partial L}{\partial X_2} &= 4 + X_1 - 10\lambda = 0 \\ \frac{\partial L}{\partial \lambda} &= 50 - 5X_1 - 10X_2 = 0 \end{aligned} \tag{2-16}$$

Solving the three equations in (2-16) for X_1, X_2, and λ, we find that

$$X_1 = 5$$
$$X_2 = \tfrac{5}{2}$$
$$\lambda = \tfrac{9}{10}$$

That is, if the second-order condition is satisfied, the consumer will maximize his utility subject to the budget constraint by consuming 5 units of X_1 and $\frac{5}{2}$ units of X_2. At that point, the consumer's marginal utility of income is $\frac{9}{10}$. Turning to the second-order condition, we find that the relevant bordered Hessian determinant

$$\begin{vmatrix} U_{11} & U_{12} & -P_1 \\ U_{21} & U_{22} & -P_2 \\ -P_1 & -P_2 & 0 \end{vmatrix} = \begin{vmatrix} 0 & 1 & -5 \\ 1 & 0 & -10 \\ -5 & -10 & 0 \end{vmatrix} = 100$$

is positive, signifying that we indeed have a maximum at $X_1 = 5$ and $X_2 = \frac{5}{2}$.

Demand functions

The preceding analysis of the consumer's utility maximization problem and its solution provides us with one approach to the derivation of an individual demand function, i.e., a function which relates the amount of a particular commodity that a consumer will purchase to the price of the commodity when the consumer's income is held constant and the prices of all other commodities remain unchanged. In this section, with the aid of cardinal utility theory, we outline three derivations of demand functions: a general method, a two-variable special case, and a graphical method. The reader who is well acquainted with the principles of economics may wish to skip this section.

General method By solving the $n + 1$ equations contained in (2-6) and (2-7) we can obtain the individual consumer's demand function for each of the n commodities available to him. For example, the consumer's demand function for the ith commodity can be obtained by solving for X_i. In general, the demand function for the ith commodity will be of the following form:

$$X_i = X_i(P_1, P_2, \ldots, P_i, \ldots, P_n, Y) \tag{2-17}$$

where $i = 1, 2, \ldots, n$. That is, for a given income Y and for given prices of all other commodities, the quantity of the ith commodity consumed by the individual consumer will depend on the price of the ith commodity. Although the exact shape of the demand function for the ith commodity depends upon the parameters and functional nature of the consumer's utility function (2-3), it is generally assumed that demand curves have negative slopes, i.e., the higher the price, the smaller the quantity demanded. (See Figure 2-1.) In certain exceptional cases, such as inferior goods, speculative commodities, and consumption for prestige, the slope of the demand function may be positive. We will discuss the case of inferior goods later in this chapter.

A special case A popular example of the aforementioned method of deriving demand functions is the case involving only two commodities X_1, X_2 in which the utility function is of the form $U = \log_e X_1 + \log_e X_2$. The Lagrangian function is defined as

$$L = \log_e X_1 + \log_e X_2 + \lambda(Y - P_1X_1 - P_2X_2) \tag{2-18}$$

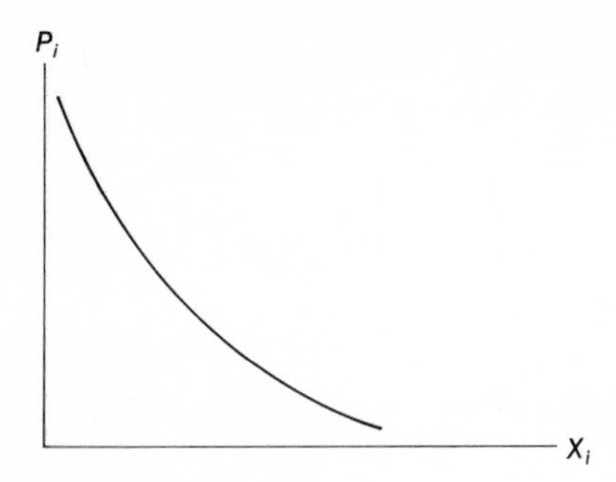

FIGURE 2-1
A demand function

Taking partial derivatives we obtain the following equations:

$$\frac{\partial L}{\partial X_1} = \frac{1}{X_1} - \lambda P_1 = 0$$

(2-19) $$\frac{\partial L}{\partial X_2} = \frac{1}{X_2} - \lambda P_2 = 0$$

$$\frac{\partial L}{\partial \lambda} = Y - P_1X_1 - P_2X_2 = 0$$

Solving for X_1 and X_2 we obtain the demand functions for commodities X_1 and X_2 respectively

(2-20) $$X_1 = \frac{Y}{2P_1} \qquad X_2 = \frac{Y}{2P_2}$$

It should be noted that both of these demand curves have negative slopes, since the utility function $U = \log_e X_1 + \log_e X_2$ has the property of diminishing marginal utility for each commodity. Although diminishing marginal utility will yield a negatively sloping demand curve, diminishing marginal utility is not required in order to have a negatively sloping demand curve. For example, the following two utility functions

(2-21) $$U = X_1X_2$$

and

(2-22) $$U = X_1^2X_2^2,$$

neither of which has the property of diminishing marginal utility, each yield demand functions identical to (2-20). (The reader should verify this statement.)

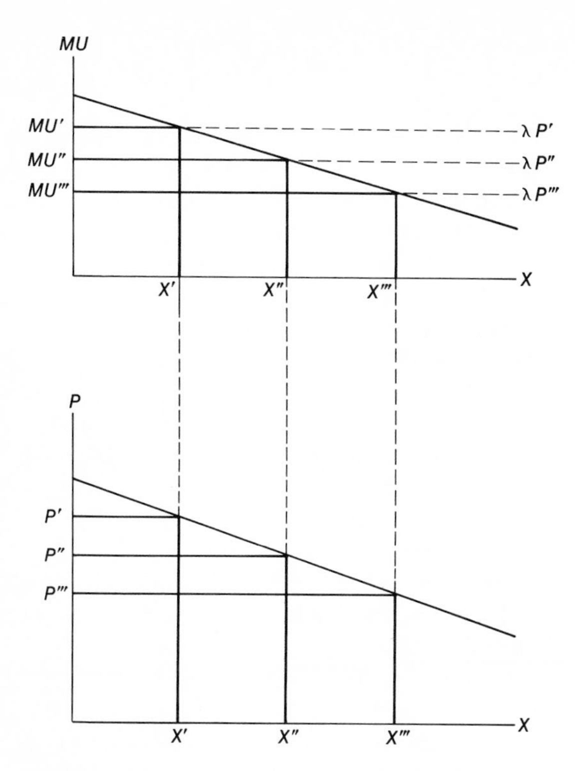

FIGURE 2-2

Graphical derivation of a demand function

Graphical method Following tradition, we also include a graphical derivation of the demand function for a particular commodity. From (2-6) we can write

$$\frac{MU}{P} = \lambda \tag{2-23}$$

We then plot the marginal utility function for the commodity which is assumed to be a declining linear function of X. (The linearity assumption is arbitrary.) The upper portion of Figure 2-2 contains the graph of a declining marginal utility function. Equation (2-23) can be rewritten as

$$P = \frac{MU}{\lambda} \tag{2-24}$$

(The marginal utility of income λ is assumed to be positive.) Each value of X determines a unique value of MU in the upper half of Figure 2-2, and each value of MU determines a unique value of P according to (2-24). The lower half of Figure 2-2 contains the demand function for the commodity, i.e., the price P associated with each value of X.

Measurement of cardinal utility

Our utility model of demand was based on the existence of a measurement of subjective utility on an absolute scale, i.e., a measurement of cardinal utility. Whether or not it is possible to obtain a cardinal measurement of utility has been the subject of heated debate in economics for a number of years. One school of thought questions "the validity of the introspective data of neoclassical cardinal utility," and maintains that "all consumer behavior can be described in terms of preferences, or rankings, in which the consumer need only state which of two collections of goods he prefers, without reporting on the magnitude of any numerical index of the strength of this preference" [10, p. 183]. A second school of thought holds that the previous statement makes it appear that the controversy over cardinal utility assumptions and the theory of consumer behavior rests on problems associated with the collection of data. The advocates of this second school of thought argue that it is not a problem of whether or not the consumer can provide the analyst with the required information, but whether or not the consumer himself behaves on the basis of such information. A theory which assumes that the consumer behaves on the basis of information about the cardinal utilities of goods is less desirable than one which reaches the same conclusion with less restrictive assumptions. The "indifference curve" approach to demand theory (discussed in the next section) arose as a direct result of these criticisms of the cardinal utility approach. However, von Neumann and Morgenstern [76] have taken a somewhat different approach to this problem by constructing a utility index which possesses at least some cardinal properties. We hasten to add that controversy still surrounds the von Neumann-Morgenstern index with respect to whether it should be considered a cardinal or an ordinal measure of utility.

The construction of the von Neumann-Morgenstern index is based on the relaxation of the assumption of complete certainty and the following five assumptions concerning the behavior of individuals [1,7,8,10,28,31,36,62,68,74, 76,78,108,109]:

1. If an individual prefers alternative A_1 to alternative A_2 and also prefers alternative A_2 to alternative A_3, then he prefers A_1 to A_3. If an individual is indifferent between A_1 and A_2 and also indifferent between A_2 and A_3, then he is indifferent between A_1 and A_3.
2. If alternative A_1 is preferred to alternative A_2 and alternative A_2 is preferred to A_3, then there exists some probability P, $0 < P < 1$, that the individual is indifferent between A_2 with complete certainty and a lottery ticket offering alternatives A_1 and A_3 with probabilities P and $1 - P$ respectively.
3. If the individual is indifferent between alternatives A_1 and A_2, if A_3 is any alternative whatever, and if one lottery ticket L_1 offers alternatives A_1 and A_3 with probabilities P and $1 - P$ respectively and another L_2 the

alternatives A_2 and A_3 with the same probabilities P and $1 - P$, then the individual is indifferent between L_1 and L_2.

4. If an individual prefers alternative A_1 to A_2 and if two lottery tickets, L_1 and L_2, both yield the same alternatives, A_1 and A_2, then the individual prefers lottery ticket L_1 if and only if the probability of winning A_1 is greater for L_1 than for L_2.
5. An individual must make a choice between two lottery tickets, L_1 and L_2. L_1 offers alternatives A_1 and A_2 with given probabilities. L_2 offers lottery tickets L_3 and L_4 (both offering A_1 and A_2 with some given probabilities, not necessarily equal). If the money values of A_1 and A_2 are known and the probabilities associated with L_1 and L_2 (compound probabilities in the case of L_2) are such that the expected monetary return associated with L_1 is the same as L_2, then the individual is indifferent between L_1 and L_2.

To illustrate the construction of the von Neumann-Morgenstern cardinal utility index consider the following example in which an eighteen-year-old male high school graduate is confronted with three alternatives:

A_1—go to college
A_2—join the Peace Corps
A_3—be drafted into the military

Assume that the eighteen-year-old lad prefers A_1 (college) to A_2 (Peace Corps) and A_2 (Peace Corps) to A_3 (the draft). The derivation of a utility index requires that we assign arbitrary utility indices to any two alternatives in such a manner that the higher index is assigned to the preferred alternative. In our example, we set the utility indices $U(A_1)$ and $U(A_3)$ equal to 1,000 and -100 respectively. Given arbitrary values for $U(A_1)$ and $U(A_3)$, we are interested in calculating a utility index $U(A_i)$ for any other alternative in terms of the values assigned to $U(A_1)$ and $U(A_3)$. Suppose, for example, we want to calculate $U(A_2)$ in terms of $U(A_1)$ and $U(A_3)$. Assumption 2 ensures us that there exists some probability P for which our eighteen-year-old lad is indifferent between A_2 and a chance between A_1 and A_3. That is, the utility associated with A_2 with certainty must be equal to the expected utility associated with a lottery offering A_1 and A_3 as alternatives for some value of P, or

$$U(A_2) = PU(A_1) + (1 - P)U(A_3) \tag{2-25}$$

The high school graduate could then be asked to reveal the value of P for which he is indifferent between A_2 with complete certainty and a chance between A_1 and A_3. Suppose that $P = 0.20$. Then

$$\begin{aligned} U(A_2) &= (0.2)(1{,}000) + (0.8)(-100) \\ &= 120 \end{aligned} \tag{2-26}$$

Similarly, we could calculate utility indices for alternatives $A_4, A_5, A_6, \ldots$. To construct a complete cardinal utility function for an individual it would be necessary to find utility numbers (according to the aforementioned procedure) for all possible quantities and combinations of all commodities. This topic is discussed further in Chapter 12.

AN INDIFFERENCE-CURVE MODEL OF DEMAND

Definitions

Many economists object to the notion of a cardinal measure of utility on the grounds that such a measure is impossible to achieve and unnecessary from the standpoint of deriving a theory of demand. Even the von Neumann-Morgenstern measure of cardinal utility has not been exempt from these criticisms, for it is frequently argued that the von Neumann-Morgenstern assumptions are "too strong" and need to be replaced by a weaker set of assumptions leading ultimately to a theory of demand.

With the aid of indifference-curve analysis it is possible to derive a model of demand based on a set of assumptions which are not nearly so strong as those underlying the utility model of demand. This approach assumes merely that the consumer is capable of stating which of two sets of commodities he prefers, if either. Utility is assumed to be *ordinal* rather than *cardinal.*

In the case of two commodities X_1 and X_2 the utility function is given by

$$U = U(X_1, X_2) \tag{2-27}$$

However, this time U can be measured only in an ordinal fashion. That is, we can say that combinations of X_1 and X_2 exist which can be ranked according to the degree of satisfaction which they engender on the part of the consumer. Indifference curves provide a way of depicting geometrically the notion of ordinal utility. An *indifference curve* is a locus of points which are geometrical representations of combinations of commodities (X_1 and X_2) such that the consumer is indifferent among any of these combinations. An *indifference map* is a collection of indifference curves each corresponding to a different level of satisfaction.

Two indifference curves U_1 and U_2, i.e., two levels of satisfaction, are illustrated in Figure 2-3. The consumer prefers the combination of X_1 and X_2 implied by point D to points A, B, and C, but he is indifferent among points A, B, and C. Although the utility derived from being on indifference curve U_2 is greater than that of U_1, there is no measure of cardinal utility attached to either curve. The negative of the slope of an indifference curve is the *marginal rate of substitution.* The geometrical properties of indifference curves will be discussed in greater detail in the following section.

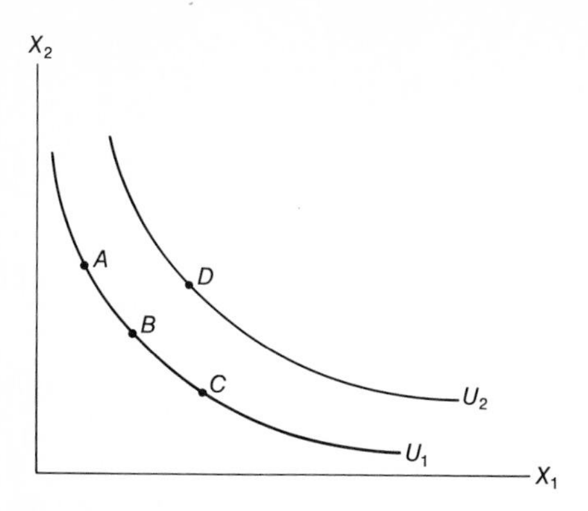

FIGURE 2-3

Indifference curves

Assumptions

We can derive a model of demand using indifference-curve analysis by making the following assumptions:

1. The consumer is confronted with a finite number of commodities whose prices are fixed and known.
2. The consumer is limited in his purchases of the various commodities by a fixed income.
3. The consumer has an *ordinal* utility function which enables him to rank different quantities and combinations of commodities according to the degree of satisfaction he derives from them.
4. The exact nature of the consumer's utility function is known to the consumer.
5. The consumer is not oversupplied with either commodity X_1 or X_2. That is, neither X_1 nor X_2 is considered to be nuisance commodity.
6. The consumer's tastes are transitive (consistent). That is, if A, B, and C are any three commodities and if A is indifferent with B and B is indifferent with C, then the consumer will be indifferent between A and C.
7. The consumer's indifference curves are characterized by a diminishing marginal rate of substitution.
8. The objective of the individual consumer is to maximize total utility subject to the constraint imposed by his limited income.
9. The consumer's utility function is independent of the utility functions of other consumers.
10. All of the commodities available to the consumer are perfectly divisible.
11. This is a static model.
12. Complete certainty is assumed.

Properties of indifference curves

Four geometrical properties of indifference curves can be derived [10, pp. 185–188] from assumptions 5, 6, and 7 above. These properties are:

1. A combination of commodities which lies on an indifference curve which is above and to the right of another represents a preferred combination of commodities (assumption 5).
2. Indifference curves slope downward and to the right (assumptions 5 and 7).
3. Indifference curves can never intersect (assumptions 5 and 6).
4. Indifference curves are convex to the origin, i.e., the absolute value of the slope of an indifference curve diminishes toward the right (assumption 7).

It was not by chance that the indifference curves illustrated in Fig. 2-3 possess all four of the aforementioned properties. We will make use of these properties in deriving a demand function in the following section.

A demand function

Returning to the special case of two commodities, consider an individual consumer whose *ordinal* utility function is given by

$$U = U(X_1, X_2) \tag{2-28}$$

where U denotes the ordinal utility or ranking on the consumer's preference scale of given combinations and quantities of X_1 and X_2. The consumer's budget constraint is

$$Y = P_1X_1 + P_2X_2 \tag{2-29}$$

The problem of the consumer is to choose some quantity of X_1 and X_2 such that he achieves as high a degree of satisfaction as possible without violating his budget constraint (2-29). The solution to this problem may be illustrated graphically by indifference curves (Figure 2-4).

The consumer is limited in his consumption of X_1 and X_2 by his income constraint (2-29). Graphically (2-29) takes the form of the straight line AB in Figure 2-4. Note that the horizontal and vertical intercepts of AB are respectively Y/P_1 and Y/P_2 and the slope of AB is given by the negative of the ratio P_1/P_2. The consumer would like to obtain as high a degree of satisfaction as possible while remaining within his budget constraint. In other words, the consumer would like to get on the highest possible indifference curve which can be reached from his income constraint AB. In Figure 2-4 it can be seen that point C, where AB is tangent to indifference curve U_2, represents the optimum purchase combination for the consumer. At point C the consumer will purchase OD units of X_2 and OE units of X_1. Point C is called an *equilibrium point* because the consumer cannot possibly increase his degree of satisfaction by moving from point C to some other point.

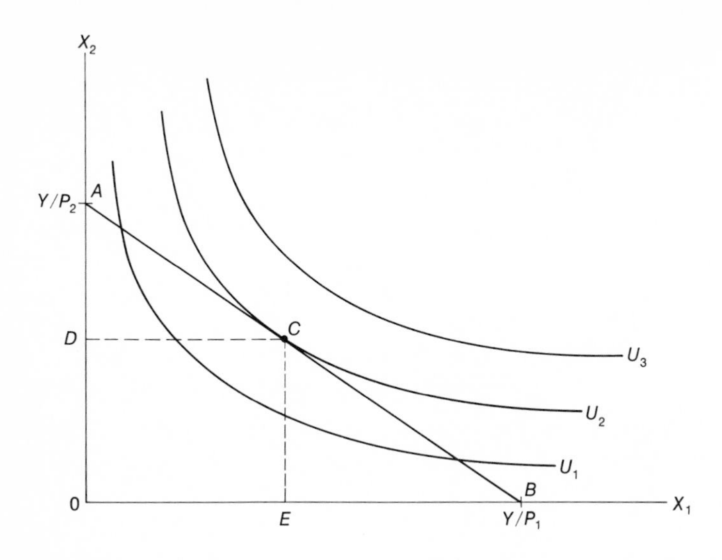

FIGURE **2-4**

Indifference-curve analysis of consumer equilibrium

At point C the slope of the income equation AB and the slope of indifference curve U_2 must, by definition, be equal. The slope of AB is $-P_1/P_2$ and the slope of U_2 is dX_2/dX_1. Therefore, the equilibrium condition is

$$-\frac{dX_2}{dX_1} = \frac{P_1}{P_2} \tag{2-30}$$

which states that the marginal rate of substitution of commodity 1 for commodity 2 must equal the price ratio P_1/P_2. But this equilibrium condition is identical with the eqilibrium condition (2-13) which we previously derived using cardinal rather than ordinal utility. Thus we find that in equilibrium, the consumer's behavior is the same whether we postulate a cardinal or an ordinal utility function.

The derivation of a demand function using indifference-curve analysis follows in a straightforward manner from the preceding discussion. Again it is convenient to consider the two-commodity case, where X_1 and X_2 are the two commodities in question. (Some authors prefer to treat X_2 as though it were money and let $P_2 = 1$.) Suppose that for a given price of X_2, P_2, and an initial price of X_1, P_1', the consumer is in equilibrium and consumes quantities X_1' and X_2' of the two commodities as illustrated by Fig. 2-5. If the price of X_1 drops to P_1'' while holding Y and P_2 constant, the income line AB will rotate to the right about point A to the new position AC and a new equilibrium will be established with the consumer purchasing X_1'' units of X_1. If the price were

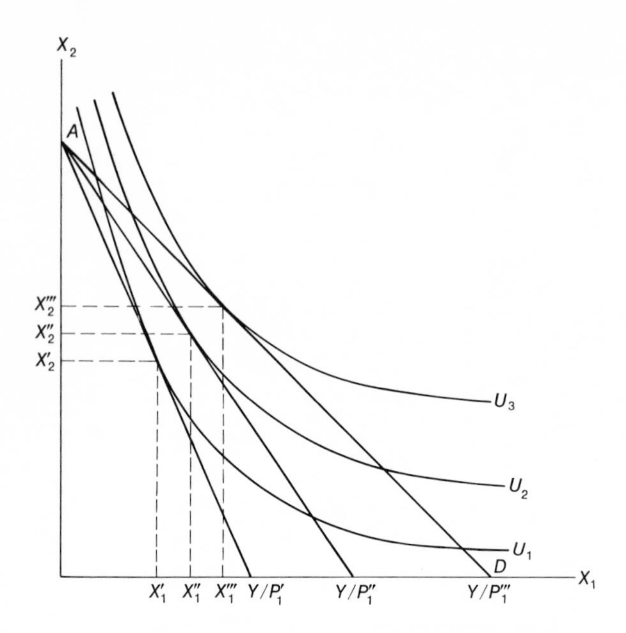

FIGURE 2-5

Derivation of a demand function using indifference-curve analysis.

to drop to P_1''' another equilibrium point would be established with the consumer purchasing X_1''' units of X_1. Similarly we could determine the equilibrium quantity of X_1 consumed for each price level for X_1. If we plot these price-quantity values, the result is a demand function for X_1. Demand curves are generally assumed to slope downward and to the right. In the following section we will discuss the role of "income" and "substitution" effects in the analysis of the slope of demand functions.

Substitution and income effects

Previously in this chapter we have indicated that the effect of a price change on the consumption of a given commodity depends on both an "income effect" and a "substitution effect." In this section, we consider the magnitude and direction of substitution and income effects of price changes.

For the two-commodity case, the first-order condition for maximization takes the following form:

$$U_1 - \lambda P_1 = 0 \tag{2-31}$$

$$U_2 - \lambda P_2 = 0 \tag{2-32}$$

$$Y - P_1X_1 - P_2X_2 = 0 \tag{2-33}$$

The second-order condition requires that the relevant bordered Hessian determinant (2-34) be positive:

$$\begin{vmatrix} U_{11} & U_{12} & -P_1 \\ U_{21} & U_{22} & -P_2 \\ -P_1 & -P_2 & 0 \end{vmatrix} > 0 \tag{2-34}$$

Define (2-31) as a new function, say ϕ. That is,

$$\phi = U_1 - \lambda P_1 = 0 \tag{2-35}$$

Now take the total differential of ϕ with respect to the variables of interest, i.e., X_1, X_2, P_1, P_2, λ, and Y (see the Appendix to this chapter for details on this technique).

$$d\phi = \frac{\partial\phi}{\partial U_1}\frac{\partial U_1}{\partial X_1}\,dX_1 + \frac{\partial\phi}{\partial U_1}\frac{\partial U_1}{\partial X_2}\,dX_2 + \frac{\partial\phi}{\partial P_1}\,dP_1 + \frac{\partial\phi}{\partial\lambda}\,d\lambda = 0 \tag{2-36}$$

or,

$$U_{11}\,dX_1 + U_{21}\,dX_2 - \lambda\,dP_1 - P_1\,d\lambda = 0 \tag{2-37}$$

Performing similar operations on (2-32) and (2-33), we get:

$$U_{12}\,dX_1 + U_{22}\,dX_2 - \lambda\,dP_2 - P_2\,d\lambda = 0 \tag{2-38}$$

$$-P_1\,dX_1 - X_1\,dP_1 - P_2\,dX_2 - X_2\,dP_2 + dY = 0 \tag{2-39}$$

Since we are interested in obtaining the effect of given changes in P_1, P_2, and Y on X_1, X_2, and λ, we rewrite (2-37), (2-38), and (2-39) in the following form to facilitate solving the three-equation system for dX_1, dX_2, and $d\lambda$ in terms of dP_1, dP_2, and dY (since $U_{12} = U_{21}$, we have exchanged the two in the first two equations):

$$U_{11}\,dX_1 + U_{12}\,dX_2 - P_1\,d\lambda = \lambda\,dP_1 \tag{2-40}$$

$$U_{21}\,dX_1 + U_{22}\,dX_2 - P_2\,d\lambda = \lambda\,dP_2 \tag{2-41}$$

$$-P_1\,dX_1 - P_2\,dX_2 + 0\,d\lambda = -dY + X_1\,dP_1 + X_2\,dP_2 \tag{2-42}$$

Observe that the coefficients of equations (2-40)–(2-42) are identical with those of the bordered Hessian determinant (2-34).

Before continuing our analysis, we must digress briefly to review Cramer's Rule (see [17, pp. 113–115] and [111, p. 347]) for solving simultaneous linear equations of the form

$$\begin{aligned} a_{11}X_1 + a_{12}X_2 + a_{13}X_3 &= b_1 \\ a_{21}X_1 + a_{22}X_2 + a_{23}X_3 &= b_2 \\ a_{31}X_1 + a_{32}X_2 + a_{33}X_3 &= b_3 \end{aligned} \tag{2-43}$$

According to Cramer's Rule, if we define a determinant D

(2-44) $$D = \begin{vmatrix} a_{11} & a_{12} & a_{13} \\ a_{21} & a_{22} & a_{23} \\ a_{31} & a_{32} & a_{33} \end{vmatrix}$$

with cofactors

(2-45) $$D_{11} = (-1)^{1+1}\begin{vmatrix} a_{22} & a_{23} \\ a_{32} & a_{33} \end{vmatrix}, \qquad D_{12} = (-1)^{1+2}\begin{vmatrix} a_{21} & a_{23} \\ a_{31} & a_{33} \end{vmatrix}, \text{ etc.}$$

then,

(2-46) $$X_1 = \frac{\begin{vmatrix} b_1 & a_{12} & a_{13} \\ b_2 & a_{22} & a_{23} \\ b_3 & a_{32} & a_{33} \end{vmatrix}}{D} = \frac{b_1 D_{11} + b_2 D_{21} + b_3 D_{31}}{D}$$

(2-47) $$X_2 = \frac{\begin{vmatrix} a_{11} & b_1 & a_{13} \\ a_{21} & b_2 & a_{23} \\ a_{31} & b_3 & a_{33} \end{vmatrix}}{D} = \frac{b_1 D_{12} + b_2 D_{22} + b_3 D_{32}}{D}$$

(2-48) $$X_3 = \frac{\begin{vmatrix} a_{11} & a_{12} & b_1 \\ a_{21} & a_{22} & b_2 \\ a_{31} & a_{32} & b_3 \end{vmatrix}}{D} = \frac{b_1 D_{13} + b_2 D_{23} + b_3 D_{33}}{D}$$

Applying Cramer's rule to equations (2-40), (2-41), and (2-42) we obtain

(2-49) $$dX_1 = \frac{\lambda\, dP_1 D_{11} + \lambda\, dP_2 D_{21} + (-dY + X_1\, dP_1 + X_2\, dP_2) D_{31}}{D}$$

(We omit dX_2 and $d\lambda$, since we are primarily interested in dX_1.) Dividing both sides of Eq. (2-49) by dP_1 and assuming that income Y and the price of X_2 do not change, i.e.,

(2-50) $$dY = dP_2 = 0,$$

we obtain

(2-51) $$\frac{\partial X_1}{\partial P_1} = \frac{\lambda D_{11}}{D} + \frac{X_1 D_{31}}{D}$$

Dividing both sides of (2-49) by dY and assuming $dP_1 = dP_2 = 0$, we get

(2-52) $$\frac{\partial X_1}{\partial Y} = -\frac{D_{31}}{D}$$

Equation (2-51) is of particular interest to us for it is the well-known *Slutsky equation* [46,93], which yields the total effect on the consumer's purchases of X_1 as P_1 changes. In order to analyze the first term of (2-51), i.e., $\lambda D_{11}/D$, it is necessary to perform the following conceptual experiment. Assume that a given change in P_1 is accompanied by a corresponding change in income such that the consumer is neither better off nor worse off than before the price change. That is, a change in the price of X_1 is accompanied by a corresponding change in Y such that

$$dU = U_1\,dX_1 + U_2\,dX_2 = 0 \qquad \text{or} \qquad \frac{U_1}{U_2} = -\frac{dX_2}{dX_1} \tag{2-53}$$

This implies that the consumer remains on the same indifference curve, although he has moved to a new position of equilibrium as a result of the price change. But in equilibrium we know from (2-11) that

$$\frac{P_1}{P_2} = \frac{U_1}{U_2} \tag{2-54}$$

By substitution of (2-54) into (2-53) we obtain

$$P_1\,dX_1 + P_2\,dX_2 = 0 \quad \text{or} \quad -P_1\,dX_1 - P_2\,dX_2 = 0 \tag{2-55}$$

Substituting (2-55) into (2-42), we find that

$$-dY + X_1\,dP_1 + X_2\,dP_2 = 0 \tag{2-56}$$

From (2-49) and the derivation of (2-51) we find that

$$\left(\frac{\partial X_1}{\partial P_1}\right)_{dU=0} = \frac{\lambda D_{11}}{D} \tag{2-57}$$

By substitution of (2-57) and (2-52) into (2-51), we obtain

$$\frac{\partial X_1}{\partial P_1} = \left(\frac{\partial X_1}{\partial P_1}\right)_{dU=0} - X_1\left(\frac{\partial X_1}{\partial Y}\right)_{dP_1=dP_2=0} \tag{2-58}$$

Equation (2-58) is the final form of the *Slutsky equation*. The first term of (2-58) is the so called *substitution effect* of a change in the price of X_1. It represents the rate at which the consumer will substitute X_1 for other commodities when the price of X_1 changes, while remaining on a given indifference curve. The second term in (2-58) is the *income effect* of a change in the price of X_1. It denotes the rate of change in the consumption of X_1 per unit change in real income caused by the price change of X_1. The sum of the substitution and income effects gives the total effect on the consumption of X_1 induced by a change in the price of P_1. In a similar manner, we could compute substitution and income effects for changes in the price of X_2.

Of particular interest is the direction of the substitution effect and the income effect. The sign of the substitution effect can be easily obtained from (2-57). We know by assumption that

$$D = \begin{vmatrix} U_{11} & U_{12} & -P_1 \\ U_{21} & U_{22} & -P_2 \\ -P_1 & -P_2 & 0 \end{vmatrix} > 0 \tag{2-59}$$

because the bordered Hessian determinant, which is equal to D, must be positive for utility to be at a maximum. Furthermore,

$$D_{11} = (-1)^{1+1} \begin{vmatrix} U_{22} & -P_2 \\ -P_2 & 0 \end{vmatrix} = -P_2^2 < 0 \tag{2-60}$$

Therefore

$$\left(\frac{\partial X_1}{\partial P_1}\right)_{dU=0} < 0 \tag{2-61}$$

since λ, the marginal utility of income, is assumed to be positive. We have thus demonstrated that the sign of the *substitution effect* is *always negative* (so long as our assumptions hold). If a decrease in P_1 is accompanied by a change in income such that the consumer remains on the same indifference curve, his consumption of X_1 will increase.

The sign of the income effect, $-X_1(\partial X_1/\partial Y)_{dP_1=dP_2=0}$, is usually assumed to be negative. When this is the case the combined effect (2-58) of a change in price on the change in quantity demanded will be such that an increase in price will lead to a decrease in the quantity demanded. That is, $\partial X_1/\partial P_1$ will be negative. However, a positive income effect is a logical possibility.

A commodity for which the income effect is positive is said to be an *inferior good.* (An increase in income causes a decrease in quantity purchased.) In the case of an inferior good the sign of $\partial X_1/\partial P_1$ will depend on the relative magnitudes of the substitution and income effects. If the substitution effect is greater than the income effect (in the case of an inferior good), then $\partial X_1/\partial P_1$ will still be negative. Alternatively, if the magnitude of the positive income effect is greater than that of the substitution effect, we will have an upward-sloping demand curve where $\partial X_1/\partial P_1$ is positive. From equation (2-58) it is obvious that the smaller the quantity of X_1 the less important will be the income effect.

As an example of an inferior good with a positive income effect which dominates the substitution effect, consider the case of a poor textile worker in the South who spends a large portion of his income for cornmeal. If the price of cornmeal drops, the textile worker who may be tired of eating corn bread (made from cornmeal) may purchase less cornmeal with his increased real income and buy some steak and "white lightning" (made from corn liquor). In this case, the slope of the textile worker's demand curve for cornmeal may actually be positive. This case is known in the literature as *Giffen's paradox.*

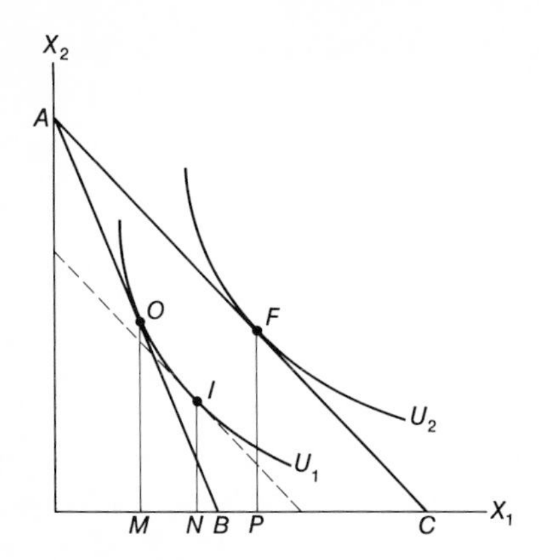

FIGURE **2-6**

Income and substitution effects for a normal good

Although a necessary condition for Giffen's paradox to hold for a particular commodity is that the commodity be an inferior good, it is not a sufficient condition.

We shall conclude this section with a graphical illustration of the income and substitution effects. Figure 2-6 shows the original equilibrium, point O, when the price ratio is given by the slope of AB. Now assume that the price of X_1 falls (the price of X_2 being constant), thereby shifting the price-ratio line to AC. For the new price ratio the equilibrium is attained at point F. Clearly the *fall* in price of X_1 has *increased* the quantity of X_1 purchased, by an amount MP. Hence the good is *not* subject to Giffen's paradox, $\partial X_1/\partial P_1 < 0$.

The total movement from O to F can be conceived as the sum of two movements: (1) a movement from O to I, the *substitution effect*, and (2) a movement from I to F, the *income effect*. The movement from O to I demonstrates the effect of a change in the price ratio *only* (I is the point of tangency between the dashed line, representing the new price ratio, and the indifference curve U_1, indicating that the level of total utility is held constant). The movement from I to F shows the effect of an increase in income, the price ratio being held constant.

Finally, we can compare the relative magnitudes of the two effects. Of course, for a price decrease the substitution effect will *always* be a positive increment of X_1. The distance on the horizontal axis MN is the substitution effect in terms of units of X_1. Similarly, NP is the income effect, and $MN + NP = MP$, the total effect. Since NP is also a positive increment to X_1, the income effect reinforces the substitution effect (X_1 is a *normal good*). However, if the indifference curves were such that point P fell between M and N, the income effect would subtract from the substitution effect, and X_1 would be considered to be an *inferior good*. And, if point P happened to lie to the left of point M, the good would be both inferior and subject to Giffen's paradox. That is, the *direction* of the income effect would not only be in opposition to the substitution effect, it would also be greater in *magnitude*.

A REVEALED-PREFERENCE MODEL OF DEMAND

Within the framework of static equilibrium there exists yet a third model of demand which has recently gained acceptability among neoclassical economists. This approach to demand theory is called the theory of "revealed preference." The major contributors to the theory of revealed preference are Samuelson [84,85], Houthakker [54], and Hicks [5]. Since the logic of revealed-preference theory is fairly intricate, we shall merely summarize some of the main points of this theory. The reader who is particularly interested in this subject should consult the references [41,50,54,84,85].

The advantage of the revealed-preference approach is that the consumer does not have to provide the theorist with his indifference map. Rather, the theorist is able to construct the indifference map by observing the consumer's market behavior. For example, by observing that the consumer in Figure 2-4 buys OD units of X_2 and OE units of X_1 when the price ratio is as shown, the theorist infers that the consumer prefers that combination of goods to any other combination either on the line AB or below AB. In other words, the consumer *reveals his preferences* by his market behavior. Of course, many market "experiments" are required to construct the entire indifference map.

Hicks' version of the revealed-preference model of demand is based on the following assumptions [50]:

1. The consumer is confronted with a finite number of commodities whose prices are fixed and known.
2. The consumer is limited in his purchases of the various commodities by a fixed income.
3. The consumer behaves according to a scale of preferences [21].
4. The preference ordering is a *weak ordering* [21].
5. The consumer always prefers more of a commodity to less of it [21].
6. The consumer's preference scale is independent of the preference scales of other consumers.
7. This is a static model.
8. Complete certainty is assumed.

Assumption 4 may require some additional explanation. Hicks explains *weak ordering* by contrasting it with *strong ordering*.

> . . . If we are to think of the consumer as only ordering a finite, and perhaps quite small, number of alternatives, it is clearly possible that he may order them strongly, having a definite preference for *A* over *B*, *B* over *C*, and so on. It is not necessary that there should be any indifferent positions. Further, if the whole order is a strong one, it is sufficient to say that he always chooses the most

preferred position open to him, and his choice is explained; preference is always sufficient to explain choice. If his ordering is weak, it is possible that there may be two (or more) positions which stand together at the top of his list; choice between two such positions remains unexplained [50, pp. 20–21].

On the basis of the aforementioned eight assumptions Hicks derives a revealed-preference model of demand which is characterized by negative-sloping demand functions. He demonstrates that in order to have an exception to the "law of demand" (consumption tends to increase when the price decreases, all other things being equal), three conditions must be fulfilled:

(i) the commodity must be an inferior good, with a negative income elasticity of significant size,
(ii) the substitution effect must be small, and
(iii) the proportion of income spent upon the inferior good must be large.

These conditions are completely consistent with the implications of the Slutsky equation (2-58).

MARKET CLASSIFICATION

In Chapter 1 we described a theory of the firm which assumed that the firm has access to three different types of information—product-demand information, factor-supply information, and production-technology information. Thus far we have concerned ourselves with models describing the behavior of individual consumers. An understanding of the nature of demand information available to the firm requires the development of market-demand models, i.e., models that explain the aggregate behavior of all consumers with regard to a particular product. For the sake of completeness, we shall describe the relatively simple-minded process by which one goes about deriving a market demand function.

If we let (1) X_{ij} denote the quantity of the jth commodity demanded by the ith consumer, (2) P_j denote the price of the jth commodity, and (3) Y_i denote the income of the ith consumer, then the ith consumer's demand function for the jth commodity can be expressed as

$$X_{ij} = X_{ij}(P_1, P_2, \ldots, P_n, Y_i) \qquad (i = 1, 2, \ldots, m; j = 1, 2, \ldots, n) \tag{2-62}$$

To analyze the behavior of the jth market we assume that all prices other than P_j are given. If the ith consumer's income remains unchanged, then the quantity, X_{ij}, he demands of the jth commodity depends only on P_j and may be expressed as

$$X_{ij} = X_{ij}(P_j) \qquad (i = 1, 2, \ldots, m; j = 1, 2, \ldots, n) \tag{2-63}$$

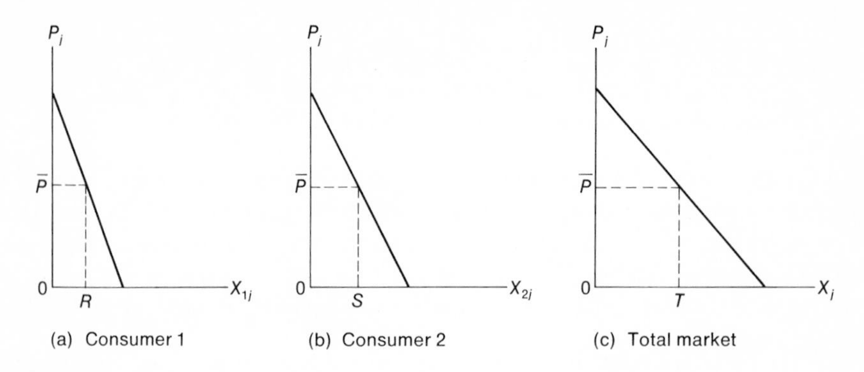

FIGURE **2-7**

Derivation of a market-demand model for a two-consumer market for the jth commodity.

The aggregate or market demand X_j for the jth product for a given price $\overline{P}$ is the sum of the quantities demanded by the m individual consumers

$$X_j = \sum_{i=1}^{m} X_{ij}(\overline{P}) = X_j(\overline{P}) \qquad (j = 1, 2, \ldots, n; \text{ over all } \overline{P}) \tag{2-64}$$

Equation (2-64) is illustrated in Figure 2-7 for a market consisting of only 2 consumers. Parts (a) and (b) of Figure 2-7 are respectively the demand curves for consumer 1 and 2 for the jth commodity. Part (c) is the aggregate demand function. Note that for a given price $\overline{P}$ the total quantity demanded by both consumers (OT in part c) is the sum of the quantity demanded by consumer 1 (OR in part a) and the quantity demanded by consumer 2 (OS in part b).

Having outlined the manner in which market-demand functions are derived, we now turn to a taxonomic system for classifying the different types of market-demand functions the firm is likely to encounter. Market-demand models are most often classified on the basis of (1) the "importance" of the individual firm in relation to the total market, (2) the homogeneity of the products sold in a particular market, and (3) the "elasticity" of demand.[2] We shall consider four different types of market-demand models:

1. Perfect competition
2. Pure monopoly
3. Monopolistic competition
4. Duopoly and oligopoly

[2] The elasticity of demand ϵ at a point on a demand curve is defined as the rate of percentage change in the quantity of commodity X demanded divided by the rate of percentage change in the price of X. That is,

$$\epsilon = -\frac{P}{X}\frac{dX}{dP}$$

It is conventional to include the minus sign in the definition of ϵ in order to make the numerical value positive (since dX/dP is normally negative).

In each case we will simply define the model and state the major assumptions on which the model rests. We shall approach market classification strictly from the point of view of economic theory. The reader who is interested in applying these market-demand models to industries in the real world should consult the literature on *industrial organization.* (The two books by Bain [5,6] and the book by Caves [15] are particularly worthy of consideration.) More will be said about this matter in Chapter 5.

Most of the concepts outlined in this section are quite elementary, and the reader who is knowledgeable in principles of economics may wish to skip over most of the material contained herein.

Perfect Competition

A firm is said to be operating in a perfectly competitive market if the following assumptions hold:

1. *Product homogeneity.* The product of any one firm is identical to the product of every other firm in the market. Consumers are, therefore, indifferent as to the firm from which they make purchases.
2. *Many firms.* There is a sufficiently large number of firms in the market each of which is so small relative to the total market that a single firm cannot exert a perceptible influence on the market price.
3. *Many consumers.* There is a sufficiently large number of consumers in the market, each of which is so small relative to the total market that a single consumer cannot exert a perceptible influence on the market price.
4. *Freedom of entry.* Both firms and consumers are free to enter the market and depart from it.
5. *Perfect information.* Both firms and consumers possess perfect knowledge about the quality and the nature of the product and the prevailing market price.
6. *No collusion.* Collusion among firms or consumers is strictly prohibited.

At the risk of getting ahead of ourselves, some mention should be made of how the market price is determined in a competitive market. The market price is determined at the intersection of the market-demand curve and the market-supply curve. Although we will discuss the derivation of the market-supply curve in detail in Chapter 5, for the moment we shall define it as a schedule of the quantities of a given product which firms would be willing to supply at each different price.

In Fig. 2-8, the market price $\bar{P}$ is determined by the intersection of the market demand curve DD and the market-supply curve SS. The market is said to be in *stable equilibrium* at the price $\bar{P}$. It is in equilibrium because at this price the quantity demanded is equal to the quantity firms wish to supply. It is *stable* because for prices slightly higher than $\bar{P}$, forces are set into operation which tend to force the price back down to $\bar{P}$ (the quantity firms wish to sell exceeds

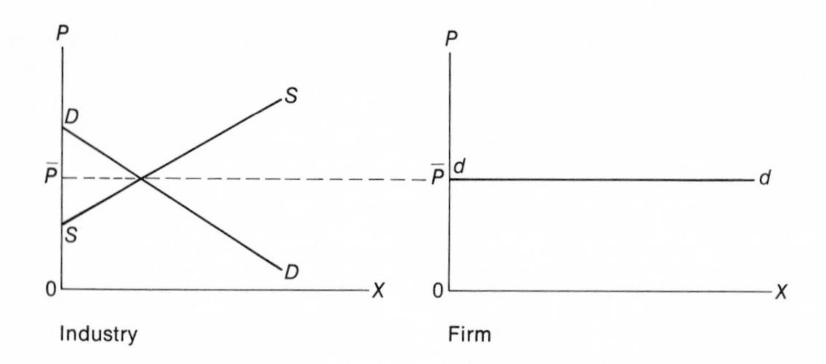

FIGURE **2-8**

Determination of the market price in a competitive market.

the quantity demanded, and firms cut their prices). For prices slightly lower than $\overline{P}$, the price should be driven back up to $\overline{P}$. An *unstable equilibrium* exists at the intersection price if, for small departures from this price, forces are set into operation which tend to move the price *away* from equilibrium. The reader can easily construct supply and demand schedules having appropriate slopes to illustrate unstable equilibrium. More will be said about equilibrium in Chapter 5.

The right side of Figure 2-8 shows that a typical firm in the industry faces a perfectly elastic demand curve *dd* at the given market price $\overline{P}$. Clearly, a firm in a perfectly competitive market has no power over price: its output decision does not influence price. Strictly speaking, the firm may be said to have an infinitesimal effect on price because the firm's demand curve is merely a magnification of the industry demand curve around the equilibrium price $\overline{P}$. However, it is certainly acceptable to ignore the infinitesimal slope, and treat the demand curve of a perfectly competitive firm as horizontal.

Monopoly

An economic model of a market with the following characteristics is denoted in economic theory as a monopoly.

1. A single firm is the sole producer of some given product.
2. There are no close *substitutes* for the product produced by the monopolistic firm.[3] The cross-elasticity of demand ϵ_{ij} between the monopolist's product i and any other product j must be less than or equal to some arbitrarily small constant k, i.e.,

$$\epsilon_{ij} = \frac{dX_i/X_i}{dP_j/P_j} \leq k \quad \text{for all} \quad j \neq i \tag{2-65}$$

[3] The concept of cross-elasticity of demand, defined in (2-65) below, is useful here. If $\epsilon_{ij} > 0$, then products i and j are said to be *substitutes*. If $\epsilon_{ij} < 0$, then i and j are *complements*.

The second characteristic of a monopoly is tantamount to assuming that the firm's behavior is completely independent of the behavior of other firms in other markets. There is no fear of retaliation from firms in other industries.

For the pure monopolist there is no distinction between the market-demand curve and the demand curve of the firm. The demand curve of the monopolist has the same properties as the market-demand curve for a perfectly competitive market. His demand curve is of the general form

$$X = X(P) \tag{2-66}$$

where dX/dP is negative (by the law of demand). Since (2-66) is a single-valued function of price, the inverse of (2-66) may be expressed as a single-valued function of the quantity X which the firm sells at different prices, with $dP/dX < 0$:

$$P = P(X) \tag{2-67}$$

With the firm operating in a perfectly competitive market, changes in the quantity of sales leave price unaffected. This is not so with the monopolist. Increased sales can only be achieved if price is reduced. The monopolist can maximize his revenue with respect to either price or quantity of output, but not both. Once he specifies a level of output (price), then price (level of output) is uniquely determined by the monopolist's demand curve.

Total revenue for the monopolist is defined by

$$TR(X) = P \cdot X \tag{2-68}$$

if we use (2-67) as our demand function. Average revenue can be obtained by dividing both sides of (2-68) by X,

$$AR(X) = \frac{TR(X)}{X} = P \tag{2-69}$$

The average revenue curve for the pure monopolist is identical to the market-demand curve. By differentiating total revenue with respect to output we obtain marginal revenue,

$$MR(X) = \frac{dTR}{dX} = P + X\frac{dP}{dX} \tag{2-70}$$

Since $dP/dX < 0$ it follows that

$$MR < AR = P \tag{2-71}$$

for the pure monopolist, as illustrated in Figure 2-9. Marginal revenue can also be related to the elasticity of demand ϵ by the following equation

$$\begin{aligned} MR(X) &= P + X\frac{dP}{dX} \\ &= P\left(1 + \frac{X\,dP}{P\,dX}\right) \\ &= P\left(1 - \frac{1}{\epsilon}\right) \end{aligned} \tag{2-72}$$

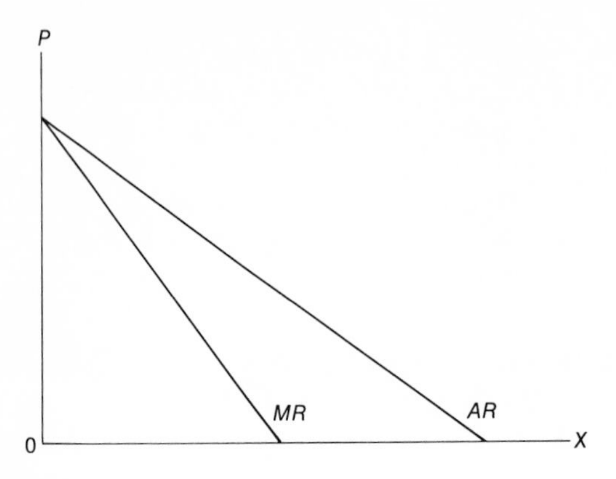

FIGURE **2-9**

Average revenue and marginal revenue for a monopolist.

Notice that if $\epsilon > 1$, equation (2-72) indicates that $MR > 0$. Hence, an increase in X (with a price decrease) would bring about an *increase* in total revenue. Table 2-1 summarizes these results (for an increase in X) for various values of demand elasticity.

Thus, we see that the point elasticity of demand is unitary when $MR = 0$. Graphically, the point on the AR curve in Figure 2-9 directly above the intersection of the MR curve and the horizontal axis is of unit elasticity. Furthermore, points on the AR curve to the right of the intersection (where $MR < 0$) are of less than unit elasticity (inelastic). Points to the left (where $MR > 0$) are of greater than unit elasticity (elastic). In the case of a concave total revenue function total revenue will be at a maximum where $\epsilon = 1$. For a firm in a perfectly competitive market $\epsilon = \infty$. Therefore

$$MR = P \tag{2-73}$$

Monopolistic competition

The concept of monopolistic (or imperfect) competition was first developed by Robinson [80] and Chamberlin [16] in the 1930's. It was used to describe a particular type of market which lies between the two extremes of perfect com-

TABLE **2-1**

Elasticity	Marginal revenue	Total revenue
$\epsilon > 1$	$MR > 0$	Increasing
$\epsilon < 1$	$MR < 0$	Decreasing
$\epsilon = 1$	$MR = 0$	Neither increasing nor decreasing

petition and pure monopoly. The need for this term arose from the empirical observation by economists that there are very few pure monopolies in the real world because there are relatively few products for which close substitutes do not exist. Likewise, it was observed that there are very few products for which the assumption of perfect homogeneity among products is valid. What is in fact observed is a wide spectrum of products, "some of which have relatively few good substitutes and some of which have many good, but not perfect substitutes" [33].

Consider the case of the R. J. Reynolds Tobacco Company, which has an absolute monopoly in the production and sale of Winston cigarettes. Philip Morris or any other cigarette-producing firm could manufacture cigarettes which are exactly identical to Winstons, but they could not label their cigarettes Winstons. However, there is nothing to prevent these other firms from producing cigarettes and calling them Kent, Marlboro, Lark, etc. Just as Reynolds has a monopoly with respect to Winstons, P. Lorillard has an absolute monopoly with respect to Kents, and Liggett and Myers has a monopoly on Larks. Each firm has a monopoly with respect to its own brand of a given product, but the various brands of this product produced by other firms are close substitutes. There is intense personal competition among the firms in terms of advertising, marketing, promotion, and packaging.

> Two important points can be gleaned from this example. First, the products are *heterogeneous* rather than homogeneous; hence perfect, and impersonal, competition cannot exist. Second, although heterogeneous, the products are only slightly differentiated. Each is a very close substitute for the other; hence competition exists but it is a *personal* competition among rivals who are well aware of each other.
>
> This general type of market is characterized by product differentiation; and product differentiation, in turn, characterizes most American markets. There is not one homogeneous type of automobile; nor, for that matter, are there homogeneous types of soap, men's suits, television sets, grocery stores, magazines, or motels [33].

Product differentiation has been defined by Chamberlin as follows:

> A general class of products is differentiated if any significant basis exists for distinguishing the goods (or services) of one seller from those of another. Such a basis may be real or fancied, so long as it is of any importance whatever to buyers, and leads to a preference for one variety of the product over another....
>
> Differentiation may be based upon certain characteristics of the product itself, such as exclusive patented features; trade-marks; trade names; peculiarities of the package or container, if any; or singularity in quality, design, color, or style. It may also exist with respect to the conditions surrounding its sale [16, p. 56].

In general, monopolistic competition is characterized by a market structure in which there are many firms selling differentiated products which are close substitutes (but not exact substitutes) for each other;

> ... any adjustment of price ... by a single producer spreads its influence over so many of his competitors that the impact felt by any one is negligible and does not

> lead him to any readjustment of his own situation. A price cut, for instance, which increases the sales of him who made it, draws inappreciable amounts from the markets of each of his many competitors, achieving a considerable result for the one who cut, but without making incursions upon the market of any single competitor sufficient to cause him to do anything he would not have done anyway [16, p. 83 and 21, pp. 208–209].

The demand curve for the product of the firm under monopolistic competition

> . . . may be expected to have a negative slope, even though the firm is as small as one operating under conditions of pure competition. For customers will have different degrees of loyalty to the firms from whom they make their purchases. A small reduction in one firm's price may only attract its competitors most mercurial customers. But, as larger and larger price reductions are instituted, it may acquire more and more customers from its rivals by drawing on customers who are less anxious to switch [10, pp. 321–322].

Duopoly and oligopoly

An *oligopoly* is a market in which the number of firms is small enough for the behavior of one firm to affect the behavior of other firms in the market. (A *duopoly* is simply a special case of oligopoly in which there are only *two* firms in the market.) Under the assumptions of oligopolistic competition, changes in the price and output of a given firm will affect the prices which other firms in the market charge and the quantity of output which they can sell. In other words, an oligopoly is characterized by a sufficiently small number of firms such that each firm reacts or responds to changes in price and output of all other firms in the market.

Unlike perfect competition, pure monopoly, and monopolistic competition, the behavior of firms in an oligopolistic market cannot be described by a single set of assumptions which are widely accepted by most economists. This lack of a unified theory of oligopoly can at least be partially explained by (1) the interdependence of firms in an oligopoly and (2) the possibility of collusion among firms.

The interdependence of firms in an oligopoly makes it almost impossible to determine the demand curve for a particular firm within the framework of static equilibrium.

> The oligopolistic seller's demand curve will be indeterminate when he cannot predict what the reactions of his rivals will be to price and output changes on his part. The output that the one firm can sell if it changes its price depends upon the manner in which other firms react to its price change. The range of possible reactions is fairly broad. Rivals may just meet the price change, they may change price in the same direction but by less than the change of the original seller, they may undercut the price change, they may improve the quality of their products, they may engage in extensive advertising campaigns, or they may react in many other ways. Inability of the individual seller to predict which reactions will occur and in what degree amounts to inability to determine the demand curve faced by him [61, p. 92].

For this reason, most of the more interesting models of oligopolistic behavior that have been developed by economists have been dynamic or probabilistic models. Game theory and behavioral models appear to be particularly apropos to oligopolistic and duopolistic markets.

An important possible consequence of oligopolistic interdependence—collusion among firms—provides an additional complicating factor in the analysis of demand curves of oligopolists. Under oligopoly a wide variety of behavioral patterns may emerge. To the extent that it is legally permissible to do so, firms may decide to cooperate in making pricing decisions. In some notable cases—e.g., the conspiracy case involving electrical equipment manufacturers in 1961—the law has apparently not served as a particularly severe constraint against collusion. On the other hand, firms may engage in "cutthroat" competition and fight each other to the death. Even when agreements do exist among oligopolists, they tend eventually to break down because of the basic conflicting interests among firms.

A variety of models have been developed to describe the behavior of oligopolistic markets. We shall briefly outline the major behavioral assumptions underlying some of these models. In later chapters we will subject some of these models to a more critical analysis.

1. *The Cournot model* The first explicit oligopoly model to be published appeared in 1838 under the name of a French mathematician, Augustin Cournot [22]. Cournot's model assumed that each firm attempts to maximize its own profit by making its output decision on the assumption that the other firms will not alter their output. In other words, Cournot assumed that the *conjectural variations* of each firm were equal to zero. (Conjectural variation represents one firm's conjecture of how the other firms' output will change as a result of a change in its own output.)

2. *The Collusion model* The collusion model assumes that all n firms in an n-firm oligopoly act jointly to maximize their combined profits. The demand function resulting from this type of behavior is identical to that of a monopolist. An interesting facet of the collusion model is the manner in which side payments are made among the competing firms to induce those who would be better off without collusion to join in the conspiracy.

3. *The Stackelberg model* [98,99] Heinrich von Stackelberg, a German economist, has developed a duopoly model which makes use of the concepts of "followership" and "leadership." In the Cournot model, for example, all firms act as followers. When a firm behaves as a leader it acts as though the other firm were behaving like a follower.

4. *The market-shares model* The market-shares model assumes that one firm in an n-firm oligopoly always desires to maintain a constant share of the total market, i.e., a fixed share of the total output of the market, regardless of the impact that this strategy has on its short-run profits. Through the use of this strategy the firm with the fixed market share hopes to derive the long-run advantages associated with a constant share of the total market. In maximizing

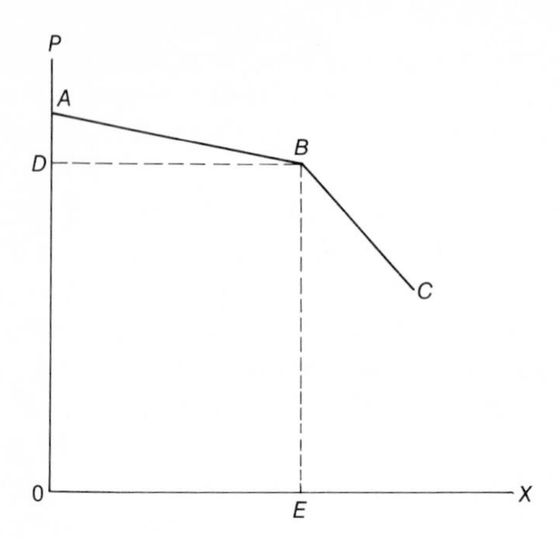

FIGURE **2-10**

A kinked-demand curve

their own profits the other firms in the market utilize the knowledge that one firm is attempting to maintain a fixed share of the market.

5. *The kinked-demand-curve model* A popular textbook model of the behavior of an oligopolistic firm is the so called "kinked-demand-curve model." Developed by Sweezy [110] this model assumes that the oligopolistic firm's conjectured demand curve is of the general form illustrated by Figure 2-10.

The rationale underlying this model is as follows. Suppose that an oligopolist's current price-quantity combination is given by point *B* in Figure 2-10. If the firm lowers its price, it is argued that its competitors will respond with equivalent price reductions of their own or else face the loss of customers to the firm initiating the price reduction. Thus the section of the firm's conjectured demand curve indicated by *BC* is likely to be relatively inelastic, i.e., a price reduction is likely to lead to less than proportionate increases in the quantity demanded. On the other hand, if the firm raises its price then its competitors will be ecstatic over the new customers which they attract from the firm that has increased its price. There will be little incentive for the other firms to raise their prices. Hence section *AB* of the firm's conjectured demand curve will be relatively elastic. It should be pointed out that this simple-minded graphical model has been found to yield rather poor results when subjected to empirical analysis [102]. Furthermore, the model has the serious deficiency of failing to explain how point *B* was originally reached.

6. *The dominant-firm model* [21, p. 241] Cohen and Cyert have described a model which avoids special assumptions about conjectural variations of the different firms in the market. It assumes that one firm is so powerful that it is the market leader. "The basic operating assumption is *the dominant firm sets the price and allows the minor firms to sell all they can at that price; the dominant firm sells the rest*" [21, p. 241].

7. *The barometric-firm model* "Another pattern of price leadership . . . occurs when one firm conventionally is the first to announce price changes which are usually followed by the other firms in the industry" [21, p. 244]. Cohen and Cyert have described this situation as one of *barometric price leadership.*

8. *Game-theory models* With the publication in 1944 of *Theory of Games and Economic Behavior* by von Neumann and Morgenstern [76] the basis for an entirely new approach to the analysis of the behavior of oligopolies was created. The article by Hurwicz [55] represents one of the earliest attempts to apply game theory to an oligopolistic market. Chapter 17 is devoted to game-theory models of the firm.

OTHER MODELS OF DEMAND

Within the framework of static equilibrium we have described three general types of demand models: (1) models of individual demand, (2) market-demand models, and (3) firm-demand models. In a textbook on the theory of the firm written before the advent of the electronic computer and the new mathematical techniques in the fields of "management science" and "operations research," it would have been appropriate to conclude our chapter on demand models at this point without fear of omitting anything of great consequence. As a result of a number of recent developments in the fields of computer science, numerical analysis, econometrics, mathematics and statistics, several other models of demand have emerged which merit our consideration. Although these topics will be treated in detail in later sections, we shall briefly summarize four other models of demand in this chapter:

1. Multivariable demand models
2. Dynamic demand models
3. Probabilistic demand models
4. Behavioral demand models

Multivariable demand models

In all of the demand models described in this chapter the quantity demanded, whether for an individual or a total market, has been expressed as a function of a single independent variable, namely price. Price was also the only independent variable which was treated explicitly in our demand models for the firm under perfect competition, pure monopoly, monopolistic competition, and oligopoly. Yet we know very well that the quantity of a given product which can be sold at a particular time (with the exception of a perfectly competitive market) is likely to depend on a host of variables and not just the price of the particular product. Other factors that may affect the sales of a product might include:

1. Prices of other substitute products
2. Income of consumers
3. Advertising and promotion expenditures
4. Quality of the product
5. Advertising expenditures of competitors
6. Quality of competitors' products
7. Service provided to customers
8. Delivery times
9. Changes in the values of the above variables over time
10. Lagged values of the above variables
11. Brand loyalty
12. Packaging

This list is by no means complete, and the reader will surely think of other variables that affect the demand for certain products.

The basic approach of econometric models of demand is to express the quantity demanded of a particular product as a function of a set of independent variables whose parameters can then be estimated from existing time-series and cross-sectional data via standard econometric estimating techniques. The problems associated with econometric demand models are complex and numerous. Since this book is concerned with theoretical models of the firm (i.e., economic theory rather than econometrics) we shall not go into a digression on econometrics. The reader interested in the econometric determination of multivariable demand relationships should consult Baumol [10, Chap. 10], Goldberger [43], Johnston [56], Klein [57], or Malinvaud [67].

Dynamic demand models

With the exception of some of the oligopolistic models which were briefly summarized in this chapter, all other models were based on the assumption that the parameters and variables describing these models would not vary over time. Or at least we assumed that we were looking at a given demand model at a particular point in time. Although many economists are quite comfortable in analyzing the dynamic world in which we live with a set of completely static models, others, like Robinson, raise serious doubts about the efficacy of this approach:

> But to use the equilibrium concept one has to keep it in its place, and its place is strictly in the preliminary stages of an analytical argument, not in the framing of hypotheses to be tested against the facts, for we know perfectly well that we shall not find facts in a state of equilibrium [81, p. 81].

The quantity of a firm's product which will be demanded at a particular time is indeed likely to be a time-dependent process. For example, the number of automobiles sold in June by General Motors will probably depend on (1) the number sold in May, (2) the number sold last year and the year before, (3) the amount spent on advertising last month as well as two months ago, and other time-related variables. In Chapter 11 we will analyze several different dynamic models of the firm involving time-dependent demand functions with built-in feedback effects.

Probabilistic demand models

Under some circumstances we may not be able to quantify the relationship between a firm's sales at a given price and other variables affecting demand. This may be due to a lack of data or insufficient knowledge about the variables which affect sales of a particular product. However, we may be able to treat the quantity demanded at a given price as a random variable and obtain an approximation for its probability distribution as well as estimates of the mean and variance of demand. In other words, we assume that the firm cannot say with complete certainty how many units of output it will sell during a particular time interval at a given price. Demand is said to be a random process. (See Chu and Naylor [18].)

This assumption appears to be at least partially borne out in the real world, for the total sales of a firm depend not only on the prevailing market price but also on the effects of advertising and promotional expenditures, the marketing strategies of competitors, the national economy, and other factors over which it may be able to exercise little or no control. It has been found that for some firms it may be possible to find a probability density function describing the behavior of demand, or equivalently a probability density function describing the frequency with which orders are received by the firm at given price levels.

In Chapter 14 we shall investigate a model in which the firm is assumed to possess some degree of monopolistic power which enables it to at least partially control the pattern of demand. That is, by changing either price or advertising and promotional expenditures the firm can affect either the probabilty distribution or the expected value of demand.

Behavioral demand models

Recently, microeconomic theory in general and the theory of demand in particular have been attacked by G. P. E. Clarkson and others of the "Carnegie Tech school of economic thought" on the grounds that it is impossible to employ microeconomic theory to generate empirically significant predictions about the behavior of consumers or firms, and that microeconomic theory is unable to meet the normal requirements employed in empirical science [20, p. 5]. Referring specifically to the theory of demand, Clarkson has stated that

> . . . the basic postulates of utility theory cannot in their present state be empirically confirmed. Consequently, the theory of utility is not refutable by empirical test. Since the concepts of the theory of demand depend for their empirical content on the empirical validity of utility theory, it would also appear that the theory of demand is not subjectable to a process of empirical confirmation [20, p. 79].

These criticisms (and others) of traditional microeconomic theory have given rise to the behavioral approach to the theory of the firm of Cyert and March [24] and others. To illustrate what is meant by a behavioral model of the firm, consider Cyert and March's requirements for a behavioral model of an oligopoly. They contend that

> . . . a behavioral model of oligopoly behavior should emphasize adaptation, problem solving, uncertainty avoidance, and incomplete rationalization of decisions. It should tend to de-emphasize explicit omniscience and goal clarity [24, p. 280].

Based on Newell, Shaw, and Simon's [77] theory of human problem solving, Clarkson [20] has developed the rudiments of a theory of individual consumer behavior, "designed to serve as a basis for the microreduction of the theory of demand to observable decision-making behavior." The objective of the theory of human problem solving is "to explain the process of human problem solving by identifying the types of decision processes that humans employ while solving a variety of problems" [20, p. 110]. These processes are defined in part by three postulates which state that for each problem solver there exists

1. A control system consisting of a number of *memories* which contain symbolized information and are interconnected by various ordering relations. . . .
2. A number of *primitive information processes*, which operate on the information in the memories. . . .
3. A perfectly definite set of rules for combining these processes into whole *programs* of processing . . . [77].

Clarkson's model of individual consumer behavior is based on a set of four main decision processes with the following characteristics:

> (a) The consumer's main decision processes should be roughly the same no matter what category of commodities is being selected from at any one period of time, (b) these decision processes should be constructed so that they are largely independent of the subject matter of any one category of commodities, and (c) some special decision processes will be needed for each category of commodities to allow the basic set of decision processes to be applied to the particular decisions that occur only within each of the separate categories [20, p. 126].

The decision processes included in Clarkson's behavioral model of demand are:

1. . . . the consumer's decision to buy a particular set of commodities with cash or cash equivalents, or by managing to pay for them by a set of monthly payments.
2. . . . the process that enables the consumer to select one set of commodities from the available alternatives.
3. . . . a set of decision processes that allows the theory to adjust its selections in accordance with some expectations about the future behavior of prices, and other variables that are considered important.
4. . . . a set of processes that resolve the various conflicting situations that might arise [20, pp. 126–133].

SUMMARY

In this chapter we have developed a number of alternative models of product demand. In Chapters 3 and 4 we will describe and analyze production and cost models respectively. These models of demand, production, and cost will serve as the basic elements in an integrated theory of the firm which will be set forth in Chapter 5. Throughout Chapters 2–5 we treat the firm as though it were operating under conditions of complete certainty and static equilibrium.

BIBLIOGRAPHY

[1] ALCHIAN, ARMEN A. "The Meaning of Utility Measurements," *American Economic Review*, **XLIII** (March, 1953), 26–50.

[2] ALLEN, R. G. D. "The Nature of Indifference Curves," *Review of Economic Studies*, **I** (1933–34), 110–121.

[3] ALLEN, R. G. D. *Mathematical Analysis for Economists*. London: Macmillan and Co., 1956.

[4] AMERICAN ECONOMIC ASSOCIATION. *Readings in Industrial Organization and Public Policy*. Homewood, Ill.: Richard D. Irwin, 1958.

[5] BAIN, JOE S. *Barriers to New Competition*. Cambridge: Harvard University Press, 1956.

[6] BAIN, JOE S. *Industrial Organization*. New York: John Wiley & Sons, 1959.

[7] BAUMOL, WILLIAM J. "The Neumann-Morgenstern Utility Index—An Ordinalist View," *Journal of Political Economy*, **LIX** (1951), 61–66.

[8] BAUMOL, WILLIAM J. "The Cardinal Utility Which Is Ordinal," *Economic Journal*, **LXVII** (1958), 665–672.

[9] BAUMOL, WILLIAM J. "On the Theory of Oligopoly," *Economica*, **XXV** (August, 1958), 187–198.

[10] BAUMOL, WILLIAM J. *Economic Theory and Operations Analysis*. Englewood Cliffs, N. J.: Prentice-Hall, Inc., 1965.

[11] BECKER, GARY S. "Irrational Behavior and Economic Theory," *Journal of Political Economy*, **LXX** (February, 1962), 1–13.

[12] BISHOP, ROBERT L. "Duopoly: Collusion or Warefare?" *American Economic Review*, **L** (1960), 933–961.

[13] BLAUG, M. *Economic Theory in Retrospect*, Rev. ed. Homewood, Ill.: Richard D. Irwin, 1968.

[14] BOULDING, KENNETH E. *Economic Analysis*. New York: Harper & Brothers, 1955.

[15] CAVES, RICHARD. *American Industry: Structure, Conduct, Performance*. Englewood Cliffs, N. J.: Prentice-Hall, 1964.

[16] CHAMBERLIN, E. H. *The Theory of Monopolistic Competition*. Cambridge: Harvard University Press, 1933.

[17] CHIANG, A. C. *Fundamental Methods of Mathematical Economics*. New York: McGraw-Hill Book Co., 1967.

[18] CHU, KONG, and THOMAS H. NAYLOR. "A Dynamic Model of the Firm," *Management Science*, **XI** (May, 1965), 736–750.

[19] CLARKSON, G. P. E. *Portfolio Selection: A Simulation of Trust Investment.* Englewood Cliffs, N. J.: Prentice-Hall, Inc., 1962.

[20] CLARKSON, G. P. E. *The Theory of Consumer Demand: A Critical Appraisal.* Englewood Cliffs, N. J.: Prentice-Hall, Inc., 1963.

[21] COHEN, KALMAN J., and RICHARD M. CYERT. *Theory of the Firm: Resource Allocation in a Market Economy.* Englewood Cliffs, N. J.: Prentice-Hall, Inc., 1965.

[22] COURNOT, AUGUSTIN (trans. by N. T. Bacon). *Récherches sur les Principes Mathematiques de la Théorie des Richesses.* New York: Macmillan & Co., 1897.

[23] CYERT, RICHARD M., and JAMES G. MARCH. "Organizational Factors in the Theory of Oligopoly," *Quarterly Journal of Economics*, **LXX** (1956).

[24] CYERT, RICHARD M., and JAMES G. MARCH. *A Behavioral Theory of the Firm.* Englewood Cliffs, N. J.: Prentice-Hall, Inc., 1963.

[25] DEAN, JOEL. *Managerial Economics.* Englewood Cliffs, N. J.: Prentice-Hall, Inc., 1951.

[26] EDGEWORTH, FRANCIS Y. *Mathematical Psychics.* London: C. K. Paul & Co., 1881.

[27] EFROYMSON, CLARENCE W. "A Note on Kinked Demand Curves," *American Economic Review*, **XXXIII** (March, 1943), 98–109.

[28] ELLSBERG, D. "Classic and Current Notions of 'Measurable Utility'," *Economic Journal*, **LXIV** (September, 1954), 528–556.

[29] FELLNER, WILLIAM. *Competition Among the Few: Oligopoly and Similar Market Structures.* New York: Alfred A. Knopf, 1949.

[30] FELLNER, WILLIAM. *Modern Economic Analysis.* New York: McGraw-Hill Book Co., 1960.

[31] FERGUSON, C. E. "An Essay on Cardinal Utility," *Southern Economic Journal*, **XXV** (1958), 11–23.

[32] FERGUSON, C. E. "Substitution Effect in Value Theory: A Pedagogical Note," *Southern Economic Journal*, **XXVI** (1960), 310–314.

[33] FERGUSON, C. E. *Microeconomic Theory.* Homewood, Illinois: Richard D. Irwin, Inc., 1966.

[34] FRIEDMAN, MILTON. "The Marshallian Demand Curve," *Journal of Political Economy*, **LVII** (1949), 463–495.

[35] FRIEDMAN, MILTON. *Price Theory.* Chicago: Aldine Publishing Co., 1962.

[36] FRIEDMAN, MILTON, and L. J. SAVAGE. "The Utility Analysis of Choices Involving Risk," *Journal of Political Economy*, **LVI** (August, 1948), 279–304.

[37] FRIEDMAN, MILTON, and L. J. SAVAGE. "The Expected-Utility Hypothesis and the Measurability of Utility," *Journal of Political Economy*, **LX** (1952), 463–474.

[38] FRISCH, RAGNAR. *Maxima and Minima.* Chicago: Rand McNally, 1966.

[39] GEORGESCU-ROEGEN, NICHOLAS. "The Pure Theory of Consumer Behavior," *Quarterly Journal of Economics*, **L** (1935–36), 545–593.

[40] GEORGESCU-ROEGEN, NICHOLAS. "A Diagrammatic Analysis of Complementarity," *Southern Economic Journal*, **XIX** (July, 1952), 1–20.

[41] GEORGESCU-ROEGEN, NICHOLAS. "Choice and Revealed Preference," *Southern Economic Journal*, **XXI** (1954), 119–130.

[42] GEORGESCU-ROEGEN, NICHOLAS. "Choice, Expectations, and Measurability," *Quarterly Journal of Economics*, **LXVIII** (1954), 503–534.

[43] GOLDBERGER, A. S. *Econometric Theory*. New York: John Wiley & Sons, 1964.

[44] HALL, R. L., and C. J. HITCH. "Price Theory and Business Behavior," *Oxford Economic Papers*, No. 2 (May, 1939), 12–45.

[45] HARROD, R. F. "Doctrines of Imperfect Competition," *Quarterly Journal of Economics* (May, 1934), 442–470.

[46] HENDERSON, JAMES M., and RICHARD E. QUANDT. *Microeconomic Theory*. New York: McGraw-Hill Book Co., 1958.

[47] HICKS, J. R. "Annual Survey of Economic Theory: The Theory of Monopoly," *Econometrica*, **III** (1935), 1–20.

[48] HICKS, J. R. *Value and Capital*. Oxford: Clarendon Press, 1939.

[49] HICKS, J. R. "The Process of Imperfect Competition," *Oxford Economic Papers*, N.S. **VI** (1954), 41–54.

[50] HICKS, J. R. *A Revision of Demand Theory*. Oxford: The Oxford University Press, 1956.

[51] HICKS, J. R., and R. G. D. ALLEN. "A Reconsideration of the Theory of Value," *Economica*, **I** (February and May, 1934), 52–76, 196–219.

[52] HOTELLING, HAROLD. "Edgeworth's Taxation Paradox and the Nature of Demand and Supply Functions," *Journal of Political Economy*, **XL** (1932), 577–616.

[53] HOTELLING, HAROLD. "Demand Functions With Limited Budgets," *Econometrica*, **III** (1935), 66–78.

[54] HOUTHAKKER, H. S. "Revealed Preference and the Utility Function," *Economica*, **XVII** (May, 1950), 159–174.

[55] HURWICZ, LEONID. "The Theory of Economic Behavior," *American Economic Review*, **XXXV** (1945), 909–925.

[56] JOHNSTON, J. *Econometric Methods*. New York: McGraw-Hill Book Co., 1963.

[57] KLEIN, LAWRENCE R. *An Introduction to Econometrics*. Englewood Cliffs, N. J.: Prentice-Hall, Inc., 1962.

[58] KNIGHT, FRANK H. "Realism and Relevance in the Theory of Demand," *Journal of Political Economy*, **LII** (1944), 289–318.

[59] KUENNE, ROBERT E. *The Theory of General Economic Equilibrium*. Princeton: Princeton University Press, 1963.

[60] LANGE, OSCAR. "Complementarity and Interrelations of Shifts in Demand," *Review of Economic Studies*, **VII** (1940–41), 58–63.

[61] LEFTWICH, RICHARD H. *The Price System and Resource Allocation* (3rd ed.). New York: Holt, Rinehart and Winston, 1966.

[62] LUCE, R. DUNCAN, and HOWARD RAIFFA. *Games and Decisions*. New York: John Wiley & Sons, Inc., 1957.

[63] LYONS, IVORY L., and MANUEL ZYMELMAN. *Economic Analysis of the Firm*. New York: Pitman Publishing Corp., 1966.

[64] MACHLUP, FRITZ. "Monopoly and Competition: A Classification of Market Positions," *American Economic Review*, **XXVII** (September, 1937), 445–451.

[65] MACHLUP, FRITZ. *The Economics of Sellers' Competition*. Baltimore: Johns Hopkins Press, 1952.

[66] MACHLUP, FRITZ. *The Political Economy of Monopoly*. Baltimore: Johns Hopkins Press, 1952.

[67] MALINVAUD, E. *Statistical Methods in Econometrics*. Chicago: Rand McNally & Co., 1966.

[68] MARSCHAK, J. "Rational Behavior, Uncertain Prospects and Measurable Utility," *Econometrica*, **XVIII** (April, 1950), 111–141.

[69] MARSHALL, ALFRED. *Principles of Economics*. London: Macmillan & Co., 1890.

[70] MAUER, WILLIAM A., and THOMAS H. NAYLOR. "Monopolistic-Monopsonistic Competition: The Multi-Product, Multi-Factor Firm," *Southern Economic Journal*, **XXXI** (July, 1964), 38–43.

[71] MAYBERRY, J. P., J. E. NASH, and MARTIN SHUBIK. "A Comparison of a Duopoly Situation," *Econometrica*, **XXI** (1953), 141–154.

[72] MODIGLIANI, FRANCO. "New Developments on the Oligopoly Front," *Journal of Political Economy*, **LXVI** (1958), 215–232.

[73] MORGENSTERN, OSKAR. "Demand Theory Reconsidered," *Quarterly Journal of Economics*, **XLII** (February, 1948), 165–201.

[74] MOSTELLER, F., and P. NOGEE. "An Experimental Measurement of Utility," *Journal of Political Economy*, **LIX** (1951), 371–404.

[75] NAYLOR, THOMAS H. "Some Theoretical Models of the Firm." Unpublished Ph.D. dissertation, Department of Economics, Tulane University, New Orleans, Louisiana, 1964.

[76] NEUMANN, J. VON, and O. MORGENSTERN. *Theory of Games and Economic Behavior* (2nd ed.). Princeton, N. J.: Princeton University Press, 1947.

[77] NEWELL, A., J. C. SHAW, and H. A. SIMON. "Elements of a Theory of Human Problem Solving," *Psychological Review*, **LXV** (1958), 151–166.

[78] OZGA, S. A. "Measurable Utility and Probability—A Simplified Rendering," *Economic Journal*, **LXVI** (1956), 419–430.

[79] PARETO, VILFREDO. *Manuel d'économie politique*. Paris: V. Giard & E. Briere, 1909.

[80] ROBINSON, JOAN. *The Economics of Imperfect Competition*. London: Macmillan & Co., 1933.

[81] ROBINSON, JOAN. *Economic Philosophy*. Chicago: Aldine Publishing Co., 1963.

[82] ROTHSCHILD, K. W. "Price Theory and Oligopoly," *Economic Journal*, **LVII** (1947), 299–320.

[83] RYAN, W. J. L. *Price Theory*. London: Macmillan & Co., 1958.

[84] SAMUELSON, PAUL A. "A Note on the Pure Theory of Consumer's Behavior," *Economica*, N.S. **V** (1938), 61–71.

[85] SAMUELSON, PAUL A. "Consumption Theory in Terms of Revealed Preference," *Economica*, N.S. **XV** (1948), 243–253.

[86] SAMUELSON, PAUL A. *Foundations of Economic Analysis*. Cambridge, Mass.: Harvard University Press, 1948.

[87] SAMUELSON, PAUL A. "The Problem of Integrability in Utility Theory," *Econometrica*, **XVII** (1950), 355–385.

[88] SAMUELSON, PAUL A. "Consumption Theorems in Terms of Overcompensation Rather Than Indifference Comparisons," *Economica*, **XX** (February, 1953).

[89] SCHULTZ, HENRY. *The Theory and Measurement of Demand.* Chicago: University of Chicago Press, 1948.

[90] SHUBIK, MARTIN. "A Comparison of Treatments of a Duopoly Problem," *Econometrica*, **XXIII** (1955), 417–431.

[91] SHUBIK, MARTIN. *Strategy and Market Structure.* New York: John Wiley & Sons, Inc., 1959.

[92] SIMON, H. A. "A Behavioral Model of Rational Choice," *Quarterly Journal of Economics*, **LXIX** (February, 1955), 99–118.

[93] SLUTSKY, E. E. "On the Theory of the Budget of the Consumer," *Giornale degli Economisti*, **LI** (July, 1915), 1–20. Reprinted in Stigler, George J., and Kenneth E. Boulding (Eds.), *Readings in Price Theory.* Homewood, Ill.: Richard D. Irwin, Inc., 1952.

[94] SMITHIES, ARTHUR. "Equilibrium in Monopolistic Competition," *Quarterly Journal of Economics*, **LV** (1940), 95–115.

[95] SPENCER, MILTON H., and LOUIS SIEGELMAN. *Managerial Economics.* Homewood, Ill.: Richard D. Irwin, 1964.

[96] SPENGLER, JOSEPH J. "Kinked Demand Curves: By Whom First Used?" *Southern Economic Journal*, **XXXII** (July, 1965), 81–84.

[97] STAEHLE, H. "A Development of the Economic Theory of Price Index Numbers," *Review of Economic Studies*, **II** (1935), 163–188.

[98] STACKELBERG, H. V. "Grundlagen einer reiner Kostentheorie," *Zeitschrift für National-Oekonomie* (May, 1932).

[99] STACKELBERG, H. V. (trans. by Alan T. Peacock). *The Theory of the Market Economy.* New York: Oxford Univ. Press, 1952.

[100] STIGLER, GEORGE J. "The Limitations of Statistical Demand Curves," *Journal of American Statistical Association*, **XXXIV** (1939), 469–481.

[101] STIGLER, GEORGE J. "Notes on a Theory of Duopoly," *Journal of Political Economy*, **XLVIII** (1940), 521–541.

[102] STIGLER, GEORGE J. "The Kinky Oligopoly Demand Curve and Rigid Prices," *Journal of Political Economy*, **LV** (1947), 432–449.

[103] STIGLER, GEORGE J. *The Theory of Price.* New York: The Macmillan Co., 1949.

[104] STIGLER, GEORGE J. "The Development of Utility Theory, I," *The Journal of Political Economy*, **LVIII** (August, 1950), 307–324.

[105] STIGLER, GEORGE J. "Perfect Competition, Historically Contemplated," *Journal of Political Economy*, **LXV** (1957), 1–17.

[106] STIGLER, GEORGE J., and KENNETH E. BOULDING (Eds.). *Readings in Price Theory.* Homewood, Ill.: Richard D. Irwin, Inc., 1952.

[107] STONIER, ALFRED W., and DOUGLAS C. HAGUE. *A Textbook of Economic Theory* (3rd ed.). New York: John Wiley & Sons, 1964.

[108] STROTZ, ROBERT H. "Cardinal Utility," *American Economic Review*, **XLII** (1953), 384–397.

[109] STROTZ, ROBERT H. "The Empirical Implications of a Utility Tree," *Econometrica*, **XXV** (1957), 269–280.

[110] SWEEZY, PAUL M. "Demand Under Conditions of Oligopoly," *Journal of Political Economy*, **XLVII** (August, 1939), 568–573.

[111] TEICHROEW, DANIEL. *An Introduction to Management Science Deterministic Models*. New York: John Wiley & Sons, 1964.

[112] TRIFFIN, ROBERT. *Monopolistic Competition and General Equilibrium Theory*. Cambridge: Harvard University Press, 1949.

[113] VICKREY, WILLIAM S. *Microstatics*. New York: Harcourt, Brace & World, Inc., 1964.

[114] WALRAS, LÉON. *Abrégé des Eléments d'économie politique pure*. Paris: R. Pichon et R. Durand-Auzias, 1938.

[115] WICKSTEED, PHILIP H. "The Scope and Method of Political Economy," *The Economic Journal*, **XXIV** (1914), 1–23.

[116] WOLD, HERMAN, and LARS JUREEN. *Demand Analysis*. New York: John Wiley & Sons, 1953.

[117] WORKING, E. J. "What Do Statistical Demand Curves Show?" *Quarterly Journal of Economics*, **XLI** (1927), 212–235.

[118] YEAGER, LELAND B. "Methodenstreit Over Demand Curves," *Journal of Political Economy*, **LXVIII** (1960), 53–64.

Mathematical appendix for chapter 2

MULTIVARIABLE OPTIMIZATION

In writing this book, we have assumed that the reader has taken a course in differential and integral calculus. Although the typical introductory course in calculus treats the problem of optimizing continuous functions of a *single* variable, *multivariable* optimization problems are usually not included in such courses. For this reason, we have included this appendix. The reader who is totally unfamiliar with multivariable optimization techniques is urged to consult Chapters 11 and 12 of the excellent textbook by Chiang [17], *Fundamental Methods of Mathematical Economics*, or Chapters 9, 11, 18, and 20 of Teichroew [111], *An Introduction to Management Science Deterministic Models.*

We shall consider two different types of multivariable optimization problems: (1) unconstrained optimization and (2) constrained optimization. We shall conclude this appendix with a discussion of Lagrangian multipliers. Before turning to these problems, we should define the concept of partial differentiation.

PARTIAL DIFFERENTIATION

Consider the following generalized function of n variables

$$\phi = \phi(X_1, X_2, \ldots, X_n) \tag{2A-1}$$

The partial derivative of ϕ with respect to X_j is defined as

$$\phi_j = \frac{\partial \phi}{\partial X_j} = \lim_{\Delta X_j \to 0} \frac{\phi(X_1, \ldots, X_j + \Delta X_j, \ldots, X_n) - \phi(X_1, \ldots, X_n)}{\Delta X_j} \tag{2A-2}$$

which represents the rate of change in ϕ with respect to X_j when all other variables are held constant.

As an illustration, suppose that

$$\phi = X_1^2 + X_1 X_2 + 3X_1^2 X_2 + X_3^2 \tag{2A-3}$$

The first-order partial derivatives of ϕ with respect to X_1, X_2, and X_3 are respectively

(2A-4) $\phi_1 = 2X_1 + X_2 + 6X_1X_2$

(2A-5) $\phi_2 = X_1 + 3X_1^2$

(2A-6) $\phi_3 = 2X_3$

The *second-order* partial derivative of ϕ with respect to X_j is defined as

(2A-7) $$\phi_{jj} = \frac{\partial \phi_j}{\partial X_j} = \frac{\partial^2 \phi}{\partial X_j^2} \qquad j = 1, \ldots, n$$

We can also define the *cross* partial derivatives

(2A-8) $$\phi_{ij} = \frac{\partial \phi_j}{\partial X_i} = \frac{\partial^2 \phi}{\partial X_i \, \partial X_j} \qquad i \neq j \quad \text{and} \quad i, j = 1, \ldots, n$$

and

(2A-9) $$\phi_{ji} = \frac{\partial \phi_i}{\partial X_j} = \frac{\partial^2 \phi}{\partial X_j \, \partial X_i} \qquad i \neq j \quad \text{and} \quad i, j = 1, \ldots, n$$

Even though ϕ_{ij} and ϕ_{ji} have been separately defined, they can be shown to be identical in value if the two cross partial derivatives are both continuous. In the preceding example,

(2A-10) $\phi_{12} = 1 + 6X_1$

and

(2A-11) $\phi_{21} = 1 + 6X_1$

Another useful concept of partial differentiation is the *total differential.* The total differential of ϕ is defined as

(2A-12) $d\phi = \phi_1 \, dX_1 + \phi_2 \, dX_2 + \cdots + \phi_n \, dX_n$

It represents the general form of the equation of the tangent plane to the surface defined by $\phi = \phi(X_1, \ldots, X_n)$. The total differential indicates the amount of change in ϕ resulting from the sum of the separate small changes in all n independent variables.

The rate of change in ϕ with respect to X_i when all other variables are permitted to vary and all X_j are specified functions of X_i is called the *total derivative* of ϕ with respect to X_i. It is given by

(2A-13) $$\frac{d\phi}{dX_i} = \phi_1 \frac{dX_1}{dX_i} + \cdots + \phi_i + \cdots + \phi_n \frac{dX_n}{dX_i}$$

If ϕ is an implicit function of the form

(2A-14) $\phi(X_1, \ldots, X_n) = 0$

we can obtain $\partial X_j / \partial X_i$ by writing the total differential of ϕ (which, of course, also equals zero),

(2A-15) $d\phi = \phi_1 \, dX_1 + \cdots + \phi_n \, dX_n = 0$

and dividing by dX_i,

(2A-16) $$\phi_1 \frac{dX_1}{dX_i} + \cdots + \phi_j \frac{dX_j}{dX_i} + \cdots + \phi_i + \cdots + \phi_n \frac{dX_n}{dX_i} = 0$$

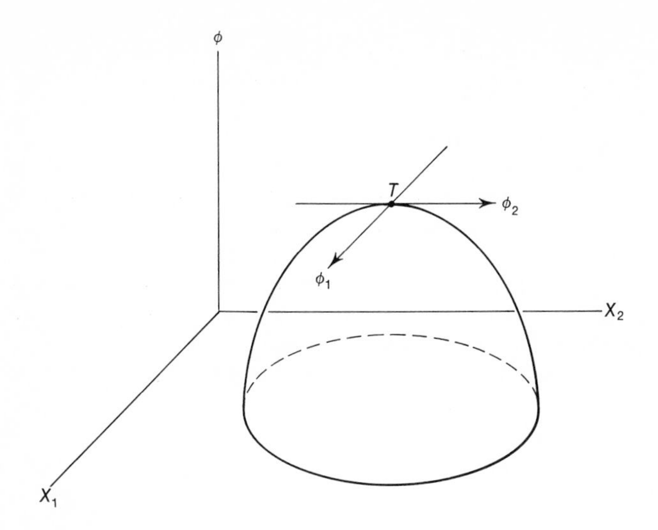

FIGURE 2A-1

Then, setting all differentials other than dX_i and dX_j equal to zero, we get

(2A-17) $$\phi_j \frac{dX_j}{dX_i} + \phi_i = 0$$

or

(2A-18) $$\frac{\partial X_j}{\partial X_i} = -\frac{\phi_i}{\phi_j}$$

Equation (2A-18) is the *implicit-function rule* of differential calculus.

UNCONSTRAINED OPTIMIZATION

Suppose we wish to find the values of the variables $X_1, X_2, \ldots, X_n$ which will optimize (maximize or minimize) the function

(2A-19) $$\phi = \phi(X_1, \ldots, X_n)$$

The necessary condition for a local optimum is that the first-order differential must be equal to zero:

(2A-20) $$d\phi = \sum_{j=1}^{n} \phi_j \, dX_j = 0$$

Since the dX_j are not necessarily zero, an equivalent condition is that *the first-order partial derivatives must all be equal to zero.* A geometrical interpretation for a maximum in the two-variable case is given in Figure 2A-1.

At the maximum point T, the partial derivative of ϕ with respect to X_2 is represented by the tangent arrow ϕ_2. Since the arrow is parallel to the X_2 axis, it has a zero slope. Similarly, the tangent arrow ϕ_1, parallel to the X_1 axis, indicates that the partial derivative of ϕ with respect to X_1 is also zero at the maximum point T. Of course, the partial derivatives would also be zero if T happened to be the minimum point in, say, a bowl. Thus (2A-20) is only a necessary, or first-order, condition for a maximum or minimum.

In the case of a maximization (minimization) problem, if ϕ is strictly concave (convex), then (2A-20) is both a *necessary* and a *sufficient* condition for a global maximum (minimum). Strict *concavity* (*convexity*) means that linear interpolation between any two points of a function gives a value less than (greater than) the value of the function at the point of interpolation.[1] If ϕ is not strictly concave for a maximization problem or strictly convex for a minimization problem, then we must examine the second-order or sufficient conditions for local maxima (minima) and then select the global maximum (minimum) from among the local ones. The second-order condition for a *local* maximum (minimum) is that the second-order total differential

$$(2A\text{-}21) \qquad d^2\phi = \sum_{j=1}^{n} \sum_{i=1}^{n} \phi_{ij}\, dX_i\, dX_j$$

be negative (positive) *regardless of the algebraic signs of the dX's* (not all dX's may be zero). In other words, ϕ must decrease in every direction from a maximum. This is the same as saying that $d\phi < 0$ for any values of the dX's (not all zero) near the maximum. And, since $d\phi = 0$ at the maximum, $d\phi$ must be *decreasing* at the maximum, or $d(d\phi) = d^2\phi < 0$.

Hence, we must ensure that $d^2\phi$ is *negative definite* for a maximum and *positive definite* for a minimum. The word "definite" is appended to mean that $d^2\phi$ must be of the indicated sign for *all* possible values of the dX's. One method for determining the negative or positive definiteness of $d^2\phi$ makes use of the *Hessian* determinant of partial derivatives (where the partial derivatives are evaluated at the point being examined).

$$(2A\text{-}22) \qquad S_n = \begin{vmatrix} \phi_{11} & \phi_{12} & \cdots & \phi_{1n} \\ \phi_{21} & \phi_{22} & \cdots & \phi_{2n} \\ \vdots & & & \\ \phi_{n1} & \phi_{n2} & \cdots & \phi_{nn} \end{vmatrix}$$

[1] For the two-dimensional case, a function is defined as *concave* if, when a straight line is drawn connecting any two points P and Q on its graph, the whole of the arc PQ, excluding the endpoints, lies on or above the straight line PQ. If the arc lies above the straight line the function is said to be *strictly concave* (see left figure).

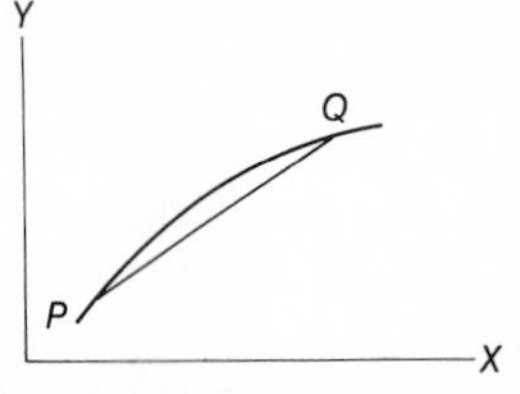

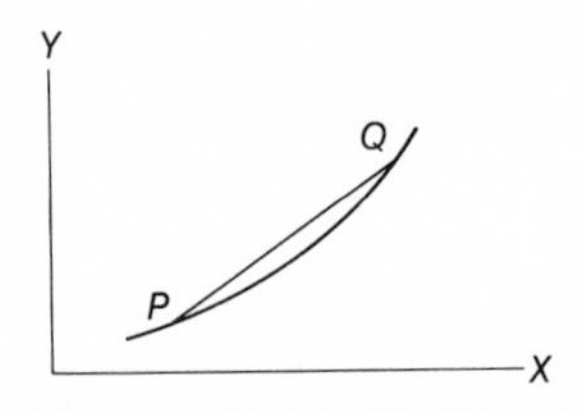

A function is defined as *convex* if, when a straight line is drawn connecting any two points P and Q on its graph, the whole of the arc PQ, excluding the endpoints, lies on or below the straight line PQ. If the arc lies below the straight line the function is said to be *strictly convex* (see right figure).

The second-order condition for a *local maximum* (i.e., $d^2\phi$ is negative definite) requires that the principal minors S_j obtained by deleting the last $(n - j)$ rows and $(n - j)$ columns of S_n alternate in sign: $S_1 < 0$, $S_2 > 0$, $S_3 < 0, \ldots, S_n(-1)^n > 0$. The second-order condition for a *local minimum* requires that the principal minors of S_n all be positive: $S_1 > 0$, $S_2 > 0, \ldots, S_n > 0$.

The value of any determinant $|A|$ may be found by the following formula:

(2A-23) $$\begin{aligned} |A| &= a_{i1}c_{i1} + a_{i2}c_{i2} + \cdots + a_{in}c_{in} \\ &= a_{1j}c_{1j} + a_{2j}c_{2j} + \cdots + a_{nj}c_{nj} \end{aligned}$$

where the a_{ij}'s are the elements of $|A|$

(2A-24) $$|A| = \begin{vmatrix} a_{11} & a_{12} & \cdots & a_{1n} \\ a_{21} & a_{22} & \cdots & a_{2n} \\ \vdots & & & \\ a_{n1} & a_{n2} & \cdots & a_{nn} \end{vmatrix}$$

The c_{ij}'s are called *cofactors* and are defined by

(2A-25) $$c_{ij} = (-1)^{i+j}|A_{ij}|$$

where $|A_{ij}|$ is a *minor* of the determinant $|A|$ obtained by deleting the ith row and jth column of $|A|$. This method of evaluating $|A|$ is called the *method of expansion by cofactors.*

To illustrate this method, consider the following example. Suppose we want to find the values of X_1, X_2, and X_3 which will optimize

(2A-26) $$\phi = -X_1^2 - X_2^2 + X_2X_3 - X_3^2 + X_1 + X_3$$

Taking the first-order partial derivatives and setting them equal to zero we obtain

(2A-27) $$\phi_1 = -2X_1 + 1 = 0$$

(2A-28) $$\phi_2 = -2X_2 + X_3 = 0$$

(2A-29) $$\phi_3 = X_2 - 2X_3 + 1 = 0$$

Solving these three equations, we find that $X_1 = \frac{1}{2}$, $X_2 = \frac{1}{3}$, and $X_3 = \frac{2}{3}$. The Hessian determinant of second-order partial derivatives is

(2A-30) $$S_3 = \begin{vmatrix} -2 & 0 & 0 \\ 0 & -2 & 1 \\ 0 & 1 & -2 \end{vmatrix}$$

The principal minors of S_3 are calculated as follows:

(2A-31) $$S_1 = -2$$

(2A-32) $$S_2 = \begin{vmatrix} -2 & 0 \\ 0 & -2 \end{vmatrix} = 4$$

(2A-33) $$S_3 = \begin{vmatrix} -2 & 0 & 0 \\ 0 & -2 & 1 \\ 0 & 1 & -2 \end{vmatrix} = -6$$

Since the principal minors of S_3 alternate in sign, we conclude that $d^2\phi$ is negative definite. Thus ϕ has a local maximum at $X_1 = \frac{1}{2}$, $X_2 = \frac{1}{3}$, and $X_3 = \frac{2}{3}$.

CONSTRAINED OPTIMIZATION

Suppose that we have an objective function

(2A-34) $$\phi = \phi(X_1, X_2, \ldots, X_j, \ldots, X_n)$$

to be optimized subject to a set of m constraints

(2A-35) $$H_i(X_1, X_2, \ldots, X_n) = 0 \qquad i = 1, 2, \ldots, m$$

where $m < n$ and where ϕ and the H_i's are assumed to be differentiable. The *Lagrangian multiplier method* is a useful method for finding the values of $X_1, X_2, \ldots, X_n$ which will solve this problem. We simply define the Lagrangian function:

(2A-36) $$L = \phi(X_1, X_2, \ldots, X_n) + \sum_{i=1}^{m} \lambda_i H_i(X_1, X_2, \ldots, X_n)$$

where the λ_i's are *Lagrangian multipliers.* The problem of maximizing or minimizing ϕ subject to (2A-35) is equivalent to finding an unconstrained maximum or minimum of L, where the X_j's and λ_i's are independent variables. The necessary condition for a maximum can be stated in either of two equivalent ways: (1) the first-order differential must be equal to zero:

(2A-37) $$dL = \sum_{j=1}^{n} \frac{\partial L}{\partial X_j} dX_j = 0$$

subject to

(2A-38) $$H_i(X_1, \ldots, X_n) = 0 \qquad i = 1, 2, \ldots, m$$

or (2) *the first-order partial derivatives of* (2A-36) *with respect to the* X_j *and the* λ_i *must all be equal to zero.*

In the case of a maximization (minimization) problem, if ϕ is strictly concave (convex) and the set of feasible solutions which satisfy (2A-35) is *convex*[2] then (2A-37) and (2A-38) are both *necessary* and *sufficient* conditions for a *global maximum (minimum)*. If these conditions do not hold, then we must examine the second-order or sufficient conditions for local optima and select the global optimum from among them.

The second-order condition for a constrained local *maximum* is

(2A-39) $$d^2L = \sum_{j=1}^{n} \sum_{k=1}^{n} \frac{\partial^2 L}{\partial X_j \, \partial X_k} dX_j \, dX_k < 0$$

for

(2A-40) $$dH_i = \sum_{j=1}^{n} \frac{\partial H_i}{\partial X_j} dX_j = 0 \qquad (i = 1, 2, \ldots, m)$$

[2] A region is said to be *convex* if a straight-line segment connecting any two points within the region lies entirely within the region.

and not all dX's equal to zero. The second-order differential of L is said to be *negative definite*, subject to $dH_i = 0$, if (2A-39) and (2A-40) are satisfied. For a local minimum, the direction of the inequality in (2A-39) must be reversed, i.e., d^2L must be *positive definite* subject to $dH_i = 0$. Whether or not d^2L is positive or negative definite (subject to $dH_i = 0$) can be determined by examining the signs of the principal minors of the *bordered Hessian determinant*, $\bar{S}_n$. This determinant has the elements $\partial^2 L/\partial X_j\, \partial X_k$ "bordered" by $\partial H_i/\partial X_j$.

In the case of a single constraint $H(X_1, X_2, \ldots, X_n) = 0$, d^2L is *negative definite* subject to

(2A-41)
$$dH = \sum_{j=1}^{n} \frac{\partial H}{\partial X_j}\, dX_j = 0$$

if and only if

$$\bar{S}_2 = \begin{vmatrix} L_{11} & L_{12} & \frac{\partial H}{\partial X_1} \\ L_{21} & L_{22} & \frac{\partial H}{\partial X_2} \\ \frac{\partial H}{\partial X_1} & \frac{\partial H}{\partial X_2} & 0 \end{vmatrix} > 0$$

(2A-42)
$$\bar{S}_3 = \begin{vmatrix} L_{11} & L_{12} & L_{13} & \frac{\partial H}{\partial X_1} \\ L_{21} & L_{22} & L_{23} & \frac{\partial H}{\partial X_2} \\ L_{31} & L_{32} & L_{33} & \frac{\partial H}{\partial X_3} \\ \frac{\partial H}{\partial X_1} & \frac{\partial H}{\partial X_2} & \frac{\partial H}{\partial X_3} & 0 \end{vmatrix} < 0$$

$$\bar{S}_4 > 0, \ldots$$

That is, negative definiteness requires that the principal minors of $\bar{S}_n$ alternate in sign. If the $\bar{S}_j$ for $(j = 2, 3, \ldots, n)$ are all negative, then d^2L subject to $dH = 0$ is positive definite. For a complete treatment of the second-order conditions for the Lagrangian method see Mathematical Appendix A of Samuelson, *Foundations of Economic Analysis* [86] and Frisch [38], *Maxima and Minima.*

Table 2A-1 summarizes the appendix thus far. Notation and symbols are as defined in the discussion above.

INTERPRETATION OF LAGRANGIAN MULTIPLIER

To conclude this appendix, we shall examine the Lagrangian multipliers λ_i more closely.

It can be shown that if the constraints (2A-35) are of the form

(2A-43) $h_i(X_1, X_2, \ldots, X_n) = B_i \qquad (i = 1, 2, \ldots, m)$

where

(2A-44) $H_i = B_i - h_i(X_1, X_2, \ldots, X_n) = 0$

then

(2A-45) $\dfrac{d\phi}{dB_i} = \lambda_i \qquad i = 1, 2, \ldots, m$

That is, the marginal change in ϕ with respect to a change in B_i (where B_i is a constant) is equal to the Lagrangian multiplier λ_i.

To illustrate this important interpretation of λ_i, consider a simple consumer utility maximization problem. The utility function is

(2A-46) $U = U(X_1, X_2)$

and the income, or budget, constraint is

(2A-47) $Y = P_1X_1 + P_2X_2$

The income available to purchase the two commodities X_1 and X_2 at prices P_1 and P_2 is given by the constant Y.

To maximize U subject to the income constraint, form the Lagrangian function

(2A-48) $L = U(X_1, X_2) + \lambda H$

where

(2A-49) $H = Y - P_1X_1 - P_2X_2 = 0$

TABLE **2A-1**

Unconstrained optima conditions

Optimize $\phi = \phi(X_1, X_2, \ldots, X_n)$

Condition	Maximum	Minimum
First-order	$\phi_j = 0$ $j = 1, \ldots, n$	$\phi_j = 0$ $j = 1, \ldots, n$
Second-order	$S_1 < 0;\ S_2 > 0,$ $S_3 < 0; \ldots$	$S_j > 0$ $j = 1, \ldots, n$

Constrained optima conditions

Optimize $\phi = \phi(X_1, X_2, \ldots, X_n)$
Subject to $H(X_1, X_2, \ldots, X_n) = 0,$
where $L = \phi + \lambda H$

Condition	Maximum	Minimum
First-order	$L_j = L_\lambda = 0$ $j = 1, \ldots, n$	$L_j = L_\lambda = 0$ $j = 1, \ldots, n$
Second-order	$\bar{S}_2 > 0;\ \bar{S}_3 < 0;$ $\bar{S}_4 > 0; \ldots$	$\bar{S}_j < 0$ $j = 2, \ldots, n$

We assume that the function U is strictly concave and we know that the set of feasible solutions is convex; hence, we need only examine first-order conditions. These conditions are

$$L_1 = \frac{\partial U}{\partial X_1} + \lambda \frac{\partial H}{\partial X_1} = 0 \tag{2A-50}$$

$$L_2 = \frac{\partial U}{\partial X_2} + \lambda \frac{\partial H}{\partial X_2} = 0 \tag{2A-51}$$

$$L_\lambda = H = 0 \tag{2A-52}$$

Solving (2A-50) and (2A-51) for λ, we obtain

$$\lambda = -\frac{\partial U/\partial X_1}{\partial H/\partial X_1} = -\frac{\partial U/\partial X_2}{\partial H/\partial X_2} \tag{2A-53}$$

Now, compare (2A-47) and (2A-49). Since Y is a constant, the only difference between the partial derivative of Y, (2A-47), with respect to, say, X_1 and the partial derivative of H, (2A-49), with respect to X_1, is the algebraic sign. Thus

$$\frac{\partial Y}{\partial X_1} = P_1 \tag{2A-54}$$

$$\frac{\partial H}{\partial X_1} = -P_1 \tag{2A-55}$$

Consequently it will always be true that

$$\frac{\partial H}{\partial X_1} = -\frac{\partial Y}{\partial X_1} \tag{2A-56}$$

and similarly

$$\frac{\partial H}{\partial X_2} = -\frac{\partial Y}{\partial X_2} \tag{2A-57}$$

Eliminating $\partial H/\partial X_1$ and $\partial H/\partial X_2$ in (2A-53) by (2A-56) and (2A-57), we obtain

$$\lambda = \frac{\partial U/\partial X_1}{\partial Y/\partial X_1} = \frac{\partial U/\partial X_2}{\partial Y/\partial X_2} = \frac{dU}{dY} \tag{2A-58}$$

Thus the Lagrangian multiplier λ is simply dU/dY, or the marginal utility of income. It measures the infinitesimal change in utility due to a small change in income Y. Thus if $\lambda > 0$, an increase in Y results in an increase in utility, and vice versa.

3

Theory of production

INTRODUCTION

In addition to product-demand information, the firm's decision makers are also assumed to possess complete knowledge of the production technology available to the firm. This implies a knowledge of (1) the inputs or factors of production going into the process, (2) the outputs or products of the process, and (3) the relationship between the inputs and the outputs. A given factor-product transformation process can be described by a production function, i.e., a function which states the explicit relationship between the factor inputs and the product outputs of the firm. In this chapter we shall be concerned primarily with production functions in which factor-product decisions are made by considering infinitesimal changes in factor-product combinations. In general, the production functions considered here shall be continuous and differentiable, and we shall assume complete certainty and static equilibrium.

This neoclassical or marginal analysis approach to production theory originated with the work of von Thunen (1826), who developed the principle that total product is maximized when resources are allocated equimarginally. Although the concept of a production function was implied by von Thunen, there was no explicit statement of a production function until 1894 when Wicksteed [62] used a production function with continuous substitution between all factors. Wicksell [61] in 1901 was among the first economists to treat the production function explicitly. In 1939 Hicks [27] developed a production function for a multiproduct, multifactor firm which has come to be the standard textbook example of neoclassical production theory. This chapter rests heavily on the assumptions of the Hicksian production function. Other more recent treatments of the production function under the assumptions of marginal analysis include the works of Carlson [4], Dano [12], Frisch [18], Menger [41], and Samuelson [50].

The book by Dano [12] is perhaps the most comprehensive treatment of this subject to date.

We shall begin by describing a general production model for a multiproduct, multifactor firm. Next we shall turn to a special case of the general model—a single-product production model. A second special case of the general model, a joint-product model, will also be discussed. Finally, six other types of production models which fall outside of the category of neoclassical, marginal-analysis models are outlined. These are:

1. Linear programming production models
2. Production models with indivisible inputs
3. Production models with durable inputs
4. Engineering production models
5. Dynamic production models
6. Probabilistic production models

A GENERAL PRODUCTION MODEL

Definitions

Consider a multiproduct, multifactor firm which uses m factors of production to produce p different products. A generalized statement of the *production function* (in implicit form) for the firm is given by

(3-1) $$Q(Z_1, \ldots, Z_p, X_1, \ldots, X_m) = 0$$

where

(3-2) $$Z_k \geq 0 \text{ are products} \qquad (k = 1, 2, \ldots, p)$$

and

(3-3) $$X_i \geq 0 \text{ are factors} \qquad (i = 1, 2, \ldots, m)$$

The dimensions of the Z_k and the X_i are physical units per unit of time.

For any given set of factors, $X_1, X_2, \ldots, X_m$, there may be several technically feasible sets of products, $Z_1, Z_2, \ldots, Z_p$. Assign arbitrary values to $p - 1$ of these products and determine the largest value of the remaining product which is consistent with equation (3-1). This will assure a single-valued production function. If all the factors and all but one of the products are assigned arbitrary values, then the remaining product is fully determined. It is further assumed that the production function is defined over the domain of non-negative factors and products and that within the domain it has continuous first- and second-order partial derivatives.

In analyzing the properties of the production function, it will be convenient to make use of three definitions: (1) the marginal product, (2) the rate of technical substitution, and (3) the rate of product transformation.

For any product a and any factor b, the *marginal product* of product a with respect to factor b is defined as

$$MP_{ab} = \frac{\partial Z_a}{\partial X_b} \qquad (a = 1, 2, \ldots, p;\ b = 1, 2, \ldots, m) \tag{3-4}$$

And, by the implicit-function rule,

$$\frac{\partial Z_a}{\partial X_b} = -\frac{\partial Q/\partial X_b}{\partial Q/\partial Z_a} \qquad (a = 1, 2, \ldots, p;\ b = 1, 2, \ldots, m) \tag{3-5}$$

The marginal product MP_{ab} measures the change in output of product a resulting from a small change in the quantity of factor b, all other factors and products being held constant.

For any two factors a and b, the *rate of technical substitution* between the two factors is defined as

$$RTS_{ab} = -\frac{\partial X_a}{\partial X_b} = \frac{\partial Q/\partial X_b}{\partial Q/\partial X_a} \qquad (a, b = 1, 2, \ldots, m) \tag{3-6}$$

Thus the *RTS* between two factors measures the number of units of one factor required to maintain constant output when one unit of the other factor is withdrawn.

For any two products a and b the *rate of product transformation* between the two products is defined as

$$RPT_{ab} = -\frac{\partial Z_a}{\partial Z_b} = \frac{\partial Q/\partial Z_b}{\partial Q/\partial Z_a} \qquad (a, b = 1, 2, \ldots, p) \tag{3-7}$$

The *RPT* between two products measures the number of units of one product which can be attained when production of the other is reduced by one unit, given a constant level of all factors.

Assumptions

In defining the above production model, we had to state some of the assumptions underlying the multifactor, multiproduct production model. We now summarize these assumptions explicitly:

1. The firm possesses a production process which is capable of transforming a maximum of m variable factors of production into p products. (There are no limitations on the availability of the factors.)
2. A continuous production function exists (with nonvanishing first- and second-order partial derivatives) which relates the set of independent factor variables to the set of independent product variables.
3. The production function is such that the quantity of output for a given product represents the maximum amount of that product which can be produced from specified factor input quantities along with specified product quantities for the remaining $p - 1$ products.

4. The exact nature of the firm's production function has been predetermined by a set of technical decisions by the firm's engineers and technicians.
5. The production function is characterized by a decreasing marginal product for all factor-product combinations ($\partial^2 Z_a / \partial X_b^2 < 0$), a decreasing rate of technical substitution between any two factors ($-\partial^2 X_a / \partial X_b^2 < 0$), and an increasing rate of product transformation between any two products ($-\partial^2 Z_a / \partial Z_b^2 > 0$).
6. All of the firm's factors and products are perfectly divisible.
7. The parameters which determine the firm's production function will not change over the time period considered.
8. The parameters which determine the production function are not permitted to be random variables.

In Chapter 5 we will use this production model to develop a general neoclassical model of the multifactor, multiproduct firm. Assumption 1 will be relaxed in Chapters 6 through 10 when we admit the use of fixed factors of production. Assumptions 2, 3, and 5 will be replaced by a set of alternative assumptions when we consider linear programming in Chapters 7 and 8. Indivisibility will be introduced in Chapter 10. Dynamic and probabilistic production models will be treated respectively in Chapters 11 and 12.

A SINGLE-PRODUCT PRODUCTION MODEL

A special case of the production function described by (3-1) is the firm which produces a single product Z from m factors of production $X_1, X_2, \ldots, X_m$. The production function for a single-product firm is given by

$$Z = Z(X_1, X_2, \ldots, X_m) \tag{3-8}$$

Consider a particular factor of production X_i with given amounts of all other factors. The marginal product of the ith factor is

$$MP_i = \frac{\partial Z}{\partial X_i} \qquad i = 1, 2, \ldots, m \tag{3-9}$$

and the average product is defined as

$$AP_i = \frac{Z}{X_i} \qquad i = 1, 2, \ldots, m \tag{3-10}$$

The law of diminishing returns

Assumption 5 of our general production model postulates a decreasing marginal product for all factor-product combinations. For a single-product production model this assumption may be restated as

$$\frac{\partial^2 Z}{\partial X_i^2} < 0 \qquad i = 1, 2, \ldots, m \tag{3-11}$$

The assumption of a declining marginal product is merely a special interpretation of what economists call the *law of diminishing returns*. Usually, this "law" permits a certain range of output over which marginal product *increases*. But, inevitably, as the amount of a variable input is increased, *other factors being held constant*, "a point is reached beyond which marginal product declines" [16, p. 115].

Equation (3-11) requires a diminishing marginal product for all output levels. This is illustrated graphically in Figure 3-1, where the production function also satisfies the definition of a *concave function*[1] (*TP* denotes total product).

Several points about the law of diminishing returns are noteworthy.

> First, a given state of technology is assumed. The law of diminishing returns says nothing about the effect of adding additional units of any one input factor, holding constant the amounts used of other input factors, when the technological processes are also being changed. Second, there must be at least one productive service whose quantity is being held constant. The law of diminishing returns says nothing about the effect on marginal product of a proportional increase in the quantities used of all productive factors. Third, it must be possible to vary the proportions in which the different input factors are combined. Finally, the law of diminishing returns is intended to be an empirical generalization. In most production processes which we can observe in the real world, the law of diminishing returns seems to hold [11, p. 111].

The law of diminishing returns is sometimes called the *law of variable proportions*. Milton Friedman has argued that this terminology is preferable because it is more general, while the former

> . . . is closely connected with the explanation of the so-called "law" in terms of fixed and variable factors of production. At bottom, however, the issue in question has little or no relation to this distinction between fixed and variable factors; it is rather concerned with the effect of varying the proportions in which different factors are employed, and all factors enter in completely symmetrical fashion [17, p. 123].

Hence, rather than interpreting Figure 3-1 as total product versus factor X_i, with all other factors fixed, Friedman would have us interpret the horizontal axis as measuring the *ratio* of say, X_a to X_b, *both* of which are variable.

An example might prove helpful at this point. Consider a manufacturing plant in which automobiles are made from capital goods (machinery) and labor. Suppose we compute the number of automobiles which can be produced as additional quantities of labor are applied to a fixed amount of capital goods. That is, suppose we have a fully equipped automobile assembly plant with no workers in the plant. Initially as we increase the number of workers employed the marginal productivity of labor is likely to increase owing to (1) specialization of labor and (2) the indivisibility of the machinery and equipment available in the assembly plant. Further increases in labor may eventually lead to smaller and smaller increases in the number of automobiles which can be produced

[1] Refer to the appendix of Chapter 2 for the definitions of convex and concave functions.

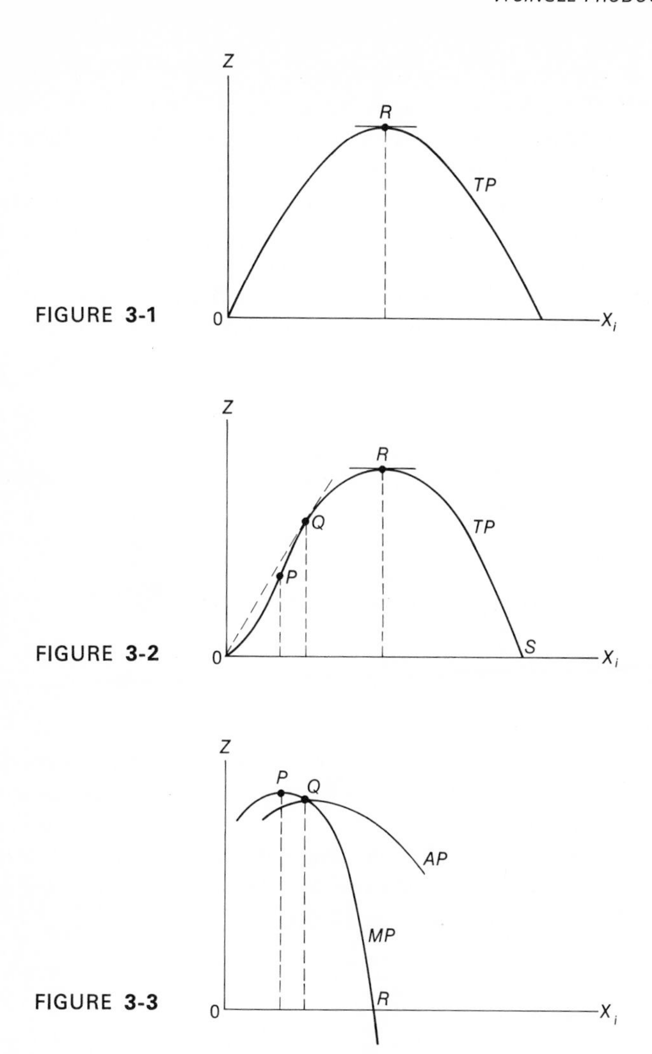

FIGURE **3-1**

FIGURE **3-2**

FIGURE **3-3**

in a given assembly plant. When this point is reached we encounter the law of diminishing returns, and marginal productivity decreases.

Figure 3-2 provides a graphical illustration. Note that the total product is increasing at an increasing rate along the segment of the production function between 0 and P. That is, the marginal product of X_i (Figure 3-3) is increasing as X_i increases. At point P on the total product curve (Figure 3-2) the shape of the production function changes from convex to concave. Marginal productivity ceases to increase, reaching a maximum at P, and begins to decrease to the right of P. However, total product is still increasing at P. Average product AP reaches a maximum at Q and then decreases with further increases in X_i. When the average product AP is just equal to the marginal product MP, the average product will have its maximum value. Total product reaches its maximum value when the marginal product is equal to zero, i.e., at point R in Figures 3-2 and 3-3. Additional increases in X_i lead to decreases in the total product.

Of course, total product would decrease only after reaching a maximum if marginal product becomes negative. A pertinent question concerns the reason for adding more of the variable factor if it decreases total product. That is, the rational firm could merely dispose of the additional units of the variable factor and thereby do better than by using them in production. However, one could argue that a negative marginal product might be plausible if disposal costs are not zero.

Output maximization

The necessary or first-order condition for output maximization for the single-product production model, where

$$Z = Z(X_1, X_2, \ldots, X_m) \tag{3-12}$$

requires that all first-order partial derivatives be equal to zero, i.e.,

$$Z_i = \frac{\partial Z}{\partial X_i} = 0 \qquad i = 1, 2, \ldots, m \tag{3-13}$$

Alternatively, the marginal productivity MP_i of each factor must be exactly equal to zero. For example, if we treat Figure 3-2 as though it were a single-factor production function, total product is maximized when marginal productivity is equal to zero at point R.

The second-order condition for a *local maximum* requires that the second-order total differential of Z be *negative definite*. We define the Hessian determinant S_m of second-order partial derivatives of Z:

$$S_m = \begin{vmatrix} Z_{11} & Z_{12} & \cdots & Z_{1m} \\ Z_{21} & Z_{22} & \cdots & Z_{2m} \\ \vdots & & & \\ Z_{m1} & Z_{m2} & \cdots & Z_{mm} \end{vmatrix} \tag{3-14}$$

Now, d^2Z will be negative definite if the principal minors S_i obtained by deleting the last $(m - i)$ rows and $(m - i)$ columns of S_m alternate in sign: $S_1 < 0$, $S_2 > 0$, $S_3 < 0, \ldots, S_m(-1)^m > 0$. If (3-12) is *strictly concave*, then Z has a global maximum at the point where (3-13) is satisfied.

A single product, two-factor production function is *strictly concave* if

$$|Z_{11}| < 0, \qquad \begin{vmatrix} Z_{11} & Z_{12} \\ Z_{21} & Z_{22} \end{vmatrix} > 0 \tag{3-15}$$

is true for *all combinations* of the two factors. Observe that Z_{11} is required to be negative. This is simply the condition that factor 1 be subject to diminishing marginal productivity. Furthermore, it follows that factor 2 must also be subject to diminishing marginal productivity. A last requirement is that $Z_{11}Z_{22} > Z_{21}^2$ (note that $Z_{21} = Z_{12}$). The cross partial Z_{21} can be interpreted as the rate of change of the marginal product of factor 1 when a small change is made in the quantity of factor 2. For example, an increase in machinery usually tends to raise the marginal product of labor.

As stated above, if the production function is *strictly concave*, then any set of X_i satisfying (3-13) corresponds to a *global maximum*. However, the conditions for *strict concavity* are rather severe. Thus, the usual textbook example of a production function, shown in Figure 3-2, does not meet these requirements. For such production functions, therefore, a number of *local maxima* may be discovered, from which the global maximum must then be selected. We should emphasize that each local maximum will satisfy the first- and second-order conditions *at the point*, but at other points the function will be convex. In other words, for some combinations of the factors, d^2Z may be *positive definite* rather than negative definite.

Isoquants

In this section we will discuss yet another way of graphically representing our single-product production model. Assume that there are only two factors, X_a and X_b. The production function is thus reduced to the following simple form:

$$Z = Z(X_a, X_b) \tag{3-16}$$

Such a production function can be represented by an *isoquant*, which is an almost exact analog of the indifference curve associated with consumer-preference theory. However, with production functions it is not necessary to restrict ourselves to ordinal measures of output as was the case with utility functions.

An *isoquant* is the locus of points which are representations of combinations of factor inputs X_a and X_b such that the level of output Z is the same for all combinations of X_a and X_b. In Figure 3-4 Z_1, Z_2, and Z_3 represent three different isoquants, i.e., three different levels of output.

Isoquants possess geometric properties which are quite similar to those of indifference curves and are based on a set of assumptions which closely parallel those underlying indifference curves. Isoquants are usually assumed to have the following properties:

1. A combination of factor inputs which lies on an isoquant Z_2 which is above and to the right of another isoquant Z_1 represents a level of output that is higher than Z_1.
2. Isoquants slope downward and to the right.
3. Isoquants can never intersect.
4. Isoquants are convex to the origin, i.e., the absolute value of the slope of an isoquant diminishes toward the right.

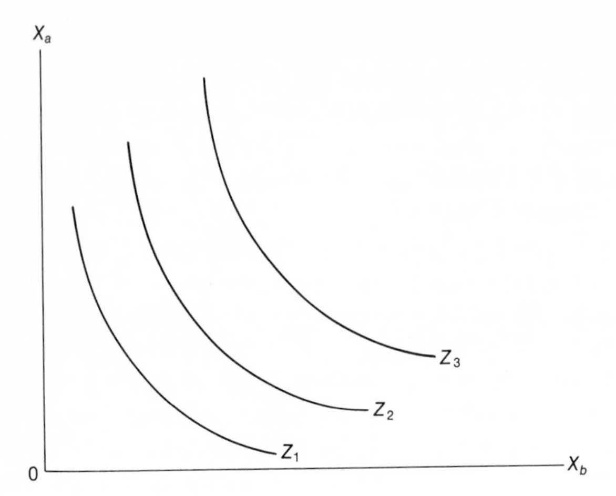

FIGURE 3-4
Isoquants

The negative of the slope of the tangent to a point on an isoquant, the *rate of technical substitution*, is the rate at which X_b must be substituted for X_a in order to maintain a given level of output. The rate of technical substitution RTS_{ab} between factors a and b can be obtained quite easily from the total differential of the production function.

$$dZ = \frac{\partial Z}{\partial X_a} dX_a + \frac{\partial Z}{\partial X_b} dX_b \tag{3-17}$$

Since $dZ = 0$ for a particular isoquant,

$$0 = \frac{\partial Z}{\partial X_a} dX_a + \frac{\partial Z}{\partial X_b} dX_b \tag{3-18}$$

then

$$\frac{dX_a}{dX_b} = -\frac{\partial Z/\partial X_b}{\partial Z/\partial X_a} = -\frac{MP_b}{MP_a} \tag{3-19}$$

And, since we define the *RTS* as the *negative* of the slope of the isoquant, we note that the *RTS* is simply the ratio of the marginal products of the two factors.

Both marginal products are assumed to be positive; hence, it follows from (3-19) that isoquants slope downward and to the right, i.e.,

$$\frac{dX_a}{dX_b} < 0 \tag{3-20}$$

The isoquants will be convex to the origin (as shown in Figure 3-4) if

$$\frac{d^2X_a}{dX_b^2} = \frac{d(dX_a/dX_b)}{dX_b} > 0 \tag{3-21}$$

By performing the indicated total differentiation, we can investigate the implicit economic assumptions made in the convexity assumption. Substituting (3-19) in (3-21), we obtain

$$\frac{d^2X_a}{dX_b^2} = \frac{d\left[-\dfrac{\partial Z/\partial X_b}{\partial Z/\partial X_a}\right]}{dX_b} = \frac{d(-Z_b/Z_a)}{dX_b} \tag{3-22}$$

And, eventually, we get[2]

$$\frac{d^2X_a}{dX_b^2} = -\frac{1}{Z_a^3}\left[Z_{bb}(Z_a)^2 - 2Z_{ba}(Z_b)(Z_a) + Z_{aa}(Z_b)^2\right] \tag{3-23}$$

The interpretations of the second-order partial derivatives are the same as discussed earlier. That is, Z_{bb}, for example, is the rate of change of the marginal product of X_b with respect to a change in the magnitude of X_b. Hence, diminishing marginal productivity with respect to both factors simply means that both Z_{bb} and Z_{aa} are negative. Since, by assumption, Z_a and Z_b are positive, the remaining unknown is Z_{ba}. Normally, we might expect an increase in the factor b to increase Z_a, thereby making Z_{ba} positive. This, combined with diminishing marginal productivity of both factors, makes

$$\frac{d^2X_a}{dX_b^2} > 0$$

The convexity property of isoquants implies that $\partial^2X_a/\partial X_b^2 > 0$. Since the *RTS* is defined as the *negative* of $\partial X_a/\partial X_b$, convexity also implies a *decreasing rate of technical substitution* between any two factors, i.e., $-\partial^2X_a/\partial X_b^2 < 0$.

A decreasing rate of technical substitution implies that the substitution of one factor for another becomes progressively more difficult as the substitution proceeds. After a certain point is reached, no further substitution is possible. It is at such a point, of course, that the isoquant become parallel to the axis.

Another measure of some usefulness in isoquant analysis is the *elasticity of substitution*. Consider, for example, isoquant Z_1 in Figure 3-4. The elasticity of substitution, e_{ab}, is a measure of the percentage change in the X_a to X_b ratio

[2] In differentiating (3-19) totally, recall that Z_b and Z_a are both functions of X_b and X_a and, in addition, X_a is itself a function of X_b (along an isoquant). Thus

$$\frac{d^2X_a}{dX_b^2} = -\frac{1}{Z_a^2}\left(Z_a\frac{dZ_b}{dX_b} - Z_b\frac{dZ_a}{dX_b}\right)$$

where

$$\frac{dZ_b}{dX_b} = Z_{bb} + Z_{ab}\frac{dX_a}{dX_b} \quad \text{and} \quad \frac{dZ_a}{dX_b} = Z_{ba} + Z_{aa}\frac{dX_a}{dX_b}$$

Of course, dX_a/dX_b can be eliminated with (3-19).

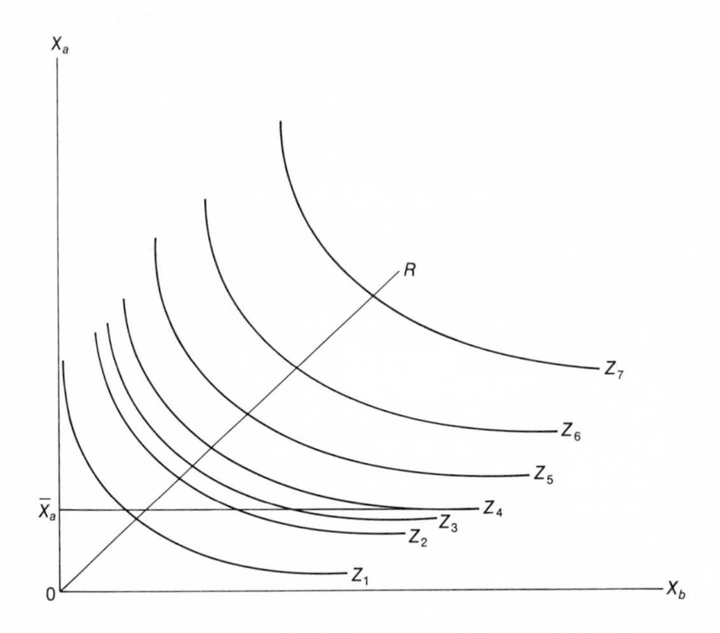

FIGURE 3-5
Returns to scale

induced by a given percentage change in the rate of technical substitution. Thus

$$e_{ab} = \frac{\dfrac{d(X_a/X_b)}{X_a/X_b}}{\dfrac{d(RTS)}{RTS}}$$

The usefulness of this concept will become more apparent in Chapter 4, where it is shown that for minimum cost a firm equates the price ratio of the factors with the *RTS*. Hence the price ratio of the factors can be substituted for *RTS* in the denominator. And e_{ab} then answers the question of the percentage change in the factor ratio induced by a given percentage change in the price ratio of the factors. For example, if the wage rate rises relative to the price of capital goods, by what percent will the firm increase its ratio of machinery to labor?

Returns of scale

An instructive use of an isoquant map is to depict *returns to scale*. Consider Figure 3-5 which represents a production function having only *two factors*, X_a and X_b. Successive higher levels of output of the *single product* are indicated by the isoquants $Z_1, Z_2, Z_3, \ldots, Z_7$.

Let the isoquants represent levels of output which are equal increments apart. For example, let $Z_1 = 100$ units of Z, $Z_2 = 200$ units, $Z_3 = 300$ units, etc. Returns to scale are indicated roughly by the distances between isoquants as measured along a ray OR from the origin. As we move from Z_1 to Z_2 to Z_3 we observe that the distance between Z_1 and Z_2 is greater than between Z_2 and Z_3. Since distance represents factor inputs, it is clear that over this range of output equal increments of output require succeedingly smaller increments of factor inputs. Thus *increasing returns to scale* are said to exist. By analogous reasoning, as we move to higher levels of output, say Z_5 to Z_6 to Z_7, *decreasing returns to scale* exist. If the isoquants were all equally spaced, implying that equal output increments entailed equal factor-input increments, *constant returns to scale* would prevail.[3]

It is important to note that we are now dealing with a problem quite different from the one we considered previously. Returns to scale concerns what happens when we increase *all* factors together. This is usually thought to be a *long-run* problem, as contrasted with the *short-run* problem of varying one factor while holding others fixed. Thus, in our earlier example of the automobile factory, the *short run* is that period during which the machinery is viewed as fixed and only labor is variable. The *long run* would be a period during which *all* factors are conceived as variable, including the machinery.

Whether a particular production function displays increasing, decreasing, or constant returns to scale is, of course, an empirical question. A large number of examples have been given in the literature to lend some empirical flavor to this question. For example, Baumol has described the case of increasing returns in warehouse construction:

> Suppose the work in building a cubical warehouse is in proportion to the number of bricks used in its construction and, within limits, the number of bricks depends strictly on the wall area of the building. It is a matter of elementary geometry that the wall and floor areas will increase as the *square* of the perimeter of the warehouse but the volume of the building (the storage area) will increase as the *cube* of the perimeter. In other words, if one doubles the land, bricks, and the bricklaying labor, one more than doubles warehouse capacity [2, p. 258].

[3] We would certainly be remiss if we omitted reference to the famous Cobb-Douglas production function. Because of its desirable properties, it has become widely used in economic analysis. For a single-product, two-factor case the function is

$$Z = AX_a^\alpha X_b^\beta$$

where A, α, and β are constants. If $\alpha + \beta = 1$, then the function displays constant returns to scale. If $\alpha + \beta > 1$, we get increasing returns to scale, and if $\alpha + \beta < 1$, we get decreasing returns to scale.

The Cobb-Douglas function is a *homogeneous function of degree* $\alpha + \beta$ because if we multiply both X_a and X_b by a constant t, we multiply the value of Z by $t^{\alpha+\beta}$. Hence, if $\alpha + \beta = 1$ we obtain constant returns to scale, e.g., multiply both X_a and X_b by 2 (double both inputs) and Z will be multiplied by 2^1, or 2 (output is doubled). The Cobb-Douglas function also has negatively sloped isoquants which are convex to the origin.

Another specific production function which has become quite useful in economic analysis is the *constant elasticity of substitution* (*CES*) *production function*. For a discussion of this function, see [1].

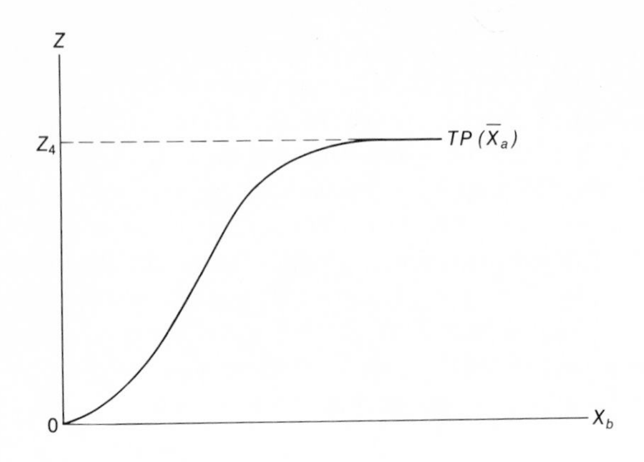

FIGURE **3-6**

Short-run production function

Before concluding this section, we should point out that the long-run problem of returns to scale can easily be related to the short-run problem of diminishing returns to one factor. For example, consider factor X_a to be capital goods (usually assumed fixed in the short run) and factor X_b to be labor, and then take the quantity of capital to be fixed at $\overline{X}_a$. Thus the horizontal line drawn at $\overline{X}_a$ in Figure 3-5 represents the short-run production function. That is, the total output of Z as a function of X_b is defined by all points on that horizontal line. If we envisage Figure 3-5 as looking down on the production "mountain" from above, then deriving the short-run production function amounts to slicing down through the mountain along the $\overline{X}_a$ line, and examining a cross section. The cross section would be of the shape in Figure 3-6.

The shape of the total product (*TP*) curve is only slightly different from the one given in Figure 3-2. In Figure 3-6, total product levels off at an output level of Z_4, indicating that the marginal product of X_b becomes zero but never becomes negative. Permitting a negative marginal product in Figure 3-2 caused *TP* to fall after reaching a maximum. Of course, we also know from Figure 3-5 that output levels off at Z_4. The isoquant representing that level of output becomes parallel to the X_b axis, indicating that further increases in X_b have no effect on output.

We could construct a family of *TP* curves similar to the one in Figure 3-6. That curve corresponds to holding X_a fixed at $\overline{X}_a$. By varying X_a or by taking slices parallel to the X_b axis (in Figure 3-5) we could construct any number of such curves.

A JOINT-PRODUCT PRODUCTION MODEL

We now turn to a second special case of our general production model (3-1) in which there are two outputs Z_a and Z_b and a single input X:

$$Q(Z_a, Z_b, X) = 0 \tag{3-24}$$

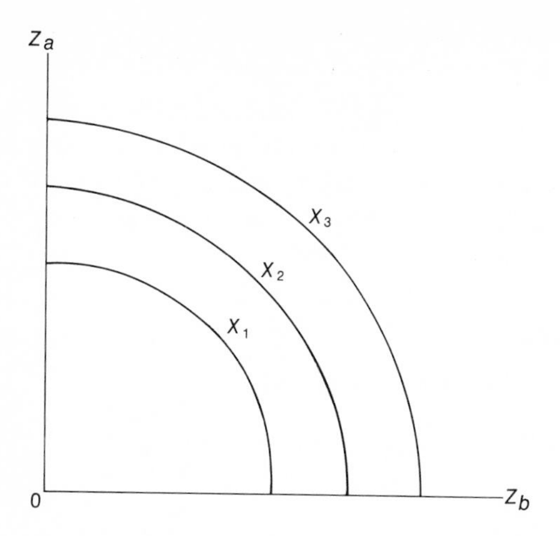

FIGURE 3-7

Production-transformation curves

If we assume that the production function can be solved for X, we can express (3-24) as

$$X = X(Z_a, Z_b) \tag{3-25}$$

where X denotes the minimum quantity of the single input required to produce Z_a units of product a and Z_b units of product b, and a and b are joint products produced in varying proportions by a single production process (factor of production). Joint products arise in firms in which the quantities of two or more products such as automobiles and trucks are technically interdependent.

Production-transformation curves provide us with a two-dimensional graphical representation of joint-product models of the type described by (3-25). A *production-transformation curve* is the locus of points which are geometrical representations of combinations of outputs Z_a and Z_b which can be produced from a given level of a single input X. Production-transformation curves are illustrated in Figure 3-7. The three production-transformation curves X_1, X_2, and X_3 represent the quantities of Z_a and Z_b.

Product transformation curves are usually assumed to have the following properties:

1. A combination of product outputs which lies on a product transformation curve X_2 which is above and to the right of another product transformation curve X_1 represents a factor input level that is higher than X_1.
2. Product transformation curves slope downward and to the right.
3. Product transformation curves can never intersect.

4. Product transformation curves are concave to the origin, i.e., the absolute slope of a product transformation curve increases towards the right.

The negative of the slope of the tangent to a point on a product transformation curve, the *rate of product transformation*, is the rate at which Z_a must be sacrificed in order to produce more Z_b without varying the input of X. The rate of product transformation RPT_{ab} between products a and b can be obtained from the total differential of the production function:

$$dX = \frac{\partial X}{\partial Z_a} dZ_a + \frac{\partial X}{\partial Z_b} dZ_b \tag{3-26}$$

Since $dX = 0$ for a given product transformation curve,

$$0 = \frac{\partial X}{\partial Z_a} dZ_a + \frac{\partial X}{\partial Z_b} dZ_b \tag{3-27}$$

and

$$\frac{dZ_a}{dZ_b} = -\frac{\partial X/\partial Z_b}{\partial X/\partial Z_a} \tag{3-28}$$

Since the *RPT* is the *negative* of the slope of the product transformation curve, $RPT = \dfrac{\partial X/\partial Z_b}{\partial X/\partial Z_a}$. Since $\partial X/\partial Z_b$ is the reciprocal of the marginal product of X with respect to Z_b and $\partial X/\partial Z_a$ is the reciprocal of the marginal product of X with respect to Z_a, the rate of product transformation also equals the ratio of the marginal product of X with respect to Z_a to the marginal product of X with respect to Z_b.

The concavity property of production-transformation curves implies that

$$\frac{\partial^2 Z_a}{\partial Z_b^2} < 0$$

Since the *RPT* is defined as the *negative* of $\partial Z_a/\partial Z_b$, concavity also implies an *increasing rate of production transformation* between any two products, i.e.,

$$-\frac{\partial^2 Z_a}{\partial Z_b^2} > 0 \tag{3-29}$$

The relation between (3-29) and diminishing marginal productivity can be analyzed in a manner similar to that used to investigate the implications of convex isoquants. The reader is urged to do so.

OTHER PRODUCTION MODELS

Thus far we have concerned ourselves with a very special class of production models, namely neoclassical marginal-analysis production models. Although we will treat several other types of production models in later chapters, it is appropriate that we at least summarize some of the proposed alternatives to the neoclassical model.

Linear programming production models

In Chapter 8 we will consider another general class of static equilibrium production models called *linear programming models*. Assumptions 2, 3, and 5 of the model described in this chapter will be replaced by the following four assumptions:

1. The firm has p independent processes or activities available, where an activity is defined as a particular way of combining a maximum of m variable factors with a maximum of n fixed factors for the production of a unit of output.
2. Each activity is characterized by a set of ratios of the quantities of the factors to the levels of each of the outputs. These ratios are constant and independent of the extent to which each activity is used.
3. The firm is constrained in its selection of activity levels by its fixed endowments of certain resources (fixed factors) required to support the p activities.
4. Two or more activities can be used simultaneously, subject to the limitations of the fixed factors available to the firm, and if this is done the quantities of the outputs and inputs will be the arithmetic sums of the quantities which would result if the activities were used separately.

Production models with indivisible inputs

The neoclassical production model outlined in this chapter is based on the assumption that all of the firm's factors of production and products are perfectly divisible. The firm's factor inputs were assumed to be perfectly divisible in acquisition and use. Indivisibility in acquisition implies that a certain factor input is indivisible in the sense that it can be obtained only in discrete units. That is, it is impossible to acquire the services of the particular factor in a quantity other than certain discrete amounts or "lumps." Indivisibility in use implies that this "lump" or "fixed factor" has to be used in combination with given amounts of other factor services if these other factors are to be efficiently employed.

The problem of indivisibility in use is treated in Chapter 8, where linear programming models of the firm are discussed. The linear programming assumption of fixed technical coefficients of production (fixed-factor proportions) is equivalent to assuming indivisibility in use. Indivisibility in acquisition and the problem of indivisible product outputs are examined in Chapter 10.

Production models with durable inputs

An implicit assumption in the production model described in this chapter was that all variable factors of production were nondurable. That is, the services of each unit of variable factor acquired by the firm were assumed to be completely exhausted during the planning period under consideration. If a variable factor service was acquired by the firm in one period it could not be used in the following period or any period thereafter.

In Chapters 15 and 16 the neoclassical production model is extended to include durable factor inputs, i.e., factor inputs whose use may be spread over time. Decisions concerning the acquisition of durable factor inputs are usually called *investment decisions* or *capital-budgeting decisions*. Several investment theories of the firm are outlined in Chapters 15 and 16.

In Chapter 1 we outlined a general theory of the firm in which factor input and product output decisions were based on three types of information: factor prices, product prices, and production technology. In order to determine if a particular durable factor should be purchased at the beginning of a planning horizon (consisting of n production periods) or during a planning horizon, and if so, in what quantities or "lumps," the profit-maximizing firm must have the following additional information (over and above the information required for single-period production decisions):

1. The conjectured useful life of the durable factor services.
2. The initial cost of one "lump" of the durable factors (capital goods).
3. The conjectured stream of revenue that will be associated with the use of the durable factors during each period of production.
4. The conjectured costs associated with the use of durable factors during each production period.
5. The conjectured product transformation function relating the durable factor services (as well as the nondurable factors) to the firm's products for each production period.
6. The conjectured discount rate over each production period.
7. The resale value of the durable factor at the end of each production period.

Given this information, the firm's multiperiod investment problem can be considered as a problem of maximizing the present worth of a conjectured stream of profit over n production periods. Although complete certainty and perfect foresight are assumed with regard to the above information, in Chapter 16 we introduce the notion of risk and uncertainty in investment decisions.

Engineering production models

Throughout the history of the development of the notion of the production function for the firm, economists have assumed that "the exact nature of the firm's production function has been predetermined by a set of technical decisions by the firm's engineers and technicians." Having disclaimed any responsibility as to the nature of the production function, economists then glibly postulate a production function which possesses the characteristics of the neoclassical model described earlier in this chapter. Unfortunately, all too few economists have chosen to ask the question, "What type of production function would an engineer use to describe the production processes of a firm?" With the exception of some early work by agricultural economists, the work of Chenery [6,7,9], Leontief [36], and Smith [54], and several other economists, there have been few attempts by economists working with engineers to subject production functions to analytical-experimental examination. (If one includes linear-programming studies in the category of analytical-experimental production studies, then the list of exceptions will be increased somewhat.)

As an analytical tool for analyzing the behavior of the complex technology of the modern production process, the neoclassical production model is usually completely nonoperational. For example, any attempt to describe the transportation of energy in the form of heat or electricity or material in the form of natural gas, petroleum, petroleum products, water, etc., requires a set of production models which differ considerably from the model described in this chapter. Smith [54, pp. 24–37] describes a number of interesting engineering production functions for such processes as electrical transmission, heat transmission, and gas transmission. Other production processes, to mention only a few, which are likely to require special attention include the production and transmission of electrical energy, multiple-pass regeneration processes, batch-reactor chemical processes, and processes involving reaction kinetics. If the economist is to understand and explain the behavior of such processes, he must become better acquainted with engineering concepts. This represents an area of research which is likely to yield high returns to both students and practitioners in the field of economics, business administration, and engineering.

Dynamic production models

The neoclassical production model is completely static. Neither the parameters which describe the production function nor the form of the production function itself are permitted to change over the time period considered. Yet we know very well that the nature of production processes (parameters and functional form) does change over time. Production processes which do change over time and are characterized by complex feedback mechanisms in which a portion of the output of the process in period T is fed back into the process as part of its input in period $T + K$ are called *dynamic processes*. Forrester in his book *Industrial Dynamics* has defined a dynamic model as "a description of how to generate the actions that are to be taken progressively through time." In Chapters 11 and 14 we consider several dynamic production models. As an example of a dynamic production model consider the following model proposed by Dorfman:

> If we consider a production program as continuous over a number of periods of time, specify the quantity of each input and output that becomes available at the beginning of each period as a function of activities in earlier periods, and seek to determine the level of each process in each period, the framework of a

dynamic analysis results. A genuine dynamic quality is imparted to the analysis when the limitations on the activities of any period are expressed in terms of the results of previous periods. In this way a feedback is introduced into the system, and the successive periods are linked together by a set of linear difference equations which determine the maximum rate of growth of the system, the level of operation of each process during each period, and any inherent tendency to cyclical behavior [13, p. 89].

Probabilistic production models

Complete certainty is another explicit assumption underlying the production model which was described in this chapter. The parameters of the production function were assumed to be fixed and known. Output is completely determined by the rate of factor inputs. In Chapter 14 we consider production models in which the rate of output depends on the rate of factor inputs as well as one or more random variables which are not under the complete control of management. In that chapter we also investigate models in which some of the parameters of the production function are random variables.

BIBLIOGRAPHY

[1] ARROW, K. J., H. B. CHENERY, B. S. MINHAS, and R. M. SOLOW. "Capital-Labor Substitution and Economic Efficiency," *Review of Economics and Statistics* (August, 1961), 225–250.

[2] BAUMOL, WILLIAM J. *Economic Theory and Operations Analysis.* Englewood Cliffs, N. J.: Prentice-Hall, Inc., 1965.

[3] BOULDING, KENNETH E., and W. ALLEN SPIVEY (Eds.). *Linear Programming and the Theory of the Firm.* New York: The Macmillan Co., 1960.

[4] CARLSON, SUNE. *A Study of the Theory of Production.* New York: Kelley & Millman, 1956.

[5] CASSELS, J. M. "On the Law of Variable Proportions," in *Explorations in Economics.* New York: McGraw-Hill Book Co., 1936.

[6] CHENERY, HOLLIS B. "Engineering Bases of Economic Analysis." Unpublished Ph.D. dissertation, Harvard University, Cambridge, Mass., 1949.

[7] CHENERY, HOLLIS B. "Engineering Production Functions," *Quarterly Journal of Economics*, **LXIII** (November, 1949), 507–531.

[8] CHENERY, HOLLIS B. "Overcapacity and the Acceleration Principle," *Econometrica*, **XX** (January, 1952), 1–28.

[9] CHENERY, HOLLIS B. "Process and Production Functions from Engineering Data," in Wassily Leontief (Ed.), *Studies in the Structure of the American Economy.* New York: Oxford University Press, 1953.

[10] CHU, KONG, and THOMAS H. NAYLOR. "A Dynamic Model of the Firm," *Management Science*, **XI** (May, 1965), 736–750.

[11] COHEN, KALMAN J., and RICHARD M. CYERT. *Theory of the Firm: Resource Allocation in a Market Economy.* Englewood Cliffs, N. J.: Prentice-Hall, Inc., 1965.

[12] DANO, SVEN. *Industrial Production Models.* New York: Springer-Verlag, 1966.

[13] DORFMAN, ROBERT. *Applications of Linear Programming to the Theory of the Firm.* Berkeley: University of California Press, 1951.

[14] DORFMAN, ROBERT, PAUL A. SAMUELSON, and ROBERT M. SOLOW. *Linear Programming and Economic Analysis.* New York: McGraw-Hill Book Co., 1958.

[15] FERGUSON, C. E. "Transformation Curve in Production Theory," *Southern Economic Journal,* **XXIX** (1962), 96–102.

[16] FERGUSON, C. E. *Microeconomic Theory.* Homewood, Ill.: Richard D. Irwin, Inc., 1966.

[17] FRIEDMAN, MILTON. *Price Theory.* Chicago: Aldine Publishing Co., 1962.

[18] FRISCH, RAGNAR. *Theory of Production.* Chicago: Rand McNally, 1965.

[19] FRISCH, RAGNAR. *Maxima and Minima: Theory and Economic Applications.* Chicago: Rand McNally, 1966.

[20] FURUBOTN, ERIK G. "The Adaptability of Fixed Productive Services in the Short Run," *Southern Economic Journal,* **XXVIII** (April, 1962), 329–339.

[21] GEORGESCU-ROEGEN, NICHOLAS. "Fixed Coefficients of Production and the Marginal Productivity Theory," *Review of Economic Studies,* **III** (1935), 40–49.

[22] GROSSE, ANNE P. "The Technological Structure of the Cotton Textile Industry," in Wassily Leontief (Ed.), *Studies in the Structure of the American Economy.* New York: Oxford University Press, 1953.

[23] HEADY, EARL O. "An Econometric Investigation of the Technology of Agricultural Production Functions," *Econometrica,* **XXV** (April, 1957), 249–268.

[24] HEADY, EARL O., and JOHN PESEK. "Expansion Paths for Some Production Functions," *Econometrica,* **XXVIII** (1960).

[25] HENDERSON, JAMES M., and RICHARD E. QUANDT. *Microeconomic Theory.* New York: McGraw-Hill, 1958.

[26] HENDERSON, JOHN S. "Marginal Productivity Analysis—A Defect and a Remedy," *Econometrica,* **XXI** (January, 1953), 155–168.

[27] HICKS, J. R. *Value and Capital.* Oxford: Clarendon Press, 1939.

[28] ICHIMURA, S. "A Critical Note on the Definition of Related Goods," *Review of Economic Studies,* **XVIII** (1950–51), 179–183.

[29] JEVONS, WILLIAM STANLEY. *The Theory of Political Economy,* 1871.

[30] KALDOR, NICHOLAS. "The Equilibrium of the Firm," *Economic Journal,* **XLIV**, (March, 1934), 60–76.

[31] KALDOR, NICHOLAS. "Limitational Factors and the Elasticity of Substitution," *Review of Economic Studies,* **IV** (1937), 162–165.

[32] KOOPMANS, TJALLING C. (Ed.). *Activity Analysis of Production and Allocation.* New York: John Wiley & Sons, 1951.

[33] KOOPMANS, TJALLING C. *Three Essays on the State of Economic Science.* New York: McGraw-Hill Book Co., 1957.

[34] KUENNE, ROBERT E. *The Theory of General Economic Equilibrium.* Princeton: Princeton University Press, 1963.

[35] LEONTIEF, WASSILY W. *The Structure of American Economy 1919–1939.* 2nd ed. New York: Oxford University Press, 1951.

[36] LEONTIEF, WASSILY W. (Ed.). *Studies in the Structure of the American Economy.* New York: Oxford University Press, 1953.

[37] LEONTIEF, WASSILY W. "The Structure of the U.S. Economy," *Scientific American*, **CCXII**, No. 4 (April, 1965), 25–35.

[38] LEVINE, R.A., and RAINEY, R. B. "Random Variations and Sampling Models in Production Economics," *Journal of Political Economy*, **LXVIII** (June, 1960), 219–231.

[39] MACHLUP, FRITZ. "On the Meaning of the Marginal Product," in *Explorations in Economics*. New York: McGraw-Hill Book Co., 1936.

[40] MAKOWER, HELEN. *Activity Analysis and the Theory of Economic Equilibrium*. New York: St. Martin's Press, 1957.

[41] MENGER, KARL. "The Properties of the Production Function," in O. Morgenstern (Ed.), *Economic Activity Analysis*. New York: John Wiley & Sons, 1954.

[42] MODIGLIANI, FRANCO, and FRANZ E. HOHN. "Production Planning Over Time and the Nature of the Expectation and Planning Horizon," *Econometrica* **XXIII** (January, 1955), 46–66.

[43] MORGENSTERN, O. (Ed.). *Economic Activity Analysis*. New York: John Wiley & Sons, 1954.

[44] NAYLOR, THOMAS H. "Some Theoretical Models of the Firm." Unpublished Ph.D. dissertation, Department of Economics, Tulane University, New Orleans, Louisiana, 1964.

[45] NAYLOR, THOMAS H. "A Kuhn-Tucker Model of the Multi-Product, Multi-Factor Firm," *Southern Economic Journal*, **XXXI** (April, 1965), 324–330.

[46] NAYLOR, THOMAS H. "The Theory of the Firm: A Comparison of Marginal Analysis and Linear Programming," *Southern Economic Journal*, **XXXII** (January, 1966), 263–274.

[47] PFOUTS, RALPH W. "The Theory of Cost and Production in the Multi-Product Firm," *Econometrica*, **XXIX** (October, 1961), 650–658.

[48] ROBINSON, JOAN. *The Economics of Imperfect Competition*. London: Macmillan & Co., 1933.

[49] ROBINSON, JOAN. "The Production Function," *Economic Journal*, **LXV** (1955), 67–71.

[50] SAMUELSON, PAUL A. *Foundations of Economic Analysis*. Cambridge: Harvard University Press, 1947.

[51] SCHWEYER, HERBERT E. *Process Engineering Economics*. New York: McGraw-Hill Book Co., 1955.

[52] SHEPHARD, RONALD W. *Cost and Production Functions*. Princeton, N. J.: Princeton University Press, 1953.

[53] SCHULTZ, HENRY. "Marginal Productivity and the General Pricing Process," *Journal of Political Economy*, **XXXVII** (1929), 505–551.

[54] SMITH, VERNON L. *Investment and Production*. Cambridge, Mass.: Harvard University Press, 1961.

[55] STIGLER, GEORGE J. "Production and Distribution Theories in the Short Run," *Journal of Political Economy*, **XLVII** (1939), 307–327.

[56] STIGLER, GEORGE J. *Production and Distribution Theories: The Formative Period*. New York: Macmillan & Co., 1946.

[57] VON THUNEN, J. H. *Der Isolierte Staat*, 1826.

[58] WALTERS, A. A. "Production and Cost Functions: An Econometric Survey," *Econometrica*, **XXXI** (1963), 1–66.

[59] WELDON, J. C. "The Multi-Product Firm," *Canadian Journal of Economics and Political Science*, **XIV** (1948), 176–190.

[60] WHITIN, T. M., and PESTON, M. H. "Random Variations, Risk, and Returns to Scale," *Quarterly Journal of Economics*, **LXVIII** (November, 1954), 603–612.

[61] WICKSELL, KNUT. *Lectures on Political Economy*. London: Routledge and Kegan Paul, 1934.

[62] WICKSTEED, PHILIP H. *An Essay on the Co-ordination of the Laws of Distribution*. London: Macmillan, 1894.

4

Theory of cost

INTRODUCTION

In the preceding two chapters we have considered two of the three types of information which the firm's decision makers are assumed to possess: product-demand information and production-technology information. The third type of information which is assumed to be available—factor-supply information—is considered in this chapter. Factor-supply information can take one of two alternative forms depending on the relative importance of the firm as a buyer of factors of production.

If for a particular factor input the firm is one of a large number of buyers of that factor and is unable to influence the price it must pay in order to obtain that factor, then the market for the factor is said to be *perfectly competitive*. When factors are purchased in a perfectly competitive market the firm must accept factor prices as fixed and beyond its control. The unskilled labor market faced by a small firm in a large industrial city is an example of a competitive factor market.

Although the assumption of a perfectly competitive factor market is no doubt a reasonable assumption for some factor inputs purchased by some firms, it is clearly not valid for all factors for all firms. An alternative case arises when the firm's purchases of a factor are large enough to influence the unit price of that factor. If a firm is the sole purchaser of a particular factor of production, the firm is said to be a *monopsonist*. If a firm is one of a relatively small number of purchasers of a given factor input and is able to influence the price it pays for the factor by varying the amount of the factor it purchases, then the firm is said to be an *oligopsonist*. We shall use the term *monopsonistic competition* as an all-inclusive term to describe any factor market in which a firm can affect factor prices by adjusting the quantity of its purchases of a given factor. Whenever monopsonistic competition occurs for a particular factor we must postulate the supply situation surrounding the given factor.

Hence if the firm faces a competitive market for a particular factor, we shall assume that the unit price for that factor is fixed and known by the firm's decision makers. On the other hand, if the firm behaves as a monopsonist with regard to its purchases of a particular factor, we shall assume that the factor-supply function for the given factor is known.

In the following section we utilize our knowledge of factor-supply conditions to develop the concept of cost. We also define a *cost equation* as a functional relationship relating total cost to the quantity of the various factors of production purchased by the firm. Although the firm's decision makers may be able to make considerable use of *cost equations*, a more useful form of cost information is the *cost function.* A *cost function* is an equation which expresses total cost as a function of production output (outputs) rather than factor-input quantities. Four alternative cost functions are considered in this chapter:

1. A single-product competitive model
2. A multiproduct competitive model
3. A single-product monopsonistic model
4. A multiproduct monopsonistic model

THE CONCEPT OF COST

Costs are defined by economists in terms of forgone alternatives or opportunities. The cost of a given factor of production is the maximum value that the factor could earn in an alternative use. Equivalently, the cost of using a particular factor input to produce a given product is the value of the best opportunity which is forgone in not using the factor input in an alternative way.

Confusion sometimes arises between the way in which economists view costs and the way accountants view costs. *Accounting costs* or *explicit costs* are those outlays of the firm which we usually think of as expenses. Expenses include all reductions in assets such as payments for wages and salaries, outlays for materials, and explicit payments for rent and interest. If a firm produces a particular product Z, its owners (who are assumed to be separate from management) incur certain accounting costs by purchasing the resources necessary to produce Z. The owners also incur some imputed or opportunity costs, and a complete accounting of profit or loss requires that these imputed costs be taken into consideration. The pure economic profit that the owners of the firm earn by producing product Z may be conceptualized as the difference between accounting profit[1] and what could be earned by the best alternative use of the owners' money.

If the firm is confronted with a perfectly competitive factor-input market for each of its factors of production, then total cost C can be expressed as a linear function of its factor-input quantities:

$$C = C_1X_1 + C_2X_2 + \cdots + C_iX_i + \cdots + C_mX_m \tag{4-1}$$

[1] Accounting profit is equal to total revenue minus accounting costs.

where C_i denotes the unit price of the ith factor input. Under perfect competition the C_i's are fixed and known. If the market for the ith factor is monopsonistic, then C_i may be a function of the rate of input of X_i:

$$C_i = C_i(X_i) \tag{4-2}$$

or more generally,

$$C_i = C_i(X_1, X_2, \ldots, X_m) \tag{4-3}$$

We shall call equations (4-1), (4-2), and (4-3) *cost equations*, since total cost is expressed as a function of the firm's factor-input quantities.

Although the firm's decision makers may be able to make considerable use of *cost equations* relating total cost to factor inputs, there exists an alternative way of representing costs, which, from the standpoint of the type of information desired by the profit-maximizing firm, is more incisive than the cost equation. The alternative to the cost equation is the *cost function*, which expresses total cost as a function of output. If the product prices or demand functions are known for each product produced by the firm, and if total cost is expressed as a function of the quantities of these products produced by the firm, then total profit can be expressed as a function of output only.

A SINGLE-PRODUCT COMPETITIVE MODEL

Constrained cost minimization

A firm produces a single product Z from m factors of production $X_1, X_2, \ldots, X_m$. The firm's production function

$$Z = Z(X_1, X_2, \ldots, X_m) \tag{4-4}$$

satisfies all of the assumptions of the single-product production model described in Chapter 3. The firm's cost equation takes the following form

$$C = C_1X_1 + C_2X_2 + \cdots + C_mX_m + F = \sum_{i=1}^{m} C_iX_i + F \tag{4-5}$$

where C_i is the competitive price of the ith factor input and F is the value of total cost at zero output rate. Assume that the objective of the firm is to minimize the total cost C of maintaining a prescribed output level $\bar{Z}$. That is, the firm wishes to minimize (4-5) subject to

$$\bar{Z} = Z(X_1, X_2, \ldots, X_m) \tag{4-6}$$

where $\bar{Z}$ is any positive value of Z.

Again using the Lagrangian multiplier method, we define the function

$$L = \sum_{i=1}^{m} C_iX_i + F + \lambda[\bar{Z} - Z(X_1, X_2, \ldots, X_m)] \tag{4-7}$$

where λ is a Lagrangian multiplier. Setting the partial derivatives of L with respect to the X_i's and λ equal to zero, we obtain

$$L_i = C_i - \lambda Z_i = 0 \qquad i = 1, 2, \ldots, m \tag{4-8}$$

$$L_\lambda = \bar{Z} - Z(X_1, X_2, \ldots, X_m) = 0 \tag{4-9}$$

Following the procedure outlined in the appendix to Chapter 2, it is easy to show that the Lagrangian multiplier is equal to marginal cost (see also, Samuelson [38, pp. 67–68]):

$$\frac{dC}{dZ} = \lambda \tag{4-10}$$

Equation (4-8) may be rewritten as

$$\frac{1}{\lambda} = \frac{Z_i}{C_i} \qquad i = 1, 2, \ldots, m \tag{4-11}$$

which states that the marginal productivity of the last dollar must be the same for each factor [38, p. 60]. It follows from (4-11) that for any two factors a and b,

$$\frac{Z_a}{Z_b} = \frac{C_a}{C_b} \qquad a, b = 1, 2, \ldots, m \tag{4-12}$$

and by the implicit-function rule,

$$-\frac{\partial X_a}{\partial X_b} = \frac{C_b}{C_a} \qquad a, b = 1, 1, \ldots, m \tag{4-13}$$

where $-\partial X_a/\partial X_b$ is the marginal rate of substitution between factors a and b.

The second-order conditions for constrained cost minimization require that the principal minors of the bordered Hessian determinant $\bar{S}_m$ be negative, where

$$\bar{S}_m = \begin{vmatrix} -\lambda Z_{11} & -\lambda Z_{12} & \cdots & -\lambda Z_{1m} & -Z_1 \\ -\lambda Z_{21} & -\lambda Z_{22} & \cdots & -\lambda Z_{2m} & -Z_2 \\ \vdots & & & & \\ -\lambda Z_{m1} & -\lambda Z_{m2} & \cdots & -\lambda Z_{mm} & -Z_m \\ -Z_1 & -Z_2 & \cdots & -Z_m & 0 \end{vmatrix}$$

Equation (4-13) states that when optimum quantities of any two factors a and b are utilized in the production process, the ratio of their factor prices must be equal to their rate of technical substitution.

Consider a special case of the single-product firm in which only two factors a and b are required to produce a single product. The production function is given by

$$Z = Z(X_a, X_b) \tag{4-14}$$

We can represent the firm's constrained cost-minimization problem graphically through the use of isoquants in Figure 4-1. The isoquants Z_1, Z_2, and Z_3 are

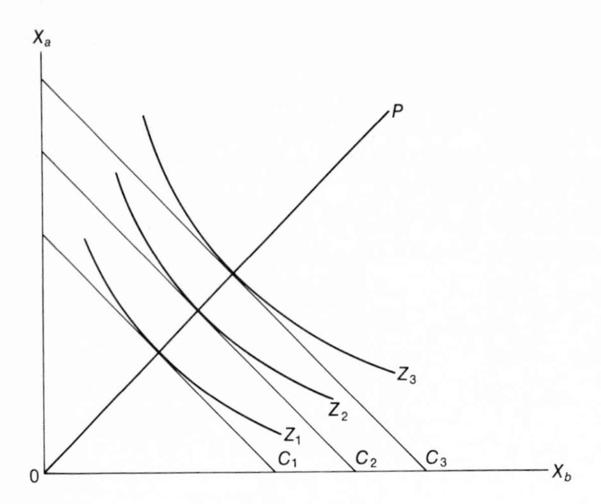

FIGURE 4-1

assumed to possess the four properties outlined in Chapter 3. The straight lines C_1, C_2, C_3 are called *isocost* lines and represent the locus of combinations of X_a and X_b which result in a total cost of $\bar{C}$. For example, every combination of X_a and X_b which lies on the isocost line C_2 yields a total cost of C_2.

Suppose the firm's decision makers want to minimize the cost of producing a particular quantity of output Z_1. This is equivalent to saying that the firm wants to find the combination of X_a and X_b which lies on isoquant Z_1 and is on the isocost line closest to the origin. The optimum combination of X_a and X_b lies at the point of tangency between the isoquant Z_1 and the isocost line C_1. At that point the slope of the isoquant $\partial X_a/\partial X_b$ is just equal to the slope of the isocost line $-C_b/C_a$ or

$$RTS_{ab} = \frac{-\partial X_a}{\partial X_b} = \frac{C_b}{C_a} \tag{4-15}$$

The locus of tangency points (OP in Figure 4-1) for all values of $\bar{Z}$ is called the *expansion path*. The goal of cost minimization implies that only those factor-input combinations which lie on the expansion path will be selected. The expansion path is an implicit function of X_a and X_b:

$$H(X_a, X_b) = 0 \tag{4-16}$$

If Z is homogeneous of degree K (where K is a constant), i.e., if

$$Z(tX_a, tX_b) = t^K Z(X_a, X_b) \tag{4-17}$$

where t is any real positive number, then it can be shown that the expansion path will be *linear* [19, pp. 62–64]. Hence, in general, the expansion path will *not* be linear. Figure 4-1 is, therefore, a special case.

Theory of short-run cost functions

The *short run* is a term used by economists to describe a period of time sufficiently short to prevent the firm from varying the quantities of some of its factor inputs. In the short run, some of the firm's factor inputs such as buildings, land, heavy equipment, etc. are *fixed*. These factors are called *fixed factors* of production. Factors which are not fixed and vary with output are called *variable factors*.

The logic of the solution to the cost-minimization problem described in the preceding section provides the basis for the derivation of short-run cost functions. Consider the system of equations consisting of the production function (4-4), the cost equation (4-5), and the set of m first-order cost minimization conditions (4-8):

$$Z = Z(X_1, X_2, \ldots, X_m) \tag{4-18}$$

$$C = \sum_{i=1}^{m} C_i X_i + F \tag{4-19}$$

$$C_i - \lambda Z_i = 0 \qquad i = 1, 2, \ldots, m \tag{4-20}$$

This system of $m + 2$ equations in $m + 3$ unknowns ($X_1, X_2, \ldots, X_m, Z, C$, and λ) can be reduced to a single equation in which total cost C is an explicit function of the quantity of output Z plus the cost of the fixed factors F:

$$C = C(Z) + F \tag{4-21}$$

Equation (4-21) is called a *cost function*, where C denotes the minimum cost of producing any given amount of output Z. The following special cost functions can be derived from (4-21).

Total cost function Although total cost functions may take on many different forms, depending on the characteristics of the production function, (4-21) represents the general form of the total cost function. A special form of cost function, the cubic cost function, possesses many of the properties which economists have associated with the "typical" firm:

$$TC = AZ^3 - BZ^2 + CZ + D \tag{4-22}$$

where A, B, C, and D are positive constants.

Figure 4-2 contains a graphical illustration of a cubic cost function. Note that the total cost function increases initially at a decreasing rate and then at an increasing rate with increases in output. The shape of the cost function changes from concave to convex as output increases. This implies that the cost function in our example was derived from a production function whose properties are consistent with the "law of variable proportions."

Total fixed cost function Fixed costs are those costs that are independent of output. They might include depreciation, rent, and the salaries of executives. In the short run these costs remain constant for all possible values of Z. For our

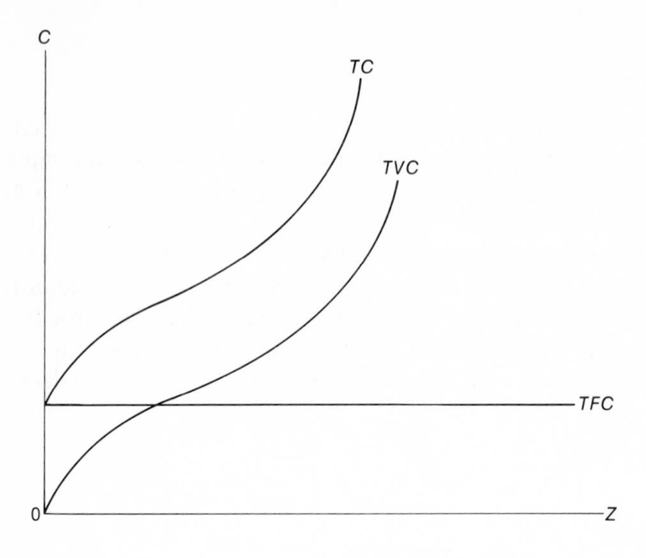

FIGURE 4-2

cubic total cost function, total fixed cost TFC is equal to D. More generally, from (4-21),

$$TFC = F \tag{4-23}$$

Total variable cost function Total variable cost TVC is defined as the difference between total cost TC and total fixed cost TFC. In general, again using (4-21),

$$TVC = C(Z) \tag{4-24}$$

and for our cubic total cost function,

$$TVC = AZ^3 - BZ^2 + CZ \tag{4-25}$$

Total variable cost is, therefore, the part of total cost which varies with the rate of output. The relationship between the total cost function, the total fixed cost function, and the total variable cost function is illustrated graphically in Figure 4-2.

Average total cost function Average total cost ATC is the total cost per unit of output,

$$ATC = \frac{TC}{Z} \tag{4-26}$$

The average total cost function associated with (4-22) is illustrated in Figure 4-3. The typical textbook average cost function decreases, reaches a minimum, and then increases. The minimum value of ATC can be obtained geometrically from the total cost function by finding the straight line passing through the origin of

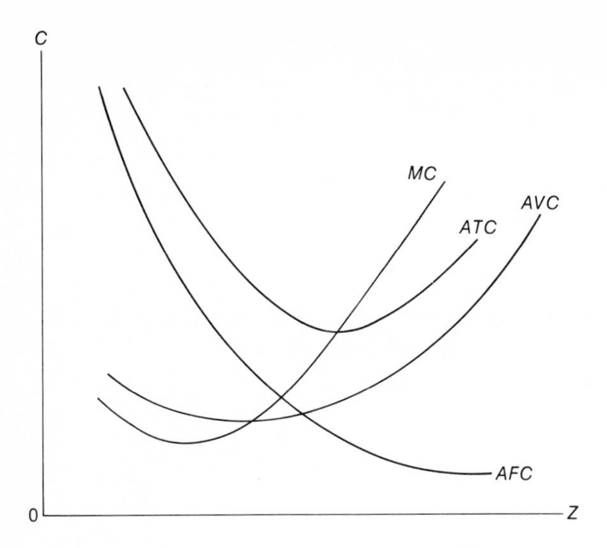

FIGURE 4-3

Figure 4-2 which is tangent to TC. The output associated with the point of tangency is the output at which average total cost is minimized. Alternatively, the minimum value of ATC can be found by setting $d(ATC)/dZ$ equal to zero.

Average fixed cost function Average fixed cost AFC is simply total fixed cost per unit of output

$$AFC = \frac{TFC}{Z} \tag{4-27}$$

The average fixed cost function is shown in Figure 4-3. Since the fixed cost is spread over a larger number of units as output is increased, the AFC curve will be a rectangular hyperbola regardless of the shape of the total cost function.

Average variable cost function Average variable cost AVC is total variable cost per unit of output

$$AVC = \frac{TVC}{Z} = ATC - AFC \tag{4-28}$$

The relationship among the three average cost functions is illustrated in Figure 4-3. With increases in output AVC decreases, reaches a minimum, and then increases. The average variable cost function reaches a minimum before the average total cost function does. Since AVC is a part of ATC, AVC is below ATC in Figure 4-3. The minimum value of AVC can be obtained geometrically from the total variable cost function by finding the straight line passing through the origin of Figure 4-2 which is tangent to TVC. The output at the point of tangency is the output at which average variable cost is minimized.

Marginal-cost function Marginal cost MC is the rate of change of total cost with respect to output

$$MC = \frac{d(TC)}{dZ} \tag{4-29}$$

or

$$MC = \frac{d(TVC)}{dZ} \tag{4-30}$$

since the derivatives of total fixed cost is zero. We can derive the following interesting relationship between MC, ATC, and AVC.

ATC will be a minimum when

$$\frac{d(ATC)}{dZ} = 0 \tag{4-31}$$

or

$$\frac{d(TC/Z)}{dZ} = \frac{Z[d(TC)/dZ] - TC}{Z^2} = 0 \tag{4-32}$$

Rewriting (4-32) we get

$$\frac{d(TC)}{dZ} = \frac{TC}{Z} \tag{4-33}$$

or

$$MC = ATC \tag{4-34}$$

That is, ATC is equal to MC when ATC is at a minimum (see Figure 4-3). Similarly, we can show that AVC is equal to MC when AVC is at a minimum.

Theory of long-run cost functions

The short run was defined as a period of time in which some of the firm's factors of production are fixed. In the *long run* all of the firm's factors of production are variable. The derivation of long-run cost functions is a logical extension of the derivation of short-run cost functions.

The firm's conjectured production function in the long run is given by

$$Z = Z(X_1, X_2, \ldots, X_m, Y_1, Y_2, \ldots, Y_n) \tag{4-35}$$

where the X_i's are the same variable factors which appeared in (4-18) and the Y_j's are the factors which were assumed to be fixed in the short run. Although the Y_j's were fixed in (4-18), they are variable in (4-35). The long-run cost equation is

$$C = \sum_{i=1}^{m} C_i X_i + F(Y_1, Y_2, \ldots, Y_n) \tag{4-36}$$

Note that F is no longer a constant as was the case in (4-19). It is now simply the total cost associated with the factors which in the short run were assumed to be held constant but are variable in the long run. To minimize the total cost of producing a given output level $\bar{Z}$ subject to the production constraint (4-35) we define the Lagrangian function

$$L = \sum_{i=1}^{m} C_i X_i + F + \lambda[\bar{Z} - Z(X_1, \ldots, X_m, Y_1, \ldots, Y_n)]$$

Taking partial derivatives and setting them equal to zero, we obtain for any output Z,

$$C_i - \lambda \frac{\partial Z}{\partial X_i} = 0 \qquad i = 1, 2, \ldots, m \tag{4-37}$$

$$\frac{\partial F}{\partial Y_j} - \lambda \frac{\partial Z}{\partial Y_j} = 0 \qquad j = 1, 2, \ldots, n \tag{4-38}$$

$$\bar{Z} - Z(X_1, X_2, \ldots, X_m, Y_1, Y_2, \ldots, Y_n) = 0 \tag{4-39}$$

Combining these equations with (4-36), we have $m + n + 2$ equations in $m + n + 3$ unknowns. Solving for C in terms of Z, we obtain the long-run total cost function

$$C = C(Z) \tag{4-40}$$

where C denotes the minimum cost of producing any given amount of output Z. Since there are no fixed factors in the long run, no fixed cost term is present in (4-40). Long-run average cost and marginal cost can be obtained directly from (4-40), since

$$TC = TVC = C \tag{4-41}$$

That is,

$$ATC = AVC = \frac{C}{Z} \tag{4-42}$$

and

$$MC = \frac{dC}{dZ} \tag{4-43}$$

As in the case of the short run, the shape of long-run cost functions depends on (1) the properties of the production function and (2) factor-input costs. If the long-run ATC has a minimum, the long-run MC will be equal to the long-run ATC at the minimum value of the ATC. From the above analysis, it can be seen that the derivation of long-run cost functions follows logically from that of short-run cost functions.

As an instructive exercise, the reader may wish to derive a long-run cost function for a *specific* production function and cost equation. One good example

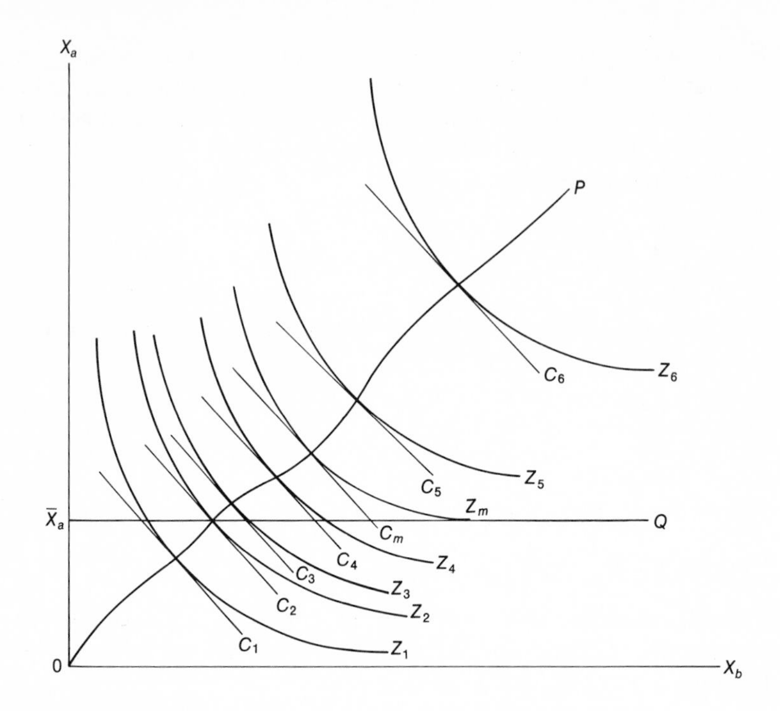

FIGURE 4-4

would be the well-known Cobb-Douglas production function for the two-factor case:

$$Z = AX_a^{\alpha}X_b^{\beta} \qquad (A, \alpha, \beta \text{ positive constants})$$

Given fixed prices for the two factors and $\beta = 1 - \alpha$ (thereby specifying constant returns to scale), the long-run total cost function is of the form

$$C = KZ$$

where K is a constant. For an explicit derivation of the above cost function, see Henderson and Quandt [19, p. 66].

Isoquant analysis

Using isoquant analysis, we can demonstrate the relation between the long-run and short-run cost functions graphically. Assume we wish to derive these functions for the production function given by (4-14). Furthermore, we take the prices of the two factors to be fixed (i.e., determined in competitive markets). In other words, we have a single-product, two-factor competitive model. Figure 4-4 illustrates the derivation of the expansion path OP for this model. The expansion path in Figure 4-4 is nonlinear to indicate the general case. Of course,

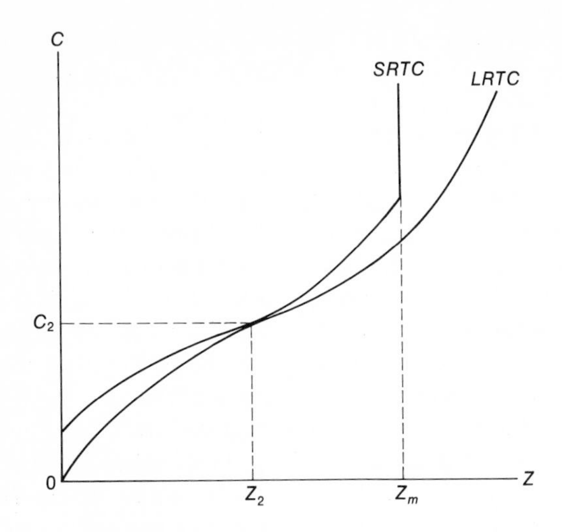

FIGURE **4-5**

as we have seen earlier, if the production function is homogeneous, the expansion path must be a straight line.

The path OP is a *long-run* expansion path. The next question concerns the analogous function in the *short run*, i.e., a "short-run expansion path." In the short run, the quantity of factor X_a is considered to be fixed at $\bar{X}_a$. Clearly, the horizontal line $\bar{X}_aQ$ defines the short-run expansion path: to increase output in the short run, the firm can only increase the quantity of X_b, since X_a is fixed at $\bar{X}_a$.

Finally, we can derive the desired long-run and short-run cost functions. The long-run expansion path OP in Figure 4-4 provides the information for the long-run cost function and the short-run path $\bar{X}_aQ$ for the short-run cost function. For example, one point on OP is the tangency point between isoquant Z_2 and isocost line C_2. This point is plotted in Figure 4-5, where we measure total cost vertically and total output horizontally. In a like manner, all other points on the long-run expansion path OP are plotted resulting in the long-run cost function *LRTC*.

The next step is to perform the same operation for the short-run function: transfer the cost-output values defined by each point on $\bar{X}_aQ$ in Figure 4-4 to Figure 4-5. The result is the short-run cost function *SRTC*. Observe in Figure 4-4 that the two expansion paths have one point in common, i.e., the intersection point which corresponds to an output of Z_2 and a cost of C_2. In Figure 4-5, this same point is the tangency point between *SRTC* and *LRTC*. Notice that at all other output levels *SRTC* exceeds *LRTC*. This follows, of course, from the fact that, in the long run, all factors are variable; consequently, each level of output is produced at minimum possible cost. In the short run, however, the firm does not have perfect flexibility, and is constrained by the invariability of factor X_a.

Several other properties of Figure 4-5 are noteworthy. The short-run cost function has a positive intercept on the C axis, while the long-run function begins at zero. This reflects the fact that fixed costs exist only in the short run. Also, *SRTC* becomes vertical at an output level of Z_m, while *LRTC* merely begins to increase at an increasing rate. The explanation for these two phenomena is totally different. The *SRTC* function rises because of the law of diminishing returns, i.e., the application of more and more X_b to the fixed quantity of the other factor, $\bar{X}_a$. The *LRTC* function rises because of the assumption that decreasing returns to scale prevail at relatively high output levels.

A further exercise is left to the reader. First, construct the *SRTC* functions corresponding to a number of other fixed levels of X_a. These other functions should each be tangent to the *LRTC* function at different output levels. (It should be apparent to the reader that the *LRTC* function may be conceived of as the "envelope curve" to all possible *SRTC* functions.) Second, derive graphically the long-run and short-run average and marginal cost functions from Figure 4-5. A hint is that the tangency point in Figure 4-5 implies that long-run and short-run *marginal* costs are equal at output Z_2 (the slopes to the total cost functions are equal), and that long-run and short-run total *average* costs are equal at the same output (the slope of a straight line from the origin to the tangency point measures average cost).

A MULTIPRODUCT COMPETITIVE MODEL

Up to this point our analysis of cost functions has been limited to the case where the firm produces a single product. The concept of the short-run cost function can easily be extended to the multifactor firm by redefining the production function as

$$Q(Z_1, \ldots, Z_p, X_1, \ldots, X_m) = 0 \tag{4-44}$$

where Z_k denotes the kth product. In order to minimize the cost of producing given amounts of outputs $\bar{Z}_1, \bar{Z}_2, \ldots, \bar{Z}_p$ we define the Lagrangian function

$$L = \sum_{i=1}^{m} C_i X_i + F + \lambda Q(\bar{Z}_1, \bar{Z}_2, \ldots, \bar{Z}_p, X_1, \ldots, X_m) \tag{4-45}$$

Taking partial derivatives and setting them equal to zero, we obtain

$$C_i + \lambda \frac{\partial Q}{\partial X_i} = 0 \qquad i = 1, \ldots, m \tag{4-46}$$

$$\lambda \frac{\partial Q}{\partial \bar{Z}_k} = 0 \qquad k = 1, \ldots, p \tag{4-47}$$

$$Q(\bar{Z}_1, \ldots, \bar{Z}_p, X_1, \ldots, X_m) = 0 \tag{4-48}$$

Note that equation (4-46) is identical to equations (4-8) and (4-20) of the single-product model. In (4-47) the Langrangian multiplier λ is assumed to be positive. The partial derivative of Q with respect to $\bar{Z}_k$ will indeed be equal to zero, since Q is defined as zero. By appending the cost equation

$$C = \sum_{i=1}^{m} C_i X_i + F \tag{4-49}$$

to the system of equations described by (4-45), (4-46), and (4-47) we obtain the following total cost function:

$$C = C(\bar{Z}_1, \bar{Z}_2, \ldots, \bar{Z}_p) + F \tag{4-50}$$

where C denotes the minimum total cost of producing output quantities $\bar{Z}_1, \bar{Z}_2, \ldots, \bar{Z}_p$.

Pfouts [34] has treated the theory of cost for multiproduct firms in considerable detail. Long-run cost functions can be derived in a straightforward manner for the multiproduct firm.

A SINGLE-PRODUCT MONOPSONISTIC MODEL

In the preceding sections the firm was assumed to purchase all of its variable factors of production in perfectly competitive markets. The prices of variable factors were fixed and known. We now turn our attention to the case where the firm cannot purchase unlimited amounts of a particular factor input at a uniform price. *Monopsonistic competition* is said to exist when the price which the firm must play for a given factor input depends on the number of units purchased. The factor price C_i of the ith variable factor is of the form

$$C_i = C_i(X_i) \qquad i = 1, 2, \ldots, m \tag{4-51}$$

The total cost equation is still

$$C = \sum_{i=1}^{m} C_i X_i + F \tag{4-52}$$

where C_i is now defined by (4-51).

To minimize (4-52) subject to

$$\bar{Z} = Z(X_1, \ldots, X_m) \tag{4-53}$$

equation (4-8) is replaced by

$$C_i + \frac{\partial C_i}{\partial X_i} \cdot X_i - \lambda Z_i = 0 \qquad i = 1, \ldots, m \tag{4-54}$$

This is the only change in the equilibrium conditions. The difference arising due to the firm's monopsonistic power is the term $(\partial C_i/\partial X_i) \cdot X_i$, which appears in

(4-54) but not (4-8). From (4-52), (4-53), and (4-54) we can derive a cost function for the monopsonistic firm using the same approach that we took with the competitive firm:

$$C = C(Z) + F \tag{4-55}$$

However, it is unlikely that the *linear* isocost curves (illustrated in Figure 4-1) for the competitive model will apply in the monopsonistic case.

A MULTIPRODUCT MONOPSONISTIC MODEL

By combining the analysis of the preceding two sections we can derive a cost function for the multiproduct monopsonistic firm. We leave the development of this model to the reader.

BIBLIOGRAPHY

[1] ANDREWS, P. W. S. *Manufacturing Business.* New York: The Macmillan Co., 1949.

[2] APEL, HANS. "Marginal Cost Constancy and Its Implications," *American Economic Review*, **XXXVIII** (December, 1948), 870–885.

[3] BAUMOL, WILLIAM J. *Economic Theory and Operations Analysis.* Englewood Cliffs, N. J.: Prentice-Hall, Inc., 1965.

[4] BECKMAN, M. J. "Fixed Technological Cost Coefficients and the Short-Run Cost Curve," *Kyklos*, **IX** (1956), 384–386.

[5] BISHOP, R. L. "Cost Discontinuities, Declining Costs and Marginal Analysis," *American Economic Review*, **XXXVIII** (1948), 607–617.

[6] BREMS, HANS. "A Discontinuous Cost Function," *American Economic Review*, **XLIII** (September, 1952), 577–586.

[7] CARTTER, ALLAN M. *Theory of Wages and Employment.* Homewood, Ill.: Richard D. Irwin, Inc., 1959.

[8] COHEN, KALMAN J., and RICHARD M. CYERT. *Theory of the Firm: Resource Allocation in a Market Economy.* Englewood Cliffs, N. J.: Prentice-Hall, Inc., 1965.

[9] DANO, SVEN. *Industrial Production Models.* New York: Springer-Verlag, 1966.

[10] DOUGLAS, PAUL H. *The Theory of Wages.* New York: Macmillan Co., 1934.

[11] EITEMAN, W. J. "Factors Determining the Location of the Least Cost Point," *American Economic Review*, **XXXVII** (December, 1947), 910–918.

[12] EITEMAN, W. J. "The Least Cost Point, Capacity, and Marginal Analysis," *American Economic Review*, **XXXVIII** (December, 1948), 899–904.

[13] EITEMAN, W. J., and G. E. GUTHRIE. "The Shape of Average Cost Curves," *American Economic Review*, **XLII** (December, 1952), 832–838.

[14] ELLIS, HOWARD S., and WILLIAM FELLNER. "External Economics and Diseconomies," in George J. Stigler and Kenneth E. Boulding (Eds.), *Readings in Price Theory*. Homewood, Ill.: Richard D. Irwin, Inc., 1952.

[15] FERGUSON, C. E. *Microeconomic Theory.* Homewood, Ill.: Richard D. Irwin, Inc., 1966.

[16] FRIEDMAN, MILTON. *Price Theory.* Chicago: Aldine Publishing Co., 1962.

[17] HAINES, W. W. "Capacity Production and the Least Cost Point," *American Economic Review*, **XXXVIII** (September, 1948), 617–624.

[18] HEADY, EARL O., and JOHN PESEK. "Expansion Paths for Some Production Functions," *Econometrica*, **XXVIII** (1960).

[19] HENDERSON, JAMES M., and RICHARD E. QUANDT. *Microeconomic Theory.* New York: McGraw-Hill, 1958.

[20] HICKS, JOHN R. *The Theory of Wages.* London: Macmillan & Co., 1930.

[21] HICKS, JOHN R. *Value and Capital.* Oxford: Clarendon Press, 1946.

[22] HIRSHLEIFER, JACK. "An Exposition of the Equilibrium of the Firm: Symmetry Between Product and Factor Analysis," *Economica*, **XXIX** (August, 1962), 263–268.

[23] JOHNSTON, J. *Statistical Cost Analysis.* New York: McGraw-Hill Book Co., 1960.

[24] LEFTWICH, RICHARD H. *The Price System and Resource Allocation* (3rd ed.). New York: Holt, Rinehart and Winston, 1966.

[25] LESOURNE, JACQUES. *Economic Analysis and Industrial Management.* Englewood Cliffs, N. J.: Prentice-Hall, Inc., 1963.

[26] MAKOWER, H., and WILLIAM J. BAUMOL. "The Analogy Between Producer and Consumer Equilibrium Analysis," *Economica*, **XVII** (1950), 63–80.

[27] MAUER, WILLIAM A., and THOMAS H. NAYLOR. "Monopolistic-Monopsonistic Competition: The Multi-Product, Multi-Factor Firm," *Southern Economic Journal*, **XXXI** (July, 1964), 38–43.

[28] MEYER, J. R. "Some Methodological Aspects of Statistical Costing as Illustrated by the Determination of Rail Passenger Costs," *American Economic Review*, **XLVIII** (May, 1958), 209–222.

[29] MEYER, J. R., A. R. FERGUSON, and G. H. BORTS. "Statistical Cost Function," *American Economic Review*, **XLVIII** (May, 1958), 209–238.

[30] NATIONAL BUREAU OF ECONOMIC RESEARCH. *Cost Behavior and Price Policy.* New York: National Bureau of Economic Research, 1943.

[31] PAULSON, W. E. "Characteristics of the Marginal Cost Curve," *Journal of Farm Economics*, **XXX** (August, 1948), 467–499.

[32] PFOUTS, RALPH W. "Distribution Theory in A Certain Case of Oligopoly and Oligopsony," *Metroeconomica*, **VII** (1955).

[33] PFOUTS, RALPH W. "The Theory of Cost and Production in the Multi-Product Firm," *Econometrica*, **XXIX** (October, 1961), 650–658.

[34] PFOUTS, RALPH W. "Multi-Product Firms Vs Single-Product Firms: The Theory of Cost and Production," *Metroeconomica*, **XVI** (1964), 51–66.

[35] ROBINSON, JOAN. *The Economics of Imperfect Competition.* London: Macmillan & Co., 1933.

[36] ROLPH, E. "The Discounted Marginal Productivity Doctrine," *Journal of Political Economy*, **XLVII** (1939), 542–556.

[37] RUSSELL, R. R. "On the Demand Curve for a Factor of Production," *American Economic Review*, **LIV** (1964), 726–732.

[38] SAMUELSON, PAUL A. *Foundations of Economic Analysis.* Cambridge: Harvard University Press, 1947.

[39] SHEPHARD, RONALD W. *Cost and Production Functions.* Princeton, N. J.: Princeton University Press, 1953.

[40] STAEHLE, HANS. "The Measurement of Statistical Cost Functions: An Appraisal of Some Recent Contributions," in George J. Stigler and Kenneth E. Boulding (Eds.), *Readings in Price Theory.* Homewood, Ill.: Richard D. Irwin, Inc., 1952.

[41] STIGLER, GEORGE J. "Production and Distribution Theories in the Short Run," *Journal of Political Economy*, **XLVII** (1939), 305–327.

[42] STIGLER, GEORGE J. *Production and Distribution Theories: The Formative Period.* New York: Macmillan & Co., 1946.

[43] VICKREY, WILLIAM S. *Microstatics.* New York: Harcourt, Brace & World, Inc., 1964.

[44] VINER, JACOB. "Cost Curves and Supply Curves," in George J. Stigler and Kenneth E. Boulding (Eds.), *Readings in Price Theory.* Homewood, Ill.: Richard D. Irwin, Inc., 1952.

[45] WALTERS, A. A. "Production and Cost Functions: An Econometric Survey," *Econometrica*, **XXXI** (1963), 1–66.

[46] WELDON, J. C. "The Multi-Product Firm," *Canadian Journal of Economics and Political Science*, **XIV** (1948), 176–190.

[47] WILES, P. J. "Empirical Research and Marginal Analysis," *Economic Journal*, **LX** (September, 1950), 513–530.

5

Marginal analysis models of the firm

INTRODUCTION

In Chapter 1 we outlined a general conceptual framework for economic theories of the firm which included as elements (1) goals, (2) a production transformation process, (3) information, and (4) decisions. The purpose of this chapter is to describe and analyze several alternative economic models of the firm within the general class of "marginal analysis" models. Recall from Chapter 1 that marginal analysis models are those models in which choices between alternative factor-product combinations are made on the basis of infinitesimal changes in factor-product combinations. Under marginal analysis the firm's demand function, production function, and cost equation are all continuous. Furthermore, the first and second partial derivatives of these functions are assumed to exist.

The models considered in this chapter are all *holistic* models as contrasted with *behavioral* models. Holistic models view the firm as a "unified acting entity or organism" [60, p. 18] in which input and output decisions are made simultaneously in the light of some given objective of the firm as a whole and in the light of given product-demand information, production-technology information, and factor-supply information. Behavioral models conceive of the firm as the "confluence of several streams of interrelated behavior" [60, p. 18]. We shall investigate the properties of behavioral models of the firm in Chapter 18.

Before turning to specific marginal analysis models of the firm, it may be useful to relate the above four elements to neoclassical (marginal analysis) models in general. First, consider the question of *goals*. Although we have considered a number of different goals in developing (within the framework of marginal analysis) theories of demand, production, and cost, we have not treated these goals as though they were the goals of the firm as a whole. For example, in Chapter 2 we considered a goal of the consumer—utility maximization. In Chapters 3 and 4 we analyzed models in which production maximization and cost minimization were explicit objectives. To be sure, certain individuals within a given firm may have as their goals output maximization or cost minimization. Following tradition, we shall assume for most of the models outlined in this chapter that these goals are superseded by the goal of *profit maximization.*

Second, the *production transformation process* for each of the models considered in this chapter can be represented by a continuous production function. The single-product and multiproduct models to be described are based on the assumptions of the single-product production function and the multiproduct production function, respectively, of Chapter 3. In other words, the production transformation processes for each of the models treated in this chapter are essentially the same.

Third, although the *information* describing the production technology for each of the neoclassical models considered here is identical, there are differences among these models in terms of the nature of the product-demand and factor-supply information available to management. With regard to product-demand information we shall consider five cases: perfect competition, monopoly, monopolistic competition, duopoly, and oligopoly. All of these were defined in Chapter 2. Perfect competition and monopsonistic competition were selected to illustrate alternative forms of factor-cost information.

Fourth, all of the models described in this chapter are concerned with two different types of *decisions*—input decisions and output decisions. The input decisions are "Which factors of production to buy?" and "In what quantities should these factors be purchased?" The output decisions are "Which products to produce?" and "In what quantities should they be produced and sold?" It is assumed throughout the analysis in this chapter that these decisions are made simultaneously rather than independently. In other words, the theories of demand, production, and cost which were treated independently in Chapters 2, 3, and 4 are now integrated into a unified theory of the firm.

In addition to the assumption of a common production function, all of the models included in this collection of marginal analysis models are based on: (1) static equilibrium, (2) complete certainty, and (3) perfect divisibility of factor inputs and product outputs.

After examining five single-product models and a multiproduct model, we shall digress briefly to give some empirical and descriptive content to the theory. Then we shall conclude this chapter with a critical evaluation of marginal analysis models of the firm. We shall identify some of the leading critics of the traditional (marginal analysis) approach to the theory of the firm and outline some of their views on the "conventional wisdom." In addition, several defenses of the orthodox theory will be presented.

THE SINGLE-PRODUCT FIRM

Perfect competition

Consider a firm which produces a single product Z and sells this product in a perfectly competitive market characterized by: (1) product homogeneity, (2) many firms, (3) many consumers, (4) freedom of entry, (5) perfect information, and (6) no collusion. The market price P for the competitive firm's product is determined by the intersection of the market demand function and the market supply function. The firm's total cost function is given by

(5-1) $$TC = TC(Z)$$

The firm's profit π is by definition equal to the difference between total revenue TR and total cost TC:

(5-2) $$\pi = TR - TC$$

(5-3) $$\pi = P \cdot Z - TC(Z)$$

Total profit will be maximized when the derivative of profit with respect to output is equal to zero:

(5-4) $$\frac{d\pi}{dZ} = P - \frac{d(TC)}{dZ} = 0$$

or when marginal cost MC is equal to price:

(5-5) $$MC = P$$

Graphically (5-5) will hold when the slope of the firm's total cost function is equal to the slope of the total revenue function. In Figure 5-1 total profit is at a maximum at output Z_0—i.e., when the vertical distance between TR and TC is a maximum. Total profit is measured by the vertical distance ST. In examining Figure 5-1 we note that MC also equals P at output Z_1, but total profit is clearly not at a maximum. In fact, total profit is negative and at a minimum at output Z_1. To guarantee that total profit is maximized when $MC = P$, the second derivative of profit must be negative:

(5-6) $$\frac{d^2\pi}{dZ^2} = \frac{-d^2TC}{dZ^2} < 0$$

or

(5-7) $$\frac{d(MC)}{dZ} > 0$$

In Figure 5-1 the slope of MC is less than zero to the left of R and greater than zero to the right of R. (There is no significance attached to the fact that TR happens to intersect TC at R in our graph.)

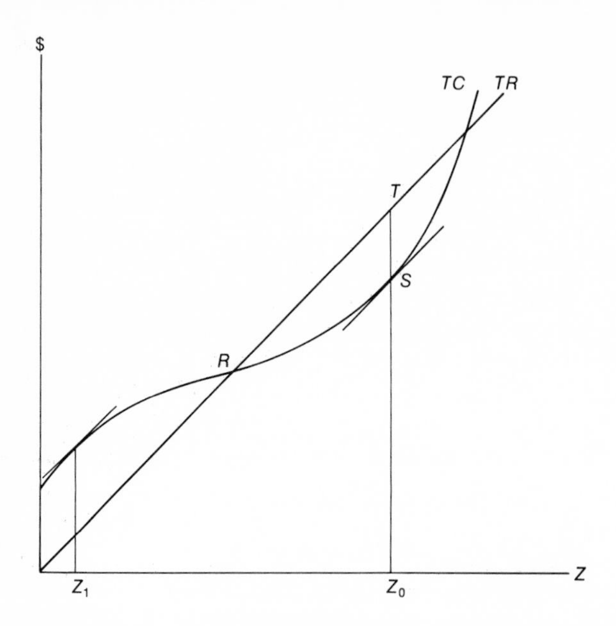

FIGURE **5-1**

Profit maximization for the perfectly competitive firm

Over the *short run*, when the firm cannot vary its fixed factors of production and hence its total cost function is fixed, the firm will have no incentive to change its rate of output from the level at which $MC = P$. Total profit will decrease when output is either increased above Z_0 or decreased below Z_0 in Figure 5-1. Hence, the firm is said to be in *short-run equilibrium* when output is such that $MC = P$. However, in the short run the firm may end up making either a profit or a loss (negative profit). Suppose, for example, the market price is P_1 in Figure 5-2 (thus the horizontal line at P_1 is the firm's demand curve). Since the price is greater than average total cost, the firm will make a positive profit. But if the price level is P_2 or P_3 the firm will operate at a loss, i.e., total cost will be less than total revenue. Figure 5-2 suggests an important limitation to our profit-maximization rule (that the firm should produce that level of output at which $MC = P$). If price falls below average variable cost, AVC, the firm's profit will be greater (i.e., its loss will be less) if it produces no output at all than if it produces a positive output. Hence our short-run,profit-maximization decision rule should be modified as follows:

Rule If P is greater than AVC, produce that level of output at which $MC = P$. If P is less than or equal to AVC, produce nothing.

There is one further minor qualification for this rule. If price drops below AVC temporarily, but is expected to rise above AVC very soon, then the shut-

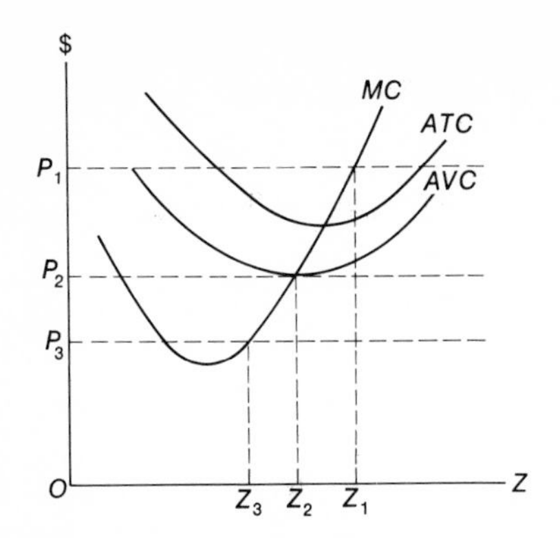

FIGURE **5-2**

Short-run equilibrium for the perfectly competitive firm

down and start-up costs which the firm would incur by stopping production and later resuming production may exceed the out-of-pocket losses which the firm would incur by producing some positive quantity of output. When this is true the firm should still produce something [26, p. 100].

On the basis of the preceding analysis we conclude that the positively sloping portion of the firm's short-run marginal cost curve represents the competitive firm's *short-run supply function*. The firm's short-run supply function is only defined above the point of minimum average variable cost. Below that point the firm will produce nothing.

The short-run supply curve for an entire competitive industry is simply the lateral sum of the short-run supply curves for all of the firms in the industry. Since the short-run supply function of each firm in the industry has a positive slope, it follows that the industry short-run supply function will also have a positive slope. In the short run, the industry supply function is fixed. This is attributable to two factors. First, the supply functions (*MC* curves) of all of the firms in the industry are fixed in the short run. Second, in the short run there is not sufficient time and opportunity for new firms to enter, or for existing firms to leave the industry.

Next let us turn to the situation which confronts a competitive industry in the long run. In the long run, all factors of production are variable, and there is sufficient time for new firms to enter the industry and for existing firms to leave. What are the implications of these new assumptions for the behavior of a competitive industry? Figure 5-3 sheds some light on this question. First, consider the right-hand side of Figure 5-3, which shows the long-run marginal cost curve, *MC*, and the average total cost curve, *ATC*, for a typical firm in a competitive industry. Both *MC* and *ATC* are derived from the firm's long-run

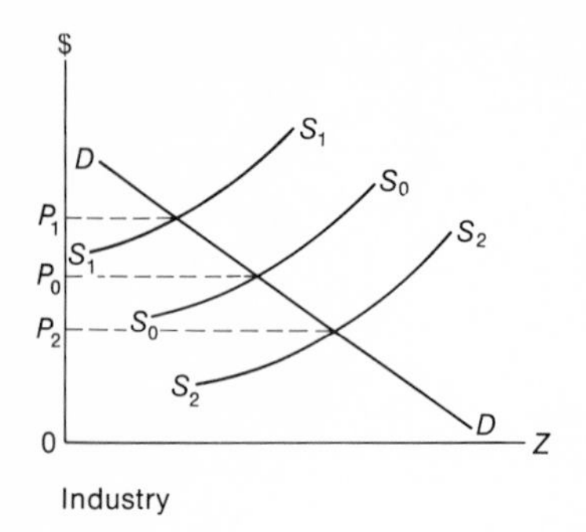

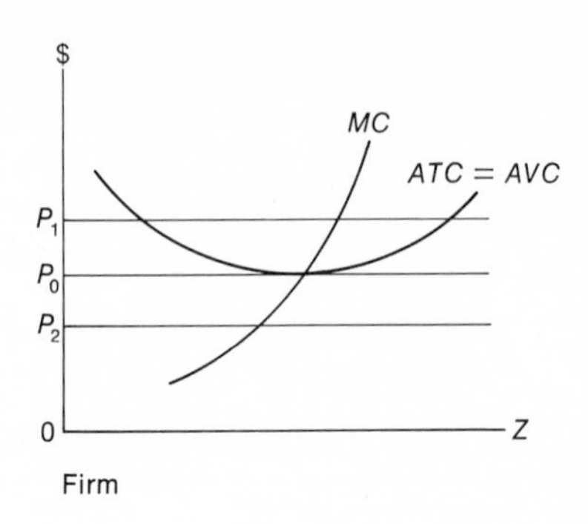

FIGURE **5-3**

Long-run equilibrium for a perfectly competitive firm and industry

total cost function, which was defined in Chapter 4. Since there are no fixed factors in the long run, average total cost is equal to average variable cost.

Next we turn to the left-hand side of Figure 5-3. The industry demand curve is given by DD. Suppose that the industry supply is S_1S_1. The market price therefore will be P_1, and looking at the right-hand side of Figure 5-3 we see that firms will make positive profits. But with free entry into the industry, new firms will be induced to enter it, and the industry supply of Z will increase. That is, the supply curve will shift downward to the right, and the market price will drop with each increase in supply. Profits will be squeezed down toward zero or to the point where no additional firms will be attracted into the industry. Thus an equilibrium position will be established at price P_0.

Alternatively, suppose that the industry supply curve were S_2S_2 rather than S_1S_1. Firms would be operating at a loss. This would result in an exodus of firms from the industry, a reduction in supply, a higher market price, and higher profits. As more firms leave the industry, losses will be eliminated and profit will approach zero. Of course, zero *economic* profit does not mean zero *accounting* profit. Rather, it means that *accounting* profit is *normal.* Normal accounting profit is just sufficient to pay entrepreneurs a return on their investment equal to the return they could earn from their best alternative investment opportunity.

Therefore the long-run equilibrium conditions for a perfectly competitive industry are (1) that every firm in the industry maximize profit, i.e., $P = MC$ and (2) that long-run minimum ATC (including normal profit) for every firm in the industry be just equal to the market price P,

(5-8) $$ATC = P$$

If this latter condition does not hold then firms will either be entering or leaving the industry. Only when (5-8) holds and firms are earning "normal accounting profit" will the number of firms in the industry remain constant. Combining the short-run equilibrium condition $P = MC$ with the long-run equilibrium condition $ATC = P$, we get

$$P = MC = ATC \tag{5-9}$$

where MC and ATC are now long-run costs rather than short run. But ATC is equal to MC at the point of minimum ATC. In summary, the long-run equilibrium condition for a competitive market is for the market price to be equal to long-run MC and minimum ATC for all firms in the industry.

The firm's long-run supply function is simply that portion of its increasing long-run MC curve which lies above long-run AVC (which is equal to ATC). If price falls below minimum ATC then zero output is produced. The long-run supply function for the industry is somewhat more complex. Thus far we have assumed that long-run costs are unaffected by the entry or exit of firms. But clearly this is a very special case, for it implies that factor costs remain constant regardless of the quantities of the factors demanded. An industry which is characterized by fixed factor prices is called a *constant-cost* industry. There are two other logical possibilities—*increasing-cost* industries and *decreasing-cost* industries. In an *increasing-cost industry* an increase in the industry's output as a whole may bid up the prices of the factor inputs and/or may cause an unfavorable shift in a firm's production functions, both of which tend to increase the total cost of firms in the industry. In a *decreasing-cost industry* increases in output for the industry as a whole lead to favorable technological change and/or the discovery of cheaper sources of raw materials, both of which tend to reduce the total costs of firms in the industry. The *long-run supply* curve for a competitive industry is obtained by adding the individual supply functions of the firms in the industry. Remember, however, that in the long run the supply function of a firm depends on the output of all other firms in the industry. The *long-run supply* curve for the industry may have a constant, positive, or negative slope depending respectively on whether it is a constant-, increasing-, or decreasing-cost industry.

Monopoly

A monopolist is the sole producer of a single product Z for which there are no close substitutes. There are restrictions preventing new firms from entering the industry (which consists of one firm). The demand curve for the monopolist is equivalent to the market demand function in a competitive market. The monopolist cannot sell unlimited quantities of its output at a given price.

Increases in sales can only be achieved by reductions in the price charged by the monopolist. The monopolist's demand curve may be expressed as

$$P = P(Z) \tag{5-10}$$

where

$$\frac{dP}{dZ} < 0$$

or

$$AR = AR(Z) \tag{5-11}$$

where AR denotes average revenue. Total revenue is defined as

$$TR(Z) = P(Z) \cdot Z \tag{5-12}$$

Recall from Chapter 2 that for the monopolist, marginal revenue MR is less than average revenue AR. The monopolist's profit function is defined by

$$\pi = TR(Z) - TC(Z) \tag{5-13}$$

For the monopolist, the necessary condition for profit maximization is that

$$\frac{d\pi}{dZ} = \frac{dTR}{dZ} - \frac{dTC}{dZ} = 0 \tag{5-14}$$

or

$$MR = MC \tag{5-15}$$

that is, marginal revenue must equal marginal cost. A sufficient condition for profit maximization is that the firm's profit function be strictly concave over all Z. That is, the second derivative of profit with respect to output must be negative:

$$\frac{d^2\pi}{dZ^2} < 0 \tag{5-16}$$

The second derivative of the firm's profit function will be negative if the firm's marginal revenue function is decreasing and if its cost function behaves in a certain prescribed manner. In Chapter 2 we learned that it is customary to assume a decreasing marginal revenue function. The firm's marginal costs may either increase or decrease with increases in output. However, if marginal costs are decreasing, the absolute value of the rate of decrease must be less than the rate of decrease of the marginal revenue function.

The optimum level of output $\bar{Z}$ for the monopolist can be found by solving (5-14) or (5-15) for Z. It is assumed that $AR(\bar{Z}) \geq AVC(\bar{Z})$ or otherwise the firm will produce nothing in the short run. The monopolist's optimum selling

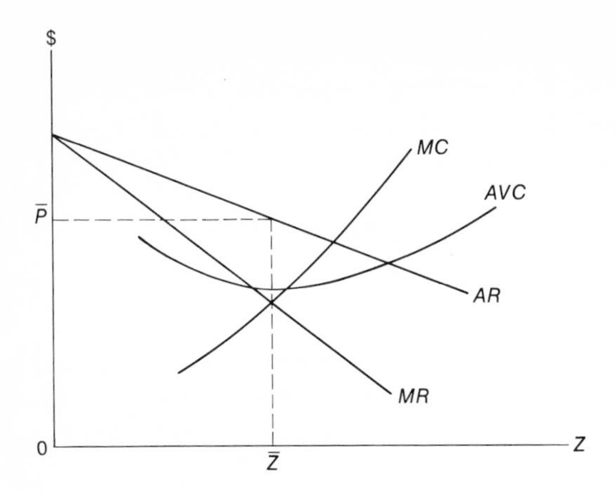

FIGURE 5-4
The monopolist's optimum price–output decision

price $\bar{P}$ can be found by substituting $\bar{Z}$ into (5-10) or (5-11). Figure 5-4 illustrates graphically the monopolist's optimum price–output decision.

The concept of the supply function is meaningless for the monopolist. The supply function was previously defined in Chapter 2 as the locus of the quantities of a given product which the firm will supply at different market prices. Since the monopolist (and not the market) sets the market price it makes little sense to ask what quantity the monopolist will produce if the price of the product is given.

Our analysis of the behavior of the monopolist has been limited to the short run. However, since firms are not free to enter the industry, the analysis of the monopolist's behavior in the long run is of limited interest. The long run differs from the short run only in terms of the possible shapes of the monopolist's cost function.

In order to apply microeconomic theory to the problems of antitrust policy we would need to go much further into the topic of monopoly than space allows. For example, one might ask what the relationship is between the long-run behavior of the monopolist and the feasibility of the assumption of no entry. To put it another way, some of the most interesting problems associated with real-world phenomena are assumed away by microeconomic theory.

Since we have not set as our goal a complete treatise on monopoly models of the firm, we shall only briefly mention three well-known extensions of the model described in this section: (1) *discriminating monopoly* [46], (2) *bilateral monopoly* [46], and (3) *multiplant monopoly* [46]. A *discriminating monopolist* charges different prices to different customers for the same product. A necessary condition for discrimination is that the monopolist be able to completely separate his customers into groups. Furthermore, discrimination is only profitable if group demand functions have different elasticities. A classic example is the doctor who charges higher prices to rich patients than to poor ones, for the same care. A *bilateral monopolist* is a single purchaser without competition (*monopsonist*) buying from a monopolist. A *multiplant monopolist* sells his product, which he can produce in two or more plants, in a single market.

Monopolistic competition

In Chapter 2 we stated that monopolistic competition is a term used to describe market situations which lie somewhere between the two extremes of perfect competition and pure monopoly. Five of the assumptions of perfect competition are retained: (1) many firms, (2) many consumers, (3) freedom of entry, (4) perfect information, and (5) no collusion. The assumption of product homogeneity is dropped. That is, each firm is assumed to produce a product which is differentiated from that of its competitors, but the degree of differentiation is slight.

The demand curve for a monopolistically competitive firm is assumed to be downward-sloping, and the decision makers of a typical firm are assumed to behave as though their actions had no effect upon the behavior of competitors. In the short run, firms will maximize profit by maintaining an output level at which MC is equal to MR. This condition is necessary and sufficient for profit maximization if the firm's marginal profit function is decreasing, as was the case with a pure monopoly.

With freedom of entry, as under perfect competition, both profits and losses will approach zero in the long run. That is, the firm's demand curve will be driven toward tangency with the long-run average total cost curve,

(5-17) $$AR = ATC$$

Figure 5-5 shows graphically the long-run equilibrium position of the monopolistically competitive firm. At output level $\bar{Z}$

(5-18) $$MR = MC$$

and

(5-19) $$AR = ATC$$

and the equilibrium price is $\bar{P}$. Note that the point of tangency between AR and ATC lies above minimum ATC. It is easy to demonstrate mathematically that the long-run marginal cost curve in Figure 5-5 intersects MR at the same output level $\bar{Z}$ for which AR is tangent to ATC [26, p. 215].

Duopoly and oligopoly

Unlike in the cases of perfect competition, pure monopoly, and monopolistic competition there is no unified theory of oligopoly or its special case duopoly.

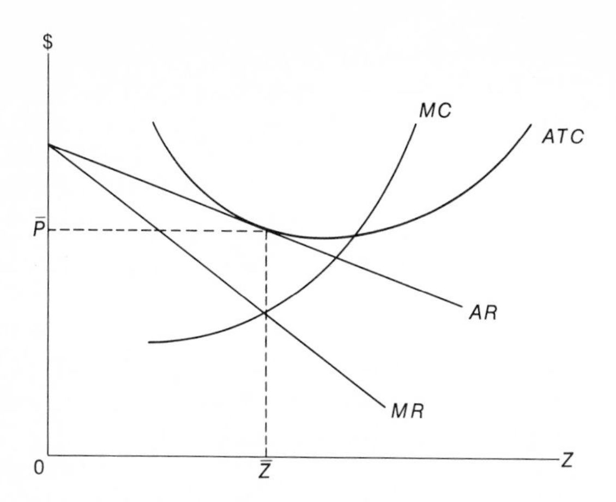

FIGURE 5-5

Long-run equilibrium for a firm under monopolistic competition

When the number of firms in a market is small enough for the behavior of one firm to affect the behavior of other firms in the market, a plethora of theories may be considered to explain the exact nature of the interdependence of firms and the possibilities for collusion. Within the neoclassical framework we can identify two general classes of models of oligopolistic behavior—(1) conjectural-variation models and (2) price-leadership models. In order to provide the reader with the general scope and nature of neoclassical oligopoly models we shall briefly outline the basic structure of four *conjectural variation* models: (1) the Cournot model, (2) the Stackelberg model, (3) the market-shares model, and (4) the kinked-demand model. In Chapter 2 we summarized the underlying logical structure of two price-leadership models—the dominant-firm model [26, p. 241] and the barometric-firm model [26, p. 244]. These two models will not be considered further. Chapters 17 and 18 will focus on some recent extensions of oligopoly theory. Chapter 17 will treat game theoretical models of the type proposed by Martin Shubik [80] and others. The work of Cyert and March [33] and others with behavioral models of oligopoly will be discussed in Chapter 18.

Conjectural variations To illustrate the concept of conjectural variations we shall consider a three-firm oligopoly. However, our analysis can easily be extended to a duopoly or an n-firm oligopoly. Assume that three firms produce and sell a single homogeneous product at the same market price P. Let Z_1, Z_2, and Z_3 denote the output of firms 1, 2, and 3 respectively, where

$$Z = Z_1 + Z_2 + Z_3 \tag{5-20}$$

is the total output of all three firms. The industry demand function is given by

(5-21) $$P = P(Z) = P(Z_1, Z_2, Z_3)$$

Total revenue TR_i for the ith firm is

$$\begin{aligned} TR_i &= P \cdot Z_i \qquad\qquad i = 1, 2, 3 \\ &= TR_i(Z_1, Z_2, Z_3) \end{aligned}$$

Total profit π_i for the ith firm is defined as

(5-22) $$\pi_i = TR_i - TC_i(Z_i) \qquad i = 1, 2, 3$$

where TC_i is the total cost function of the ith firm. Assuming that each firm maximizes its own profit, we differentiate (5-22) with respect to each firm's output and set the resulting derivatives equal to zero:

(5-23) $$\frac{d\pi_1}{dZ_1} = \frac{\partial TR_1}{\partial Z_1} + \frac{\partial TR_1}{\partial Z_2} \cdot \frac{dZ_2}{dZ_1} + \frac{\partial TR_1}{\partial Z_3} \cdot \frac{dZ_3}{dZ_1} - \frac{dTC_1}{dZ_1} = 0$$

(5-24) $$\frac{d\pi_2}{dZ_2} = \frac{\partial TR_2}{\partial Z_1} \cdot \frac{dZ_1}{dZ_2} + \frac{\partial TR_2}{\partial Z_2} + \frac{\partial TR_2}{\partial Z_3} \cdot \frac{dZ_3}{dZ_2} - \frac{dTC_2}{dZ_2} = 0$$

(5-25) $$\frac{d\pi_3}{dZ_3} = \frac{\partial TR_3}{\partial Z_1} \cdot \frac{dZ_1}{dZ_3} + \frac{\partial TR_3}{\partial Z_2} \cdot \frac{dZ_2}{dZ_3} + \frac{\partial TR_3}{\partial Z_3} - \frac{dTC_3}{dZ_3} = 0$$

We can solve equations (5-23), (5-24), and (5-25) for Z_1, Z_2, and Z_3 if we know either the functional forms or the values of dZ_1/dZ_2, dZ_1/dZ_3, dZ_2/dZ_1, dZ_2/dZ_3, dZ_3/dZ_1, and dZ_3/dZ_2. These derivatives are called *conjectural variations.* Depending on the assumptions that we make regarding the exact nature of conjectural variations, we can formulate a variety of different oligopoly models.

The Cournot model Cournot's model assumes that each of the three firms in the oligopolistic industry maximizes profit on the assumption that the other two firms will not alter their output. In other words, this model assumes that the conjectural-variation terms in equations (5-23), (5-24), and (5-25) are all zero. This implies that each firm in the industry produces at an output level which equates marginal revenue and marginal cost,

(5-26) $$MR_i = MC_i \qquad i = 1, 2, 3$$

If the second-order conditions for each firm hold, i.e., if

(5-27) $$\frac{\partial^2 \pi_i}{\partial Z_i^2} < 0 \qquad i = 1, 2, 3$$

or

(5-28) $$\frac{dMR_i}{dZ_i} < \frac{dMC_i}{dZ_i} \qquad i = 1, 2, 3$$

then (5-26) can be solved for Z_1, Z_2, and Z_3, and the solution will be an equilibrium solution for the three-firm market. In Chapter 17, we shall reconsider the Cournot model as an example of a two-person, nonconstant-sum game. Also, we shall expose the basic fallacy of the Cournot behavioral assumptions.

Reaction functions which express the output of each oligopolist as a function of the outputs of the other competing firms can be obtained by solving the first equation in (5-26) for Z_1, the second equation for Z_2, and the third equation for Z_3.

$$\begin{aligned} Z_1 &= \psi_1(Z_2, Z_3) \\ Z_2 &= \psi_2(Z_1, Z_3) \\ Z_3 &= \psi_3(Z_1, Z_2) \end{aligned} \tag{5-29}$$

The reaction function for firm 1 yields a relationship between Z_1 and the output levels for firms 2 and 3 with the property that for any specified values of Z_2 and Z_3 the corresponding value of Z_1 maximizes the profit of firm 1. The reaction functions for firms 2 and 3 have a similar interpretation. A set of values for Z_1, Z_2, and Z_3 which satisfy all three reaction functions constitute an equilibrium solution.

Two special cases of the Cournot model merit brief consideration—the Edgeworth model [37] and the collusion model [46].

Edgeworth's model, developed in 1883, expresses conjectural variations in terms of price changes rather than output changes. It assumes that oligopolists behave as though their rivals would maintain a constant price. A variation of the Cournot model is the *collusion model* in which all three firms act jointly to maximize their combined profits. This is equivalent to assuming that the three firms merge into a single monopoly. Conjectural variations are the same as they were for the Cournot model but the objective is to maximize total industry profits rather than the profits of the three separate firms. This model is usually associated with the name of E. H. Chamberlin [21].

The Stackelberg model [85,86] The concepts of "leadership" and "followership" have been introduced into duopoly theory by Heinrich von Stackelberg. The Cournot model is a special case of the Stackelberg model in which both firms behave as followers. That is, under the Cournot assumptions firm 1 maximizes its profit function $\pi_1(Z_1, Z_2)$ with respect to Z_1 on the assumption that $dZ_2/dZ_1 = 0$. Firm 2 maximizes $\pi_2(Z_1, Z_2)$ with respect to Z_2 on the assumption that $dZ_1/dZ_2 = 0$. Firm 1 is said to be a leader, according to Stackelberg, if it maximizes $\pi_1[Z_1, \psi_2(Z_1)]$ with respect to Z_1, where $\psi_2(Z_1)$ is firm 2's reaction function. Firm 2's reaction function represents the optimal value of Z_2 when firm 2 is a follower. This implies that the conjectural variation term of firm 1 is

$$\frac{dZ_2}{dZ_1} = \frac{d\psi_2(Z_1)}{dZ_1} \tag{5-30}$$

Firm 2 is a leader if it maximizes $\pi_2[\psi_1(Z_2), Z_2]$ with respect to Z_2, where

$$\frac{dZ_1}{dZ_2} = \frac{d\psi_1(Z_2)}{dZ_2} \tag{5-31}$$

is firm 2's conjectural variation term: These definitions can also be extended to the case of a three-firm oligopoly or, for that matter, an n-firm oligopoly. All three firms in our three-firm oligopoly behaved as followers with the Cournot models. We could call firm 1 a leader (with respect to firms 2 and 3) if it maximized $\pi_1[Z_1, \psi_2(Z_1, Z_3), \psi_3(Z_1, Z_2)]$, where firm 1's conjectural variation terms are

$$\frac{dZ_2}{dZ_1} = \frac{d\psi_2(Z_1, Z_3)}{dZ_1} \tag{5-32}$$

and

$$\frac{dZ_3}{dZ_1} = \frac{d\psi_3(Z_1, Z_2)}{dZ_1} \tag{5-33}$$

In the case of a duopoly, each firm calculates its conjectured maximum profit from both leadership and followership and then chooses to behave according to the strategy (i.e., leadership or followership) which yields the greater conjectured profit. Four possible cases may arise.

1. Firm 1 behaves as a follower.
   Firm 2 behaves as a follower.
2. Firm 1 behaves as a leader.
   Firm 2 behaves as a leader.
3. Firm 1 behaves as a follower.
   Firm 2 behaves as a leader.
4. Firm 1 behaves as a leader.
   Firm 2 behaves as a follower.

If both firms behave as followers as in case 1, then the Cournot solution will be obtained. If both firms behave as leaders (case 2), then the solution will be unstable and no specific outcome can be predicted in advance. This case is called *Stackelberg disequilibrium* or *warfare*. Unless the two firms enter into a collusive agreement or one of the firms succumbs to the leadership of the other, the market will be characterized by instability with regard to prices and output. A type of economic warfare in which each firm attempts to take advantage of the other will exist so long as the market is in Stackelberg disequilibrium. (See the article by Bishop [12], for a thorough discussion of warfare in duopoly.) If one firm behaves as a leader and the other as a follower (cases 3 and 4), then a stable solution will result if the first- and second-order conditions for a maximum are satisfied.

The market-shares model In the case of a duopoly the market-shares model assumes that one firm, say firm 2, always desires to maintain a constant share k of the total market

$$k = \frac{Z_2}{Z_1 + Z_2} \tag{5-34}$$

Solving (5-34) for Z_2, and assuming that firm 2's conjectural variation term is

$$\frac{dZ_1}{dZ_2} = 0 \tag{5-35}$$

we obtain for firm 2's output

$$Z_2 = \frac{kZ_1}{1 - k} \tag{5-36}$$

Firm 1 utilizes its knowledge of firm 2's market-share goal in maximizing its own profit. Substitution from (5-36) for Z_2, yields firm 1's profit function

$$\pi_1 = \pi_1[Z_1, kZ_1/(1 - k)] \tag{5-37}$$

Firm 1 maximizes (5-37) with respect to Z_1. Its conjectural variation term, from (5-36), is

$$\frac{dZ_2}{dZ_1} = \frac{k}{1 - k} \tag{5-38}$$

The kinked-demand model The kinked-demand model, which was described in detail in Chapter 2, can also be formulated in terms of conjectural variations. (See [26, pp. 253–254].)

THE MULTIPRODUCT FIRM[1]

The models outlined in the preceding section were restricted to the single-product firm. The factor-input side of the firm was ignored by virtue of the fact that for each model a cost function relating total cost to output was postulated. We now turn our attention to the multiproduct, multifactor firm. Specifically, the objectives of this section are: (1) to define a mathematical model of a firm which may purchase factors as a monopsonist and/or perfect competitor, and sell products as a monopolist and/or perfect competitor; (2) to derive and interpret the traditional set of optimality conditions (necessary conditions for profit maximization) for the firm; (3) to present and explain a concise table which conveniently cross classifies these optimality conditions depending on the buying and selling conditions facing the firm; and (4) to state the economic significance of the concavity requirements for global optimality for the firm.

Our model rests upon the following set of assumptions:

1. There exists a total revenue function which relates the output quantities of the firm's p products to total revenue. This function is fixed and known.
2. There exists a total cost equation which relates the factor-input quantities of the firm's m variable factors to total cost. This function is fixed and known.

[1] This section is taken from a paper by William A. Mauer and Thomas H. Naylor, "Monopolistic-Monopsonistic Competition: The Multi-Product, Multi-Factor Firm," *Southern Economic Journal*, XXXI (July 1964), pp. 38–43.

3. The objective of the firm is to maximize profit subject to the technical constraints imposed by its production function.
4. The firm possesses a production process which is capable of transforming a maximum of m variable factors of production into p products. (There are no limitations on the availability of the factors.)
5. A continuous production function exists (with nonvanishing first- and second-order partial derivatives) which relates the set of independent factor variables to the set of independent product variables.
6. The production function is such that the quantity of output produced for a given product represents the maximum amount of that product which can be produced from specified factor input quantities along with specified product quantities for the remaining $p - 1$ products.
7. The exact nature of the firm's production function has been predetermined by a set of technical decisions by the firm's engineers and technicians.
8. The production function is characterized by a decreasing marginal product for all factor-product combinations, a decreasing rate of technical substitution between any two factors, and an increasing rate of product transformation between any two products.
9. All of the firm's factors and products are perfectly divisible.
10. The parameters which determine the firm's total revenue function, production function, and total cost equation will not change over the time period which is being considered.
11. The parameters which determine the firm's total revenue function, production function, and total cost equation are not permitted to be random variables.

A mathematical model of the firm

Consider a firm whose production process transforms any finite number of factors into any finite number of products. The firm may purchase factors as a monopsonist or perfect competitor, and sell products as a monopolist or perfect competitor.

The factor-product transformation process for the firm is given by

$$Q(Z_1, \ldots, Z_p, X_1, \ldots, X_m) = 0 \tag{5-39}$$

where

$$Z_k \geq 0 \text{ are products} \qquad (k = 1, \ldots, p) \tag{5-40}$$

and

$$X_i \geq 0 \text{ are factors} \qquad (i = 1, 2, \ldots, m) \tag{5-41}$$

It is further assumed that the production function is defined over the domain of non-negative factors and products and that within the domain of definition it has continuous first- and second-order partial derivatives.

Let TR denote the firm's total revenue function and TC its total cost equation,

(5-42) $$TR = TR(Z_1, \ldots, Z_p)$$

(5-43) $$TC = TC(X_1, \ldots, X_m)$$

The firm's total profit function is then defined as

(5-44) $$\pi = TR - TC$$

Profit maximization and optimality conditions

The objective of the firm is to maximize total profit subject to the technical constraints imposed by its production function, which is assumed to be given. This maximization problem may be solved by the straightforward Lagrangian method by letting

(5-45) $$L = TR - TC + \lambda Q$$

where λ is a Lagrangian multiplier. Using a single subscript on L, Q, TR, and TC to denote partial differentiation, the necessary conditions for profit maximization, i.e., the vanishing of the $(p + m + 1)$ partial derivatives, are given by the following:

(5-46) $$L_k = TR_k + \lambda Q_k = 0 \qquad (k = 1, 2, \ldots, p)$$

(5-47) $$L_i = -TC_i + \lambda Q_i = 0 \qquad (i = 1, 2, \ldots, m)$$

(5-48) $$L_\lambda = Q(Z_1, \ldots, Z_p, X_1, \ldots, X_m) = 0$$

Assuming solutions exist, select any two equations (e.g., a and b) from among the p equations of (5-46) and solve for λ,

(5-49) $$\lambda = -\frac{TR_a}{Q_a}$$

(5-50) $$\lambda = -\frac{TR_b}{Q_b}$$

Equating these two expressions and rewriting them, we obtain

(5-51) $$\frac{TR_a}{TR_b} = \frac{Q_a}{Q_b}$$

But by the implicit-function rule

(5-52) $$\frac{Q_a}{Q_b} = -\frac{\partial Z_b}{\partial Z_a}$$

Therefore we can write (5-52) as

(5-53) $$\frac{TR_a}{TR_b} = -\frac{\partial Z_b}{\partial Z_a}$$

But TR_a fulfills the requirement of the well-known definition of the marginal revenue for product a (MR_a), while TR_b corresponds to the marginal revenue for product b (MR_b). Equation (5-53) may now be written as

$$\frac{MR_a}{MR_b} = -\frac{\partial Z_b}{\partial Z_a} \tag{5-54}$$

Equation (5-54) states that when optimum quantities of a and b are being produced the ratio of their marginal revenues must be equal to the rate of product transformation between the two products.

If we had selected two equations from (5-47), instead of (5-46), then (5-53) would have become

$$\frac{TC_a}{TC_b} = -\frac{\partial X_b}{\partial X_a} \tag{5-55}$$

But TC_a fulfills the requirements of the familiar definition of the *marginal factor cost* of factor a (MFC_a), while TC_b corresponds to the marginal factor cost of factor b (MFC_b).[2] Equation (5-55) may now be written as

$$\frac{MFC_a}{MFC_b} = -\frac{\partial X_b}{\partial X_a} \tag{5-56}$$

Equation (5-56) indicates that when optimum quantities of a and b are consumed in the production process, the ratio of their marginal costs must be equal to their rate of technical substitution.

Finally, if we select one equation from the p equations in (5-46) and one from the m equations in (5-47), then (5-51) becomes

$$TC_a = TR_b \frac{\partial Z_b}{\partial X_a} \tag{5-57}$$

or

$$MFC_a = MR_b \frac{\partial Z_b}{\partial X_a} \tag{5-58}$$

which indicates that optimality requires the marginal factor cost of factor a to be equal to the marginal revenue product of b with respect to a.

Thus we have a set of optimality conditions for production for a firm which buys factors under monopsonistic conditions and sells products under monopolistic conditions.

Table of optimality conditions

Now that we have developed the optimality conditions for a firm acting under monopsonistic and monopolistic conditions, a straightforward process allows us to state similar conditions for the firm confronted with different combinations

[2] We use the term *marginal factor cost* (MFC_i) to denote the partial derivative of the total cost *equation* with respect to the ith factor. The term *marginal cost* refers to the partial derivative of the total cost *function* with respect to the kth product (MC_k). Recall that the total cost equation is a function of factor input variables and the total cost function is a function of the firm's output variables.

of perfect, monopsonistic, and monopolistic competition in its buying and selling, since under perfect competition

(5-59) $\qquad MR_k = P_k \qquad (k = 1, \ldots, p)$

(5-60) $\qquad MFC_i = C_i \qquad (i = 1, \ldots, m)$

where P_k is the price of the kth product and C_i is the price of the ith factor. (Both P_k and C_i are given to the firm under perfect competition.) Accordingly, Table 5-1 indicates the rate of product transformation (between two products), the marginal revenue product (for a product with respect to a factor), and the rate of technical substitution (between two factors) for all possible cases of perfect and imperfect (monopsonistic and monopolistic) competition facing the firm in its purchases of factors of production and sales of product.

The four possible cases which might confront the firm include:

Case 1. Perfectly competitive conditions for factor purchases and product sales.

Case 2. Imperfectly competitive conditions for factor purchases and product sales.

Case 3. Perfectly competitive conditions for factor purchases and imperfectly competitive conditions for product sales.

Case 4. Imperfectly competitive conditions for factor purchases and perfectly competitive conditions for product sales.

TABLE **5-1**

Optimality conditions

Case	Rate of product transformation	Marginal revenue product	Rate of technical substitution
1	$\frac{P_a}{P_b} = -\frac{\partial Z_b}{\partial Z_a}$ $(a, b = 1, \ldots, p)$	$C_a = P_b \frac{\partial Z_b}{\partial X_a}$ $(a = 1, \ldots, m)$ $(b = 1, \ldots, p)$	$\frac{C_a}{C_b} = -\frac{\partial X_b}{\partial X_a}$ $(a, b = 1, \ldots, m)$
2	$\frac{MR_a}{MR_b} = -\frac{\partial Z_b}{\partial Z_a}$ $(a, b = 1, \ldots, p)$	$MFC_a = MR_b \frac{\partial Z_b}{\partial X_a}$ $(a = 1, \ldots, m)$ $(b = 1, \ldots, p)$	$\frac{MFC_a}{MFC_b} = -\frac{\partial X_b}{\partial X_a}$ $(a, b = 1, \ldots, m)$
3	$\frac{MR_a}{MR_b} = -\frac{\partial Z_b}{\partial Z_a}$ $(a, b = 1, \ldots, p)$	$C_a = MR_b \frac{\partial Z_b}{\partial X_a}$ $(a = 1, \ldots, m)$ $(b = 1, \ldots, p)$	$\frac{C_a}{C_b} = -\frac{\partial X_b}{\partial X_a}$ $(a, b = 1, \ldots, m)$
4	$\frac{P_a}{P_b} = -\frac{\partial Z_b}{\partial Z_a}$ $(a, b = 1, \ldots, p)$	$MFC_a = P_b \frac{\partial Z_b}{\partial X_a}$ $(a = 1, \ldots, m)$ $(b = 1, \ldots, p)$	$\frac{MFC_a}{MFC_b} = -\frac{\partial X_b}{\partial X_a}$ $(a, b = 1, \ldots, m)$

Sufficient conditions for profit maximization

Although we have established a set of necessary conditions for profit maximization under four possible competitive conditions, we are not assured of a local maximum, for local minima and stationary values will also satisfy these first-order conditions. Hence we must impose a set of sufficient (second-order) conditions for profit maximization. The sufficiency conditions require that the bordered Hessian determinants be negative definite.

We must now turn to the concavity requirements for assuring that the local maxima achieved via the Lagrangian method are in fact global optima. In order for the Lagrangian method to yield global maxima it it necessary for the firm's profit function and production function to be strictly concave.

A strictly concave profit function implies that the firm's revenue function is strictly concave and that the firm's cost function behaves in a certain prescribed manner. The firm's revenue function will be strictly concave only if we can assume that increases in output will yield diminishing marginal returns, i.e., the firm possesses a decreasing marginal-revenue function. The firm's marginal costs may either increase or decrease with increases in output. However, if marginal costs are decreasing, the absolute value of their rate of decrease must be less than or equal to the rate of decrease of the marginal-revenue function.

A strictly concave production function must satisfy the following desiderata: (1) a decreasing marginal rate of substitution between any two factors; (2) a decreasing marginal product for all factor-product combinations; and (3) an increasing marginal rate of product transformation between any two products.

If, and only if, all of the above concavity requirements are satisfied, we can say with complete certainty that the results obtained through the use of the Lagrangian method are in fact global maxima.

MARKET ORGANIZATION IN THE UNITED STATES

Heretofore we have restricted our discussion to highly abstract theoretical models of firms. A major way of classifying the models has been by market structure. For example, we have discussed firms operating in competitive, monopolistic, and oligopolistic markets. In this section, we shall interrupt the exposition of pure theory in order to relate and contrast the theoretical models with actual market structures in the United States.

The theoretical classification of markets has been primarily by the number of sellers. A market with many sellers is competitive, one with few sellers is oligopolistic, and one with a single seller is monopolistic. In real life, however, other important characteristics of markets are relevant in explaining the behavior of firms in an industry. We list six of the more important *elements of market structure* here [20, p. 16]:

1. Concentration
2. Product differentiation

3. Barriers to entry of new firms
4. Growth rate of market demand
5. Price elasticity of market demand
6. Ratio of fixed to variable costs in the short-run

Although each of the above elements would warrant discussion if space permitted, we shall consider only the first.

Concentration refers to the empirical question of the number of firms in a given industry. Thus a highly concentrated industry would be one in which only a few firms were sellers—corresponding to the theoretical model of oligopoly. A relatively unconcentrated industry would approach the competitive model.

A *concentration ratio* is a fairly crude measure of the place a particular market occupies in the spectrum extending from pure monopoly at one extreme to pure competition at the other.

Many technical problems arise in the measurement of concentration. We can only discuss briefly some of the problems here, but for an exhaustive discussion the reader should consult the book by Bain [5]. The usual concentration ratio for an industry is obtained by dividing total sales (or some other size variable) of the four largest sellers by total sales of the industry. The arbitrary number four is used because the census may not disclose data for a smaller number of firms. Two problems are immediately apparent: (1) what is the "correct" variable of size: sales, value added, employment, or assets? and (2) what is the "correct" delimitation of the industry?

Of the variables of size listed above, many economists consider value added (or income generated) as the best single measure of economic size [1]. However, there are data-collection difficulties associated with obtaining value added by firms. Sales is the most easily available measure, but its use ignores the extent of vertical integration. Rather than discuss these measures further, we again refer the interested reader to Bain [5].

The problem of delimiting the industry has arisen in a number of antitrust cases, e.g., the Alcoa case [87, p. 19] and the du Pont cellophane case [87, p. 41]. It is understandable why this should be so. For example, if cellophane, Saran, Glassine, and polyethylene are all products in the "flexible packaging materials market," then du Pont (the sole supplier of cellophane) is not a monopolist and, consequently, does not violate the Sherman Act provision which makes "monopolization" illegal. But if cellophane is the *only* product in the "cellophane market," du Pont is indeed guilty! Fortunately for du Pont the court held that the "flexible packaging materials market" was the relevant market.

Stigler has suggested the following economic criteria for delimiting an industry:

> An industry should embrace the maximum geographical area and the maximum variety of productive activities in which there is strong long-run substitution. If buyers can shift on a large scale from product or area *B* to *A*, then

> the two should be combined. If producers can shift on a large scale from *B* to *A*, again they should be combined.
>
> Economists usually state this in an alternative form: All products or enterprises with large long-run cross-elasticities of either supply or demand should be combined into a single industry [90, p. 4].

Adelman has observed that the concentration ratio "suffers from the arbitrary element in the choice of numbers, and also wastes all the available information about the structure of the group itself. There is certainly a difference in structure between two industries, each with a concentration ratio of (say) 0.50, but with the largest firm in one industry having 15 percent of total output, and the largest firm in the second industry having 40 percent" [1, p. 273].

Adelman also cautioned that concentration ratios

> . . . must be modified by quite a number of additional facts before we are justified in saying anything much about the structure of the market. If substitutes are close, entry easy, etc., the boundaries of the market mean little, and fewness is more apparent than real. There is no logical connection between concentration and any behavior pattern in any instance. But, as a general statistical matter, the greater the concentration the lower the odds in favor of competitive behavior. Therefore, though a concentration ratio tells us little about a given industry at a given time, groups of concentration ratios, permitting comparison in time and space, do give us some solid information, and hence the most important use of concentration is in comparison: over time; or among countries, or regions, or industries at the same time [2, p. 7].

In order to give the reader some notion of the degree of concentration in American industry, we present Table 5-2.

Apparently, the steam engines and turbines industry corresponds to an oligopoly: the four largest firms account for 93 percent of sales. Cigarettes should also probably be classified as an oligopoly. But how far down the list do we descend until we reach monopolistic competition, or pure competition?

TABLE **5-2**

Concentration ratios in selected American industries, 1963

Industry	Total number of companies	Percent of value of shipments accounted for by four largest
Steam engines and turbines	17	93
Primary copper	13	85
Cigarettes	7	80
Typewriters	17	76
Tires and inner tubes	105	70
Computing and related machines	213	67
Envelopes	180	32
Book printing	662	19
Games and toys	767	15
Dresses	4577	6

Source: *Concentration Ratios in Manufacturing Industry 1963*, report of the Subcommittee on Antitrust and Monopoly, U.S. Senate Judiciary Committee, 89th Cong., 2nd Sess. (Washington, D.C., 1966), Table 3.

Another question arises in examining Table 5-2. What is the explanation for the fact that some industries are more concentrated than others? We might suggest that one important factor is the extent of *economies of scale* in relation to market demand. That is, if a firm's long-run average cost curve reaches its minimum point only at a relatively large output, say, one-fourth of total industry output, then it is reasonable to expect high concentration. Of course this is but one of many factors.

Further discussion of this and related issues is unfortunately beyond the scope of this book. However, for an excellent introductory discussion of industrial organization and public policy, the reader should consult Caves [20]. An examination of the efficiency of market organizations from the viewpoint of society belongs to the theory of welfare economics. A good discussion of welfare economics is contained in Ferguson [42]. We now turn to an evaluation of the theoretical models of the firm presented in the earlier sections.

A CRITICAL APPRAISAL OF THE NEOCLASSICAL MODEL

For each model discussed thus far in this chapter, we have stated the assumptions underlying the model, formulated the model, and derived certain conclusions from the model by the use of mathematical or graphical manipulations. No attempt has been made to evaluate qualitatively any of the models outlined in this chapter. We now turn to a critical evaluation of the neoclassical model of the firm.

In spite of its widespread acceptance among economists, the neoclassical model has been unable to escape vigorous attacks from some rather articulate foes. Criticisms have ranged from expressions of doubt about the cognitive and motivational assumptions underlying the model to the assertion that the type of firm implied by the neoclassical model has few of the characteristics which we have come to identify with actual business firms [33, p. 8]. Studies by Hall and Hitch [44], as well as Lester [58,59], have attempted to show that businessmen take into account factors that are quite different from the concepts employed in marginal analysis and the neoclassical model. Others have attempted to show that it is hardly conceivable that businessmen can obtain the information that marginal analysis assumes they have at their disposal. Neoclassical theory

> . . . views the firm as an impersonal "black box" which responds automatically to changes in the external world. The firm incurs costs, pays wages, sets prices, etc., in such a manner as to maximize its profits. This theory . . . works quite well in predicting long-run trends in prices and costs in industries that are reasonably competitive. And it is a very useful framework within which to construct [a] model. In particular, the variables in which economists are interested (price, output, etc.) and the factors which influence these variables are essential for any study of the firm. There are many important questions, however, which the economic theory of the firm has left largely unanswered (whether from lack of interest on the part of economists or from lack of suitable analytical tools is not relevant here) [15, p. 4].

There is a definite need for models of the firm which incorporate a much greater degree of realism and complexity than the neoclassical model. These alternative theories should provide answers to questions such as (1) What are the effects of organizational structure on managerial behavior? (2) How are resources allocated within firms? (3) What effect does uncertainty have on decision making? (4) What factors influence the firm's growth rate? (5) How does the firm interact with its external environment?

One of the more interesting and perhaps well-known debates between marginalists and antimarginalists, the Lester-Machlup controversy, was published in a series of articles by the *American Economic Review* in 1946 and 1947. Lester [58,59], a labor economist who was somewhat disturbed by some of the conclusions that seemed to emerge from the marginal doctrine, represented the antimarginalists' point of view, while Machlup [63,64] defended marginalism. Even today, Machlup's defense of marginalism probably remains one of the most lucid verbal statements of the neoclassical theory of the firm ever published. In reply to Lester's scathing denunciation of marginalism, Machlup said, "Unable to see how marginal analysis can be applied to their material, these critics have concluded that marginalism should be discarded. It can be shown, however, that the alleged inapplicability of marginal analysis is often due to a failure to understand it, to faulty research techniques, or to mistaken interpretations of findings" [63, p. 84]. Although Machlup pointed out a number of fallacies in Lester's work, he by no means succeeded in giving marginal analysis a clean bill of health.

Unfortunately, many of the critics of marginal analysis have failed to see its essentially tautological nature. Given the assumptions of profit maximization and rationality, the marginal conditions follow as simple mathematical tautologies. Hence much of the criticism of marginal analysis has been ill-considered.

> Even though some of these criticisms have attacked the wrong things, nevertheless the dissatisfaction which they represent is well grounded. . . . A theory which assumes knowledge of what cannot be known is clearly defective as a guide to actual behavior. What must be known, however, in order to maximize profits in a situation of imperfect markets and multi-variable production functions is a whole set of functional relationships, such as demand and supply functions, which are not given by immediate experience, and often are not even given by the most refined analysis of past data. If a firm cannot know what its marginal costs and marginal revenues are, it is useless to advise it to act so as to bring them to equality [17, p. 5].

Criticisms of neoclassical theory

In this section we shall summarize a number of the more important criticisms which have been aimed at the neoclassical model. In the following section we will consider some of the defenses which have been put forth in behalf of the neoclassical model.

Goals The fundamental behavioral assumption underlying the neoclassical model is that the firm's decision makers maximize profits in a manner which is "objectively rational." That is, the firm's managers select from the set of all possible behavior alternatives that alternative which will lead to maximum profits. Although this assumption is widely accepted by both economists and businessmen alike it has come under attack from a variety of sources. For example,

> The assumption of rationality implies the existence of the "economic man," an assumption which has been called into increasing question by studies in psychology, business sociology, and institutional economics. The assumption of some formal kind of maximization demands an inordinate amount of information about supply, demand, and the physical conditions of production. The assumption that the quantity to be maximized is measurable slurs over the wealth of inchoate psychic considerations which influence every economic decision [35, p. 80].

Challenges to the profit-maximization assumption have taken four different forms. *First*, it is argued that profit is simply one of many possible goals of the firm's decision makers. Other goals might include functional goals such as production goals, inventory goals, sales goals, and market-share goals or alternatively personal goals such as salary, security, status, power, prestige, social service, professional excellence, and utility. We will consider Baumol's sales-maximization goal and Williamson's utility-maximization goal in Chapter 18. *Second*, some critics do not deny the importance of profit but question the assumption of maximization. Simon [82] and Margolis [68] have argued that the profit-maximizing goal should be replaced by a profit-sufficing goal for the firm. They contend that the firm's decision makers aspire to a satisfactory level of profits but not an optimum level. A *third* group of critics argue that because of uncertainty and imperfect information it is impossible for firms to maximize profits. The assumption of imperfect information combined with a goal of profit maximization is tantamount to assuming subjectively rational behavior (rather than objectively rational behavior) on the part of the firm. *Fourth*, some economists contend that firms are nonrational. That is, given a payoff function which may be expressed in terms of profit, utility, or some other measure, the firm's decision makers select alternative courses of action which do not maximize their payoff functions.

Perfect knowledge The neoclassical model assumes that the firm possesses perfect information about the nature of its total revenue function, production, and total cost equation. "It assumes that there is a well-organized system for the acquisition and dissemination of relevant information to the firm and within the firm, whether this be concerning technical processes, human relations, the markets for products and raw materials, or facilities of production" [22, p. 208]. Bonini [15] argues that we cannot examine the behavior of the firm independent of its information and control system. It has been suggested by Cleland that the assumption of perfect knowledge be replaced by the assumption that "the normal information system is unorganized, distorted, and full of noise and that the acquisition and dissemination of relevant information to the firm and within the firm is a problem that must be solved internally" [22, p. 209]. Others have argued that

> . . . information is not given to the firm but must be obtained, that alternatives are searched for and discovered sequentially, and that the order in which the environment is searched determines to a substantial extent the decisions that will be made. In this way, the theory of choice and the theory of search become closely intertwined and take on prime importance in a general theory of decision making [33, p. 10].

Complete certainty By assuming complete certainty with regard to the parameters which determine the firm's total revenue function, production function, and total cost equation, the neoclassical model evades some of the most critical problems which confront management, namely, *risk*, and *uncertainty*.

> Knight and others have made familiar the notion that the heart of the entrepreneur's function is to shoulder the risks of economic enterprise and to assume the responsibility for reaching decisions in areas of ignorance. These risks result specifically from the fact that the relevant economic functions are not, and in the nature of the case cannot be, known [35, p. 90].

Knight has stated that

> With the introduction of uncertainty—the fact of ignorance and the necessity of actions based upon opinion rather than knowledge—into this Eden-like situation, its character is entirely changed. . . . With uncertainty present doing things, the actual execution of activity, becomes in a real sense a secondary part of life, the primary problem or function is deciding what to do and how to do it.
>
> In the first place, goods are produced for a market, on the basis of entirely impersonal prediction of wants, not for the satisfaction of the wants of the producers themselves. The producer takes the responsibility of forecasting the consumers' wants. In the second place, the work of forecasting and at the same time a large part of the technological direction and control of production are still further concentrated upon a very narrow class of the producers, and we meet with a new economic functionary, the entrepreneur [54, p. 268].

The problem of uncertainty is treated in detail in Chapter 12.

Decision-making process Under the assumptions of neoclassical theory, the firm decides how much to produce and which factor inputs to purchase by equating various price ratios with the rate of product transformation, the rate of technical substitution, and the marginal product for all factor-product combinations. Some economists have asserted that firms do not make decisions by the rules of marginal calculus, but instead use a series of rules of thumb or heuristics to make decisions.

Hall and Hitch [44] and others have suggested that firms use full-cost or markup rules to determine selling prices. That is, price is determined by marking up average variable cost by a fixed percentage. The markup is assumed to cover fixed costs and some profit. Although the concept of markup pricing met with a cool reception by marginalists initially, recent studies by Cyert and March [33] and others indicate that it is widely used by business firms. A decision rule for making output decisions has been proposed by Eiteman [40]. Eiteman's rule uses inventory turnover as an estimator of demand and hence as a guide for making output decisions.

One of the most interesting models of the firm which assumes managers rely on heuristics in making decisions is the department-store model developed by Cyert and March [33]. This model assumes that price and output decisions are made independently via a set of specific decision rules in the light of a sales objective and a markup objective. Models of this type are discussed in Chapter 18.

Organization The neoclassical model of the firm

> . . . has few of the characteristics we have come to identify with actual business firms. It has no complex organization, no problems of control, no standard operating procedures, no budget, no controller, no aspiring "middle management." To some economists it has seemed implausible that a theory of an organization can ignore the fact that it is one [33, p. 8].

Cleland [22, p. 209] has suggested that the decision process of the firm is determined by the organizational structure of the firm which in turn determines the firm's information system. Boulding [17] went one step further and proposed that "organization theory" be integrated into the economic theory of the firm.

> The traditional economic concept of the actor is that of the *person*—a single consumer or producer, directing his behavior toward this or that variable as the conditions which surround him change. We have been increasingly aware that most decisions are made in a framework of organization, even though it remains true that decisions are actually made by persons. A person acting in a role, however, is not the same thing as a person acting on his own behalf. . . . The life of any individual therefore can be conceived as a series of intersecting roles, in each of which he plays a somewhat different part. An organization then comes to be visualized as a network of interacting roles, tied together by lines of communication, both formal and informal. These lines of communication may have several significant dimensions, involving not only the quantity and quality of the communications themselves, but also the degree of authority which they bear and the probable impact on the behavior of both sender and recipient. A role itself is created partly by the communications which have impinged on it in the past, partly by the idiosyncrasies of the present occupant. As each new occupant accepts a role a barrage of role-informing communications impinges on him, modifying his previous concept of the role; however, persons are not merely passive occupants of roles, but themselves actively change and even create roles [17, p. 11–12].

Production process The neoclassical model assumes a continuous, strictly concave production function which is completely determined by the firm's engineers and technicians. All of the firm's factors and products are perfectly divisible. Baumol, in advocating the use of mathematical programming as an alternative approach to the theory of production, has aptly summarized a broad range of criticisms of the marginalists' concept of the production function.

> In at least one sense, the programming analysis digs deeper than does neoclassical theory. . . . The neoclassical theory assumes that the optimal technical production processes have somehow already been determined before the economic theorist goes to work on the problem. This premise is an integral part of the very concept of the production function, for, by definition, that function tells us what is the largest possible output which can be obtained for every input combination. That is, it assumes that optimal processes are employed to make those inputs go as far as possible. . . . The choice of an optimal combination of production processes, i.e., of an optimal technological arrangement, is no trivial task. It is, however, one which can be handled by the methods of mathematical programming.
>
> A second reason why it is desirable to reexamine production decision making from a programming standpoint is that the orientation of the programmer and that of the businessman have a great deal in common. In industry one never hears of concepts such as the production function or the marginal product, even though it is true that these ideas must lie somewhere behind much of management's thinking. Programming theory, though it is, of course, rather abstract and still quite removed from everyday managerial parlance, brings us much closer to the language and the viewpoint of the business world [9, p. 271].

Chapters 6 through 10 treat mathematical programming models of the firm.

Static equilibrium The firm's total revenue function, production function, and cost equation are assumed to be unchanging under the assumptions of the neoclassical model. The behavior of the firm is described in terms of comparative statics. This implies that the firm starts in one equilibrium position, and when changes occur adjusts to another equilibrium position after a sufficient lapse of time. With static equilibrium, problems of growth rates, dynamic feedback effects, capital accumulation, capital budgeting, etc., are assumed away. Dissatisfaction with the neoclassical world of static equilibrium is widespread.

> There is also a psychological element in the survival of equilibrium theory. There is an irresistible attraction about the concept of equilibrium—the almost silent hum of a perfectly running machine; the apparent stillness of the exact balance of counteracting pressures; the automatic smooth recovery from a chance disturbance. Is there perhaps something Freudian about it? We have to look for a psychological explanation to account for the powerful influence of an idea that is intellectually unsatisfactory [76, pp. 80–81].

The stationary assumption of the neoclassical model should be replaced by a growth assumption in which the wants, state of technology, and the body of knowledge are assumed to be changeable and changing [22, p. 209]. There is a definite need for a dynamic theory of the firm in which there is no limit on the supply of resources available to the firm, a theory in which the growth of the firm may be described by means of the increase in its capacity. Dynamic models of the firm will be considered in Chapter 11.

Environment The scope of economic activity included in neoclassical models of the firm by economists is obviously a matter of choice. These models relate to a single enterprise. Boulding has defined the larger environment of the firm as follows:

> Externally the larger environment consists of attitudes and opinions related to the firm on the part of government, other organizations, and the public at large. Internally the larger environment consists of such factors as morale, self-confidence, and the attitudes toward the firm of those most intimately connected with it [17, pp. 15–18].

The models discussed in this chapter have completely ignored the larger environment of the firm. They have assumed that the wants, resources, and the body of knowledge are independent of one another and of the actions of the firm [22, p. 208]. No consideration has been given to the moral, social, or ethical implications of the profit-maximizing firm. The entire analysis has been oriented toward one very small unit of the economy, the individual firm. Furthermore, no effort has been made to ascertain the relationship between the firm and the economy as a whole or to resolve any conflicts that may arise between the objectives of the firm and the objectives of the economy.[3]

> It may be that most of the extensions of the theory of the firm which I have outlined can be summed up in terms of the difference between the traditional "small firm" of classical theory and the "large firm" which has become so important a part of the modern economy. In the large firm, matters of organization, of politics, and of social responsibility which are present only in embryo in the small firm blossom into large and visible problems. General Motors is clearly a "political" organization both in its internal and external relations in the way that a small farming or retailing firm is not. Nevertheless, these problems are present in embryo even in the small firm, and it may be that as we study the problems of large-scale organization we will throw light even on the problem of the economic behavior of the person and the family, for every human is in himself an organization of cells far more complex than General Motors. What we are witnessing, therefore, is not so much a revolution in the theory of the firm as a deepening and broadening, in which the broadening itself leads to a deepening, all of which we hope will lead to better understanding of the complex systems of human behavior in the framework of both small organizations and large [17, p. 17].

Defense of neoclassical theory

Needless to say, when a theory such as the neoclassical theory of the firm which traces its lineage back to 1838 is challenged, its advocates do not quietly retreat into the background, never to be heard from again. In fact, each new attack on marginalism by the revisionists seems to have brought forth a resounding counterattack from the marginalists. In this section we summarize some of the arguments which have been put forth in support of orthodoxy.

First, Friedman argues that the critics of marginal analysis have missed the point by their preoccupation with the validity of the assumptions of models.

[3] An excellent book on this topic is John Kenneth Galbraith, *The New Industrial State*, Houghton Mifflin Company, 1967.

According to Friedman the validity of a model depends not on the validity of the assumptions on which the model rests, but rather on the ability of the model to predict the behavior of the dependent variables which are treated by the model.

> The difficulty in the social sciences of getting new evidence for this class of phenomena and of judging its conformity with the implications of the hypothesis makes it tempting to suppose that other, more readily available, evidence is equally relevant to the validity of the hypothesis—to suppose that hypotheses have not only "implications" but also "assumptions" and that the conformity of these "assumptions" to "reality" is a test of the validity of the hypothesis different from or additional to the test by implications. This widely held view is fundamentally wrong and productive of much mischief. Far from providing an easier means for sifting valid from invalid hypotheses, it only confuses the issue, promotes misunderstanding about the significance of empirical evidence for economic theory, produces a misdirection of much intellectual effort devoted to the development of consensus on tentative hypotheses in positive economics [43, p. 14].

Friedman claims that neoclassical theory has been a successful predictive device.

Although the notion that conformity to observed behavior is a desirable check on the validity of an economic model is indeed an appealing methodological position, Friedman has by no means escaped criticism for maintaining such a position. For example, Blaug argues that "Friedman's position is unassailable until it is realized that he is insisting on empirical testing of predictions as the sole criterion of validity; he seems to be saying that it makes no difference whatever to what extent the assumptions falsify reality" [13, pp. 612–613].

Critics of Friedman's brand of positive economics (e.g., Koopmans) as applied to "verification by accuracy of predictions" argue that to state a set of assumptions, and then to exempt a subclass of their implications from verification, is a curiously roundabout way of specifying the content of a theory that is regarded as open to empirical refutation [55, p. 139]. "It leaves one without an understanding of the reasons for the exemptions" [55, p. 139].

Second, a number of economists have defended marginalist positions by attempting to demonstrate the validity of the assumptions underlying the neoclassical model. Machlup's [63] defense of marginalism is based on the claim that the neoclassical assumptions are plausible. His argument is based on the assertion that cost and revenue functions are subjective.

> It should hardly be necessary to mention that all the relevant magnitudes involved—cost, revenue, profit—are subjective—that is, perceived or fancied by the men whose decisions or actions are to be explained (the businessmen)—rather than "objective." . . . Marginal analysis of the firm should not be understood to imply anything but subjective estimates, guesses and hunches [63].

Others have attempted to show empirically (by questionnaires) that the assumptions of marginal analysis are valid [36].

Third, although business firms may not objectively pursue marginal calculations in making decisions, in the long-run only those firms will survive which make decisions which are consistent with neoclassical theory. Therefore the neoclassical model may be used to predict the behavior of surviving firms. This argument has been made by Alchian [3]:

> . . . The economist, using the present analytical tools developed in the analysis of the firm under certainty, can predict the more adaptable and viable types of economic interrelationships that will be induced by environmental change even if individuals themselves are unable to ascertain them. That is, although individual participants may not know their cost and revenue situations, the economist can predict the consequences of higher wage rates, taxes, government policy, etc. Like the biologist, the economist predicts the effects of environmental changes on the surviving class of living organisms; the economist need not assume that each participant is aware of, or acts according to, his cost and demand situation. These are concepts for the economist's use and not necessarily for the individual participant's, who may have other analytic or customary devices, which, while of interest to the economist, serve as data and not as analytic methods [3].

Fourth, to incorporate many of the changes in the theory of the firm which have been proposed by the revisionists would result in models which are admittedly more "realistic" but mathematically intractable. Therefore it is better to stay with the traditional models which are somewhat more manageable.

This concludes our survey of marginal-analysis models of the firm. In the next part of the book we shall consider a second approach to the theory of the firm, i.e., mathematical-programming models.

BIBLIOGRAPHY

[1] ADELMAN, M. A. "The Measurement of Industrial Concentration," *Review of Economics and Statistics*, **XXXIII** (1951), 269–296.

[2] ADELMAN, M. A. "Industrial Concentration," a statement to the Subcommittee on Antitrust and Monopoly, U.S. Senate Judicial Committee, September 10, 1964.

[3] ALCHIAN, A. A. "Uncertainty, Evolution, and Economic Theory," *Journal of Political Economy*, **LVIII** (June, 1950), 211–221.

[4] BAILEY, M. J. "Price and Output Determination by a Firm Selling Related Products," *American Economic Review*, **XLIV** (March, 1954), 82–93.

[5] BAIN, JOE. *Industrial Organization*. New York: John Wiley & Sons, 1959.

[6] BAUMOL, WILLIAM J. "On the Theory of Oligopoly," *Economica*, **XXV** (August, 1958), 187–198.

[7] BAUMOL, WILLIAM J. *Business Behavior, Value and Growth*. New York: Macmillan & Co., 1959.

[8] BAUMOL, WILLIAM J. "On the Theory of the Expansion of the Firm," *American Economic Review*, **LII** (December, 1962), 1078–1087.

[9] BAUMOL, WILLIAM J. *Economic Theory and Operations Analysis*. Englewood Cliffs, N. J.: Prentice-Hall, Inc., 1965.

[10] BAUMOL, WILLIAM J., and RICHARD E. QUANDT. "Rules of Thumb and Optimally Imperfect Decisions," *American Economic Review*, **LIV** (March, 1964), 23–46.

[11] BECKER, GARY S. "Irrational Behavior and Economic Theory," *Journal of Political Economy*, **LXX** (February, 1962), 1–13.

[12] BISHOP, ROBERT L. "Duopoly: Collusion or Warfare?" *American Economic Review*, **L** (1960), 933–961.

[13] BLAUG, M. *Economic Theory in Retrospect*. Homewood, Ill.: Richard D. Irwin, Inc., 1962.

[14] BODENHORN, D. "A Note on the Theory of the Firm," *Journal of Business*, **XXXII** (April, 1959).

[15] BONINI, CHARLES P. *Simulation of Information and Decision Systems in the Firm*. Englewood Cliffs, N. J.: Prentice-Hall, Inc., 1963.

[16] BOULDING, KENNETH E. "Implications for General Economics of More Realistic Theories of the Firm," *American Economic Review*, **XLII** (May, 1952), 35–44.

[17] BOULDING, K. E. "The Present Position of the Theory of the Firm," in K. E. Boulding and W. Allen Spivey (Eds.), *Linear Programming and the Theory of the Firm*. New York: Macmillan, 1960.

[18] BOULDING, K. E., and W. A. SPIVEY (Eds.). *Linear Programming and the Theory of the Firm*. New York: Macmillan, 1960.

[19] CARLSON, SUNE. *A Study of the Theory of Production*. New York: Kelley and Millman, 1956.

[20] CAVES, RICHARD. *American Industry: Structure, Conduct, Performance*. Englewood Cliffs, N. J.: Prentice-Hall, 1964.

[21] CHAMBERLIN, E. H. *The Theory of Monopolistic Competition*. Cambridge: Harvard University Press, 1933.

[22] CLELAND, SHERRILL. "A Short Essay on a Managerial Theory of the Firm," in K. E. Boulding and W. A. Spivey (Eds.), *Linear Programming and the Theory of the Firm*. New York: Macmillan, 1960.

[23] CLEMENS, E. W. "Price Discrimination and the Multi-Product Firm," *Review of Economic Studies*, **XIX** (1951–52), 1–11.

[24] COASE, R. H. "The Nature of the Firm," in *Readings in Price Theory*. Homewood, Ill.: Richard D. Irwin, Inc., 1952.

[25] COHAN, AVERY B. "The Theory of the Firm: A View on Methodology," *Journal of Business*, **XXXVI** (July, 1963), 316–324.

[26] COHEN, KALMAN J., and RICHARD M. CYERT. *Theory of the Firm: Resource Allocation in a Market Economy*. Englewood Cliffs, N. J.: Prentice-Hall, Inc., 1965.

[27] COOPER, W. W. "Theory of the Firm: Some Suggestions for Revision," *American Economic Review*, **XXXIX** (December, 1949).

[28] COOPER, W. W. "A Proposal for Extending the Theory of the Firm," *Quarterly Journal of Economics*, **LXV** (1951), 87–109.

[29] COURNOT, AUGUSTIN (trans. by N. T. Bacon). *Récherches sur les Principes Mathematiques de la Théorie des Richesses*. New York: Macmillan and Co., 1897.

[30] CYERT, R. M., and J. G. MARCH. "Organizational Structure and Pricing Behavior in an Oligopolistic Market," *American Economic Review*, **XLV** (March, 1955), 129–139.

[31] CYERT, R. M., and J. G. MARCH. "Organizational Factors in the Theory of Oligopoly," *Quarterly Journal of Economics*, **LXX** (1956), 44–46.

[32] CYERT, R. M., and J. G. MARCH. "Research on a Behavioral Theory of the Firm," in *Contributions to Scientific Research in Management*. The Proceedings of the Scientific Program following the Dedication of the Western Data Processing Center, Graduate School of Business Administration, University of California, Los Angeles, January 29–30, 1959.

[33] CYERT, R. M., and J. G. MARCH. *A Behavior Theory of the Firm*. Englewood Cliffs, N. J.: Prentice-Hall, 1963.

[34] CYERT, R. M., H. A. SIMON, and D. B. TROW. "Observation of a Business Decision," *The Journal of Business*, **XXIX** (1956), 237–248.

[35] DORFMAN, ROBERT. *Applications of Linear Programming to the Theory of the Firm*. Berkeley: University of California Press, 1951.

[36] EARLY, J. S. "Marginal Policies of 'Excellently Managed' Companies," *American Economic Review*, **XLVI** (1956), 44–70.

[37] EDGEWORTH, FRANCIS Y. *Mathematical Psychics*. London: C. K. Paul & Co., 1881.

[38] EDGEWORTH, FRANCIS Y. "La teoria pura del monopolio," *Giornale degli Economisti*, **XV** (1897), 13–31.

[39] EFROYMSON, CLARENCE W. "A Note on Kinked Demand Curves," *American Economic Review*, **XXXIII** (March, 1943), 98–109.

[40] EITEMAN, W. J. *Price Determination*. Bureau of Business Research Report No. 16, Ann Arbor, Michigan, 1949.

[41] FELLNER, WILLIAM. *Competition Among the Few: Oligopoly and Similar Market Structures*. New York: Alfred A. Knopf, 1949.

[42] FERGUSON, C. E. *Microeconomic Theory*. Homewood, Ill.: Richard D. Irwin, Inc., 1966.

[43] FRIEDMAN, MILTON. *Essays in Positive Economics*. Chicago: University of Chicago Press, 1953.

[44] HALL, R. L., and C. J. HITCH. "Price Theory and Business Behavior," *Oxford Economic Papers*, No. 2 (May, 1939), 12–45.

[45] HARROD, R. F. "Doctrines of Imperfect Competition," *Quarterly Journal of Economics*, **XLVIII** (May, 1934), 442–470.

[46] HENDERSON, JAMES M., and RICHARD E. QUANDT. *Microeconomic Theory*. New York: McGraw-Hill Book Co., 1958.

[47] HICKS, J. R. "Annual Survey of Economic Theory: The Theory of Monopoly," *Econometrica*, **III** (1935), 1–20.

[48] HICKS, J. R. *Value and Capital*. Oxford: Clarendon Press, 1939.

[49] HICKS, J. R. "The Process of Imperfect Competition," *Oxford Economic Papers*, N.S. **VI** (1954), 41–54.

[50] HIRSHLEIFER, JACK. "An Exposition of the Equilibrium of the Firm: Symmetry Between Product and Factor Analysis," *Economica*, **XXIX** (August, 1962), 263–268.

[51] JEVONS, WILLIAM STANLEY. *The Theory of Political Economy*, 1871.

[52] KALDOR, NICHOLAS. "The Equilibrium of the Firm," *Economic Journal*, **XLIV** (March, 1934), 60–76.

[53] KATONA, G. *Psychological Analysis of Economic Behavior*. New York: McGraw-Hill Book Co., 1961.

[54] KNIGHT, F. H. *Risk, Uncertainty and Profit*. Boston: Houghton, Mifflin, 1921.

[55] KOOPMANS, TJALLING C. *Three Essays on the State of Economic Science*. New York: McGraw-Hill Book Co., 1957.

[56] KRUPP, S. R. "Theoretical Explanation and the Nature of the Firm," *Western Economic Journal*, **I** (Summer, 1963), 191–204.

[57] KUENNE, ROBERT E. *The Theory of General Economic Equilibrium*. Princeton: Princeton University Press, 1963.

[58] LESTER, R. A. "Shortcomings of Marginal Analysis for Wage-Employment Problems," *American Economic Review*, **XXXVI** (March, 1946), 63–82.

[59] LESTER, R. A. "Marginalism, Minimum Wages, and Labor Markets," *American Economic Review*, **XXXVII** (March, 1947), 135–148.

[60] MCGUIRE, JOSEPH M. *Theories of Business Behavior*. Englewood Cliffs, N. J.: Prentice-Hall, Inc., 1964.

[61] MCGUIRE, JOSEPH M., JOHN S. Y. CHIU, and ALVAR O. ELBING. "Executive Incomes, Sales, and Profits," *American Economic Review*, **LII** (September, 1962), 753–761.

[62] MACHLUP, FRITZ. "Monopoly and Competition: A Classification of Market Positions," *American Economic Review*, **XXVII** (September, 1937), 445–451.

[63] MACHLUP, FRITZ. "Marginal Analysis and Empirical Research," *American Economic Review*, **XXXVI** (September, 1946), 519–554.

[64] MACHLUP, FRITZ. "Rejoinder to an Antimarginalist," *American Economic Review*, **XXXVII** (March, 1947), 148–154.

[65] MACHLUP, FRITZ. *The Economics of Sellers' Competition*. Baltimore: Johns Hopkins Press, 1952.

[66] MACHLUP, FRITZ. "Theories of the Firm: Marginalist, Behavioral, Managerial," *American Economic Review*, **LVII** (March, 1967), 1–33.

[67] MARCH, J. G., and H. A. SIMON. *Organizations*. New York: John Wiley & Sons, 1958.

[68] MARGOLIS, JULIUS. "The Analysis of the Firm: Rationalism, Conventionalism, and Behaviorism," *Journal of Business*, **XXXI** (July, 1958), 187–199.

[69] MARSHALL, ALFRED. *Principles of Economics*. London: Macmillan & Co., 1890.

[70] MAUER, WILLIAM A., and THOMAS H. NAYLOR. "Monopolistic-Monopsonistic Competition: The Multi-Product, Multi-Factor Firm," *Southern Economic Journal*, **XXXI** (July, 1964), 38–43.

[71] MAYBERRY, J. P., J. E. NASH, and MARTIN SHUBIK. "A Comparison of Treatments of a Duopoly Situation," *Econometrica*, **XXI** (1953), 141–154.

[72] MODIGLIANI, FRANCO. "New Developments on the Oligopoly Front," *Journal of Political Economy*, **LXVI** (1958), 214–232.

[73] NAYLOR, THOMAS H. "Some Theoretical Models of the Firm," unpublished Ph.D. dissertation, Department of Economics, Tulane University, New Orleans, Louisiana, 1964.

[74] PAPANDREOU, A. G. "Problems in the Theory of the Firm," in *Survey of Contemporary Economics*, Vol. II. Homewood, Ill.: Richard D. Irwin, Inc., 1952.

[75] PHILLIPS, ALMARIN. "Operations Research and the Theory of the Firm," *Southern Economic Journal*, **XXVIII** (April, 1962), 357–364.

[76] ROBINSON, JOAN. *Economic Philosophy*. Chicago: Aldine Publishing Co., 1963.

[77] ROTHSCHILD, K. W. "Price Theory and Oligopoly," *Economic Journal*, **LVII** (1947), 299–320.

[78] SAMUELSON, PAUL A. *Foundations of Economic Analysis*. Cambridge: Harvard University Press, 1948.

[79] SCITOVSKY, T. "A Note on Profit Maximization and its Implications," *Review of Economic Studies*, **XI** (1943), 57–60.

[80] SHUBIK, MARTIN. *Strategy and Market Structure*. New York: John Wiley & Sons, 1959.

[81] SIMON, H. A. "A Behavioral Model of Rational Choice," *Quarterly Journal of Economics*, **LXIX** (February, 1955), 99–118.

[82] SIMON, H. A. "Theories of Decision-Making in Economics," *American Economic Review*, **XLIX** (June, 1959), 253–283.

[83] SIMON, H. A. "New Developments in the Theory of the Firm," *American Economic Review*, **LII** (May, 1962), 1–15.

[84] SMITHIES, ARTHUR. "Equilibrium in Monopolistic Competition," *Quarterly Journal of Economics*, **LV** (1940), 95–115.

[85] STACKELBERG, H. V. "Grundlagen einer reiner Kostentheorie," *Zeitschrift für National-Oekonomie* (May, 1932).

[86] STACKELBERG, H. V. (trans. by Alan T. Peacock). *The Theory of the Market Economy*. New York: Oxford University Press, 1952.

[87] STELZER, IRWIN M. *Selected Antitrust Cases* (3rd ed.). Homewood, Ill.: Richard D. Irwin, Inc., 1966.

[88] STIGLER, GEORGE J. "Notes on a Theory of Duopoly," *Journal of Political Economy*, **XLVIII** (1940), 521–541.

[89] STIGLER, GEORGE J. "The Kinky Oligopoly Demand Curve and Rigid Prices," *Journal of Political Economy*, **LV** (1947), 432–449.

[90] STIGLER, G. J. *Introduction in Business Concentration and Price Policy*. Princeton: Princeton University Press, 1955.

[91] SWEEZEY, PAUL M. "Demand Under Conditions of Oligopoly," *Journal of Political Economy*, **XLVII** (August, 1939), 568–573.

[92] TRIFFIN, ROBERT. *Monopolistic Competition and General Equilibrium Theory*. Cambridge: Harvard University Press, 1949.

[93] WALRAS, LEON. *Abrege des Elements d'économie politique pure*. Paris: R. Pichon et R. Durand-Auzias, 1938.

[94] WELDON, J. C. "The Multi-Product Firm," *Canadian Journal of Economics and Political Science*, **XIV** (1948), 176–190.

[95] WHITE, C. MICHAEL. "Multiple Goals in the Theory of the Firm," in K. E. Boulding and W. Spivey (Eds.), *Linear Programming and the Theory of the Firm*. New York: Macmillan, 1960.

[96] WILLIAMSON, OLIVER E. "Managerial Discretion and Business Behavior," *American Economic Review*, **LIII** (December, 1963), 1032–1057.

[97] WILLIAMSON, OLIVER E. *The Economics of Discretionary Behavior: Managerial Objectives in a Theory of the Firm*. Englewood Cliffs, N. J.: Prentice-Hall, Inc., 1964.

[98] WINTER, SIDNEY G. "Economic Natural Selection and the Theory of the Firm," *Yale Economic Essays* (Spring, 1964), 225–272.

PART 3

Mathematical programming models of the firm

6

The mathematical programming problem of the firm

INTRODUCTION

Without exception, the solutions to all of the optimization models described in the preceding four chapters were obtained through the use of *classical* optimization techniques. In each model some objective function

(6-1) $$\phi = \phi(X_1, X_2, \ldots, X_j, \ldots, X_n)$$

was optimized (maximized or minimized) subject to a set of m constraints

(6-2) $$H_i(X_1, X_2, \ldots, X_n) = 0 \qquad i = 1, 2, \ldots, m$$

where $m < n$ and where ϕ and H_i were assumed to be differentiable.

The Lagrangian multiplier method has proved to be useful for solving problems which can be formulated in this manner. Unfortunately, attempts to apply this method to certain types of economic models of the firm can lead to at least three kinds of problems. First, economic variables are usually assumed to be non-negative. That is, negative values are usually considered to be nonsensical. With the Lagrangian method it is quite possible to obtain negative values which satisfy the first- and second-order optimality conditions. When non-negative solutions are required, we must turn to other methods. Second, if the objective function ϕ and all of the constraints H_i for a particular model are linear, then the partial derivatives $\partial\phi/\partial X_j$ and $\partial H_i/\partial X_j$ are constants and the necessary conditions for a maximum or a minimum cannot possibly be satisfied. "This reflects the fact that a linear function has no finite maximum or minimum—unless the variables are further constrained, for example, by non-negativity requirements, in which case we also run into the difficulty mentioned above" [32, p. 194]. Third, one or more of the constraints for a model of the firm may take the form of inequalities,

(6-3) $$H_i(X_1, \ldots, X_n) \geq 0 \qquad i = 1, 2, \ldots, m$$

One alternative is to disregard the inequalities (i.e., treat them as equations) and apply the Lagrangian method. However, it may turn out that there are no feasible solutions to the model when the inequality constraints are all replaced by equations. Hence the Lagrangian method breaks down. As an alternative we might transform all inequality constraints into equations through the use of surplus variables S_i,

(6-4) $$H_i(X_1, \ldots, X_n) - S_i = 0 \qquad i = 1, 2, \ldots, m$$

Since (6-4) is merely an identity which defines S_i, it imposes no restriction on the variables $X_1, X_2, \ldots, X_n$ unless we add the non-negativity constraint,

(6-5) $$S_i \geq 0 \qquad i = 1, 2, \ldots, m$$

The non-negativity constraint (6-5) ensures that the inequality in (6-3) is not reversed. Unfortunately, this takes us back to our original problem regarding non-negative variables. With the Lagrangian method we have no assurance that (6-5) will be satisfied.

These three problems with the Lagrangian method—(1) non-negativity requirements, (2) linear objective functions and constraints, and (3) inequalities—provide the rationale for the use of the collection of mathematical techniques known as *mathematical programming*. Mathematical programming was designed specifically to circumvent these problems. Economic models which are characterized by non-negativity requirements, linear objective functions and constraints, and inequalities can all be solved with mathematical programming techniques.[1]

THE MATHEMATICAL PROGRAMMING PROBLEM

The general problem of mathematical programming may be stated as the problem of determining the values of n variables $X_1, X_2, \ldots, X_n$ which will maximize or minimize the function

(6-6) $$Z = \phi(X_1, X_2, \ldots, X_n)$$

subject to m constraints of the form

(6-7) $$h_i(X_1, X_2, \ldots, X_n) \begin{pmatrix} \leq \\ = \\ \geq \end{pmatrix} B_i \qquad i = 1, 2, \ldots, m$$

and to non-negativity constraints

(6-8) $$X_j \geq 0 \qquad j = 1, 2, \ldots, n$$

[1] There are indeed other problems connected with the use of the Lagrangian method. In particular, it cannot handle dynamic models or models which are characterized by uncertainty and risk. Dynamic programming and stochastic programming, two special cases of mathematical programming, will be considered in Chapters 11 and 12 respectively. In this chapter, and the remaining chapters in this section, we shall restrict ourselves to models of the firm which assume complete certainty and static equilibrium.

In (6-7), one and only one of the symbols $\leq$, $=$, $\geq$ holds for each equation.[2] The number of equations m may be greater than, less than, or equal to the number of variables n.

If both the objective function (6-6) and all of the constraints (6-7) are linear, then we have the important special case of mathematical programming known as a *linear programming* problem. If the objective function is nonlinear and the constraints are either linear or nonlinear, then we have a *nonlinear programming* problem. Finally, if some or all of the variables in a mathematical programming problem are required to take on only discrete or integral values, then we have an *integer programming* problem.

Before turning to a survey of linear, nonlinear, and integer programming models we shall formulate a mathematical programming model of the firm and with the aid of the Kuhn-Tucker theorem [83] derive the optimality conditions for the model and interpret their economic significance.

A MATHEMATICAL PROGRAMMING MODEL OF THE FIRM

The model described in this section is a transitional model, designed to enable one to move gradually in a stepwise manner from marginal analysis models to linear and nonlinear programming models of the firm. It is essentially an extension of the profit-maximization model of the multiproduct, multifactor firm (described in Chapter 5) to include both fixed and variable factors of production. (In the original model only variable factors were considered.) In addition, all variables are assumed to be non-negative. Otherwise, the assumptions underlying this model are the same as those of the multifactor, profit-maximization model of Chapter 5.

The model[3]

Consider a firm which uses m variable factors and n fixed factors to produce p different products, where

(6-9) X_{ik} = quantity of the ith variable factor used in the production of the kth product ($i = 1, \ldots, m$; $k = 1, \ldots, p$).

(6-10) Y_{jk} = quantity of the jth fixed factor used in the production of the kth product ($j = 1, \ldots, n$; $k = 1, \ldots, p$).

(6-11) Z_k = quantity of the kth product ($k = 1, \ldots, p$).

(6-12) Y_j = quantity of the jth fixed factor which is currently available to the firm ($j = 1, \ldots, n$).

[2] We use h_i rather than H_i when we place the constant, B_i, on the right-hand side. For example, $H_i = B_i - h_i \geq 0$ for $h_i \leq B_i$.

[3] This model is taken from Thomas H. Naylor, "A Kuhn-Tucker Model of the Multi-Product, Multi-Factor Firm," *Southern Economic Journal*, XXXI (April 1965), pp. 324–330.

The firm's production function is given by

(6-13) $$Q(Z_1, \ldots, Z_p, X_{11}, \ldots, X_{mp}, Y_{11}, \ldots, Y_{np}) = 0$$

Furthermore, the total consumption of the jth fixed factor in the production of the p products cannot exceed the quantity of the firm's currently available jth fixed factor

(6-14) $$\sum_{k=1}^{p} Y_{jk} \leq Y_j \qquad (j = 1, \ldots, n)$$

Let R denote the firm's total revenue function and let C denote its total variable cost equation,

(6-15) $$R = R(Z_1, \ldots, Z_p)$$

(6-16) $$C = C(X_{11}, \ldots, X_{mp})$$

Pfouts has suggested that "transferring units of fixed factors from the production of one product to that of another ordinarily entails a cost" [104, p. 652–653]. This type of cost does not belong in either the category of variable costs or fixed costs, for "these costs do not change continuously with the output of a particular product, but they do change as the product-mix of the firm is changed" [104, p. 652]. This type of conversion cost may be written as

(6-17) $$K = K(Y_{11}, \ldots, Y_{np})$$

Then $\partial K/\partial Y_{jk}$, which is assumed to be positive, denotes the cost of converting a small amount of the jth fixed factor into the production of the kth product.

Finally, F is defined to be fixed costs other than K.

(6-18) $$F = \text{fixed costs}$$

The firm's profit function is now defined as

(6-19) $$\pi = R - C - K - F$$

The objective of the firm is to maximize (6-19) subject to (6-13) and (6-14) and the additional constraint that all of the variables must be non-negative.

At this point it may be observed that the straightforward Lagrangian method is no longer applicable because of the non-negativity requirement and the inequality constraints imposed by (6-14). Hence, to analyze the properties of our mathematical programming model of the firm we need a more sophisticated mathematical tool—the Kuhn-Tucker theorem.

The Kuhn-Tucker theorem [83]

The Kuhn-Tucker theorem, which is in reality a set of theorems, is a convenient mathematical tool for describing the optimality conditions of functions constrained by equalities and inequalities rather than just equalities. This rather powerful theorem provides the theoretical basis for many of the existing linear and nonlinear programming computational algorithms. For example, Wolfe's [128] simplex algorithm for quadratic programming is a direct consequence of the Kuhn-Tucker theorem. However, in the present case we are concerned primarily with the use of the Kuhn-Tucker theorem as an expository device for economic analysis.

The Kuhn-Tucker theorem may be applied to the problem of finding the extreme values of a function

$$\phi = \phi(X_1, \ldots, X_n) \tag{6-20}$$

where the variables are constrained by inequalities of the following form:

$$H_i(X_1, \ldots, X_n) \geq 0 \qquad i = 1, \ldots, m \tag{6-21}$$

Although the theorem is equally applicable to both minimization and maximization problems, we will consider only the maximization problem.

In order for the theorem to be operative, it is necessary to assume that the objective function (6-20) and the constraints (6-21) are concave and differentiable. There is an additional minor restriction on the constraints to eliminate the possibility of a singular point on the frontier of the constraints.[4]

The formulation of the Lagrangian function for this constrained maximization problem is straightforward:

$$L = \phi(X_1, \ldots, X_n) + \sum_{i=1}^{m} \lambda_i H_i(X_1, \ldots, X_n) \tag{6-22}$$

for

$$X_j \geq 0 \text{ and } \lambda_i \geq 0 \qquad (j = 1, \ldots, n;\ i = 1, \ldots, m)$$

To ensure the existence of a constrained maximum at X_j° and λ_i° it is necessary and sufficient that a "saddle point" exist at the extreme value.

The set of X_j° and λ_i° is called a *saddle point* of the function $L(X_j, \lambda_i)$ if $X_j^\circ \geq 0$, $\lambda_i^\circ \geq 0$ and

$$L(X_j, \lambda_i^\circ) \leq L(X_j^\circ, \lambda_i^\circ) \leq L(X_j^\circ, \lambda_i)$$

for all $X_j \geq 0$ and $\lambda_i \geq 0$. It may be helpful to imagine an actual saddle-shaped function, $L(X, \lambda)$, in three dimensions. Then, the saddle point is that center point in the saddle seat which corresponds to a maximum along the X-axis (λ constant at λ°) and to a minimum along the λ-axis (X constant at X°).

[4] This minor condition is satisfied if $L(X_1, \ldots, X_n, \lambda_1^\circ, \ldots, \lambda_m^\circ)$ is a concave function in $X_1, \ldots, X_n$ and $L(X_1^\circ \ldots, X_n^\circ, \lambda_1, \ldots, \lambda_m)$ is a convex function of $\lambda_1, \ldots, \lambda_m$. The symbol X_j° means that X_j takes that value at which ϕ is maximized.

To ensure the existence of a saddle point, it is necessary and sufficient that the following conditions hold:

(6-23) $$\left.\frac{\partial L}{\partial X_j}\right|_{X_j = X_j^\circ} \leq 0 \qquad (j = 1, \ldots, n)$$

(6-24) $$\sum_{j=1}^{n} \left.\frac{\partial L}{\partial X_j}\right|_{X_j = X_j^\circ} \cdot X_j^\circ = 0$$

(6-25) $$X_j^\circ \geq 0 \qquad (j = 1, \ldots, n)$$

(6-26) $$\left.\frac{\partial L}{\partial \lambda_i}\right|_{\lambda_i = \lambda_i^\circ} \geq 0 \qquad (i = 1, \ldots, m)$$

(6-27) $$\sum_{i=1}^{m} \left.\frac{\partial L}{\partial \lambda_i}\right|_{\lambda_i = \lambda_i^\circ} \cdot \lambda_i^\circ = 0$$

(6-28) $$\lambda_i^\circ \geq 0 \qquad (i = 1, \ldots, m)$$

The strict inequality will hold for condition (6-23) only when $X_j^\circ = 0$. Similarly, the strict inequality will hold for condition (6-26) only if $\lambda_i^\circ = 0$, i.e., if the ith constraint is not binding. (For the reader who would like to see the conditions applied to a numerical example, Chapter 9 provides such an illustration.)

Application of the Kuhn-Tucker theorem

In order for the Kuhn-Tucker theorem to apply to the profit-maximization problem of the firm, it is necessary that (6-19), (6-13), and (6-14) be *concave* and *differentiable*. The firm's revenue function is characterized by the fact that increases in output yield diminishing marginal returns. Both C and K, the firm's cost equations, are assumed to behave in the following manner. Marginal costs may either increase or decrease with increases in output. However, if marginal costs are decreasing, the absolute value of the rate of decrease must be less than or equal to the rate of decrease of the marginal revenue function. The firm's profit function (6-19) will be concave if the above conditions are fulfilled. Furthermore, the production function (6-13) is assumed to be differentiable and obeys the law of diminishing returns. This follows, of course, if the production function is concave. The fixed factor constraints (6-14) are linear and may be considered as both concave and convex. Hence both the objective function of the firm and its related constraints satisfy the concavity requirements of the Kuhn-Tucker theorem.

Next, the Lagrangian function for the firm's constrained profit-maximization problem is formulated;

(6-29) $$L = R - C - K - F + \lambda Q + \sum_{j=1}^{n} \mu_j \left(Y_j - \sum_{k=1}^{p} Y_{jk} \right)$$

(Both λ and the μ_j are Lagrangian multipliers.) Corresponding to conditions (6-23) through (6-28), the following conditions, (6-30) through (6-35), must be satisfied to ensure a constrained maximum at X_{ik}°, Y_{jk}°, Z_{k}°, λ°, and μ_{j}°, $(i = 1, \ldots, m; j = 1, \ldots, n; k = 1, \ldots, p)$.

(6-30a) $$\frac{\partial L}{\partial Z_k} = \frac{\partial R}{\partial Z_k} + \lambda \frac{\partial Q}{\partial Z_k} \leq 0 \qquad (k = 1, \ldots, p)$$

(6-30b) $$\frac{\partial L}{\partial X_{ik}} = -\frac{\partial C}{\partial X_{ik}} + \lambda \frac{\partial Q}{\partial X_{ik}} \leq 0 \qquad (i = 1, \ldots, m; k = 1, \ldots, p)$$

(6-30c) $$\frac{\partial L}{\partial Y_{jk}} = -\frac{\partial K}{\partial Y_{jk}} + \lambda \frac{\partial Q}{\partial Y_{jk}} - \mu_j \leq 0 \qquad (j = 1, \ldots, n; k = 1, \ldots, p)$$

(6-31) $$\sum_{k=1}^{p} \left(\frac{\partial R}{\partial Z_k} + \lambda \frac{\partial Q}{\partial Z_k}\right) \cdot Z_k^{\circ} + \sum_{i=1}^{m} \sum_{k=1}^{p} \left(-\frac{\partial C}{\partial X_{ik}} + \lambda \frac{\partial Q}{\partial X_{ik}}\right) \cdot X_{ik}^{\circ}$$
$$+ \sum_{j=1}^{n} \sum_{k=1}^{p} \left(-\frac{\partial K}{\partial Y_{jk}} + \lambda \frac{\partial Q}{\partial Y_{jk}} - \mu_j\right) \cdot Y_{jk}^{\circ} = 0$$

(6-32a) $$Z_k^{\circ} \geq 0 \qquad (k = 1, \ldots, p)$$

(6-32b) $$X_{ik}^{\circ} \geq 0 \qquad (i = 1, \ldots, m; k = 1, \ldots, p)$$

(6-32c) $$Y_{jk}^{\circ} \geq 0 \qquad (j = 1, \ldots, n; k = 1, \ldots, p)$$

(6-33a) $$\frac{\partial L}{\partial \lambda} = Q \geq 0$$

(6-33b) $$\frac{\partial L}{\partial \mu_j} = Y_j - \sum_{k=1}^{p} Y_{jk} \geq 0 \qquad (j = 1, \ldots, n)$$

or

$$\sum_{k=1}^{p} Y_{jk} \leq Y_j \qquad (j = 1, \ldots, n)$$

(6-34) $$Q \cdot \lambda^{\circ} + \sum_{j=1}^{n} \left(Y_j - \sum_{k=1}^{p} Y_{jk}\right) \cdot \mu_j^{\circ} = 0$$

(6-35a) $$\lambda^{\circ} \geq 0$$

(6-35b) $$\mu_j^{\circ} \geq 0 \qquad (j = 1, \ldots, n)$$

(Note that the partial derivatives in (6-30), (6-31), (6-33), and (6-34) are assumed to be evaluated at the optimum values of the variables in the model, as was the case with (6-23), (6-24), (6-26), and (6-27).)

Economic interpretation

We now turn to a detailed analysis of the economic significance of conditions (6-30) through (6-35). Whenever possible we will compare these results with those of the profit-maximization model of the multifactor, multiproduct firm described in Chapter 5.

Before interpreting the economic implications of these mathematical statements it is necessary to define in economic terms the Lagrangian multipliers

λ and μ_j. The interpretation of λ is facilitated if we treat the symbol Q as though it were an arbitrary product (for example Z_1), although in reality it is merely a symbol denoting the implicit form of the production function. If Q is interpreted in this manner, then λ corresponds to the imputed value or shadow price of Q. The interpretation of μ_j is more straightforward than that of λ. The μ_j's are simply the values imputed to the firm's fixed factors of production, i.e., the opportunity costs (per unit) associated with each fixed factor.

Condition (6-30a) may be rewritten as

$$\frac{\partial R}{\partial Z_k} \leq -\lambda \frac{\partial Q}{\partial Z_k} \qquad (k = 1, \ldots, p) \tag{6-36}$$

In this form it states that the marginal revenue (or price in the case of perfect competition) of the kth product must be less than or equal to the marginal imputed cost of producing the kth product. Whenever the equality holds for (6-36) for a particular product, this implies that the product is being produced at an optimum level. If the equality holds over all k, then for any two products a and b,

$$\frac{MR_a}{MR_b} = -\frac{\partial Z_b}{\partial Z_a} \tag{6-37}$$

This is the familiar requirement of marginal analysis that when optimum quantities of a and b are being produced the ratio of their marginal revenues must be equal to the rate of product transformation of the two products. However, if the inequality holds for (6-36), then the profit-maximizing firm will not choose to produce the kth product, for the marginal imputed cost of producing the kth product exceeds the marginal revenue of the kth product. Furthermore, if the marginal revenue exceeds the imputed marginal cost of a particular product, the firm should increase the level of output of that product to the point where marginal revenue equals imputed marginal cost.

Condition (6-30b) may be rewritten as

$$\frac{\partial C}{\partial X_{ik}} \geq \lambda \frac{\partial Q}{\partial X_{ik}} \qquad (i = 1, \ldots, m;\ k = 1, \ldots, p) \tag{6-38}$$

In this form it states that the marginal factor cost (or price in the case of perfect competition) of the ith variable factor used in the production of the kth product must be greater than or equal to the marginal value imputed to the use of one unit of the ith variable factor in the production of the kth product. Whenever the equality holds for (6-38), the ith variable factor is being utilized at an optimum level with regard to the kth product. If the equality holds over all m variable factors for a particular product k, then for any two variable factors a and b,

$$\frac{MFC_a}{MFC_b} = -\frac{\partial X_{bk}}{\partial X_{ak}} \qquad (k = 1, \ldots, p) \tag{6-39}$$

This is the marginal analysis requirement that when optimum quantities of a and b are consumed in the production of the kth product, the ratio of their marginal factor costs must be equal to their rate of technical substitution.

However, if the inequality holds for (6-38), then the profit-maximizing firm will not utilize the ith variable factor in the production of the kth product, for the marginal factor cost of using the ith variable factor in the production of the kth product exceeds the marginal value imputed to the use of one unit of the ith variable factor in the production of the kth product. Furthermore, if the marginal value imputed to the use of the ith variable factor in the production of the kth product is greater than the marginal factor cost of the ith variable factor, then the level of usage of the ith factor in the kth product should be increased.

If the equality holds for both (6-36) and (6-38) over all i and k, and if we select any particular variable factor a and any particular product b, then

$$MFC_{ab} = MR_b \cdot \frac{\partial Z_b}{\partial X_{ab}} \tag{6-40}$$

(MFC_{ab} denotes the marginal factor cost of factor a in producing product b.) This is the optimality requirement that the marginal factor cost of factor a must be equal to the marginal revenue product of b with respect to a.

Condition (6-30c) is of particular interest, since it has no theoretical counterpart in the marginal analysis model of Chapter 5. It is convenient to rewrite the expression in the following form:

$$\lambda \frac{\partial Q}{\partial Y_{jk}} - \frac{\partial K}{\partial Y_{jk}} \leq \mu_j \qquad (j = 1, \ldots, n; k = 1, \ldots, p) \tag{6-41}$$

Condition (6-41) states that the marginal value imputed to the use of one unit of the jth fixed factor in the production of the kth product minus the marginal cost of converting one unit of the jth fixed factor into the production of the kth product must be less than or equal to the marginal value imputed to the jth fixed factor. If the equality holds for (6-41), then the jth fixed factor is being utilized at an optimum level with regard to the kth product. If the inequality holds for (6-41), then the jth fixed factor will not be utilized in the production of the kth product. Furthermore, if the direction of the inequality is reversed, the firm should increase the level of usage of the jth fixed factor in the production of the kth product.

It should be observed, however, that if excess capacity exists in the jth fixed factor, then the corresponding constraint is not binding, and (6-41) becomes

$$-\frac{\partial K}{\partial Y_{jk}} + \lambda \frac{\partial Q}{\partial Y_{jk}} = 0 \qquad (j = 1, \ldots, n; k = 1, \ldots, p) \tag{6-42}$$

From the analysis of conditions (6-30a), (6-30b), and (6-30c) it follows that the requirements for (6-31) are also fulfilled; for either

$$\frac{\partial R}{\partial Z_k} + \lambda \frac{\partial Q}{\partial Z_k} = 0 \qquad \text{or} \qquad Z_k^\circ = 0$$

either

$$-\frac{\partial C}{\partial X_{ik}} + \lambda \frac{\partial Q}{\partial X_{ik}} = 0 \qquad \text{or} \qquad X_{ik}^\circ = 0$$

and either

$$-\frac{\partial K}{\partial Y_{jk}} + \lambda \frac{\partial Q}{\partial Y_{jk}} - \mu_j = 0 \qquad \text{or} \qquad Y_{jk}^{\circ} = 0$$

But to ascertain the economic significance of (6-31), it must be rewritten as

$$\sum_{k=1}^{p} \frac{\partial R}{\partial Z_k} \cdot Z_k^{\circ} - \sum_{i=1}^{m} \sum_{k=1}^{p} \frac{\partial C}{\partial X_{ik}} \cdot X_{ik}^{\circ} - \sum_{j=1}^{n} \sum_{k=1}^{p} \frac{\partial K}{\partial Y_{jk}} \cdot Y_{jk}^{\circ} = \sum_{j=1}^{n} \sum_{k=1}^{p} \mu_j Y_{jk}^{\circ} - \lambda \left[\sum_{k=1}^{p} \frac{\partial Q}{\partial Z_k} \cdot Z_k^{\circ} + \sum_{i=1}^{m} \sum_{k=1}^{p} \frac{\partial Q}{\partial X_{ik}} \cdot X_{ik}^{\circ} + \sum_{j=1}^{n} \sum_{k=1}^{p} \frac{\partial Q}{\partial Y_{jk}} \cdot Y_{jk}^{\circ} \right] \tag{6-43}$$

Equation (6-43) states that the firm's total profit must be equal to the imputed cost of its scarce resources, or equivalently that the firm's profit after paying the imputed cost of its scarce resources must be equal to zero. This zero profit condition should not be confused with the zero profit requirement for long-run equilibrium under perfect competition.

> In imputation, zero profits is an accounting requirement. If accounting prices [imputed prices] are set up which do not completely exhaust profits, these prices do not impute profits completely to the scarce inputs which were used to obtain the outputs. The accounting prices must then be increased to eliminate these unimputed profits.[5]

Conditions (6-32a), (6-32b), and (6-32c) are satisfied by the assumption of economic feasibility. Equation (6-13), the firm's production function, indicates that the equality will always hold for condition (6-33a). Furthermore, if there is an excess supply of the jth fixed factor, the inequality will hold for condition (6-33b), and μ_j will be equal to zero. The equality will hold if the jth fixed factor is not in excess supply. Therefore, condition (6-34) must necessarily hold. Since $Q = 0$, equation (6-34) may be rewritten as

$$\sum_{j=1}^{n} \mu_j Y_j^{\circ} = \sum_{j=1}^{n} \sum_{k=1}^{p} \mu_j Y_{jk}^{\circ} \tag{6-44}$$

Equation (6-44) indicates that the total value imputed to the scarce resources available to the firm must be equal to the total value of the scarce resources used in manufacturing operations. Finally, the Lagrangian multipliers are assumed to be non-negative, i.e., conditions (6-35a) and (6-35b) are satisfied.

Summary

We have shown that the Kuhn-Tucker theorem is an extremely useful device for interpreting the optimality conditions of the multiproduct, multifactor firm which utilizes both fixed and variable factors of production. The Kuhn-Tucker

[5] See [8], first edition (1962), p. 92.

theorem has also been found to be useful in comparing marginal analysis models of the multiproduct, multifactor firm with mathematical programming models of the firm. In one sense the model described in this section is a transitional model, designed to enable one to move gradually and in a stepwise manner from marginal analysis models of the firm to mathematical programming models of the firm. Although our model contains most of the important characteristics found in marginal analysis models, it also contains three characteristics found in mathematical programming models but not in marginal analysis models: (1) non-negativity requirements, (2) fixed factors of production, and (3) inequality constraints.

A SURVEY OF MATHEMATICAL PROGRAMMING MODELS

The general problem of mathematical programming was previously defined as the problem of finding the extreme values of the function $\phi(X_1, \ldots, X_n)$ subject to the $m + n$ constraints $h_i(X_1, \ldots, X_n)\{\leq, =, \geq\}B_i$ for $(i = 1, \ldots, m)$ and $X_j \geq 0$ for $(j = 1, \ldots, n)$. In this and the following four chapters three widely used (although not mutually exclusive) subsets of mathematical programming are considered: linear programming, nonlinear programming, and integer programming. Linear programming (Chapters 7 and 8) is a special case of mathematical programming in which ϕ and h_i are linear functions. Nonlinear programming (Chapter 9) includes the case in which ϕ and/or the h_i are nonlinear functions. Integer programming (Chapter 10) refers to that class of mathematical programming problems in which solutions must be expressed as integers.

Since the scope of Part III of this book is limited to the firm under complete certainty and static equilibrium, two other important classes of mathematical programming problems, stochastic programming (Chapter 12) and dynamic programming (Chapter 11), will not be considered until later. Stochastic programming includes those cases in which the parameters of ϕ and h_i are random variables. For a complete survey of the literature on stochastic programming, see Madansky [93]. Among the more important contributions to the literature on stochastic programming are the papers by Charnes and Cooper [25], Dantzig [34,39,41], Elmaghraby [53], Evers [54], Kataoka [81], Madansky [90,91,92,93], Tintner [115,116], and Vajda [118].

Dynamic programming refers to a mathematical method of analysis which is used to solve multistage decision problems, i.e., problems in which decisions generated in stage 1 become conditions for stage 2, etc. Production scheduling is an example of a multistage decision problem; for the amount one plans to produce this month is partially dependent on how much one produced last month, because of the possible accumulation or reduction of backlog.

The essential characteristic of dynamic programming is that optimum solutions are reached in a stepwise manner. Given the conditions of stage 1 an optimum solution is determined. Then the optimum solution from stage 1 is integrated with stage 2 to arrive at a new optimum solution. The optimum solution of stage 2 is then integrated with stage 3 to arrive at a new optimum solution. This procedure is continued over all stages. At each stage the optimum solution from the preceding stage is carried forward as a condition for the stage in question. Mathematical techniques have been developed to handle lengthy multistage decision problems involving nonlinearity and uncertainty, as well as problems involving linearity and complete certainty. The books by Bellman [11] and Bellman and Dreyfus [12] contain excellent surveys of the theory and application of dynamic programming.

Linear programming

The model Linear programming is a mathematical technique which yields the optimum solution to problems defined by a linear objective function subject to a set of linear constraints. Mathematically, the problem of linear programming may be stated as one of optimizing (maximizing or minimizing) a linear objective function of the following form:

(6-45) $$Z = \sum_{j=1}^{n} C_j X_j$$

subject to linear constraints of the form

(6-46) $$\sum_{j=1}^{n} a_{ij} X_j \begin{pmatrix} \leq \\ = \\ \geq \end{pmatrix} B_i \qquad (i = 1, \ldots, m),$$

and

(6-47) $$X_j \geq 0 \qquad (j = 1, \ldots, n)$$

where C_j, a_{ij}, and B_i are all constants.

Solution techniques In 1947 Dantzig, while working for the United States Air Force [33,38], developed a practical numerical procedure called the "simplex method" for solving linear programming problems. Given a linear programming problem, an initial—or basic feasible—solution is obtained. The simplex method determines whether or not the solution can be improved by introducing a "new" variable into the solution and removing one of the "old" variables from the solution. If improvement is possible, a new solution is obtained. It is then tested to determine whether it is an optimum solution; if it is not, further substitutions are made. This solution evaluation procedure continues until it is no longer possible to improve the solution further, indicating that an optimum solution has been found. Thus, the simplex method is an iterative technique which successively improves the basic feasible solution until an optimum solution is found. In Chapter 7 we examine two variations of the simplex method—the primal-simplex method and the dual-simplex method.

Applications Let us consider a preliminary application of linear programming to the theory of the firm. This initial formulation of the linear programming problem of the firm will be defined according to the method found most frequently in the literature. However, in Chapter 8 this approach is modified so as to conform to the notation and terminology of the marginal analysis models of Chapter 5. Only then will it be possible to achieve a meaningful comparison of linear programming and conventional marginal analysis.

Consider a firm which has n independent activities (or processes) available, where an activity is defined to be a particular way of combining factor inputs for the production of an output. Activities may represent different methods for the production of a single product or the production of distinct products. The definition of an activity presupposes that the firm has previously made a technical decision as to the way of combining inputs for varying output levels.

Let X_j, where $(j = 1, \ldots, n)$, denote the level of the firm's jth activity $(X_j \geq 0)$. The objective of the firm is to maximize total net revenue Z, which is assumed to be a linear function of the firm's activity levels:

$$Z = \sum_{j=1}^{n} P_j X_j \tag{6-48}$$

where P_j denotes the net revenue of a unit level of the jth activity of the firm. (Net revenue is assumed to be net of variable cost.)

The firm is constrained in its selection of activity levels by its fixed endowments of inputs required to support the n activities. These constraints may be such that (1) the capacities of the various components of fixed plant may be limited; (2) the inputs for some activities may be produced within the firm, in which case activities that produce these inputs must be in balance with activities that consume them; (3) certain outputs may be usable only in rigidly fixed proportions. In other cases constraints may take the form of (4) quality specifications for some or all products; (5) minimum quantities of inputs or outputs, set by contractual obligations or other considerations; (6) financial constraints [47, p. 161]. If B_i denotes the fixed endowment of the firm's ith input and B_i is a linear function of the independent activity levels (X_j's), then the constraints imposed on the activity levels are given by

$$\sum_{j=1}^{n} a_{ij} X_j \leq B_i \qquad (i = 1, \ldots, m) \tag{6-49}$$

where a_{ij} is the quantity of B_i required to support a unit level of the jth activity.

In summary, the assumptions upon which the linear programming formulation of the problem of the firm rests are (1) perfect competition, (2) linearity, (3) divisibility, (4) additivity, and (5) finiteness.

1. *Perfect Competition.* The price of a unit level of the jth activity is fixed and known.

2. *Linearity*. By definition, in linear programming each process is characterized by certain ratios of the quantities of the inputs to each other and to the quantities of each of the outputs. These ratios are defined to be constant and independent of the extent to which the process is used [45].
3. *Divisibility*. It is assumed that any process can be used at any positive level so long as sufficient resources are available; indivisibilities and "lumpiness" in production are ignored [45].
4. *Additivity*. It is assumed that two or more processes can be used simultaneously, within the limitations of available resources, and that if this is done the quantities of the outputs and inputs will be the sums of the quantities which would result if the several processes were used individually [45].
5. *Finiteness*. It is assumed that the number of processes available is finite [45].

Linear programming has been successfully applied to a wide variety of specific industrial problems. The following examples are typical of these applications.[6]

The products of many firms are subject to seasonal sales fluctuations, e.g., of oil-refining companies. For such companies widely fluctuating production rates have proved extremely costly, whereas uniform production rates build up inventories that incur excessive storage costs. Through the use of linear programming these companies can establish a production schedule that will satisfy demand as well as minimize both the costly effects of fluctuating production rates and the excessive inventory carrying charges resulting from a uniform production rate.

Further applications in this area involve finding the best uses of production capacity and the best basis for assigning production to a number of manufacturing or producing centers. Excess-capacity problems involve selecting from among a group of potential products that set of products which will both utilize the capacity and maximize the contribution to profit and overhead. Assigning production to a number of producing points with due consideration to the initial location of raw materials, plant production capacities, demand requirements, and final destination of products is a type of problem that is easily solved by linear programming. It is similar to the task of assigning production to processes in a plant where the products have varying production periods and are not equally efficient. In this instance linear programming will provide for the optimum allocation of products among different processes in accordance with some objective, such as minimum processing time.

There are numerous instances in which certain basic components are combined to produce a product having a certain set of specifications. Examples of this type of problem can be found in the blending of gasolines, the mixing

[6] For a comprehensive bibliography of linear programming applications see: V. Riley and S. Gass, *Linear Programming and Associated Techniques* (Baltimore: Johns Hopkins Press, 1958).

of cattle feeds, and the mixing of meats to produce sausages or other meat products. A problem in oil refineries, for example, is to select a number of crude-oil products to be blended into different grades of gasoline. The basic products have certain common characteristics, such as octane rating, vapor pressure indices, and distillation temperatures. Considering the demand for gasoline of varying specifications and the supply conditions for the crude-oil products, linear programming can determine the mixture of crudes that will yield maximum profit, minimum cost, or some other optimum. The cattle-feed problem consists in minimizing the cost of producing a feed that meets certain nutritional requirements.

Processes requiring inputs that are available at different quanties, qualities, and prices present a purchasing problem that can be solved for a least-cost objective. An oil refinery which purchases all of its crude oil from outside sources uses linear programming with a profit-maximizing objective to determine which crudes should be purchased. The model considers output requirements and specifications, crude oils on hand, and processing costs in the evaluation of this problem.

Whether to make a product component or purchase it from an outside source is another problem area in which linear programming can be of assistance. The factors that are considered in a problem of this type are: process and product requirements, production and purchasing costs, selling costs, overhead costs, and either a profit or cost objective to be optimized.

The route that a salesman should follow in order to minimize distance traveled in covering a specified territory is also a problem that can be solved by linear programming. Under certain conditions linear programming can be used to solve a variety of different routing problems involving origin-destination schemes. For example, we may have empty boxcars at various locations (origins) and requests for boxcars at other locations (destinations). Given the cost of moving empty boxcars, linear programming will yield the optimum assignment of empty boxcars from origins to destinations. This technique is also useful in determining the location of additional warehousing facilities and the allocation of products to machines.

Another class of problems involves assigning facilities to jobs in a manner that embodies some performance objective. Thus problems of assigning products to facilities in which the costs of producing each product will vary with the facility chosen can be solved by linear programming. This technique can also be used to assign workers to jobs offering a quantitative measure of the workers' effectiveness.

Linear programming has also been used to solve problems of optimizing executive compensation programs, location of and management of river-dam projects, farm management, contract awards, traffic control, scheduling of military tanker fleets, minimizing trim losses in paper mills, balancing assembly-line operations, and optimizing investment portfolio allocations for both individual and institutional investors.

An example model Consider a firm which has facilities for assembling two different types of television sets.[7] These facilities can be used to assemble both black-and-white and color sets. At the present time the firm is producing only one model of each type of set. The black-and-white set retails for $198 and contributes $15 to profit and overhead, whereas the color set sells for $499.95 at the retail level and contributes $45 to profit and overhead. Both the black-and-white sets and the color sets are 21-inch table models.

The television manufacturer is concerned with the problem of deciding how to best utilize his production facilities so as to maximize profits. Since both labor skills and plant and equipment are completely interchangeable with regard to the production of the two types of television sets, varying quantities of both black-and-white and color sets may be produced on the same day. The present demand for television sets is such that the company can sell as many sets as it can produce.

The objective of the firm is to produce that quantity of black-and-white sets X_1 and color sets X_2 that will maximize total contribution to profit and overhead subject to the constraints imposed by the capacity of the existing assembly plant. The profit function is given by π:

$$\pi = 15X_1 + 45X_2 \tag{6-50}$$

The production of television sets involves the assembly of approximately 1000 components to a metal chassis base and the insertion of the chassis and the speaker into a cabinet. The process consists of three essential steps: (1) subassembly, or the fabrication of major components; (2) set assembly, or the insertion of the chassis and speaker into a cabinet; and (3) final inspection and testing.

Most of the major components of television sets are prepared on separate subassembly lines prior to movement to the main assembly lines. However, speakers, cabinets, and transformers are purchased from outside suppliers. With the exception of color picture tubes, the manufacturer always carries an inventory consisting of a sufficient number of components to satisfy the daily production requirements for both black-and-white and color television sets. The plant has a daily production capacity of only 50 color picture tubes, and technical requirements prevent the purchase of color tubes from outside suppliers (in the short run). This constraint on the production of color sets may be expressed algebraically as

$$X_2 \leq 50 \tag{6-51}$$

This inequality indicates that the number of units of X_2 must be less than or equal to 50, where 50 is the daily supply of color picture tubes.

Each black-and-white set requires 1 man-hour of set assembly time, whereas a color set requires 1.6 man-hours. The plant employs 30 men for an eight-hour shift to perform the set assembly operations. Since the plant is in operation for

[7] This model was taken from [103].

only one shift per day, the capacity of the set assembly line is (8×30) or 240 man-hours per day. The set assembly constraint may be expressed as

(6-52) $$1.0X_1 + 1.6X_2 \leq 240$$

This relation indicates that the number of units of X_1 multiplied by the 1.0 man-hours that each unit of X_1 requires on the set assembly line plus the number of units of X_2 multiplied by the 1.6 man-hours that each unit of X_2 requires on the set assembly line must be less than or equal to 240, the amount of labor capacity measured in man-hours per day, available for set assembly operations.

Black-and-white sets each require 0.5 man-hours of testing and final inspection, whereas color sets require 2.0 man-hours. The inspection capacity of the plant is 162 man-hours per day. Mathematically, the inspection constraint may be expressed as

(6-53) $$0.5X_1 + 2.0X_2 \leq 162$$

The problem of the firm is to determine the non-negative values of X_1 and X_2 which will maximize π subject to the constraints imposed by the present production facilities of the assembly plant, i.e., (6-51), (6-52), and (6-53). In the following chapter we will solve this linear programming problem.

Nonlinear programming

The model The problem of nonlinear programming is one of finding the values of $X_1, \ldots, X_n$ which will maximize or minimize

(6-54) $$Z = \phi(X_1, \ldots, X_n)$$

subject to m constraints of the form

(6-55) $$h_i(X_1, \ldots, X_n)\begin{pmatrix} \leq \\ = \\ \geq \end{pmatrix}B_i \qquad i = 1, \ldots, m$$

and to n non-negativity constraints

(6-56) $$X_j \geq 0 \qquad j = 1, \ldots, n$$

The most general form of nonlinear programming problem (and the most difficult case to solve) is the case where both ϕ and h_i are nonlinear. Most of the research on nonlinear programming has focused on problems characterized by nonlinear objective functions and *linear constraints*. However, the computational techniques for finding optimum solutions have not been developed, even for this special case of nonlinear programming, except for the case where ϕ has very special properties. Two special cases of (6-54) and (6-55) are of particular interest. In both of these the constraints are assumed to be linear. In the first case, the objective function ϕ can be written as the sum of n separate functions, each of which is a function of a single variable,

(6-57) $$Z = \phi(X_1, \ldots, X_n) = \phi_1(X_1) + \cdots + \phi_n(X_n)$$

Functions which can be written in the form of (6-57) are said to be *separable*. Additional restrictions must be imposed on the $\phi_j(X_j)$ in order to guarantee an optimum solution. In the second case, the objective function can be expressed as the sum of a linear function and quadratic function,

$$(6\text{-}58)\qquad \begin{aligned} Z &= \phi(X_1, \ldots, X_n) \\ &= C_1X_1 + \cdots + C_nX_n + D_{11}X_1^2 + D_{12}X_1X_2 \\ &\qquad + \cdots + D_{1n}X_1X_n + \cdots + D_{nn}X_n^2 \end{aligned}$$

(To ensure the existence of an optimum solution certain restrictions must be imposed on the D_{ij}'s.) Nonlinear programming problems of this type are called *quadratic programming problems*. As an example of quadratic programming, we might consider the problem of determining the non-negative values of X_1 and X_2 that will minimize

$$(6\text{-}59)\qquad Z = X_1^2 + 3X_2^2 - 4X_1 - 6X_2$$

subject to the constraint that

$$(6\text{-}60)\qquad X_1 + 2X_2 \leq 4$$

Solution techniques Historically, the development of nonlinear programming techniques has closely followed the development of linear programming. Much of the recent work in nonlinear programming can be traced back to the development of the Kuhn-Tucker theorem [83] in 1951. This important theorem laid the foundation for much of the recent work in nonlinear programming. Among the presently available nonlinear programming techniques are (1) separable programming, (2) quadratic programming, (3) gradient techniques, (4) decomposition methods, and (5) cutting-plane methods.[8] Most of these require "convexity" in order to guarantee that convergence will occur. In the case of a maximization problem "convexity" means that the objective function is *concave* and the set of feasible solutions, i.e., solutions which satisfy the constraints, is convex. Alternatively, "convexity" implies a convex objective function for a minimization problem and a convex region of feasibility.

Next we shall briefly consider five nonlinear programming techniques.

Charnes and Lemke [28] developed an approximation method in 1954 for treating minimization problems with separable objective functions and linear constraints. In 1963 C. E. Miller [97] developed a generalized *separable programming* algorithm capable of handling separable nonlinear constraints as well as separable objective functions. The idea underlying separable programming is to develop linear approximations for nonlinear objective functions and constraints and solve the resulting reformulated problem as a linear programming problem.

Since 1955 a number of different techniques have been proposed for solving *quadratic programming problems*, i.e., problems of optimizing a quadratic

[8] See Philip Wolfe, "Methods of Nonlinear Programming" [131] for a comprehensive survey of nonlinear programming techniques.

objective function subject to a set of linear constraints. Among the more important contributions to the literature are the papers by Barankin and Dorfman [7], Beale [9,10], Boot [13,14,15,16,17], Dorn [48,49], Frank and Wolfe [57], Hildreth [77], Houthakker [79], Lemke [89], Markowitz [94], Moore and Whinston [98], Theil and Van De Panne [113], Van De Panne [121], and Wolfe [128]. The book by Boot [13] and Chapter 7 of Hadley's book [73] contain excellent summaries of the literature on quadratic programming.

A third classification of nonlinear programming techniques includes the techniques known as "creeping" or *gradient methods*. Some of these methods can handle nonlinear objective functions and constraints. "Geometrically, they involve our sliding around the feasible region, always in a continuous motion (no jumps) and always uphill on the profit and downhill on the cost function" [8, p. 142]. There are several different types of gradient methods: (1) direct differential gradient methods [20,23], (2) Lagrangian differential gradient methods [4,131], (3) projected-gradient methods [59,88,106,107,127, 134], and (4) reduced gradient methods [131].

Two other nonlinear programming techniques are the *decomposition procedure* [131] and the *cutting-plane method* of Kelley [82] and Wolfe [129]. Computer programs using the cutting-plane method have been written by Dornheim [52] and Griffith and Stewart [71]. The books by Abadie [1], Boot [13], and Hadley [73] and the papers by Wolfe [131,132] are recommended for an in-depth survey of nonlinear programming techniques.

Applications The applications of nonlinear programming to the economic theory of the firm are so obvious that little space need be devoted to their description. In general, if we append (1) non-negativity requirements and (2) inequality constraints to the models described in Chapters 2–5, then each of these models becomes a nonlinear programming problem. This is precisely what we did in this chapter in developing the example of a mathematical programming model of the firm. Note that this model is characterized by a nonlinear objective function (6-19) and a set of constraints consisting of a nonlinear production function (6-13) and a set of fixed-factor limitations expressed in the form of linear inequalities (6-14). Indeed, we can say that nonlinear models are the rule rather than the exception in economics.

An example model An automobile plant manufactures automobiles and trucks.[9] The plant is organized into four departments: (1) sheet-metal stamping, (2) engine assembly, (3) final automobile assembly, and (4) final truck assembly —raw materials, labor, and other inputs being available at constant prices within the demand range of the plant. Monthly department capacities are given as follows:

Metal stamping	25,000 autos or	35,000 trucks
Engine assembly	33,333 autos or	16,667 trucks
Auto assembly	22,500 autos	
Truck assembly		15,000 trucks

[9] This example was taken from Dorfman, Samuelson, and Solow [47], p. 96.

If we let X_1 denote the number of automobiles sold and X_2 denote the number of trucks sold in one month, then the firm's net profit (net of variable cost) function is given by

$$\pi = \left(625 - \frac{X_1}{60}\right)X_1 + 250X_2 \tag{6-61}$$

$$= 625X_1 + 250X_2 - \frac{X_1^2}{60}$$

This net profit function reflects the fact that the demand function for automobiles slopes downward but the demand curve for trucks does not. The constraints for this nonlinear programming problem may be expressed in the form of the following linear inequalities:

$$\begin{aligned} 0.00400X_1 + 0.00286X_2 &\leq 100 \\ 0.00300X_1 + 0.00600X_2 &\leq 100 \\ 0.00444X_1 \qquad\qquad &\leq 100 \\ 0.00667X_2 &\leq 100 \end{aligned} \tag{6-62}$$

Since the objective function is both separable and quadratic and the constraints are linear, this problem may be solved by either separable programming or quadratic programming techniques.

Integer programming

Integer programming (or discrete programming, as it is sometimes called) is merely a special case of mathematical programming in which the solution variables are required to take on integral values. Integer programming must be used when one or more of the firm's factors or products is indivisible and the assumption of perfect divisibility is no longer reasonable. In the models described in Chapters 2–5 all of the firm's factors and products were assumed to be perfectly divisible in *acquisition* and in *use*.

Indivisibility in acquisition implies that a certain factor of production is indivisible in the sense that it can be obtained only in discrete units. That is, it is impossible to acquire the services of the particular factor in a quantity other than certain discrete amounts or "lumps." Indivisibility in use implies that this "lump" or "fixed factor" has to be used in combination with given amounts of other factor services if these other factors are to be efficiently employed. The assumption of constant factor proportions in linear programming models of the firm is tantamount to assuming a type of indivisibility in use.

The case of indivisibility in acquisition may be illustrated by the airline that operates a fleet of five DC-8 aircraft, but cannot acquire a fraction of a DC-8. The firm can purchase DC-8's in integral units only. Furthermore, it cannot hire $\frac{5}{8}$ of a pilot. Pilots are indivisible. Although the services of DC-8's and airline pilots can be varied in extremely small increments, it is not possible to acquire a fractional part of either a DC-8 or a pilot.

Many factor services that the firm uses may be assumed to be indivisible in acquisition. The quantity of the factor may be incapable of continuous variation for purely technical reasons, such as the case with DC-8's. The services rendered by a DC-8 must be of a certain minimum quantity if it is to do the work for which it was designed. Indivisibility may also arise for reasons that are both technical and institutional. For example, it may not be legally possible to hire labor service in units of less than one week or one month. Whether or not the degree of indivisibility is significant depends in part on the number of units of the particular factor that the firm is using. If an airline operates a fleet of 150 aircraft, then the degree of indivisibility of aircraft will not be highly significant or at least not so significant as it would be if the firm were a small charter airline with only three aircraft. The concept of indivisibility in acquisition also depends on the units in which the factor inputs are measured. In general, with durable factors (like DC-8's) that yield their services over more than one planning period, the computational problems associated with indivisibility will be more significant if factor inputs are measured in terms of the number of factors rather than in terms of the services they render. The factor of production, DC-8 transportation services, may be measured in number of DC-8's or in seat-miles or ton-miles. Indivisibility is likely to be more significant (in the sense of computational difficulties and economic consequences) if transportation service is measured in terms of the number of DC-8's available rather than seat-miles.

Prior to 1958 there existed no computational procedure that would guarantee integral solutions to mathematical programming problems. In 1958 Gomory [65] developed a method for solving integer linear programming problems called the "Method of Integer Forms" or the "cutting-plane" method. Although this method yields an optimum integer solution in a finite number of steps, it requires considerably more steps to reach an optimum solution than does the straightforward simplex method. Hence, one must choose between the simplex method with its nonintegral solutions and the "cutting-plane" method with its integral solutions but more complicated computational procedure. As a result, mathematicians are working on alternative methods of solving integer linear programming problems with the goal of improving computational efficiency, i.e., eliminating the number of computational steps required to reach an optimum solution.[10] For example, Martin [70], who has developed and successfully tested an "accelerated Euclidian algorithm" for solving integer linear programming problems, claims to have solved much larger problems than those attempted by Gomory. In 1960, Gomory [66] developed a method for solving mixed (integer-continuous) variable linear programming problems. Among the important contributions to the literature on integer linear programming are the works of Dantzig [35,36]; Dantzig, Fulkerson, and Johnson [40]; Glover [64]; Gomory [65,66,67]; Gomory and Baumol [68]; Gomory and Hoffman [69];

[10] For a comprehensive survey of the recent developments in integer programming, see the papers by Balinski [6] and Gomory [67].

Land and Doig [86]; Markowitz and Manne [96]. The paper by Gomory and Baumol [68] and Chapter 8 of Baumol [8] contain excellent treatments of the economic interpretation of integer linear programming problems. The book by Weingartner [124] applies integer linear programming to the problem of capital budgeting.

At the present time there are several alternative approaches for solving integer nonlinear programming problems, each of which is extremely complex mathematically and computationally. One of these involves approximating both the objective function and constraints by separable linear functions and then applying one of the linear integer programming methods to the transformed linear programming problem. A second method has been proposed by Kunzi and Oettli [85] for solving integer quadratic programming problems. Kelley [82] has suggested yet a third method which treats the general nonlinear integer programming problem. Only limited computational experience has been reported with the latter two techniques.

BIBLIOGRAPHY

[1] ABADIE, J. *Nonlinear Programming*. Amsterdam: North-Holland, 1967.

[2] APOSTOL, T. M. *Mathematical Analysis*. Reading, Mass.: Addison-Wesley, 1957.

[3] ARROW, KENNETH J., and ALAIN C. ENTHOVEN. "Quasi-Concave Programming," *Econometrica*, **XXIX** (October, 1961), 779–800.

[4] ARROW, KENNETH J., LEONID HURWICZ, and HIROFUMI UZAWA. *Studies in Linear and Non-Linear Programming*. Stanford: Stanford University Press, 1958.

[5] BABBAR, M. M. "Distributions of Solutions of a Set of Linear Equations," *Journal of the American Statistical Association*, **L** (September, 1955), 854–864.

[6] BALINSKI, M. L. "Integer Programming, Methods, Uses, Computation," *Management Science*, **XII** (November, 1965), 253–313.

[7] BARANKIN, E. W., and R. DORFMAN. "On Quadratic Programming," *University of California Publications in Statistics*, **II** (1958), 285–318.

[8] BAUMOL, WILLIAM J. *Economic Theory and Operations Analysis*. Englewood Cliffs, N. J.: Prentice-Hall, Inc., 1965.

[9] BEALE, E. M. L. "On Optimizing a Convex Function Subject to Linear Inequalities," *Journal of the Royal Statistical Society*, **XVII** (1955), 173–184.

[10] BEALE, E. M. L. "On Quadratic Programming," *Naval Research Logistics Quarterly*, **VI** (1959), 227–243.

[11] BELLMAN, RICHARD. *Dynamic Programming*. Princeton, N. J.: Princeton University Press, 1957.

[12] BELLMAN, R., and S. DREYFUS. *Applied Dynamic Programming*. Princeton, N. J.: Princeton University Press, 1962.

[13] BOOT, JOHN C. G. *Quadratic Programming*. Chicago: Rand McNally, 1964.

[14] BOOT, JOHN C. G. "Notes on Quadratic Programming: The Kuhn-Tucker and Theil-Van de Panne Conditions, Degeneracy, and Equality Constraints," *Management Science*, **VIII** (1961), 85–98.

[15] BOOT, JOHN C. G. "On Trivial and Binding Constraints in Programming Problems," *Management Science*, **VIII** (1962), 419–441.

[16] BOOT, JOHN C. G. "Binding Constraint Procedures of Quadratic Programming," *Econometrica*, **XXXI** (1963), 464–498.

[17] BOOT, JOHN C. G. "On Sensitivity Analysis in Convex Quadratic Programming Problems," *Operations Research*, **XI** (1963), 771–786.

[18] BOULDING, KENNETH E. "The Present Position of the Theory of the Firm," in Kenneth E. Boulding and W. Allen Spivey (Eds.), *Linear Programming and the Theory of the Firm*. New York: Macmillan, 1960.

[19] BOULDING, KENNETH E., and W. ALLEN SPIVEY (Eds.). *Linear Programming and the Theory of the Firm*. New York: The Macmillan Co., 1960.

[20] BROWN, R. R. *Gradient Methods for the Computer Solution of System Optimization Problems*, M.I.T., Department of Electrical Engineering, WADC Technical Note 57-159, September, 1957.

[21] BURGER, E. "On Extrema with Side Conditions," *Econometrica*, **XXIII** (October, 1955), 451–452.

[22] CARR, CHARLES R., and CHARLES W. HOWE. *Quantitative Decision Procedures in Management and Economics*. New York: McGraw-Hill Book Co., 1964.

[23] CARROLL, C. W. "The Created Response Surface Technique for Optimizing Nonlinear Restrained Systems," *Operations Research*, **IX** (March–April, 1961), 169–184.

[24] CHARNES, A., and W. W. COOPER. "Non-Linear Power of Adjacent Extreme Point Methods in Linear Programming," *Econometrica*, **XXV** (January, 1957), 132–153.

[25] CHARNES, A., and W. W. COOPER. "Chance-Constrained Programming," *Management Science*, **VI** (1959), 73–79.

[26] CHARNES, A., and W. W. COOPER. *Management Models and Industrial Applications of Linear Programming*. New York: John Wiley & Sons, 1961.

[27] CHARNES, A., W. W. COOPER, and G. H. SYMONDS. "Cost Horizons and Certainty Equivalents: An Approach to Stochastic Programming of Heating Oil," *Management Science*, **IV** (1958).

[28] CHARNES, A., and CARTON LEMKE. "Minimization of Non-Linear Separable Convex Functionals," *Naval Research Logistics Quarterly*, **I** (1954), 301–312.

[29] CHUNG, AN-MIN. *Linear Programming*. Columbus, Ohio: Charles E. Merrell Co., 1959.

[30] COURANT, R. *Differential and Integral Calculus*, Vol. II. New York: Interscience, 1936.

[31] DANO, SVEN. *Linear Programming in Industry: Theory and Applications*. Wien: Springer-Verlag, 1960.

[32] DANO, SVEN. *Industrial Production Models*. New York: Springer-Verlag, 1966.

[33] DANTZIG, GEORGE B. *A Procedure for Maximizing a Linear Function Subject to Linear Inequalities*. Washington: Headquarters, U.S. Air Force, Comptroller, 1948.

[34] DANTZIG, GEORGE B. "Linear Programming under Uncertainty," *Management Science*, **I** (1955), 197–206.

[35] DANTZIG, GEORGE B. "Note on Solving Linear Programs in Integers," *Naval Research Logistics Quarterly*, **VI** (1959), 75–76.

[36] DANTZIG, GEORGE B. "On the Significance of Solving Linear Programming Problems with Some Integer Variables," *Econometrica*, **XXVIII** (January, 1960), 30–44.

[37] DANTZIG, GEORGE B. "Compact Basis Triangularization for the Simplex Algorithm," in Robert L. Graves and Philip Wolfe (Eds.), *Recent Advances in Mathematical Programming*. New York: McGraw-Hill Book Co., 1963.

[38] DANTZIG, GEORGE B. *Linear Programming and Extensions*. Princeton: Princeton University Press, 1963.

[39] DANTZIG, GEORGE B., and R. W. COTTLE. "Positive (Semi-) Definite Programming," in J. Abadie (Ed.), *Nonlinear Programming*. Amsterdam: North-Holland, 1967.

[40] DANTZIG, GEORGE B., D. R. FULKERSON, and S. JOHNSON. "Solution of a Large-Scale Traveling-Salesman Problem," *Journal of the Operations Research Society of America*, **II** (1954), 393–410.

[41] DANTZIG, GEORGE B., and A. MADANSKY. "On the Solution of Two-Stage Linear Programs Under Uncertainty," in *Proceedings of the Fourth Berkeley Symposium on Mathematical Statistics and Probability*. Berkeley: University of California Press, 1961.

[42] DANTZIG, GEORGE B., A. ORDEN, and P. WOLFE. "Notes on Linear Programming: Part 1—The Generalized Simplex Method for Minimizing a Linear Form Under Uncertainty Restraints," The RAND Corporation, RM-1268, November 19, 1953.

[43] DANTZIG, GEORGE B., and M. B. SHAPIRO. *Solving the Chemical Equilibrium Problem Using the Decomposition Principle*, The RAND Corporation, P-2056, August 10, 1960.

[44] DENNIS, J. B. *Mathematical Programming and Electrical Networks*. Cambridge: Technology Press, 1959.

[45] DORFMAN, ROBERT. *Application of Linear Programming to the Theory of the Firm*. Berkeley: University of California Press, 1951.

[46] DORFMAN, ROBERT. "Mathematical or Linear, Programming: A Nonmathematical Exposition," *American Economic Review*, **XLIII** (December, 1953), 797–825.

[47] DORFMAN, ROBERT, PAUL A. SAMUELSON, and ROBERT SOLOW. *Linear Programming and Economic Analysis*. New York: McGraw-Hill Book Co., 1958.

[48] DORN, W. S. "Duality in Quadratic Programming," *Quarterly of Applied Mathematics*, **XVIII** (1960), 155–162.

[49] DORN, W. S. "On Lagrangian Multipliers," *Operations Research*, **IX** (1961), 95–104.

[50] DORN, W. S. "Self-Dual Quadratic Programs," *Journal of the Society for Industrial and Applied Mathematics*, **IX** (1961), 51–54.

[51] DORN, W. S. "Non-Linear Programming—A Survey," *Management Science*, **IX** (January, 1963), 171–208.

[52] DORNHEIM, F. R. "Optimization Subject to Nonlinear Constraints Using the Simplex Method and its Application to Gasoline Blending," Sinclair Research Laboratories, Harvey, Illinois, paper presented at Optimization Techniques Symposium, New York University, May 18, 1960.

[53] ELMAGHRABY, S. E. "An Approach to Linear Programming Under Uncertainty," *Operations Research*, **VII** (March–April, 1959), 208–216.

[54] EVERS, WILLIAM H. "A New Model for Stochastic Linear Programming," *Management Science*, **XIII** (May, 1967).

[55] FIACCO, A. V., and G. P. MCCORMICK. "The Sequential Unconstrained Minimization Technique for Nonlinear Programming," *Management Science*, **X** (January, 1964), 360–366.

[56] FORSYTHE, G. "Computing Constrained Minima with Lagrange Multipliers," *Journal of the Society for Industrial and Applied Mathematics*, **III** (1955), 173–178.

[57] FRANK, MARQUERITE, and PHILIP WOLFE. "An Algorithm for Quadratic Programming," *Naval Research Logistics Quarterly*, **VI** (March–June, 1956), 95–110.

[58] FREUND, R. J. "The Introduction of Risk into a Programming Model," *Econometrica*, **XXIV** (1956), 253–263.

[59] FRISCH, RAGNAR. "The Multiplex Method for Linear Programming," Universetetets Socialokønomiske Institut (Oslo), Memorandum, October, 1955.

[60] FISCH, RAGNAR. *Maxima and Minima*. Chicago: Rand McNally, 1966.

[61] GALE, D. "The Basic Theorems of Real Linear Equations, Inequalities, Linear Programming and Game Theory," *Naval Research Logistics Quarterly*, **III** (1956), 193–200.

[62] GALE, DAVID. *The Theory of Linear Economic Models*. New York: McGraw-Hill Book Co., 1960.

[63] GASS, SAUL. *Linear Programming: Methods and Applications*. New York: McGraw-Hill Book Co., 1958.

[64] GLOVER, FRED. "Generalized Cuts in Diophantine Programming," *Management Science*, **XIII** (November, 1966), 254–268.

[65] GOMORY, RALPH E. "Outline of an Algorithm for Integer Solutions to Linear Programs," *Bulletin of the American Mathematical Society*, **LXIV** (September, 1958), 275–278.

[66] GOMORY, RALPH E. "An Algorithm for the Mixed Integer Problem," RM-2597, The RAND Corporation, 1960.

[67] GOMORY, RALPH E. "An Algorithm for Integer Solutions to Linear Programs," in Robert L. Graves and Philip Wolfe (Eds.), *Recent Advances in Mathematical Programming*. New York: McGraw-Hill Book Co., 1963.

[68] GOMORY, RALPH E., and WILLIAM J. BAUMOL. "Integer Programming and Pricing," *Econometrica*, **XXVIII** (July, 1960), 521–550.

[69] GOMORY, RALPH E., and A. J. HOFFMAN. "On the Convergence of An Integer Programming Process," *Naval Research Logistics Quarterly*, **X** (1963), 121–123.

[70] GRAVES, ROBERT L., and PHILIP WOLFE (Eds.). *Recent Advances in Mathematical Programming*. New York: McGraw-Hill Book Co., 1963.

[71] GRIFFITH, R. E., and R. A. STEWART. "A Nonlinear Programming Technique for the Optimization of Continuous Processing Systems," *Management Science*, **VII** (1961), 370–393.

[72] HADLEY, G. *Linear Programming*. Reading, Mass.: Addison-Wesley Publishing Co., 1962.

[73] HADLEY, G. *Nonlinear and Dynamic Programming*. Reading, Mass.: Addison-Wesley, 1964.

[74] HADLEY, G., and T. M. WHITIN. *Analysis of Inventory Systems*. Englewood Cliffs, N. J.: Prentice-Hall, 1963.

[75] HANCOCK, H. *Theory of Maxima and Minima*. New York: Dover, 1960.

[76] HARTLEY, H. O. "Nonlinear Programming by the Simplex Method," *Econometrica*, **XXIX** (April, 1961), 223–237.

[77] HILDRETH, C. "A Quadratic Programming Procedure," *Naval Research Logistics Quarterly*, **XIV** (1957), 79–85.

[78] HOLT, C., F. MODIGLIANI, J. MUTH, and H. SIMON. *Planning Production, Inventories, and Work Force*. Englewood Cliffs, N. J.: Prentice-Hall, Inc., 1960.

[79] HOUTHAKKER, H. S. "The Capacity Method of Quadratic Programming," *Econometrica*, **XXVIII** (1960), 62–87.

[80] HOWARD, R. *Dynamic Programming and Markov Processes*. Cambridge: Technology Press, 1960.

[81] KATAOKA, S. "A Stochastic Programming Model," *Econometrica*, **XXXI** (January–April, 1963), 181–196.

[82] KELLEY, J. E. "The Cutting-Plane Method for Solving Convex Programs," *Journal of the Society for Industrial and Applied Mathematics*, **VIII** (December, 1960), 703–712.

[83] KUHN, H. W., and A. TUCKER. "Nonlinear Programming," in J. Neyman (Ed.), *Proceedings of the Second Berkeley Symposium on Mathematical Statistics and Probability*. Berkeley: University of California Press, 1951.

[84] KUNZI, H. P., and W. DRELLE. *Nonlinear Programming*. Waltham, Mass.: Blaisdell Publishing Co., 1966.

[85] KUNZI, H. P., and WERNER OETTLI. "Integer Quadratic Programming," in R. L. Graves and P. Wolfe (Eds.), *Recent Advances in Mathematical Programming*. New York: McGraw-Hill Book Co., 1963.

[86] LAND, A. H., and A. G. DOIG. "An Automatic Method of Solving Discrete Programming Problems," *Econometrica*, **XXVIII** (1960), 497–512.

[87] LAVI, ABRAHIM, and THOMAS P. VOGL. *Recent Advances in Optimization Techniques*. New York: John Wiley & Sons, 1966.

[88] LEMKE, C. "The Constrained Gradient Method of Linear Programming," *Journal of the Society for Industrial and Applied Mathematics*, **IX** (1961), 1–17.

[89] LEMKE, C. "A Method for Solution of Quadratic Programs," *Management Science*, **VIII** (1962), 442–453.

[90] MADANSKY, ALBERT. "Inequalities for Stochastic Linear Programming Problems," *Management Science*, **VI** (1960), 197–204.

[91] MADANSKY, ALBERT. "Methods of Solution of Linear Programs Under Uncertainty," *Operations Research*, **X** (July–August, 1962), 463–471.

[92] MADANSKY, ALBERT. "Dual Variable in Two-Stage Linear Programming Under Uncertainty," *Journal of Mathematical Analyses and Applications*, **VI** (February, 1963), 98–108.

[93] MADANSKY, ALBERT. "Linear Programming Under Uncertainty," in Robert L. Graves and Philip Wolfe (Eds.), *Recent Advances in Mathematical Programming*. New York: McGraw-Hill Book Co., 1963.

[94] MARKOWITZ, HARRY M. "The Optimization of a Quadratic Function Subject to Linear Constraints," *Naval Research Logistics Quarterly*, **III** (1956), 111–133.

[95] MARKOWITZ, H. *Portfolio Selection* (Cowles Foundation Monograph No. 16). New York: John Wiley & Sons, 1959.

[96] MARKOWITZ, HARRY M., and ALAN S. MANNE. "On the Solution of Discrete Programming Problems," *Econometrica*, **XXV** (January, 1957), 84–85.

[97] MILLER, C. E. "The Simplex Method for Local Separable Programming," in R. Graves and P. Wolfe (Eds.), *Recent Advances in Mathematical Programming*. New York: McGraw-Hill Book Co., 1963.

[98] MOORE, J. H., and A. B. WHINSTON. "Experimental Methods in Quadratic Programming," *Management Science*, **XIII** (September, 1966), 58–76.

[99] MORGENSTERN, O. *Economic Activity Analysis*. New York: John Wiley & Sons, 1954.

[100] NAYLOR, THOMAS H. "A Kuhn-Tucker Model of the Multi-Product, Multi-Factor Firm," *Southern Economic Journal*, **XXXI** (April, 1965), 324–330.

[101] NAYLOR, THOMAS H. "The Theory of the Firm: A Comparison of Marginal Analysis and Linear Programming," *Southern Economic Journal*, **XXXII** (January, 1966), 263–274.

[102] NAYLOR, THOMAS H. "The Economic Theory of the Firm: Three Tools of Analysis," *Quarterly Review of Economics and Business*, **V** (Winter, 1965), 33–49.

[103] NAYLOR, THOMAS H., and EUGENE T. BYRNE. *Linear Programming*. Belmont, California: Wadsworth Publishing Co., 1963.

[104] PFOUTS, RALPH W. "The Theory of Cost and Production in the Multi-Product Firm," *Econometrica*, **XXIX** (October, 1961), 650–658.

[105] PHIPPS, C. G. "Maxima and Minima under Restraint," *American Mathematics Monthly*, **LIX** (1952), 230–235.

[106] ROSEN, J. B. "The Gradient Projection Method for Nonlinear Programming, Part I. Linear Constraints," *Journal of the Society for Industrial and Applied Mathematics*, **IX** (1960), 181–217.

[107] ROSEN, J. B. "The Gradient Projection Method for Nonlinear Programming, Part II. Nonlinear Constraints," *Journal of the Society for Industrial and Applied Mathematics*, **IX** (1961), 514–532.

[108] RUBIN, W. *Principles of Mathematical Analysis*. New York: McGraw-Hill Book Co., 1953.

[109] SIMON, H. A. "Dynamic Programming Under Uncertainty with a Quadratic Function," *Econometrica*, **XXIV** (1956), 74–81.

[110] SPANG, H. A. "A Review of Minimization Techniques for Nonlinear Functions," *Journal of the Society for Industrial and Applied Mathematics*, **IV** (1962), 343–365.

[111] SPIVEY, W. ALLEN. *Linear Programming*. New York: The Macmillan Co., 1963.

[112] THEIL, H. "A Note on Certainty Equivalence in Dynamic Planning," *Econometrica*, **XXV** (1957), 346–349.

[113] THEIL, H., and C. VAN DE PANNE. "Quadratic Programming as an Extension of Classical Quadratic Maximization," *Management Science*, **VII** (1960), 1–20.

[114] THOMPSON, G. L., W. W. COOPER, and ABRAHAM CHARNES. "Characterizations by Chance-Constrained Programming," in Robert L. Graves and Philip Wolfe (Eds.), *Recent Advances in Mathematical Programming*. New York: McGraw-Hill Book Co., 1963.

[115] TINTNER, G. "Stochastic Linear Programming With Applications to Agricultural Economics," *Proceedings of the Second Symposium on Linear Programming*. Washington, D.C.: National Bureau of Standards, 1955.

[116] TINTNER, G. "A Note on Stochastic Linear Programming," *Econometrica*, **XXVIII** (April, 1960), 490–495.

[117] TUCKER, A. W. "Linear and Nonlinear Programming," *Operations Research*, **V** (1957), 244–257.

[118] VAJDA, S. "Inequalities in Stochastic Linear Programming," *Bulletin of the International Statistical Institute*, **XXXVI** (1958), 357–363.

[119] VAJDA, S. *Readings in Linear Programming*. New York: John Wiley & Sons, 1958.

[120] VAJDA, S. *Mathematical Programming*. Reading, Mass.: Addison-Wesley, 1961.

[121] VAN DE PANNE, C. "Programming with a Quadratic Constraint," *Management Science*, **XII** (July, 1966), 798–815.

[122] WAGNER, H. "On the Distribution of Solutions in Linear Programming Problems," *Journal of the American Statistical Association*, **LIII** (1958), 161–163.

[123] WEGNER, P. "A Nonlinear Extension of the Simplex Method," *Management Science*, **VII** (1960), 43–55.

[124] WEINGARTNER, H. M. *Mathematical Programming and the Analysis of Capital Budgeting Problems*. Englewood Cliffs, N. J.: Prentice-Hall, Inc., 1963.

[125] WILDE, D. J. *Optimum Seeking Methods*. Englewood Cliffs, N. J.: Prentice-Hall, 1964.

[126] WILDE, D. J., and C. S. BEIGHTLER. *Foundations of Optimization*. Englewood Cliffs, N. J.: Prentice-Hall, 1967.

[127] WITZGALL, C. *Gradient-Projection Methods for Linear Programming*. Princeton University and International Business Machines Corporation, Report No. 2, August, 1960.

[128] WOLFE, PHILIP. "The Simplex Method for Quadratic Programming," *Econometrica*, **XXVII** (1959), 382–398.

[129] WOLFE, PHILIP. "Accelerating the Cutting-Plane Method for Nonlinear Programming," *Journal of the Society for Industrial and Applied Mathematics*, **IX** (September, 1961), 481–488.

[130] WOLFE, PHILIP. *Recent Developments in Nonlinear Programming*, The RAND Corporation, R-401-PR, May, 1962.

[131] WOLFE, PHILIP. "Methods of Nonlinear Programming," in Robert L. Graves and Philip Wolfe (Eds.), *Recent Advances in Mathematical Programming*. New York: McGraw-Hill Book Co., 1963.

[132] WOLFE, PHILIP. "Methods of Nonlinear Programming," in J. Abadie (Ed.), *Nonlinear Programming*. Amsterdam: North-Holland, 1967.

[133] ZOUTENDIJK, G. "Maximizing a Function in a Convex Region," *Journal of the Royal Statistical Society*, **XXI** (1959), 338–355.

[134] ZOUTENDIJK, G. *Methods of Feasible Directions*. Amsterdam: Elsevier Publishing Co., 1960.

7

Linear programming

INTRODUCTION

In this chapter we shall develop the mathematics of linear programming. Insofar as many excellent books are available on this subject [10,14,15,17], the reader is referred to them for a more rigorous development. The purpose of this chapter is to provide the reader who is not trained in the mathematics of the technique with enough knowledge to understand the following chapters. Furthermore, some of the examples presented will illustrate the wide variety of industrial applications of linear programming.

As we saw in Chapter 6, linear programming is a mathematical technique which can be used to solve problems having the following structure:
Maximize (minimize)

$$Z = C_1X_1 + C_2X_2 + \cdots + C_nX_n \tag{7-1}$$

subject to

$$\begin{aligned} a_{11}X_1 + a_{12}X_2 + \cdots + a_{1n}X_n &\le B_1 \\ a_{21}X_1 + a_{22}X_2 + \cdots + a_{2n}X_n &\le B_2 \\ &\vdots \\ a_{m1}X_1 + a_{m2}X_2 + \cdots + a_{mn}X_n &\le B_m \end{aligned} \tag{7-2}$$

and

$$X_i \ge 0 \qquad (i = 1, \ldots, n) \tag{7-3}$$

where the a_{ij}, B_i, and C_j are constants. Observe that the inequalities in (7-2) are not required to be of the form shown; multiplication by -1 could convert a "greater than" inequality to a "less than" inequality. It is also possible to have equalities as well as inequalities.

It should be emphasized that in this chapter we shall consider only the *linear* programming technique. We are restricting ourselves to a special class of mathematical programming techniques—that class in which the *objective function*, (7-1), and the *constraint conditions*, inequality system (7-2), are linear. The conditions (7-3) are known as *non-negativity conditions*.

Before reviewing the mathematical concepts which we shall use, it should be instructive to pose a simple linear programming problem and solve it graphically.

AN EXAMPLE PROBLEM

Consider a firm producing product X. The firm operates in a purely competitive market; hence, it can sell all of the X that it can produce at a constant price of P. Production of X is limited by two factors: (1) labor and (2) machine capacity. Notice that we are dealing with a short-run optimizing problem: quantities of labor and machine capacity are assumed to be fixed. For those who may be disturbed by the assumption that the amount of labor is a fixed quantity, assume that labor is hired under a long-term contract. The firm has 200 man-hours of labor and 90 hours of machine capacity.

The product can be produced in two ways: (1) a labor-intensive process in which one unit of X requires 5 man-hours and 1 machine-hour, and (2) a capital-intensive process in which one unit of X requires 1 man-hour and 2 machine-hours. We will also assume that other *variable* inputs are required in the two processes, and that process 1 has a variable cost per unit of X of VC_1 and, similarly, process 2 has a variable cost VC_2.

The firm's short-run problem is to maximize the contribution to profit and overhead, π. Or, cast in the structure of a linear programming problem, the objective function becomes

$$\text{(7-4)} \qquad \text{maximize } \pi = (P - VC_1)X_1 + (P - VC_2)X_2$$

where

$$X_1 = \text{quantity of } X \text{ produced by process 1}$$

$$X_2 = \text{quantity of } X \text{ produced by process 2}$$

The constraints state that the firm cannot use more man-hours or machine-hours than are available. Thus

$$\text{(7-5)} \qquad \begin{aligned} 5X_1 + 1X_2 &\leq 200 \quad \text{labor constraint} \\ 1X_1 + 2X_2 &\leq \ \ 90 \quad \text{machine constraint} \end{aligned}$$

And, of course, we require

$$\text{(7-6)} \qquad X_1 \geq 0, \ X_2 \geq 0$$

To simplify the calculations, we shall assume that both $(P - VC_1)$ and $(P - VC_2)$ are equal to 1. The objective function reduces to

$$\pi = X_1 + X_2$$

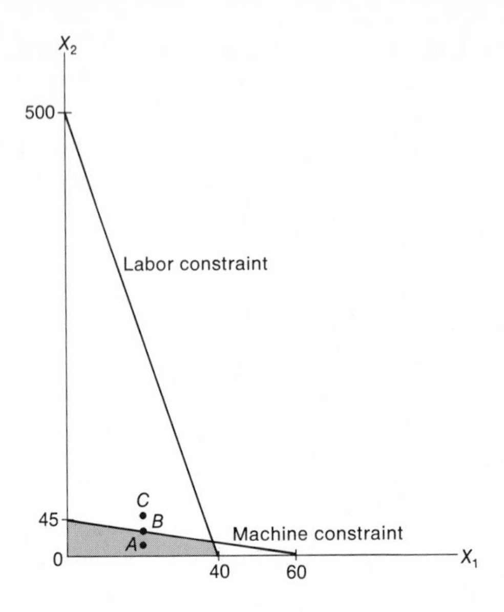

FIGURE 7-1

In Figure 7-1 the levels of the processes are plotted on the axes, X_1 and X_2. Observe that the two constraint conditions are plotted as if they were equalities rather than inequalities. The reason will become clear as we proceed.

The *feasible region* is indicated by shading the area bounded by the two constraints and the axes. It is that region which includes all possible combinations of X_1 and X_2 which violate neither the constraint conditions nor the non-negativity conditions. It is obvious that any point in Figure 7-1 represents a particular combination of values for the levels of the two processes. For example, consider point *A*, which is defined by $X_1 = 20$ and $X_2 = 20$. Substituting these values into system (7-5),

$$5(20) + 20 = 120 \leq 200 \qquad \text{labor constraint}$$

$$20 + 2(20) = 60 \leq 90 \qquad \text{machine constraint}$$

shows that point *A* is clearly feasible. In fact, point *A* represents a particular operating level of the two processes which involves unused quantities of the two inputs. That is, there are 80 excess man-hours of labor and 30 excess machine-hours. This is easy to see in Figure 7-1, since point *A* lies in the interior of the feasible region.

Point *B*, which lies on the boundary of the feasible region, has coordinates $X_1 = 20$ and $X_2 = 35$. From the figure it is evident that machine capacity is being used fully (point *B* lies on the machine constraint boundary). That this is correct can also be demonstrated by substituting the process levels corresponding to point B into the constraint conditions:

$$5(20) + 35 = 135 \leq 200 \qquad \text{labor constraint}$$

$$20 + 2(35) = 90 = 90 \qquad \text{machine constraint}$$

Finally, consider point C, which has coordinates $X_1 = 20$ and $X_2 = 50$. Since point C lies outside the feasible region, we would expect at least one of the constraints to be violated. Figure 7-1 shows that the machine constraint is violated (since it is a "less than" inequality constraint, all points to the right and vertically upward from the constraint line violate it). Notice that the labor constraint is not violated. This is shown by substitution into the constraint conditions:

$$5(20) + 50 = 150 \leq 200 \qquad \text{labor constraint}$$

$$20 + 2(50) = 120 > 90 \qquad \text{machine constraint}$$

Next we construct a series of iso-π lines. A particular iso-π line is the locus of all combinations of the process levels which result in the same π. Since

$$\pi = X_1 + X_2$$

to construct a particular iso-π line we simply substitute the particular value of π into the objective function, and plot the resulting equation. Hence, for a π level of K, we plot

$$X_2 = K - X_1$$

In Figure 7-2 we superimpose a series of iso-π lines on the same feasible region developed in Figure 7-1. Since we have assumed that the firm wishes to maximize π, it is clear that it will choose that point in the feasible region which also lies on the iso-π line corresponding to the highest value of π. Point T meets both of these tests and is therefore the solution (iso-π lines represent greater values of π the farther their distance from the origin).

The fact that the optimal point T is determined by the intersection of the two constraint lines suggests an algebraic solution procedure (viewing the two constraint conditions as equations, their simultaneous solution gives the coordinates of point T). Since the number of linear programming problems which can be solved graphically is greatly restricted (problems in which there are only two or three variables), it seems prudent to investigate algebraic techniques. Here we shall give a heuristic approach to the algebraic procedure; later, after introducing some linear algebra concepts, we shall turn to a more careful algebraic development.

Notice that the feasible region is bounded by straight lines, and is, in fact, a convex polygon. Furthermore, the objective function is also a straight line. Of course this should not be surprising, since we have restricted ourselves to *linear* programming. It is reasonable, therefore, to expect that the optimal

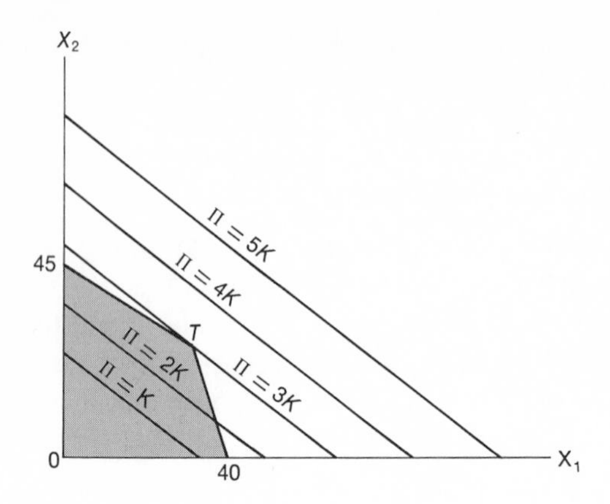

FIGURE **7-2**

solution will lie on the boundary of the feasible region and it will be a corner point (or extreme point) of the convex feasible region. These expectations are verified by an imagined graphical analysis of the type in Figure 7-2 for various shapes of feasible regions and objective functions.

Only if the objective function is parallel to a boundary line can we envisage a point on the boundary other than a corner point as being optimal. Even in this case, a point at the corner of the region would also be optimal. That is to say, the firm would be indifferent between any point on the boundary and a corner point. This is illustrated in Figure 7-3.

If the objective function were such as to make the slope of the iso-π lines as shown in Figure 7-3, all points on the boundary TB would yield the same value for the objective function. Since the firm would be indifferent between T and a point C (any point on TB other than T or B), we can make the following statement. The optimal point can be considered to occur always at a corner point of the feasible region. Of course, we have not proved this statement; our argument has only provided an intuitive explanation for a very important theorem in linear programming. Its importance is the fact that, in searching for an optimal solution, we no longer need to examine each of the infinite number of points in the feasible region; we need examine only the finite number of corner points.

Making use of this last theorem, we can now proceed to solve the problem algebraically. Since each corner point is determined by the intersection of two sides of the feasible region, it is possible to obtain the coordinates of all corner points by solving simultaneously the equations for the appropriate sides. Once all corner points are known, and since we know the optimal point must be a corner point, it becomes a simple task to substitute each corner point into the objective function in order to find the optimal one. We should note that it is a simple task in this example, because there are only four corner points; however, for problems with many variables it is no longer simple.

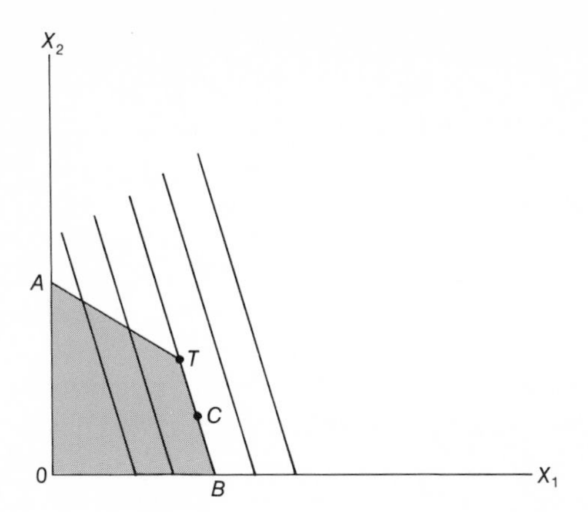

FIGURE **7-3**

The simplex method, which we shall discuss later, is a systematic procedure which greatly reduces the number of corner points which must be tested. It is helpful to think of the simplex method as a way of moving from corner point to corner point in such a fashion as to always increase the value of the objective function. Upon reaching a corner point which has the property that no further moves will increase the objective function, one has reached the optimal solution.

Recall that in our example the constraint conditions are inequalities, not equations. It is necessary to introduce a new concept to convert the inequalities into equations, the *slack variable* (or *surplus variable* for "greater than" inequalities). The name, of course, describes its function perfectly. It can be conceived as a variable to measure the amount of excess or unused capacity.

To illustrate, we add a slack variable to each of the constraint inequalities:

$$\begin{aligned} 5X_1 + 1X_2 + S_1 &= 200 \qquad \text{labor constraint} \\ 1X_1 + 2X_2 + S_2 &= \ \ 90 \qquad \text{machine constraint} \end{aligned} \tag{7-7}$$

We also require S_1 and S_2 to be zero or positive. For example, note that for point T, the optimal point, both constraints are used fully (point T lies on both constraint lines in Figure 7-2). If each coordinate of point T were increased by one, both constraints would be violated. That is to say, the coordinates of the new point, T', would represent levels of X_1 and X_2 such that *more* than 200 man-hours of labor and *more* than 90 machine-hours would be required. And, for the system of equations (7-7) to hold, S_1 and S_2 would necessarily be negative. Hence the requirement that they be non-negative is obvious.

Before turning to the determination and evaluation of each of the corner points, we must point out one further concept which will be developed more fully later. The system of equations (7-7) represents the typical system in linear programming problems: a system of simultaneous equations in which there are more unknowns than there are equations. Specifically, there are four unknowns, X_1, X_2, S_1, and S_2, and two equations. There are, of course, an infinite number of combinations of values of the four unknowns which will satisfy the two equations. For example, assign arbitrary values to any two of the unknowns and the system becomes one of two equations in two unknowns. As is well known, a system of equations with the same number of equations as unknowns has a unique solution (assuming the equations are independent and consistent).

We shall now state another important theorem of linear programming: If any two unknowns are set equal to zero and if the remaining two equations in two unknowns are solved, the values of the two unknowns, if non-negative, will correspond to a corner point of the feasible region. (It is important to note that not all of the solutions so obtained will be non-negative; hence they will not correspond to corner points.)

By the formula for combinations, there are six different ways in which we can choose two unknowns from four so as to set the selected two equal to zero. The solutions corresponding to the six ways are called *basic solutions*. However, two of the ways give solutions which violate the non-negativity conditions, *viz*., setting X_1 and S_1 equal to zero and setting X_2 and S_2 equal to zero. Referring to Figure 7-1, these two solutions correspond to the intersection of the labor-constraint line with the X_2 axis and the intersection of the machine-constraint line with the X_1 axis; both points are clearly nonfeasible, since in the first case S_2 will be less than zero and in the second case S_1 is less than zero. Since two of the six solutions are nonfeasible, it follows that there are four corner points. The four feasible, or corner-point solutions, are known as *basic feasible solutions*.

At last we can turn to the algebraic solution of the example problem. We set two variables equal to zero, solve the system of equations (7-7) for the values of the other two variables, and then insert the values of the variables into the objective function to determine the value of π. The results for each of the four basic feasible solutions are tabulated:

Variables set equal to zero	Simultaneous solution of equation (7-7)	Corresponding corner point in figure 7-3	Value of objective function
$X_1, X_2 = 0$	$S_1 = 200, \quad S_2 = 90$	0	0
$X_1, S_2 = 0$	$X_2 = 45, \quad S_1 = 155$	*A*	45
$X_2, S_1 = 0$	$X_1 = 40, \quad S_2 = 50$	*B*	40
$S_1, S_2 = 0$	$X_1 = 34.4, X_2 = 27.8$	*T*	62.2

Clearly, the value of the objective function at point T is the largest value for any of the corner points, or basic feasible solutions. Hence, this is the optimal solution. The firm should produce 34.4 units of X by process 1 and 27.8 units of X by process 2 in order to maximize π.

This appears to be a convenient place to summarize the simplex method. One theorem stated that we need not evaluate all feasible solutions, but we need evaluate only all *basic* feasible solutions (corner points). In cases of *many* variables there would be *many* basic feasible solutions; so many that it could be extremely time consuming to evaluate each. The simplex method is designed to cope with this problem. The simplex algorithm is a systematic way of moving from one basic feasible solution to another, omitting the evaluation of solutions which do not increase the value of the objective function as much as others. For example, if we started at point O we might move to point A, and then directly to point T, omitting point B altogether. Before turning to the next section of this chapter, the reader who is not familiar with the basic concepts of linear algebra may wish to consult the mathematical appendix at the end of the chapter.

LINEAR PROGRAMMING FUNDAMENTALS

Let us begin by restating the general linear programming problem in vector notation (after all inequalities have been converted into equations).

Maximize (or minimize)

$$Z = \mathbf{c}'\mathbf{x} \tag{7-8}$$

subject to

$$X_1\mathbf{a}_1 + X_2\mathbf{a}_2 + \cdots + X_n\mathbf{a}_n = \mathbf{b} \tag{7-9}$$

and

$$\mathbf{x} \geq \mathbf{0} \tag{7-10}$$

where

$\mathbf{c}'$ is a row vector, $(C_1, C_2, \ldots, C_n)$

$\mathbf{x}$ is a column vector, $\begin{bmatrix} X_1 \\ X_2 \\ \vdots \\ X_n \end{bmatrix}$

$\mathbf{b}$ is a column vector, $\begin{bmatrix} B_1 \\ B_2 \\ \vdots \\ B_m \end{bmatrix}$

$\mathbf{0}$ is an n-dimensional null column vector

$\mathbf{a}_j$ is the column vector of coefficients of the variable X_j for $j = 1, 2, \ldots, n$

$$\begin{bmatrix} a_{1j} \\ a_{2j} \\ \vdots \\ a_{mj} \end{bmatrix}$$

Hereafter we shall refer only to a maximizing problem. However, it should be pointed out that the above formulation describes a minimization problem as well, since maximizing $-Z$ is the same as minimizing Z.

Definitions

1. A *feasible solution* to the problem is a vector $\mathbf{x}$ which satisfies conditions (7-9) and (7-10).
2. A *basic feasible solution* is a feasible solution with no more than m positive X_i. That is, the number of positive variables in the solution is no greater than the number of constraints. If the number of positive X_i is exactly m, the solution is a *nondegenerate basic feasible solution.*
3. A *maximum feasible solution* is a feasible solution which maximizes equation (7-8).

Assumptions

In the analysis to follow we shall make five assumptions.

1. None of the equations represented by (7-9) are redundant. As we shall see later, the conversion of inequalities into equations and other adjustments made to obtain an initial basic feasible solution necessarily makes $r(\mathbf{A}) \equiv m$ (where $\mathbf{A}$ is the matrix composed of the n column vectors $\mathbf{a}_j$).
2. The equations are consistent. This of course ensures the existence of a solution.
3. A feasible solution to the problem exists. Since a feasible solution exists, a basic feasible solution exists also. (For proof, see Hadley [15, p. 80].)
4. The solution set is bounded. This ensures that the maximum feasible solution is finite.
5. Every basic feasible solution is nondegenerate.

The first four assumptions should hold true for linear programming problems which are formulated properly. Redundancy in the original inequality constraints can occur, but, as discussed earlier, it has no effect on the solution. Redundancy merely increases the computational problem. A formulation error could cause the fourth assumption to be violated; we shall see later how the simplex method signals this condition. The problem created when degeneracy occurs is of theoretical importance and will be discussed later. Degeneracy, of course, means that the basic feasible solution contains *less* than m positive solution variables (see definition 2).

Theorems

1. The set of all feasible solutions to the linear programming problem is a convex set. (For proof, see Gass [14, p. 46].)

2. The objective function (7-8) will assume a maximum at an extreme point of the convex set of feasible solutions. (For proof, see Gass [14, p. 47].)

The importance of Theorems 1 and 2 should be emphasized. They tell us that in searching for the maximum feasible solution, we need examine only the extreme points of the set of feasible solutions. Since there is a finite number of extreme points, we know that our search for the maximum can be greatly reduced. For example, if the set of feasible solutions to the problem happened to be one of the convex sets in Figure 7A-2 (in the appendix to this chapter), we need examine only each of the corner points (A, B, C, and D); we do *not* need to examine the infinite number of points contained in the interior of those sets (or points on the boundaries other than corner points).[1]

The following two theorems are proved in Gass [14, pp. 49–50].

3. If a set of m vectors $\mathbf{a}_1, \mathbf{a}_2, \ldots, \mathbf{a}_m$ can be found that are linearly independent and such that

$$X_1\mathbf{a}_1 + X_2\mathbf{a}_2 + \cdots + X_m\mathbf{a}_m = \mathbf{b}$$

and all $X_i \geq 0$, then the point

$$\mathbf{x} = \begin{bmatrix} X_1 \\ X_2 \\ \vdots \\ X_m \\ 0 \\ 0 \\ \vdots \\ 0 \end{bmatrix}$$

is an extreme point of the convex set of feasible solutions. $\mathbf{x}$ is an n-dimensional vector whose last $n - m$ elements are zero.

4. If $\mathbf{x}$ is an extreme point of the convex set of feasible solutions, then the vectors associated with positive X_i form a linearly independent set. Hence, at most, m of the X_i are positive.

[1] It is possible that points on the boundary could have the same value in the objective function as the adjacent extreme points, but never greater. See Figure 7-3 for a graphical illustration.

Theorems 3 and 4 tell us that every basic feasible solution corresponds to an extreme point. Considering Theorem 2, we now know that the maximum feasible solution will be a basic feasible solution. Hence, if we can find some method to generate all basic feasible solutions, we can evaluate each in the objective function and simply select that solution which gives the largest value to the objective function as the maximum solution.

Generating basic feasible solutions

Fortunately, Dantzig [8] has developed a systematic procedure, the simplex method, for generating and evaluating basic feasible solutions. This procedure has the great virtue of skipping over basic feasible solutions which do not increase the value of the objective function as much as others, thereby reducing computational effort. Before examining the simplex method, we shall tackle the problem of generating basic feasible solutions. (This is an integral part of the simplex method, but for clarity we shall treat it separately.)

This section will deal with the mechanics of how, given an initial basic feasible solution, we can generate another. The basic idea is simple. The basis is changed by one vector at a time. Remember that there are exactly m positive variables in a basic feasible solution; the remaining $n - m$ variables are all equal to zero. Hence we set a variable that is positive in solution I equal to zero in solution II, and permit a variable that is zero in I to be positive in II.

Another way to describe the generation of solution II from I is to say that we enter a new vector, say $\mathbf{a}_p$, into the basis to replace a solution I basis vector, say $\mathbf{a}_h$. Of course, X_h was positive and X_p was zero in I; in II, X_h becomes zero and X_p becomes positive.

Vector to remove Let the given basic feasible solution be:

$$\mathbf{x} = \begin{bmatrix} X_1 \\ X_2 \\ \vdots \\ X_m \\ 0 \\ 0 \\ \vdots \\ 0 \end{bmatrix}$$

So,

$$X_1\mathbf{a}_1 + X_2\mathbf{a}_2 + \cdots + X_m\mathbf{a}_m = \mathbf{b} \tag{7-11}$$

Since the vectors $\mathbf{a}_1, \mathbf{a}_2, \ldots, \mathbf{a}_m$ are linearly independent, we can express every vector in m-space (known as *requirements space*) as a linear combination of these basis vectors.

Suppose we decide to enter a vector not currently in the basis into the basis, say $\mathbf{a}_p$ (in the next section we shall determine precisely which vector to enter). First we should determine how many units of $\mathbf{a}_1, \mathbf{a}_2, \ldots, \mathbf{a}_m$ must be removed for each unit of $\mathbf{a}_p$ in order not to violate the constraints. This information is given by the equation below in which we express $\mathbf{a}_p$ as a linear combination of the basis vectors:

$$\mathbf{a}_p = Y_{1p}\mathbf{a}_1 + Y_{2p}\mathbf{a}_2 + \cdots + Y_{mp}\mathbf{a}_m \tag{7-12}$$

Next we should determine how much $\mathbf{a}_p$ to insert (or, the value of X_p). Let the correct amount be δ. Then, multiplying both sides of (7-12) by δ, we obtain

$$\delta\mathbf{a}_p = \delta Y_{1p}\mathbf{a}_1 + \delta Y_{2p}\mathbf{a}_2 + \cdots + \delta Y_{mp}\mathbf{a}_m \tag{7-13}$$

or

$$\delta\mathbf{a}_p - \delta Y_{1p}\mathbf{a}_1 - \delta Y_{2p}\mathbf{a}_2 - \cdots - \delta Y_{mp}\mathbf{a}_m = 0 \tag{7-14}$$

Next, add equation (7-14) to the left-hand side of equation (7-11).

$$X_1\mathbf{a}_1 + X_2\mathbf{a}_2 + \cdots + X_m\mathbf{a}_m + \delta\mathbf{a}_p - \delta Y_{1p}\mathbf{a}_1 - \delta Y_{2p}\mathbf{a}_2 - \cdots - \delta Y_{mp}\mathbf{a}_m = \mathbf{b} \tag{7-15}$$

Rearranging (7-15) and combining terms,

$$(X_1 - \delta Y_{1p})\mathbf{a}_1 + (X_2 - \delta Y_{2p})\mathbf{a}_2 + \cdots + (X_m - \delta Y_{mp})\mathbf{a}_m + \delta\mathbf{a}_p = \mathbf{b} \tag{7-16}$$

Observe that in (7-16) we have a feasible solution with $\mathbf{a}_p$ in the solution. Thus, we have accomplished half of the process: we have entered a new vector into the basis. We have made X_p, which was formerly zero, some positive value δ. Next, in order to complete the process of generating a new *basic* feasible solution, we must remove a vector that was in the original basis (a basis can contain only m linearly independent vectors). Or, what is the same thing, we must make one of the coefficients of the initial basis vectors zero.

At first glance it would appear to be a simple matter to meet this requirement. Since δ is still an unknown, we merely need to select a value for δ to make one of the $\mathbf{a}_j$ coefficients zero. Two possibilities would be

$$\delta = X_1/Y_{1p}$$
$$\delta = X_2/Y_{2p} \qquad \text{where} \quad Y_{1p}, Y_{2p} > 0$$

The restriction that Y_{1p} and Y_{2p} be positive is made clear by reference to (7-16). If, say, $Y_{1p} \le 0$, then no matter what positive value δ is given, the coefficient of $\mathbf{a}_1$ cannot be made zero.

However, the matter is somewhat more complicated. We cannot overlook the non-negativity conditions which require all $X_i \ge 0$. Although either of the two possibilities would meet the requirement of making an X_i zero, we might also violate the requirement that all X_i be non-negative. Consequently, we must choose δ to be the *minimum* of all

$$X_i/Y_{ip} \quad \text{for all} \quad i = 1, 2, \ldots, m \qquad \text{for which} \quad Y_{ip} > 0$$

In this way we force one of the X_i to be zero and prevent any from becoming negative. Hence if the X_i/Y_{ip} meeting the above criterion is X_h/Y_{hp}, then $\mathbf{a}_h$ becomes the vector that should be removed. If a tie for minimum exists, the new solution will be degenerate. We shall return to this problem later.

Example Making use of the example posed at the beginning of this chapter, we can clarify the process of generating new basic feasible solutions. The example can be formulated as

$$\text{maximize } \pi = X_1 + X_2 \tag{7-17}$$

subject to

$$X_1\begin{bmatrix}5\\1\end{bmatrix} + X_2\begin{bmatrix}1\\2\end{bmatrix} + S_1\begin{bmatrix}1\\0\end{bmatrix} + S_2\begin{bmatrix}0\\1\end{bmatrix} = \begin{bmatrix}200\\90\end{bmatrix} \tag{7-18}$$

and

$$X_1, X_2, S_1, S_2 \geq 0 \tag{7-19}$$

Take the initial basic feasible solution to be

$$200\begin{bmatrix}1\\0\end{bmatrix} + 90\begin{bmatrix}0\\1\end{bmatrix} = \begin{bmatrix}200\\90\end{bmatrix} \tag{7-20}$$

That is, $X_1 = 0$, $X_2 = 0$, $S_1 = 200$, and $S_2 = 90$. Suppose we decide to enter vector $\begin{bmatrix}5\\1\end{bmatrix}$ into the basis. Then, as in (7-12), we write

$$\begin{bmatrix}5\\1\end{bmatrix} = \alpha\begin{bmatrix}1\\0\end{bmatrix} + \beta\begin{bmatrix}0\\1\end{bmatrix}$$

Clearly, solving for α and β yields $\alpha = 5$ and $\beta = 1$. So,

$$\begin{bmatrix}5\\1\end{bmatrix} = 5\begin{bmatrix}1\\0\end{bmatrix} + 1\begin{bmatrix}0\\1\end{bmatrix}$$

or, as in (7-14),

$$\delta\begin{bmatrix}5\\1\end{bmatrix} - 5\delta\begin{bmatrix}1\\0\end{bmatrix} - \delta\begin{bmatrix}0\\1\end{bmatrix} = 0 \tag{7-21}$$

Adding (7-21) to the left-hand side of equation (7-20), rearranging, and combining terms, we obtain

$$(200 - 5\delta)\begin{bmatrix}1\\0\end{bmatrix} + (90 - \delta)\begin{bmatrix}0\\1\end{bmatrix} + \delta\begin{bmatrix}5\\1\end{bmatrix} = \begin{bmatrix}200\\90\end{bmatrix} \tag{7-22}$$

Two possibilities exist for values of δ which would remove one of the initial basis vectors (or make S_1 or S_2 zero):

$$\delta = 200/5 = 40$$

$$\delta = 90$$

Note, however, that if we choose $\delta = 90$ the coefficient of vector $\begin{bmatrix}1\\0\end{bmatrix}$, i.e., variable S_1 becomes negative, or -250. This is inadmissible by (7-19). Hence, we choose the minimum $\delta = 40$. And, our new basic feasible solution becomes

$$0\begin{bmatrix}1\\0\end{bmatrix} + 50\begin{bmatrix}0\\1\end{bmatrix} + 40\begin{bmatrix}5\\1\end{bmatrix} = \begin{bmatrix}200\\90\end{bmatrix}$$

or $S_1 = 0$, $S_2 = 50$, $X_1 = 40$, and $X_2 = 0$.

Vector to enter We shall continue to assume that we are given a basic feasible solution. The problem of obtaining an initial basic feasible solution is deferred until later.

In the last section we discussed a method for selecting the vector to remove from the basis when entering a new vector. Here we want to answer another question: *which* nonbasis vector should enter the basis?

A basic feasible solution to the general linear programming problem of equations (7-8), (7-9), and (7-10) is:

$$\mathbf{x} = \begin{bmatrix}X_1\\X_2\\\vdots\\X_m\\0\\0\\\vdots\\0\end{bmatrix}$$

and

$$X_1\mathbf{a}_1 + X_2\mathbf{a}_2 + \cdots + X_m\mathbf{a}_m = \mathbf{b}$$

Let $\mathbf{c}_b' = (C_1, C_2, \ldots, C_m)$; that is, the objective function coefficients of the positive variables in the solution. Further, let

$$\mathbf{x}_b = \begin{bmatrix}X_1\\X_2\\\vdots\\X_m\end{bmatrix}$$

Then the scalar product, $\mathbf{c}_b'\mathbf{x}_b$, gives the value of the objective function, Z, for this solution.

Any vector in the requirements space, $\mathbf{a}_j$, can now be expressed as a unique linear combination of the basis vectors. Thus

$$\mathbf{a}_j = Y_{1j}\mathbf{a}_1 + Y_{2j}\mathbf{a}_2 + \cdots + Y_{mj}\mathbf{a}_m \tag{7-23}$$

The interpretation of the scalars $Y_{1j}, Y_{2j}, \ldots, Y_{mj}$ is important. If we want to enter one unit of $\mathbf{a}_j$ into the solution, then to continue to satisfy the restraints, we must remove Y_{ij} units of $\mathbf{a}_1$, Y_{2j} units of $\mathbf{a}_2, \ldots$, and Y_{mj} units of $\mathbf{a}_m$. If the sign of a Y_{ij} is negative, the interpretation should be that adding one unit of $\mathbf{a}_j$

permits us to add Y_{ij} units of the vector in question. Now define the scalar product

$$Z_j = \mathbf{c}_b'\mathbf{y}_j \qquad \text{where } \mathbf{y}_j = \begin{bmatrix} Y_{1j} \\ Y_{2j} \\ \vdots \\ Y_{mj} \end{bmatrix} \tag{7-24}$$

The quantity Z_j is the reduction in the value of the objective function due to the adjustment of existing basis vectors in order to accommodate one unit of $\mathbf{a}_j$. Of course, Z_j does not provide all the information we need. Adding one unit of $\mathbf{a}_j$ also has a direct effect on the objective function. This direct effect is given by C_j. Hence in assessing the desirability of adding a particular vector to the basis we should examine the *total* effect on the objective function of adding one unit. Thus we should compare the $C_j - Z_j$ values for all potential replacement vectors.

There are three possibilities in comparing the $C_j - Z_j$:

1. If $C_j - Z_j \leq 0$ for $j = 1, \ldots, n$ then the current solution is the maximum feasible solution.
2. If at least one $C_j - Z_j > 0$ then the current solution is not the maximum. It is also required that at least one $Y_{ij} > 0$ for $\mathbf{a}_j$ corresponding to a $C_j - Z_j > 0$. The reason for this is made clear in 3.
3. If a $C_j - Z_j > 0$ for $\mathbf{a}_j$ with all $Y_{ij} \leq 0$, then we are confronted with the problem of an *unbounded solution.* The reason is that a negative Y_{ij} means that, rather than having to remove units of the vector from the basis to accommodate a new vector, we can *add* more of the existing vector (a zero Y_{ij} can be interpreted quite similarly). Hence, if all $Y_{ij} \leq 0$, we are not limited in any way. If one unit of $\mathbf{a}_j$ increases the objective function by $C_j - Z_j$, then we can increase Z without bound by increasing $\mathbf{a}_j$. Obviously such a situation reflects an error in formulation.

Let us now return to 2. If more than one $C_j - Z_j > 0$, we must choose one of these $\mathbf{a}_j$ as the replacing vector. Here we follow the rule that we choose that $\mathbf{a}_j$ which produces the greatest increase in Z per unit. Thus we find the largest positive $C_j - Z_j$, say $C_p - Z_p$. Then $\mathbf{a}_p$ is the new vector to enter the basis. If there is a tie for largest, any arbitrary selection device is adequate.

In summary, we have developed a procedure for determining which vector to remove and which vector to enter in moving from one basic feasible solution to another.

Simplex tables

We are now in a position to apply the rules derived above to the example problem. In doing the calculations it is advantageous to make systematic use of simplex tables in order to reduce the probability of error. In the following discussion we continue to defer the problem of obtaining the initial basic feasible solution. However, it is instructive to note the ease with which one can get a first solution when the constraints are all "less than" inequalities—as is the case in the example.

The problem is to maximize

$$\pi = X_1 + X_2$$

subject to

$$\begin{aligned} 5X_1 + 1X_2 &\leq 200 \\ 1X_1 + 2X_2 &\leq \ 90 \\ X_1, X_2 &\geq 0 \end{aligned}$$

As before, we add slack variables to convert the inequalities into equations (here, we shall use X_3 to represent the slack variable in the first constraint rather than S_1 in order to conform to the symbols in this section; similarly, X_4 in lieu of S_2).

$$\text{maximize } \pi = X_1 + X_2 + 0X_3 + 0X_4 \tag{7-25}$$

subject to

$$\begin{aligned} 5X_1 + 1X_2 + 1X_3 + 0X_4 &= 200 \\ 1X_1 + 2X_2 + 0X_3 + 1X_4 &= 190 \\ X_1, X_2, X_3, X_4 &\geq 0 \end{aligned} \tag{7-26}$$

In vector notation:

$$\text{maximize } \pi = \mathbf{c}'\mathbf{x} \tag{7-27}$$

subject to

$$X_1\mathbf{a}_1 + X_2\mathbf{a}_2 + X_3\mathbf{a}_3 + X_4\mathbf{a}_4 = \mathbf{b} \tag{7-28}$$

and

$$\mathbf{x} \geq 0 \tag{7-29}$$

where

$$\mathbf{c}' = (1, 1, 0, 0)$$

$$\mathbf{x} = \begin{bmatrix} X_1 \\ X_2 \\ X_3 \\ X_4 \end{bmatrix} \qquad \mathbf{b} = \begin{bmatrix} 200 \\ 90 \end{bmatrix}$$

$$\mathbf{a}_1 = \begin{bmatrix} 5 \\ 1 \end{bmatrix}, \quad \mathbf{a}_2 = \begin{bmatrix} 1 \\ 2 \end{bmatrix}, \quad \mathbf{a}_3 = \begin{bmatrix} 1 \\ 0 \end{bmatrix}, \quad \mathbf{a}_4 = \begin{bmatrix} 0 \\ 1 \end{bmatrix}$$

Observe that the vectors $\mathbf{a}_3$ and $\mathbf{a}_4$ form an identity matrix of order m. It will always be true when all constraints are "less than" inequalities that the vectors associated with the slack variables will form an identity matrix. The identity matrix permits us to obtain a basic feasible solution quite easily. Thus, referring back to equation (7-28) since $\mathbf{a}_1$ and $\mathbf{a}_2$ are nonbasis vectors, $X_1 = 0$ and $X_2 = 0$. By inspection the initial solution is $X_3 = 200$ and $X_4 = 90$,

$$X_3\mathbf{a}_3 + X_4\mathbf{a}_4 = \mathbf{b}$$

or

$$200\begin{bmatrix}1\\0\end{bmatrix} + 90\begin{bmatrix}0\\1\end{bmatrix} = \begin{bmatrix}200\\90\end{bmatrix}$$

Now we take the above information and rearrange it into the useful format as shown in Table 7-1.

The first row, C_j, is simply $\mathbf{c}'$ and the first column, C_i, is $\mathbf{c}_b$ (the objective function coefficients of the basis variables). The second column, labeled "Basis," contains the basis vectors $\mathbf{a}_3$ and $\mathbf{a}_4$. The remaining columns contain numbers which, when multiplied by the basis vectors, yield the vectors at the head of the columns. These numbers, or scalars, correspond to the Y_{ij} given in equation (7-23). To illustrate, we can write the following five vector equations immediately from observation of Table 7-1:

$$
\begin{aligned}
\mathbf{a}_1 &= 5\mathbf{a}_3 + 1\mathbf{a}_4 \\
\mathbf{a}_2 &= 1\mathbf{a}_3 + 2\mathbf{a}_4 \\
\mathbf{a}_3 &= 1\mathbf{a}_3 + 0\mathbf{a}_4 \\
\mathbf{a}_4 &= 0\mathbf{a}_3 + 1\mathbf{a}_4 \\
\mathbf{b} &= 200\mathbf{a}_3 + 90\mathbf{a}_4
\end{aligned}
\tag{7-30}
$$

The numbers in the Z_j and $C_j - Z_j$ rows were derived from the definitions of those variables as given in the preceding section. Thus,

$$Z_1 = \mathbf{c}_b'\mathbf{y}_1 \qquad \text{where } \mathbf{y}_1 = \begin{bmatrix}5\\1\end{bmatrix}$$

so

$$Z_1 = (0)(5) + (0)(1) = 0$$

Since $C_1 = 1$, then $C_1 - Z_1 = 1 - 0 = 1$.

We can interpret these quantities easily. The loss, or reduction in the objective function, due to adjusting existing basis variables sufficiently to accommodate one unit of $\mathbf{a}_1$ is Z_1, or 0. Since one unit of $\mathbf{a}_1$ adds C_1, or 1, to the objective

TABLE 7-1

C_i \\ C_j	Basis	1 $\mathbf{a}_1$	1 $\mathbf{a}_2$	0 $\mathbf{a}_3$	0 $\mathbf{a}_4$	$\mathbf{b}$
0	$\mathbf{a}_3$	(5)	1	1	0	200
0	$\mathbf{a}_4$	1	2	0	1	90
	Z_j	0	0	0	0	0
	$C_j - Z_j$	1	1	0	0	

function, the total effect on π is $C_1 - Z_1 = 1$. The value of π is given by the Z_j corresponding to the column headed by **b**. For the first solution, $\pi = 0$.

Next we turn to the construction of Table 7-2, or generating the second basic feasible solution. First, we must determine the vector to be entered in the basis (the vector, $\mathbf{a}_p$, as discussed earlier). We know that we have not reached the maximum feasible solution, because there is at least one $C_j - Z_j > 0$. Since both $C_1 - Z_1$ and $C_2 - Z_2$ are equal to 1, and this is the largest positive $C_j - Z_j$, we can enter either $\mathbf{a}_1$ or $\mathbf{a}_2$. Arbitrarily, we choose $\mathbf{a}_1$.

At this point we need to make clear the notational scheme we shall follow in regard to the Y_{ij}. It is conventional to view Y_{ij} as the element in the ith row and jth column. However, it would appear to be less confusing in this case to let the first subscript of Y refer to the *number of the vector* heading that row and, similarly, to let the second subscript refer to the *number of the vector* heading that column. Hence, in Table 7-1, Y_{31} refers to element 5.

The vector to be removed is determined by computing the values of X_i/Y_{i1} for all i for which $Y_{i1} > 0$. The X_i are the current basis variables (the numbers given in the **b** column in Table 7-1) and the Y_{i1} are the numbers in the entering vector, $\mathbf{a}_1$, column in Table 7-1. Thus,

$$\frac{X_3}{Y_{31}} = \frac{200}{5} = 40$$
$$\frac{X_4}{Y_{41}} = \frac{90}{1} = 90$$

The minimum, $X_3/Y_{31} = 40$, corresponds to $\mathbf{a}_3$. Hence, to generate Table 7-2, we shall enter $\mathbf{a}_1$ and remove $\mathbf{a}_3$ from the basis. The basis for Table 7-2 will consist of $\mathbf{a}_1$ and $\mathbf{a}_4$. The element that lies in the entering vector column and departing vector row is called the *pivot element*. In Table 7-1 the pivot element is circled. We shall also circle the pivot element in succeeding tables.

Recall that the numbers in each vector's column are the multipliers of the basis vectors which enable us to express each particular vector as a linear combination of the basis vectors. We can derive the numbers for the new table as follows. From Table 7-1, $\mathbf{a}_1 = 5\mathbf{a}_3 + \mathbf{a}_4$ [the first equation in (7-30)]. Next, solve for $\mathbf{a}_3$:

$$\mathbf{a}_3 = \tfrac{1}{5}(\mathbf{a}_1 - \mathbf{a}_4) \tag{7-31}$$

Substitute equation (7-31) in each of the equations in (7-30) in order to eliminate $\mathbf{a}_3$. The result is the system of equations (7-32) which is in the desired form: each vector is expressed as a unique linear combination of the new basis vectors, $\mathbf{a}_1$ and $\mathbf{a}_4$:

$$\begin{aligned}
\mathbf{a}_1 &= 1\mathbf{a}_1 + 0\mathbf{a}_4 \\
\mathbf{a}_2 &= \tfrac{1}{5}\mathbf{a}_1 + \tfrac{9}{5}\mathbf{a}_4 \\
\mathbf{a}_3 &= \tfrac{1}{5}\mathbf{a}_1 - \tfrac{1}{5}\mathbf{a}_4 \\
\mathbf{a}_4 &= 0\mathbf{a}_1 + 1\mathbf{a}_4 \\
\mathbf{b} &= 40\mathbf{a}_1 + 50\mathbf{a}_4
\end{aligned} \tag{7-32}$$

Table 7-2 can easily be constructed from (7-32).

Clearly, we are moving in the proper direction. The value of π has increased from 0 in Table 7-1 to 40 in Table 7-2. However, the positive $C_2 - Z_2 = \frac{4}{5}$ indicates that this is not the maximum feasible solution, and a further iteration, or table, is called for.

Rather than going through the trouble of manipulating the vector equations each time, it would be desirable from a computational standpoint to obtain mechanical rules which would permit us to calculate the new $\overline{Y}_{ij}$ directly from the old Y_{ij}. Let Y_{ij} refer to the old table and $\overline{Y}_{ij}$ refer to the new table.

By following the procedure used in obtaining the Y_{ij} for Table 7-2, the rules below can be specified. Let $\mathbf{a}_p$ be the entering vector and $\mathbf{a}_h$ the departing vector. Thus, element Y_{hp} is the pivot element. For $j = 1, \ldots, n + 1$ (column $n + 1$ is the $\mathbf{b}$ column):

$$\overline{Y}_{pj} = \frac{Y_{hj}}{Y_{hp}} \tag{7-33}$$

$$\overline{Y}_{ij} = Y_{ij} - Y_{ip}\left[\frac{Y_{hj}}{Y_{hp}}\right] \qquad \text{for } i = 1, \ldots, m;\ i \neq p \tag{7-34}$$

Finally, let us construct Table 7-3 using these rules. Since $\mathbf{a}_2$ in Table 7-2 has the largest positive $C_j - Z_j$, it becomes the entering vector. The departing vector is found by comparing

$$X_1/Y_{12} = 40/\tfrac{1}{5} = 200$$
$$X_4/Y_{42} = 50/\tfrac{9}{5} = 27.8$$

Hence, $\mathbf{a}_4$ is the vector to be removed. The new basis becomes $\mathbf{a}_1$ and $\mathbf{a}_2$. To calculate the $\overline{Y}_{ij}$ for Table 7-3, we simply use equations (7-33) and (7-34). To illustrate, we calculate the $\overline{Y}_{2j}$ (i.e., the $\overline{Y}_{pj}$ using (7-33)):

$$\begin{aligned}
\overline{Y}_{21} &= 0/\tfrac{9}{5} &&= 0 \\
\overline{Y}_{22} &= \tfrac{9}{5}/\tfrac{9}{5} &&= 1 \\
\overline{Y}_{23} &= -\tfrac{1}{5}/\tfrac{9}{5} &&= -\tfrac{1}{9} \\
\overline{Y}_{24} &= 1/\tfrac{9}{5} &&= \tfrac{5}{9} \\
\overline{Y}_{25} &= 50/\tfrac{9}{5} &&= 27.8
\end{aligned}$$

TABLE **7-2**

C_i \ C_j		1	1	0	0	
C_i	Basis	$\mathbf{a}_1$	$\mathbf{a}_2$	$\mathbf{a}_3$	$\mathbf{a}_4$	$\mathbf{b}$
1	$\mathbf{a}_1$	1	$\frac{1}{5}$	$\frac{1}{5}$	0	40
0	$\mathbf{a}_4$	0	$\circled{\frac{9}{5}}$	$-\frac{1}{5}$	1	50
	Z_j	1	$\frac{1}{5}$	$\frac{1}{5}$	0	40
	$C_j - Z_j$	0	$\frac{4}{5}$	$-\frac{1}{5}$	0	

We calculate the $\bar{Y}_{1j}$ using (7-34). Notice that calculations may be made easier by recognizing that the $\bar{Y}_{pj}$, which have just been calculated, may be substituted in (7-34) for the ratios Y_{hj}/Y_{hp}. Hence

$$\begin{aligned}
\bar{Y}_{11} &= 1 - \tfrac{1}{5}(0) &&= 1\\
\bar{Y}_{12} &= \tfrac{1}{5} - \tfrac{1}{5}(1) &&= 0\\
\bar{Y}_{13} &= \tfrac{1}{5} - \tfrac{1}{5}(-\tfrac{1}{9}) &&= \tfrac{2}{9}\\
\bar{Y}_{14} &= 0 - \tfrac{1}{5}(\tfrac{5}{9}) &&= -\tfrac{1}{9}\\
\bar{Y}_{15} &= 40 - \tfrac{1}{5}(27.8) &&= 34.4
\end{aligned}$$

After calculating the Z_j and $C_j - Z_j$ from the definition given earlier, we can complete Table 7-3.

Table 7-3 represents the maximum feasible solution, since there are no $C_j - Z_j > 0$. The value of the objective function is $\pi = 62.2$, and the variables have the following values: $X_1 = 34.4$, $X_2 = 27.8$, $X_3 = 0$, $X_4 = 0$. This solution is identical with the solution obtained graphically at the beginning of the chapter. Of course, the important point of comparison is that the simplex method is not limited to problems of two or three variables as is the graphical method.

It would be instructive for the reader to interpret the values $C_3 - Z_3$ and $C_4 - Z_4$. We shall discuss this important idea in a later section.

Only two major items remain to complete the development of the simplex method: (1) obtaining the *initial* basic feasible solution, and (2) degeneracy. Following these two items we shall present a brief treatment of duality and the dual simplex method.

Initial basic feasible solution

In the example problem, obtaining an initial basic feasible solution was simple. The reason was that the constraints were all "less than" inequalities. And, after introducing a slack variable in each constraint, the coefficients of the slack variables formed an identity matrix which served as the initial basis.

By convention the **b** components are all made non-negative. For example, if the constraint

$$3X_1 - 2X_2 \leq -100 \tag{7-35}$$

TABLE 7-3

C_i \ C_j		1	1	0	0	
C_i	Basis	$\mathbf{a}_1$	$\mathbf{a}_2$	$\mathbf{a}_3$	$\mathbf{a}_4$	**b**
1	$\mathbf{a}_1$	1	0	$\frac{2}{9}$	$-\frac{1}{9}$	34.4
1	$\mathbf{a}_2$	0	1	$-\frac{1}{9}$	$\frac{5}{9}$	27.8
	Z_j	1	1	$\frac{1}{9}$	$\frac{4}{9}$	62.2
	$C_j - Z_j$	0	0	$-\frac{1}{9}$	$-\frac{4}{9}$	

were formulated, we should multiply through by -1 before beginning the simplex method. Or,

$$-3X_1 + 2X_2 \geq 100 \tag{7-36}$$

is obtained in the conversion of -100 to 100.

This introduces the "greater than" inequality. As discussed before, to convert the inequality (7-36) into an equation, we subtract a surplus variable. Hence

$$-3X_1 + 2X_2 - 1S_1 = 100 \tag{7-37}$$

Unfortunately, the coefficient of S_1 is -1, and this prevents the vector associated with S_1 from being part of an identity matrix. And this, in turn, requires us to look elsewhere for an initial basis.

The problem is easily overcome by the following procedure which applies equally to constraints formulated originally as equations. The procedure is to introduce *artificial variables* (and artificial vectors). Suppose, for example, the original constraints are

$$\begin{aligned} 5X_1 + 2X_2 &\geq 20 \\ 2X_1 + 5X_2 &= 35 \end{aligned} \tag{7-38}$$

Since both of the **b** components are non-negative, the first step is to subtract a surplus variable from the left-hand side of the first constraint. Thus

$$\begin{aligned} 5X_1 + 2X_2 - 1S_1 &= 20 \\ 2X_1 + 5X_2 + 0S_1 &= 35 \end{aligned} \tag{7-39}$$

Clearly, there is not an identity matrix available to serve as the initial basis. To see this, we observe the detached coefficients, or matrix **A**:

$$\begin{bmatrix} 5 & 2 & -1 \\ 2 & 5 & 0 \end{bmatrix}$$

To remedy this we add artificial variables to both equations:

$$\begin{aligned} 5X_1 + 2X_2 - 1S_1 + 1A_1 + 0A_2 &= 20 \\ 2X_1 + 5X_2 + 0S_1 + 0A_1 + 1A_2 &= 35 \end{aligned} \tag{7-40}$$

Now matrix **A** contains a desired identity matrix:

$$\begin{bmatrix} 5 & 2 & -1 & 1 & 0 \\ 2 & 5 & 0 & 0 & 1 \end{bmatrix}$$

Immediately, we can obtain a basic solution, *viz.*, $A_1 = 20$, $A_2 = 35$, and X_1, X_2, and S_1 all equal zero. Of course, we have changed the problem, and this solution is *not* a feasible solution to the original problem. This is corrected by assigning objective function coefficients to the artificial variables in such a way that the artificial variables will be driven from the solution. For example, in a maximizing problem, the objective function coefficient is made to be a very large negative number (large relative to the coefficients of the other variables). Hence the simplex method will ensure that the artificial variable is zero in the maximal solution, and thereby collapses the contrived problem back into its original form.

In summary, if all constraints are "less than" inequalities (after ensuring that **b** is non-negative), the coefficients of the slack variables provide us with an identity matrix which serves as the basis for the initial basic feasible solution. If, however, "greater than" inequality constraints are present, artificial variables are introduced to provide the identity matrix. Hence we start with an initial basic solution which is not feasible; but by assigning appropriate objective function coefficients to the artificial variables we ensure that the optimal solution will be feasible. It should be noted that the important point is to obtain an identity submatrix in the **A** matrix; hence if by chance one is present before artificial variables are added, an initial basic feasible solution is obtainable immediately. An example of the use of artificial variables is given in the duality section.

Degeneracy

Throughout our development of the simplex method we assumed that every basic feasible solution was nondegenerate. That is, we assumed that none of the basis variables were ever zero—or, what is the same thing, that **b** could never be expressed as a linear combination of fewer than m linearly independent vectors where $r(\mathbf{A}) = m$. Here we want to discuss briefly what could bring about a degenerate solution.

The degeneracy problem is illustrated easily by referring back to the discussion of the choice of the vector to be replaced in generating a new basic feasible solution. The rule for the choice was stated as follows: Choose the minimum of all

$$X_i / Y_{ip} \qquad \text{for all } i = 1, 2, \ldots, m$$

where

$$Y_{ip} > 0$$

$\mathbf{a}_p$ is the entering vector

But if by chance a tie should exist for the minimum, two X_i will become zero. Hence, there will be fewer than m positive X_i in the solution, and degeneracy is said to exist.

The major theoretical problem posed by degeneracy is the possibility of cycling.

> When degeneracy is present, the objective function may not change when we move from one basic feasible solution to another. Then we can no longer be sure that no basis will be repeated. In fact, we may get into a situation where we cycle forever, repeating the same sequence of bases, and never reach an optimal solution [15, p. 174].

In practice, however, no problem has ever been known to cycle [14, p. 116]. A contrived problem which demonstrates cycling is given in Gass [14, p. 119]. Furthermore, computer codes for solving linear programming problems normally are not designed to avoid the possibility of cycling. Although two methods have been developed to eliminate the possibility of cycling (one by Charnes [4] and the other by Dantzig, Orden, and Wolfe [9]), we shall not present them here. Owing to the negligible practical possibility of cycling, we shall simply rely upon *any* arbitrary method for breaking the tie in the choice of the vector to be replaced.

DUALITY

The dual problem

Duality refers to the fact that every linear programming problem has associated with it another linear programming problem. If the original problem is called the *primal* problem, then the associated problem is called the *dual* problem. It is immaterial which is called the primal and which is called the dual.

Baumol has colorfully described the relationship between the primal and the dual as follows:

> Suppose a mischievous gremlin were let loose on this linear programming problem and decided that he would turn everything he possibly could on its head. For the word "maximize" he would substitute "minimize." For the symbol $\geq$ he would substitute $\leq$. . . . [3, p. 104]

Rather than continuing with Baumol's description of every item which is "turned on its head," we can illustrate the relationship by our example problem.

Arbitrarily, we shall call the original problem the primal. That is, the primal problem is to

$$\text{maximize} \quad \pi = X_1 + X_2 \tag{7-41}$$

subject to

$$\begin{aligned} 5X_1 + 1X_2 &\leq 200 \\ 1X_1 + 2X_2 &\leq 90 \\ X_1, X_2 &\geq 0 \end{aligned} \tag{7-42}$$

The dual problem becomes

$$\text{minimize} \quad V = 200W_1 + 90W_2 \tag{7-43}$$

subject to

$$\begin{aligned} 5W_1 + 1W_2 &\geq 1 \\ 1W_1 + 2W_2 &\geq 1 \\ W_1, W_2 &\geq 0 \end{aligned} \tag{7-44}$$

New variables have been introduced in the dual, *viz.*, W_1 and W_2. For the moment, we simply state that these variables are "accounting prices" or "shadow prices" of the resources used. Hence W_1 is the shadow price of labor and W_2 is the shadow price of machine capacity. The shadow price of labor is a measure of the contribution to π of one additional unit of labor. Similarly, W_2 is the marginal profitability of machine capacity.

The objective function of the dual (7-43) can be interpreted as the valuation of the firm's resources. That is, from the primal we see that the firm has available 200 man-hours of labor and 90 machine-hours. Multiplying these quantities by their accounting prices and adding gives us a measure of the valuation of the firm's resources.

The constraints (7-44) are interpreted as follows. Referring to activity 1 in the primal, we observe that to produce one unit of X_1 requires 5 man-hours and 1 machine-hour (i.e., 5 and 1 are the components of the first column of the matrix **A**). The primal's objective function shows that every unit of X_1 contributes 1 to π. Hence the first constraint of the dual states that the accounting value of the resources needed to produce one unit of X_1 must be $\geq$ the unit profit which can be derived from one unit of X_1 in the market. The dual's second constraint can be interpreted similarly for X_2. It should be noted that the primal's **A** matrix is transposed to obtain the corresponding matrix of the dual. Thus the dual's matrix of coefficients is $\mathbf{A}'$ (by coincidence in our example, $\mathbf{A} \equiv \mathbf{A}'$).

We can now state the following theorem (for proof, see Gass [14, p. 84]):

Duality Theorem If either the primal or the dual problem has a finite optimum solution, then the other problem has a finite optimum solution, and the values of the objective functions are equal.

This theorem makes the surprising statement that the maximum value of π is equal to the minimum value of V. Hence (as computed earlier), since the maximum value of π is 62.2, it follows that the minimum valuation of the firm's resources is also 62.2. In other words, the values of the shadow prices W_1 and W_2 are of just the right amount to exactly exhaust π.

To demonstrate the close relationship between the primal and the dual more clearly, we shall present the simplex method solution to the dual, and then compare the optimum solutions of the primal and the dual. Solving the dual by the simplex method also has the advantage of illustrating minimizing problems and the use of artificial variables.

We must add two *surplus* variables, W_3 and W_4, and two *artificial* variables, W_5 and W_6, to the objective function and constraints of the dual. In the objective function, the coefficients of W_5 and W_6 are both of a magnitude M, where M is a very large number. Thus

$$\text{minimize} \quad V = 200W_1 + 90W_2 + 0W_3 + 0W_4 + MW_5 + MW_6 \tag{7-45}$$

subject to

$$\begin{aligned} 5W_1 + 1W_2 - 1W_3 + 0W_4 + 1W_5 + 0W_6 &= 1 \\ 1W_1 + 2W_2 + 0W_3 - 1W_4 + 0W_5 + 1W_6 &= 1 \\ W_1, W_2, W_3, W_4, W_5, W_6 &\geq 0 \end{aligned} \tag{7-46}$$

Following the simplex method discussed earlier, we can solve the dual problem. The three simplex tables (Tables 7-4, 7-5, and 7-6) are presented without further explanation (we use $\mathbf{w}_j$ to represent the requirements space vector associated with the variable W_j).

Table 7-6 gives the optimum solution to the dual problem. To facilitate the comparison of the solution of the dual problem with the solution to the primal problem see Table 7-3 on page 193.

Of course, the first point to note is that maximum π (in primal) = minimum V (in dual) = 62.2. The shadow prices of labor and machine capacity, W_1 and W_2, are given in the dual solution as $\frac{1}{9}$ and $\frac{4}{9}$ respectively. Notice that these values also appear in the primal solution (Table 7-3) as negative values in the $C_j - Z_j$ row. In the primal table they can be interpreted easily. For example, the $-\frac{1}{9}$ in the $\mathbf{a}_3$ column means that if one unit of $\mathbf{a}_3$ were entered in the solution,

TABLE 7-4

C_i \ C_j		200	90	0	0	M	M	
C_i	Basis	$\mathbf{w}_1$	$\mathbf{w}_2$	$\mathbf{w}_3$	$\mathbf{w}_4$	$\mathbf{w}_5$	$\mathbf{w}_6$	$\mathbf{b}$
M	$\mathbf{w}_5$	(5)	1	-1	0	1	0	1
M	$\mathbf{w}_6$	1	2	0	-1	0	1	1
	Z_j	$6M$	$3M$	$-M$	$-M$	M	M	$2M$
	$C_j - Z_j$	$200 - 6M$	$90 - 3M$	M	M	0	0	

TABLE 7-5

C_i \ C_j		200	90	0	0	M	M	
C_i	Basis	$\mathbf{w}_1$	$\mathbf{w}_2$	$\mathbf{w}_3$	$\mathbf{w}_4$	$\mathbf{w}_5$	$\mathbf{w}_6$	$\mathbf{b}$
200	$\mathbf{w}_1$	1	$\frac{1}{5}$	$-\frac{1}{5}$	0	$\frac{1}{5}$	0	$\frac{1}{5}$
M	$\mathbf{w}_6$	0	($\frac{9}{5}$)	$\frac{1}{5}$	-1	$-\frac{1}{5}$	1	$\frac{4}{5}$
	Z_j	200	$40 + \frac{9}{5}M$	$\frac{1}{5}M - 40$	$-M$	$40 - \frac{1}{5}M$	M	$40 + \frac{4}{5}M$
	$C_j - Z_j$	0	$50 - \frac{9}{5}M$	$40 - \frac{1}{5}M$	M	$\frac{6}{5}M - 40$	0	

TABLE 7-6

C_i \ C_j		200	90	0	0	M	M	
C_i	Basis	$\mathbf{w}_1$	$\mathbf{w}_2$	$\mathbf{w}_3$	$\mathbf{w}_4$	$\mathbf{w}_5$	$\mathbf{w}_6$	$\mathbf{b}$
200	$\mathbf{w}_1$	1	0	$-\frac{2}{9}$	$\frac{1}{9}$	$\frac{2}{9}$	$-\frac{1}{9}$	$\frac{1}{9}$
90	$\mathbf{w}_2$	0	1	$\frac{1}{9}$	$-\frac{5}{9}$	$-\frac{1}{9}$	$\frac{5}{9}$	$\frac{4}{9}$
	Z_j	200	90	-34.4	-27.8	34.4	27.8	62.2
	$C_j - Z_j$	0	0	34.4	27.8	$M - 34.4$	$M - 27.8$	

π would be reduced by $\frac{1}{9}$. But $\mathbf{a}_3$ is the vector associated with the variable X_3, and X_3 is the slack variable in the labor constraint. Hence adding one unit of X_3 is equivalent to removing one man-hour of labor; thus, if removing one man-hour of labor reduces π by $\frac{1}{9}$, it must also be true that adding one man-hour increases π by $\frac{1}{9}$. This confirms our interpretation of W_1 in the dual as the shadow price, or marginal profitability, of labor. By a similar line of reasoning W_2 can be interpreted to be the shadow price of machine capacity.

Although there are other interesting relationships between the primal and the dual which we could explore, we shall terminate our discussion here. For more complete discussions, the reader is referred to [12, Chapter 7] and to [3, Chapter 6].

Before turning to a brief summary of the dual-simplex method, we should point out that there are some practical advantages of duality also. In our discussion thus far we have been concerned with interpretation. That is, we have pointed out that for every resource allocation problem (the primal), there is an associated pricing problem (the dual). But in addition there may be computational advantages in solving the dual in lieu of the primal. For example, if the primal has more constraints than variables, then the dual might be easier to solve, since it would have fewer constraints. Another important practical application of duality is in sensitivity analysis: the analysis of the effect of changing parameters after the optimal solution has been obtained. For a good illustration of duality and sensitivity analysis, see Spivey [17, p. 171].

The dual-simplex method

The dual-simplex method is another algorithm for solving linear programming problems. It is particularly useful in solving integer programming problems (discussed in Chapter 10).

The reason for its usefulness is as follows. In solving integer programming problems one usually obtains an optimal solution by the simplex method, ignoring the requirement that the variables must be integers. Of course, a requirement for the solution to be maximal is that all of the $C_j - Z_j$ must be ≤ 0. The next step in the integer programming solution procedure is to introduce a new constraint. If the constraint is added in such a way as to keep all $C_j - Z_j \leq 0$ while making the solution nonfeasible (a nonfeasible solution has some $X_i < 0$), then the dual-simplex method is appropriate.

In other words, the dual-simplex method starts with a basic, but not feasible, solution which meets the requirement that all $C_j - Z_j \leq 0$. It then moves from basic solution to basic solution in such a way as to keep all $C_j - Z_j \leq 0$. Eventually, provided no basis has to be repeated, the optimal solution will be obtained (when all solution variables become ≥ 0).

In essence, the dual-simplex method deals with the primal problem as if the simplex method were being applied simultaneously to the dual problem. That is, the criteria for entering and removing a vector are those for the dual of the primal problem being solved.

Here we shall merely list the rules for the dual-simplex method. For a more complete treatment, the reader is referred to Hadley [15, p. 242].

1. Begin with a basic solution with one or more $X_i < 0$ for $i = 1, \ldots, m$ (where these X_i are the m variables associated with basis vectors) and with all $C_j - Z_j \leq 0$.
2. The vector to be removed is determined by finding the minimum of all $X_i < 0 \quad \text{for } i = 1, \ldots, m$.
   Let X_h be the minimum, then $\mathbf{a}_h$ should be removed.
3. The vector to be entered is determined by finding the minimum of all $(C_j - Z_j)/Y_{hj} \quad \text{for } Y_{hj} < 0$.
   Let the minimum be $(C_p - Z_p)/Y_{hp}$, then $\mathbf{a}_p$ should be entered. If a tie exists, any arbitrary rule can be used to break it. Degeneracy is indicated if the minimum is zero; cycling is theoretically possible, but we shall ignore that possibility.
4. The transformation from solution to solution is made in the same way as in the simplex method.

TWO EXAMPLE PROBLEMS[2]

A production problem

In Chapter 6 we formulated a linear programming problem for a television manufacturer whose objective is to determine the quantity of black-and-white television sets X_1 and color television sets X_2 which will maximize the profit function

$$\pi = 15X_1 + 45X_2 \tag{7-47}$$

subject to the following constraints imposed by the existing production facilities:

$$\begin{aligned} X_2 &\leq 50 \\ 1.0X_1 + 1.6X_2 &\leq 240 \\ 0.5X_1 + 2.0X_2 &\leq 162 \end{aligned} \tag{7-48}$$

Introducing slack variables S_1, S_2, and S_3 the problem may be restated as one of maximizing

$$\pi = 15X_1 + 45X_2 + 0S_1 + 0S_2 + 0S_3 \tag{7-49}$$

subject to

$$\begin{aligned} 1.0X_2 + S_1 &= 50 \\ 1.0X_1 + 1.6X_2 + S_2 &= 240 \\ 0.5X_1 + 2.0X_2 + S_3 &= 162 \end{aligned} \tag{7-50}$$

[2] These two examples were taken from Naylor and Byrne [16], Chapter 4.

Table 7-7 contains the initial simplex table for this problem. For clarity, rather than using vector notation in the table as we did earlier in the chapter, we shall substitute the symbol of the associated variable. We denote the column of right-hand side constants with B.

Table 7-8 represents the final simplex table and indicates that the optimum production plan for the firm calls for the production of 15 black-and-white sets and 35 color sets yielding a total profit of $4,335. Note that the shadow prices for set assembly capacity and final testing capacity are $6.25 and $17.50 respectively.

A blending problem

As an example of a cost-minimization problem which is typical of a broad class of linear programming problems known as "blending problems" consider the case of a soap manufacturer who finds he cannot satisfy the demand for one of his powdered laundry soap products during a particular week. The firm is faced with a loss of sales, amounting to 1,000 pounds, simply because its production capacity is inadequate. Although this situation is only temporary, the firm does have a way of satisfying the excess demand.

Specifically, the firm is considering buying powdered soap from two other manufacturers and blending them into a soap that would at least meet the specifications of the soap presently being marketed by the company. That this is possible has been established through previous experience. The soap company wants to know how much soap 1 and soap 2 to purchase in order to satisfy

TABLE 7-7

C_i \ C_j		15	45	0	0	0	
C_i	Basis	X_1	X_2	S_1	S_2	S_3	B
0	S_1	0	(1.0)	1	0	0	50
0	S_2	1.0	1.6	0	1	0	240
0	S_3	0.5	2.0	0	0	1	162
	Z_j	0	0	0	0	0	0
	$C_j - Z_j$	15	45	0	0	0	

TABLE 7-8

C_i \ C_j		15	45	0	0	0	
C_i	Basis	X_1	X_2	S_1	S_2	S_3	B
45	X_2	0	1	0	$-\frac{5}{12}$	$\frac{10}{12}$	35
0	S_1	0	0	1	$\frac{5}{12}$	$-\frac{10}{12}$	15
15	X_1	1	0	0	$\frac{20}{12}$	$-\frac{16}{12}$	184
	Z_j	15	45	0	6.25	17.50	4335
	$C_j - Z_j$	0	0	0	-6.25	-17.50	

demand and provide a product that is identical with the present product. The firm can purchase soap 1 and soap 2 for \$0.10 and \$0.08 per pound, respectively.

To the consumer the three most important characteristics of powdered laundry soap are washing power, sudsiness, and hardness. By analyzing certain chemical and physical characteristics of soap it is possible actually to measure the respective characteristics of a particular soap product. Research indicates that the particular soap in question must have a washing-power factor of at least 6.5, a sudsiness factor of at least 3.0, and a hardness factor no greater than 4.0.

Table 7-9 shows the characteristics of the two soaps being considered for blending purposes.

The firm's research department has determined that the characteristics of the two soaps combine linearly by weight when blended. In other words, if equal weights of soap 1 and soap 2 are combined, the resulting blend will have the following characteristics: washing power, 7.5; sudsiness, 4.0; and hardness, 3.0.

As can be seen, this particular blend has the required characteristics. However, it does not represent the minimum cost blend. If we let X_1 denote the quantity of soap 1 (in pounds) and X_2 denote the quantity of soap 2 (in pounds) used in the blend, the objective of the firm is to minimize the cost function:

$$Z = 0.10X_1 + 0.08X_2 \tag{7-51}$$

The washing-power constraint may be expressed algebraically by the inequality

$$\frac{6X_1}{1000} + \frac{9X_2}{1000} \geq 6.5 \tag{7-52}$$

The expression $X_1/1000$ denotes the fraction of the total blend having a washing power of 6.0, and $X_2/1000$ the fraction having a washing power of 9.0. Therefore (7-52) states that the quantities of soap 1 and soap 2 must be such that a blend will be produced whose washing-power factor is at least 6.5. Alternatively, the weighted average of the washing-power factor of the blend must be at least 6.5. The sudsiness and hardness constraints may be expressed respectively as

$$\frac{2X_1}{1000} + \frac{6X_2}{1000} \geq 3 \tag{7-53}$$

and

$$\frac{1X_1}{1000} + \frac{5X_2}{1000} \leq 4 \tag{7-54}$$

TABLE **7-9**

	Soap 1	Soap 2
Washing power	6	9
Sudsiness	2	6
Hardness	1	5

A fourth constraint, which recognizes the demand situation, must be added—the total weight of the blend must be equal to the total weight demanded:

$$X_1 + X_2 = 1{,}000 \tag{7-55}$$

When both sides of the washing-power, sudsiness, and hardness constraints are multiplied by 1,000, the four constraints become

$$\begin{aligned} 6X_1 + 9X_2 &\geq 6{,}500 \\ 2X_1 + 6X_2 &\geq 3{,}000 \\ 1X_1 + 5X_2 &\leq 4{,}000 \\ 1X_1 + 1X_2 &= 1{,}000 \end{aligned} \tag{7-56}$$

Introducing the appropriate slack and artificial variables, the constraints may be rewritten as

$$\begin{aligned} 6X_1 + 9X_2 - S_1 + A_1 &= 6{,}500 \\ 2X_1 + 6X_2 - S_2 + A_2 &= 3{,}000 \\ 1X_1 + 5X_2 + S_3 \qquad &= 4{,}000 \\ 1X_1 + 1X_2 \qquad + A_3 &= 1{,}000 \end{aligned} \tag{7-57}$$

Table 7-10 is the initial simplex table. Table 7-11 is the final simplex table indicating that the soap firm should purchase 250 pounds of soap 1 and 750

TABLE **7-10**

C_i \ C_j		0.10	0.08	0	M	0	M	0	M	
C_i	Basis	X_1	X_2	S_1	A_1	S_2	A_2	S_3	A_3	B
M	A_1	6	9	−1	1	0	0	0	0	6,500
M	A_2	2	(6)	0	0	−1	1	0	0	3,000
0	S_3	1	5	0	0	0	0	1	0	4,000
M	A_3	1	1	0	0	0	0	0	1	1,000
	Z_j	$9M$	$16M$	$-M$	M	$-M$	M	0	M	$10{,}500M$
	$C_j - Z_j$	$0.10 - 9M$	$0.08 - 16M$	M	0	M	0	0	0	

TABLE **7-11**

C_i \ C_j		0.10	0.08	0	M	0	M	0	M	
C_i	Basis	X_1	X_2	S_1	A_1	S_2	A_2	S_3	A_3	B
0.10	X_1	1	0	0	0	0	0	$-\frac{1}{4}$	$\frac{5}{4}$	250
0.08	X_2	0	1	0	0	0	0	$\frac{1}{4}$	$-\frac{1}{4}$	750
0	S_2	0	0	0	0	1	−1	1	1	2000
0	S_1	0	0	1	−1	0	0	$\frac{3}{4}$	$\frac{21}{4}$	1750
	Z_j	0.10	0.08	0	0	0	0	−0.005	0.10	85
	$C_j - Z_j$	0	0	0	M	0	M	0.005	$M - 0.10$	

pounds of soap 2. The cost of these purchases is \$85. Note that the $C_j - Z_j$ value for A_3 in Table 7-11 is $M - 0.10$. The value of M is such that it far exceeds 0.10, thus making $M - 0.10$ a positive quantity.

Several blending problems are contained in the set of linear programming case studies in Naylor and Byrne [16].

BIBLIOGRAPHY

[1] ARROW, KENNETH J., LEONID HURWICZ, and HIROFUMI UZAWA. *Studies in Linear and Non-Linear Programming*. Stanford: Stanford University Press, 1958.

[2] BAUMOL, WILLIAM J. "Activity Analysis in One Lesson," *American Economic Review*, **XLVIII** (December, 1958), 837–873.

[3] BAUMOL, WILLIAM J. *Economic Theory and Operations Analysis*. Englewood Cliffs, N. J.: Prentice-Hall, Inc., 1965.

[4] CHARNES, A., W. W. COOPER, and A. HENDERSON. *An Introduction to Linear Programming*. New York: John Wiley & Sons, 1953.

[5] CHARNES, A., and W. W. COOPER. *Management Models and Industrial Applications of Linear Programming*. New York: John Wiley & Sons, 1961.

[6] CHUNG, AN-MIN. *Linear Programming*. Columbus, Ohio: Charles E. Merrill Co., 1959.

[7] DANO, SVEN. *Linear Programming in Industry: Theory and Applications*. Wien: Springer-Verlag, 1960.

[8] DANTZIG, GEORGE B. *A Procedure for Maximizing a Linear Function Subject to Linear Inequalities*. Washington: Headquarters, U.S. Air Force, Comptroller, 1948.

[9] DANTZIG, G. B., A. ORDEN, and P. WOLFE. "The Generalized Simplex Method for Minimizing a Linear Form under Linear Inequality Restraints," *Pacific Journal of Mathematics*, **5** (1955), 183–195.

[10] DANTZIG, GEORGE B. *Linear Programming and Extensions*. Princeton: Princeton University Press, 1963.

[11] DORFMAN, ROBERT. "Mathematical, or Linear, Programming: A Nonmathematical Exposition," *American Economic Review*, **XLIII** (December, 1953), 797–825.

[12] DORFMAN, ROBERT, PAUL A. SAMUELSON, and ROBERT SOLOW. *Linear Programming and Economic Analysis*. New York: McGraw-Hill Book Co., 1958.

[13] GARVIN, WALTER W. *Introduction to Linear Programming*. New York: McGraw-Hill Book Co., 1960.

[14] GASS, SAUL. *Linear Programming: Methods and Applications*. New York: McGraw-Hill Book Co., 1964.

[15] HADLEY, G. *Linear Programming*. Reading, Mass.: Addison-Wesley Publishing Co., 1962.

[16] NAYLOR, THOMAS H., and EUGENE T. BYRNE. *Linear Programming*. Belmont, California: Wadsworth Publishing Co., 1963.

[17] SPIVEY, W. ALLEN. *Linear Programming*. New York: The Macmillan Co., 1963.

[18] VAJDA, S. *Readings in Linear Programming*. New York: John Wiley & Sons, 1958.

[19] VAJDA, S. *Mathematical Programming*. Reading, Mass.: Addison-Wesley, 1961.

Mathematical appendix for chapter 7

LINEAR ALGEBRA

Vector A vector is an ordered set of numbers. The best explanation is probably an illustration. A column vector **v** is denoted by

$$\begin{bmatrix} v_1 \\ v_2 \\ v_3 \end{bmatrix}$$

and a row vector **v**′ is denoted by

$$(v_1, v_2, v_3)$$

Vector **v** is said to lie in three-dimensional space, or simply three-space. A vector with two components, say **w**, $\begin{bmatrix} w_1 \\ w_2 \end{bmatrix}$ lies in two-space.

Vectors with the same number of components may be added or subtracted. For example, the sum of two vectors **w** and **y** is shown below:

$$\begin{bmatrix} w_1 \\ w_2 \end{bmatrix} + \begin{bmatrix} y_1 \\ y_2 \end{bmatrix} = \begin{bmatrix} w_1 + y_1 \\ w_2 + y_2 \end{bmatrix}$$

Vector addition is commutative and associative.

The *scalar product* of two *n*-component vectors, **w** and **y**, is defined to be the scalar, $\mathbf{w} \cdot \mathbf{y}$:

$$w_1 y_1 + w_2 y_2 + \cdots + w_n y_n = \sum_{i=1}^{n} w_i y_i$$

One other operation with vectors which will be useful is the multiplication of vectors by scalars. For the scalar, *a*, and the vector **w**, the scalar product of *a* and **w** is the vector **z**, where

$$\mathbf{z} = \begin{bmatrix} aw_1 \\ aw_2 \end{bmatrix}$$

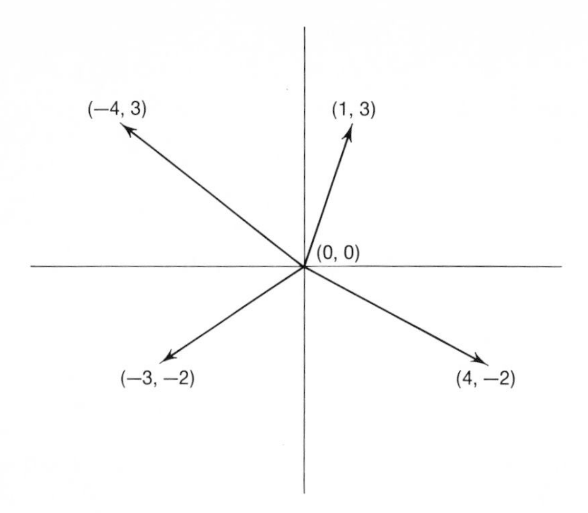

FIGURE **7A-1**

Vector space The totality of all vectors of n components makes up the n-dimensional vector space. It is usually helpful to think of vectors in terms of their geometrical counterparts, at least for two- and three-dimensional vectors. For example, consider some two-dimensional vectors: (1, 3), (4, −2), (−3, −2), (−4, 3), and (0, 0). If we use the Cartesian coordinate system, and take the first component to measure horizontal distance and the second to measure vertical distance, then we can plot the vectors in Figure 7A-1. The two-dimensional vector space can be conceived as the totality of all points in the plane.

Linear combination A linear combination is obtained by performing scalar multiplication and vector addition on a set of vectors. Thus, $\mathbf{x}$ is a linear combination of the vectors $\mathbf{w}$ and $\mathbf{y}$ (β and δ are scalars).

$$\mathbf{x} = \beta\mathbf{w} + \delta\mathbf{y}$$

A set of vectors all of which belong to the same vector space is said to be *linearly dependent* if one of the vectors is the *null* vector (all components zero) or if one can be expressed as a linear combination of the others. If not, the set of vectors is said to be *linearly independent*.

In two-space, there can be only two independent vectors in a set. The vectors (0, 1) and (1, 0) are two independent vectors. Every other vector in two-space can be expressed as a linear combination of these two vectors. The vector (m, n), for example, could be written as $m(1, 0) + n(0, 1) = (m, n)$. Notice that every pair of vectors in two-space is not necessarily linearly independent. The two vectors, (0, 1) and (0, 2), are linearly dependent. The reason is that (0, 2) can be expressed as a linear combination of (0, 1), *viz.*, (0, 2) = 2(0, 1). It is impossible, on the other hand, to express (0, 1) as a linear combination of (1, 0); hence, these two vectors are linearly independent.

Similarly, in three-space, every vector can be expressed as a linear combination of three independent vectors. In n-space every vector can be expressed as a linear combination of n independent vectors. Thus every set of $n + 1$ vectors is linearly dependent.

Basis Any set of n linearly independent vectors in n-space is a basis for n-space. Thus the vectors (0, 1) and (1, 0) form a basis for two-space. The vectors (0, 2) and (4, 0) also form a basis for two-space. Hence a basis is not unique.

Any vector in n-space can be expressed uniquely as a linear combination of the vectors of a given basis. For proof, see Hadley [15, p. 43].

Matrix A matrix is a rectangular array of real numbers written as follows:

$$\mathbf{A} = \begin{bmatrix} a_{11} & a_{12} & \cdots & a_{1n} \\ a_{21} & a_{22} & \cdots & a_{2n} \\ \vdots & & & \\ a_{m1} & a_{m2} & \cdots & a_{mn} \end{bmatrix}$$

The above matrix is called an $m \times n$ matrix because it has m rows and n columns. A double subscript is used to denote the location of any element, a_{ij} (a_{ij} is located in the ith row and the jth column). The matrix can also be conceived of as either n column vectors or m row vectors.

Two matrices are equal if and only if their corresponding elements are equal. Two matrices of the same order (i.e., with the same number of rows and columns) may be added by adding corresponding elements. Scalar multiplication of a matrix is defined to be the multiplication of each element in the matrix by the scalar.

The product of two matrices **AB** is defined if and only if **A** has the same number of columns as **B** has rows. For example, let **A** be an $m \times p$ matrix and **B** a $p \times n$ matrix. Then, **AB** is the matrix of order $m \times n$ with any element, c_{ij}, as given below:

$$c_{ij} = a_{i1}b_{1j} + a_{i2}b_{2j} + \cdots + a_{ip}b_{pj}$$

It is important to observe that the product **BA** is not defined, since the number of columns of **B** is not equal to the number of rows of **A**. In general, matrix multiplication is not commutative (**AB** is not generally equal to **BA**). For example,

$$\mathbf{A} = \begin{bmatrix} 2 & 5 \\ 1 & 0 \end{bmatrix} \qquad \mathbf{B} = \begin{bmatrix} 1 & 2 & 4 \\ 6 & 3 & 1 \end{bmatrix}$$

$$\mathbf{AB} = \begin{bmatrix} 32 & 19 & 13 \\ 1 & 2 & 4 \end{bmatrix} \qquad \mathbf{BA} \text{ is not defined}$$

The *identity* matrix is a square matrix (the number of rows equals the number of columns) having the number 1 for its diagonal elements and zeros elsewhere. The identity matrix of order 3 is

$$\mathbf{I} = \begin{bmatrix} 1 & 0 & 0 \\ 0 & 1 & 0 \\ 0 & 0 & 1 \end{bmatrix}$$

where the order equals the number of columns or rows. Notice that if A is any matrix, then

$$\mathbf{AI} = \mathbf{IA} = \mathbf{A}$$

The *transpose* of a matrix **A**, written **A**′, is the matrix obtained by interchanging the rows and columns of **A**. Thus if

$$\mathbf{A} = \begin{bmatrix} a_{11} & a_{12} \\ a_{21} & a_{22} \end{bmatrix}, \qquad \text{then } \mathbf{A}' = \begin{bmatrix} a_{11} & a_{21} \\ a_{12} & a_{22} \end{bmatrix}$$

Matrix rank The rank of a matrix is closely related to the concept of linearly independent vectors. If **A** is an $m \times n$ matrix, the row rank of the matrix is the maximum number of linearly independent row vectors. Similarly, the column rank of **A** is the maximum number of linearly independent column vectors. Furthermore, the column rank is always equal to the row rank of a particular matrix; hence we shall simply speak of *matrix rank*. We shall write $r(\mathbf{A})$ to indicate the rank of matrix **A**.

Determining the rank of a matrix is rather tedious if the matrix is of a high order. We shall not pursue this problem here; for one method, the reader is referred to Spivey [17, p. 77].

Inverse of a matrix For a square matrix **A**, a matrix **B** which satisfies

$$\mathbf{AB} = \mathbf{BA} = \mathbf{I}$$

is called the inverse of **A**. The inverse of **A** is normally written $\mathbf{A}^{-1}$. Only square matrices can have inverses. Furthermore, only those square matrices whose rank equals their order can have inverses; these matrices are also referred to as *nonsingular* matrices.

The inverse of a nonsingular matrix **A** can be calculated from the formula

$$\mathbf{A}^{-1} = \frac{1}{|\mathbf{A}|} \operatorname{adj} \mathbf{A}$$

The "adj **A**" represents the adjoint matrix of **A**. If **C** is the matrix of cofactors of **A** (see the appendix to Chapter 2 for a definition of cofactor), then **C**′ is the adjoint of **A**. $|\mathbf{A}|$ denotes the determinant of **A**.

SIMULTANEOUS LINEAR EQUATIONS

We can now begin to use some of the linear algebra concepts to shed some light upon the solutions to simultaneous linear equations—the heart of solving linear programming problems.

Although the constraints of linear programming problems are often stated as linear inequalities, we shall limit our discussion to linear equations. The reason is that the solution to a set of inequalities is difficult to handle; and, fortunately, we may avoid this difficulty. Inequalities can be converted into equations by the use of slack (or surplus) variables. Furthermore, the problem is not altered, since a non-negative solution to the converted set of equations is a non-negative solution to the corresponding set of linear inequalities. For a clear geometrical explanation of this important property, see Spivey [17, p. 97].

The constraint inequality $\alpha X + \beta Y \leq c$ can be transformed into an equality by adding the slack variable Z to the left-hand side: $\alpha X + \beta Y + Z = c$. If the inequality were of the opposite sense, we would subtract a surplus variable from the left-hand side. It is important to note that the slack (or surplus) variable must be restricted to be non-negative. (The coefficients of slack and surplus variables in the objective function of a programming problem are always zero; hence they can have no effect on the value of that function.)

Consider the equations

$$1X_1 + 0X_2 = 3$$
$$0X_1 + 1X_2 = 5$$

We can write these equations more compactly either in vector notation,

$$X_1\mathbf{a}_1 + X_2\mathbf{a}_2 = \mathbf{b}$$

where

$$\mathbf{a}_1 = \begin{bmatrix}1\\0\end{bmatrix}, \quad \mathbf{a}_2 = \begin{bmatrix}0\\1\end{bmatrix}, \quad \text{and } \mathbf{b} = \begin{bmatrix}3\\5\end{bmatrix}$$

or, in matrix notation,

$$\mathbf{Ax} = \mathbf{b}$$

where

$$\mathbf{A} = \begin{bmatrix}1 & 0\\0 & 1\end{bmatrix}, \quad \mathbf{x} = \begin{bmatrix}X_1\\X_2\end{bmatrix}, \quad \text{and } \mathbf{b} = \begin{bmatrix}3\\5\end{bmatrix}$$

Solving the equation can be viewed as finding those scalars, X_1 and X_2, which permit us to express $\mathbf{b}$ as a linear combination of $\mathbf{a}_1$ and $\mathbf{a}_2$. Since $\mathbf{a}_1$ and $\mathbf{a}_2$ are linearly independent (see earlier discussion), they form a basis in two-space. Furthermore, we know that any vector in two-space can be expressed *uniquely* as a linear combination of the vectors of a given basis. Hence the solution, $X_1 = 3$ and $X_2 = 5$, is unique.

Next, consider the equation

$$X_1\mathbf{a}_1 + X_2\mathbf{a}_2 + X_3\mathbf{a}_3 = \mathbf{b}$$

where $\mathbf{a}_3$ is added to the equation and is $\begin{bmatrix}2\\2\end{bmatrix}$.

Since in two-space every set of three (or more) vectors must be linearly dependent, we know that there is no unique set of scalars, X_1, X_2, and X_3, which will satisfy the equation. For example, X_3 could assume *any* value, and values for X_1 and X_2 could be found to satisfy the equation. We have a set of equations with more unknowns than equations—the typical linear programming problem.

The two examples illustrate two possible outcomes in solving a set of equations: a unique solution and an infinite number of solutions. There is one further possibility: no solution. Of course, such an outcome is not expected if the constraints are formulated properly, but an error in formulation can lead to such a result. If there is no solution to a set of linear equations, they are said to be *inconsistent*. A geometrical illustration of a two-variable, two-equation case would be two parallel lines (there would be no solution because the lines would never intersect).

If we have a matrix equation

$$\mathbf{Ax} = \mathbf{b}$$

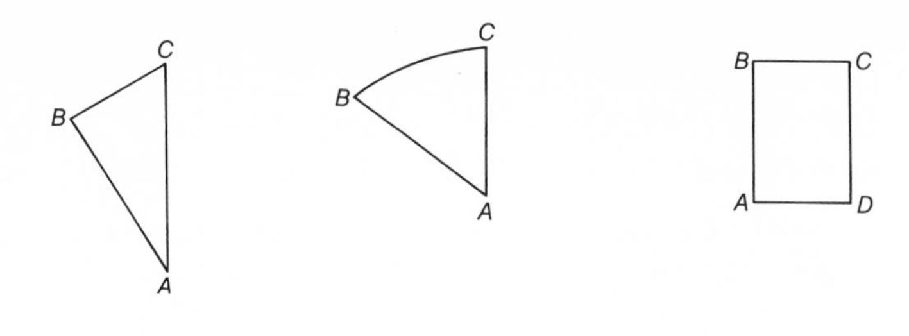

FIGURE 7A-2

we can test it for consistency by comparing the rank of **A** with the rank of a matrix $\mathbf{A}_b$, where $\mathbf{A}_b$ is defined as

$$\mathbf{A}_b = (\mathbf{A}, \mathbf{b})$$

That is, the column vector **b** becomes an additional column of the matrix **A**, and is known as the *augmented* matrix of the system. Now, if $r(\mathbf{A}) < r(\mathbf{A}_b)$, the system of equations is inconsistent, that is, no solution exists. If $r(\mathbf{A}) = r(\mathbf{A}_b)$, the system is consistent. It is not possible for $r(\mathbf{A}) > r(\mathbf{A}_b)$ because $\mathbf{A}_b$ contains **A**.

In summary, the typical linear programming problem has constraint equations which have an infinite number of solutions. The other two possibilities—a single solution and no solution—are rare. (If there is but a single solution, there is no problem of choice, and linear programming becomes irrelevant.)

Before leaving the discussion of simultaneous linear equations, we should mention the problem of *redundancy*. If we have a consistent set of equations, but the rank of **A** is less than the number of equations, then there are *redundant* equations. That is, if the number of equations is m and $r(\mathbf{A}) = k$ where $m > k$, then $m - k$ equations are linear combinations of the remaining k equations. These redundant equations could be dropped from the system with no effect on the solution. However, the simplex method is so designed that the redundant equations do no harm if they are not discovered and dropped.

Convex sets A set is simply a collection of distinct objects. Although the concept is quite general and could refer to the set of Duke University professors, our use of the concept will be in regard to sets of points or vectors. For example, the two-dimensional vector space can be envisaged as the set of all linear combinations of the two independent vectors (0, 1) and (1, 0).

A *convex* set in two-space can be defined as follows. A set of vectors, S, is convex if and only if for every pair of vectors in S the *convex combination* $k\mathbf{x} + (1 - k)\mathbf{y}$ is also an element of S (where **x** and **y** are any two vectors in S and $0 \leq k \leq 1$). Geometrically, this definition can be interpreted as stating that a set of points (vectors) is convex if, for any two points in the set, a straight-line segment connecting the points lies entirely within the set. Some examples are shown in Figure 7A-2.

Although the above discussion refers to convex sets in two-space, the concept is easily extended to n-space. Thus a set of vectors S in n-space is convex if, and only if, for every pair of vectors belonging to S the linear combination $k\mathbf{x} + (1 - k)\mathbf{y}$ is also an element of S (as before, **x** and **y** are any two vectors in S and $0 \leq k \leq 1$).

The corner points of the convex sets shown in Figure 7A-2 (points A, B, C, and D) are known as *extreme points*. Formally, a point, say point **a**, is an extreme point of the convex set S if and only if there do not exist two points **e** and **f** in S such that

$$\mathbf{a} = k\mathbf{e} + (1 - k)\mathbf{f}$$

where $0 < k < 1$. Observe that the inequalities on k are strict. Clearly, if the inequalities on k are weak, **a** could be written as $k\mathbf{a} + (1 - k)\mathbf{f}$ where $k = 1$. Hence extreme points are points which do not lie on line segments joining two other points in the set.

8

Linear programming models of the firm

INTRODUCTION

Heretofore in presenting models of the firm we have assumed that the relevant functions were smooth and continuous. Thus the traditional marginal analysis employing differential calculus was presented. In this chapter, as an alternative formulation, we shall make use of the mathematical technique discussed in the last chapter.

Linear programming permits us to examine the theory of production from a somewhat different point of view.

> This point of view, as compared with that of the traditional smooth marginal analysis, involves a shift in the focus of attention. Instead of seeking the optimal combination of inputs and outputs, we seek the optimal combinations of levels of activities. Thus the linear programming analysis provides more information than the marginal approach; it not only defines a goal in terms of optimal quantities of inputs and outputs, but it also gives specific directions for achieving this goal in terms of the various activities available to the firm [6, p. 141].

This chapter is divided into two main sections. The first section analyzes a simple model of a firm which produces a single product by two processes, or activities. Graphical methods are used to obtain the profit-maximizing solution. The second section formulates algebraically a general linear programming model of the firm and compares the optimality conditions with those of the the general marginal analysis model. To conclude the chapter we consider a simple example of the *decomposition principle.*

SINGLE-PRODUCT, TWO-ACTIVITY MODEL

We consider here the example problem given in Chapter 7 as the basic model. This should prove advantageous since it will permit a comparison between the conventional linear programming solution technique, as given there, and the solution to be given here in the context of the theory of the firm.

The following assumptions are relevant:

1. The firm has two independent activities available. An activity is defined as a particular way of combining the two fixed factors for the production of a unit of output. Each activity has a variable cost per unit of output associated with it which is constant and independent of the level of the activity.
2. The firm operates in a purely competitive product market. Hence it can sell all of the product, X, that it can produce at a fixed and known price of P.

Assumption 2 requires a bit of discussion. We are restricting models in this chapter to those meeting the mathematical requirements of linear programming. One requirement is that the objective function be *linear*. Since the objective function is the profit function, and one term is revenue, a moment's reflection will reveal the necessity for the first assumption. Revenue can be written as

$$\text{Revenue} = PX \tag{8-1}$$

Now if the firm is an imperfect competitor, it faces a sloping demand curve. Let the demand curve be

$$P = a - bX \qquad \text{where } b \neq 0 \tag{8-2}$$

Substituting the demand curve, (8-2), in (8-1), we get

$$\text{Revenue} = aX - bX^2 \tag{8-3}$$

Hence if P is not fixed, or independent of X, the objective function becomes nonlinear. We shall present nonlinear programming models of the firm in Chapter 9. We now return to the remaining assumptions of our present model.

3. The firm is concerned with a *short*-run optimization problem. It possesses quantities of two factors of production which are fixed for the problem at hand and its objective is to maximize profit.
4. The production function, as defined by the two activities, is homogeneous of degree one. That is, constant returns to scale prevail: increasing each of the factors in, say, activity 1 by a multiplier m results in an increase in X produced by that activity by the same multiplier m.
5. The firm is constrained in its selection of activity levels by its fixed endowments of the two factors.
6. The two activities can be used simultaneously; if this is done, the quantities of the outputs and inputs will be the arithmetic sum of the quantities which would result if the activities were used separately.
7. The exact nature of the firm's activities has been predetermined by a set of technical decisions by the firm's engineers and technicians.
8. The firm's factors and products are perfectly divisible. (This assumption will be relaxed in Chapter 10, where we consider integer programming.)

9. Neither the factor prices, product prices, nor the coefficients which determine the firm's activities (input-output coefficients) will change over the time period considered. (This is a static model.)
10. Neither the factor prices, product prices, nor the coefficients which determine the firm's activities are permitted to be random variables. (Complete certainty is assumed.)

The following symbols will be used:

X = the number of units of output
X_1 = the level or number of units of X produced by the first activity
X_2 = the level or number of units of X produced by the second activity
P = the price per unit of X
VC_1 = the variable cost per unit of X_1
VC_2 = the variable cost per unit of X_2

The following parameters are applicable:

(a) Activity 1 requires 5 man-hours and 1 machine-hour to produce 1 unit of X.
(b) Activity 2 requires 1 man-hour and 2 machine-hours to produce 1 unit of X.
(c) The firm is endowed with 200 man-hours of labor.
(d) The firm is endowed with 90 machine-hours of machine capacity.
(e) $P = 2$ per unit of X, $VC_1 = 1$ per unit of X_1, and $VC_2 = 1$ per unit of X_2.

The profit function π of the firm is

$$\pi = (P - VC_1)X_1 + (P - VC_2)X_2 \tag{8-4}$$

or

$$\pi = X_1 + X_2$$

The constraints are

$$\begin{aligned} 5X_1 + 1X_2 &\leq 200 \\ 1X_1 + 2X_2 &\leq 90 \end{aligned} \tag{8-5}$$

And the non-negativity conditions are

$$X_1 \geq 0, \; X_2 \geq 0 \tag{8-6}$$

In the previous chapter we solved the above problem in the conventional linear programming manner. The optimal solution was found both by graphical analysis and by the simplex method. The optimal combination of the two activities calls for the production of 34.4 units of X by activity 1 and 27.8 units of X by activity 2. Hence maximum profit is given by equation (8-4), or 62.2. [Note that

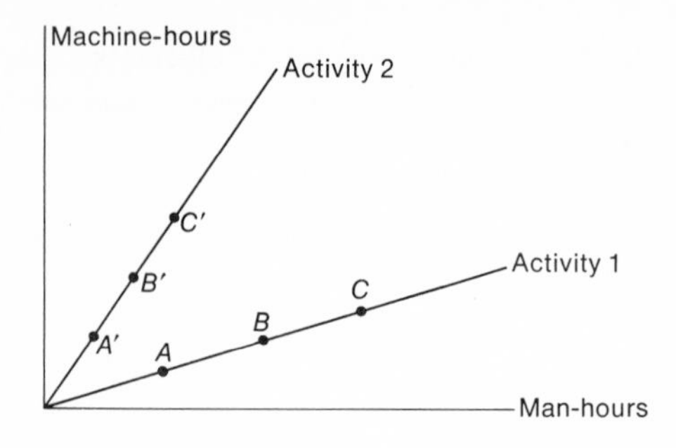

FIGURE **8-1**

by virtue of the values of the parameters specified in (e), total output is also 62.2 units.]

Our objective here will be to solve the problem again. However, we will do so in a manner which permits us to compare the linear programming model with the marginal analysis model. In this way, we shall be able to highlight the basic differences between the two models.

Production function

We start by examining the production function. An isoquant map is the usual graphical presentation of the production function. Hence in Figure 8-1 we show the first step in the derivation of the isoquant map for our model.

As is conventional, the factors are shown on the axes. Furthermore, each activity is represented by a ray from the origin. Observe that the slope of a ray represents the ratio of the factors which define that activity.

The coordinates of the points A, B, and C and the corresponding values of X_1 in Fig. 8-1 are given below:

Point	Man-hours	Machine-hours	X_1
A	10	2	2
B	15	3	3
C	20	4	4

Since activity 1 is defined by the requirement that 5 man-hours must be combined with 1 machine-hour to produce 1 unit of X, it is clear that all three points lie on the ray. Also, one may easily calculate that A corresponds to a production by activity 1 of 2 units of X. Similarly, B corresponds to a level of 3 units of X, and C to 4 units of X. Thus one restriction on the applicability of linear programming models is suggested: the production process must have the property of constant returns to scale.

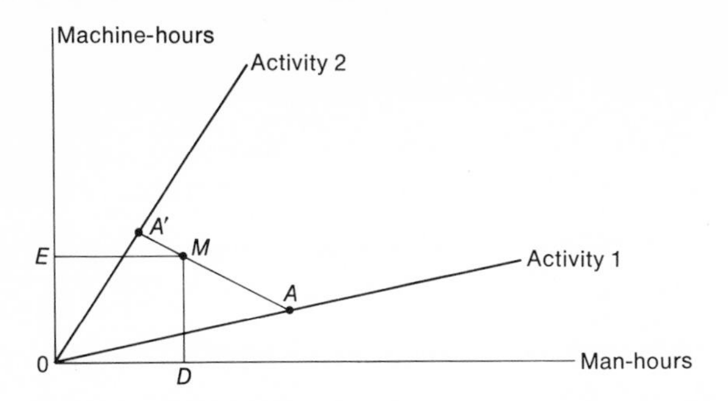

FIGURE **8-2**

Points A', B', and C' in the figure lie on the ray representing activity 2. The coordinates and associated values of X_2 are given below:

Point	Man-hours	Machine-hours	X_2
A'	2	4	2
B'	3	6	3
C'	4	8	4

We now have two points on each of three isoquants. That is, A and A' lie on the isoquant representing an output of 2 units of X, B and B' lie on the $X = 3$ isoquant, and C and C' lie on the $X = 4$ isoquant. Another requisite of the production function is also apparent: the overall production function consists of a finite number of processes, each characterized by fixed proportions of the inputs.

Point A is one production plan for producing a total output of 2 units, *viz.*, activity 1 operates at a level of 2 units and activity 2 operates at the zero level. Similarly, A' is another production plan for producing a total output of 2 units; here, activity 2 is at the level $X_2 = 2$, and activity 1 is shut down. The next question concerns the possibility of using activities 1 and 2 simultaneously to produce a total output of 2 units.

It can be shown that the straight-line segment connecting points A and A' is the locus of all combinations of activities 1 and 2 which produce a combined output of 2 units [1, p. 277]. To see this, refer to Figure 8-2.

Point M, which is located on $A'A$ such that $A'M/A'A = 0.3$, represents that combination of activities 1 and 2 for which 0.6 units of X are produced by activity 1 and 1.4 units of X are produced by activity 2. The rule is quite general: if $A'M/A'A = k$, then k times 2 units of X are produced by activity 1 and $(1 - k)$ times 2 units of X are produced by activity 2.

Two units of X can be produced by the production plan specified by M. This plan requires OD units of labor and OE units of machine capacity;

1.4 units of X are produced by activity 2 and 0.6 units by activity 1. Furthermore, it is a simple matter to determine the factor quantities required by each activity:

Activity 1

$$(5 \text{ man-hours per unit of } X)\ 0.6 \text{ units} = 3 \text{ man-hours}$$

$$(1 \text{ machine-hour per unit of } X)\ 0.6 \text{ units} = 0.6 \text{ machine-hours}$$

Activity 2

$$(1 \text{ man-hour per unit of } X)\ 1.4 \text{ units} = 1.4 \text{ man-hours}$$

$$(2 \text{ machine-hours per unit of } X)\ 1.4 \text{ units} = 2.8 \text{ machine-hours}$$

Summarizing, we have the input requirements for M:

	Man-hours	Machine-hours
Activity 1	3.0	0.6
Activity 2	1.4	2.8
Total	4.4 (= OD)	3.4 (= OE)

If point M should represent the optimal production plan, we then could report the following information: (1) total output, (2) the levels of each of the two activities, (3) the factor inputs required by each activity, and (4) the aggregate factor inputs (4.4 man-hours and 3.4 machine-hours). Here it is appropriate to point out that the linear programming model provides more information than does marginal analysis. The marginal analysis model would only provide information of types (1) and (4) above.

To illustrate the point made above more forcefully, let us consider Figure 8-3.

As discussed in Chapter 3, the typical marginal analysis isoquant can be drawn as shown in Figure 8-3(a). Marginal analysis would view each point (on an isoquant) as a different activity. If point M is given as the optimal operating point, we would view the factor input ratio of M as defining a particular activity. However, the linear programming isoquant in Figure 8-3(b), given that M is the optimal point, would permit us to derive more information, *viz.*, items (1) through (4) enumerated earlier. That is, M would be conceived of as a combination of two activities.

We should call attention to one other point in regard to Figure 8-3b. The isoquant shown includes segments parallel to the axes, which have not been explained. These parallel segments simply show that further additions of the factors are redundant and cannot increase output when the other factor is fixed.

We should emphasize that, on these grounds, we are not criticizing marginal analysis and extolling the virtues of linear programming. We feel that each model is useful, and the choice of models depends upon the purpose of the investigator. For an investigator interested in the problems of market-price determination, marginal analysis may be appropriate, while if the firm is the subject,

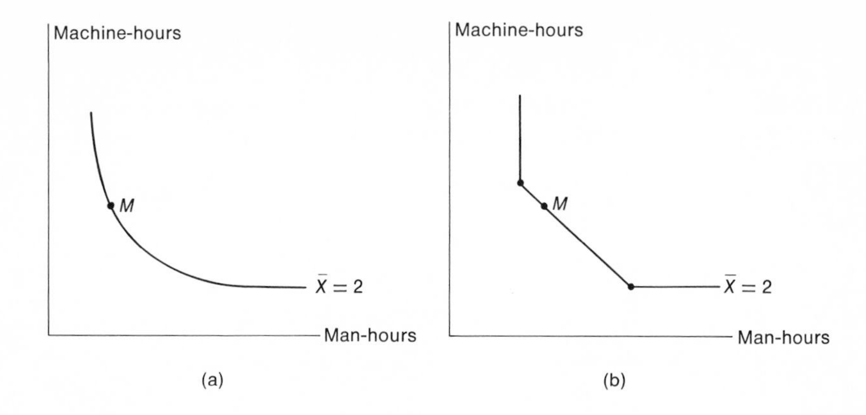

FIGURE **8-3**

(a) Marginal analysis isoquant; (b) linear programming isoquant.

linear programming may provide better insight. It might be added that marginal analysis, envisaging the production function as a infinite number of activities, might be better suited for long-run analysis wherein all types of productive processes are, in principle, conceivable. Linear programming, viewing the firm as possessing only a finite number of alternative processes, might be more suitable for short-run analysis.

Profit-maximizing solution

Figure 8-4 shows the complete isoquant map. The reader should observe and make sure that he understands why the isoquants are spaced equal distances apart for equal output differences. A feature of our earlier assumption that the profit function coefficients of X_1 and X_2 are each 1 is that the isoquants can be viewed as isoprofit curves. Thus the firm's objective of maximizing profit can be reduced to maximizing output.

To obtain the profit-maximizing production plan, the feasible region has been superimposed on the isoprofit map. The endowment of 200 man-hours of labor is indicated by the vertical line cutting the horizontal axis at point D. All points lying on that vertical line or to the left represent combinations of the two activities which do not require more than 200 man-hours of labor. Similarly, the horizontal line intersecting the machine-hours axis at point E indicates the machine capacity endowment of 90 machine-hours. Hence the rectangular area $OEMD$ defines the feasible region: only points on the boundaries or in the interior of the rectangle are feasible.

The firm's problem has now been effectively solved. The firm seeks that point in the feasible region that also lies on the highest possible isoprofit curve. Clearly this is point M.

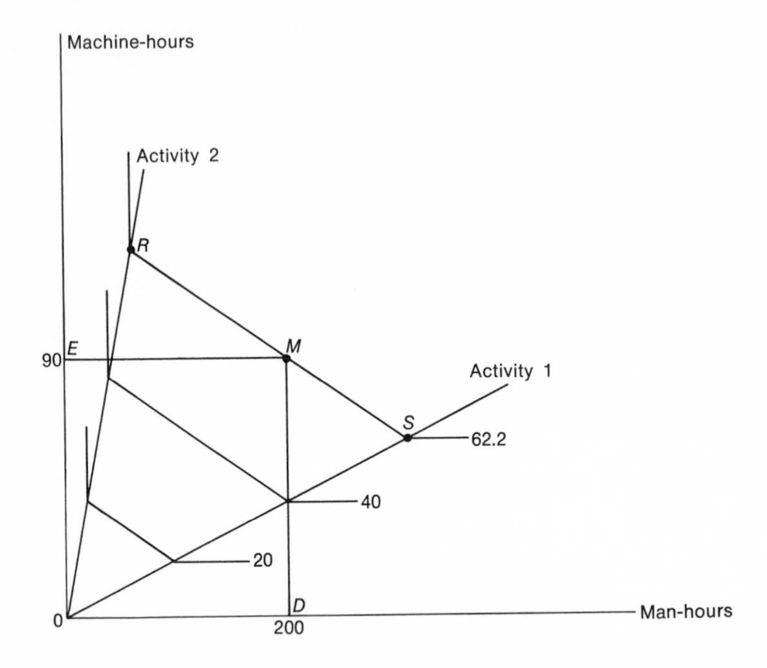

FIGURE **8-4**

Once point M has been determined, it is a simple matter to determine the levels of the two activities. Maximum profit is 62.2; and, of course, maximum output is 62.2 units. Thus activity 2 operates at a level of $(MS/RS)\cdot(62.2)$ units and activity 1 operates at a level of $(RM/RS)\cdot(62.2)$ units. The inputs to each activity are easily found once the level of each is known, as was demonstrated earlier.

Cost curves

As a further step in the comparison of linear programming and marginal analysis, it will be useful to derive the cost curves. The characteristic shapes of marginal analysis short-run cost curves are shown in Figure 8-5 (refer to Chapter 4).

For the parameters assumed for the linear programming model, the cost curves are simple to derive. Both activities have the same variable costs per unit output; thus the curves would be horizontal up to maximum output, and then vertical. They are depicted in Figure 8-6.

To make the derivation somewhat more interesting, let us assign different variable costs to the two activities. For example, let

$$VC_1 = 1 \text{ per unit of } X_1 \text{ and } VC_2 = 2 \text{ per unit of } X_2$$

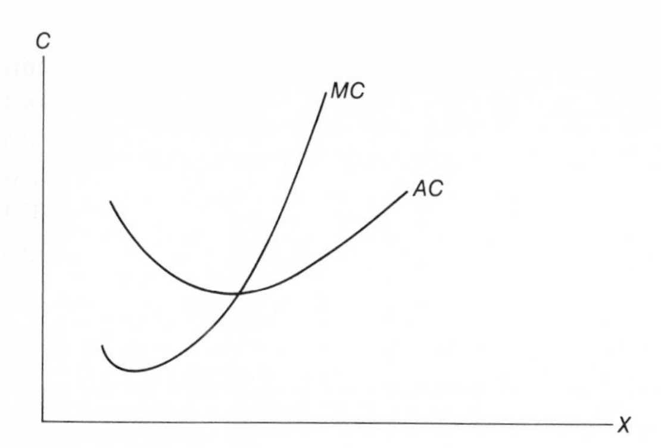

FIGURE 8-5

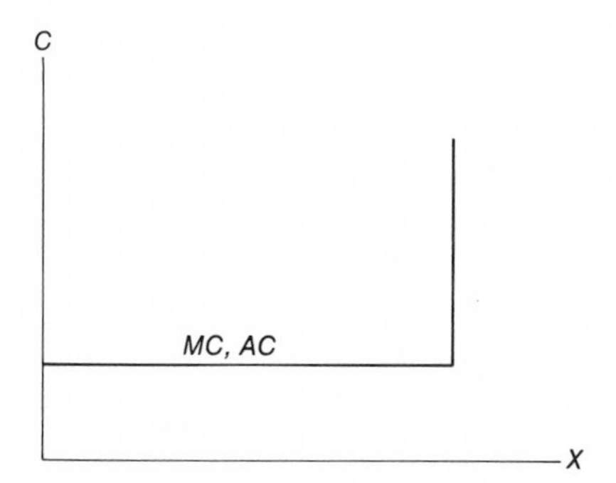

FIGURE 8-6

Clearly, activity 1 will be brought into operation before activity 2. Thus for low outputs the firm's marginal cost curve will be horizontal at $VC_1 = 1$. That is, the firm will operate activity 1 alone as output increases from zero to the maximum capacity which activity 1 can produce alone. We can determine this output by finding the minimum of

$$\frac{200 \text{ man-hours}}{5 \text{ man-hours per unit of } X_1} = 40 \text{ units of } X_1$$

and

$$\frac{90 \text{ machine-hours}}{1 \text{ machine-hour per unit of } X_1} = 90 \text{ units of } X_1$$

Hence the firm's endowment of 200 man-hours of labor limits the output of activity 1 to 40 units of X. The marginal cost curve is horizontal at 1 per unit for the output range from 0 to 40. (See Figure 8-7.)

The next problem is to find the marginal cost for outputs above 40 units. From our earlier analysis we know that maximum output of the firm is 62.2 units. Also, we know that the firm operates the two activities in combination to produce the maximum output. Our next step is to calculate the marginal cost for the 41st unit. And, as we shall see, the marginal cost for the 41st unit will be equal to that of the 42nd unit, and so on, until we reach maximum output of 62.2 units.

To produce one more unit of output when the firm is producing 40 units by activity 1 requires a reduction in output by activity 1. The reason is simple. At $X_1 = 40$ all of the labor endowment is in use. Activity 1 must be reduced to free enough labor for activity 2 to produce the additional unit *plus* the activity 1 output reduction. This is possible because activity 2 is relatively more efficient in the use of labor than is 1.

Let ΔX be the reduction in output of activity 1 necessary to release enough labor for activity 2 to produce $(\Delta X + 1)$ units. Then total output will be

	Output produced
Activity 1	$40 - \Delta X$
Activity 2	$\Delta X + 1$
Total	41

By definition, the marginal cost of the 41st unit is the net change in total cost due to increasing output from 40 to 41 units. Thus

$$MC_{41} = VC_2(\Delta X + 1) - VC_1(\Delta X) \tag{8-7}$$

The value of ΔX can be found from the equation which states that the amount of labor released by activity 1 is equal to the amount of labor required by activity 2. Or

$$(5 \text{ man-hours per unit of } X_1)\Delta X \text{ units} = (1 \text{ man-hour per unit of } X_2)(\Delta X + 1) \text{ units} \tag{8-8}$$

Solving,

$$\Delta X = \frac{1}{4}$$

Substituting $\Delta X = \frac{1}{4}$ in (8-7), we get

$$MC_{41} = 2.25$$

To obtain MC_{42} the same procedure would be required, and thus $MC_{42} = 2.25$. Consequently, marginal cost is constant at 2.25 for the range of outputs greater than 40 units up to maximum output. At maximum output marginal cost becomes vertical, indicating that physical capacity has been reached. Knowing the marginal cost function, average cost can be derived. We shall not derive it here but simply present it in Figure 8-7.

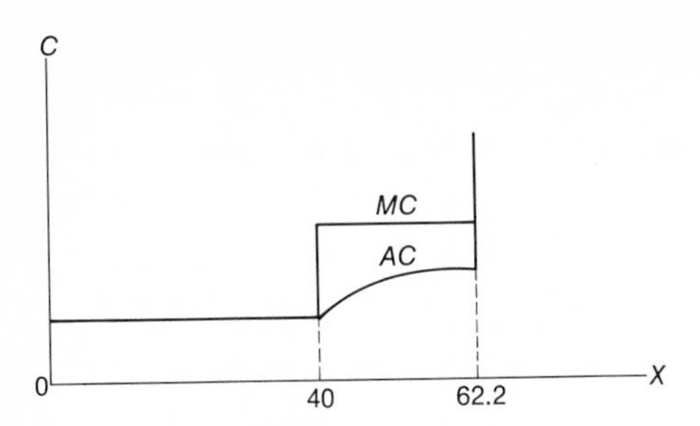

FIGURE **8-7**

Marginal cost and average cost coincide except for the output range where $40 < X < 62.2$. In summary, the short-run cost curves of marginal analysis and linear programming both rise as capacity is approached. However, where marginal analysis curves are smooth and continuous, linear programming curves rise by discontinuous jumps. The reader interested in a further graphical comparison of marginal analysis and linear programming, *viz.*, the derivation of average and marginal revenue product curves, is referred to Baumol [1, p. 291]. For a graphical treatment of a wide variety of linear programming models, see Wu and Kwang [2, pp. 94–157].

Marginal profitability of fixed input

In marginal analysis, the short-run, profit-maximizing solution may be described mathematically by letting

P = fixed price per unit of X

K = units of fixed input

L = units of variable input

W = fixed cost per unit of L

Then the short-run profit function is given by

$$\pi = PX - WL \tag{8-9}$$

The firm's production function is

$$X = f(K, L)$$

and the firm has available $\bar{K}$ units of input K. The cost of $\bar{K}$ is "sunk" in the short run, and thereby irrelevant. However, it may be highly relevant to know how much an *additional* unit of K is worth to the firm. This value is given by the Lagrangian multiplier, λ, when the above problem is formulated as follows:

$$\text{maximize} \quad G = Pf(K, L) - WL + \lambda(\bar{K} - K) \tag{8-10}$$

Using a single subscript on G and f to denote partial differentiation, the necessary conditions for profit maximization are:

(8-11) $$G_L = Pf_L - W = 0$$

(8-12) $$G_K = Pf_K - \lambda = 0$$

(8-13) $$G = \bar{K} - K = 0$$

Assuming that solutions exist and that the second-order conditions for maximization are satisfied, equations (8-11), (8-12), and (8-13) can be solved for the optimal values of L, K, and λ.

The Lagrangian multiplier λ is equal to Pf_K. That is, λ equals the product price times the marginal product of K, where $K = \bar{K}$ and L is at its optimal value. In other words, λ is a measure of the contribution to profit of an (infinitesimal) increase in K. The firm would be willing to pay λ for a small increase in K. Now let us turn to the linear programming model and consider the corresponding concept in that form of analysis.

In linear programming models the marginal profitabilities, or shadow prices, of the inputs are calculated simultaneously with the values of the activity levels. The shadow prices are the linear programming analogs of Lagrangian multipliers. The shadow price of an input measures the contribution to profit of a unit increase in the resource.

The shadow prices of labor and machine capacity were calculated in Chapter 7, and were found to be $\frac{1}{9}$ and $\frac{4}{9}$ respectively. In other words, if the firm could obtain an additional man-hour for less than $\frac{1}{9}$, it would be profitable to do so. Similarly, it would be profitable to purchase a machine-hour at any price below $\frac{4}{9}$. Chapter 7 also pointed out that shadow prices become the "activity levels" (solution variables) when the dual problem is formulated.

COMPARISON OF GENERAL MARGINAL ANALYSIS AND LINEAR PROGRAMMING MODELS[1]

In this section we will further delineate some of the differences underlying the marginal analysis and linear programming approaches to the theory of the firm. We will compare the marginal analysis model of the multiproduct, multifactor firm developed in Chapter 5 with a similar linear programming model of the firm.

Marginal analysis model

For convenience, we will repeat the assumptions underlying the marginal analysis model:

1. The prices of the firm's products are fixed and known.
2. The prices of the firm's factors are fixed and known.

[1] This section is based on Thomas H. Naylor, "The Theory of the Firm: A Comparison of Marginal Analysis and Linear Programming," *The Southern Economic Journal*, **XXXII** (January, 1966), pp. 263–273.

3. The objective of the firm is to maximize profit subject to the technical constraints imposed by its production function.
4. The firm possesses a production process which is capable of transforming a maximum of m variable factors of production into p products. (There are no limitations on the availability of the factors.)
5. A continuous production function exists (with nonvanishing first-order and second-order partial derivatives) which relates the set of independent factor variables to the set of independent product variables.
6. The production function is such that the quantity of output produced for a given product represents the maximum amount of that product which can be produced from specified factor-input quantities along with specified product quantities for the remaining $p - 1$ products.
7. The exact nature of the firm's production function has been predetermined by a set of technical decisions by the firm's engineers and technicians.
8. The production function is characterized by a decreasing marginal product for all factor-product combinations, a decreasing rate of technical substitution between any two factors, and an increasing rate of product transformation between any two products.
9. All of the firm's factors and products are perfectly divisible.
10. The parameters which determine the firm's total revenue function, production function, and total-cost equation will not change over the time period considered.
11. The parameters which determine the firm's total revenue function, production function, and total cost equation are not permitted to be random variables.

It should be pointed out that we have made one change in repeating the assumptions from Chapter 5. Here we require perfect competition in both the product markets and the factor markets (assumptions 1 and 2). The reason is, of course, that *linear* programming requires linear functions, and these in turn require perfect competition. Refer to the first section of this chapter for a more elaborate discussion.

The optimality conditions for the marginal analysis model of the firm may be derived in a straightforward manner by use of the Lagrangian multiplier method. These optimality conditions take the form of the following economic decision rules:

Rule 1 The price ratio of any two products must equal the marginal rate of product transformation between the two products.

Rule 2 The price ratio of any two factors must equal the marginal rate of technical substitution between the two factors.

Rule 3 The price ratio of any factor-product combination must equal the marginal product for the particular factor-product combination.

Linear programming model

Our linear programming model of the multiproduct, multifactor firm rests on the following set of assumptions:

1. The firm has p independent activities available, where an activity is defined as a particular way of combining a maximum of m variable factors for the production of a unit of output. A unit of output is analogous to a unit of product, but the firm may produce more than one product. Since a given product may be produced by several different activities each using different factor-input ratios, the number of activities may exceed the number of products.
2. The prices of the firm's variable factors and products are fixed and known. (Perfect competition is assumed.)
3. The objective of the firm is to maximize profit subject to the constraints imposed by the nature of its activities and the amounts of fixed factors which are available.
4. Each activity is characterized by a set of ratios of the quantities of the factors to the levels of each of the outputs. These ratios are constant and independent of the extent to which each activity is used. (The firm's production functions are homogeneous of degree one, i.e., constant returns to scale are assumed.)
5. The firm is constrained in its selection of activity levels by its fixed endowments of certain resources (fixed factors) required to support the p activities. (The firm's fixed factors are perfectly divisible in use, but there is an upper limit on the total quantity of each fixed factor available.)
6. Two or more activities can be used simultaneously, subject to the limitations of the fixed factors available to the firm, and if this is done the quantities of the outputs and inputs will be the arithmetic sums of the quantities which would result if the activities were used separately.
7. The exact nature of the firm's activities has been predetermined by a set of technical decisions by the firm's engineers and technicians.
8. All of the firm's factors and products are perfectly divisible. (This assumption may, of course, be relaxed if one desires to formulate an integer linear programming model.)
9. Neither the factor prices, product prices, nor the coefficients which determine the firm's activities (input-output coefficients) will change over the time period considered.
10. Neither the factor prices, product prices, nor the coefficients which determine the firm's activities are permitted to be random variables.

Production-function comparisons

Since most of the differences of marginal analysis and linear programming models concern the production function, it seems appropriate to explore this concept in some detail.

Under the assumptions of conventional marginal analysis, the firm's production function is said to be a function of the quantities of fixed and variable factors which are used in the firm's production process. For any given factor quantities, the dependent variable represented by the function is usually defined as the maximum quantity of the particular product that can be produced, in a given state of technology, from the specified factor quantities.

The marginal analysis production function implies that a physical maximization of output for given levels of input has already been achieved. In essence this implies that the profit-maximization problem of the firm is a two-stage problem. The first stage consists of deriving a method for achieving the *physical* maximization presupposed in the definition of the production function. That is, stage 1 is equivalent to determining the technology for the firm. The second stage is merely the problem of maximizing total profit subject to the conditions imposed by the production function.

It should be pointed out that the first of the firm's two decision problems can be solved independently of the second, but the second problem must either be solved simultaneously with the first problem or after the solution to the first problem has been obtained.

The distinction between the types of problems for which conventional marginal analysis and linear programming are best suited may be clarified by further examining the nature of the two different types of productive decisions made by the firm. The firm is assumed to have certain fixed factors at its disposal and access to variable factors through the open market.

The first decision is usually considered to be technical. That is, the firm must decide on the technology to be applied in the production of the set of product possibilities available to it. This involves determining the maximum quantity of output for each product variable attainable from specified factor quantities along with other specified product quantities.

Once technology is determined or fixed by the previous decision, the second decision is concerned with which products should be produced, and in what quantities, so as to maximize total profit. It should be remembered that at this point a decision to produce a particular set of products at a particular output level automatically determines the level of factor usage for the firm; for the production function prescribes the exact proportions for each level of output for all possible product combinations.

The marginal analysis model of the firm is concerned only with the second type of decision problem; for it assumes that the firm's technological problem has already been solved. Dorfman has summarized some of the difficulties involved in attempting to solve the second of the firm's two decision problems by marginal analysis.

> ... Machinery, and especially the more advanced types, is likely to be inflexible with regard to the factors which must be combined with it and with regard to the rate and character of its output. Thus, when it has been determined to use a certain number of units of a specific machine, several of the other variables in the production function have been determined at the same time. It

> will not then be possible to move freely from point to point on the production surface except in an indirect manner.
>
> The type of decision which faces a firm using industrial processes is therefore essentially different from the decisions contemplated by marginal analysis. The firm may decide the extent to which to use each of the types of equipment it owns at any time. In that case any variation in the use of equipment implies simultaneous variation in the use of factors complementary to that equipment. The firm may choose among a number (generally finite) of ways of applying its equipment. Or it may select among a number of types of equipment offered for its purchase. All of these decisions differ in two respects from the kind of decisions treated by marginal analysis. First, they affect the quantities of a group of distinct inputs and outputs simultaneously. Second, the range of choice does not lie along a continuous scale, but involves selection among discrete alternatives. The effects of such decisions are therefore not adequately expressed by the theoretical operation of partial differentiation with respect to the quantities of separate inputs and outputs [4, p. 10].

In other words, the difficulty in solving the firm's second decision problem (profit maximization subject to the constraints imposed by the production function) stems from the fact that the solution of the firm's technological problem may yield a production function which does not possess such properties as continuity, concavity, and nonzero first- and second-order partial derivatives. Marginal analysis may not be at all appropriate for solving the second type of decision problem in industrial environments similar to those outlined by Dorfman. Linear programming was devised specifically to circumvent the difficulties described by Dorfman in solving the firm's second-stage decision problem.

Furthermore, linear programming can handle both decision problems simultaneously. That is, linear programming determines both the quantities of the products to be produced *and* the optimal technological arrangement of productive activities.

In the final analysis the principal difference between the assumptions underlying marginal analysis models and linear programming models of the firm lies in the definition of an "activity." The salient differences have been summarized by Dorfman as follows.

> . . . The [activity] of linear programming is a more specifically defined concept than the production function of marginal analysis. Indeed, a production function is a family of [activities] which use the same factors and turn out the same products. If we compare any two points on a production surface, if the internal ratios of the inputs and outputs at the two points are the same they will represent different levels of the same [activity], otherwise they will represent different [activities]. The production function thus is a tool for exhibiting and comparing different but related [activities]. What it fails to present adequately is the consequence of using several [activities] in parallel, and such combinations of [activities] are characteristic of modern industry [4, p. 15].

We turn now to the explicit formulation of the linear programming model.

A linear programming model of the firm

Consider a firm that has p independent activities available, where an activity is defined as a particular way of combining a maximum of m variable factors with a maximum of n fixed factors for the production of a unit of output. We then let

Z_k = the level of the kth activity $(k = 1, \ldots, p)$
X_{ik} = the total quantity of the ith variable factor required by the kth activity $(i = 1, \ldots, m; k = 1, \ldots, p)$
Y_{jk} = the total quantity of the jth fixed factor required by the kth activity $(j = 1, \ldots, n; k = 1, \ldots, p)$
Y_j = the quantity of the jth fixed factor currently available to the firm $(j = 1, \ldots, n)$
a_{ik} = the quantity of the ith variable factor required by one unit of the kth activity $(i = 1, \ldots, m; k = 1, \ldots, p)$
b_{jk} = the quantity of the jth fixed factor required by one unit of the kth activity $(j = 1, \ldots, n; k = 1, \ldots, p)$
P_k = the competitive price per unit of the kth activity $(k = 1, \ldots, p)$
C_i = the competitive price per unit of the ith variable factor $(i = 1, \ldots, m)$
K_{jk} = the cost of converting one unit of the jth fixed factor for use in the kth activity $(j = 1, \ldots, n; k = 1, \ldots, p)$[2]

The firm's profit function may then be stated as

$$\pi = \sum_{k=1}^{p} P_k Z_k - \sum_{i=1}^{m} \sum_{k=1}^{p} C_i X_{ik} - \sum_{j=1}^{n} \sum_{k=1}^{p} K_{jk} Y_{jk} \tag{8-14}$$

By definition, in linear programming each activity is characterized by certain ratios of the quantities of the factors to each other and to the levels of each of the outputs. These ratios are defined to be constant and independent of the extent to which each activity is used. Hence it becomes necessary to impose the following constraints on our problem.

$$X_{ik} = a_{ik} Z_k \qquad (i = 1, \ldots, m; k = 1, \ldots, p) \tag{8-15}$$

$$Y_{jk} = b_{jk} Z_k \qquad (j = 1, \ldots, n; k = 1, \ldots, p) \tag{8-16}$$

These two constraints are tantamount to assuming that the firm's production functions are homogeneous of degree one. The firm is constrained in its selection of activity levels by its fixed endowments of certain resources required to support the p activities.

$$\sum_{k=1}^{p} Y_{jk} \leq Y_j \qquad (j = 1, \ldots, n) \tag{8-17}$$

[2] The nature of this type of conversion cost was first outlined by Pfouts [14].

In summary, the mathematical problem of the firm is one of determining those values of Z_k, X_{ik}, and Y_{jk} which will maximize:

$$\pi = \sum_{k=1}^{p} P_k Z_k - \sum_{i=1}^{m} \sum_{k=1}^{p} C_i X_{ik} - \sum_{j=1}^{n} \sum_{k=1}^{p} K_{jk} Y_{jk} \tag{8-18}$$

subject to

$$X_{ik} = a_{ik} Z_k \qquad (i = 1, \ldots, m;\ k = 1, \ldots, p) \tag{8-19}$$

$$Y_{jk} = b_{jk} Z_k \qquad (j = 1, \ldots, n;\ k = 1, \ldots, p) \tag{8-20}$$

$$\sum_{k=1}^{p} Y_{jk} \leq Y_j \qquad (j = 1, \ldots, n) \tag{8-21}$$

Although this constrained optimization problem can be solved by the simplex method, our principal concern here is not with the technique of solving the problem, but rather with the interpretation of the solution in the light of existing economic theory. The Kuhn-Tucker theorem provides a convenient mathematical tool for describing the optimality conditions for our linear programming model of the firm. (For a formal statement of the Kuhn-Tucker theorem, see Chapter 6 and [9].)

Since both the objective function and the constraints in our linear programming model are linear, the concavity requirements of the Kuhn-Tucker theorem are automatically fulfilled. Next we must formulate the Lagrangian function for our model:

$$L = \pi + \sum_{j=1}^{n} \mu_j \left(Y_j - \sum_{k=1}^{p} Y_{jk} \right) + \sum_{i=1}^{m} \sum_{k=1}^{p} \nu_{ik} (X_{ik} - a_{ik} Z_k) + \sum_{j=1}^{n} \sum_{k=1}^{p} \omega_{jk} (Y_{jk} - b_{jk} Z_k) \tag{8-22}$$

(The symbols μ_j, ν_{ik}, and ω_{jk} denote Lagrangian multipliers.) Conditions (8-23)–(8-30) correspond to the necessary and sufficient conditions of the Kuhn-Tucker theorem for a constrained maximum at Z_k°, X_{ik}°, Y_{jk}°, μ_j°, ν_{ik}°, and ω_{jk}°.

$$P_k \leq \sum_{i=1}^{m} \nu_{ik} a_{ik} + \sum_{j=1}^{n} \omega_{jk} b_{jk} \qquad (k = 1, \ldots, p) \tag{8-23a}$$

$$-C_i \leq -\nu_{ik} \qquad (i = 1, \ldots, m;\ k = 1, \ldots, p) \tag{8-23b}$$

$$\omega_{jk} - K_{jk} \leq \mu_j \qquad (j = 1, \ldots, n;\ k = 1, \ldots, p) \tag{8-23c}$$

$$\sum_{k=1}^{p} P_k Z_k^\circ - \sum_{i=1}^{m} \sum_{k=1}^{p} C_i X_{ik}^\circ - \sum_{j=1}^{n} \sum_{k=1}^{p} K_{jk} Y_{jk}^\circ = \sum_{j=1}^{n} \sum_{k=1}^{p} \mu_j b_{jk} Z_k^\circ \tag{8-24}$$

$$Z_k^\circ \geq 0 \qquad (k = 1, \ldots, p) \tag{8-25a}$$

$$X_{ik}^\circ \geq 0 \qquad (i = 1, \ldots, m;\ k = 1, \ldots, p) \tag{8-25b}$$

$$Y_{jk}^\circ \geq 0 \qquad (j = 1, \ldots, n;\ k = 1, \ldots, p) \tag{8-25c}$$

(8-26a) $$\sum_{k=1}^{p} Y_{jk} \leq Y_j \qquad (j = 1, \ldots, n)$$

(8-26b) $$X_{ik} \geq a_{ik}Z_k \qquad (i = 1, \ldots, m;\ k = 1, \ldots, p)$$

(8-26c) $$Y_{jk} \geq b_{jk}Z_k \qquad (j = 1, \ldots, n;\ k = 1, \ldots, p)$$

(8-27) $$\sum_{j=1}^{n} \mu_j^\circ Y_j = \sum_{j=1}^{n} \sum_{k=1}^{p} Y_{jk}\mu_j^\circ$$

(8-28a) $$\mu_j^\circ \geq 0 \qquad (j = 1, \ldots, n)$$

(8-28b) $$\nu_{ik}^\circ \geq 0 \qquad (i = 1, \ldots, m;\ k = 1, \ldots, p)$$

(8-28c) $$\omega_{jk}^\circ \geq 0 \qquad (j = 1, \ldots, n;\ k = 1, \ldots, p)$$

An economic interpretation

Having outlined a set of necessary and sufficient conditions for profit maximization for our linear programming model of the firm, we now turn to an economic interpretation of these results. In addition we shall compare these results with the economic interpretation of the optimality conditions of the marginal analysis model of the firm.

Before interpreting the economic implications of the optimality conditions for the linear programming model, we should discuss the Lagrangian multipliers μ_j, ν_{ik}, and ω_{jk}. These multipliers are the prices imputed to the firm's factors of production, that is, the prices the firm would be willing to pay for a marginal unit of a particular factor. The marginal value imputed to the jth fixed factor is denoted by μ_j. The marginal value imputed to the ith variable factor used in the kth activity is denoted by ν_{ik}. The marginal value imputed to the jth fixed factor used in the kth activity is denoted by ω_{jk}.

In the analysis of the economic implications of (8-23a) there is no exactly analogous relationship for the familiar requirement of conventional marginalism which states that when optimum quantities of any two products are being produced the ratio of their prices must be equal to their rate of product transformation. The difficulty stems from the fact that the main emphasis of linear programming is on the "activity" rather than on particular products and factors. A particular product may be produced by several different activities each using different factor-input ratios. Furthermore, the production of a single end product may require several stages of production, each of which corresponds to a separate activity. Unless we specify which activities are associated with each of the different products, the rate of product transformation between any two products will not be defined. Since we have not chosen to assign each activity in our model to a particular product, the rate of product transformation is not defined in our analysis. By assigning each activity to a particular product it would then be possible to define the rate of product transformation between any two products, but the mathematical complexity of the analysis would be increased considerably by the addition of a third subscript to each of the input-output coefficients (a_{ik} and b_{jk}).

Condition (8-23a) states that the price per unit of the kth activity must be less than or equal to the sum of the imputed costs of the fixed and variable factors used to produce one unit of the kth activity.[3] This is equivalent to stipulating that positive profits are not permitted for any activity of the given technology. Activities that are unprofitable under these imputed prices are not considered as claimants for the scarce resources in question. This means that if the market price of the kth activity is less than its imputed price, the kth activity will not be utilized. Activities that break even are acceptable alternatives in combination with or as substitutes for those already in use. That is, if the market price of the kth activity is equal to the imputed price of the fixed and variable factors used in its production, then the kth activity may be utilized at that level.

Equation (8-23a) is actually analogous to the familiar result of marginal analysis in which optimality requires that marginal revenue (or price) be equated with marginal cost. In this case, if the price of the kth activity equals the marginal imputed cost of the kth activity, the kth activity will be utilized at that level.

Condition (8-23b) states that if the ith variable is used by the kth activity the factor price must be equal to the marginal value imputed to the ith variable factor with regard to the kth activity. The competitive market analog of (8-23b) under marginal analysis is the requirement that the usage of a particular factor for a particular product be carried to the point where the price of the factor is just equal to the value of the marginal product for the particular product. If the price of the ith factor exceeds the marginal value imputed to the ith variable factor with regard to the kth activity, the factor will not be utilized by the kth activity. The market analog to this case stipulates that factors are not utilized at levels in which their factor costs exceed the value of their marginal product. If the price of the ith variable factor is less than the marginal value imputed to the ith variable factor with regard to the kth activity, then the level of usage of the ith factor in the kth activity should be increased. Furthermore, the condition of the marginal analysis model that when optimum quantities of the variable factors are used in the production of a particular product, the ratio of their factor prices must be equal to their rate of technical substitution does not hold here, because the marginal rate of substitution is not defined in our linear programming model. The reason that the marginal rate of substitution is not defined again stems from the fact that we have not assigned product labels to the activities in our model. If we had assigned each activity to the production of one of the firm's products and if there were several activities capable of turning out the same product, each with its own input proportions, then there would exist piecewise linear isoproduct curves connecting corresponding points on

[3] Here we are using the term "imputed cost" to mean a valuation based on alternative factor uses *internal* to the firm. In conventional economic theory the term "imputed cost" usually refers to a valuation based on alternative factor uses *external* to the firm.

the different activity rays and the slopes of these segments would be the marginal rates of substitution.

Condition (8-23c) states that the marginal value of the jth fixed factor used in the kth activity minus the marginal cost of converting one unit of the jth fixed factor into the kth activity must be less than or equal to the marginal value imputed to one unit of the jth fixed factor. There is no analog to this condition in the marginal analysis model, for the marginal analysis model contains no fixed factors of production. If the equality holds for (8-23c), then the jth fixed factor is being utilized at an optimum level with regard to the kth activity. If the inequality holds for (8-23c), then the jth fixed factor will not be utilized in the kth activity. Furthermore, if the direction of the inequality is reversed, then the firm should increase the level of usage of the jth fixed factor in the kth activity. If excess capacity exists in the jth fixed factor, then $\omega_{jk} - K_{jk} = 0$.

The familiar optimality requirement of marginal analysis that the price ratio of any factor-product combination must be equal to the marginal product for the particular factor-product combination is not discernible in our linear programming model. Although the term "value imputed to an activity" is analogous to the term "value of the marginal product" which is used in marginal analysis, the term "marginal product" is not defined under the assumptions of our linear programming model. Again this can be attributed to the fact that we have not specified which products are produced by the firm's different activities.

By utilizing equations (8-15) and (8-16) and the definition of profit per unit of the kth activity, condition (8-23) can also be expressed as

$$(8\text{-}29) \qquad P_k - \sum_{i=1}^{m} C_i a_{ik} - \sum_{j=1}^{n} K_{jk} b_{jk} \leq \sum_{j=1}^{n} \mu_j b_{jk} \qquad (k = 1, \ldots, p)$$

This is the mathematical formulation of the linear constraints of the *dual problem* of linear programming which states that the profit per unit of the kth activity cannot exceed the imputed cost per unit of the kth activity. The dual problem of the firm may be expressed as

$$(8\text{-}30) \qquad \text{minimize} \quad T = \sum_{j=1}^{n} \mu_j Y_j$$

subject to

$$(8\text{-}31) \qquad \sum_{j=1}^{n} \mu_j b_{jk} \geq P_k - \sum_{i=1}^{m} C_i a_{ik} - \sum_{j=1}^{n} K_{jk} b_{jk} \qquad (k = 1, \ldots, p)$$

The saddle-point values (Z_k°, X_{ik}°, Y_{jk}°, μ_j°, ν_{ik}°, ω_{jk}°) of the Lagrangian function L possess the following interesting characteristics. The objective function, π, of the primal problem is maximized at Z_k°, X_{ik}°, Y_{jk}°, while the objective function of the dual problem T is minimized at μ_j°, ν_{ik}°, ω_{jk}°, and $\pi^\circ = T^\circ$. (The proof is omitted.)

The primal problem which is the main subject matter of this section involves maximization, while the dual problem involves minimization. The former involves activity levels no greater than resources permit, the other an imputed price no lower than the amounts necessary to allocate all profits. The dual problem of the firm is to find prices for its scarce resources which will minimize the total imputed cost of these resources to the firm, and yet involve an imputed cost per unit of the kth activity which is no less than the profit per unit for the kth activity. The discussion of conditions (8-23a) and (8-23b) has indicated that through these two properties of the dual problem of linear programming the imputed prices provide criteria for decisions as to which activities are to be used by the firm. These criteria can also be applied tentatively to activities not represented in the technology from which the imputed prices were computed.

Condition (8-24) states that the firm's profits after paying the imputed costs to its scarce resources must be zero.

Conditions (8-25a) through (8-25c) are satisfied by the assumption of economic feasibility. Condition (8-26a) is merely a statement to the effect that the total usage of the jth fixed factor in the production of the firm's p activities cannot exceed the currently available quantity of the firm's jth fixed factor. The equalities will hold for (8-26b) and (8-26c), since they were defined accordingly. Condition (8-27) indicates that the values imputed to the scarce resources available to the firm must be equal to the value of the scarce resources used in manufacturing operations. The Lagrangian multipliers are required to be nonnegative.

For the purpose of comparison with the marginal analysis model of the firm, the optimality conditions for our linear programming model of the firm may be summarized in the form of the following decision rules:

Rule 1 The unit price of each activity must be less than or equal to the sum of the imputed costs of the fixed and variable factors used to produce one unit of that activity.

Rule 2 For each variable factor-activity combination the unit price of the given variable factor must be greater than or equal to the marginal value imputed to the variable factor with regard to the given activity.

Rule 3 The cost of converting one unit of a given fixed factor for use in a given activity must be greater than or equal to the net marginal value imputed to the given fixed factor used in the given activity, i.e., the marginal value imputed to a unit of the given fixed factor used in the given activity minus the marginal value imputed to one unit of the fixed factor.

Rule 4 The firm's total profit after paying the costs of its scarce resources (fixed factors) must be equal to zero.

Rule 5 The total value imputed to the scarce resources available to the firm must be equal to the imputed value of the scarce resources used by the firm in manufacturing operations.

In this section we have shown that there are a number of differences between conventional marginal analysis models of the firm and linear programming models of the firm. Our objective was to spell out in considerable detail exactly what some of these differences are. As a result of this investigation we have found that the principal differences between the two models lies in the assumptions underlying them and the economic implications of their optimality conditions.

THE DECOMPOSITION PRINCIPLE

Consider a linear programming model of the firm in which the problem of the firm is expressed in the form

$$\text{maximize} \quad \pi = P_1X_1 + P_2X_2 + P_3X_3 + P_4X_4 \tag{8-32}$$

subject to

$$\begin{aligned} a_{11}X_1 + a_{12}X_2 + a_{13}X_3 + a_{14}X_4 &\leq B_1 \\ a_{21}X_1 + a_{22}X_2 + a_{23}X_3 + a_{24}X_4 &\leq B_2 \\ a_{31}X_1 + a_{32}X_2 \qquad\qquad\qquad\qquad &\leq B_3 \\ a_{41}X_1 + a_{42}X_2 \qquad\qquad\qquad\qquad &\leq B_4 \\ a_{53}X_3 + a_{54}X_4 &\leq B_5 \end{aligned} \tag{8-33}$$

where X_j denotes the level of the jth activity, P_j is the net contribution to profit and fixed cost of the jth activity, a_{ij} is the quantity of the ith fixed factor required by one unit of the jth activity, and B_i is the quantity of the ith fixed factor which is presently available.

This type of linear programming problem arises whenever some of the firm's fixed factors can be used by only one set of the firm's activities. An example of this type of situation would be a firm with multiple plants that have fixed factors which are unique to each of the plants, e.g., special types of equipment, certain labor skills, etc. In addition, the multiplant firm possesses a number of fixed factors such as a central computer, top management, and a sales force which may be pooled.

Suppose in our example model that we have two plants (1 and 2). Fixed factors 1 and 2 have been pooled and are available in either plant 1 or 2. Fixed factors 3 and 4 are available only in plant 1 and fixed factor 5 is available only in plant 2. Activities 1 and 2, which require the use of fixed factors 1, 2, 3, and 4, can take place only in plant 1. Activities 3 and 4 can take place only in plant 2.

The structure of this problem implies that it may be possible to treat the firm's overall problem as two subproblems and perhaps reduce computational effort. Consequently, it is possible in principle "to plan the overall operation of an organization without the central staff having full knowledge of the technology of each part" [3, p. 462]. This approach to linear programming is called the *decomposition principle* of linear programming. An excellent treatment of this topic is given by Dantzig [3, Chapter 23].

BIBLIOGRAPHY

[1] BAUMOL, WILLIAM J. *Economic Theory and Operations Analysis*. Englewood Cliffs, N. J.: Prentice-Hall, 1965.

[2] BOULDING, KENNETH E., and W. ALLEN SPIVEY (Eds.). *Linear Programming and the Theory of the Firm*. New York: Macmillan Co., 1960.

[3] DANTZIG, GEORGE B. *Linear Programming and Extensions*. Princeton, N. J.: Princeton University Press, 1963.

[4] DORFMAN, ROBERT. *Application of Linear Programming to the Theory of the Firm*. Berkeley, Calif.: University of California Press, 1951.

[5] DORFMAN, ROBERT. "Mathematical, or 'Linear,' Programming," *American Economic Review*, **XLIII** (December, 1953), 797–825.

[6] DORFMAN, ROBERT, PAUL A. SAMUELSON, and ROBERT SOLOW. *Linear Programming and Economic Analysis*. New York: McGraw-Hill Book Co., 1958.

[7] KOOPMANS, TJALLING C. (Ed.). *Activity Analysis of Production and Allocation*. New York: John Wiley & Sons, 1951.

[8] KOOPMANS, TJALLING C. *Three Essays on the State of Economic Science*. New York: McGraw-Hill Book Co., 1957.

[9] KUHN, H. W., and A. TUCKER. "Nonlinear Programming," in J. Neyman (Ed.), *Proceedings of the Second Berkeley Symposium on Mathematical Statistics and Probability*. Berkeley, Calif.: University of California Press, 1951.

[10] MAUER, WILLIAM A., and THOMAS H. NAYLOR. "Monopolistic-Monopsonistic Competition: The Multi-Product, Multi-Factor Firm," *Southern Economic Journal*, **XXXI** (July, 1964), 38–43.

[11] MENGER, KARL. "The Properties of the Production Function," in O. Morgenstern (Ed.), *Economic Activity Analysis*. New York: John Wiley & Sons, 1954.

[12] NAYLOR, THOMAS H. "A Kuhn-Tucker Model of the Multi-Product, Multi-Factor Firm," *Southern Economic Journal*, **XXXI** (April, 1965), 324–330.

[13] NAYLOR, THOMAS H. "The Theory of the Firm: A Comparison of Marginal Analysis and Linear Programming," *Southern Economic Journal*, **XXXII** (January, 1966), 263–274.

[14] PFOUTS, RALPH W. "The Theory of Cost and Production in the Multi-Product Firm," *Econometrica*, **XXIX** (October, 1961), 650–658.

[15] SIMONNARD, MICHEL. *Linear Programming*. Englewood Cliffs, N. J.: Prentice-Hall, 1966.

9

Nonlinear programming models of the firm

INTRODUCTION

The models of the firm discussed in the preceding chapter all included the assumption that the firm faced a perfectly elastic demand curve, i.e., the firm was a perfect competitor. In this chapter we will relax that assumption. We will formulate a model in which the firm will be able to influence price by its output decision. However, in moving from the competitive to the monopolistic model we must first discuss a new programming technique—nonlinear programming. Actually, it would be more accurate to refer to nonlinear programming as a *collection* of techniques. (The reader should not infer that nonlinearities in economics are restricted to demand and revenue functions, for we have already encountered nonlinear utility, production, and cost functions in this book.)

The plan of this chapter is as follows. First we shall survey some of the problems which can arise when nonlinearities are permitted. Second, we shall formulate a simple two-product monopoly model. The equilibrium output decision of the firm will be determined graphically, and then the graphical solution will be used to illustrate the Kuhn-Tucker conditions. A second nonlinear programming problem—a production-scheduling problem—is then formulated to illustrate the use of the Kuhn-Tucker theorem to solve a cost-minimization problem. To conclude the chapter, the monopoly model will be solved by the technique of quadratic programming. As will be discussed, quadratic programming is a solution procedure that is applicable only to a particular type of nonlinear programming problems.

A SURVEY OF PROBLEMS DUE TO NONLINEARITIES

The general nonlinear programming problem is to determine the values of n variables $X_1, X_2, \ldots, X_n$ which will maximize or minimize the function

(9-1) $$Z = \phi(X_1, X_2, \ldots, X_n)$$

subject to m constraints of the form

(9-2) $$h_i(X_1, X_2, \ldots, X_n)\begin{pmatrix} \geq \\ = \\ \leq \end{pmatrix}B_i \qquad i = 1, 2, \ldots, m$$

and to the non-negativity constraints

(9-3) $$X_j \geq 0 \qquad j = 1, 2, \ldots, n$$

In (9-2), one and only one of the symbols $\begin{pmatrix} \geq \\ = \\ \leq \end{pmatrix}$ holds for each equation. The number of equations m may be greater than, less than, or equal to n, the number of variables.

Nonlinear objective function

As one might guess, methods for solving nonlinear programming problems are generally more difficult conceptually than are the methods for linear programming problems. At the present time a number of methods exist for solving nonlinear problems, each depending to an important degree upon the exact nature of the objective function and the constraints. First let us consider problems in which the constraints (9-2) are all linear. This means that the feasible region is a convex set just as in linear programming.[1] Figure 9-1 shows one such feasible region. However, if we permit (9-1), the objective function, to be nonlinear, we may obtain *curved* isoprofit contours. In three dimensions, the objective function would be a hill with point A as the very top point. Thus the profit-maximizing solution would clearly be point T.

Observe that the optimal point no longer coincides with an extreme point of the feasible region. That is, an algorithm such as the simplex method of linear programming, which moves from one extreme point to another *ignoring all other feasible points*, is not appropriate here. One might think that what is needed is a method for evaluating all points on the boundary in addition to the extreme points. Unhappily, this too would be insufficient. Consider what

[1] Recall from earlier chapters that a *convex set* is a set of points such that a straight-line segment connecting any two points in the set lies entirely within the set. The reader should not confuse a convex *set* with a convex *function* (or a concave function). The convexity or concavity of functions was discussed in the mathematical appendix to Chapter 2. For example, a function is strictly convex if linear interpolation between any two points of the function gives a value greater than the value of the function at the point of interpolation.

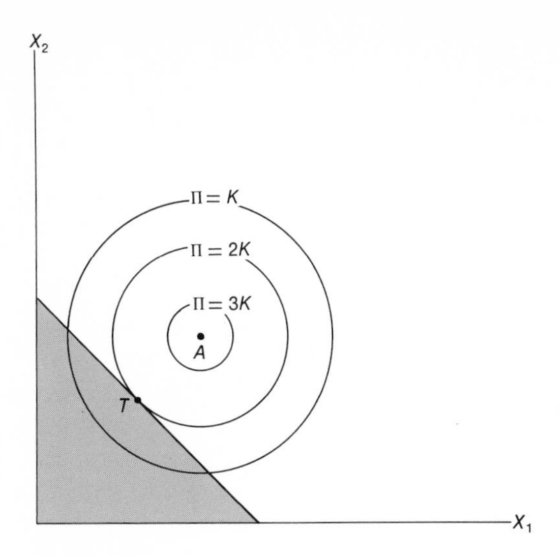

FIGURE **9-1**

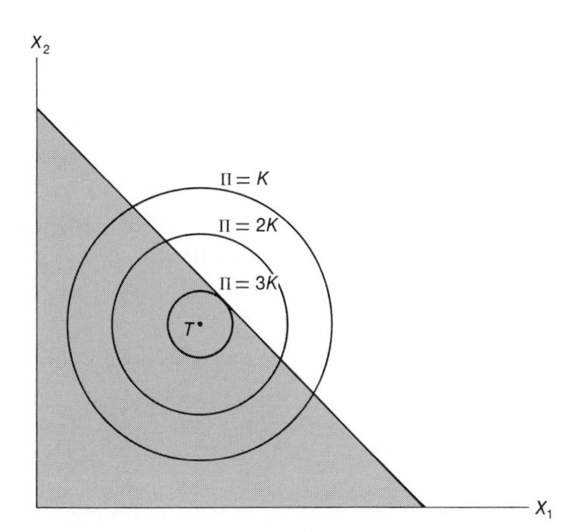

FIGURE **9-2**

happens to the optimal point when the constraint in Figure 9-1 is shifted to the location shown in Figure 9-2. Now it is not even true that the optimal point lies on a boundary: the optimal point T now lies in the *interior* of the feasible region.

As another illustration of problems that might arise with nonlinear objective functions, consider the possibility of local optimal points. In Figure 9-3 there

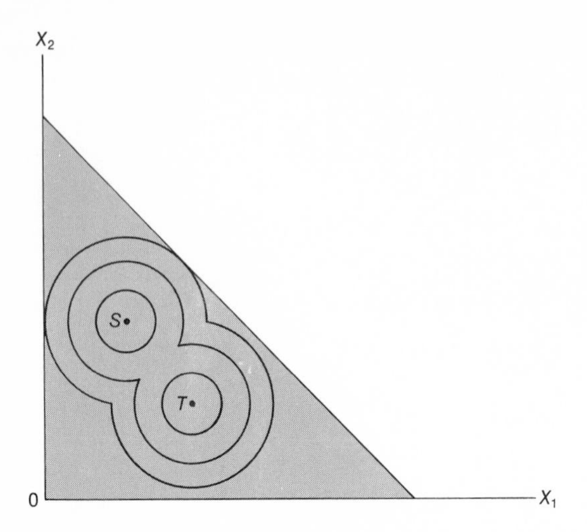

FIGURE **9-3**

are two hilltops, points S and T. Each point is a local optimal point in the sense that small movements in any direction away from the points result in a diminution of profit. If we happened to arrive at point S by a technique like the simplex method, we would view S as the solution even though the profit at T is higher than at S.

This last problem is particularly difficult. Of course, in principle the classical calculus optimization techniques provide the answer. Locate all stationary points (points where the first-order differential is zero) in the feasible region, evaluate the objective function for all points corresponding to local maxima (points where the second-order differential is negative), and then select the global maximum from the local maxima. However, in practice many of the algorithms avoid the problem by concentrating on objective functions which have only one hilltop. Or, what is the same thing, they concentrate on objective functions which are concave for maximizing problems (and convex for minimizing problems).

Here we shall only mention the possibility that the objective function of a maximizing problem is convex (or concave in a minimizing problem). Of course this would be the mathematical counterpart of the increasing-returns problem in economic theory. The problem can be demonstrated by re-examining Figure 9-2. Imagine that point T represents the bottom of a cup. That is, invert the hilltop, thereby making the objective function convex rather than concave. Thus isoprofit contours represent higher levels of profit the larger the diameter of the contour. Graphically, the global maximum would probably occur at a corner point of the feasible region, but this is by no means the case for less well-behaved convex objective functions.

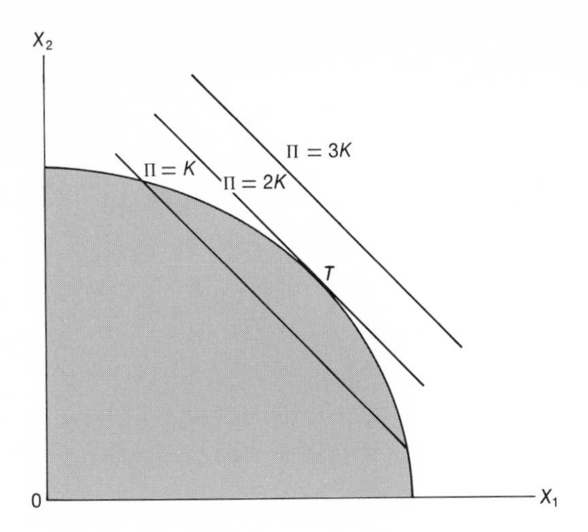

FIGURE **9-4**

Although in general the increasing-returns problem is quite difficult to solve, a method for solving such problems using integer programming techniques is discussed in Chapter 10.

Nonlinear constraints

Next, consider what happens when we reverse the assumptions and permit the constraints to be nonlinear while keeping the objective function linear. Two main cases can arise. In the first case, the nonlinear constraints continue to define a convex set of feasible solutions. This will be true, for example, if the constraints are all concave functions and ≥ 0. (For a proof of this, see Carr and Howe [10, p. 243].) Figure 9-4 illustrates the simplest possible case of a nonlinear constraint defining a convex feasible region. Notice that the linear isoprofit contours determine the optimal point to be T. Point T lies on the boundary of the constraint rather than at an extreme point of the feasible region.

In the second main case, the nonlinear constraints do *not* define a convex set of feasible solutions. This is illustrated in Figure 9-5. The problem of local optimal points again arises. Since any small movement away from point S decreases profit, that point is a local maximum. Thus computational techniques which examine the value of the objective function for small movements in any direction might mislead us into thinking that S is the global solution. In fact, the global solution is point T. As is the case when local optima arise for nonlinear objective functions, the problem of nonconvex feasible regions is often handled by avoiding it—that is, by assuming that the constraints define a convex feasible region.

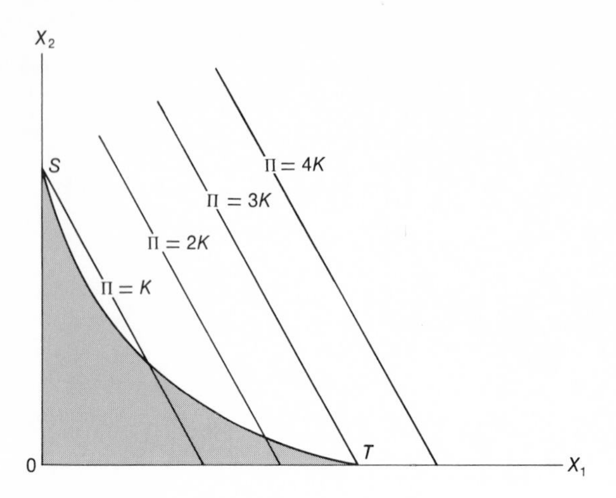

FIGURE **9-5**

In view of the many possible types of nonlinear programming problems, it is no surprise that there are many types of solution procedures. Actually there are a number of types of nonlinear problems for which no successful solution techniques are yet available. In the remainder of this chapter we shall limit our discussion to perhaps the "best-behaved" nonlinear problem. This problem will have a second-degree polynomial objective function. The objective function will be concave (thereby ruling out the problem of multiple optima) with linear constraints (thereby defining a convex set of feasible solutions).

For a further discussion of nonlinear programming techniques, the reader is referred to our introductory discussion in Chapter 6 and to the comprehensive surveys by Wolfe [48,49].

TWO-PRODUCT, TWO-ACTIVITY MONOPOLY MODEL

The model to be discussed here will possess a number of the characteristics of the single-product, two-activity model described in Chapter 8. The major difference is that product price there was assumed to be a constant (the firm was a perfect competitor), while here we shall consider the price of the product to depend upon the level of output of the firm (the firm is a monopolist).

Another small difference is that there we considered the firm to have two processes available for producing a single product, and here, for variety, we shall consider the output of each process (activity) to be a different product.

The following *assumptions* are made:

1. The firm has two independent activities available. An activity is defined as a particular way of combining the two fixed factors for the production of a unit of output. Activity 1 produces product 1 and activity 2 produces

product 2. Each activity could have a variable cost per unit output associated with it. However, for simplicity we shall assume that the variable cost is zero for each activity.

2. The firm faces downward-sloping demand curves in each product market. The two demand curves are:

$$P_1 = 10 - 0.1X_1$$
$$P_2 = 20 - 0.2X_2 \tag{9-4}$$

where

P_i = price per unit of the ith product ($i = 1, 2$)
X_i = quantity in units of the ith product ($i = 1, 2$)

3. The firm is concerned with a short-run optimization problem. It possesses quantities of two factors of production which are fixed for the problem at hand, and its objective is to maximize profit.
4. The production function as defined by the two activities is homogeneous of degree one. That is, constant returns to scale prevail: increasing each of the factors in, say, activity 1 by a multiplier m results in an increase in output produced by that activity by the same multiplier m.
5. The firm is constrained in its selection of activity levels by its fixed endowments of the two factors.
6. The two activities can be used simultaneously; if this is done, the quantities of the outputs and inputs will be the arithmetic sum of the quantities that would result if the activities were used separately.
7. The exact nature of the firm's activities has been predetermined by a set of technical decisions by the firm's engineers and technicians.
8. The firm's factors and products are perfectly divisible. (This assumption is relaxed in Chapter 10, where we consider integer programming.)
9. Neither the factor prices, product prices, nor the coefficients which determine the firm's activities (input-output coefficients) will change over the time period considered. (This is a static model.)
10. Neither the factor prices, product prices, nor the coefficients which determine the firm's activities are permitted to be random variables. (Completely certainty is assumed.)

The following parameters are applicable:

(a) Activity 1 requires 5 man-hours and 1 machine-hour to produce one unit of X_1
(b) Activity 2 requires 1 man-hour and 2 machine-hours to produce one unit of X_2
(c) The firm is endowed with 200 man-hours of labor.
(d) The firm is endowed with 90 machine-hours of machine capacity.
(e) The demand curves are given by equation (9-4) above.

The profit function of the firm is

$$\pi = (10 - 0.1X_1)X_1 + (20 - 0.2X_2)X_2 \tag{9-5}$$

or, equivalently,

$$\pi = 750 - 0.1(X_1 - 50)^2 - 0.2(X_2 - 50)^2 \tag{9-6}$$

The constraints are

$$\begin{aligned} 5X_1 + 1X_2 &\leq 200 \quad \text{labor constraint} \\ 1X_1 + 2X_2 &\leq \ \ 90 \quad \text{machine constraint} \end{aligned} \tag{9-7}$$

or, equivalently,

$$\begin{aligned} H_l &= 200 - 5X_1 - 1X_2 \geq 0 \quad \text{labor constraint} \\ H_m &= \ \ 90 - 1X_1 - 2X_2 \geq 0 \quad \text{machine constraint} \end{aligned} \tag{9-8}$$

In the future, we shall refer to the labor constraint as H_l and the machine constraint as H_m. To be consistent with the terminology of (9-2), we have defined H_l, for example, as $B_l - h_l \geq 0$ where $h_l = 5X_1 + 1X_2$ and $B_l = 200$. The nonnegativity conditions are:

$$X_1 \geq 0, \ X_2 \geq 0 \tag{9-9}$$

Graphical solution

The equilibrium solution can easily be obtained graphically. Figure 9-6 shows that the optimal point is point T. Reading the coordinates of point T from the graph, one finds that the firm should produce 30 units of X_1 and 30 units of X_2 in order to maximize profit. Profits for this output decision would be 630.

It should prove instructive to consider how one might use classical calculus techniques to obtain the solution. Unfortunately, the Lagrangian multiplier method requires that the constraints be equations rather than inequalities. Nevertheless, we can follow a procedure which makes use of the Lagrange method. In the process we can gain insight into the Kuhn-Tucker conditions which provide the basis for a number of nonlinear algorithms.

First we will ignore the constraints. The necessary condition for a maximum is that the partial derivatives of π with respect to X_1 and X_2 equal zero. This gives us two equations in two unknowns:

$$\begin{aligned} \pi_{X_1} &= -0.2(X_1 - 50) = 0 \\ \pi_{X_2} &= -0.4(X_2 - 50) = 0 \end{aligned} \tag{9-10}$$

The simultaneous solution of the two equations is $X_1 = 50$, $X_2 = 50$. Since the π function is strictly concave (the second-order differential is negative for all

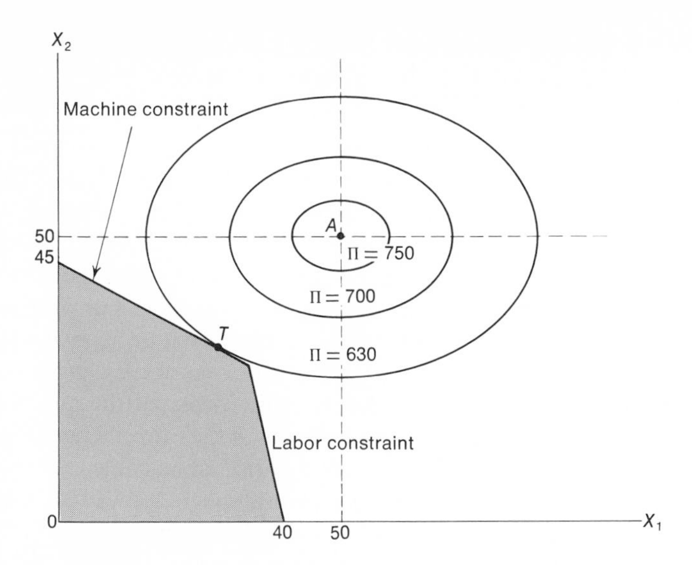

FIGURE **9-6**

values of the $X_i)^2$, this point corresponds to the unconstrained maximum (point A in Figure 9-6). Clearly this point is nonfeasible. This can be checked by substituting $X_1 = 50$, $X_2 = 50$ in the constraints (9-7).

The important observation is that either one or both of the constraints will be binding in the optimal solution. But if a constraint is binding, we can consider it to be an equation rather than an inequality. Hence if we could know the constraints that would be binding in the optimal solution beforehand, we could apply the Lagrange-multiplier method. The major problem then turns out to be to find out which constraints will be binding. Here the Kuhn-Tucker conditions are helpful. However, before turning to these conditions let us finish the problem with the tools at hand.

Having solved our model graphically, we are in the fortunate situation of knowing which constraints will be binding in the optimal solution. Figure 9-6 shows that the machine-capacity constraint is binding; i.e., the machine-capacity inequality holds as an equation. Since the labor constraint is not binding, we can simply drop it. Thus we form the conventional Lagrangian function:

$$L = 750 - 0.1(X_1 - 50)^2 - 0.2(X_2 - 50)^2 + \lambda_m(90 - X_1 - 2X_2) \tag{9-11}$$

[2] Or, what is the same thing, the Hessian determinants alternate in sign (negative, then positive) for all values of the X_i. Thus

$$|-0.2| = -0.2 < 0 \qquad \text{and} \qquad \begin{vmatrix} -0.2 & 0 \\ 0 & -0.4 \end{vmatrix} = 0.08 > 0$$

Taking partial derivatives of L with respect to X_1, X_2, and λ_m, setting each equal to zero, and solving the three equations for the three unknowns, yields

$$X_1 = 30, \quad X_2 = 30, \quad \text{and} \quad \lambda_m = 4$$

Since the function is of the proper shape (concave), the above values correspond to the profit-maximizing solution. One further point should be noted. The Langrangian multiplier λ_m, which corresponds to the machine constraint, is positive. Whenever a constraint is binding in the optimal solution, its corresponding Lagrangian multiplier is positive (it could, in rare cases, be zero). Concisely, referring to the machine constraint as H_m, we have the product $H_m\lambda_m = 0$ in an optimal solution. The economic interpretation of λ_m is also of interest. The instantaneous rate of change of profit with respect to a change in the endowment of machine capacity is 4. That is, if we increased the quantity of machine-hours very slightly, we would increase profit at the rate of 4 per hour. Thus λ_m is the marginal imputed value, or accounting price, of machine capacity. Of course, the imputed value of the Lagrangian multiplier associated with the labor constraint is zero (we possess redundant labor), and thus a small increase in labor availability would be of zero value. Finally, observe that in the optimal solution, $H_l\lambda_l = 0$, where H_l refers to the labor constraint ($H_l = 200 - 5(30) - 1\,(30) = 20$).

The Kuhn-Tucker conditions

The Kuhn-Tucker conditions, which were stated for the general case in Chapter 6, equations (6-23) through (6-28), are the mathematical basis for nonlinear programming solution techniques. Consequently, to understand these conditions better, let us write out the conditions for our particular problem.

The problem is to maximize

$$L = 750 - 0.1(X_1 - 50)^2 - 0.2(X_2 - 50)^2 + \lambda_l(200 - 5X_1 - X_2) + \lambda_m(90 - X_1 - 2X_2) \tag{9-12}$$

and the Kuhn-Tucker conditions, that is, the conditions that X_1 and X_2 must satisfy for profit maximization, are

$$\frac{\partial L}{\partial X_1} = -0.2(X_1 - 50) - 5\lambda_l - \lambda_m \leq 0$$
$$\frac{\partial L}{\partial X_2} = -0.4(X_2 - 50) - \lambda_l - 2\lambda_m \leq 0 \tag{9-13}$$

$$[-0.2(X_1 - 50) - 5\lambda_l - \lambda_m]X_1 + [-0.4(X_2 - 50) - \lambda_l - 2\lambda_m]X_2 = 0 \tag{9-14}$$

$$X_1 \geq 0, \; X_2 \geq 0 \tag{9-15}$$

$$\frac{\partial L}{\partial \lambda_l} = 200 - 5X_1 - X_2 \geq 0$$
$$\frac{\partial L}{\partial \lambda_m} = 90 - X_1 - 2X_2 \geq 0 \tag{9-16}$$

$$(200 - 5X_1 - X_2)\lambda_l + (90 - X_1 - 2X_2)\lambda_m = 0 \tag{9-17}$$

(9-18) $\lambda_l \geq 0, \ \lambda_m \geq 0$

For our particular problem the above conditions are necessary *and* sufficient. Our objective function is concave, and the set of feasible solutions is convex.

Some of the above conditions should be familiar to the reader on the basis of the discussion in the preceding section. For example, equation (9-17) simply states that the Lagrangian multiplier associated with a constraint that is binding in the optimal solution will be positive (since the constraint will equal zero) and, if the constraint is not binding (and therefore not equal to zero), then the Lagrangian multiplier must be zero. Conditions (9-18) state that the imputed values of the resources can never be negative in an optimal solution. If one were negative, the solution would not be optimal because the firm could increase profit by using less of that resource.

The major "new" conditions are equations (9-13) and (9-14). Here we will merely give a rough economic rationale for these requirements. Of course, the only thing new about (9-13) is the substitution of inequalities for equalities. But (9-14) is completely new. In fact, (9-14) is analogous to (9-17). The requirement in (9-17) is that if a constraint is not binding (nonzero), then the corresponding Lagrangian multiplier must be zero, and vice versa. Equation (9-14) requires that if $\partial L/\partial X_1$ is nonzero, then X_1 must be zero and vice versa. But let us look more closely at $\partial L/\partial X_1$. The first term, $-0.2(X_1 - 50)$, is the marginal profitability of X_1. That is, it gives the rate of increase of π for a small increase in X_1. Call it the "marginal π of X_1." Next, consider the second term, $5\lambda_l$. We have discussed the interpretation of the λ's before. They can be interpreted as the marginal imputed values of the resources. Thus, if we think of λ_l as the marginal imputed value of labor, and we multiply λ_l by 5 (where 5 is the rate of labor hours required per unit production of X_1), then the product can be interpreted as the imputed value of labor per unit of X_1. Refer to this component as "imputed value of labor/X_1." Similarly, the third term becomes the "imputed value of machines/X_1." Thus, $\partial L/\partial X_1$ can be written as a word equation:

(9-19) $$\text{(Marginal profit of } X_1) - \text{(imputed value of labor)}/X_1 - \text{(imputed value of machines)}/X_1 \leq 0$$

Now we can interpret equation (9-14). If $\partial L/\partial X_1$ is negative, this means that the imputed value of the resources used to produce X_1, or the opportunity cost of X_1, *exceeds* the marginal profit of X_1. Clearly in such a case X_1 should not be produced. But this is exactly what (9-14) requires. Conversely, if the marginal profit exactly equals the imputed value (note that marginal profit can never exceed imputed value, by (9-13)), then X_1 should be produced, and again (9-14) would be satisfied.

To take this explanation one step further, we will substitute in (9-14) the actual optimal values of X_1, X_2, λ_l, and λ_m which were determined earlier. That is, $X_1 = 30$, $X_2 = 30$, $\lambda_l = 0$, and $\lambda_m = 4$. Thus

$$\frac{\partial L}{\partial X_1} = 4 - 5(0) - 4 = 0$$

and

$$\frac{\partial L}{\partial X_2} = 8 - 0 - 2(4) = 0$$

Substitution in (9-14) yields

$$(0)30 + (0)30 = 0$$

Use of the Kuhn-Tucker conditions in obtaining solutions

In the preceding discussion the Kuhn-Tucker conditions were viewed as statements which define the optimal solution. That is, they specify properties of the optimal solution, but they say nothing about *how to obtain* the optimal solution. Here we shall examine the conditions with the objective of learning what assistance they can give toward finding the optimal solution. This section should also provide a useful transition to the discussion of the quadratic programming algorithm.

Our approach will be to list all of the various combinations of the variables which must be either zero or nonzero. For example, from (9-17) we know that either λ_l will be zero, or that the labor constraint H_l (i.e., $\partial L/\partial\lambda_l$) will be zero. Similarly, either λ_m or the machine constraint H_m will be zero. We will ignore the rare possibility that both λ and its associated restraint will be zero.

We have the same "either-or" situation with regard to condition (9-14). That is, either X_1 will be zero or $\partial L/\partial X_1$ will be zero, and similarly for X_2 and $\partial L/\partial X_2$. Again, we ignore the unlikely possibility that both X_i and $\partial L/\partial X_i$ will be zero simultaneously. We summarize the various possibilities in Table 9-1.

TABLE **9-1**

Case number	$\partial L/\partial X_1$	$\partial L/\partial X_2$	X_1	X_2	H_l	H_m	λ_l	λ_m
1	0	0	$\neq 0$	$\neq 0$	0	0	$\neq 0$	$\neq 0$
2	0	$\neq 0$	$\neq 0$	0	0	0	$\neq 0$	$\neq 0$
3	$\neq 0$	0	0	$\neq 0$	0	0	$\neq 0$	$\neq 0$
4	$\neq 0$	$\neq 0$	0	0	0	0	$\neq 0$	$\neq 0$
5	0	0	$\neq 0$	$\neq 0$	0	$\neq 0$	$\neq 0$	0
6	0	$\neq 0$	$\neq 0$	0	0	$\neq 0$	$\neq 0$	0
7	$\neq 0$	0	0	$\neq 0$	0	$\neq 0$	$\neq 0$	0
8	$\neq 0$	$\neq 0$	0	0	0	$\neq 0$	$\neq 0$	0
9	0	0	$\neq 0$	$\neq 0$	$\neq 0$	0	0	$\neq 0$
10	0	$\neq 0$	$\neq 0$	0	$\neq 0$	0	0	$\neq 0$
11	$\neq 0$	0	0	$\neq 0$	$\neq 0$	0	0	$\neq 0$
12	$\neq 0$	$\neq 0$	0	0	$\neq 0$	0	0	$\neq 0$
13	0	0	$\neq 0$	$\neq 0$	$\neq 0$	$\neq 0$	0	0
14	0	$\neq 0$	$\neq 0$	0	$\neq 0$	$\neq 0$	0	0
15	$\neq 0$	0	0	$\neq 0$	$\neq 0$	$\neq 0$	0	0
16	$\neq 0$	$\neq 0$	0	0	$\neq 0$	$\neq 0$	0	0

By way of a very inefficient procedure, we can use the Kuhn-Tucker conditions to find the solution. We do this by solving for the values of the variables corresponding to each possibility in Table 9-1. Of course the procedure continues only until the optimal solution is determined. We should recognize the optimal solution easily. It will be the *only* set of values of the variables that satisfies all of the Kuhn-Tucker conditions. Again, we should emphasize that satisfying the Kuhn-Tucker conditions is a *sufficient* condition for a maximum only when the objective function is concave and the feasible solution set is convex.

Clearly this computational procedure is inefficient. Even for this two-variable, two-constraint case we may need to evaluate as many as *sixteen* possibilities, or cases. We shall see in the next section (by employing the simplex method) that the quadratic programming algorithm provides the answer to the computational problem.

Since we already know the optimal solution, we will not be quite so foolish as to work through the cases in numerical order. The reader should observe that case 9 defines the optimal solution. However, to illustrate the procedure we shall examine case 1. This case specifies that $\partial L/\partial X_1$, $\partial L/\partial X_2$, H_l, and H_m all equal zero. Since H_l and H_m are zero, this means that both constraints are binding, and thereby they become equations rather than inequalities (conditions (9-16)). Also, since $\partial L/\partial X_1$ and $\partial L/\partial X_2$ equal zero, we obtain two more equations from condition (9-13). Hence we have four equations in four unknowns:

$$\begin{aligned} H_l &= 200 - 5X_1 - X_2 = 0 \\ H_m &= 90 - X_1 - 2X_2 = 0 \\ \partial L/\partial X_1 &= -0.2(X_1 - 50) - 5\lambda_l - \lambda_m = 0 \\ \partial L/\partial X_2 &= -0.4(X_2 - 50) - \lambda_l - 2\lambda_m = 0 \end{aligned}$$

The simultaneous solution is

$$\begin{aligned} X_1 &= 34.4 \\ X_2 &= 27.8 \\ \lambda_l &= -10 \\ \lambda_m &= -49.4 \end{aligned}$$

Clearly this is not the optimal solution. Both λ's are negative, and this violates Kuhn-Tucker condition (9-18).

Now let us jump directly to case 9, the case defining the optimal solution. From $H_m = 0$, $\partial L/\partial X_1 = 0$, and $\partial L/\partial X_2 = 0$, we obtain three equations in three unknowns:

$$\begin{aligned} H_m &= 90 - X_1 - 2X_2 = 0 \\ \partial L/\partial X_1 &= -0.2(X_1 - 50) - \lambda_m = 0 \\ \partial L/\partial X_2 &= -0.4(X_2 - 50) - 2\lambda_m = 0 \end{aligned}$$

The simultaneous solution is

$$X_1 = 30$$

$$X_2 = 30$$

$$\lambda_m = 4$$

$$\lambda_l = 0$$

This is the optimal solution because these values of the variables satisfy all of the Kuhn-Tucker conditions.

A PRODUCTION-SCHEDULING PROBLEM

To illustrate the minimizing problem, let us turn to a production-scheduling problem of the firm. In order to apply the Kuhn-Tucker conditions to a numerical example, we will construct a quite simplified model.

Assume that the firm faces a decision as to the number of units of output X to produce in January and February. At the end of January enough units of X must be on hand to supply regular customers a total of 100 units. Furthermore, at the end of February, the required quantity must be 200 units. For simplicity, we assume that the firm ceases business at that time.

The production cost in a given month is a simple function of output. Thus

$$C = 2X^2 \tag{9-20}$$

where

C = total production cost

X = units of output

In addition to the production cost, units produced in January which are not sold until February incur an inventory cost of 8 per unit. Taking the initial inventory to be zero, we formulate the total cost function

$$C = 2X_1^2 + 2X_2^2 + 8(X_1 - 100) \tag{9-21}$$

where

X_1 = units produced in January

X_2 = units produced in February

Thus, we wish to minimize (9-21) subject to the constraints

$$\begin{aligned} X_1 &\geq 100 \quad &\text{January demand} \\ X_1 + X_2 &\geq 300 \quad &\text{February demand} \end{aligned} \tag{9-22}$$

and

$$X_1,\ X_2 \geq 0 \tag{9-23}$$

Before going further, we should pause to state the Kuhn-Tucker conditions for a minimizing problem. Of course, one method of solution would be to transform the above problem into a *maximizing* problem. Maximizing $-C$ is equivalent to minimizing C.

For the two-variable, two-constraint case, the Kuhn-Tucker conditions for a minimum can be stated as follows.

$$\text{minimize} \quad C = C(X_1, X_2) \tag{9-24}$$

subject to

$$\begin{aligned} H_1(X_1, X_2) &\leq 0 \\ H_2(X_1, X_2) &\leq 0 \end{aligned} \tag{9-25}$$

and

$$X_1,\ X_2 \geq 0 \tag{9-26}$$

Form the Lagrangian function L,

$$L = C + \lambda_1 H_1 + \lambda_2 H_2 \tag{9-27}$$

Then

$$\begin{aligned} \frac{\partial L}{\partial X_1} &= \frac{\partial C}{\partial X_1} + \lambda_1 \frac{\partial H_1}{\partial X_1} + \lambda_2 \frac{\partial H_2}{\partial X_1} \geq 0 \\ \frac{\partial L}{\partial X_2} &= \frac{\partial C}{\partial X_2} + \lambda_1 \frac{\partial H_1}{\partial X_2} + \lambda_2 \frac{\partial H_2}{\partial X_2} \geq 0 \end{aligned} \tag{9-28}$$

$$\frac{\partial L}{\partial X_1} \cdot X_1 + \frac{\partial L}{\partial X_2} \cdot X_2 = 0 \tag{9-29}$$

$$X_1 \geq 0,\ X_2 \geq 0 \tag{9-30}$$

$$\begin{aligned} \frac{\partial L}{\partial \lambda_1} &= H_1 \leq 0 \\ \frac{\partial L}{\partial \lambda_2} &= H_2 \leq 0 \end{aligned} \tag{9-31}$$

$$H_1 \lambda_1 + H_2 \lambda_2 = 0 \tag{9-32}$$

$$\lambda_1 \geq 0,\ \lambda_2 \geq 0 \tag{9-33}$$

If the objective function (9-24) is convex and the constraints define a convex set of feasible solutions, then the Kuhn-Tucker conditions, (9-28)–(9-33), are both necessary and sufficient for a minimum. The constraints (9-25) will define a convex set if H_1 and H_2 are both convex functions.

It is easy to show that the objective function in our example is convex. If the second-order differential of C is positive for all combinations of X_1 and X_2, then C is a convex function. But an equivalent condition for the positive definiteness of d^2C is for all Hessian determinants to be positive (see the appendix to Chapter 2):

$$S_1 = |C_{11}| > 0$$

$$S_2 = \begin{vmatrix} C_{11} & C_{12} \\ C_{21} & C_{22} \end{vmatrix} > 0$$

Hence, C is convex, since

$$S_1 = |4| > 0$$

$$S_2 = \begin{vmatrix} 4 & 0 \\ 0 & 4 \end{vmatrix} = 16 > 0$$

Since linear functions are both convex and concave, H_1 and H_2 are convex and thereby define a convex set of feasible solutions. Consequently, the pair of X_1 and X_2 values which satisfies the Kuhn-Tucker conditions also specifies the production plan which minimizes total cost. Thus the Lagrangian function is

$$L = 2X_1^2 + 2X_2^2 + 8(X_1 - 100) + \lambda_1(100 - X_1) + \lambda_2(300 - X_1 - X_2)$$

and

$$4X_1 + 8 - \lambda_1 - \lambda_2 \geq 0 \qquad \text{(9-28a)}$$
$$4X_2 - \lambda_2 \geq 0$$

$$(4X_1 + 8 - \lambda_1 - \lambda_2)X_1 + (4X_2 - \lambda_2)X_2 = 0 \qquad \text{(9-29a)}$$

$$X_1 \geq 0, \ X_2 \geq 0 \qquad \text{(9-30a)}$$

$$100 - X_1 \leq 0 \qquad \text{(9-31a)}$$
$$300 - X_1 - X_2 \leq 0$$

$$(100 - X_1)\lambda_1 + (300 - X_1 - X_2)\lambda_2 = 0 \qquad \text{(9-32a)}$$

$$\lambda_1 \geq 0, \ \lambda_2 \geq 0 \qquad \text{(9-33a)}$$

By trial and error, we can obtain the optimal values of X_1 and X_2. For example, assume that λ_1 and λ_2 are both nonzero. Then the inequalities (9-31a) become

$$100 - X_1 = 0$$

$$300 - X_1 - X_2 = 0$$

and

$$X_1 = 100, \ X_2 = 200$$

Since both X_1 and X_2 are positive, the inequalities (9-28a) become

$$4X_1 + 8 - \lambda_1 - \lambda_2 = 0$$

$$4X_2 - \lambda_2 = 0$$

and

$$\lambda_1 = -392, \ \lambda_2 = 800$$

But a *negative* λ_1 is not permitted by (9-33a). As a second trial, assume that λ_1 is zero but λ_2 is nonzero. Also, assume that both X_1 and X_2 are positive. (Common sense suggests this alternative.) Hence we can write three equations:

$$300 - X_1 - X_2 = 0$$

$$4X_1 + 8 - \lambda_1 - \lambda_2 = 0$$

$$4X_2 - \lambda_2 = 0$$

Since we have assumed that λ_1 is zero, we have three equations in three unknowns. The simultaneous solution is:

$$X_1 = 149$$

$$X_2 = 151$$

$$\lambda_2 = 604$$

This solution defines the minimum-cost solution, since it satisfies the Kuhn-Tucker conditions. Thus the firm should produce 149 units in January and 151 in February to minimize total cost. The value of λ_1 is zero, indicating that small changes in the January demand constraint in (9-22) will not affect total cost. This is obvious in view of the fact that the optimal plan calls for producing 149 units when only 100 are needed. The positive value of λ_2 indicates that an increase in the February demand constraint in (9-22) will have a positive impact on cost. Of course, if inventory cost were zero, the firm would produce 150 units in each month. The positive cost of producing units in January for demand in February is the explanation for producing fewer units in January than in February.

QUADRATIC PROGRAMMING

In this section we will describe a particular quadratic programming algorithm, and work through the profit-maximization model given earlier as an example. The algorithm we will describe was devised by Wolfe [45]. However, the version given below is a slight modification by Carr and Howe [10].

The essence of the Wolfe algorithm is made clear by referring to the Kuhn-Tucker conditions (9-13) and (9-16). Because the objective function was a second-degree polynomial (the sum of a linear form and a quadratic form), equation (9-13), which results from differentiating (9-12), is linear. The conditions (9-16) will also be linear because they are the result of differentiating (9-12) with respect to λ_i, and the linear constraints were the coefficients of the λ_i in (9-12). Hence the Kuhn-Tucker conditions become a set of linear inequalities subject to the side conditions (9-14) and (9-17) and the usual non-negativity conditions.

Now, if we transform the inequalities in (9-13) and (9-16) into equalities by adding slack and surplus variables, we obtain the set of equations

$$\begin{aligned} -0.2(X_1 - 50) - 5\lambda_l - \lambda_m + V_1 &= 0 \\ -0.4(X_2 - 50) - \lambda_l - 2\lambda_m + V_2 &= 0 \end{aligned} \quad (9\text{-}34)$$

$$\begin{aligned} 200 - 5X_1 - X_2 - W_l &= 0 \\ 90 - X_1 - 2X_2 - W_m &= 0 \end{aligned} \quad (9\text{-}35)$$

The side conditions (9-14) and (9-17) can be expressed as

$$V_1X_1 + V_2X_2 = 0 \quad (9\text{-}36)$$

$$W_l\lambda_l + W_m\lambda_m = 0 \quad (9\text{-}37)$$

Thus (9-34) and (9-35) give us four equations in eight variables, and (9-36) and (9-37) require that at least four of the variables equal zero. If a maximal solution exists, it must be a *basic solution* to the set of four equations. (This result is due to Barankin and Dorfman [5].) But the simplex algorithm of linear programming is designed to examine basic solutions to systems of linear equations. Furthermore, the slack and surplus variables V_1, V_2, W_l, and W_m must be non-negative to prevent a reversal of the inequalities, and the Kuhn-Tucker conditions (9-15) and (9-18) require the remaining variables to be non-negative. Accordingly, we know that the maximal solution, if it exists, will be a basic feasible solution to the set of equations (9-34) and (9-35).

Of course, there will be a unique basic feasible solution only if the second-order conditions are satisfied. But these conditions are satisfied by ensuring that the problem is indeed of the quadratic programming form. Namely, the objective function must be a concave second-degree polynomial, and the constraints must be linear (for a minimizing problem the objective function must be convex).

It follows that we are interested in finding the basic feasible solution to (9-34) and (9-35). This is somewhat different from the ordinary linear programming problem. There we examine successive basic feasible solutions until we reach that solution which optimizes an objective function. Here we seek merely to find *the* basic feasible solution.

We shall accomplish this goal by making use of artificial variables—that is, we shall obtain an initial basic solution to the problem by the artificial-variable technique described in Chapter 7. Recall that the procedure involves adding artificial variables in order to obtain an initial basis. The initial basic solution will therefore be nonfeasible with regard to the original constraints (though feasible with regard to the artificial problem). By assigning unfavorable coefficients to the artificial variables in the objective function, we are assured that the artificial variables will be driven from the solution (equated to zero) by the logic of the simplex method. Then when all artificial variables are zero we will have a basic solution which is feasible with regard to the original constraints.

In a linear programming problem we would normally expect more iterations to be required before reaching the *optimal* basic feasible solution. However, in quadratic programming, once we eliminate all artificial variables and obtain a basic feasible solution, we also have our optimal solution.

There is a further difference between the two which is important. We must not violate the side conditions (9-36) and (9-37) when selecting the entering variable for a new simplex table. For example, if X_1 happened to be in the basic solution, and the $C_j - Z_j$ associated with V_1 indicated that V_1 should be the entering variable, we could not enter that variable. Rather, we would select the next most favorable entering variable which would not violate the side conditions.

We shall now work through the monopoly model using the algorithm described above.

For convenience we shall state the problem once more:

$$\text{maximize} \quad \pi = 750 - 0.1(X_1 - 50)^2 - 0.2(X_2 - 50)^2 \tag{9-38}$$

subject to

$$\begin{aligned} 5X_1 + 1X_2 &\leq 200 \\ 1X_1 + 2X_2 &\leq 90 \end{aligned} \tag{9-39}$$

and

$$X_1 \geq 0, \; X_2 \geq 0 \tag{9-40}$$

Earlier, we added slack and surplus variables to Kuhn-Tucker conditions (9-13) and (9-16) and obtained (9-34) and (9-35). Transferring the constant terms in (9-34) and (9-35) to the right-hand side, and multiplying each equation through by -1, we get

$$\begin{aligned} 0.2X_1 + 5\lambda_l + \lambda_m - V_1 &= 10 \\ 0.4X_2 + \lambda_l + 2\lambda_m - V_2 &= 20 \end{aligned} \tag{9-41}$$

$$\begin{aligned} 5X_1 + X_2 + W_l &= 200 \\ X_1 + 2X_2 + W_m &= 90 \end{aligned} \tag{9-42}$$

Now we shall add an artificial variable to each equation.

$$\begin{aligned} 0.2X_1 + 5\lambda_l + \lambda_m - V_1 + A_1 &= 10 \\ 0.4X_2 + \lambda_l + 2\lambda_m - V_2 + A_2 &= 20 \\ 5X_1 + X_2 + W_l + A_l &= 200 \\ X_1 + 2X_2 + W_m + A_m &= 90 \end{aligned}$$

The initial basic solution is then obtained by setting X_1, X_2, λ_l, λ_m, V_1, V_2, W_l, and W_m equal to zero. Hence

$$A_1 = 10$$

$$A_2 = 20$$

$$A_l = 200$$

$$A_m = 90$$

For computational purposes [10] it is convenient to utilize a two-phase procedure for driving the artificial variable out of the solution. In phase 1 the artificial variables A_l and A_m, which are associated with the linear constraints (9-42), are driven from the solution. The artificial variables A_1 and A_2, which are associated with (9-43), are driven out of the solution in phase 2.

Phase 1

We form the objective function for *phase 1* by assigning the coefficient 1 to the artificial variables A_l and A_m, and a zero coefficient to all other variables. Thus when the objective function is minimized, i.e., equal to zero, both A_l and A_m will have been driven from the solution. Both to ensure that the side conditions

$$V_1X_1 + V_2X_2 = 0$$

$$W_l\lambda_l + W_m\lambda_m = 0$$

are not violated, and to facilitate computation, the algorithm does not permit λ_l, λ_m, V_1, V_2, W_l, and W_m to be entering variables in this first phase.

The first simplex table is given below. (For clarity, rather than using vector notation in the table as we did in Chapter 7, we shall substitute the symbol of the associated variable.) We denote the column of right-hand side constants by B.

TABLE **9-2**

C_i \ C_j		0	0	0	0	0	0	0	0	0	0	1	1	
	Basis	X_1	X_2	λ_l	λ_m	V_1	V_2	W_l	W_m	A_1	A_2	A_l	A_m	B
0	A_1	0.2	0	5	1	−1	0	0	0	1	0	0	0	10
0	A_2	0	0.4	1	2	0	−1	0	0	0	1	0	0	20
1	A_l	5	1	0	0	0	0	1	0	0	0	1	0	200
1	A_m	1	2	0	0	0	0	0	1	0	0	0	1	90
	Z_j	6	3	0	0	0	0	1	1	0	0	1	1	290
	$C_j - Z_j$	−6	−3	0	0	0	0	−1	−1	0	0	0	0	

Table 9-2 indicates that the nonbasic variable X_1 should be substituted for the basic variable A_l. Applying the rules of the simplex method, the new solution is given by the values of the basic variables:

TABLE **9-3**

$A_1 =$	2
$A_2 =$	20
$X_1 =$	40
$A_m =$	50

Of course, the value of the objective function is not minimized yet; it is equal to 50. The second table (we will not construct it here) indicates that X_2 should replace A_m to give the new basic solution:

TABLE **9-4**

$A_1 =$	3.1
$A_2 =$	8.9
$X_1 =$	34.4
$X_2 =$	27.8

Phase 2

Thus the first objective function has been reduced to zero: the artificial variables A_l and A_m have been driven from the solution. Now, we must eliminate A_1 and A_2. To do this, we form the *phase 2* objective function by assigning the coefficient 1 to A_1 and A_2, and proceed to minimize this function. Again we must continue to satisfy the side conditions at each change of basis:

TABLE **9-5**

$\lambda_l =$	0.6
$A_2 =$	8.3
$X_1 =$	34.4
$X_2 =$	27.8

TABLE **9-6**

$\lambda_m =$	3.1
$A_2 =$	2.7
$X_1 =$	34.4
$X_2 =$	27.8

The final table values are:

TABLE **9-7**

$\lambda_m =$	4.0
$W_1 =$	20.4
$X_1 =$	30.0
$X_2 =$	30.0

The solution in Table 9-7 constitutes a basic feasible solution to the original Kuhn-Tucker constraints (before adding the artificial variables). Hence, these are the values of the variables which maximize the quadratic programming problem. This solution, of course, is the same as determined earlier in the chapter by graphical means.

The particular quadratic programming algorithm which we have described in this chapter is a modified version of Wolfe's [45] simplex method for quadratic programming. The reader may also wish to consult other references on quadratic programming including Barankin and Dorfman [5], Boot [6,7,8,9], Frank and Wolfe [19], Hildreth [26], Houthakker [28], and Theil and Van De Panne [38]. Also, we have not considered the dual problem of nonlinear programming. This problem has been treated by Balinski and Baumol [4], Dorn [14], and Wolfe [47].

SUMMARY

In this chapter we have attempted to give the reader some flavor of nonlinear programming and its applicability to the theory of the firm. Our approach was to select one particular nonlinear programming technique (quadratic programming), and to develop it in some depth. Since the number of techniques is now quite large, and new developments are being made continuously, we could not possibly include an in-depth discussion of the entire field of nonlinear programming in one chapter. For the reader who would like a more comprehensive treatment of nonlinear programming techniques, we recommend Abadie [1], Hadley [23], Künzi and Krelle [31], and Wolfe [48,49].

BIBLIOGRAPHY

[1] ABADIE, J. *Nonlinear Programming*. Amsterdam: North-Holland, 1967.

[2] ARROW, KENNETH J., LEONID HURWICZ, and HIROFUMI UZAWA. *Studies in Linear and Non-Linear Programming*. Stanford: Stanford University Press, 1958.

[3] BAUMOL, WILLIAM J. *Economic Theory and Operations Analysis*. Englewood Cliffs, N. J.: Prentice-Hall, Inc., 1965.

[4] BALINSKI, M. L., and W. J. BAUMOL. "The Dual in Nonlinear Programming and Its Economic Interpretation," *Review of Economic Studies* (to be published).

[5] BARANKIN, E. W., and R. DORFMAN. "On Quadratic Programming," *University of California Publications in Statistics*, **II** (1958), 285–318.

[6] BOOT, J. C. G. *Quadratic Programming*. Chicago: Rand McNally, 1960.

[7] BOOT, J. C. G. "Notes on Quadratic Programming: The Kuhn-Tucker and Theil-Van de Panne Conditions, Degeneracy, and Equality Constraints," *Management Science*, **VIII** (1961), 85–98.

[8] BOOT, J. C. G. "On Trivial and Binding Constraints in Programming Problems," *Management Science*, **VIII** (1962), 419–441.

[9] BOOT, J. C. G. "Binding Constraint Procedures of Quadratic Programming," *Econometrica*, **XXXI** (1963), 464–498.

[10] CARR, CHARLES R., and CHARLES W. HOWE. *Quantitative Decision Procedures in Management and Economics*. New York: McGraw-Hill Book Co., 1964.

[11] DANTZIG, GEORGE B. *Linear Programming and Extensions*. Princeton: Princeton University Press, 1963.

[12] DANTZIG, G. B., and R. W. COTTLE. "Positive (Semi-) Definite Programming," in J. Abadie (Ed.), *Nonlinear Programming*. Amsterdam: North-Holland, 1967.

[13] DORFMAN, ROBERT, PAUL A. SAMUELSON, and ROBERT SOLOW. *Linear Programming and Economic Analysis*. New York: McGraw-Hill Book Co., 1958.

[14] DORN, W. S. "Duality in Quadratic Programming," *Quarterly of Applied Mathematics*, **XVIII** (1960), 155–162.

[15] DORN, W. S. "On Lagrangian Multipliers," *Operations Research*, **IX** (1961), 95–104.

[16] DORN, W. S. "Non-Linear Programming—A Survey," *Management Science*, **IX** (January, 1963), 171–208.

[17] FIACIO, A. V., and G. P. MCCORMICK. "The Sequential Unconstrained Minimization Technique for Nonlinear Programming," *Management Science*, **X** (January, 1964), 360–366.

[18] FORSYTHE, G. "Computer Constrained Minima with Lagrange Multipliers," *Journal of the Society for Industrial and Applied Mathematics*, **III** (1955), 173–178.

[19] FRANK, MARGUERITE, and PHILIP WOLFE. "An Algorithm for Quadratic Programming," *Naval Research Logistics Quarterly*, **VI** (March–June, 1956), 95–110.

[20] FRISCH, RAGNER. *Maxima and Minima*. Chicago: Rand McNally, 1966.

[21] GRAVES, ROBERT L., and PHILIP WOLFE (Eds.). *Recent Advances in Mathematical Programming*. New York: McGraw-Hill Book Co., 1963.

[22] GRIFFITH, R. E., and R. A. STEWART. "A Nonlinear Programming Technique for the Optimization of Continuous Processing Systems," *Management Science*, **VII** (1961), 370–393.

[23] HADLEY, G. *Nonlinear and Dynamic Programming*. Reading, Mass.: Addison-Wesley, 1964.

[24] HANCOCK, H. *Theory of Maxima and Minima*. New York: Dover, 1960.

[25] HARTLEY, H. O. "Nonlinear Programming by the Simplex Method," *Econometrica*, **XXIX** (April, 1961), 223–237.

[26] HILDRETH, C. "A Quadratic Programming Procedure," *Naval Research Logistics Quarterly*, **XIV** (1957), 79–85.

[27] HOLT, C., F. MODIGLIANI, J. MUTH, and H. SIMON. *Planning Production, Inventories, and Work Force*. Englewood Cliffs, N. J.: Prentice-Hall, Inc., 1960.

[28] HOUTHAKKER, H. S. "The Capacity Method of Quadratic Programming," *Econometrica*, **XXVIII** (1960), 62–87.

[29] KENDRICK, DAVID A. *Programming Investment in the Process Industries*. Cambridge: Technology Press, 1967.

[30] KUHN, H. W., and A. TUCKER. "Nonlinear Programming," in J. Neyman (Ed.), *Proceedings of the Second Berkeley Symposium on Mathematical Statistics and Probability*. Berkeley: University of California Press, 1951.

[31] KUNZI, H. P., and W. KRELLE. *Nonlinear Programming*. Waltham, Mass.: Blaisdell Publishing Co., 1966.

[32] LAVI, ABRAHIM, and THOMAS P. VOGL. *Recent Advances in Optimization Techniques*. New York: John Wiley & Sons, 1966.

[33] NAYLOR, THOMAS H. "A Kuhn-Tucker Model of the Multi-Product, Multi-Factor Firm," *Southern Economic Journal*, **XXXI** (April, 1965), 324–330.

[34] ROSEN, J. B. "The Gradient Projection Method for Nonlinear Programming, Part I. Linear Constraints," *Journal of the Society for Industrial and Applied Mathematics*, **IX** (1960), 181–217.

[35] ROSEN, J. B. "The Gradient Projection Method for Nonlinear Programming, Part II. Nonlinear Constraints," *Journal of the Society for Industrial and Applied Mathematics*, **IX** (1961), 514–532.

[36] SAATY, THOMAS L., and JOSEPH BRAM. *Nonlinear Mathematics*. New York: McGraw-Hill Book Co., 1964.

[37] SPANG, H. A. "A Review of Minimization Techniques for Nonlinear Functions," *Journal of the Society for Industrial and Applied Mathematics*, **IV** (1962), 343–365.

[38] THEIL, H., and C. VAN DE PANNE. "Quadratic Programming as an Extension of Classical Quadratic Maximization," *Management Science*, **VII** (1960), 1–20.

[39] VAJDA, S. *Mathematical Programming*. Reading, Mass.: Addison-Wesley, 1961.

[40] VAN DE PANNE, C. "Programming with a Quadratic Constraint," *Management Science*, **XII** (July, 1966), 798–815.

[41] WEGNER, P. "A Nonlinear Extension of the Simplex Method," *Management Science*, **VII** (1960), 43–55.

[42] WILDE, D. J. *Optimum Seeking Methods*. Englewood Cliffs, N. J.: Prentice-Hall, 1964.

[43] WILDE, D. J., and C. S. BEIGHTLER. *Foundations of Optimization*. Englewood Cliffs, N. J.: Prentice-Hall, 1967.

[44] WITZGALL, C. *Gradient-Projection Methods for Linear Programming*. Princeton University and International Business Machines Corporation, Report No. 2, August, 1960.

[45] WOLFE, P. "The Simplex Method for Quadratic Programming," *Econometrica*, **XXVII** (1959), 382–398.

[46] WOLFE, P. "Accelerating the Cutting-Plane Method for Nonlinear Programming," *Journal of the Society for Industrial and Applied Mathematics*, **IX** (September, 1961), 481–488.

[47] WOLFE, P. "A Duality Theorem for Nonlinear Programming," *Quarterly of Applied Mathematics*, **XIV** (1961), 239–244.

[48] WOLFE, P. "Methods of Nonlinear Programming," in Robert L. Graves and P. Wolfe (Eds.), *Recent Advances in Mathematical Programming*. New York: McGraw-Hill Book Co., 1963.

[49] WOLFE, P. "Methods of Nonlinear Programming," in J. Abadie (Ed.), *Nonlinear Programming*. Amsterdam: North-Holland, 1967.

[50] ZOUTENDIJK, G. *Methods of Feasible Directions*. Amsterdam: Elsevier Publishing Co., 1960.

10

Integer programming and problems of the firm

INTRODUCTION

In some problems of the firm, noninteger values of economic variables have no meaning. Capital budgeting provides an example. A firm may have to choose among a number of different investment projects. The profit function may include a number of variables, each of which represents a different project. If the variable takes on the value 1, the project is undertaken; if the variable takes on the value 0, the project is bypassed. Clearly a variable assuming the value 0.7 would be meaningless.

Another example is the problem of indivisibility in input acquisition. In the not unusual situation where equipment is available with only discrete capacities, the solution must not specify equipment of "in-between" capacities. Electric generator units are normally manufactured only with capacities of 150, 200, and 250 kilowatts. For an expected demand of 215 kilowatts, a unit of 250 kilowatts of capacity would have to be purchased.

Integer linear programming is a mathematical technique which is designed to handle problems of this type. More specifically, integer *linear* programming is linear programming with the proviso that some, or all, variables must be integers. Of course, one could also consider integer *nonlinear* programming problems, but we shall not do so here.

In this chapter we shall consider a number of applications of integer programming to problems of the firm (hereafter we omit the adjective linear). As will be seen, integer programming can be used to solve some problems which are not obviously of the integer programming structure. Following the discussion of applications, we will describe the solution technique and use it to work a numerical example. Finally, we will discuss the interpretation of integer programming dual variables.

APPLICATIONS

Indivisibility of inputs and outputs

As was discussed in Chapter 6, some inputs may not be available in continuous values. The example given there was the airline company which operates a fleet of five DC-8 aircraft, but cannot acquire a fraction of a DC-8. It must add another "whole" DC-8 if it desires to increase its fleet. Furthermore, the company cannot hire another $\frac{5}{8}$ of a pilot per aircraft should it wish to do so.

The relative importance of indivisibility in economic theory is by no means a settled issue. On the one hand Ryan argues that

> . . . Indivisibility of the kind we have described is seldom important: it is always a matter of degree and frequently the result of how we define input. Further, a firm can generally vary the quantities of the services of durable goods that it uses more or less continuously by hiring these from other firms [24, p. 86].

However, Markowiz and Manne contend just the opposite.

> . . . In reality, there is no lack of indivisibilities. . . . Not only are these conditions typical of such natural monopolies as bridges, electric power grids, and communications networks, they are also characteristic of setup time problems in machine shops, of learning curves in aircraft production, of carload and airline shipments, and so on [23, p. 84].

Throughout the remainder of this chapter it will be assumed that technological and institutional indivisibilities do in fact exist, but that their degree of importance varies widely, depending on the particular situation.

One might think that from a practical viewpoint an integer programming technique is unnecessary. It might be argued that it is sufficient to round off noninteger variables. This is probably correct if the rounding is small relative to the values of the variables involved. However, in certain cases such rounding can result in solutions that are quite different from the optimal *integer* solution.

To illustrate this point, consider the following problem, which might be faced by a shipbuilder.

$$\text{(10-1)} \qquad \text{maximize} \quad \pi = 3X + 4Y$$

subject to

$$\text{(10-2)} \qquad \begin{aligned} 2X + Y &\leq 6 \\ 2X + 3Y &\leq 9 \end{aligned}$$

and

$$X \geq 0, \quad Y \geq 0$$

where X and Y are integers. The firm must decide how many ocean liners X and how many tankers Y should be produced to maximize profit π. The firm is constrained in its choice by the two inequalities, (10-2). The two constraints

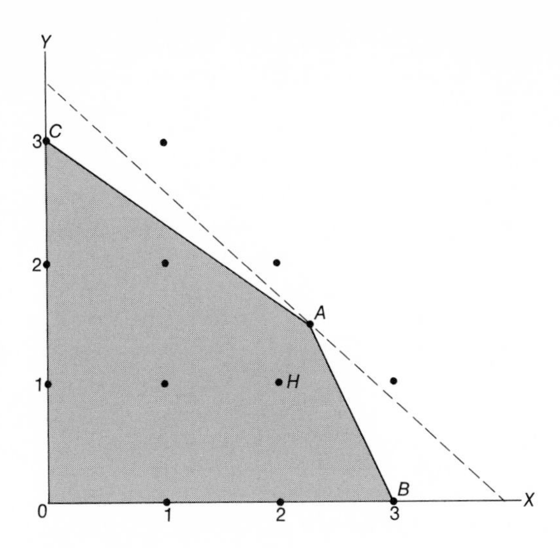

FIGURE 10-1

could represent resource availabilities of, say, machinery and labor. The problem is shown graphically in Figure 10-1.

The feasible region for the ordinary linear programming problem (disregarding the integrality requirements) is given in the figure by the area $AB0C$. The objective function, shown as the dashed line, attains its highest value at point A. The values of X and Y corresponding to A are

$$X = 2.25 \quad Y = 1.50 \tag{10-3}$$

and

$$\pi = 3(2.25) + 4(1.50) = 12.75$$

In other words, (10-3) gives the optimal number of ocean liners and tankers for profit maximization *if the firm could make fractions of ships.* Since we assume that this is not possible, one solution might be to round off 2.25 ocean liners to 2 ocean liners, and to round off 1.50 tankers to 1 tanker.

The "rounded" solution permits a profit of

$$\pi = 3(2) + 4(1) = 10$$

The reader may check to see that the constraints, (10-2), are satisfied. It should be pointed out that in some problems rounding might violate the constraints.

But this solution is not the optimal integer solution. The optimal integer solution is

$$X = 0 \quad Y = 3 \tag{10-4}$$

and, for these values of X and Y,

$$\pi = 3(0) + 4(3) = 12$$

This can be seen graphically by envisaging a leftward movement of the objective function until the first *feasible* integer solution is reached (the integer solutions are indicated by the black dots in Figure 10-1). Thus the objective function would reach point C ($X = 0$, $Y = 3$) well before reaching point H ($X = 2$, $Y = 1$).

This simple example illustrates that rounding can sometimes be very costly. Rounding would have led to a profit of 10 when a profit of 12 was possible.

Fixed costs

An important application of integer programming is in the case of fixed costs. That is, in producing a particular product there are usually some costs that are inherent in the production process and not dependent upon the number of units produced. This type of cost introduces nonlinearity into the objective function and renders linear programming useless. Although the method is not obvious the problem can be cast into the integer programming framework, and thereby solved. We shall alter our example to demonstrate the application of integer programming. But first we shall examine the total cost function for n products.

In general, a cost function characterized by a fixed component may be represented as

$$C_j = \begin{cases} \alpha_j + \beta_j X_j & \text{if } X_j > 0 \\ 0 & \text{if } X_j = 0 \end{cases} \tag{10-5}$$

where

C_j = total cost of output j

α_j = fixed cost of output j

β_j = variable cost of output j

X_j = quantity of output j

We now define a new variable δ_j to be either equal to 0 or 1 according as X_j is 0 or positive:

$$\delta_j = \begin{cases} 1, & X_j > 0 \\ 0, & X_j = 0 \end{cases} \tag{10-6}$$

The total cost function to be minimized for the n products is

$$C = \sum_{j=1}^{n} [\alpha_j(\delta_j) + \beta_j X_j] \tag{10-7}$$

Observe that the function is linear only for positive values of X_j. At the origin there is a discontinuity of magnitude α_j. However, by the introduction of the artificial integer variable δ_j, the nonlinear objective function has been transformed into one solvable by integer programming.

Let us examine the nature of the constraints necessary to ensure that δ_j takes on the proper value at the proper time. This can be done easily by using the example discussed earlier. The problem was to maximize profit, where profit was given by (10-1) subject to the constraints (10-2). Assume further that there is a fixed cost of 2 associated with X, and a fixed cost of 3 associated with Y. That is, if *any positive quantity* of X is produced, a fixed cost of 2 must be subtracted from profit; and, similarly, if Y is produced at all, a fixed cost of 3 must be subtracted from profit. Hence the profit function must be written as

$$\pi = 3X + 4Y - 2\delta_x - 3\delta_y \tag{10-8}$$

where

$$\begin{cases} \delta_x = 1, & \text{then} \quad X > 0 \\ \delta_y = 1, & \text{then} \quad Y > 0 \end{cases}$$
$$\begin{cases} \delta_x = 0, & \text{then} \quad X = 0 \\ \delta_y = 0, & \text{then} \quad Y = 0 \end{cases}$$

The problem now becomes one of constructing constraints to ensure that the above conditions are met. To do this, consider first the two possibilities that violate the above stipulations.

$$\text{(A)} \quad \begin{cases} X = 0, & \text{when} \quad \delta_x = 1 \\ Y = 0, & \text{when} \quad \delta_y = 1 \end{cases}$$

$$\text{(B)} \quad \begin{cases} X > 0, & \text{when} \quad \delta_x = 0 \\ Y > 0, & \text{when} \quad \delta_y = 0 \end{cases}$$

Possibility (A) is clearly unacceptable. But after closer examination we conclude that this possibility will never occur. The reason is that the objective function coefficients of δ_x and δ_y are very unfavorable relative to the coefficients of X and Y. In a maximizing problem, X and Y will always enter the solution before δ_x and δ_y. Hence we do not need explicit constraints to prevent the occurrence of (A).

Possibility (B) does require explicit constraints. Clearly in a maximizing process δ_x and δ_y would always be set equal to zero. Each reduces profit. To avoid (B), we add the constraints

$$\begin{aligned} X - L_x\delta_x &\leq 0 \\ Y - L_y\delta_y &\leq 0 \end{aligned} \tag{10-9}$$

The coefficients L_x and L_y are arbitrarily large numbers. The only requirement is that L_y, for example, must be large enough to permit the satisfaction of the constraint for any value of Y allowed by the other constraints; the constraints (10-2) permit Y to vary from 0 to 6. Hence we could set $L_y = 6$, or

$$Y - 6\delta_y \le 0 \tag{10-10}$$

If Y is positive, (10-10) requires δ_y to equal 1. Since Y can never exceed 6, (10-10) can always be satisfied by $\delta_y = 1$.

In addition to (10-9), we must also constrain δ_x and δ_y to 0 and 1. By solving the problem with integer programming techniques, we ensure that the variables are integers. However, we must include the constraints

$$\begin{aligned} \delta_x &\le 1 \\ \delta_y &\le 1 \end{aligned} \tag{10-11}$$

to control the range of the variables.

Thus the problem of fixed costs as defined in this example may be handled by solving the following integer programming problem.

$$\text{maximize} \quad \pi = 3X + 4Y - 2\delta_x - 3\delta_y \tag{10-12}$$

subject to

$$\begin{aligned} 2X + Y &\le 6 \\ 2X + 3Y &\le 9 \\ X - L_x\delta_x &\le 0 \\ Y - L_y\delta_y &\le 0 \\ \delta_x &\le 1 \\ \delta_y &\le 1 \end{aligned} \tag{10-13}$$

and all variables are non-negative integers.

Before turning to a specific technique for solving integer programming problems of the type described in this section, we shall briefly consider the problem of increasing returns (which was described in Chapter 9) as well as an integer programming approach to its solution.

Increasing returns

The possibility of increasing returns has always been a problem in economic theory. Increasing returns renders marginal analysis almost intractable. As an illustration, Figure 10-2 shows a particular isoquant from a production function which displays increasing returns to specialization. That is, higher values of an input are associated with ever-increasing marginal yields.

Clearly the isoquant has the "wrong" curvature. It is a contour taken from a three-dimensional production function that has a "valley" running in the uphill direction. Hence the production function is convex. As discussed in Chapter 9,

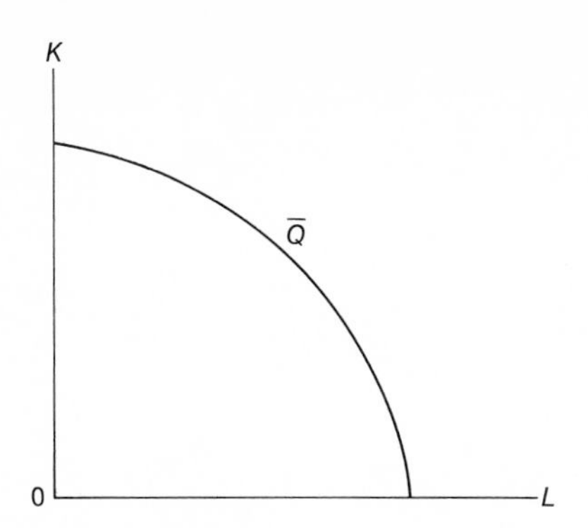

FIGURE **10-2**

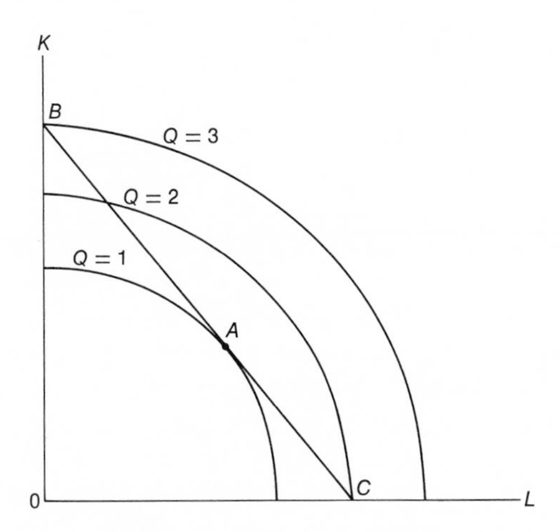

FIGURE **10-3**

calculus and programming methods are normally of little use when we seek to *maximize* a *convex* objective function. (Of course, the same applies when we seek to *minimize* a *concave* function.)

Figure 10-3 illustrates the failure of the marginal tangency conditions. In the normal case, when the firm seeks to maximize output for a given cost, the point of tangency between the isocost (or budget) line and an isoquant determines the optimal allocation of inputs. The marginal condition in Figure 10-3 would specify that point A is optimal, with $Q = 1$. Movement in either direction along the isocost line BC would increase Q. In fact, movement to point B would maximize Q. We fully understand the reason: the second-order conditions would indicate that A is a point of minimum Q rather than maximum Q.

More important, once we leave point A and move along the cost line, we find that output increases until we reach point B or C. Depending upon which

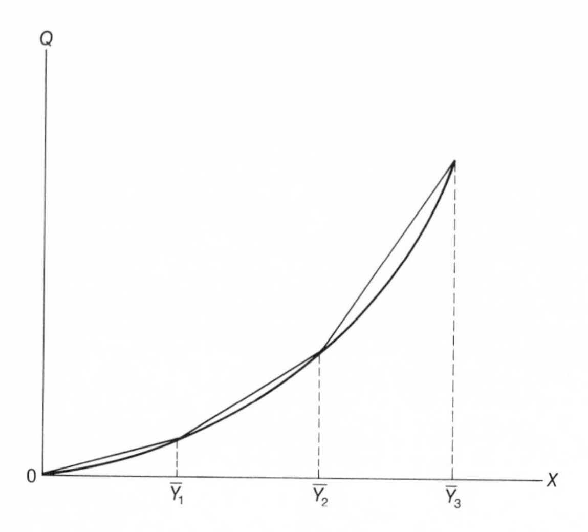

FIGURE **10-4**

direction we follow upon leaving A, we will select one of the two points as the optimum. But if we select point C as the optimum, we will be incorrect: point B is the *global* optimum while point C is but a *local* optimum. The problem of determining the global optimum is made difficult by increasing returns.

Markowitz and Manne [23] have suggested a method for solving such problems. Basically, their approach is to reformulate the problem as an integer programming problem. The nonlinear objective function is approximated by a piecewise linear function. Artificial integer variables are introduced to adjust the "wrong" shape of the objective function. Thus the converted problem is one of maximizing a linear function over a convex feasible region; and this ensures us that a local optimum will also be a global optimum.

We will describe the Markowitz and Manne technique for a simple production function with one input and increasing returns. Let the function be as shown in Figure 10-4. Thus $Q = f(X)$ for $0 \leq X \leq \overline{Y}_3$ and $dQ/dX > 0$, $d^2Q/dX^2 > 0$.

The curve can be approximated by linear segments. In Figure 10-4 the domain of X is divided into three arbitrary intervals demarcated by the constants $\overline{Y}_1$, $\overline{Y}_2$ and $\overline{Y}_3$. The accuracy of approximation could be improved to any desired degree by increasing the number of intervals. Now, denoting the slopes of the linear segments by $\overline{S}_1$, $\overline{S}_2$, and $\overline{S}_3$, and denoting the continuous input variables within each interval by X_1, X_2, and X_3, we can write a linear production function as

$$Q = \overline{S}_1 X_1 + \overline{S}_2 X_2 + \overline{S}_3 X_3 \tag{10-14}$$

The difficulty due to the increasing-returns phenomenon (i.e., $\overline{S}_3 > \overline{S}_2 > \overline{S}_1$) is that the linear programming algorithm will tend to bring in the X_i with the highest slope first, then the next highest, and so on. This is because the X_i with the highest slope, or $\bar{S}_i$, increases the objective function at the greatest rate. But of course this is illegitimate. Production must begin at zero and increase; it cannot begin at maximum output and decrease!

This is the problem that the artificial integer variables, δ_i (taking on values of 0 or 1), solve. By defining certain constraints involving the artificial variables, it is possible to ensure that the X_i will be employed in the proper sequence. That is, the integer variables ensure that output begins at zero and increases, rather than the absurdity of the reverse production order.

To do this we must include the following constraints:

$$\begin{aligned} &\delta_1 > (1/\bar{Y}_1)X_1 \\ &\delta_2 \geq [1/(\bar{Y}_2 - \bar{Y}_1)]X_2 \\ &\delta_3 \geq [1/(\bar{Y}_3 - \bar{Y}_2)]X_3 \\ &\delta_1, \delta_2, \delta_3 = 0 \text{ or } 1 \end{aligned} \tag{10-15}$$

The above constraints require $\delta_i = 1$ if X_i is positive. They also limit the range of the X_i to the proper intervals. Thus X_2 can vary continuously between 0 and $(\bar{Y}_2 - \bar{Y}_1)$. The constraints below are necessary to complete the technique.

$$\begin{aligned} &\delta_2 \leq (1/\bar{Y}_1)X_1 \\ &\delta_3 \leq [1/(\bar{Y}_2 - \bar{Y}_1)]X_2 \end{aligned} \tag{10-16}$$

Consider what happens when X_3 is positive (obviously, X_3 is the most attractive X_i to enter, since its objective function coefficient is the highest—but it is nonsensical for X_3 to be positive *unless* X_1 and X_2 are at their maximum values). A positive value of X_3 requires $\delta_3 = 1$ (by 10-15), and this ensures that $X_2 = \bar{Y}_2 - \bar{Y}_1$ (by 10-16)—its maximum value. Furthermore, a positive value of X_2 requires $\delta_2 = 1$ (by 10-15), and this ensures that $X_1 = \bar{Y}_1$ (by 10-16) —its maximum value. Hence the effect of this system of constraints is to rule out impossible production plans.

In principle we have a scheme for handling the problem of increasing returns. We can locate a *global* optimum just as we do in conventional optimizing problems. However, there are some disadvantages which should be mentioned. One is the computational problem. We will have more to say about this problem in integer programming later. Another disadvantage is that the function must be *separable* for this technique to work. That is, if $Q = f(X, Y)$, then we must be able to write $Q = g(X) + h(Y)$.

Other applications

Rather than giving further detailed discussions of integer programming applications, we refer the reader to the excellent survey by Dantzig [6]. In addition, for a thorough discussion of the usefulness of integer programming in capital budgeting, see Weingartner [25] and the brief discussion of the Weingartner model in Chapter 15.

INTEGER PROGRAMMING SOLUTION TECHNIQUE

Integer programming (or discrete programming, as it is sometimes called), is merely a special case of linear programming in which the solution variables are required to take on integral values. Prior to 1958 there existed no computational procedure that would guarantee integral solutions to linear programming problems. But in 1958 Gomory developed a method for solving such problems, which he calls the Method of Integer Forms, or the "cutting-plane" method [11]. Although this method will arrive at an optimal integer solution in a finite number of steps, it requires considerably more steps to reach an optimum solution than does the straightforward simplex method. Hence, one must choose between the straightforward simplex method with its nonintegral solutions and the "cutting-plane" method with its integral solutions but more complicated computational procedure.

Gomory's Method of Integer Forms takes as its starting point the optimum continuous solution to a linear programming problem that has been solved by the simplex method. If this solution is not an integer solution (and there is no reason to expect that it would be an integer solution), then an additional linear constraint must be incorporated into the linear programming problem. This additional constraint is constructed according to a certain rule developed by Gomory, namely the "cutting-plane" rule. The new linear programming problem is then reoptimized via the dual simplex method. This procedure is then repeated until an optimum solution is reached which is also an integer solution. Due to the nature of the constraints which are added after each reoptimization takes place, an optimum integral solution is guaranteed in a finite number of steps.

We shall now describe Gomory's algorithm in detail. We will limit our discussion to the *all-integer* problem. That is, we shall consider an integer programming problem in which *all variables* must take on integer values in the solution. Gomory has also developed an algorithm for solving a *mixed-integer–continuous-variable* problem [12]. For a good exposition of this algorithm, the reader is referred to Hadley [16]. Perhaps the most effective algorithms for solving mixed-integer problems are of the *branch and bound* type, and these are rather different from the Gomory algorithm [1,21,22].

Let us state the general integer programming problem in vector notation (after all inequalities have been converted into equations).

(10-17) maximize (or minimize) $Z = \mathbf{c}'\mathbf{x}$

subject to

(10-18) $X_1\mathbf{a}_1 + X_2\mathbf{a}_2 + \cdots + X_n\mathbf{a}_n = \mathbf{b}$

and

(10-19) $\mathbf{x} \geq \mathbf{0}$ and all integer

where

$$\mathbf{c}' = \text{a row vector, } (C_1, C_2, \ldots, C_n)$$

$$\mathbf{x} = \text{a column vector, } \begin{bmatrix} X_1 \\ X_2 \\ \vdots \\ X_k \\ \vdots \\ X_n \end{bmatrix}$$

$$\mathbf{b} = \text{a column vector, } \begin{bmatrix} B_1 \\ B_2 \\ \vdots \\ B_k \\ \vdots \\ B_m \end{bmatrix}$$

$\mathbf{0}$ = an n-dimensional null column vector

$\mathbf{a}_j$ = column vector of coefficients of the variable X_j for $j = 1, 2, \ldots, n$

$$\begin{bmatrix} a_{1j} \\ a_{2j} \\ \vdots \\ a_{kj} \\ \vdots \\ a_{mj} \end{bmatrix}$$

Let the optimal basic feasible solution to the problem be as given below (*where we have ignored the integrality requirement*):

$$\mathbf{x} = \begin{bmatrix} X_1 \\ X_2 \\ \vdots \\ X_k \\ \vdots \\ X_m \\ 0 \\ 0 \\ \vdots \\ 0 \end{bmatrix}$$

and

$$X_1\mathbf{a}_1 + X_2\mathbf{a}_2 + \cdots + X_k\mathbf{a}_k + \cdots + X_m\mathbf{a}_m = \mathbf{b}$$

Let $\mathbf{c}_b' = (C_1, C_2, \ldots, C_k, \ldots, C_m)$; that is, the objective function coefficients of the positive variables in the solution. Further, let

$$\mathbf{x}_b = \begin{bmatrix} X_1 \\ X_2 \\ \vdots \\ X_k \\ \vdots \\ X_m \end{bmatrix}$$

Then the scalar product $\mathbf{c}_b'\mathbf{x}_b$ gives the value of the objective function Z for this solution.

Any vector in requirements space $\mathbf{a}_j$ can be expressed as a unique linear combination of the basis vectors. Thus,

$$\mathbf{a}_j = Y_{1j}\mathbf{a}_1 + Y_{2j}\mathbf{a}_2 + \cdots + Y_{kj}\mathbf{a}_k + \cdots + Y_{mj}\mathbf{a}_m \tag{10-20}$$

Now, if components of $\mathbf{x}_b$ are integers, we have the optimal integer solution. However, assume that X_k is *not* an integer. Then consider the equation

$$X_k = B_k - \sum_{j=m+1}^{n} Y_{kj}X_j \tag{10-21}$$

This equation can be written directly from the simplex table. Notice that it is simply the kth row of the table. In order to make this clear, let us return to our example problem:

$$\text{maximize} \quad \pi = 3X + 4Y \tag{10-22}$$

subject to

$$\begin{aligned} 2X + Y &\leq 6 \\ 2X + 3Y &\leq 9 \end{aligned} \tag{10-23}$$

and

$$X \geq 0, \quad Y \geq 0$$

where X and Y are integers.

In vector notation (after adding slack variables):

$$\text{maximize} \quad \pi = \mathbf{c}'\mathbf{x} \tag{10-24}$$

subject to

$$X\mathbf{a}_1 + Y\mathbf{a}_2 + S_1\mathbf{a}_3 + S_2\mathbf{a}_4 = \mathbf{b} \tag{10-25}$$

and

$$\mathbf{x} \geq 0 \quad \text{and all integer}$$

where

$$\mathbf{c}' = (3, 4, 0, 0)$$

$$\mathbf{x} = \begin{bmatrix} X \\ Y \\ S_1 \\ S_2 \end{bmatrix}$$

$$\mathbf{b} = \begin{pmatrix} 6 \\ 9 \end{pmatrix}$$

and

$$\mathbf{a}_1 = \begin{pmatrix} 2 \\ 2 \end{pmatrix} \quad \mathbf{a}_2 = \begin{pmatrix} 1 \\ 3 \end{pmatrix} \quad \mathbf{a}_3 = \begin{pmatrix} 1 \\ 0 \end{pmatrix} \quad \mathbf{a}_4 = \begin{pmatrix} 0 \\ 1 \end{pmatrix}$$

Table 10-1 is the simplex table corresponding to the optimal solution when we *ignore the integer requirement*. For ease of interpretation, we will use the variable symbols rather than the corresponding vector symbols. This solution corresponds to point A in Figure 10-1.

Finally, we can illustrate (10-21) by example. Since the optimal solution, $X = 2\frac{1}{4}$, $Y = 1\frac{1}{2}$, is not an integer solution, we select the variable with the largest fractional part ($Y = 1\frac{1}{2}$). This criterion seems to work well in practice, but is not always most efficient. Hence, we write the Y equation (given by the second row of the simplex table):

$$0X + 1Y - \tfrac{1}{2}S_1 + \tfrac{1}{2}S_2 = 1\tfrac{1}{2}$$

or, after rearranging to comply with (10-21),

$$Y = 1\tfrac{1}{2} - (-\tfrac{1}{2}S_1 + \tfrac{1}{2}S_2) \tag{10-21a}$$

We now return to the general discussion. The Y_{kj} and B_k can be decomposed into the sum of a positive or negative integer (or zero) and a *non-negative fractional part*. That is,

$$Y_{kj} = W_{kj} + F_{kj} \qquad \text{for } j = m + 1, \ldots, n \tag{10-26}$$

and

$$B_k = W_k + F_k$$

where W is an integer and F is a non-negative fraction.

TABLE **10-1**

C_i \ C_j		3	4	0	0	
C_i	Basis	X	Y	S_1	S_2	B
3	X	1	0	$\frac{3}{4}$	$-\frac{1}{4}$	$2\frac{1}{4}$
4	Y	0	1	$-\frac{1}{2}$	$\frac{1}{2}$	$1\frac{1}{2}$
	Z_j	3	4	$\frac{1}{4}$	$\frac{5}{4}$	$12\frac{3}{4}$
	$C_j - Z_j$	0	0	$-\frac{1}{4}$	$-\frac{5}{4}$	

Example:

(10-26a)
$$-\tfrac{1}{2} = -1 + \tfrac{1}{2} \qquad \text{variable } S_1 \text{ coefficient}$$
$$\tfrac{1}{2} = 0 + \tfrac{1}{2} \qquad \text{variable } S_2 \text{ coefficient}$$

and

$$1\tfrac{1}{2} = 1 + \tfrac{1}{2} \qquad \text{value of } B$$

Substituting (10-26) into (10-21) gives

(10-27)
$$X_k = W_k - \sum_{j=m+1}^{n} W_{kj}X_j + F_k - \sum_{j=m+1}^{n} F_{kj}X_j$$

Now for any *integer* solution the sum of the last two terms on the right-hand side of (10-27) must be an integer. We need not worry about the remaining terms, for they will necessarily be integers. Hence

$$F_k - \sum_{j=m+1}^{n} F_{kj}X_j \qquad \text{must be an integer}$$

Since F_k is a positive fraction ($0 < F_k < 1$), and since the second term in the expression cannot be negative (by definition of the F_{kj}), it is clear that for any integer solution

(10-28)
$$F_k - \sum_{j=m+1}^{n} F_{kj}X_j \leq 0$$

That is, the expression cannot be a positive integer. Hence, every feasible solution to the *integer* problem must satisfy (10-28).

Example:

(10-28a)
$$\tfrac{1}{2} - (\tfrac{1}{2}S_1 + \tfrac{1}{2}S_2) \leq 0$$

The example (10-28a) makes it clear that the optimum solution obtained by ignoring the integer constraint violates (10-28). That is, in the optimal solution, S_1 and S_2 both equal zero, and thus

$$\tfrac{1}{2} - (\tfrac{1}{2}(0) + \tfrac{1}{2}(0)) > 0$$

The constraint (10-28) is the "cutting plane" of Gomory. It reduces the set of feasible solutions, but does *not* exclude any *integer* feasible solutions.

We shall illustrate the next step by example. The new constraint can be converted into an equation by introducing a new slack variable, S_3:

(10-29)
$$-\tfrac{1}{2}S_1 - \tfrac{1}{2}S_2 + S_3 = -\tfrac{1}{2}$$

Now we want to incorporate this new constraint into the problem. It is instructive to observe what this new constraint does graphically. By substitution

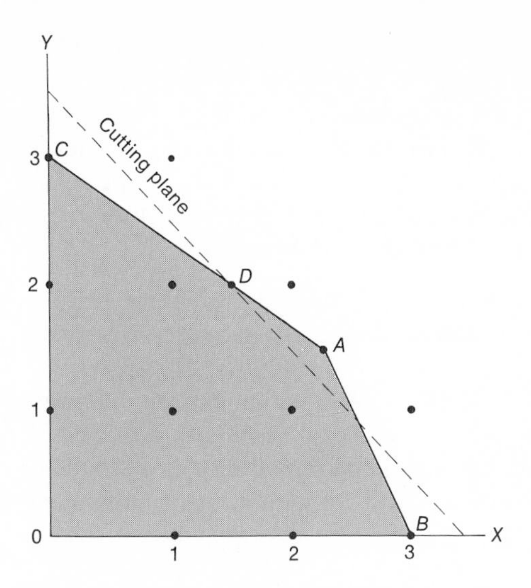

FIGURE 10-5

from the original constraints, we can express (10-29) in terms of the variables X and Y (recognizing that $S_3 = 0$ when (10-29) is satisfied exactly). Thus

$$-\tfrac{1}{2}[6 - 2X - Y] - \tfrac{1}{2}[9 - 2X - 3Y] = -\tfrac{1}{2}$$

and

$$Y = 3\tfrac{1}{2} - X$$

Hence, we can graph (10-29) in Figure 10-5 as the dashed line. The original feasible region is the shaded area, and point A is the noninteger optimal solution.

Two facts should be noted. First, the new constraint cuts away or reduces the original feasible solution so as to include in the "cutaway" portion the optimal noninteger solution (point A). Second, in reducing the feasible region, none of the originally feasible integer solutions become nonfeasible.

The new constraint (10-29) can easily be included in a new simplex table. It becomes the last row of Table 10-2. We must also add a new column for the new slack variable, S_3.

TABLE 10-2

C_i \ C_j		3	4	0	0	0	
	Basis	X	Y	S_1	S_2	S_3	B
3	X	1	0	$\frac{3}{4}$	$-\frac{1}{4}$	0	$2\frac{1}{4}$
4	Y	0	1	$-\frac{1}{2}$	$\frac{1}{2}$	0	$1\frac{1}{2}$
0	S_3	0	0	$-\frac{1}{2}$	$-\frac{1}{2}$	1	$-\frac{1}{2}$
	Z_j	3	4	$\frac{1}{4}$	$\frac{5}{4}$	0	$12\frac{3}{4}$
	$C_j - Z_j$	0	0	$-\frac{1}{4}$	$-\frac{5}{4}$	0	

At first glance one might think Table 10-2 represents an optimal solution: there are no positive elements in the $C_j - Z_j$ row. However, observe that a solution variable is negative, $S_3 = -\frac{1}{2}$. This means that Table 10-2 represents a *nonfeasible* basic solution. But this is precisely the situation in which the *dual simplex method* is appropriate. The reader is referred to Chapter 7 for a discussion of this method. For convenience, the three-step procedure for selection of the entering and departing vectors is reproduced below:

1. Begin with a basic solution with one or more $X_i < 0$ for $i = 1, \ldots, m$ (where these X_i are the m variables associated with basis vectors) and with all $C_j - Z_j \leq 0$.
2. The vector to be removed is determined by finding the minimum of all $X_i < 0$ for $i = 1, \ldots, m$.
   Let X_h be the minimum, then $\mathbf{a}_h$ should be removed.
3. The vector to be entered is determined by finding the minimum of all $(C_j - Z_j)/Y_{hj}$ for $Y_{hj} < 0$.

Let the minimum be $(C_p - Z_p)/Y_{hp}$, then $\mathbf{a}_p$ should be entered. If a tie exists, any arbitrary rule can be used to break it.

The dual simplex algorithm indicates that S_3 should be removed from the solution ($S_3 = -\frac{1}{2}$ is the minimum of the negative solution values). And, S_1 should replace S_3 in the solution, since its $(C_j - Z_j)/Y_{hj}$ is the minimum for all negative Y_{hj} in the S_3 row. That is,

$$-\tfrac{1}{4}/-\tfrac{1}{2} = \tfrac{1}{2} \qquad \text{variable } S_1 \text{ column}$$

$$-\tfrac{5}{4}/-\tfrac{1}{2} = \tfrac{5}{2} \qquad \text{variable } S_2 \text{ column}$$

Hence computation by the usual simplex routine gives Table 10-3.

Table 10-3 represents a new optimal basic feasible solution (all $C_j - Z_j \leq 0$ and all solution variables are non-negative). This solution corresponds to point D in Figure 10-5. Unfortunately, we note that $X = \frac{3}{2}$ in this solution, which still violates the integrality requirement. Consequently we must introduce a further Gomory "cutting plane."

This second Gomory constraint can be shown to be

$$-\tfrac{1}{2}S_3 + S_4 = -\tfrac{1}{2} \tag{10-30}$$

TABLE **10-3**

C_i \ C_j	Basis	3 X	4 Y	0 S_1	0 S_2	0 S_3	B
3	X	1	0	0	-1	$\frac{3}{2}$	$\frac{3}{2}$
4	Y	0	1	0	1	-1	2
0	S_1	0	0	1	1	-2	1
	Z_i	3	4	0	1	$\frac{1}{2}$	$12\frac{1}{2}$
	$C_j - Z_j$	0	0	0	-1	$-\frac{1}{2}$	

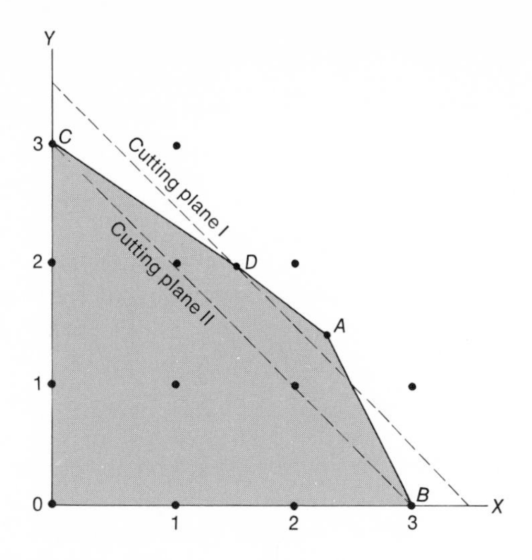

FIGURE **10-6**

where S_4 is the second Gomory slack variable. In terms of X and Y, (10-30) can be written as

$$Y = 3 - X$$

Graphically, we can show (10-30) in Figure 10-6 as "Cutting Plane II." Again, the constraint slices off a portion of the feasible region—including the optimal point corresponding to Table 10-3 (point D), but not including any integer solutions that were originally feasible.

Adding the constraint (10-30) to the problem necessitates an expanded table, Table 10-4.

The application of the dual-simplex method is again appropriate. Replacing S_4 with S_3, and applying the simplex routine, we get Table 10-5.

Table 10-5 corresponds to the optimal integer solution (point C in Figure 10-6). There are no positive $C_j - Z_j$, and all solution variables are non-negative

TABLE **10-4**

C_i \ C_j		3	4	0	0	0	0	
	Basis	X	Y	S_1	S_2	S_3	S_4	B
3	X	1	0	0	-1	$\frac{3}{2}$	0	$\frac{3}{2}$
4	Y	0	1	0	1	-1	0	2
0	S_1	0	0	1	1	-2	0	1
0	S_4	0	0	0	0	$-\frac{1}{2}$	1	$-\frac{1}{2}$
	Z_j	3	4	0	1	$\frac{1}{2}$	0	$12\frac{1}{2}$
	$C_j - Z_j$	0	0	0	-1	$-\frac{1}{2}$	0	

integers. Hence, the values of the variables, when constrained to be integers, are

$$X = 0$$

$$Y = 3$$

and

$$\pi = 3(0) + 4(3) = 12$$

Observe that the $C_j - Z_j$ row, the dual variables or shadow prices, are also integers. We now turn to a brief discussion of the interpretation of the dual variables of an integer programming problem.

INTEGER DUAL PRICES

One of the byproducts of the solution to an integer programming problem by the Method of Integer Forms is of particular interest in studying the theory of the firm. The imputed values or dual prices of integer linear programming problems possess some peculiarities that are quite different from those of continuous linear programming problems. Gomory and Baumol [14] have made an extensive comparison between the dual prices for continuous linear programming problems and integer linear programming problems, the results of which are summarized briefly below.

Like the simplex method, the Method of Integer Forms yields a dual problem whose solution imputes prices to the scarce inputs. A number of the characteristics of these dual prices are similar to those found in continuous linear programming problems.

However, the integer dual prices possess a number of unique characteristics. First, the dual prices themselves will be integers. Second, the dual prices are to some extent arbitrary, varying with the procedure by which they are computed. Third, the dual prices will tend to impute zero prices to a number of resources to which the economist will want to assign a higher value.[1] Fourth, the dual

TABLE **10-5**

Optimal integer solution

C_i \ C_j		3	4	0	0	0	0	
	Basis	X	Y	S_1	S_2	S_3	S_4	B
3	X	1	0	0	−1	0	3	0
4	Y	0	1	0	1	0	−2	3
0	S_1	0	0	1	1	0	−4	3
0	S_3	0	0	0	0	1	−2	1
	Z_j	3	4	0	1	0	1	12
	$C_j - Z_j$	0	0	0	−1	0	−1	

[1] In the example problem, an economist would probably be unwilling to assign a price of zero to the resource corresponding to the constraint, $2X + Y \leq 6$; but this is the dictum of Table 10-5.

price of a resource will not always be equal to its marginal revenue product, and, in fact, the entire concept of the marginal revenue product of an input itself becomes somewhat ambiguous [2,14].

The preceding summary has been concerned with the dual prices of the original fixed factors of the firm. Of particular interest is the economic interpretation of the dual prices associated with the additional Gomory constraints. According to Baumol, "these may be viewed as a measure of the opportunity cost of indivisibility—e.g., the loss imposed on the businessman by the lack of a unit of artificial capacity which prevents him from obtaining four-tenths of a case to fill up that last empty bit of space in his warehouse" [2, p. 165]. Needless to say, there is no theoretical counterpart to these imputed costs of indivisibility in the continuous linear programming problem, since all variables are assumed to be perfectly divisible.

BIBLIOGRAPHY

[1] BALINSKI, M. L. "Integer Programming: Methods, Uses, Computation," *Management Science*, **XII** (November, 1965), 253–313.

[2] BAUMOL, WILLIAM J. *Economic Theory and Operations Analysis*. Englewood Cliffs, N. J.: Prentice-Hall, Inc., 1965.

[3] CARR, CHARLES R., and CHARLES W. HOWE. *Quantitative Decision Procedures in Management and Encounter*. New York: McGraw-Hill Book Co., 1964.

[4] CHUNG, AN-MIN. *Linear Programming*. Columbus, Ohio: Charles E. Merrill Co., 1959.

[5] DANTZIG, GEORGE B. "Note on Solving Linear Programs in Integers," *Naval Research Logistics Quarterly*, **VI** (1959), 75–76.

[6] DANTZIG, GEORGE B. "On the Significance of Solving Linear Programming Problems with Some Integer Variables," *Econometrica*, **XXVIII** (January, 1960), 30–44.

[7] DANTZIG, GEORGE B. *Linear Programming and Extensions*. Princeton: Princeton University Press, 1963.

[8] DANTZIG, GEORGE B., D. R. FULKERSON, and S. JOHNSON. "Solution of a Large-Scale Traveling-Salesman Problem," *Journal of the Operations Research Society of America*, **II** (1954), 393–410.

[9] DRIEBEEK, NORMAN J. "An Algorithm for the Solution of Mixed Integer Programming Problems," *Management Science*, **XII** (March, 1966), 576–587.

[10] GLOVER, FRED. "Generalized Cuts in Diophantine Programming," *Management Science*, **XIII** (November, 1966), 254–268.

[11] GOMORY, RALPH E. "Outline of an Algorithm for Integer Solutions to Linear Programs," *Bulletin of the American Mathematical Society*, **LXIV** (September, 1958), 275–278.

[12] GOMORY, RALPH E. "An Algorithm for the Mixed Integer Problem," RM-2597, The RAND Corporation, 1960.

[13] GOMORY, RALPH E. "An Algorithm for Integer Solutions to Linear Programs," in Robert L. Graves and Philip Wolfe (Eds.), *Recent Advances in Mathematical Programming*. New York: McGraw-Hill Book Co., 1963.

[14] GOMORY, RALPH E., and WILLIAM J. BAUMOL. "Integer Programming and Pricing," *Econometrica*, **XXVIII** (July, 1960), 521–550.

[15] GOMORY, RALPH E., and A. J. HOFFMAN. "On the Convergence of An Integer Programming Process," *Naval Research Logistics Quarterly*, **X** (1963), 121–123.

[16] HADLEY, G. *Nonlinear and Dynamic Programming*. Reading, Mass.: Addison-Wesley, 1964.

[17] HILLIER, FREDERICK S., and GERALD J. LIEBERMAN. *Introduction to Operations Research*. San Francisco: Holden-Day, Inc., 1967.

[18] KELLEY, J. E. "The Cutting-Plane Method for Solving Convex Programs," *Journal of the Society for Industrial and Applied Mathematics*, **VIII** (December, 1960), 703–712.

[19] KENDRICK, DAVID A. *Programming Investment in the Process Industries*. Cambridge, Mass.: Technology Press, 1967.

[20] KUNZI, HANS P., and WERNER OETTLI. "Integer Quadratic Programming," in R. L. Graves and P. Wolfe (Eds.), *Recent Advances in Mathematical Programming*. New York: McGraw-Hill Book Co., 1963.

[21] LAND, A. H., and A. G. DOIG (Eds.). "An Automatic Method of Solving Discrete Programming Problems," *Econometrica*, **XXVIII** (1960), 497–521.

[22] LAWLER, E. L., and D. E. WOOD. "Branch and Bound Methods, a Survey," *Operations Research*, **XIV** (July–August, 1966).

[23] MARKOWITZ, HARRY M., and ALAN S. MANNE. "On the Solution of Discrete Programming Problems," *Econometrica*, **XXV** (January, 1957), 84–85.

[24] RYAN, W. J. L. *Price Theory*. London: Macmillan & Co., Ltd., 1962.

[25] WEINGARTNER, H. M. *Mathematical Programming and the Analysis of Capital Budgeting Problems*. Englewood Cliffs, N. J.: Prentice-Hall, Inc., 1963.

PART 4

Dynamic and probabilistic models of the firm

11

Dynamic models of the firm

INTRODUCTION

All of the models considered thus far in this book have been static-equilibrium models. By looking at the firm at a particular point in time rather than over time we have in effect abstracted away the variable time. In this chapter we shall introduce the variable time into our models of the firm.

We shall investigate a class of models in which decisions made in period t_0 affect the behavior of the firm in periods $t_1, t_2, \ldots, T$, where T is the planning horizon of the firm. With the introduction of the variable time, the analysis becomes extremely complex. Unfortunately, classical optimization techniques and mathematical programming are suitable for solving only certain special cases of dynamic problems. Hence we must draw on higher forms of mathematics, namely differential equations, the calculus of variations, Pontryagin's maximum principle, and dynamic programming.

We begin by defining the standard dynamic problem. Then we consider three special cases of the standard problem: (1) differential equations, (2) Pontryagin's maximum principle, and (3) calculus of variations. Example models of the firm illustrating each of these three techniques are described. Finally, a brief section on dynamic programming is included.

The reader who is seriously interested in dynamic models should consult the excellent book by Connors and Teichroew [15].

THE STANDARD DYNAMIC PROBLEM

The standard dynamic problem [15, p. 5] is to optimize the functional

$$\phi = \int_{t_0}^{t_1} Z[Y_1(t), \ldots, Y_m(t); X_1(t), \ldots, X_n(t); t]\, dt \tag{11-1}$$

subject to

$$\frac{dY_i(t)}{dt} = f_i[Y_1(t), \ldots, Y_m(t); X_1(t), \ldots, X_n(t); t] \quad i = 1, 2, \ldots, m \tag{11-2}$$

and

$$Y_i(t_0) = Y_i^0 \quad i = 1, 2, \ldots, m \tag{11-3}$$

The $Y_i(t)$'s are referred to individually as *state variables* and collectively as the *trajectory* of the system. The $X_j(t)$'s are the *control functions* which determine the behavior of the system and are chosen from a set of admissible functions. The planning period begins at t_0 and ends at t_1. The problem is to choose control functions $X_j(t)$, $j = 1, \ldots, n$ from the set of admissible control functions so that the trajectory $Y_i(t)$, $i = 1, \ldots, m$ optimizes ϕ, i.e., (11-1).

SYSTEMS ANALYSIS [15]

As a first approach to the solution to the standard dynamic problem, we assume that the objective function ϕ given by (11-1) is not known explicitly to the decision maker. However, the decision maker is assumed to have some nonquantified criteria in mind which he desires the firm to achieve. Among the criteria which might be used by the firm's decision makers to evaluate alternative decision rules and policies (control functions) are: (1) "good performance at minimum cost," (2) "stable operations," (3) "rapid response to input," (4) "satisficing" [15, p. 6]. (Satisficing means ascertaining a policy or decision rule which is "good enough" although it is not necessarily optimal.) With this approach the decision maker desires to satisfy one or more criteria of the type previously mentioned for the firm which can be described by

$$\frac{dY_i(t)}{dt} = f_i[Y_1(t), \ldots, Y_m(t); X_1(t), \ldots, X_n(t); t] \quad i = 1, 2, \ldots, m \tag{11-4}$$

and

$$Y_i(t_0) = Y_i^0 \quad i = 1, 2, \ldots, m \tag{11-5}$$

The state variables $Y_1, Y_2, \ldots, Y_m$ might include such variables as profit, production, inventory, sales, market share, to mention only a few.

The control functions (decision rules) $X_j(t), j = 1, \ldots, n$, are selected on the basis of hunches, trial and error, and simple guesses. The decision maker selects a set of control parameters X_j, $j = 1, 2, \ldots, n$, the system of simultaneous differential equations (11-4) are solved, and the behavior of the state variables Y_i, $i = 1, 2, \ldots, m$, is examined. If the behavior of the firm is consistent with the predetermined criteria set forth by the decision maker, then the control functions are accepted. If the behavior of the firm is not satisfactory, the parameters and/or form of the control functions are changed and the system of differential equations is re-solved. The behavior of the firm is reexamined, etc. [15, p. 6].

Analytical solutions are available for linear systems of simultaneous differential equations of the form

$$\frac{dY_i(t)}{dt} = \sum_{i=1}^{m} a_{ij}(t)Y_i + \sum_{j=1}^{n} b_{ij}(t)X_j + g_i(t) \qquad i = 1, \ldots, m \tag{11-6}$$

and have been treated in the literature by Allen [2], Holt, Modigliani, Muth, and Simon [27,28], Simon [36], and Tustin [42]. Analytical solutions to systems of nonlinear differential equations are extremely complex and difficult to achieve. For this reason numerical analysis and computer-simulation techniques [18] have in many cases proved to be the only practical way of solving complex nonlinear systems of differential equations.

It is not our intention to present a treatise on differential equations, since a number of excellent references are available on this topic including the books by Allen [4], Bellman and Cook [10], Coddington and Levinson [14], and Kaplan [32]. However, in order to provide the reader with some notion of how this approach can be applied in practice, we shall consider a simple example involving a single differential equation in one variable. (This model was developed by Teichroew [39, pp. 228–231].)

Consider a monopolist who produces a single product and sells the product at a price P in a market which can absorb no more than M dollars of the product per unit of time (without lowering the price).

1. If the firm does no advertising, its rate of sales $S(t)$ at any point in time will decrease at a rate ($\lambda > 0$) proportional to the rate of sales at that time. The change in the rate of sales is given by

$$\frac{dS(t)}{dt} = -\lambda S(t) \tag{11-7}$$

If $S(t) = S_0$ when $t = 0$, then it can be shown that

$$S(t) = S_0 e^{-\lambda t} \tag{11-8}$$

Equation (11-8) is said to be the solution of (11-7) and indicates that sales decrease exponentially with time, depending on the value of λ.

2. If the firm advertises, the rate of sales will increase at a rate proportional to the rate of advertising, but this increase affects only that proportion of the market which is not already purchasing the product. The first assumption controls the other part of the market. If we let

$$A = \text{rate of advertising} \tag{11-9}$$

$$\gamma = \text{a constant } (\gamma > 0) \tag{11-10}$$

$$[1 - (S(t)/M)] = \text{part of the market affected by advertising} \tag{11-11}$$

then

$$\frac{dS(t)}{dt} = -\lambda S(t) + \gamma A[1 - (S(t)/M)] \tag{11-12}$$

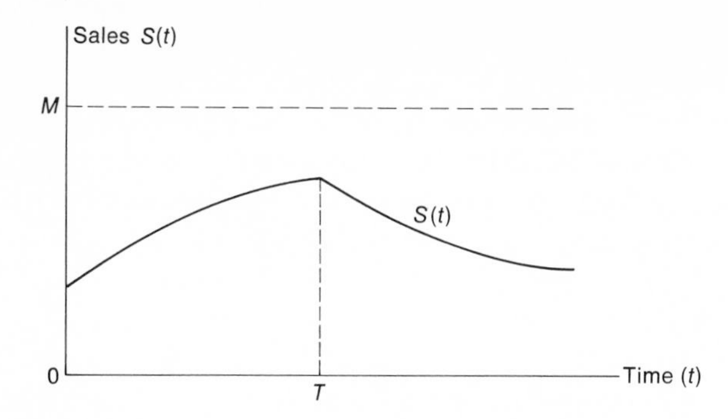

FIGURE 11-1

In this case we have a single state variable S and a single control variable A. If we again assume that $S(t) = S_0$ when $t = 0$, then the solution to (11-12) is given by

$$S(t) = \frac{M\gamma A}{M\lambda + \gamma A} + \left[S_0 - \frac{M\gamma A}{M\lambda + \gamma A}\right]e^{-[\lambda + (\gamma A/M)]t} \tag{11-13}$$

The decision maker can now determine analytically the effect of alternative advertising policies on sales. Consider the case where advertising is constant for a given period and is then stopped. Let a denote the total amount spent on advertising. Then

$$\begin{aligned} A(t) &= a/T \qquad 0 \le t \le T \\ &= 0 \qquad T < t \end{aligned} \tag{11-14}$$

Then from (11-13)

$$\begin{aligned} S(t) &= \frac{M\gamma a}{TM\lambda + \gamma a} + \left[S_0 - \frac{M\gamma a}{TM\lambda + \gamma a}\right]e^{-[\lambda + (\gamma a/TM)]t} \qquad 0 \le t \le T \\ &= S(T)e^{-\lambda(t-T)} \qquad T < t \end{aligned} \tag{11-15}$$

since (11-8) applies for $t > T$. The graph of $S(t)$ is shown in Figure 11-1.

The decision maker can now experiment with the parameters a and T in order to determine the "most satisfactory" time path of sales. Of course, the desired time path of sales would depend upon factors which we are not prepared to introduce here. For example, the rate of interest would need to be considered in establishing the proper exchange rate between dollars at different points in time. (This will be discussed in Chapters 15 and 16.)

CALCULUS OF VARIATIONS

The fundamental problem of the calculus of variations is concerned with finding functions $Y_1(t), \ldots, Y_n(t)$ from the class of admissible functions with fixed end points

$$(Y_1^0, \ldots, Y_n^0), (Y_1^1, \ldots, Y_n^1) \tag{11-16}$$

such that the functional

$$\phi = \int_{t_0}^{t_1} Z\left(t, Y_1, \ldots, Y_n, \frac{dY_1}{dt}, \ldots, \frac{dY_n}{dt}\right) dt \tag{11-17}$$

is an extremum (optimal time path) [15]. If (11-17) is rewritten as

$$\phi = \int_{t_0}^{t_1} Z(t, Y_1, \ldots, Y_n, X_1, \ldots, X_n)\, dt \tag{11-18}$$

the fundamental problem of the calculus of variations can be viewed as a special case of the standard dynamic problem in which the control functions X_j, $j = 1, \ldots, n$, are the time derivatives $dY_j/dt, j = 1, \ldots, n$. The problem becomes one of optimizing (11-18) subject to

$$\frac{dY_j}{dt} = X_j \qquad j = 1, \ldots, n \tag{11-19}$$

$$Y_i(t_0) = Y_j^0 \qquad j = 1, \ldots, n \tag{11-20}$$

$$Y_i(t_1) = Y_j^1 \qquad j = 1, \ldots, n \tag{11-21}$$

A necessary condition for an extremum is that the Y_j's satisfy the Euler equations

$$Z_{Y_j} - \frac{dZ_{\dot{Y}_j}}{dt} = 0 \qquad j = 1, \ldots, n \tag{11-22}$$

where

$$Z_{Y_j} = \frac{\partial Z}{\partial Y_j} \tag{11-23}$$

$$Z_{\dot{Y}_j} = \frac{\partial Z}{\partial \dot{Y}_j} \tag{11-24}$$

and

$$\dot{Y}_j = \frac{dY_j}{dt} \tag{11-25}$$

(For a complete treatment of the sufficiency conditions for an extremum, see Connors and Teichroew [15].)

In this section we shall concern ourselves with the problem of optimizing (11-17) subject to (11-19), (11-20), (11-21), and the additional m constraints

$$\psi_i\left[Y_1(t), \ldots, Y_n(t), \frac{dY_1}{dt}, \ldots, \frac{dY_n}{dt}\right] = 0 \qquad i = 1, \ldots, m \leq n \tag{11-26}$$

Introducing the shorthand notation $Z[t, Y(t), \dot{Y}(t)]$ and $\psi_i[Y(t), \dot{Y}(t)]$ for the values defined respectively by (11-17) and (11-26), we can express our constrained optimization in the equivalent form of optimizing

$$\phi^* = \int_{t_0}^{t_1} L[t, Y(t), \lambda(t), \dot{Y}(t)]\, dt \tag{11-27}$$

where

$$L = Z + \sum_{i=1}^{m} \lambda_i(t)\psi_i[Y(t), \dot{Y}(t)] \tag{11-28}$$

Note that the λ_i functions play a role which is analogous to the Lagrangian multiplier of classical optimization techniques. The functions $Y_1(t), \ldots, Y_n(t)$, which make ϕ an extremum subject to (11-26), satisfy the Euler equations for (11-27). The Euler equations yield $n + m$ simultaneous equations

$$L_{Y_j} - \frac{dL_{\dot{Y}_j}}{dt} = 0 \qquad j = 1, \ldots, n \tag{11-29}$$

$$L_{\lambda_i} \equiv \psi_i[Y(t), \dot{Y}(t)] = 0 \qquad i = 1, \ldots, m \tag{11-30}$$

These equations are sufficient to determine the extremals $Y_j(t)$, $j = 1, \ldots, n$, and $\lambda_i(t)$, $i = 1, \ldots, m$, provided that at least one of the determinants

$$\begin{vmatrix} \dfrac{\partial\psi_1}{\partial\dot{Y}_1} & \cdots & \dfrac{\partial\psi_1}{\partial\dot{Y}_m} \\ \vdots & \cdots & \vdots \\ \dfrac{\partial\psi_m}{\partial\dot{Y}_1} & \cdots & \dfrac{\partial\psi_m}{\partial\dot{Y}_m} \end{vmatrix} \neq 0 \tag{11-31}$$

for some m of the variables $\dot{Y}_j$, $j = 1, \ldots, n$.

To illustrate the applicability of the calculus of variations to the theory of the firm we have included an example model. Consider a firm which produces a product Z from two factors X_1 (a current input) and X_2 (a capital input).[1] The prices of X_1 and X_2 are C_1 and C_2 respectively. The firm's planning horizon is T years. We assume that the output requirements $Z(t)$ for the firm are a function of time and are known with complete certainty over the planning horizon. The firm is to choose the level of investment outlay X_2 to be made initially, and the rate of consumption of current input $X_1(t)$ at each instant over T. The production process is constrained by a production function of the form

$$Z(t) = f[X_1(t), X_2] \tag{11-32}$$

[1] This model was taken almost verbatim from pp. 283–286 of Vernon L. Smith, *Investment and Production* [38].

It is further assumed that no output can be produced without some positive amount of each input. The problem of the firm is to choose $X_1(t) \geq 0$ and $X_2 \geq 0$ so as to minimize

$$C = \int_0^T C_1 X_1(t)\, dt + C_2 X_2 \tag{11-33}$$

subject to (11-32). An equivalent problem is to minimize

$$C^* = \int_0^T (C_1 X_1(t) + \lambda\{Z(t) - f[X_1(t), X_2]\})\, dt + C_2 X_2 \tag{11-34}$$

with respect to the *extremal* $X_1(t)$ and the *scalar variable* X_2.

Note that (11-34) is simply a special case of the standard constrained optimization problem of the calculus of variations given by (11-27), where

$$L = C_1 X_1(t) + \lambda\{Z(t) - f[X_1(t), X_2]\} \tag{11-35}$$

We apply the Euler equation directly to (11-34) to minimize C^* with respect to the extremal $X_1(t)$

$$\frac{\partial L}{\partial X_1(t)} = C_1 - \lambda f_1 = 0 \tag{11-36}$$

where

$$f_1 = \frac{\partial f}{\partial X_1(t)}$$

Note that (11-36) was obtained by straightforward scalar differentiation, since L in (11-35) does not contain any time derivatives of $X_1(t)$. We apply the condition

$$\frac{\partial C^*}{\partial X_2} = 0 \tag{11-37}$$

in minimizing (11-34) with respect to the scalar X_2,

$$\frac{\partial C^*}{\partial X_2} = -\int_0^T \lambda f_2\, dt + C_2 = 0 \tag{11-38}$$

where $f_2 = \partial f / \partial X_2$. From the production function (11-32) and the necessary conditions for cost minimization (11-36) and (11-38) it is possible to determine (if they exist) the optimal consumption path of current input $X_1^\circ(t)$, the optimal level of investment X_2°, and the function

$$\lambda^\circ = \lambda[C_1, C_2, T, Z_0^T(t)] \tag{11-39}$$

By eliminating λ from (11-36) and (11-38) we get

$$-\int_0^T \frac{C_1 f_2}{f_1}\, dt + C_2 = 0 \tag{11-40}$$

The ratio f_2/f_1 is the amount by which the consumption of X_1 is decreased (increased) at time t if the initial installation of capital X_2 is increased (decreased) infinitesimally. The ratio $C_1 f_2/f_1$ is the rate of savings in the cost of the current input per unit increase in X_2. Therefore the integral of $C_1 f_2/f_1$ over the interval $0 \leq t \leq T$ is the total savings in current input cost per unit increase in capital investment. Equation (11-40) states that investment is expanded, given the time path of output requirements, until the total current input cost saved from the last increment of capital equals the cost of that increment of capital. By integrating (11-40) in combination with (11-32), we can determine $X_1^\circ(t)$ and X_2°. We can then solve (11-36) for λ°. The solution to our cost-minimization problem may, therefore, be expressed as

$$X_1^\circ(t) = X_1[C_1, C_2, T, Z_0^T(t)] \tag{11-41}$$

$$X_2^\circ = X_2[C_1, C_2, T, Z_0^T(t)] \tag{11-42}$$

$$\lambda^\circ = \lambda[C_1, C_2, T, Z_0^T(t)] \tag{11-43}$$

where λ is the instantaneous (or short-run) marginal operating cost function.

In addition to the book by Connors and Teichroew [15], a number of other good books on the calculus of variations are available including Akhiezer [1], Bliss [13], Elsgolc [16], Fox [19], Gelfand and Fomin [20], Hestenes [24], and Weinstock [43].

PONTRYAGIN'S MAXIMUM PRINCIPLE

Pontryagin's maximum principle [17,31,35] treats the standard dynamic problem, which was previously defined by Equations (11-1), (11-2), and (11-3). That is, we want to choose control functions $X_1(t), \ldots, X_n(t)$ which optimize

$$\phi = \int_{t_0}^{t_1} Z[Y_1(t), \ldots, Y_m(t), X_1(t), \ldots, X_n(t); t]\, dt \tag{11-44}$$

subject to

$$\frac{dY_i(t)}{dt} = f_i[Y_1(t), \ldots, Y_m(t), X_1(t), \ldots, X_n(t); t] \qquad i = 1, \ldots, m \tag{11-45}$$

$$Y_i(t_0) = Y_i^0 \qquad i = 1, 2, \ldots, m \tag{11-46}$$

We assume that Z and the f_i's are continuous in the variables $Y_1, \ldots, Y_m$, $X_1, \ldots, X_n$, and t and have continuous first-order partial derivatives with respect to $Y_1, \ldots, Y_m$.

Suppose that we define a *new* state variable Y_{m+1}, where

$$Y_{m+1} = \int_{t_0}^{t} Z[Y_1(t), \ldots, Y_m(t), X_1(t), \ldots, X_n(t); t]\, dt \tag{11-47}$$

$$Y_{m+1}(t_0) = 0 \qquad t_0 \leq t \leq t_1 \tag{11-48}$$

It follows that Y_{m+1} satisfies the differential equation

$$\frac{dY_{m+1}(t)}{dt} = Z[Y_1(t), \ldots, Y_m(t), X_1(t), \ldots, X_n(t); t] \qquad t_0 \le t \le t_1 \tag{11-49}$$

Our problem can therefore be transformed without loss in generality into one of optimizing

$$\phi = \sum_{i=1}^{m+1} C_i Y_i(t_1) \tag{11-50}$$

where $C_i = 0$ for $i = 1, \ldots, m$ and $C_{m+1} = 1$.

To solve the problem of finding the optimum control functions $X_1^\circ(t), \ldots, X_n^\circ(t)$ and the corresponding trajectory $Y_1^\circ(t), \ldots, Y_m^\circ(t)$, $t_0 \le t \le t_1$, we introduce m functions $W_1(t), \ldots, W_m(t)$ and a *Hamiltonian* function H which satisfy the conditions

$$H = \sum_{i=1}^{m} W_i f_i \tag{11-51}$$

$$\frac{dW_i}{dt} = \frac{-\partial H}{\partial Y_i} = -\sum_{j=1}^{m} W_j \frac{\partial f_j}{\partial Y_i} \qquad i = 1, \ldots, m \tag{11-52}$$

$$W_i(t_1) = C_i \qquad i = 1, \ldots, m \tag{11-53}$$

[To simplify the notation, the m used in (11-51), (11-52), and (11-53) includes the new variable defined by (11-48).]

The optimum control-vector function $X^\circ(t)$, which makes ϕ a maximum or a minimum, is the control-vector function which renders the Hamiltonian function H, (11-51), a maximum or a minimum for $t_0 \le t \le t_1$. A necessary condition for ϕ to be an extremum with respect to $X(t)$ is

$$\frac{\partial H}{\partial X_j} = 0 \qquad j = 1, \ldots, n \tag{11-54}$$

Once the control-vector function $X(t)$ is selected, the adjoint vector function $W(t)$ is uniquely determined by (11-52) and (11-53) and the initial conditions $Y_i(t_0) = Y_i^0$, $i = 1, \ldots, m$.[2]

To illustrate the applicability of Pontryagin's maximum principle to the theory of the firm, consider the following example model developed by Hwang, Fan, and Erickson [31].

Forecasting is used by a manufacturing firm to design production rules which anticipate and prepare for sales fluctuations. A buffer inventory is maintained so that errors in sales forecasts will not cause stockouts or will not

[2] The preceding two paragraphs are based on [31], p. 753.

force rapid changes in the rate of production. The rate of change in finished-goods inventories is equal to the difference between the production and sales rates:

(11-55) $$\frac{dI(t)}{dt} = P(t) - S(t)$$

where $I(t)$, $P(t)$, and $S(t)$ denote respectively the inventories, production, and sales at time t. We assume that for a given price, the sales function $S(t)$ is known with complete certainty over time.

The rate of cost for holding inventories and stockouts is given by the quadratic cost function $C_I(I(t) - I^*)^2$, and the rate at which production costs are incurred is given by $C_P(P(t) - P^*)^2$, where C_I and C_P are constants, and I^* and P^* denote the desired inventory level and production level respectively for the firm. Both I^* and P^* are assumed to be constants. The total cost incurred over a planning period of length T is given by

(11-56) $$C_T = \int_0^T \{C_I(I(t) - I^*)^2 + C_P(P(t) - P^*)^2\}\, dt$$

The problem is to find the production plan which will minimize (11-56) subject to the constraint imposed by (11-55).

To solve this problem let

(11-57) $$Y_1(t) = I(t)$$

(11-58) $$X(t) = P(t)$$

We can rewrite (11-57) as

(11-59) $$\frac{dY_1}{dt} = X(t) - S(t) \qquad Y_1(0) = Y_1^0$$

where $S(t)$ is a certain fixed function.

We introduce the new variable $Y_2(t)$ such that

(11-60) $$Y_2(t) = \int_0^t \{C_I(Y_1(t) - I^*)^2 + C_P(X(t) - P^*)^2\}\, dt$$

$$Y_2(0) = 0 \qquad 0 \le t \le T$$

It follows that $Y_2(t)$ satisfies the differential equation

(11-61) $$\frac{dY_2(t)}{dt} = C_I(Y_1 - I^*)^2 + C_P(X - P^*)^2 \qquad 0 \le t \le T$$

The problem is, therefore, transformed into one of minimizing

(11-62) $$\phi = C_1 Y_1(T) + C_2 Y_2(T)$$

where $C_1 = 0$ and $C_2 = 1$. Defining the Hamiltonian function H according to (11-51), (11-52), and (11-53), we obtain

(11-63) $$H(W_1, W_2, Y_1, Y_2, X) = W_1(X - S) + W_2[C_I(Y_1 - I^*)^2 + C_P(X - P^*)^2]$$

(11-64) $$\frac{dW_1}{dt} = \frac{-\partial H}{\partial Y_1} - 2W_2C_I(Y_1 - I^*) \qquad W_1(T) = 0$$

(11-65) $$\frac{dW_2}{dt} = \frac{-\partial H}{\partial Y_2} = 0 \qquad W_2(T) = 1$$

Solving (11-65) for W_2 yields

(11-66) $$W_2(t) = 1 \qquad 0 \leq t \leq T$$

Therefore the Hamiltonian can be written as

(11-67) $$H = W_1(X - S) + C_I(Y_1 - I^*)^2 + C_P(X - P^*)^2$$

Pontryagin's maximum principle states that (11-67) must be a minimum with respect to X. The values of Y_1, Y_2, W_1, and W_2 are considered as fixed. The optimum production plan may be obtained from (11-54) as

(11-68) $$\frac{\partial H}{\partial X} = W_1 + 2C_P(X - P^*) = 0$$

or

(11-69) $$W_1(t) = -2C_P(X(t) - P^*)$$

Combining (11-69) and (11-64) yields

(11-70) $$X(T) = P^*$$

and

(11-71) $$-2C_P\frac{dX}{dt} = -2C_I(Y_1 - I^*)$$

or

(11-72) $$C_I(Y_1(t) - I^*) - C_P\frac{dX}{dt} = 0$$

$$X(T) = P^*$$

Equations (11-72) and (11-59) are a pair of simultaneous differential equations in the two unknown functions Y_1 $(= I)$ and X $(= P)$.

The solutions to (11-72) and (11-59) are given by

(11-73) $$Y_1(t) = A_1e^{\lambda t} + A_2e^{-\lambda t} + \overline{Y}_1$$

(11-74) $$X(t) = A_1e^{\lambda t} - A_2\lambda e^{-\lambda t} + \frac{d\overline{Y}_1}{dt} + S(t)$$

where $\lambda^2 = C_I/C_P$.

A_1 and A_2 are constants which are determined by the initial conditions, and $\bar{Y}_1$ is the particular solution of the equation to be determined by the forms and/or values of functions I^*, P^*, and S. (Techniques for solving simultaneous differential equations are described in Allen [4].)

DYNAMIC PROGRAMMING

A goal of completeness dictates that we should at least mention another important approach to dynamic economic models—*dynamic programming*. Dynamic programming is a collection of mathematical techniques for solving certain types of sequential decision problems [30, p. 317]. Unlike systems analysis, calculus of variations, and Pontryagin's maximum principle, there does not exist a standard dynamic programming problem.

> Rather, dynamic programming is a general type of approach to problem solving, and the particular equations used must be developed to fit each individual situation. Therefore, a certain degree of ingenuity and insight into the general structure of dynamic programming problems is required to recognize when a problem can be solved by dynamic programming procedures, and how it can be done [26, p. 239].

Hillier and Lieberman [26, pp. 243–244] have summarized the basic features which characterize dynamic programming problems:

> 1. The problem can be divided up into stages, with a policy decision required at each stage.
> 2. Each stage has a number of states associated with it.
> 3. The effect of the policy decision at each stage is to transform the current state into a state associated with the next stage (possibly according to a probability distribution).
> 4. Given the current state, an optimal policy for the remaining stages is independent of the policy adopted in previous stages.
> 5. The solution procedure begins by finding the optimal policy for each state of the last stage.
> 6. A recursive relationship is available which identifies the optimal policy for each state with n stages remaining, given the optimal policy for each state with $(n - 1)$ stages remaining.
> 7. Using this recursive relationship, the solution procedure moves backward stage by stage—each time finding the optimal policy for each state of that stage—until it finds the optimal policy when starting at the initial stage [26, pp. 243–244].

A number of applications of dynamic programming to the solution of managerial decision problems have been proposed including optimum investment programs, production scheduling, equipment replacement problems, etc. Among the references available on dynamic programming are Bellman [6,9], Bellman and Dreyfus [11], Hadley [22], Howard [29,30], and Simon [37].

BIBLIOGRAPHY

[1] AKHIEZER, N. E. *The Calculus of Variations.* Watham, Mass.: Blaisdell Publishing Company, 1962.

[2] ALLEN, R. G. D. "The Engineer's Approach to Economic Models," *Economica,* **XXIII** (1955), 158–168.

[3] ALLEN, R. G. D. *Mathematical Analysis for Economists.* London: Macmillan and Co., 1956.

[4] ALLEN, R. G. D. *Mathematical Economics.* New York: Macmillan and Co., 1960.

[5] ATHANS, M., and P. L. FALB. *Optimal Control, An Introduction to the Theory and Its Applications.* New York: McGraw-Hill Book Co., 1966.

[6] BELLMAN, R. *Dynamic Programming.* Princeton, N. J.: Princeton University Press, 1957.

[7] BELLMAN, R. *Adaptive Control Processes.* Princeton: Princeton University Press, 1961.

[8] BELLMAN, R. *Mathematical Optimization Techniques.* Berkeley: University of California Press, 1963.

[9] BELLMAN, R. "Dynamic Programming and Mathematical Economics," The RAND Corp., RM-3539-PR, March, 1963.

[10] BELLMAN, R., and K. L. COOK. *Differential-Difference Equations.* New York: Academic Press, 1963.

[11] BELLMAN, R., and S. DREYFUS. *Applied Dynamic Programming.* Princeton, N. J.: Princeton University Press, 1962.

[12] BERKOVITZ, L. D. "A Survey of Certain Aspects of the Mathematics of Control Problems," The RAND Corp., RM-3309-PR, December, 1962.

[13] BLISS, G. A. *Lectures on the Calculus of Variations.* Chicago: University of Chicago Press, 1963.

[14] CODDINGTON, E. A., and N. LEVINSON. *Theory of Ordinary Differential Equations.* New York: McGraw-Hill Book Co., 1955.

[15] CONNORS, M. M., and DANIEL TEICHROEW. *Optimal Control of Dynamic Operations Research Models.* Scranton, Pa.: International Textbook Co., 1967.

[16] ELSGOLC, L. E. *Calculus of Variations.* Oxford: Pergamon Press, 1961.

[17] FAN, L. T. *The Continuous Maximum Principle—A Study of Complex Systems Optimization.* New York: John Wiley & Sons, 1966.

[18] FORRESTER, JAY W. *Industrial Dynamics.* New York: The M.I.T. Press and John Wiley & Sons, Inc., 1961.

[19] FOX, CHARLES. *An Introduction to the Calculus of Variations.* London: Oxford University Press, 1950.

[20] GELFAND, I. M., and S. V. FOMIN. *Calculus of Variations.* Englewood Cliffs, N. J.: Prentice-Hall, 1963.

[21] GOLDBERG, S. *Introduction to Difference Equations.* New York: John Wiley & Sons, 1958.

[22] HADLEY, G. *Nonlinear and Dynamic Programming.* Reading, Mass.: Addison-Wesley, 1964.

[23] HENDERSON, JAMES M., and RICHARD E. QUANDT. *Microeconomic Theory.* New York: McGraw-Hill Book Co., 1958.

[24] HESTENES, MAGNUS R. *Calculus of Variations and Optimal Control Theory.* New York: John Wiley & Sons, 1966.

[25] HICKS, J. R. *Value and Capital.* Oxford: Clarendon Press, 1939.

[26] HILLIER, F. S., and G. J. LIEBERMAN. *Introduction to Operations Research.* San Francisco: Holden-Day, 1967.

[27] HOLT, CHARLES C., FRANCO MODIGLIANI, and JOHN F. MUTH. "Derivation of a Linear Decision Rule for Production and Employment," *Management Science*, **II** (January, 1956), 159–177.

[28] HOLT, C., F. MODIGLIANI, and H. SIMON. *Planning Production, Inventories, and Work Force.* Englewood Cliffs, N. J.: Prentice-Hall, 1960.

[29] HOWARD, R. *Dynamic Programming and Markov Processes.* Cambridge: Technology Press, 1960.

[30] HOWARD, RONALD A. "Dynamic Programming," *Management Science*, **XII** (January, 1966), 317–348.

[31] HWANG, C. L., L. T. FAN, and L. E. ERICKSON. "Optimum Production Planning by the Maximum Principle," *Management Science*, **XIII** (May, 1967), 751–755.

[32] KAPLAN, WILFRED. *Ordinary Differential Equations.* Reading, Mass.: Addison-Wesley, 1964.

[33] KURZ, MORDECAI. "Optimal Paths of Capital Accumulation Under the Minimum Time Objective," *Econometrica*, **XXXIII** (January, 1965), 42–66.

[34] MURPHY, ROY E. *Adaptive Processes in Economic Systems.* New York: Academic Press, 1965.

[35] PONTRYAGIN, L. S., *et al. The Mathematical Theory of Optimal Processes.* New York: Interscience Publishers, 1962.

[36] SIMON, H. A. "On the Application of Servomechanism Theory in the Study of Production Control," *Econometrica*, **XX** (1952), 247–268.

[37] SIMON, H. A. "Dynamic Programming Under Uncertainty with a Quadratic Function," *Econometrica*, **XXIV** (1956), 74–81.

[38] SMITH, VERNON L. *Investment and Production.* Cambridge, Mass.: Harvard University Press, 1961.

[39] TEICHROEW, DANIEL. *An Introduction to Management Science Deterministic Models.* New York: John Wiley & Sons, 1964.

[40] THEIL, HENRI. *Optimal Decision Rules for Government and Industry.* Chicago: Rand McNally, 1964.

[41] TOU, J. T. *Modern Control Theory.* New York: McGraw-Hill Book Co., 1964.

[42] TUSTIN, A. *The Mechanism of Economic Systems.* New York: James H. Heineman, 1953.

[43] WEINSTOCK, ROBERT. *Calculus of Variations.* New York: McGraw-Hill Book Co., 1952.

[44] WILDE, D. *Optimum Seeking Methods.* Englewood Cliffs, N. J.: Prentice-Hall, 1964.

12

Models of the firm under risk and uncertainty*

RISK AND UNCERTAINTY DEFINED

All of the models of the firm described thus far in this book rest on the assumption that the firm's decision makers behave as though the firm's demand function, production function, and factor costs are all known with *complete certainty*. Cohen and Cyert [17] have proposed a useful way of classifying the general features of decision problems which will facilitate a comparison of the models described in this chapter with those models which have already been outlined in Chapters 1–11. Cohen and Cyert argue that whenever a decision maker is faced with a decision problem, the following elements are all present:

1. There is a set of two or more *possible behavior alternatives* which represents the range of different decisions which a decision maker can conceivably make.
2. There is a set of two or more *behavior alternatives that the decision maker actually considers*. These alternatives will generally be discovered as a result of overt search behavior by the decision maker. The search behavior may discover only a subset of the set of possible behavior alternatives specified in (1), although in some decision problems the set of behavior alternatives actually considered may coincide with the set of possible behavior alternatives.
3. There is a set of two or more possible future states of affairs which represent the *possible outcomes* which can conceivably result from the decision maker's actions in this situation. [These outcomes may exist objectively or they may exist subjectively in the mind of the decision maker.]
4. There is a *pay-off function* which represents the subjective value of the utility which the decision maker places upon each possible future state of

* The author of this chapter is Eugene T. Byrne, Jr.

affairs. This pay-off function defines a partial ordering on the set of possible future states of affairs. In some cases, the payoff function may be represented by a cardinal function, in other cases, by an ordinal function.

5. The decision maker possesses some degree of *information about which of the possible outcomes may actually occur* if he chooses any particular behavior alternative. This information may either be complete, in which case each of the decision maker's behavior alternatives will correspond to a unique outcome; or this information may be incomplete, in which case there is at least one behavior alternative to which there correspond two or more possible outcomes. When this information is incomplete, there may be *information as to the probability that a particular outcome will occur* if the decision maker selects a particular alternative [17, pp. 306–307].

In the models of the firm which have been presented in the preceding eleven chapters we have assumed that the firm's decision makers behave as though they possess complete information which relates a single outcome to each alternative course of action. That is, we have considered only the case where decisions are made under conditions of complete certainty.

In the absence of certainty, the decision maker no longer envisages a one-to-one relationship between alternative courses of action and outcomes [1]. Knight [42] has proposed that decision problems under conditions of *noncertainty* be classified as either decision making under *risk* or decision making under *uncertainty*. If the decision maker is able to calculate *objectively* the probability that a given outcome will be associated with a particular course of action then the decision making is said to take place under conditions of *objective risk*. If on the other hand the decision maker has no objective basis for calculating the probabilities associated with the various action-outcome combinations but still has some intuitive feeling as to the approximate magnitude of these probabilities, then decision making is said to take place under conditions of *subjective risk*. If the decision maker is unable to calculate (either objectively or subjectively) the probabilities associated with the different action-outcome combinations with which he is associated, then we have decision making under *uncertainty*.

PROBABILITY

As was indicated in the preceding section, whenever the future value of a variable is not known with certainty at least two possibilities exist. First, the exact values a variable can assume can be specified with certainty along with the proportions in which such values occur. This would be the case, for example, when a perfect die is tossed. Second, the lack of certainty with regard to the values and proportions for a variable may be recognized but completely unspecifiable. This could be the case for the values of some demographic variables a century from now. The latter case could be characterized as a state of complete ignorance.

If these two possibilities are regarded as the end points on a continuum of measurement, the problem of expressing the possible values of variables is clear. That is, a given situation may provide insufficient information about the underlying process to permit exact specification of future values (in contrast with the case of the perfect die), yet there may be enough information to permit estimation of such values. In other words, the situation is not one of complete ignorance. Where there is some information, the procedure used to estimate values need not, and in fact usually will not, be unique for all individuals.

The foregoing discussion suggests that there ought to be ways to express the possible values of variables in the absence of complete certainty. The objective of this section is to evaluate alternative means of expression and to select the means that provides maximum consistency within a framework of business decision making under less than perfect certainty. The evaluation concludes in favor of a means of expression that is not represented by either of the extremes mentioned in the beginning of this section.

When an individual is asked to provide information about the values a variable may assume at some point in the future, a number of responses are possible. The individual may state "I think it will be greater than x." Or he may state "there is a 50–50 chance that the value will be between x and y." Another possible statement is, "the variable will have an expected value of μ, a standard deviation of σ units, and will be normally distributed." A fourth statement might be, "I have no way of associating a value with the variable x." Each of these statements represents varying degrees of confidence about the future. Yet it is only the third kind of statement that provides a precise measure capable of incorporation into a mathematical framework for decision making. The general body of knowledge which gives mathematical rigor to statistical estimation is called *probability theory*.

Fortunately there is general agreement on the mathematical properties of probabilities. However, there is no general agreement on the definition of probability. Some see probability as a property of empirical phenomena [70], others see it as an extension of logic [40], while still others see it as the degree of confidence that an individual has in the truth of a particular proposition [72].

Thus we have the immediate task of evaluating the different definitions of probability. The general criterion for selecting a particular definition will be the extent to which it can contribute to the general problem of choosing among alternative courses of action for the firm.

We shall consider two alternative views of probability—the *objectivist* view and the *subjectivist* view.

The objectivist view

The objectivist view had its beginning with the *Ars Conjectandi* of Bernoulli, generally regarded as the founder of the classical school of mathematical probability [40].

If one seeks to find a clear-cut definition of objective probability by examining the works of the early writers, such as Bayes and Laplace, it becomes obvious that such works are quite vague. For example, it is not clear whether the early writers on this subject felt that probability concepts can be applied only to situations that approximate the results obtainable from idealized processes, such as coin tossing and the like, or whether judgment can be permitted to enter into probability concepts, such as situations where reference to an idealized process may not be possible. Despite its vagueness, there was rather general acceptance of the Principle of Indifference or Insufficient Reason, which states that events should be regarded as equally likely unless there are reasons to the contrary [69]. With this as a starting point, "Probability is the ratio of the number of favorable cases to the total number of equally likely cases" [86]. The requirement that the definition of probability be founded on the Principle of Insufficient Reason was rejected by later writers, notably von Mises [86], Knight [42], and Reichenbach [70]. These writers generally regarded probability as the relative frequency of some kind of event in a sequence of events that can be repeated without limit and which tends to a fixed limit [86]. Even so, it is difficult to find sufficient agreement among probability theorists to give a single definition of objective probability. However, Savage has given a statement of the objective position that is adequate for our purposes.

> Objectivist views hold that some repetitive events, such as tosses of a penny, prove to be in reasonably close agreement with the mathematical concept of independently repeated random events, all with the same probability. According to such views, evidence for the quality of agreement between the behavior of the repetitive event and the mathematical concept, and for the magnitude of the probability that applies (in case any does), is to be obtained by observation of some repetitions of the events, and from no other source whatsoever [72].

The basic features of objective probability are contained in this definition. These features and their implications for a theory of decision making will now be discussed.

First we notice that the objectivist position relies on the repetitiveness of events. Second, there is great reliance upon the ability of empirical systems to converge to the true probability. In other words, objectivists conclude that probability is an objective property of those physical systems that are capable of repetition. The decision-making implications should be clear. By relying upon a frequency definition the objectivist cannot allow single events to be defined probabilistically. For the objectivist there is no such thing as the probability that on a given toss of a coin there will be a head or a tail. The coin will either be a head or it will not. Certainly there are many situations in business and elsewhere that would find such a restriction undesirable [3].

The second feature of objective probability is the reliance upon convergence in empirical systems. Many writers feel that this is a particularly vexing requirement. One reason is that, as Fellner states,

> A person may watch drawings of odd and even, or of red and black, to the end of his days, and yet he will not observe the theoretical value of any frequency in the sense in which he observes that a number is odd or a color is red [30].

Even more strongly, Fellner considers it "objectionable to state without qualification that the convergence of some frequency ratio is observable" [30]. On this same point, Arrow, among others, has observed that this requirement effectively admits subjectivity into what has been set up as a wholly objective measure [3,30,72]. In other words, if there is a repetitive physical system, at what point does one conclude that there is correspondence between the system and some mathematical system? Clearly this point is not objectively determined.

A final point on the objectivist position concerns the role of a decision maker. It is generally agreed that objectivists require that all reasonable men be in agreement about the probability inherent in a given physical system. There is consequently no place for personal differences within the objectivist framework.

On the basis of the preceding discussion it seems reasonable to remove objective probability from serious consideration as a tool for use in decision making. Few if any business situations are clearly repetitive and there are certainly many business situations that are one (or few) of a kind. Finally, it seems fairly obvious that personal differences play a significant role in decision making [91]. Any theory that is set in a decision-making framework should not rule out the possibility that disagreement is possible even when the same information is available to reasonable men.

The foregoing criticisms of objective probability have been levied with a *single* criterion in mind. Namely, to what extent does the measure of noncertainty fit into a decision theoretic framework? The conclusion is that the objectivist measure fails to satisfy the criterion.[1]

Having eliminated the need for further consideration of decision making under objective risk in this book, we now turn our attention to decision making under subjective risk.

The subjectivist view

The subjectivist (or personalist) view of probability is of fairly recent origin. Despite some hints on the nonobjective character of probability that can be found among earlier writers, Laplace and Bayes for example, Ramsey [43], de Finetti [43], and Savage [72] are recognized for their conception and formalization of subjective probability. This view defines probability as a measure of the degree of confidence that a particular individual has in the truth of a particular proposition. Beginning with the proposition that there is a simple ordering among acts, Savage proves a number of theorems and introduces additional postulates to arrive at the theorem that a simple ordering as applied to events is a qualitative probability. Furthermore, Savage proves that this

[1] However, some objectivists would consider this form of attack to be improper. The purpose of any philosophical system is to predict. Given this objective, it is less clear that objective probability concepts are not useful. However, even at this level it is quite possible to raise the same objections, and some that have not been raised, to the objectivist position [30,72].

qualitative probability has a numerical equivalent that has the mathematical properties ordinarily attributed to probabilities.

At this point it is useful to make a few observations about subjective probability. These observations are intended to establish the superiority of subjective probability as the measure of noncertainty in a decision framework. At the same time, criticisms directed against the subjective position will be evaluated.

The definition of subjective probability makes it clear that personal differences among individuals are recognized and accepted. The theory does not require that all reasonable men agree. Thus even if it were possible to consider two individuals as having roughly the same experience and information, it is not a requirement that their probability estimates be the same [73]. The absence of this requirement does lend substantial support to the use of subjective probability as part of a framework for decision making under noncertainty.

The goal of subjective probability theory is also an important feature. Whereas the objectivist goal is largely predictive, the subjectivist goal is consistency in decision making. When an individual states his feelings about the states of nature, these can be transformed into numerical values that obey the laws of mathematical probability. These laws permit the description of complex events in terms of the simple event probabilities given by individuals. For example, assume an individual associates a subjective probability of 0.4 with the event "a head on a single toss of a coin." Using the laws of mathematical probability, the probability of "two heads in succession" is 0.16. Prior to these calculations, the individual may have associated a probability of 0.25 with this latter event, which would not be consistent with the probability he associated with the simple event "a head on a single toss of a coin." While the theory does not state exactly how to remove the observed inconsistency, it has been recognized. One possibility, in this case, is to hold the probability of the simple event and correct the probability of the complex event.

The translation of an individual's feelings about the states of nature has so far been discussed only generally. The procedure used to obtain the numerical values that are subjective probabilities will now be discussed.

On the grounds that there is often substantial difference between what an individual says he will do and what he actually does, subjective probabilities are to be obtained by behavioral interrogation [72]. That is, an individual is presented with a series of (probabilistic) alternatives among which he must make actual choices. This has also been the form of a number of experimental investigations into subjective probability. Savage's gamble method and Schlaifer's standard lottery method are prominent behavioral interrogation techniques. For present purposes it is sufficient to illustrate the Savage procedure [72].

Assume that the outcomes from a proposed advertising program can be usefully described by two, all-inclusive, terms: "effective" and "ineffective." To obtain the decision maker's subjective probabilities for these two outcomes we proceed as follows. Present the decision maker the *real-world gamble*: receive $0 if the advertising program turns out to be "ineffective" or receive $10 if the advertising program turns out to be "effective." At the same time present the decision maker the *hypothetical gamble*: a box is known to contain four red balls and six black balls. If a red ball is drawn from the box you will receive $0, if a black ball is drawn you will receive $10. The decision maker is then asked to select either the real-world gamble or the hypothetical gamble. If he selects the hypothetical gamble the proportion of red and black balls in the box is changed. Assume that it is changed to contain three red balls and seven black balls. If the decision maker now expresses indifference between the real-world gamble and the hypothetical gamble, his subjective probabilities for the two outcomes of the proposed advertising program are determined—namely, the subjective probability for the outcome "ineffective" is 0.3 and the subjective probability for the outcome "effective" is 0.7. Notice that it is not required that the set of outcomes be restricted to "ineffective" and "effective." Varying measures of effectiveness for the proposed program could have been employed.

This method of obtaining subjective probabilities emphasizes the probability of single events. The objectivist position cannot offer single-event probabilities. Considering that it is desirable to be able to measure an individual's feelings about the occurrence of an event, the subjectivist position is therefore preferred.

Notice that the information that a decision maker must possess is reduced when the subjectivist position is adopted. With this position, the information required is no more or less than the individual has at the moment that probabilities are to be obtained.[2] In contrast to this, if the objectivist position is to be used at all, a process must be repetitive. Furthermore, a number of observations are required before any probabilities can be assessed. Finally, if the certainty framework of previous chapters is considered, the perfect-certainty assumption requires information which is most often not available at the specific instance of business decision making. Few if any cases can be presented where information is perfect.

The technique outlined above for obtaining subjective probabilities has led to some question about the quality of subjective probabilities [72]. An individual may be much more confident about one subjective probability estimate than he is of another. Therefore it is suggested that second-order probabilities (i.e., probabilities on the probabilities) are appropriate. This suggestion can be treated in two ways. First, it is difficult to see the logical conclusion of such an argument. That is, if second-order probabilities are appropriate, why should not third,

[2] Of course there are instances in which additional information would change the subjective probabilities presently associated with the outcomes of noncertain proposals. Even in this case, the methods for evaluating the usefulness of additional information rely upon the information currently available to the decision maker. See Grayson [32].

fourth, etc., probabilities be considered? The intractability of the suggestion is apparent. Second, and in support of the first evaluation, the degree of confidence associated with subjective probabilities is to be found in the initial probabilities themselves. Thus if two individuals are considering the same proposal, a measure of confidence for the subjective probabilities could be the variance. For the individual with the greater confidence there would be a lesser value for the variance. In other words, the inference can be made that individuals do not suppress their feelings when they are being asked to make choices. Whatever confidence they may have regarding outcomes is completely contained in the derived probabilities.

Perhaps more significant is the suggestion by Fellner that individuals "slant" or reassess probabilities according to their ultimate disposition [25,29,30,68]. Thus an individual will give a different probability to an event if his immediate superior will use it, rather than if his ultimate superior will use it. Despite some interesting experimental support for this assertion, there is room for doubt that it destroys the probability view that has been discussed here. That is, the suggestion may be more appropriate to game theoretic concepts than it is to a subjective probability concept. It is also possible that while "slanting" may in fact occur, the consistency desideratum could eliminate its impact because "slanted" probabilities are not required to have the properties ordinarily attributed to probabilities. Yet it is also entirely feasible that a clever individual, upon considering the ultimate disposition of his subjective probabilities, could produce different subjective probabilities for the same events. This does not involve any real contradiction, since the basis for arriving at subjective probabilities is never at question. So long as the individual's choices conform to the mathematics of probability there is no concern about the basis for assigning these probabilities [30].

Summary

The purpose of this section has been to evaluate presently existing views on probability. The criterion used in the evaluation is to what extent does each view support a framework of business decision making under noncertainty.

On this basis then the subjectivist viewpoint is clearly superior to the objectivist view when consistency in decision making is desired. This position is supported by the fact that (1) business situations are not always characterized by repetitiveness of events and (2) it does not seem desirable to force agreement among reasonable individuals.

It should be emphasized that adopting the subjectivist viewpoint merely provides the basis for describing the noncertainty attending potential choices. In the remainder of this book whenever we refer to decision models under risk we shall always mean subjective rather than objective risk.

DECISION CRITERIA UNDER RISK

Given a decision problem under conditions of subjective risk, what criteria might the decision maker use in choosing among alternative courses of action? It is this question to which this section is addressed. We shall consider four different criteria for decision making under risk:

1. Risk discounting.
2. Expected value.
3. Certainty equivalents.
4. Utility theory.

Risk discounting

To illustrate the use of risk discounting, assume that the outcome from two alternatives is measured by net income = revenue − cost, where revenue is a random variable. Assuming that the mean of the revenue distribution is known, the decision maker will apply a correction factor to the mean prior to calculating net income. The magnitude and direction of the correction depend on some measure of the dispersion and the decision maker's attitude toward risk. Thus if a decision maker has a desire to avoid risk, the correction factor will be negative and will be larger the greater the degree of dispersion. For a decision maker with a preference for risk, the correction factor will be positive and will increase as dispersion increases. In either case a single value for revenue is obtained and the net income is calculated for both alternatives. The alternative with the maximum value for net income is chosen. This approach to decision making is known as *risk discounting.*

Although this example is admittedly simple, it does illustrate the fact that individuals may not act the same way when faced with identical conditions. Further, while this example uses net income as a decision criterion and revenue as the random variable, the approach is similar to that of other variables. When the decision criterion is stated in terms of a single value and there exist random variables that enter into the definition of the criterion, then risk discounting is often a useful procedure.

Unfortunately there are no established techniques for implementing risk discounting. A decision maker who is contemplating the use of risk discounting is not provided with guidelines as to whether his attitude is one of preference or aversion. It could be said that the decision maker gazes at a probability distribution for a random variable, and after a sufficient length of time the "correction" factor will appear, as if by magic. Even if an individual is certain that his attitude is one of risk aversion he is given no hint whatever on the magnitude of the correction factor. Finally, the individual is never completely certain from one decision to the next whether he is applying risk discounting in any consistent manner. One method of avoiding these many conflicts is to employ a criterion that exhibits risk neutrality. This criterion is called expected value optimization to which we now turn.

Expected value

The concept of expected value is best illustrated by reference to a simple example. To describe a chance prospect A, assume a random variable X can take on the discrete values 1, 2, 3, 4, 5, 6 with associated probabilities $p_1, p_2, \ldots, p_6$ such that

$$\sum_{i=1}^{6} p_i = 1 \tag{12-1}$$

If there are monetary payoffs associated with the values of the variable, that is, there are amounts $S_1, S_2, S_3, S_4, S_5, S_6$, then the expected value of the chance prospect is defined as

$$E_A = \sum_{i=1}^{6} p_i S_i \tag{12-2}$$

Suppose, for example, that we have

i	p_i	S_i
1	0.2	−1
2	0.2	0
3	0.2	+1
4	0.2	+2
5	0.1	+3
6	0.1	+4

then the expected value is

$$E_A = 0.2(-1) + 0.2(0) + 0.2(1) + 0.2(2) + 0.1(3) + 0.1(4) = 1.1 \tag{12-3}$$

In order to illustrate how the concept of expected value is used as a criterion, assume there is a second-chance prospect such that

$$E_B = \sum_{i=1}^{6} p_i S_i = 2.0 \tag{12-4}$$

Under the expected value-maximization criterion the prospect B is preferred to the prospect A. In fact B is preferred to A if

$$E_B > E_A \tag{12-5}$$

If a number of prospects are being considered then the prospect with the highest expected value is preferred above all others.

In general, for n proposals with expected values E_i, $i = 1, 2, \ldots, n$, the most preferred proposal has E_i a maximum and the least preferred has E_i a minimum. The expected value of a combination of projects has an expected value equal to the sum of the expected values of proposals in the combination. Considering any two combinations, the preferred combination has highest expected value.

Referring again to the calculation of the expected value of prospect A, it should be noticed that E_A does not correspond to any of the payoffs S_i. This is not unexpected, since the expectation is not defined in terms of any single outcome. In fact, the calculation of expected value and the use of expected value maximization as a decision criterion is based upon the application of the Law of Large Numbers[3] whereby the expected value is reduced to a quasi-certain value, in the long run.

Thus the criterion was designed for use in a repetitive environment, such as gambling or insurance. However, even in repetitive situations the criterion may not be defensible. This can be illustrated by a simple example. Assume an individual can choose between the *status quo* and a chance prospect that offers $S_1 = \$1{,}000$ with $p_1 = 0.5$ and $S_2 = -\$1{,}000$ with $p_2 = 0.5$. The chance prospect has the expected value

$$E_C = 0.5(1{,}000) + 0.5(-1{,}000) = 0 \qquad (12\text{-}6)$$

while we assume that the *status quo* has a mathematical expectation of zero. If expected value maximization is used as the decision criterion, an individual would be indifferent between these alternatives. Yet it is clear that the chance prospect offers the *possibility* of substantial losses or gains at the end of many trials. Because of this it is very unlikely that an individual would be indifferent between the chance prospect and the *status quo*. For a single trial involving the chance prospect there would be either a gain of \$1,000 or a loss of \$1,000. Again it is unlikely that an individual would be indifferent between the chance prospect and the *status quo*. Largely on these grounds it is suggested that ". . . the classification of chance prospects as a function of the mathematical expectation of corresponding gains. . . ." [57] should be rejected as a decision criterion when the circumstances surrounding a decision invalidate the Law of Large Numbers.

The use of expected value maximization is also criticized because the Law of Large Numbers requires successive trials to be independent, and this is rarely satisfied in a business environment.

However, it is the failure of the criterion to consider extreme values that evokes the greatest dissatisfaction. That is, there are chance prospects for which the expected value is theoretically infinite, yet no reasonable individual will accept the prospect over the outright receipt of any reasonable amount of money.

[3] The Law of Large Numbers states that if in n identical trials X occurs k times, and if n is very large, then k/n approaches the probability p of X.

The classic example of course is the discussion of a coin-tossing game by Bernoulli [9]. The game, now known as the St. Petersburg game, can be formulated as follows: if a fair coin is tossed until a head appears to end the game, and an individual is paid 2^{n-1} dollars if the head appears on the nth toss, how much would an individual pay for the privilege of playing the game? Clearly the expected value is

$$EV = \sum_{n=1}^{\infty} \left(\frac{1}{2}\right)^n 2^{n-1} = \frac{1}{2} \sum_{n=1}^{\infty} 1^{n-1} = \infty \tag{12-7}$$

Yet almost no reasonable individual would prefer EV if he could exchange it for the certain receipt of any large sum of money.

A number of solutions to the problem are possible. One solution is that individuals tend to regard very small probabilities as equivalent to zero. Thus in the St. Petersburg game, the probability of a head appearing on the nth toss, where n is very large, is $(\frac{1}{2})^n$. This probability is regarded as zero. Therefore the value of the game is finite.

Bernoulli, however, proposes a substitute to expected monetary gain. This substitute, called the expected utility or moral expectation, is based on the proposition that "... any increase in wealth, no matter how insignificant, will always result in an increase in utility which is inversely proportionate to the quantity of goods already possessed" [9]. Bernoulli also presents a suggestion by Cramer that "... the moral value of goods be directly proportionate to the square root of their mathematical quantities ..." [9]. In both cases, the value of the St. Petersburg game is reduced to approximately the same (small) amounts of money. Significantly, neither Bernoulli nor Cramer suggest actually measuring utility. Yet they are credited with the insight that led to the development of the modern theory of utility. This theory will be discussed shortly.

Our discussion so far has demonstrated that expected value maximization lacks many essential features as a criterion for decision making under risk.

Certainty equivalents

Continued discussion of the problems of decision making under risk has led many economists to postulate risk aversion as a behavioral assumption. The essence of the certainty equivalent approach is that it overcomes the assumption that preferences are linear in money. Assume a decision maker is confronted by a probability distribution of net income from a given proposal. Following Lutz and Lutz, the entrepreneur is assumed to desire a balance between the expected net income and some measure of dispersion. Let the mean of the probability distribution represent the expected value and the standard deviation represent the dispersion. Now, a decision maker is risk-averse if, for the same mean value, he prefers a smaller standard deviation to a larger one or if, for the same standard deviation, he prefers a larger mean value to a smaller one. Furthermore, "According to whether his *aversion* to risk is strong or weak, either he

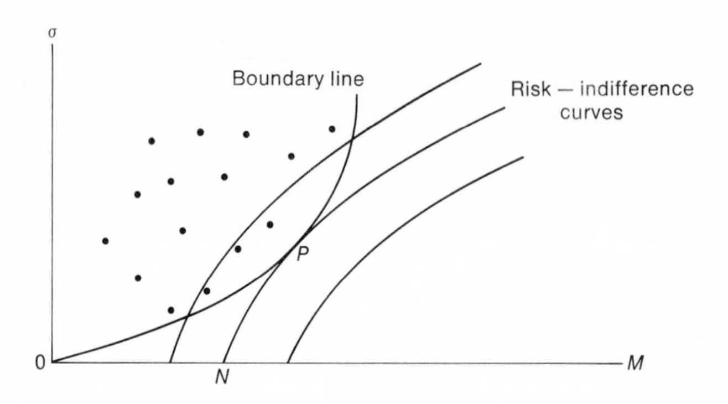

FIGURE 12-1

σ-M risk-indifference curves

may prefer a low mean (or modal) value combined with a smaller dispersion to a higher mean (or modal) value combined with a larger dispersion, or he may prefer the opposite" [47]. Based on these assumptions, we can present a set of mean (M) and standard deviation (σ) risk-indifference curves. Assuming that as the standard deviation increases a larger compensating increase in M is required, the risk-indifference curves would be concave to the M axis as in Figure 12-1. Figure 12-1 also reveals a *boundary line* or efficient set of proposals for decision based on the assumption that the decision maker is risk-averse. This is obtained by noting that the σ-M plane contains numerous points, each corresponding to a different proposal. Comparing any point between the boundary line and the vertical axis with any point on the boundary line reveals that points on the boundary line have maximum M for a given value of σ *and* minimum σ for a given value of M. Thus if there is any point not on a proposed boundary line which has a greater M for the given value of σ or a smaller σ for the same M, then this point becomes a point on the boundary.

In Figure 12-1 the proposal represented by point P is optimal. Point N, with $M = ON$, is the equivalent certain amount of this proposal, since $\sigma = 0$ at this point. Of course, a different set of risk-indifference curves will change the optimal point P and its equivalent.

A number of objections can be raised against the certainty equivalence approach or the manner in which it is used. The first objection, which is also the most destructive, concerns the exact manner in which a choice is made among proposals on the boundary line. The usual assumption regarding the attitude toward risk is that of risk aversion and a decreasing marginal rate of substitution of σ for M [44,75]. This implies concave risk-indifference curves and a boundary line as in Figure 12-1.

However much agreement there is on the shape of the curves no attempt is made to specify methods for deriving a set of σ-M risk-indifference curves for an individual. In effect, there is no way to choose among the proposals on the boundary line. The usual choice of risk aversion as the attitude toward risk is itself questionable and is one objection to the manner in which the certainty equivalent approach is most often used. There appears to be quite general agreement that decision makers commonly possess an attitude toward risk which can best be described as a combination of preference for and aversion to risk [31,56]. That is, for some ranges of outcomes, a decision maker may exhibit risk preference, while for others he may exhibit risk aversion.

Another objection that can be raised against the certainty equivalence approach is that users generally neglect the portfolio aspect of business decisions. That is, the approach generally considers the problem as the choice among single opportunities, whereas empiricism appears to suggest that the problem is to choose among portfolios, or combinations of opportunities. This aspect has received greater attention with respect to capital investment problems and is evidenced by the work of Markowitz, Sharpe, and others, discussed at greater length in Chapter 16. The main points of interest here are that (1) the usual assumption is that of risk-aversion, and (2) some relation between expected value and dispersion is employed to specify a decision-making function. Total risk aversion is a relatively strong assumption about a decision maker's attitude toward risk. This shortcoming can be overcome by considering the criterion of expected utility maximization.

Utility theory

In our discussion of the St. Petersburg paradox we noted that both Bernoulli and Cramer were able to resolve the problem by involving utility notions. However, the introspective nature of the Bernoulli-Cramer cardinal utility eventually resulted in the demise of cardinal utility. The work of Hicks and Allen [36] in developing the theory of ordinal utility apparently ended the controversy. Savage, working with the foundations provided by Ramsey [29], and von Neumann and Morgenstern [87], advanced and popularized the development in the early 1950's. Since the superiority of ordinal utility had apparently been demonstrated, the use of these seemingly latter-day versions of cardinal utility resulted in confusion among some economists [6]. The confusion was reduced and attacks by ordinalists generally diminished when it was realized that von Neumann-Morgenstern measurable utility was not a rebirth of the economist's concept of cardinal utility [78]. The latter concept considered utility as a psychic quantity that was measurable up to a positive linear transformation, if not actually, then in principle. The von Neumann-Morgenstern utility, also measurable up to a positive linear transformation, is not a psychic quantity and can only be used to determine choices (i.e., preferences) in situations defined probabilistically. The common property of the two utilities—uniqueness up to a positive linear transformation—is merely a mathematical fact for cardinal measures and cannot be used to conclude that the two concepts of utility are the same. If U is a cardinal index then

$$U^* = \rho U + \alpha, \qquad \rho > 0 \tag{12-8}$$

is a positive linear transformation of U. Given U there are an infinite number of indexes that will maintain the intensity of preferences. To illustrate that intensity of preferences is not changed under a positive linear transformation, assume that a decision maker's preferences for A, B, and C are defined, in ascending order, by the numbers 3, 5, 9 as presented below. First differences, denoted by $\Delta_1 U$, are also given:

	U	$\Delta_1 U$
A	3	
B	5	2
C	9	4

If the index U^* is constructed from

$$U^* = 2U + 1 \tag{12-9}$$

the new index numbers are 7, 11, and 19 for A, B, and C, respectively. These appear below along with their first differences, denoted by $\Delta_1 U^*$.

	U^*	$\Delta_1 U^*$
A	7	
B	11	4
C	19	8

As before, the first differences indicate that C is preferred to B by twice as much as B is preferred to A.

The fact that von Neumann-Morgenstern utility, as a measure, is not unlike other measures is made clear by reference to temperature scales. If a crucible of water is heated the temperature may register 203° on a Fahrenheit scale. However, assuming no heat loss, the temperature of the water would be 95° on a Centigrade scale. Thus the measure of the heat of the water depends on the scale that is used and is not a property of the water itself.

The significant difference between the two concepts of cardinal utility may be seen most readily by reference to an example. This example will also provide a second illustration of the procedure for obtaining a von Neumann-Morgenstern utility. (An earlier illustration appeared in Chapter 2.) Consider that the decision maker is confronted by the following chance prospect: he may receive \$0 with probability $\frac{1}{2}$ or \$20 with probability $\frac{1}{2}$; i.e., the outcomes depend on the toss of a fair coin. We arbitrarily assign zero utility to the gain of \$0 and one utile to the gain of \$20. The utility of the gamble then is $(\frac{1}{2})(0) + (\frac{1}{2})(1) = \frac{1}{2}$. Assume the decision maker states that he would be indifferent between the receipt of \$3 for certain and the outcome for the toss of the fair coin. Then his utility for \$3 is $\frac{1}{2}$, the same as the expected utility of the coin-toss alternative. In terms of a utility function, three points have been obtained, viz., \$0 with utility equal to zero, \$3 with utility equal to $\frac{1}{2}$, and \$20 with utility equal to one. This procedure of confronting the decision maker with simple chance prospects is repeated until the utility curve is specified between \$0 and \$20. By similar methods, the utility function may be extended.

Once a decision maker's utility function has been specified, it can be used to make decisions where alternatives are specified in terms of chance prospects. Thus for any decision maker whose preferences can be described by a von Neumann-Morgenstern utility, the choice among chance alternatives is made on the basis of expected utility. For example, if there are two prospects, A whose outcomes are $a_1, a_2, \ldots, a_n$ with associated probabilities $p_1, p_2, \ldots, p_n$ and B whose outcomes are $b_1, b_2, \ldots, b_n$ with associated probabilities $q_1, q_2, \ldots, q_n$, then A is chosen if

$$\text{(12-10)} \qquad U_A = \sum_{i=1}^{n} U_i p_i > U_B = \sum_{i=1}^{n} U_i q_i$$

where the U_i's are the utilities of the outcomes. This procedure of assigning utilities to outcomes and selecting among chance alternatives on the basis of maximum expected utility is termed the expected utility maxim.

It is particularly significant that the procedure for obtaining a von Neumann-Morgenstern utility does not require the decision maker to specify the utility of some amount of money, e.g., $3. All that is required is for the decision maker to specify the amount of money which, if received with certainty, would make him indifferent between that amount and the chance prospect. Thus the von Neumann-Morgenstern utility does not rely on any psychological quantity that a decision maker must produce by intuitive introspection.

Although it appears that the controversy surrounding the nature of von Neumann-Morgenstern utility has ended, the expected utility maxim has not been universally accepted. Fortunately, the expected utility maxim is usually presented as a consequence of a set of axioms of rational behavior. These axioms appear readily acceptable to many economists, and the most forceful objections to the maxim are found in observations on the behavior of seemingly rational individuals. Thus in relatively simple situations individuals have (apparently undeniably) failed to act in a manner which is consistent with the maxim.

The major line of defense against such examples rests with the matter of consistency. Raiffa [68], for example, points out that his initial choices, to an example presented by Ellsberg [25], were in conflict with the Savage axioms, but that he would have been willing to pay a premium to remove this inconsistency. Others have argued that observed inconsistencies of this type are the result of irrational behavior on the part of the decision maker. It is clear then that proponents of the expected utility maxim do not require that every decision maker will or must act in accordance with the maxim. What is suggested is that the axioms present a method whereby a decision maker can be provided with his own preferences and the method for allowing these preferences to determine choice. If the decision maker acts in violation of the maxim, he is not being consistent with his stated preferences.

If decision makers are at all times rational, i.e., if they wish to be consistent with their own preferences, and if they can always make coherent choices in

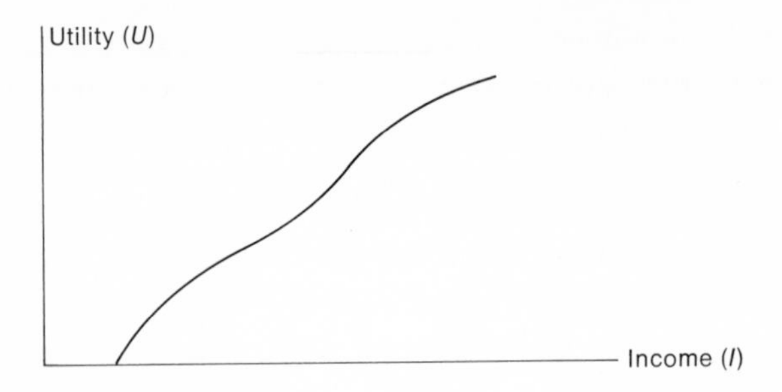

FIGURE 12-2

Friedman-Savage utility function

relatively uncomplicated situations, the expected utility maxim would be a descriptive and predictive system. Of course, this is not to be expected and innumerable situations can be hypothesized to refute any such claim. On the other hand, there appears to be a desire for consistency in the face of uncertainty when decision problems are taken seriously and properly understood.

The normative implications of the theory of utility having been established, we must now inquire into the possible properties of utility functions. The previous discussion of certainty equivalence models carried the implication that aversion to risk is the usual assumption. The initial hypothesis concerning the shape of the utility function was presented by Friedman and Savage [31].

Friedman and Savage require a utility function that will embody five essential behavioral features of individual (consumer) units:

1. Consumer units prefer large to small certain incomes.
2. Low-income consumer units buy, or are willing to buy, insurance.
3. Low-income consumer units buy, or are willing to buy, lottery tickets.
4. Many low-income consumer units buy, or are willing to buy, both insurance and lottery tickets.
5. Lotteries typically have more than one prize.

The authors consider the alternatives open to the consumer unit as capable of being expressed entirely in terms of money income so that total utility can be expressed as a function of money income alone.

If I represents the money income of a consumer unit per unit time and $U(I)$ the utility of that income, then the shape of the utility function shown in Figure 12-2 is consistent with all five behavioral features. For example, in order to rationalize statement (2), the utility functions of the consumer units may not be everywhere convex.

In a later article, Markowitz [56] accepts the Friedman-Savage hypothesis, as far as it goes, but is critical of the inability of the hypothesis to include consideration of other common phenomena. Markowitz also points out that

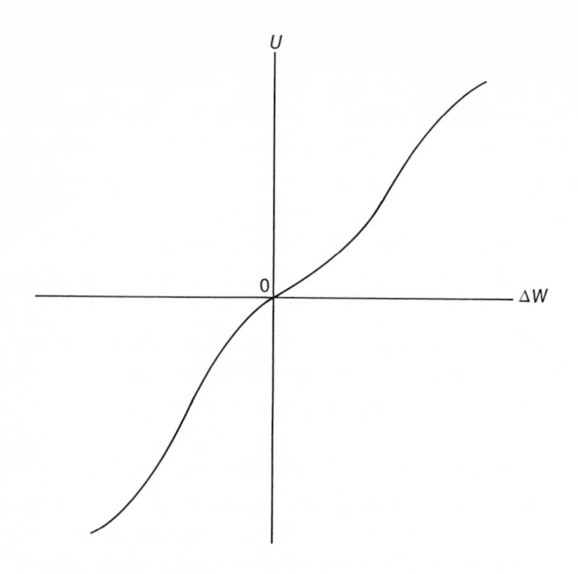

FIGURE **12-3**

Markowitz utility function

the Friedman-Savage hypothesis allows three points of behavior not generally observed:

1. Persons of middle income accepting large symmetrical bets (i.e., a 50–50 chance of a large loss or gain).
2. Moderately wealthy persons' willingness to risk large fractions of wealth at actuarially unfair odds (i.e., one whose expected gain, or loss, of wealth equals zero), and
3. Both poor and rich people consistently rejecting a fair bet [56].

Choosing to assume that income is discounted by some interest rate and to speak of the "utility of wealth," Markowitz presents the following utility function, shown as Figure 12-3, which incorporates the Friedman-Savage hypothesis and the objections raised to it.

The origin represents present wealth. Values of W to the right of the origin represent increments to current wealth, while values to the left represent decrements. Utility is positive above the origin and negative below.

There are several properties of the curve that must be noted. The utility function has three inflection points with the middle inflection point at the origin (present wealth). The distance between inflection points is a nondecreasing function of wealth. That is, the inflection points move away from the origin as wealth increases. The function is monotonically increasing but bounded (so as to avoid the St. Petersburg paradox). The function is first convex, then concave, then convex, and finally concave. Also, the utility function falls faster to the left of the origin than it rises to the right of the origin.

The implication of the Markowitz hypothesis is clear. Much of generally observed behavior is consistent with a utility function that exhibits, at the same time, risk aversion and risk preference. The inference is not to exclude a purely risk-averse or risk-seeking function. Indeed, for many decision makers acting in various business capacities, a purely risk-averse function is realistic [33].

At the same time, Grayson [32] and Weitzman [89] have produced utility functions that generally support the Markowitz hypothesis. Grayson's work is particularly relevant because some of the subjects were presented with conclusions about their attitudes toward risk based on the derived utility functions. The subjects generally agreed that the investigator's conclusions appeared to represent their preferences.

We do not suggest that it is a simple matter to derive utility functions for decision makers nor that every decision maker can be expected to cooperate fully in the matter. However, we do suggest that if decision makers desire to be consistent with their own preferences, they must be willing to devote time to the derivation of their specific utility functions. The importance of this suggestion lies in the fact that risk-indifference curves, shown in Figure 12-1, cannot be derived with known methods. Once the assumption of risk aversion is dropped and an attempt is made to define methods for measuring preferences, then risk aversion, risk seeking or some combinations of the two must also be admitted. Further, the discussion in this section indicated that it is realistic to assume that preferences are based on more than means and variances.

Summary

In this section various alternative decision criteria have been discussed. Consideration of expected value maximization, risk discounting, and selected certainty-equivalence criteria led to the conclusion that expected value maximization failed to specify decisions that were consistent with most behavior in the face of uncertainty. The risk-discounting and certainty-equivalence models incorporated somewhat more realistic behavioral assumptions; however, the final decision rules did not provide a unique decision. Investigation of the theory of utility or risk preference indicates that techniques exist for determining an individual's attitude toward risk. In addition, a desire to be consistent with one's preference will produce a decision rule that is unambiguous in the matter of choice.

DECISION CRITERIA UNDER UNCERTAINTY

Having considered the problem of decision making under risk, we now turn to the problem of decision making under uncertainty, i.e., where the probabilities associated with future outcomes are unknown. To illustrate the problem of decision making under uncertainty, consider a firm which is planning to embark

Alternatives \ Outcomes	O_1	O_2	O_3
A_1	\$12	−\$ 6	\$24
A_2	\$36	\$12	\$48
A_3	−\$ 3	\$60	\$30

FIGURE 12-4
A payoff matrix

on a major television advertising campaign. Three television networks are available for use by the firm in carrying out its television advertising campaign. These alternative networks are denoted by A_1, A_2, and A_3 respectively. Associated with each television network are three possible outcomes O_1, O_2, and O_3. These outcomes represent increments in total profit for the firm which result from the use of a particular television network for the advertising campaign. (Incremental profits are measured in millions of dollars.) The payoff matrix which the firm faces is given in Figure 12-4. Note that the payoff matrix consists of three rows, one for each alternative television network. There are also three columns, one for each possible outcome. The elements of the payoff matrix represent the increase in profit to the firm associated with every possible outcome which may occur as the result of using one of the three network alternatives. Which alternative (or alternatives) should the firm choose?

In this section we shall outline five possible criteria which the firm might use in making a decision of this type. These criteria include:

1. Bayes (Laplace).
2. Maximin.
3. Maximax.
4. Hurwicz.
5. Minimax regret.

Bayes (Laplace) criterion

The Bayes criterion states that, if we have absolutely no information about the probabilities associated with future outcomes, then we should assign equal probabilities to each of the possible outcomes and use these probabilities to compute the expected value of each alternative course of action. In our example, we would assign a probability of $\frac{1}{3}$ to each of the three outcomes O_1, O_2, and O_3. The expected profit for each alternative would be

$$E\pi_1 = \tfrac{1}{3}(12) + \tfrac{1}{3}(-6) + \tfrac{1}{3}(24) = \$10$$

$$E\pi_2 = \tfrac{1}{3}(36) + \tfrac{1}{3}(12) + \tfrac{1}{3}(48) = \$32$$

$$E\pi_3 = \tfrac{1}{3}(-3) + \tfrac{1}{3}(60) + \tfrac{1}{3}(30) = \$29$$

According to the Bayes criterion, the firm would select alternative 2. That is, it would choose television network 2 which provides an expected profit of $32.

The Bayes criterion does possess a number of obvious shortcomings. The most serious of these deficiencies is the fact that it is usually not clear in advance to the decision maker which unknown outcomes are equally probable. If in fact there are n possible outcomes and the decision maker is aware of only m of these, then his decision will be influenced considerably by the magnitude of m. Suppose there are 10 possible outcomes which may occur and the decision maker is aware of 5 of them. Applying Bayes' rule he would assign a probability of $\frac{1}{5}$ to each outcome. On the other hand, if the decision maker had known there were actually 10 outcomes, he would have assigned a probability of $\frac{1}{10}$ to each outcome.

The Bayes criterion is sometimes called "The Principle of Insufficient Reason."

> Because it is assumed that all possible states of nature are of equal probability, there is no likelihood that any one will actually occur. Thus, this principle is sometimes interpreted to mean that if there is no reason for one course of action rather than another to be taken, no action at all will occur. Because the lack of action in itself is a course of action (based on insufficient reason), this explanation hardly appears to be rational [49].

Since the Bayes criterion makes use of the expected-value concept, it also suffers from inadequacies associated with the expected-value approach. These deficiencies were pointed out earlier in this chapter.

Maximin criterion

The maximin criterion, which was first suggested by Wald, represents a very conservative approach to decision making. For each possible alternative the decision maker determines the worst possible outcome, that is, the one with the lowest payoff. He then selects that alternative whose minimum payoff is highest. In other words, the objective is to maximize one's minimum possible gains.

In our example the minimum possible payoffs associated with alternatives A_1, A_2, and A_3 are $-\$6$, $\$12$, and $-\$3$ respectively. The minimum profit of A_2 is larger than that of A_1 and A_3. Therefore, the maximin criterion would also call for the use of television network 2 by the firm for its television advertising campaign.

> In the present context the maximin strategy is somewhat less attractive than it is in a game situation, where the player has an active opponent whose interests are in direct conflict with his own. In such circumstances there can be good reason for fearing the worst. But where one's opponent is nature, who, at least in calmer moments, cannot be considered a systematic and calculating opponent, the maximin approach is rather clearly a manifestation of pure cowardice. This is not meant to imply that cowardice is necessarily irrational. On the contrary, there is much to be said for the Falstaffian position of self-preservation. There are persons

and situations where the maximin strategy is entirely appropriate, but it's well to recognize the criterion for what it is [7, p. 552].

More will be said about the maximin criterion when we discuss game theory models of the firm in Chapter 17.

Maximax criterion

Whereas the maximin criterion offers considerable appeal to the conservative decision maker, the maximax criterion is best suited for the proverbial "optimist" who looks only at the best possible outcome. This criterion can be illustrated by examining the behavior of someone who "plays the horses" and in placing his bet "to win" on a given horse looks only at the fact that his horse has won two races in the past while completely overlooking the fact that the horse did not win 73 of the 75 races in which he has run.

In our example problem (again referring to Figure 12-4) the decision maker using a maximax criterion would select alternative A_3, because it is possible to obtain a payoff of \$60 by choosing alternative A_3. The decision maker completely disregards the fact that he might also lose \$3 by selecting A_3. "The maximax criterion, which is a decision rule well suited to the temperament of a plunger, considers only the most glittering prize offered by any strategy and is blind to any other contingencies" [7, p. 553].

Hurwicz' criterion

Hurwicz has proposed a criterion which lies somewhere between the conservative extreme of the maximin criterion and the optimistic extreme of the maximax criterion. According to the Hurwicz criterion the decision maker should make use of a weighted average of the minimum and maximum payoffs of each alternative in making a decision. In our example, suppose that we assign a weight of $\alpha = \frac{1}{3}$ to the minimum payoff of each alternative and a weight of $1 - \alpha = \frac{2}{3}$ to the maximum payoff associated with each alternative. The three alternatives would be evaluated as follows:

$$A_1 = \tfrac{1}{3}(-6) + \tfrac{2}{3}(24) = \$14$$

$$A_2 = \tfrac{1}{3}(12) + \tfrac{2}{3}(48) = \$36$$

$$A_3 = \tfrac{1}{3}(-3) + \tfrac{2}{3}(60) = \$39$$

Applying the Hurwicz criterion, the firm would select alternative A_3. Of course, if the decision maker were somewhat more conservative and α were assigned a value of $\frac{2}{3}$ and $1 - \alpha$ were $\frac{1}{3}$, then A_2 would be chosen rather than A_3. Like the maximin and the maximax criteria, the Hurwicz criterion ignores information about the less extreme values of the payoffs associated with each strategy or alternative.

Outcomes / Alternatives	O_1	O_2	O_3
A_1	\$24	\$66*	\$24
A_2	\$ 0	\$48*	\$ 0
A_3	\$39*	\$ 0	\$18

FIGURE **12-5**

A regret matrix

Minimax regret criterion

The minimax regret criterion proposed by Savage focuses on the opportunity cost of an incorrect decision on the part of the decision maker. From the payoff matrix in Figure 12-4, we construct a new matrix in Figure 12-5 called a *regret matrix*. The elements in the regret matrix are computed in the following manner. The element in the ith row and the jth column of the regret matrix is the opportunity cost of choosing the ith alternative when the jth outcome is realized. For example, if the decision maker selects the first alternative A_1, and outcome O_1 actually occurs, then he forgoes \$24—the difference between the \$12 he actually receives and the \$36 he could have received if he had selected A_2. Note that the element in row 2 and column 1 is equal to \$0 because A_2 is the best alternative to have chosen, if outcome O_1 occurs. The other elements in the regret matrix are calculated in a similar manner.

The philosophy underlying this approach is the protection of the decision maker against excessive opportunity costs. To protect himself against excessive opportunity costs, the decision maker applies a *minimax* criterion to the regret matrix. The maximum possible loss in each row is denoted by an asterisk in Figure 12-5. That alternative whose row contains the smallest of the three maximum regret elements is chosen by the decision maker. In our example, A_3 will be chosen. A_3 is said to be a minimax strategy, since it minimizes the decision maker's maximum possible loss. Since the minimax regret criterion considers only the largest regret element in each row of Figure 12-5, it ignores a substantial amount of the data in the payoff matrix, not unlike the maximin, maximax, and Hurwicz criteria.

Other criteria

Two other criteria for decision making under uncertainty will be treated in Chapters 16 and 17. The Shackle criterion is discussed in Chapter 16. The mixed-strategy criterion is described in the chapter on game theory (Chapter 17).

MODELS OF THE FIRM INVOLVING RISK

A number of extensions of the economic theory of the firm have been proposed which introduce risk into the problem of the firm. We shall briefly outline two approaches to the theory of the firm under risk. First, we consider an extension of the neoclassical model. Second, we discuss linear programming models under risk. The degree of complexity of these two topics makes it impossible to treat them in detail within the confines of this textbook.

A monopolistic multiproduct model of the firm

Dhrymes has developed a monopolistic multiproduct model of the firm which is subject to a random demand component [23].

> The analytical framework is similar to that of portfolio selection and to some extent rests on modern utility theory. The objective is to study the response of the product mix of the firm to changes in the subjective disposition of the entrepreneur toward risk, to changes in the probability characteristics of the demand for the firm's products, and to changes in specific tax rates imposed on the various outputs of the firm [23].

Dhrymes found that the problem of optimization for his firm could be decomposed into two stages. In the first stage the firm decides on an optimum output mix on the basis of expected utility maximization. In the second stage, given this output mix, the firm decides on the optimum combination of inputs necessary to implement its production decision, on the basis of constrained cost minimization.

> While, essentially, the qualitative conclusions drawn from the latter aspect are quite similar to those obtained in the case of the uniproduct firm, it was found that the response of the multiproduct firm to changes in the state of uncertainty, both in terms of its attitude toward risk and changes in the parameters of the relevant distribution, is much more complex than in the case of the uniproduct firm. The same holds true of changes in specific tax rates applied to the firm's products.
>
> It is possible to obtain a special case which exactly duplicates the response of the uniproduct firm, but this is found only at the expense of very severe restrictions on the type of goods produced by the firm and on the cost and demand characteristics of its operation [23].

Linear programming under risk

The deterministic linear programming problem which was defined in Chapter 7 may be formulated as one of minimizing

(12-11) $$Z = \mathbf{c}'\mathbf{x}$$

subject to

(12-12) $$\mathbf{A}\mathbf{x} \geq \mathbf{b}$$

and

$$\mathbf{x} \geq 0 \tag{12-13}$$

where **c** and **x** are $n_1 \times 1$ vectors, **A** is an $m \times n_1$ matrix, **b** is an $m \times 1$ vector, and **0** is an $n_1 \times 1$ null vector.

The introduction of *risk* into the linear programming model implies that the coefficients of the model are no longer treated as though they were known with complete certainty. We now assume that at least some of the coefficients of **c**, **A**, and **b** are random variables, and that the probability distributions of these random variables are completely known. Indeed, this is a reasonable assumption on which to base a linear programming model of the firm, for it is unlikely that the firm's factor prices, product prices, input-output coefficients, and fixed factors will all remain fixed and known for long periods of time. What alternatives are available to us for extending the linear programming model to include the possibility of risk? We shall briefly consider three such alternatives—(1) stochastic objective functions, (2) two-stage problems, and (3) chance-constrained linear programming. Our discussion shall draw heavily on Madansky's excellent paper [53].

Stochastic objective function Suppose that risk is introduced only in the coefficients of the objective function (12-11). In this case, the optimum vector **x** lies in the convex set defined by (12-12) and (12-13), and the problem becomes one of finding a vector in this convex set which minimizes "an appropriate objective function for the risky situation" [53]. The appropriate objective function is obtained as follows:

> Consider the utility of each possible value of the objective function, that is, the utility of $\mathbf{c}'\mathbf{x}$ for each possible **c**. Then take the expected value of the utility for $\mathbf{c}'\mathbf{x}$ over the distribution of the random vector **c** as the objective function to be minimized. If the utility function is linear in the objective function, then the problem reduces to one of merely looking at the inner product of the expected value of **c** with **x**, and this now becomes a nonstochastic linear programming problem. But whatever the nature of the utility function, the problem has been converted to one which is nonstochastic [53, p. 103].

The solution to the nonstochastic problem may involve solving a complex nonlinear programming problem, since the nonstochastic program depends on the nature of the utility function which has been postulated.

Two-stage problem An alternative formulation of the linear programming problem under risk calls for the introduction of risk into the **A**-matrix or the **b**-vector in (12-12). A problem arises as to how to carry over the concept of "feasibility" to a linear programming problem whose **A** matrix and **b** vector are random variables. The *two-stage problem* represents one of several approaches which have been proposed to answer this question.

> The decision maker is supposed to choose a non-negative **x**, then observe a value of the random matrix **A** and the random vector **b**, and finally compare **Ax** with **b**. The vector **x** may or may not be feasible. But whether feasible or not, we are

> going to allow the decision maker after the fact to make another decision $\mathbf{y}$ to compensate for any discrepancies between $\mathbf{Ax}$ and $\mathbf{b}$, based on his original decision $\mathbf{x}$ and the later-observed $\mathbf{A}$ and $\mathbf{b}$, but at a penalty cost [53, p. 105].

To illustrate the two-stage problem, consider a firm which transforms n_1 factors of production denoted by the vector $\mathbf{x}$ into m products denoted by the vector $\mathbf{b}$ according to the linear transformation process $\mathbf{Ax} = \mathbf{b}$. The coefficients of $\mathbf{A}$ represent the quantity of factor j required to produce one unit of product i. At the beginning of the production period the firm decides to use some non-negative quantity of factors of production $\mathbf{x}$ to produce $\mathbf{b}$ units of the firm's m products. Total demand $\mathbf{b}$ is a random variable and is, therefore, unknown to the firm when it selects $\mathbf{x}$. $\mathbf{A}$ is a nonrandom matrix.

The vector $\mathbf{y}$ is the second-stage decision vector. The second-stage decision vector includes two different types of activities. If the quantity demanded $\mathbf{b}$ exceeds the amount produced $\mathbf{Ax}$, the firm must go into the open market and purchase commodities at a penalty cost in order to satisfy the excess demand. If the amount produced $\mathbf{Ax}$ exceeds the quantity demanded $\mathbf{b}$, then the firm will have to either store or scrap the excess inventory at a penalty cost.

The constraints for the two-stage problem are given by

$$\mathbf{Ax} + \mathbf{By} = \mathbf{b} \tag{12-14}$$

where $\mathbf{B}$ is an $m \times n_2$ matrix and $\mathbf{y}$ is an $n_2 \times 1$ vector. The vector $\mathbf{y}$ contains enough slack variables so that the inequality constraints (12-12) are equalities. $\mathbf{B}$ usually consists of elements which are zeros and plus or minus ones. Both $\mathbf{x}$ and $\mathbf{y}$ are non-negative.

To construct the objective function for the two-stage problem we let $\mathbf{f}$ denote the nonrandom penalty cost vector for $\mathbf{y}$. For given $\mathbf{A}$, $\mathbf{b}$, and $\mathbf{x}$, we must find the second-stage decision vector $\mathbf{y}$ which minimizes

$$G = \mathbf{f}'\mathbf{y} \tag{12-15}$$

subject to

$$\mathbf{By} = \mathbf{b} - \mathbf{Ax} \tag{12-16}$$

and

$$\mathbf{y} \geq \mathbf{0} \tag{12-17}$$

If we assume that the utility of the objective function is linear, the appropriate objective for the two-stage problem is to minimize $\mathbf{c}'\mathbf{x} + E \min_{\mathbf{y}} \mathbf{f}'\mathbf{y}$, where E is an expected utility operator.

Chance-constrained linear programming Chance-constrained linear programming refers to a modification of our original linear programming problem given by (12-11), (12-12), and (12-13), that specifies for each constraint a probability with which we want this constraint to be achieved [53, p. 106].

> The difference between the chance-constrained formulation and the [two-stage] formulation is that in the latter the specific contingency plans of the decision maker for each possible infeasibility are explicitly spelled out, as are the explicit costs for all the possible infeasibilities, whereas in the former these

explicit costs of the various types of infeasibility are reflected in the probabilities associated with each of the constraints. If a violation of a particular constraint is going to be costly, in the [two-stage] formulation one would have to think hard about what the actual costs of the specific contingency plan under infeasibility would be, whereas in the chance-constrained formulation one might say: If violation of this constraint is going to be very costly, I want to be 99% sure of satisfying this constraint [53, p. 106–107].

Solution techniques The reader who is interested in mathematical techniques for solving the aforementioned formulations of linear programming problems under risk should consult the papers by Charnes and Cooper [13,14], Dantzig [18,19,20,21], Elmaghraby [26], Evers [27], Kirby [41], Madansky [50,51,52,53], Tintner [82,83], Vajda [85], Wagner [88], and Wets [90]. The recent paper of Spivey [77] contains an excellent exposition of linear programming under risk.

BIBLIOGRAPHY

[1] ALCHIAN, A. A. "Uncertainty, Evolution, and Economic Theory," *Journal of Political Economy*, **LVIII** (June, 1950), 211–221.

[2] ANSOFF, H. I. "A Model for Diversification," *Management Science*, **IV** (July, 1958), 392–414.

[3] ARROW, KENNETH J. "Alternative Approaches to the Theory of Choice in Risk-Taking Situations," *Econometrica*, **XIX** (October, 1951), 404–420.

[4] BABBAR, M. M. "Distributions of Solutions of a Set of Linear Equations," *Journal of the American Statistical Association*, **L** (September, 1955), 854–864.

[5] BARON, DAVID P. "Price Uncertainty and Expected Profit Under Pure Competition," Unpublished paper, University of Indiana, September, 1967.

[6] BAUMOL, WILLIAM J. "The Neumann-Morgenstern Utility Index—An Ordinalist View," *Journal of Political Economy*, **LIX** (1951), 61–66.

[7] BAUMOL, W. J. *Economic Theory and Operations Analysis*. Englewood Cliffs, N. J.: Prentice-Hall, Inc., 1965.

[8] BELLMAN, RICHARD. *Dynamic Programming*. Princeton, N. J.: Princeton University Press, 1957.

[9] BERNOULLI, DANIEL. "Exposition of a New Theory on the Measurement of Risk," *Papers of the Imperial Academy of Sciences in Petersburg*, **V** (1738), 175–192 [trans. by Louise Sonner, *Econometrica*, **XXII** (January, 1954), 31–35].

[10] BOWMAN, EDWARD H., and ROBERT B. FETTER. *Analysis for Production Management*. Homewood, Ill.: Richard D. Irwin, 1961.

[11] BOWMAN, MARY JEAN. *Expectations, Uncertainty, and Business Behavior*. New York: Social Science Research Council, 1958.

[12] CARTER, C. F. "A Revised Theory of Expectations," *The Economic Journal*, **LXIII** (December, 1953).

[13] CHARNES, A., and W. W. COOPER. "Chance-Constrained Programming," *Management Science*, **VI** (1959), 73–79.

[14] CHARNES, A., W. W. COOPER, and G. H. SYMONDS. "Cost Horizons and Certainty Equivalents: An Approach to Stochastic Programming of Heating Oil," *Management Science*, **IV** (1958).

[15] CHERNOFF, HERMAN, and LINCOLN E. MOSES. *Elementary Decision Theory.* New York: John Wiley & Sons, 1959.

[16] CHURCHMAN, C. WEST, RUSSELL L. ACKOFF, and E. LEONARD ARNOFF. *Introduction to Operations Research.* New York: John Wiley & Sons, 1957.

[17] COHEN, KALMAN J., and RICHARD M. CYERT. *Theory of the Firm: Resource Allocation in a Market Economy.* Englewood Cliffs, N. J.: Prentice-Hall, Inc., 1965.

[18] DANTZIG, GEORGE B. "Linear Programming Under Uncertainty," *Management Science,* **I** (1955), 197–206.

[19] DANTZIG, G. B., and A. R. FERGUSON. "The Allocation of Aircraft to Routes—An Example of Linear Programming Under Uncertain Demand," *Management Science,* **III** (October, 1956), 45–73.

[20] DANTZIG, G. B., and A. MADANSKY. "On the Solution of Two-Stage Linear Programs Under Uncertainty," *Proceedings of the Fourth Berkeley Symposium on Mathematical Statistics and Probability.* Berkeley: University of California Press, 1961.

[21] DANTZIG, G. B., A. ORDEN, and P. WOLFE. "Notes on Linear Programming: Part 1—The Generalized Simplex Method for Minimizing a Linear Form Under Uncertainty Restraints," The RAND Corp., RM-1268, November 19, 1953.

[22] DEFINETTI, BRUNO. "Foresight: Its Logical Laws, Its Subjective Sources," in H. E. Kyburg and H. E. Smokler (Eds.), *Studies in Subjective Probability.* New York: John Wiley & Sons, 1964.

[23] DHRYMES, PHOEBUS J. "On the Theory of the Monopolistic Multiproduct Firm Under Uncertainty," *International Economic Review,* **V** (September, 1964), 239–257.

[24] EDGEWORTH, F. Y. "Probability," in *Encyclopedia Britannica* (11th ed.), Vol. **XXII**.

[25] ELLSBERG, DANIEL. "Risk, Ambiguity and the Savage Axioms," *Quarterly Journal of Economics,* **LXXV** (November, 1961), 643–669.

[26] ELMAGHRABY, S. E. "An Approach to Linear Programming Under Uncertainty," *Operations Research,* **VII** (March–April, 1959), 208–216.

[27] EVERS, WILLIAM H. "A New Model for Stochastic Linear Programming," *Management Science,* **XIII** (May, 1967), 680–693.

[28] FARRAR, DONALD E. *The Investment Decision Under Uncertainty.* Englewood Cliffs, N. J.: Prentice-Hall, 1962.

[29] FELLNER, WILLIAM. "Distortion of Subjective Probabilities as a Reaction to Uncertainty," *Quarterly Journal of Economics,* **LXXV** (November, 1961).

[30] FELLNER, WILLIAM. *Probability and Profit.* Homewood, Ill.: Richard D. Irwin, Inc., 1965.

[31] FRIEDMAN, MILTON, and L. J. SAVAGE. "The Utility Analysis of Choices Involving Risk," *Journal of Political Economy,* **LVI** (August, 1948), 279–304.

[32] GRAYSON, C. JACKSON. *Decisions Under Uncertainty.* Cambridge: Harvard University Press, 1960.

[33] GREEN, P. E. "Risk. Attitudes and Chemical Investment Decisions," *Chemical Engineering Progress,* **LIX** (January, 1963), 35–40.

[34] HART, A. G. "Risk, Uncertainty and the Unprofitability of Compounding Probabilities," *Studies in Mathematical Economics and Econometrics.* Chicago: University of Chicago Press, 1942.

[35] HESPOS, RICHARD F., and PAUL A. STRASSMAN. "Stochastic Decision Trees for the Analysis of Investment Decisions," *Management Science*, **XI** (August, 1965), 244–259.

[36] HICKS, J. R., and R. G. D. ALLEN. "A Reconsideration of the Theory of Value," *Economica* (February–May, 1934), 52–76 and 196–219.

[37] HYMANS, SAUL H. "The Price-Taker: Uncertainty, Utility, and the Supply Function," *International Economic Review*, **VII** (September, 1966), 346–356.

[38] JEFFREYS, HAROLD. *Theory of Probability*. Oxford: Clarendon Press, 1961.

[39] KATAOKA, S. "A Stochastic Programming Model," *Econometrica*, **XXXI** (January–April, 1963), 181–196.

[40] KEYNES, JOHN MAYNARD. *A Treatise on Probability*. London: Macmillan & Co., 1929.

[41] KIRBY, MICHAEL J. L. "The Current State of Chance-Constrained Programming," *System Research Memorandum*, No. 181, Evanston, Ill., Northwestern University, September, 1967.

[42] KNIGHT, F. H. *Risk, Uncertainty and Profit*. Boston: Houghton, Mifflin, 1921.

[43] KYBURG, HENRY E., JR., and HOWARD E. SMOKLER (Eds.). *Studies in Subjective Probability*. New York: John Wiley & Sons, 1964.

[44] LANGE, OSCAR. *Price Flexibility and Employment*. Bloomington, Ind.: Principia Press, 1952.

[45] LESOURNE, JACQUES. *Economic Analysis and Industrial Management*. Englewood Cliffs, N. J.: Prentice-Hall, 1963.

[46] LUCE, R. D., and H. RAIFFA. *Games and Decisions*. New York: John Wiley & Sons, 1957.

[47] LUTZ, FRIEDRICH, and VERA LUTZ. *Theory of Investment of the Firm*. Princeton, N. J.: Princeton University Press, 1951.

[48] MAGEE, JOHN F. "How to Use Decision Trees in Capital Investment," *Harvard Business Review*, **XLII** (September–October, 1964), 79–95.

[49] MCGUIRE, JOSEPH W. *Theories of Business Behavior*. Englewood Cliffs, N. J.: Prentice-Hall, Inc., 1964.

[50] MADANSKY, ALBERT. "Inequalities for Stochastic Linear Programming Problems," *Management Science*, **VI** (1960), 197–204.

[51] MADANSKY, A. "Methods for Solution of Linear Programs Under Uncertainty," *Operations Research*, **X** (July–August, 1962), 463–471.

[52] MADANSKY, A. "Dual Variables in Two-Stage Linear Programming Under Uncertainty," *Journal of Mathematical Analysis and Applications*, **VI** (February, 1963), 98–108.

[53] MADANSKY, A. "Linear Programming Under Uncertainty," in R. Graves and P. Wolfe (Eds.), *Recent Advances in Mathematical Programming*. New York: McGraw-Hill Book Co., 1963.

[54] MANNE, ALAN S. *Economic Analysis for Business Decisions*. New York: McGraw-Hill Book Co., 1961.

[55] MARGOLIS, JULIUS. "Sequential Decision Making in the Firm," *American Economic Review*, **L** (May, 1960), 526–533.

[56] MARKOWITZ, HARRY. "The Utility of Wealth," *The Journal of Political Economy*, **LX** (1952), 151–158.

[57] MASSE, PIERRE. *Optimal Investment Decision: Rules for Action and Criteria for Choice*. Englewood Cliffs, N. J.: Prentice-Hall, 1962.

[58] MARSCHAK, J. "Money and the Theory of Assets," *Econometrica*, **VI** (October, 1938), 311–325.

[59] MARSCHAK, J. "Rational Behavior, Uncertain Prospects and Measureable Utility," *Econometrica*, **XVIII** (April, 1950), 111–141.

[60] MILLS, EDWIN S. "Uncertainty and Price Theory," *Quarterly Journal of Economics*, **LXXIII** (February, 1959), 116–130.

[61] MOOD, A. M., and F. A. GRAYBILL. *Introduction to the Theory of Statistics.* New York: McGraw-Hill Book Co., 1963.

[62] MORRIS, WILLIAM T. "Diversification," *Management Science*, **IV** (July, 1958), 382–391.

[63] NELSON, RICHARD R. "Uncertainty, Prediction, and Competitive Equilibrium," *Quarterly Journal of Economics*, **LXXV** (February, 1961), 41–62.

[64] NEMHAUSER, GEORGE. *Introduction to Dynamic Programming*. New York: John Wiley & Sons, 1966.

[65] OI, WALTER Y. "The Desirability of Price Instability Under Pure Competition," *Econometrica*, **XXIX** (January, 1961), 58–64.

[66] PENNER, RUDOLPH. "Uncertainty and Short-Run Shifting of the Corporate Tax?" *Oxford Economic Papers*, **XIX** (March, 1967), 99–110.

[67] PRATT, JOHN W. "Risk Aversion in the Small and the Large," *Econometrica*, **XXXII** (January–April, 1964), 122–136.

[68] RAIFFA, HOWARD. "Risk, Ambiguity and the Savage Axioms: Comment," *Quarterly Journal of Economics*, **LXXV** (November, 1961).

[69] REICHENBACH, HANS. *The Theory of Probability*. Berkeley: University of California Press, 1949.

[70] REICHENBACH, H. *The Rise of Scientific Philosophy*. Berkeley: University of California Press, 1951.

[71] SAVAGE, L. J. "The Theory of Statistical Decision," *Journal of the American Statistical Association*, **XLVI** (1951), 55–67.

[72] SAVAGE, LEONARD J. *The Foundations of Statistics*. New York: John Wiley & Sons, 1954.

[73] SCHLAIFER, R. *Probability and Statistics for Business Decisions*. New York: McGraw-Hill Book Co., 1959.

[74] SENGUPTA, S. SANKAR. *Operations Research in Seller's Competition: A Stochastic Microtheory*. New York: John Wiley & Sons, 1967.

[75] SHARPE, W. F. "Capital Asset Prices: A Theory of Market Equilibrium," *Journal of Finance*, **XIX** (September, 1964), 425–442.

[76] SIMON, H. A. "A Behavioral Model of Rational Choice," *Quarterly Journal of Economics*, **LXIX** (February, 1955), 99–118.

[77] SPIVEY, W. ALLEN. "Decision Making and Probabilistic Programming," *Industrial Management Review*, **IX** (Winter, 1968), 57–67.

[78] STROTZ, ROBERT H. "Cardinal Utility," *American Economic Review*, **XLII** (1953), 384–397.

[79] SUMMERS, GEORGE W. *Financing and Initial Operations of New Firms*. Englewood Cliffs, N. J.: Prentice-Hall, 1962.

[80] THEIL, H. "A Note on Certainty Equivalence in Dynamic Planning," *Econometrica*, **XXV** (1957), 346–349.

[81] THOMPSON, G. L., W. W. COOPER, and ABRAHAM CHARNES. "Characterizations by Chance-Constrained Programming," in R. L. Graves and P. Wolfe

(Eds.), *Recent Advances in Mathematical Programming*. New York: McGraw-Hill Book Co., 1963.

[82] TINTNER, G. "A Note on Stochastic Linear Programming," *Econometrica*, **XXVIII** (April, 1960), 490–495.

[83] TINTNER, G. "Stochastic Linear Programming With Applications to Agricultural Economics," *Proceedings of the Second Symposium on Linear Programming*. Washington, D.C.: National Bureau of Standards, 1955.

[84] TISDELL, CLEM. "Uncertainty, Instability, Expected Profit," *Econometrica*, **XXXI** (January–April, 1963), 243–247.

[85] VAJDA, S. "Inequalities in Stochastic Linear Programming," *Bulletin of the International Statistical Institute*, **XXXVI** (1958), 357–363.

[86] VON MISES, RICHARD. *Probability, Statistics, and Truth*. New York: Macmillan, 1957.

[87] VON NEUMANN, JOHN, and OSKAR MORGENSTERN. *Theory of Games and Economic Behavior*. Princeton: Princeton University Press, 1940.

[88] WAGNER, H. "On the Distribution of Solutions in Linear Programming Problems," *Journal of the American Statistical Association*, **LIII** (1958), 161–163.

[89] WEITZMAN, MARTIN. "Utility Analysis and Group Behavior: An Empirical Study," *The Journal of Political Economy*, **LXXIII** (February, 1965), 18–26.

[90] WETS, REOGER. "Programming Under Uncertainty: The Complete Problem," Boeing Document DI-82-0379, Seattle, Washington: Boeing Scientific Research Laboratories, October, 1964.

[91] WILLIAMSON, OLIVER E. *The Economics of Discretionary Behavior: Managerial Objectives in a Theory of the Firm*. Englewood Cliffs, N. J.: Prentice-Hall, Inc., 1964.

PART 5

Computer simulation

13

The design of computer simulation experiments

COMPUTER SIMULATION DEFINED

The verb "to simulate" is a term which has come into vogue recently in a number of scientific disciplines to describe the ancient art of model building. Although simulation has been applied to some extremely diverse forms of model building, ranging from Renaissance paintings and sculpture to scale models of supersonic jet airliners and computer models of cognitive processes, it has come to mean something quite specific to both physical scientists and social scientists alike. The modern use of the word traces its origin to the work of von Neumann and Ulam in the late 1940's when they coined the term *Monte Carlo analysis* to apply to a numerical technique which they used to solve certain nuclear-shielding problems which were either too expensive for experimental solution or too complicated for analytical treatment. Monte Carlo analysis referred to the solution of nonprobabilistic mathematical problems by simulating a stochastic process which has moments or probability distributions satisfying the mathematical relations of the nonprobabilistic problem.

With the advent of the high-speed digital computer in the early 1950's simulation took on yet another meaning, for it had then become possible to experiment with mathematical models (describing some system of interest) on a computer. For the first time in history, social scientists found that it was possible to perform controlled, laboratory-like experiments in a manner similar to that employed by physicists, only using a computer rather than some physical process such as a nuclear reactor.

Unfortunately, there is no general consensus as to the exact meaning of "simulation." For those who prefer a strictly formal definition of simulation the one proposed by Churchman is *sine qua non.*

> "x simulates y" is true if and only if (a) x and y are formal systems, (b) y is taken to be the real system, (c) x is taken to be an approximation to the real system, and (d) the rules of validity in x are non-error-free [21].

We shall define simulation as a numerical technique for conducting experiments with certain types of mathematical and logical models describing the behavior of an economic system on a digital computer over extended periods of time. The principal difference between a simulation experiment and a "real world" experiment is that with simulation the experiment is conducted with a model of the economic system rather than with the actual economic system itself.

A RATIONALE FOR COMPUTER SIMULATION

In order to outline the rationale underlying the use of computer simulation as a vehicle of analysis for the theory of the firm, it is necessary to point out an obvious but very important similarity between marginal analysis, linear programming, and computer simulation as applied to the theory of the firm. In general, the principal motivation for using any one of these three analytical tools (with regard to the theory of the firm) is the pursuit of scientific knowledge about the behavior of the firm. When applied to economics the scientific method takes the form of the following well-known four-stage procedure: (1) observation of the economic system; (2) formulation of a mathematical model which attempts to explain the observations of the system; (3) prediction of the behavior of the system on the basis of the model by using mathematical or logical deduction, that is, by obtaining solutions to the model; and (4) performance of experiments to test the validity of the model.

For the most part the emphasis of both marginal analysis and linear programming models of the firm has been oriented toward the second and third stages of the scientific method. That is, with each of these analytical approaches a mathematical model of the firm is formulated and an optimum solution to the problem of the firm is derived by some mathematical technique. With marginal analysis and linear programming, major emphasis is placed on the deductive rather than inductive processes of the scientific method.

However, the orientation of computer simulation is somewhat different from marginal analysis and linear programming. The methodological position taken by computer simulation is that when one is dealing with economic systems it is sometimes simply not plausible to carry out one or more of the four steps of the scientific method. Although this position is similar to the methodological position in economics, which asserts that "It is impossible to conduct planned experiments in economics," it is not exactly the same. The position of those who advocate the use of computer simulation as a mode of analysis is that some form of simulation may prove to be an acceptable substitute for the step (or steps) in the scientific method which is causing the difficulty. That is, computer simulation may permit the possibility of conducting a type of pseudoexperiment on an economic system.

Looking first at the observation stage of the scientific method, we find frequently in economics that it is either impossible or extremely costly to observe the actual behavior of an economic system. For example, certain historical data such as sales data, cost data, and production data may simply not exist for a particular business firm. Or data on wages, investment, population, and productivity may be virtually nonexistent in an underdeveloped country. However, in both of these cases we may have sufficient information to formulate "meaningful" hypotheses about the probability distributions of some of these variables over time or estimates of their trends over time. We may then use an electronic computer to generate data (pseudo-observations) for the economic system of interest on the basis of the assumed probability distributions or time trends. The pseudo-observations may in turn be used by the analyst in formulating, manipulating, and testing models describing the behavior of the system as a whole. That is, we merely substitute the computer-generated data for the missing actual observations of the economic system. In many cases these simulated data may prove to be completely adequate, particularly if the model of the economic system under study is sensitive only to large changes in the values of the simulated input data.

To be sure, in the second step of the scientific method we would want to avoid completely formulating mathematical models describing the behavior of a complex economic system such as a firm, based entirely on simulated data. However, we may be willing to place considerable confidence in models of the firm formulated with the aid of data collected from empirical observations which have been supplemented by simulated data (in the case of missing data), provided the model has been subjected to extensive statistical testing in the fourth step of the scientific method.

It is the third step of this method that has provided most of the impetus for using computer simulation as a tool of analysis in economics. Even though a mathematical model can be formulated to describe a dynamic economic system operating under conditions of uncertainty, it may not be possible to obtain a solution to the model by standard analytical techniques such as the Lagrangian multiplier method or the simplex method, and in turn make predictions about the behavior of the system. Most of the problems in economics are of such a complex nature that solution techniques do not exist for solving them, or if they do exist, they may very well exceed the capabilities of our present-day electronic computers. Models used in the development of theories of the business cycle and market behavior both give rise to difficulties of this type. Since the 1930's economists have relied on solutions to differential and difference equations as the standard analytical techniques for investigating the behavior of business cycles and competitive markets. But as nonlinearities, higher-order equations, and stochastic variates are introduced into these models, solutions by straightforward analytical techniques become increasingly difficult, if not impossible. Although it may be conceptually possible to formulate a mathematical model describing the behavior of a dynamic, multiprocess firm operating under uncertainty, present-day mathematical techniques are simply incapable of yielding solutions to a problem of this magnitude. Under these circumstances economists have almost been forced to turn to numerical analysis or computer simulation as an alternative mode of analysis.

> Computer models . . . can be made as complex and realistic as our theories permit, for analytical solutions to these models are unnecessary. No matter how complicated the formulation of the model, simulation techniques enable us to trace out the consequences of the model. Hence, economic theories can be cast into a precise model without distortion of the meaning embodied in the theories, and the description of the world implied by these theories can be determined [26, p. 82].

Finally, it may be either impossible or very costly to perform experiments to test the validity of mathematical models describing the behavior of an economic system. Obviously this problem is merely a mirror image of the first problem which we discussed regarding the implementation of the scientific method. In both cases there exists a problem of insufficient data. In the first case, data available for the purpose of formulating hypotheses about the system were insufficient. However, in the fourth step of the scientific method the problem lies in obtaining numerical data to verify the mathematical model and its solution. In fact, the only difference between these two problems is in the use to which the simulated data are to be put. For example, in the first case we may be interested in simulating next year's sales data to facilitate the *formulation of a mathematical model* describing the behavior of a firm which uses sales data as one of its inputs. However, in the fourth case we may be interested in simulating next year's sales data for an entirely different reason. That is, simulated data may be used to *test* alternative *hypotheses* concerning the operation of the firm during the forthcoming year. Such hypotheses are usually called *decision rules*. In other words, simulation provides us with a tool for tracing out the effects of alternative decision rules on the behavior of the firm within the confines of a tightly controlled laboratory experiment. To be sure, it may be argued that we can do the same thing with marginal analysis and mathematical programming, but with computer simulation we can experiment with more variables, more decision rules, more complex models, and models which more nearly approximate the actual behavior of business firms; and we can do all of these things with speeds which were heretofore unattainable.

METHODOLOGY

Having defined computer simulation and indicated some of the reasons why we might choose to use this analytical tool in attacking the economic theory of the firm, we now turn to a brief summary of the methodology of computer simulation.[1] Computer simulation experiments with models of economic systems usually involve a procedure consisting of the following six steps.

1. Formulation of the problem.
2. Formulation of a mathematical model.
3. Formulation of a computer program.
4. Validation.
5. Experimental design.
6. Data analysis.

We now turn to a description of each of these six steps.

Formulation of the problem

Not unlike other forms of scientific inquiry, computer simulation experiments should begin with the formulation of a problem or an explicit statement of the objectives of the experiment, since there is little benefit to be derived from experiments that involve simulation for the sake of simulation. These objectives usually take the form of (1) questions to be answered, (2) hypotheses to be tested, and (3) effects to be estimated.

If the objective of a simulation experiment (with a model of a firm) is to obtain answers to one or more specific questions, then obviously we must attempt to specify these questions with a high degree of detail at the outset of the experiment. Among the questions or decision problems which might be solved by computer simulation are the following: Should the firm embark on a particular advertising campaign? Which of two new products will be more profitable? What effect will a downturn in the economy have on the firm's sales? Will a change in federal import quotas adversely affect the profits of the firm? Needless to say, it is not sufficient just to specify the questions that are to be answered by a simulation experiment, but we must also specify objective criteria for evaluating possible answers to these questions. For example, we must define exactly what we mean by an "optimum" production or marketing strategy if we expect to recognize such a strategy when we are confronted with it. Unless we specify precisely what is meant by a "suitable" answer to a question that has been raised, we cannot hope to achieve meaningful results from computer simulation experiments.

On the other hand, the objective of our simulation experiment may be to test one or more hypotheses about the behavior of a given firm. Is total profit more sensitive to changes in the firm's product mix or organization structure? Is there any significant difference in the effects of five alternative advertising policies on profit? In the example model which appears in the following chapter, we test the hypothesis that five alternative managerial policies have equal effects on the firm's profitability. In each case, the hypotheses to be tested as well as the criteria for "accepting" or "rejecting" them must be stated explicitly.

[1] For a comprehensive treatment of the methodology of computer simulation see Thomas H. Naylor *et al.*, *Computer Simulation Techniques*, John Wiley & Sons, New York, 1966.

Finally, our objective may be to estimate the effects of certain changes in the values of managerial decision variables on the endogenous or dependent variables describing the behavior of the firm. For example, we may wish to experiment with different factor-input quantities and estimate the expected profit associated with alternative factor-input patterns. Generally speaking, we would want to construct confidence intervals for parameter estimates of endogenous variables generated by simulation experiments, where these output variables represent the results of the use of alternative managerial policies or decision rules.

Formulation of a mathematical model

Having formulated our experimental objectives, the next step in the design of a simulation experiment is the formulation of a mathematical model relating the endogenous variables of the firm to the controllable policy variables and the exogenous variables of the firm. The exogenous variables are assumed to be determined by forces outside the control of the firm's decision makers. Some of the exogenous variables may be random variables, others may be expressed in the form of time trends. As we shall soon observe, the inclusion of random or stochastic variables in a computer model gives rise to a number of unique methodological problems which do not exist with marginal analysis and mathematical programming models.

One of the first considerations that enter into the formulation of a mathematical model of a firm is the choice of variables to be included in the model. As a general rule we encounter little or no difficulty with regard to the endogenous variables of a model of the firm because these variables are usually determined at the outset of the experiment when we formulate the objectives of the study. Most of the models described in this book contain a single endogenous variable—utility, cost, or profit. However, in Chapter 1 we indicated that our decision to concentrate on models of the firm with a single output variable was a matter of convenience, and did not imply that we believe that managers of business firms look only at a single output variable in making decisions for the firm. With marginal analysis and mathematical programming, it is necessary to reduce the problem of the firm to the optimization of a single endogenous variable such as utility, cost, or profit. With simulation we can investigate the response of a number of different endogenous variables including profit, cost, utility, production, sales, inventory levels, and market share. However, the real difficulty arises in the choice of the input (exogenous and policy) variables affecting the output variables. Too few input variables may lead to invalid models, whereas too many exogenous and policy variables may render computer simulation impossible because of insufficient computer memory or make computational programs unnecessarily complicated.

A second major consideration in the formulation of mathematical models is the complexity of the model. On the one hand it can be argued that firms are indeed quite complicated and that mathematical models which claim to describe the behavior of a firm must necessarily also be complicated. To a certain extent this is true, but on the other hand we would not want to go to the extreme of constructing complex models that require an unreasonable amount of computation time, regardless of how realistic they may be. In general we are interested in formulating mathematical models that yield reasonably accurate descriptions or predictions about the behavior of a firm, while minimizing computational and programming time. The complete interdependence of these characteristics of mathematical models cannot be overemphasized. For example, the number of variables in a model and its complexity are directly related to programming time, computation time, and validity. By altering any one of the characteristics of a model we in turn alter all of the other characteristics.

Computer programming time represents a third area of consideration in formulating mathematical models for computer simulation. The amount of time required to write a computer program for generating the time paths for the endogenous variables of a particular mathematical model depends in part on the number of variables used in the model and the complexity of the model. If some of the variables utilized in the model are stochastic in nature, then both programming time and computation time are likely to be increased significantly. The amount of effort expended in attempting to reduce programming time must of course be balanced against the questions of validity and computational speed. If the costs in terms of realism are not too great, it may even pay the analyst to formulate his model in such a manner that it satisfies the requirements of one of the simulation languages such as SIMSCRIPT [74], GPSS [49], DYNAMO [87], or SIMULATE [58]. The gains made in terms of reduced programming time may completely offset the loss in validity, which may result from such a modification.

The fourth area of interest in model building is the validity of the model or the amount of "realism" built into it. That is, does the model adequately describe the behavior of the firm in future time periods? Unless the answer to this question is "yes," the value of our model is reduced considerably, and our simulation experiment becomes merely an exercise in deductive logic.

The fifth and final consideration in formulating a computer-simulation model is its compatibility with the type of experiments that are going to be carried out with it. Since our primary objective in formulating mathematical models is to enable us to conduct simulation experiments, some thought must be given to the particular type of experimental design features that must be built into our models.

Having formulated a mathematical model describing the behavior of a firm, we must estimate the values of the statistical significance of these estimates.[2]

[2] The estimation of the parameters of economic models properly falls within the domain of the discipline of econometrics and is beyond the scope of this book. The books by Johnston [64] and Malinvaud [73] contain excellent treatments of the theory and techniques of econometrics.

Once we have formulated a model describing the behavior of a firm and have estimated its parameters on the basis of observations taken from the real world, we must make an initial value judgment concerning the adequacy of our model. That is, we must test the model. Clearly there is very little to be gained by using an inadequate model to carry out simulation experiments on a computer, because we would merely be "simulating our own ignorance."

Among the questions that we may wish to raise at this point in our procedure are the following ones.

1. Have we included any variables which are not pertinent in the sense that they contribute little to our ability to predict the behavior of the endogenous variables of the firm?
2. Have we failed to include one or more exogenous variables that are likely to affect the behavior of the endogenous variables in our system?
3. Have we inaccurately formulated one or more of the functional relationships between the firm's output and input variables?
4. Have the estimates of the parameters of the model been made properly?
5. Are the estimates of the parameters in our model statistically significant?
6. On the basis of hand calculations (since we have not yet formulated a computer program) how do the theoretical values of the endogenous variables of our model compare with historical or actual values of the endogenous variables?

If, and only if, we can answer all six of these questions satisfactorily should we proceed to step 3 and the formulation of a computer program. Otherwise we should repeat steps 1 and 2 until we obtain satisfactory answers to the aforementioned questions.

Formulation of a computer program

The formulation of a computer program for the purpose of conducting simulation experiments with a model of the firm requires that special consideration be given to three activities: (1) computer program; (2) data input and starting conditions; and (3) data generation.

Computer program The first step in writing a computer simulation program involves formulating a flow chart outlining the logical sequence of events to be carried out by the computer in generating the time paths of the endogenous variables of the model. The importance of flow charting in writing computer programs cannot be overemphasized. Next we must consider the matter of writing the actual computer code that will be used to run our experiments. In general, there are two alternatives available to us. We can either write our program in a general-purpose language such as FORTRAN, ALGOL, or PL/I, or we can use one of the new special-purpose simulation languages such as GPSS [49], SIMSCRIPT [74], DYNAMO [87], or SIMULATE [58]. The principal advantage of using a special-purpose simulation language is that they require less programming time than general-purpose compilers. These languages have been written to facilitate the programming of certain types of systems. For example, SIMULATE was designed primarily for simulating large-scale economic systems that have been formulated as econometric models consisting of large sets of equations. On the other hand, GPSS and SIMSCRIPT are particularly well suited for scheduling and waiting-line problems. Although we can reduce programming time by using a simulation language, we must usually pay a price for this benefit in terms of reduced flexibility in models and increased computer running times. Another important advantage of special-purpose simulation languages is that they usually provide error-checking techniques that are far superior to those provided by FORTRAN, ALGOL, etc. One final consideration in the development of a computer program for a simulation experiment is what kind of output reports are needed to provide the required information about the behavior of the simulated system. If we use a general-purpose language such as FORTRAN, then there will be a minimum number of restrictions imposed on the format of our output reports. However, if we use a special-purpose simulation language such as SIMSCRIPT, then we must adhere to the output format requirements of the language.

The FORTRAN language was selected for use in this book because it is a widely used computer language that closely resembles the language of mathematics and was designed primarily for scientific computation. (Although most economists are familiar with FORTRAN, relatively few economists have used the special-purpose simulation languages.) One of the principal advantages of FORTRAN is that it provides the analyst with an efficient means of writing computer programs requiring a relatively short period of instruction and no detailed knowledge of the computer itself. Furthermore, FORTRAN compilers are now available for nearly all of the computers used most often by industry, government, and colleges and universities. The FORTRAN language used in this book is not designed for any particular computer, but with minor modifications it can be adapted to the FORTRAN language of any computer having a FORTRAN compiler. For this reason the FORTRAN statements appearing in this book have deliberately been kept quite simple. The reader who is not familiar with FORTRAN may wish to consult a FORTRAN manual published by the manufacturer of the computer he is using.

Data input and starting conditions Another aspect of the computer programming phase of the development of simulation experiments is the matter of input data and starting conditions for the simulation experiments. Since simulation experiments are by their very nature dynamic experiments, a question arises as to what values should be assigned to the model's variables and parameters at the time we begin simulating the system. That is, we must break into the system at some particular point in time. When we do so, what assumptions should we make about the state of the system being simulated? Needless to say, this question is not easily answered for most systems, and the investigator must usually resort to trial-and-error methods for determining a set of initial conditions for the system that will not lead to biased results in future time periods.

Data generation A problem directly related to the one of writing computer simulation programs is the development of numerical techniques (which can be programmed on a computer) for data generation. Data used in computer simulation experiments can either be read into the computer from external sources, such as punched cards and magnetic tapes, or it may be generated internally by special subroutines. If one or more of the exogenous variables included in our model of the firm is a stochastic variable with a known probability distribution, then we are confronted with the problem of devising a process of random selection from the given probability distribution so that the results of the repetition of this process on a digital computer will give rise to a probability distribution of sampled values that corresponds to the probability distribution of the variable of interest.

In considering stochastic processes involving either continuous or discrete random variables, we define a function $F(x)$ called the *cumulative distribution* function of x, which denotes the probability that a random variable X takes on the value of x or less. If the random variable is discrete, then x takes on specific values, and $F(x)$ is a step function. If $F(x)$ is continuous over the domain of x, it is possible to differentiate this function and define $f(x) = dF(x)/dx$. The derivative $f(x)$ is called a *probability density* function. Finally, the cumulative distribution function may be stated mathematically as

$$F(x) = P(X \leq x) = \int_{-\infty}^{x} f(t)\, dt \tag{13-1}$$

where $F(x)$ is defined over the range $0 \leq F(x) \leq 1$, and $f(t)$ represents the value of the probability density function of the random variable X when $X = t$.

Uniformly distributed random variables play a major role in the generation of random variables drawn from *other* probability distributions. We will denote uniform variables by r, when $0 \leq r \leq 1$, and $F(r) = r$. Chapter 3 of [78] contains a survey of the theory and methods of generating *pseudorandom numbers* or uniformly distributed random variables on the interval (0, 1). These numbers are called pseudorandom numbers because, although they are generated from a completely deterministic recursive formula by a computer, their statistical properties coincide with the statistical properties of numbers generated by an idealized chance device that selects numbers from the unit interval (0, 1) independently and with all numbers equally likely. So long as these pseudorandom numbers can pass the set of statistical tests (frequency test, serial test, lagged product test, runs test, gap test, etc. [78]) implied by an idealized chance device, they can be treated as "truly" random even though they are not.

Since pseudorandom number generators (in the form of subroutines) are available for all computers, we shall not delve further into this topic. It will be assumed that the pseudorandom numbers used in the subroutines of this chapter

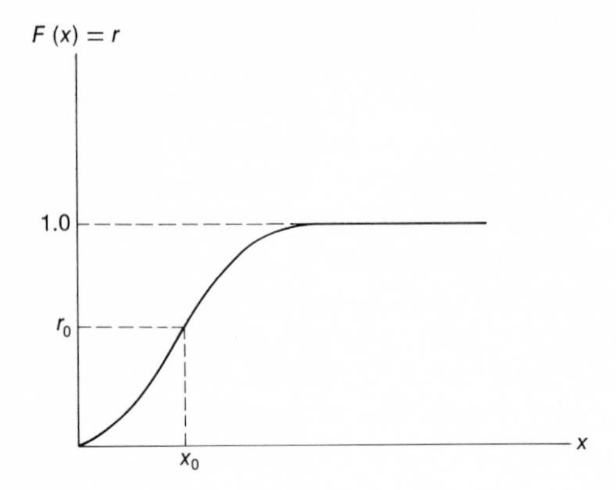

FIGURE **13-1**

A cumulative distribution function

and in the example model in the following chapter will be generated by a preprogrammed FORTRAN function. This function is denoted by R = RAND(R).

If we wish to generate random variables, x_i, from some particular statistical population whose distribution function is given by $f(x)$, we first obtain the cumulative distribution function $F(x)$. (See Figure 13-1.) Since $F(x)$ is defined over the range 0 to 1 we can generate uniformly distributed random numbers and set $F(x) = r$. It is clear that x is uniquely determined by $r = F(x)$. It therefore follows that for any particular value of r, say r_0, which we generate, it is possible to find the value of x, in this case x_0, corresponding to r_0 by the inverse function of F if it is known,

$$x_0 = F^{-1}(r_0) \tag{13-2}$$

where $F^{-1}(r)$ is the inverse transformation of r on the unit interval into the domain of x. We may summarize this method mathematically by saying that if we generate uniform random numbers corresponding to a given $F(x)$

$$r = F(x) = \int_{-\infty}^{x} f(t)\, dt \tag{13-3}$$

then

$$P(X \leq x) = F(x) = P[r \leq F(x)] = P[F^{-1}(r) \leq x] \tag{13-4}$$

and consequently $F^{-1}(r)$ is a variable which has $f(x)$ as its probability density function. This is equivalent to solving (13-3) for x in terms of r. This procedure is called the *inverse transformation* method.

Perhaps the simplest continuous probability density function is the one that is constant over the interval (a, b) and is zero otherwise. This density function

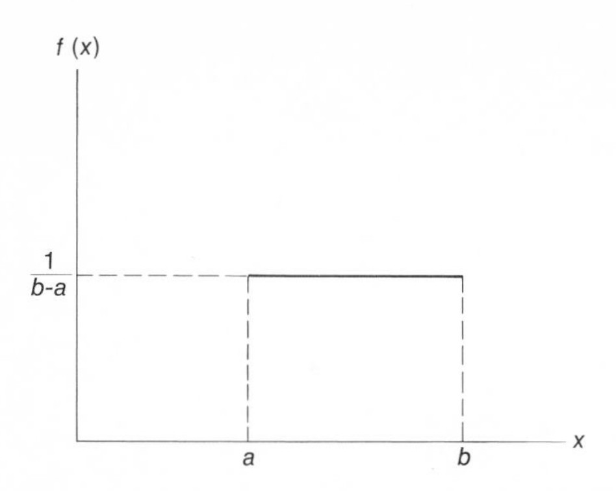

FIGURE 13-2

defines what is known as the uniform or rectangular distribution. The principal value of the uniform distribution for simulation techniques lies in its simplicity and in the fact that it can be used to generate random variables from numerous other probability distributions.

Mathematically the uniform density function is defined as

$$f(x) = \begin{cases} \dfrac{1}{b-a}, & a < x < b \\ 0, & \text{otherwise} \end{cases} \tag{13-5}$$

Here X is a random variable defined over the interval (a, b). The graph of the uniform distribution is illustrated in Figure 13-2.

The cumulative distribution function $F(x)$ for a uniformly distributed random variable X is

$$F(x) = \int_a^x \frac{1}{b-a}\,dt = \frac{x-a}{b-a} \qquad 0 \le F(x) \le 1 \tag{13-6}$$

To simulate a uniform distribution over some given domain (a, b), we must first obtain the inverse transformation for (13-6), according to (13-2).

$$x = a + (b-a)r \qquad 0 \le r \le 1 \tag{13-7}$$

We then generate a set of pseudorandom numbers corresponding to the range of cumulative probabilities, i.e., uniform random variables defined over the range 0 to 1. Each random number r determines uniquely a uniformly distributed variable x.

A graphical explanation will perhaps serve to clarify the issues here. Figure 13-3 illustrates the fact that each generated value of r is associated with one and only one value of x. For example, the specific value of the cumulative distribution function at r_0 fixes the value of x at x_0. Obviously, this procedure may be repeated as many times as one desires, each time generating a new value of x.

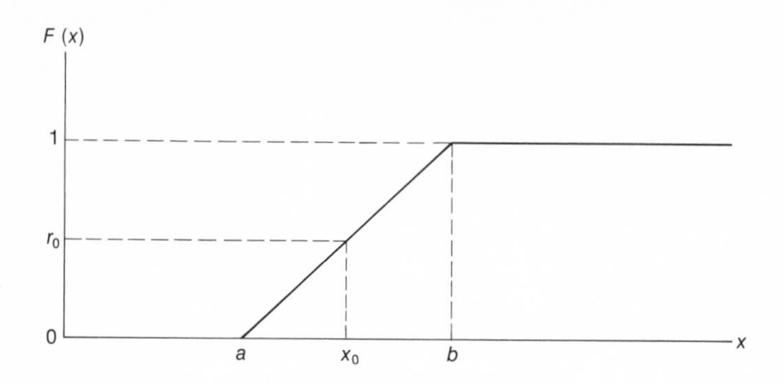

FIGURE 13-3

```
1. SUBROUNTINE UNIFRM (A, B, X)
2. R = RAND(R)
3. X = A + (B - A)*R
4. RETURN
```

FIGURE 13-4

Generation of uniform variables—FORTRAN Subroutine

Figure 13-4 contains a FORTRAN subroutine for generating a uniform distribution for a given interval (a, b). The first statement in the subroutine is an initialization statement which identifies the particular subroutine as the one called by the main program. The second statement in the subroutine is a library function which causes the variable R to be set equal to a pseudorandom number generated by the function RAND. Each time the subroutine is called a new value of R will be generated. The variable R is the FORTRAN symbol for r. The third statement in the FORTRAN subroutine transforms R from the (0, 1) interval to the (a, b) interval by use of FORTRAN arithmetic and (13-7). The fourth statement returns the generated value of X and the program control back to the main program.

Techniques for generating other probability distributions can be derived directly from the aforementioned procedure for generating uniform variates.[3] For example, the Central Limit theorem permits us to generate normally distributed random variables (with given mean and variance) by simply taking the sum of N uniform variables (see [78, Chapter 4]). Techniques for generating χ^2, t, and F distributions can be derived from the method for generating normal variables. In Chapter 14 we will derive a method for generating negative exponential variables.

[3] See [78], Chapter 4, for a complete collection of techniques and FORTRAN programs for generating random variables on a computer.

Validation [80]

The problem of validating simulation models is indeed a difficult one because it involves a host of practical, theoretical, statistical, and even philosophical [89] complexities. Validation of simulation experiments is merely part of a more general problem, namely the validation of any kind of model or hypothesis. The basic questions are, "What does it mean to validate a hypothesis?" and "What criteria should be used to establish the validity of a hypothesis?"

In general, two tests seem appropriate for validating simulation models. First, how well do the simulated values of the endogenous variables compare with known historical data, if historical data are available? Second, how accurate are the simulation model's predictions of the real system in future time periods? What are some of the practical considerations in verifying computer models? Some criteria must be devised to indicate when the time paths generated by a computer simulation model agree sufficiently with the observed or historical time paths so that agreement cannot be attributed merely to chance. Specific *measures* and *techniques* must be considered for testing the "goodness of fit" of a simulation model, that is, the degree of conformity of simulated time series to observed data. Cyert has suggested that the following measures might be appropriate [33]:

1. Number of turning points.
2. Timing of turning points.
3. Direction of turning points.
4. Amplitude of the fluctuations for corresponding time segments.
5. Average amplitude over the whole series.
6. Simultaneity of turning points for different variables.
7. Average values of variables.
8. Exact matching of values of variables.

To this list of measures we would add the probability distribution and variation about the mean (variance, skewness, kurtosis) of variables.

Within the confines of this chapter it is impossible to enumerate all of the statistical techniques available for testing the "goodness of fit" of simulation models. However, we shall list some of the more important ones and suggest a number of references which describe these tests in detail.

A. *Analysis of variance* The analysis of variance is a collection of techniques for data analysis which can be used to test the hypothesis that the mean (or variance) of a series generated by a computer simulation experiment is equal to the mean (or variance) of the corresponding observed series. Three important assumptions underlie the use of this technique—normality, statistical independence, and a common variance. The paper by Naylor, Wertz, and Wonnacott [82] describes the use of the analysis of variance in analyzing data generated by simulation experiments.

B. *Chi-square test* The chi-square test is a classical statistical test which can be used for testing the hypothesis that the set of data generated by a simulation model has the same frequency distribution as a set of observed historical data. Although this test is relatively easy to apply, it has the problem of all tests using categorical-type data, namely, the problem of selecting categories in a suitable and unbiased fashion. It has the further disadvantage that it is relatively sensitive to nonnormality.

C. *Factor analysis* Cohen and Cyert have suggested the performance of a factor analysis on the set of time paths generated by a computer model, a second factor analysis on the set of observed time paths, and a test of whether the two groups of factor loadings are significantly different from each other [29].

D. *Kolmogorov-Smirnov test* The Kolmogorov-Smirnov test is a *distribution free* (nonparametric) test concerned with the degree of agreement between the distribution of a set of sample values (simulated series) and some specified theoretical distribution (distribution of actual data). The test involves specifying the cumulative frequency distribution of the simulated and actual data. It treats individual observations separately and unlike the chi-square test does not lose information through the combining of categories.

E. *Nonparametric tests* Walsh [103] describes a host of other nonparametric tests which can be used for testing the "goodness of fit" of simulated data to real-world data.

F. *Regression analysis* Cohen and Cyert have also suggested the possibility of regressing actual series on the generated series and testing whether the resulting regression equations have intercepts which are not significantly different from zero and slopes which are not significantly different from unity [29].

G. *Spectral analysis* Data generated by computer simulation experiments are usually highly autocorrelated. When autocorrelation is present in sample data, the use of classical statistical estimating techniques (which assume the absence of autocorrelation) will lead to underestimates of sampling variances (which are unduly large) and inefficient predictions. Spectral analysis considers data arranged in a series according to historical time. It is essentially the quantification and evaluation of autocorrelated data at which spectral analysis is aimed, after the data have been transformed into the frequency domain. For purposes of describing the behavior of a stochastic variable over time, the information content of spectral analysis is greater than that of sample means and variances. Spectral analysis provides a means of objectively comparing time series generated by a computer model with observed time series. By comparing the estimated spectra of simulated data and corresponding real-world data, one can infer how well the simulation resembles the system it was designed to emulate [7,44,51,83].

H. *Theil's inequality coefficient* A technique developed by Theil has been used by a number of economists to validate simulations with econometric models [98]. Theil's inequality coefficient U provides an index which measures the degree to which a simulation model provides retrospective predictions of observed historical data. U varies between 0 and 1. If $U = 0$, we have perfect predictions. If $U = 1$, we have very bad predictions. There is no obvious reason why this technique cannot be used to validate models of the firm, as well as econometric models.

Experimental design [18,79]

In a computer simulation experiment, as in any experiment, careful thought should be given to the problem of experimental design. Although a number of researchers have considered the need to utilize experimental-design techniques with simulation experiments and have noted the extensive literature on the subject of experimental design,[4] economists have virtually ignored experimental-design considerations in carrying out simulation experiments with models of economic systems. For the most part, the existing experimental-design literature is concerned with the problems and techniques of designing real-world experiments, whereas computer simulation experiments are in effect experiments on a mathematical model.[5] The task of deciding which material in the experimental-design literature is applicable to simulation experiments is extremely difficult. This situation is likely to be particularly acute to economists who (prior to the advent of computer simulation) have had only limited opportunity to perform experiments with economic systems. Our objective in this section and the following one is to show the relationship between existing experimental-design and data-analysis techniques and the design of computer simulation experiments with models of economic systems. Before turning to a number of specific experimental-design problems, it is appropriate that we define several terms.

The two most important terms in the language of experimental design are *factor* and *response*. Both terms refer to variables. Whether a variable in a particular experiment is a factor or a response depends upon the role played by the variable in the experiment in question. To illustrate the difference between a factor and a response, suppose we have two variables, X and Y. If our experiment is designed to answer the question "How does a change in X affect Y?" then X is a factor and Y is a response. In an experiment using a computer model of a firm, a response must of necessity be an endogenous (output) variable, whereas a factor will normally be an exogenous or policy (input) variable.

For example, with a model of the firm, profit, output, or utility might be response variables. On the other hand, advertising expenditures, labor inputs, capital outlays, GNP, and per capita income might be treated as factors.

[4] Among the publications that have acknowledged the relevance and importance of experimental-design problems in designing simulation experiments are included: Burdick and Naylor [18,79], Conway [31], Naylor *et al.* [78], and Tocher [99]. In addition, Bonini [9], Cyert and March [35], Dear [37], Fishman and Kiviat [43,44], Hufschmidt [59], Jacoby and Harrison [62], Naylor, Wertz, and Wonnacott [82,83,84], and Preston and Collins [86] have considered specific experimental-design problems.

[5] The "classical" experimental-design literature includes the works of Cochran and Cox [25], Cox [32], Davies [36], Fisher [42], Quenouille [88], and Winer [104].

A large percentage of the terms and concepts in the theory of experimental design results from the classification of the factors in the experiment by the following dichotomous questions:

1. Is the factor in question controlled or not?
2. Are the values (levels) of the factor observed or not?
3. Is the effect of the factor a subject for study or is the factor included merely to increase the precision of the experiment?
4. Are the levels of the factor quantitative or qualitative?
5. Is the factor fixed or random?

A factor is *controlled* if its levels are purposefully selected by the experimenter. (In the case of economic models, the experimenter is usually called a policy maker.) Production scheduling rules and inventory control policies are subject to the control of managerial decision makers. Wars, foreign competition, labor strikes, and national disasters are factors which might affect the firm but which are not controllable by the firm's policy makers.

A factor is *observed* if its levels are observed or measured and recorded as part of the data. More often than not the observed factors consist of just the controlled factors in a particular experiment, but there are frequent exceptions. It is unwise to control a factor without observing it, but an uncontrolled factor may often be observed. For the firm, wars and strikes, although uncontrolled, can be observed. Observations on uncontrolled factors are often called *concomitant* observations. In the analysis of data concomitant observations should be treated differently from observations on controlled factors. The *analysis of covariance* is a technique of data analysis which utilizes concomitant observations. Although concomitant observations are useful, in the real world it is never possible to observe *all* the factors which might affect a given response.

The distinction between factors which are of basic interest and those which are included to increase precision is an important distinction for it serves to emphasize the fact that for almost all experiments the factors of basic interest are not the only ones to significantly affect the outcome. In the literature, controlled factors which are included to increase precision are often called *block factors* and their levels are called *blocks*. In simulation experiments there are never uncontrolled or unobserved factors. The role which uncontrolled and unobserved factors play in the real world is played in a computer simulation model by the random character of exogenous variables. The effects or variations in response which these factors cause in the real world have been incorporated in the computer simulation model in the form of experimental errors or random deviations. Once we have a model, the factors are determined, and it is not possible in an experiment on the model to identify additional factors as sources of variation.

A factor is *quantitative* if its levels are numbers which are expected to have a meaningful relationship with the response. Otherwise, a factor is *qualitative*. The amount of money spent on advertising and the size of the work force might be among the quantitative factors for a model of the firm. If part of the input to a simulation model consists of a decision rule or economic policy, and if several policies are under consideration, the policy could be a qualitative factor. We will consider an experiment in which managerial policies are qualitative factors in Chapter 14.

When an experimenter is investigating the effect of a factor on a response, he will be interested in drawing inferences with respect to a certain range or population of levels for the factor. If all the levels of interest of a particular factor are included in the experiment, that factor is said to be *fixed*. If, however, the levels of a factor that are actually included in the experiment constitute a random (or representative) sample from the population of levels in which the experimenter is interested, then the factor is said to be *random*. The notion of random factors permits inferences of a probabilistic nature to be made about factor levels which do not actually appear in the experiment.

Next we describe four problems which arise in the design of simulation experiments and identify some of the techniques which have been developed to solve them. The four experimental-design problems include: (A) the problem of stochastic convergence; (B) the problem of size; (C) the problem of motive; and (D) the multiple-response problem.

A. *The problem of stochastic convergence* Most experiments are intended to yield information about population quantities or averages such as average profit or sales for a particular managerial policy (in the case of a firm). As estimates of population averages, the sample averages we compute from several runs on a computer will be subject to random fluctuations and will not be exactly equal to the population averages. However, the larger the sample (i.e., the more runs we observe), the greater the probability that the sample averages will be very close to the population averages. The convergence of sample averages for increasing sample size is called *stochastic convergence*.

The problem of stochastic convergence is that it is slow. A measure of the amount of random fluctuation inherent in a chance quantity is its standard deviation. If σ is the standard deviation of a single observation, then the standard deviation of the average of n observations is $\sigma/\sqrt{n}$. Thus in order to halve the random error we must quadruple the sample size n; to decrease the random error by a factor ten we must increase the sample size by a factor of one hundred. It can easily happen that a reasonably small random error requires an unreasonably large sample size.

Because of the slowness of stochastic convergence we are led to seek methods other than increasing sample size to reduce random error. In real-world experiments error-reduction techniques commonly involve including factors such as blocks or concomitant variables which are not of basic interest to the experimenter. If some of these factors can be controlled or observed instead of being uncontrolled and unobserved, their effects will no longer contribute to the random error, and the standard deviation σ of a single observation will be reduced.

In a computer simulation experiment on a given model it is not possible to include more factors for error-reduction purposes. The inclusion of more factors requires a change in the model. Once the model has been specified, all the uncontrolled factors have been irretrievably absorbed in the probabilistic specification for the exogenous inputs.

There are, however, error-reduction techniques which are suitable for computer simulation experiments. They are called *Monte Carlo techniques* [22,41,53,65]. The underlying principle of Monte Carlo techniques is the utilization of knowledge about the structure of the model, properties of the probability distributions of the exogenous inputs, and properties of the observed variates actually used for inputs to increase the precision (i.e., reduce random error) in the measurement of averages for the response variables.

Hammersley and Handscomb [53] have written an excellent book on the subject of Monte Carlo techniques. Some of the techniques they discuss are importance sampling, control variates, correlation (i.e., regression methods and antithetic variate methods), and conditional Monte Carlo. The book also contains an extensive bibliography.

B. *The problem of size* What we have called the problem of size arises in both real-world and simulation experiments. It could just as easily be called "the problem of too many factors." In a factorial design for several factors the number of cells required is the product of the number of levels for each of the factors in the experiment. Thus in a four-factor experiment with a model of the firm, if we have 6 different employment policies, 5 alternative marketing plans, 5 possible inventory policies, and 10 different equipment replacement policies, then a total of $6 \times 5 \times 5 \times 10 = 1{,}500$ cells (or factor combinations) would be required for a full factorial design. If we had a ten-factor experiment and if we only used two levels for each of these factors the full factorial experiment would require $2^{10} = 1{,}024$ cells. It is clear that the full design can require an unmanageably large number of cells if more than a few factors are to be investigated.

If we require a complete investigation of the factors in the experiment, including main effects and interactions of all orders, then there is no solution to the problem of size. If, however, we are willing to settle for a less than complete investigation, perhaps including main effects and two-factor interactions, then there are designs that will accomplish our purpose yet require fewer cells than the full factorial. Fractional factorial designs, including Latin square and Greco-Latin square designs, are examples of designs which require only a fraction of the cells required by the full factorial design.

In any design which utilizes fewer cells than the full factorial there will be some *confounding* of effects. A main effect, for example, might be confounded with an interaction effect, which means that the statistic which measures the main effect is exactly the same statistic which measures the interaction effect.

Thus the statistic in question can tell us that some effect is present, but it cannot tell us whether the main effect, the interaction effect, or some combination of the two is present. Only if the interaction effect can be assumed to be zero (or at least negligibly small) are we justified in stating that the observed effect is in fact a main effect.

Experimenters are usually most interested in main effects. It is important therefore that main effects not be confounded with other main effects. In practically all of the commonly used fractional factorial designs main effects are confounded with interactions (preferably high-order interactions) and not with other main effects. If an experimenter uses one of these designs to measure main effects, he must be willing to assume, at least tentatively, that the interactions with which the main effects are confounded are zero. Few experimenters are deterred from the use of fractional factorial designs by the necessity of such assumptions. Although the assumption that a high-order interaction is zero is frequently justifiable, we suspect that in many instances the difficulty in interpreting a high-order interaction influences the experimenter's willingness to assume it zero.

The problems that arise in obtaining fractional factorial designs by confounding main effects with interactions have proved appealing to mathematical statisticians. As a result, much has been written in this area both in books and in articles in the professional journals. Tables of designs can be found in the book by Cochran and Cox [25] and in a publication in the Applied Mathematics Series of the National Bureau of Standards [46]. Bonini [9] has an example of a fractional factorial design employed in a computer simulation experiment.

So far the problem of size reduction has been discussed in an analysis-of-variance framework. As was mentioned in the section on analysis of variance, this collection of techniques for data analysis (i.e., the analysis of variance) is appropriate when the factors are qualitative. However, if the factors $X_1, X_2, \ldots, X_k$ are quantitative, and the response Y is related to the factors by some mathematical function f, then regression analysis, rather than the analysis of variance, may be an appropriate method of data analysis. The functional relationship $Y = f(X_1, \ldots, X_k)$ between the response and the quantitative factors is called the *response surface* [11,13,14,55]. Least-squares regression analysis is a method for fitting a response surface to observed data in such a way as to minimize the sum of squared deviations of the observed responses from the value predicted from the fitted response surface.

For an experiment which utilizes regression analysis to explore a response surface a factorial design or a fractional factorial design may not be optimal. Several authors, primarily Box [10–17], have developed designs called *response-surface designs* which are appropriate when response-surface exploration via regression analysis is the aim of the experiment. An important advantage of the response-surface designs in comparison with comparable factorial designs is the reduction in the required size of the experiment without a corresponding reduction in the amount of information obtained.

Response-surface designs have not been given the attention they deserve in most of the books on experimental design. An exception is chapter 8A in the second edition of the book by Cochran and Cox [25]. Fortunately, there are a number of readable journal articles on response-surface designs, including Box and Draper [13], Box and J. S. Hunter [14], and Box and W. G. Hunter [15]. The recent paper by Hill and W. G. Hunter [55] contains a survey of response-surface designs and a complete bibliography. Response-surface designs were used by Hufschmidt [59] to design a computer simulation experiment with a model of a water-resource system. Hoggatt has used response-surface designs with simulation experiments with a computer model of a market [56].

C. *The problem of motive* The experimenter should specify his objectives as precisely as possible to facilitate the choice of a design which will best satisfy his objectives. Two important types of experimental objectives can be identified: (1) the experimenter wishes to find the combination of factor levels at which the response variable is maximized (or minimized) in order to optimize some process, (2) the experimenter wishes to make a rather general investigation of the relationship of the response to the factors in order to determine the underlying mechanisms governing the process under study. The distinction between these two aims is less important when the factors are qualitative than it is when the factors are quantitative. Unless certain interactions can be assumed to be zero, the only way to find the combination of levels of qualitative factors which will produce an optimum response is to measure the response at all combinations of factor levels (i.e., the full factorial design). Even if interactions are assumed negligible in an experiment with qualitative factors, the design is likely to be the same whether the aim is to optimize or to explore.

In an experiment with quantitative factors the picture is quite different. Hence the continuity of the response surface can usually be used to guide us quickly and efficiently to a determination of the optimum combination of factor levels. There are two commonly used sampling methods for finding the optimum of a response surface: systematic sampling and random sampling. Systematic-sampling methods include: (1) the uniform-grid or factorial method; (2) the single-factor method; (3) the method of marginal analysis; and (4) the method of steepest ascent. The article by Hufschmidt contains a case study involving the use of both systematic and random sampling methods for the design of a simulation experiment. A detailed description of several of these methods can be found in Cochran and Cox [25].

When general exploration of a response surface is the aim, it is difficult to identify a "best" experimental design because general exploration is usually a less precisely specified goal than optimization. However, we can state a guiding principle: when the aim of an experiment is to further general knowledge and understanding, it is important to give careful and precise consideration to the existing state of knowledge and to questions and uncertainties upon which we desire the experimental data to shed some light. Box and W. G. Hunter [15] have written an excellent paper on the use of experiments to further general understanding, including the role played by experimental design.

D. *The multiple-response problem* This problem arises when we wish to observe many different response variables in a given experiment. The multiple-response problem occurs frequently in computer simulation experiments with economic systems. Profit, sales, cost, output, investment, to mention only a few, might all be treated as response variables in a simulation experiment with a model of the firm.

It is often possible to bypass the multiple-response problem by treating an experiment with many responses as many experiments each with a single response. Alternatively several responses could be combined (e.g., by addition) and treated as a single response. However, it is not always possible to bypass the multiple-response problem; often multiple responses are inherent in the situation under study. Unfortunately, experimental design techniques for multiple-response experiments are virtually nonexistent.

Any attempt to solve the multiple-response program is likely to require the use of utility theory. Gary Fromm [47] has taken an initial step in this direction by using utility theory to evaluate the results of policy simulation experiments with the Brookings Model. The specific problem with which Fromm was confronted was how to choose among alternative economic policies which affect a large number of different response variables in many different ways. He treated utility as a response variable and developed a discounted utility function over time which depends on the values of the endogenous variables of the model, as well as the mean, variance, skewness, and kurtosis of these variables.

Data analysis

In a well-designed experiment consideration must be given to methods of analyzing the data once they are obtained. Most of the classical experimental-design techniques described in the literature are used in the expectation that the data will be analyzed by one or both of the following two methods: analysis of variance and regression analysis. The analysis of variance is a collection of techniques for data analysis which are appropriate when qualitative factors are present, although quantitative factors are not excluded. Regression analysis is a collection of techniques for data analysis which utilizes the numerical properties of the levels of quantitative factors. From a mathematical point of view the distinction between regression analysis and the analysis of variance is somewhat artificial. For example, an analysis of variance can be performed as a regression analysis using dummy variables which can assume only the values zero or one. An excellent treatise on the application of regression analysis has been written by Draper and Smith [39]. Since the great bulk of experimental-design techniques described in the literature have the analysis of variance as the intended method of data analysis we shall investigate several special cases of analysis of variance. These techniques include the F-test, multiple comparisons, multiple rankings, spectral analysis, sequential sampling, and nonparametric methods. We shall investigate the application of each of these techniques to the analysis of data generated by simulation experiments with models of the firm.

F-test Suppose that we are interested in testing the null hypothesis that the expected profits associated with each of five managerial policies are equal. The F-test is a straightforward procedure for testing hypotheses of this type. If the null hypothesis is accepted in our example experiment, then one tentatively concludes that the sample differences between policies are attributable to random fluctuations rather than to actual differences in population values (expected profits). On the other hand, if the null hypothesis is rejected, then further analysis, such as multiple comparisons and multiple rankings, is recommended. The F-test rests on three important assumptions (1) *normality*, (2) *equality of variance*, and (3) *statistical independence*. The papers by Naylor, Wertz, and Wonnacott [82,84] contain two applications of the use of the F-test to analyze data generated by simulation experiments.

Multiple comparisons Typically, managerial decision makers are interested not only in whether alternatives differ but also in *how* they differ. Multiple comparison and multiple ranking procedures often become tools relevant to meeting the latter query, for they have been designed specifically to attack questions of how means of many populations differ.

In contrast with the analysis of variance, multiple comparison methods emphasize the use of confidence intervals rather than the testing of hypotheses. For example, if one is interested in comparing the means of different populations, then a number of $(100 - \alpha)$ percent confidence intervals for the differences between population means may be constructed. Scheffé [91] and Winer [104] have written comprehensive surveys of multiple comparison procedures. Naylor, Wertz, and Wonnacott [82,84] have applied multiple comparisons to the analysis of output data from simulation experiments.

Multiple rankings Frequently the objective of computer simulation experiments with models of the firm is to find the "best," "second best," "third best," etc., policy. Although multiple comparison methods of estimating the sizes of differences between policies (as measured by population means) are often used as a way of attempting to achieve indirectly goals of this type, multiple ranking methods represent a more direct approach to a solution of the ranking problem.

A good estimate of the rank of a set of economic policies is simply the ranking of the sample means associated with the given policies. Because of random error, however, sample rankings may yield incorrect results. With what probability can we say that a ranking of sample means represents the true ranking of the population means? It is basically this question which multiple ranking procedures attempt to answer.

Bechhofer, Dunnett, and Sobel [5] have developed a procedure for selecting a single population and guaranteeing with probability P that the selected population is the "best," provided some other condition on the parameters is satisfied. This procedure assumes normality, statistical independence, and a common *unknown variance*. It has been used by Naylor, Wertz, and Wonnacott [82] with simulation experiments with a model of a multiprocess firm to evaluate the profitability of alternative managerial plans and strategies.

Spectral analysis Spectral analysis is a statistical technique frequently employed in the physical sciences and more recently applied by economists to analyze the behavior of economic time series [7,44,51,63,83,85,100]. There are at least four reasons why we might want to consider spectral analysis as one possible technique for analyzing data generated by simulation experiments with an econometric model.

First, data generated by computer simulation experiments are usually highly autocorrelated, e.g., sales in period t are likely to be highly correlated with sales in period $t - k$. As we have stated previously, it is well known that when autocorrelation is present in sample data the use of classical statistical estimating techniques, which assume the absence of autocorrelation, will lead to underestimates of sampling variances (which are unduly large) and inefficient predictions. Several methods are available for treating this problem: (1) Simply ignore autocorrelation and compute sample means and variances over time thereby incurring the aforementioned statistical problems. (2) Divide the sample record length into intervals that are longer than the interval of major autocorrelation and work with the observations on these supposedly independent intervals [44]. This method suffers from the fact that, "the choices of sample record length and sampling interval seem to have neither enough prior nor posterior justification in most cases to make this choice much more than arbitrary" [44]. (3) Replicate the simulation experiment and compute sample means and variances across the ensemble rather than over time. This method may lead to excessive computer running time and fail to yield the type of information that is desired about a particular time series. (4) Use a technique such as spectral analysis, which is based on a model in which the probabilities of component outcomes in a time series depend on previous outcomes in the series. With spectral analysis the problems associated with methods (1) and (2) can be successfully avoided without replicating the experiment.

Second, "When we study a stochastic process, we are interested in the average level of activity, deviations from this level, and how long these deviations last, once they occur" [44]. Spectral analysis provides this kind of information.

Third, with spectral analysis it is relatively easy to construct confidence bands and to test hypotheses for the purpose of comparing the simulated results of the use of two or more alternative economic policies. Frequently it is impossible to detect differences in time series generated by simulation experiments when we restrict ourselves to simple graphical analysis. Spectral analysis provides a means of objectively comparing time series generated with a computer model.

Fourth, spectral analysis can also be used as a technique for validating an econometric model of an economic system. By comparing the estimated spectra of simulated data and corresponding real-world data we can infer how well the model resembles the system it was designed to emulate [44].

Fishman and Kiviat [44] have written a path-breaking article on the use of spectral analysis in analyzing data generated by computer simulation models. The books by Blackman and Tukey [7] and Granger and Hatanaka [51] and the papers by Jenkins [63] and Parzen [85] are recommended for obtaining the basic elements of spectral analysis. Tukey [100] has written a paper in which spectral analysis and the analysis of variance are compared in detail. Naylor, Wertz, and Wonnacott [83] have applied spectral analysis to the analysis of simulation experiments with econometric models. Spectral analysis has also been used to compare data generated by a computer model of the textile industry with corresponding real-world data as a technique of verification [81].

Sequential sampling Since computer time is not a free gift of nature, data generated by computer simulation experiments (observations) are costly. The cost of experimentation may be greatly reduced if at each stage of the simulation experiment the analyst balances the cost of additional observations (generated by the computer) against the expected gain in information from such observations. With computer simulation experiments the objective of sequential sampling is to minimize the number of observations (sample size) for obtaining the information which is required from the experiment. Rather than setting in advance the number of observations to be generated, the sample size n is considered a random variable dependent on the outcome of the first $n - 1$ observations. In terms of computer time, the cost of a simulation run is minimized by generating only enough observations to achieve the required results with predetermined accuracy.

For example, a sequential test on a model of the firm could be designed to determine if the profits obtained by using a certain investment policy in combination with various production policies differ significantly. The sequential method sets a procedure for deciding at the ith observation whether to accept a given hypothesis, reject the hypothesis, or continue sampling by taking the $(i + 1)$th observation. Such a procedure must specify for the ith observation a division of the i-dimensional space of all possible observations into three mutually exclusive and exhaustive sets: an area of preference A_i for accepting the hypothesis, an area of preference B_i for rejecting it, and an area of indifference C_i where no statement can be made about the hypothesis and further observations are necessary. The fundamental problem in the theory of sequential sampling is that of a proper choice of the sets—A_i, B_i, and C_i [76].

Although Wald's *Sequential Analysis* [101] is the best-known reference on sequential procedures, Chapter 34 of Kendall and Stuart [66] contains a comprehensive treatment of this topic. The article by Chernoff [19] is also worthy of consideration. In addition, the optimization procedures developed by Kiefer and others [68,69,70,71] offer promise in analyzing data generated by computer models.

Nonparametric methods In addition to the aforementioned techniques, numerous nonparametric techniques of data analysis are available. See the books by Siegel [96] and Walsh [103].

COMPUTER MODELS OF THE FIRM

Having outlined a methodology for designing computer simulation experiments with models of the firm, we shall now briefly describe several simulation studies involving models of the firm. The purpose of this survey is to illustrate the fact that simulation can be used to analyze a wide variety of models. In Chapter 14 we shall describe in detail an application of computer simulation to a specific model of the firm.

Cohen

In his doctoral dissertation entitled *Computer Models of the Shoe, Leather, Hide Sequence*, Kalman Cohen formulated and experimented with two mathematical models, a "one-period-change model" and a "process model," describing the aggregate behavior of shoe retailers, shoe manufacturers, and cattlehide leather tanners between 1930 and 1940 [26]. The principal exogenous variables included in Cohen's models were the Bureau of Labor Statistics consumers' price index, disposable personal income, and the stocks of hides held by hide dealers. After dividing the industry vertically into five segments—consumers, shoe retailers, shoe manufacturers, cattlehide tanners, and hide dealers, two major classes of endogenous variables were defined—price and physical flow. Among the endogenous variables analyzed by Cohen were the retailers' selling price, sales, and shoe receipts; the manufacturers' selling price, production, and leather receipts; the tanners' selling price, finished production, hide wettings, and hide receipts; and the hide dealers' selling price [26, p. vii]. Both of Cohen's models consisted of lagged simultaneous nonlinear difference equations subject to boundary constraints, with one month used as the unit of time.

> ... A "one-period-change model," is intended to explain the values of the endogenous variables for only one time period ahead into the future; this model assumes, as is usually done in econometrics, that lagged endogenous variables refer to their actually observed values. ... A "process model," is designed to explain the determination of the endogenous variables for an arbitrarily large number of future time periods. The equations of the process model, together with the observed time path of the exogenous variables, are treated as a closed dynamic system; each month, the values of the predetermined endogenous variables are the values generated by the model, not the actually observed values [26, p. vii].

A computer was used to generate the time paths from 1930 to 1940 of each endogenous variable for each of the two models. These results were in turn compared with the actual time paths of these variables. A very close correspondence was found between the simulated time paths and the actual time paths on an annual basis.

Forrester

Of the existing simulation models of the firm and industry, perhaps the "industrial dynamics" project of Jay Forrester is the most controversial [45]. Actually "industrial dynamics" is not a simulation model at all but rather a methodology for studying business and economic systems that utilize computer simulation as a tool of analysis. Forrester defines industrial dynamics as

> . . . the study of the information-feedback characteristics of industrial activity to show how organizational structure, amplification (in policies), and time delays (in decisions and actions) interact to influence the success of the enterprise. It treats the interactions between the flows of information, money, orders, materials, personnel, and capital equipment in a company, an industry, or a national economy [45, p. 13].

The industrial dynamics approach to simulation is similar to the other methods discussed in this chapter in the sense that the mathematical models used to describe a firm, an industry, or an economy must be expressed in the form of a set of lagged difference equations. However, in the case of industrial dynamics, a special computer language, DYNAMO, has been developed for writing programs for difference equation simulation models. In his book *Industrial Dynamics* Forrester describes three industrial dynamics models of the firm that have been programmed in DYNAMO. These include a production-distribution model, an advertising model, and a customer-producer-employment model. The DYNAMO output for these models takes the form of a series of graphs of the time paths of the endogenous variables of the models. In addition to the hypothetical models included in *Industrial Dynamics*, DYNAMO has also been applied to a number of simulations of firms and industries in the real world, e.g., the Sprague Electric Company, the shoe, leather, hide industry, and the textile industry.

Forrester's approach has not been widely accepted by economists or management scientists. The following statements by Forrester, to mention only a few, have done little to broaden the scope of his influence with these two groups and have not convinced them that industrial dynamics is the panacea which he claims it is. "Management science has failed to assist top management because the philosophy and objectives of management science have often been irrelevant to the manager" [45, p. 3]. "Many of the past failures in economic model building can be traced to unsound methods and to attempts to reach unachievable objectives" [45, p. 53]. Although many economists consider industrial dynamics to be an interesting approach to the analysis of the behavior of firms, few are willing to completely abandon economic theory and replace it with industrial dynamics.

A model of the textile industry

Naylor, Sasser, and Wallace [81,102] have developed a nine-equation econometric model of the U.S. textile industry to explain the behavior of the textile industry during the period 1953 through 1962. The endogenous variables of the model include apparel output and demand, textile mill products output and demand, employment, wages, profit, and investment. A computer program was written to simulate the behavior of the industry between 1953 and 1962 on the basis of the behavioral relationships implied by the model. Three different techniques were used to compare the simulated data generated by the model with actual observed data—graphical analysis, spectral analysis, and total-variance analysis. A number of simulation experiments have been conducted with the model to evaluate the impact of certain governmental policies on the U.S. textile industry.

Other computer models of the firm

In Chapter 18 we describe several other computer models of the firm including Balderston and Hoggatt's [1,2] model of the West Coast lumber industry, Bonini's [9] *Simulation of Information and Decision Systems in the Firm*, and Cyert and March's [35] behavioral models of the firm (a duopoly model, an oligopoly model, and a model of a department store).

Management games

The term "game" or "operational game" refers to a special type of simulation in which human participants act as decision makers within the framework of the system being simulated. Although the concept of gaming originated many centuries ago in the form of military war games (used for training purposes), its use in business and economics only goes back to 1956 when the American Management Association developed the first so-called management decision-making game, called the Top Management Decision Game [6]. Since 1956 hundreds of management games have been developed by various universities, business firms, and research organizations, both for research purposes and for training persons in such diverse disciplines as management, business operation, economics, organization theory, psychology, production management, finance, accounting, and marketing. These games range in degree of complexity from the relatively simple U.C.L.A. Executive Games [54] to the more complex Harvard Business School Management Simulation Game [75] and the Carnegie Tech Management Game [27,28,30,38]. The degree of realism and the level of abstraction also vary considerably among the existing management games. However, most games involve decisions which would be made only by rather high-level executives as opposed to operating employees.

Most business games are built around a hypothetical oligopolistic industry consisting of three to six firms, whose decision makers or managers are the "players" of the game. At the outset of the game each firm or "team" is allocated a specified amount of resources in the form of cash, inventories, raw materials, plant and equipment, etc. Then before each operating period (usually assumed to be a quarter) the players make decisions concerning price, output, advertising, marketing, to mention only a few possibilities. This information is then read into a computer that has been programmed on the basis of a set of mathematical models that provide a link between the operating results of the individual firms (for example sales, profits, and levels of inventory) and the individual firms' operating decision, as well as the external environment (the market). On the basis of (1) a set of operating characteristics, such as demand and cost functions, and a set of accounting formulas that have been programmed into the computer and (2) the individual decisions of each firm, operating results are generated by the computer in the form of printed reports, such as profit-and-loss statements, balance sheets, production reports, sales reports, and total industry reports at the end of each operating period. The environment can usually be changed by the administrator of the game by altering the parameters of the operating characteristics of the game. For example, it may be possible to change parameters that affect the rate of growth of the economy, the rate of taxation, the rate of depreciation of fixed assets, the industry wage rate, the prices of raw materials, and production lead time. In each case the firms find it necessary to react according to the magnitude and the nature of the change imposed by the external environment, that is, the parameters of the game. Some of the more complicated and more realistic games even permit multiple products, plants, and marketing areas, stochastic production periods, stochastic demand, labor negotiations, and the sale of common stock.

BIBLIOGRAPHY

[1] BALDERSTON, F. E., and AUSTIN C. HOGGATT. *Simulation of Market Processes.* Berkeley: Institute of Business and Economic Research, 1962.

[2] BALDERSTON, F. E., and AUSTIN C. HOGGATT. "Simulation Models: Analytic Variety and the Problem of Model Reduction," in Austin C. Hoggatt and Frederick E. Balderston (Eds.), *Symposium on Simulation Models.* Cincinnati: South-Western Publishing Co., 1963.

[3] BECHHOFER, ROBERT E. "A Sequential Multiple Decision Procedure for Selecting the Best One of Several Normal Populations with a Common Unknown Variance, and Its Use with Various Experimental Designs," *Biometrics*, **XIV** (1958), 408–429.

[4] BECHHOFER, ROBERT E., and SAUL BLUMENTHAL. "A Sequential Multiple-Decision Procedure for Selecting the Best One of Several Normal Populations with a Common Unknown Variance, II: Monte Carlo Sampling Results and New Computing Formulae," *Biometrics*, **XVIII** (March, 1962), 52–67.

[5] BECHHOFER, ROBERT E., C. W. DUNNETT, and M. SOBEL. "A Two-Sample Multiple Decision Procedure for Ranking Means of Normal Populations with a Common Unknown Variance," *Biometrika*, **XLI** (1954), 170–176.

[6] BELLMAN, RICHARD, *et al.* "On the Construction of a Multi-Person, Multi-Stage Business Game," *Operations Research*, V (1957), 469–503.

[7] BLACKMAN, R. B., and J. W. TUKEY. *The Measurement of Power Spectra.* New York: Dover Publications, Inc., 1958.

[8] BLAKE, K., and G. GORDON. "Systems Simulation with Digital Computers," *IBM Systems Journal*, **III**, No. 1 (1964), 14–20.

[9] BONINI, CHARLES P. *Simulation of Information and Decision Systems in the Firm.* Englewood Cliffs, N. J.: Prentice-Hall, Inc., 1963.

[10] BOX, G. E. P. "Multifactor Designs of First Order," *Biometrika*, **XXXIX** (1952), 49–57.

[11] BOX, G. E. P. "The Exploration and Exploitation of Response Surfaces: Some General Considerations and Examples," *Biometrics*, **X** (1954), 16–60.

[12] BOX, G. E. P., and D. W. BEHNKEN. "Some New Three Level Designs for the Study of Quantitative Variables," *Technometrics*, **II** (1960), 455–474.

[13] BOX, G. E. P., and N. R. DRAPER. "A Basis for the Selection of a Response Surface Design," *Journal of American Statistical Association*, **LIV** (1959), 622–654.

[14] BOX, G. E. P., and J. S. HUNTER. "Multi-factor Experimental Designs for Exploring Response Surfaces," *Annals of Mathematical Statistics*, **XXVIII** (1957), 195–241.

[15] BOX, G. E. P., and WILLIAM G. HUNTER. "The Experimental Study of Physical Mechanisms," *Technometrics*, **VII** (1965), 23–42.

[16] BOX, G. E. P., and K. B. WILSON. "On the Experimental Attainment of Optimum Conditions," *Journal of the Royal Statistical Society B*, **XIII** (1951), 1–45.

[17] BOX, G. E. P., and P. V. YOULE. "The Exploration and Exploitation of Response Surfaces: An Example of the Link Between the Fitted Surface and the Basic Mechanism of the System," *Biometrics*, **XI** (1955), 289–323.

[18] BURDICK, DONALD S., and THOMAS H. NAYLOR. "Design of Computer Simulation Experiments for Industrial Systems," *Communications of the ACM*, **IX** (May, 1966), 329–339.

[19] CHERNOFF, HERMAN. "Sequential Design of Experiments," *Annals of Mathematical Statistics*, **XXX** (September, 1959), 755–770.

[20] CHU, KONG, and THOMAS H. NAYLOR. "A Dynamic Model of the Firm," *Management Science*, **XI** (May, 1965), 736–750.

[21] CHURCHMAN, C. WEST. "An Analysis of the Concept of Simulation," in Austin C. Hoggatt and Frederick E. Balderston (Eds.), *Symposium on Simulation Models.* Cincinnati: South-Western Publishing Co., 1963.

[22] CLARK, C. E. "Importance Sampling in Monte Carlo Analyses," *Operations Research*, **IX** (1961), 603–620.

[23] CLARKSON, GEOFFREY P. E. *Portfolio Selection: A Simulation of Trust Investment.* Englewood Cliffs, N. J.: Prentice-Hall, Inc., 1962.

[24] CLARKSON, G. P. E., and H. A. SIMON. "Simulation of Individual and Group Behavior," *American Economic Review*, **L**, No. 5 (December, 1960), 920–932.

[25] COCHRAN, W. G., and COX, G. M. *Experimental Designs*. New York: John Wiley & Sons, 1957.

[26] COHEN, K. J. *Computer Models of the Shoe, Leather, Hide Sequence*. Englewood Cliffs, N. J.: Prentice-Hall, Inc., 1960.

[27] COHEN, KALMAN J., *et al.* "The Carnegie Tech Management Game," in Harold Guetzkow (Ed.), *Simulation in Social Science*. Englewood Cliffs, N. J.: Prentice-Hall, Inc., 1962.

[28] COHEN, KALMAN J., *et al.* *The Carnegie Tech Management Game*. Homewood, Ill.: Richard D. Irwin, 1964.

[29] COHEN, KALMAN J., and RICHARD M. CYERT. "Computer Models in Dynamic Economics, *The Quarterly Journal of Economics*, **LXXV** (February, 1961), 112–127.

[30] COHEN, KALMAN J., and ERIC RHENMAN. "The Role of Management Games in Education and Research," *Management Science*, **VII** (1961), 171–176.

[31] CONWAY, R. W. "Some Tactical Problems in Digital Simulation," *Management Science*, **X** (October, 1963), 47–61.

[32] COX, D. R. *Planning of Experiments*. New York: John Wiley & Sons, 1958.

[33] CYERT, RICHARD M. "A Description and Evaluation of Some Firm Simulations," in *Proceedings of the IBM Scientific Computing Symposium on Simulation Models and Gaming*. White Plains, N. Y.: IBM, 1966.

[34] CYERT, R. M., E. A. FEIGENBAUM, and J. G. MARCH. "Models in a Behavioral Theory of the Firm," *Behavioral Science*, **IV** (April, 1959), 81–95.

[35] CYERT, RICHARD M., and JAMES G. MARCH. *A Behavioral Theory of the Firm*. Englewood Cliffs, N. J.: Prentice-Hall, Inc., 1963.

[36] DAVIES, O. L. (Ed.). *Design and Analysis of Industrial Experiments*. New York: Hafner Publishing Co., 1960.

[37] DEAR, R. E. "Multivariate Analyses of Variance and Covariance for Simulation Studies Involving Normal Time Series," System Development Corporation, FN-5644, November, 1961.

[38] DILL, WILLIAM R., and NEIL DOPPELT. "The Acquisition of Experience in a Complex Management Game," *Management Science*, **X** (October, 1963), 30–46.

[39] DRAPER, N. R., and H. SMITH. *Applied Regression Analysis*. New York: John Wiley & Sons, 1966.

[40] DUNNETT, C. W. "A Multiple Comparison Procedure for Comparing Several Treatments with a Control," *Journal of the American Statistical Association*, **L** (1955), 1096–1121.

[41] EHRENFIELD, S., and S. BEN-TUVIA. "The Efficiency of Statistical Simulation Procedures," *Technometrics*, **IV** (May, 1962), 257–275.

[42] FISHER, RONALD A. *The Design of Experiments*. London: Oliver and Boyd, 1951.

[43] FISHMAN, GEORGE S. "Problems in the Statistical Analysis of Simulation Experiments: The Comparison of Means and the Length of Sample Records," *Communications of the ACM*, **X** (February, 1967), 94–99.

[44] FISHMAN, GEORGE S., and PHILIP J. KIVIAT. "The Analysis of Simulation-Generated Time Series," *Management Science*, **XIII** (March, 1967), 525–557.

[45] FORRESTER, JAY W. *Industrial Dynamics*. New York: The M.I.T. Press and John Wiley & Sons, Inc., 1961.

[46] "Fractional Factorial Designs for Factors at Two and Three Levels," U.S. Department of Commerce, National Bureau of Standards, *Applied Mathematics Series 58*, U.S. Government Printing Office, Washington D.C. 20025 (September 1, 1961).

[47] FROMM, GARY. "An Evaluation of Monetary Policy Instruments," Paper presented at the annual meeting of the Econometric Society, San Francisco, December, 1966.

[48] GAFARIAN, A. V., and C. J. ANCKER. "Mean Value Estimation from Digital Computer Simulation," *Operations Research* (January–February, 1966), 25–44.

[49] *General Purpose Simulator II*, Program Library, Reference 7090-CS-13X, International Business Machines Corporation.

[50] GORDON, G. "A General Purpose Systems Simulator," *IBM Systems Journal*, **I** (1962), 18–32.

[51] GRANGER, C. W. J., and M. HATANAKA. *Spectral Analysis of Economic Time Series*. Princeton, N. J.: Princeton University Press, 1964.

[52] GUPTA, S. S. "On Some Multiple Decision (Selection and Ranking) Rules," *Technometrics*, **VII** (May, 1965), 225–246.

[53] HAMMERSLEY, J. M., and D. C. HANDSCOMB. *Monte Carlo Methods*. New York: John Wiley & Sons, 1964.

[54] HENSHAW, R. C., and J. R. JACKSON. *The Executive Game*. Homewood, Ill.: Richard D. Irwin, Inc., 1966.

[55] HILL, WILLIAM J., and WILLIAM G. HUNTER. "A Review of Response Surface Methodology: A Literature Survey," *Technometrics*, **VIII** (November, 1966), 571–590.

[56] HOGGATT, AUSTIN C. "An Experimental Business Game," *Behavioral Science*, **IV** (1959), 192–203.

[57] HOGGATT, AUSTIN C. "A Simulation Study of an Economic Model," *Contributions to Scientific Research in Management*. The Proceedings of the Scientific Program following the Dedication of the Western Data Processing Center, Graduate School of Business Administration, University of California, Los Angeles, January 29–30, 1959.

[58] HOLT, CHARLES C., ROBERT W. SHIRLEY, DONALD V. STEWARD, JOSEPH L. MIDLER, and ARTHUR STROUD. "Program SIMULATE, a User's and Programmer's Manual," Social Systems Research Institute, University of Wisconsin, May, 1964 (mimeographed).

[59] HUFSCHMIDT, M. M. "Analysis of Simulation: Examination of Response Surface," in Arthur Maass *et al.* (Eds.), *Design of Water-Resource Systems*. Cambridge: Harvard University Press, 1966.

[60] "IBM Management Decision-Making Laboratory Administrator's Reference Manual," International Business Machines Corporation, B20-8099 (1963).

[61] JACKSON, R. R. P. "Queueing Systems with Phase Type Service," *Operational Research Quarterly*, **V** (1964).

[62] JACOBY, J. A., and S. HARRISON. "Multi-variable Experimentation and Simulation Models," *Naval Research Logistics Quarterly*, **IX** (1962), 121–136.

[63] JENKINS, G. M. "General Considerations in the Analysis of Spectra," *Technometrics*, **III** (May, 1961), 133–166.

[64] JOHNSTON, J. *Econometric Methods.* New York: McGraw-Hill Book Co., 1967.

[65] KAHN, HERMAN. "Use of Different Monte Carlo Sampling Techniques," The RAND Corporation, P-766, November 30, 1955.

[66] KENDALL, M. G., and ALAN STUART. *The Advanced Theory of Statistics.* Vol. II: *Inference and Relationship.* New York: Hagner Publishing Co., 1961.

[67] KENDALL, M. G., and ALAN STUART. *The Advanced Theory of Statistics.* Vol. III: *Design and Analysis, and Time-Series.* New York: Hafner Publishing Co., 1966.

[68] KIEFER, J. "Invariance, Minimax Sequential Estimation, and Continuous Time Processes," *Annals of Mathematical Statistics,* **XXVIII** (March, 1957), 573–601.

[69] KIEFER, J. "Sequential Minimax Search for a Maximum," in *Proceedings of the American Mathematical Society* (June, 1953).

[70] KIEFER, J., and J. SACKS. "Asymptotically Optimum Sequential Inference and Design," *Annals of Mathematical Statistics,* **XXXIV** (September, 1963), 705–750.

[71] KIEFER, J., and L. WEISS. "Some Properties of Generalized Sequential Probability Ratio Tests," *Annals of Mathematical Statistics,* **XXVIII** (1957), 57–75.

[72] MACLAREN, M. D., and G. MARSAGLIA. "Uniform Random Number Generators," *Journal of the ACM,* **XII** (1965), 83–89.

[73] MALINVAUD, E. *Statistical Methods in Econometrics.* Chicago: Rand McNally & Co., 1966.

[74] MARKOWITZ, H. M., BERNARD HAUSNER, and H. W. KARR. *SIMSCRIPT: A Simulation Programming Language,* The RAND Corporation, RM-3310, November, 1962.

[75] MCKENNEY, JAMES L. *Simulation Gaming for Management Development.* Boston: Graduate School of Business Administration, Harvard University, 1967.

[76] MILLER, D. W., and MARTIN K. STARR. *Inventory Control: Theory and Practice.* Englewood Cliffs, N. J.: Prentice-Hall, Inc., 1962.

[77] NAYLOR, THOMAS H. "The Economic Theory of the Firm: Three Tools of Analysis," *Quarterly Review of Economics and Business* (1966), 33–49.

[78] NAYLOR, THOMAS H., JOSEPH L. BALINTFY, DONALD S. BURDICK, and KONG CHU. *Computer Simulation Techniques.* New York: John Wiley & Sons, 1966.

[79] NAYLOR, THOMAS H., DONALD S. BURDICK, and W. EARL SASSER. "Computer Simulation Experiments with Economic Systems: The Problem of Experimental Design," *Journal of the American Statistical Association,* **LXII** (December, 1967), 1315–1337.

[80] NAYLOR, THOMAS H., and J. M. FINGER. "Verification of Computer Simulation Models," *Management Science,* **XIV** (October, 1967), 92–101.

[81] NAYLOR, THOMAS H., WILLIAM H. WALLACE, and W. EARL SASSER. "A Computer Simulation Model of the Textile Industry," *Journal of the American Statistical Association,* **LXII** (December, 1967), 1338–1364.

[82] NAYLOR, THOMAS H., KENNETH WERTZ, and THOMAS WONNACOTT. "Methods for Analyzing Data from Computer Simulation Experiments," *Communications of the ACM*, **X** (November, 1967), 703–710.

[83] NAYLOR, THOMAS H., KENNETH WERTZ, and THOMAS WONNACOTT. "Spectral Analysis of Data Generated by Simulation Experiments with Econometric Models," *Econometrica*, **XXXVII** (April, 1969).

[84] NAYLOR, THOMAS H., KENNETH WERTZ, and THOMAS WONNACOTT. "Some Methods for Evaluating the Effects of Economic Policies Using Simulation Experiments," *Review of the International Statistical Institute*, **XXXVII** (February, 1968), 184–200.

[85] PARZEN, EMANUEL. "Mathematical Considerations in the Estimation of Spectra," *Technometrics*, **III** (May, 1961), 167–190.

[86] PRESTON, LEE E., and NORMAN R. COLLINS. *Studies in a Simulated Market*, Research Program in Marketing, Graduate School of Business Administration, University of California, Berkeley, 1966.

[87] PUGH, ALEXANDER L. *DYNAMO User's Manual*. Cambridge, Mass.: Technology Press, 1963.

[88] QUENOUILLE, M. H. *The Design and Analysis of Experiments*. New York: Hafner Publishing Co., 1953.

[89] REICHENBACH, HANS. *The Rise of Scientific Philosophy*. Berkeley: University of California Press, 1951.

[90] SAATY, THOMAS L. *Elements of Queueing Theory*. New York: McGraw-Hill Book Co., 1961.

[91] SCHEFFÉ, HENRY. *The Analysis of Variance*. New York: John Wiley & Sons, 1959.

[92] SHUBIK, MARTIN. *Strategy and Market Structure*. New York: John Wiley & Sons, 1959.

[93] SHUBIK, MARTIN. "Simulation and the Theory of the Firm," in *Contributions to Scientific Research in Management*. The Proceedings of the Scientific Program following the Dedication of the Western Data Processing Center, Graduate School of Business Administration, University of California, Los Angeles, January 29–30, 1959.

[94] SHUBIK, MARTIN. "Simulation of the Industry and the Firm," *American Economic Review*, **L**, No. 5 (December, 1960), 908–919.

[95] SHUBIK, MARTIN. *Game Theory and Related Approaches to Social Behavior*. New York: John Wiley & Sons, 1964.

[96] SIEGEL, SIDNEY. *Nonparametric Statistics*. New York: McGraw-Hill Book Co., 1956.

[97] TEICHROEW, DANIEL, and JOHN F. LUBIN. "Computer Simulation: Discussion of Techniques and Comparison of Languages," *Communications of the ACM*, **IX** (October, 1966), 723–741.

[98] THEIL, H. *Economic Forecasts and Policy*. Amsterdam: North-Holland Publishing Co., 1961.

[99] TOCHER, K. D. *The Art of Simulation*. Princeton, N. J.: D. Van Nostrand Co., 1963.

[100] TUKEY, JOHN W. "Discussion Emphasizing the Connection Between Analysis of Variance and Spectral Analysis," *Technometrics*, **III** (May, 1961), 191–220.

[101] WALD, A. *Sequential Analysis.* New York: John Wiley & Sons, 1947.

[102] WALLACE, WILLIAM H., THOMAS H. NAYLOR, and W. EARL SASSER. "An Econometric Model of the Textile Industry in the United States," *Review of Economics and Statistics*, **XLX** (February, 1968), 13–22.

[103] WALSH, JOHN E. *Handbook of Nonparametric Statistics*, Vols. I and II. Princeton, N. J.: D. Van Nostrand Co., 1962 and 1965.

[104] WINER, B. J. *Statistical Principles in Experimental Design.* New York: McGraw-Hill Book Co., 1962.

14

A computer model of the firm

INTRODUCTION

In this chapter we shall apply the methodology described in Chapter 13 to a model of the firm developed by Chu and Naylor [7]. With marginal analysis and linear programming it was relatively easy to find examples which were fairly typical of their particular classification of models of the firm. However, with computer simulation the range of choice in selecting an example model is so broad that it is impossible to formulate a "typical" computer model of the firm. The reason for this difficulty stems from the fact that we have almost complete freedom of choice in selecting the assumptions on which to base a computer simulation model of the firm. The only limitations imposed on computer models are those constraints imposed by (1) existing physical limitations of present-day digital computers, and (2) limitations in the imagination and mathematical prowess of the model builder. Therefore, our choice of the following model to illustrate the application of computer simulation to the theory of the firm is necessarily quite arbitrary.

THE MODEL

The assumptions underlying the model are summarized below:

1. The firm possesses a k-stage production process capable of manufacturing a single product. Without exception, each unit of final output of the firm must pass through all k of these stages in a particular order (see Figure 14-1).
2. Each process has its own separate production function, which is independent of the production functions of the other $k - 1$ processes.

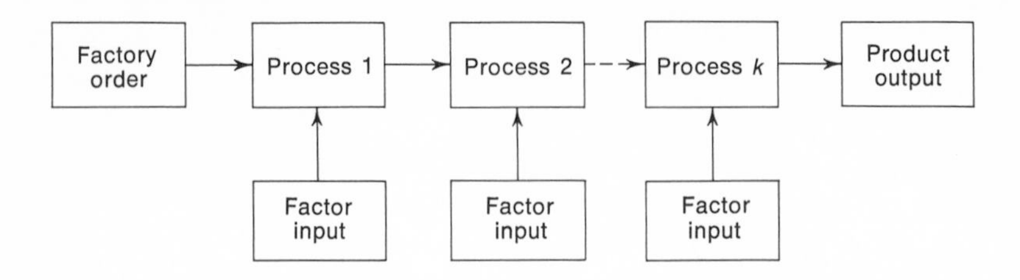

FIGURE **14-1**

Flow chart for a model of the firm

3. The rate of output (production rate) of the jth process, Q_j ($j = 1, 2, \ldots, k$), during planning period TM is a random variable. Its probability density function $f_j(q)$ is completely determined by the level of factor inputs for process j during planning period TM—which is to say that by altering its allocation of productive inputs the firm can alter the probability distributions of the Q_j. If $f_j(q)$ is determined, then obviously the expected value $E(Q_j)$ and variance Var (Q_j) for process j are also determined.
4. Although the neoclassical production function was designed to measure Q_j, the quantity of output per unit time, it is more convenient in this model to use the reciprocal relationship, $ST_j = 1/Q_j$, where ST_j denotes the time required to produce one unit of output or one production order in the jth process ($j = 1, 2, \ldots, k$). The probability density function for ST_j and its parameters are completely determined by the level of factor inputs for process j. Therefore, for each process, ST_j may be treated as a random variable with a known probability density function $f_j(ST)$, expected value ET_j, and variance VT_j. In other words, the firm cannot completely control the value of ST_j, but it can affect ET_j or VT_j, or even $f_j(ST)$ by altering the rate of factor inputs for process j. Hence for specified rates of factor input at the jth process, ST_j is a random variable which is not subject to further control by the firm.
5. The number of orders which arrive at the firm per unit time (or the quantity of output which can be sold per unit time at a particular price) is a random variable D with probability density function $f(d)$, expected value $E(D)$, and variance Var (D). Hence the firm cannot ordinarily [Var $(D) \neq 0$] predict with complete certainty the number of units it can sell at a given price during TM. However, it is able to influence $f(d)$, $E(D)$, and Var (D) by adjusting its expenditure strategies for advertising, marketing, and promotion. Demand is said to be a stochastic process, or equivalently, the time interval between the arrival of orders may be thought of as a stochastic process. In this model it is more convenient to think of the latter type of stochastic process. We define a random variable AT_i, the time interval between the arrival of the ith order and the $(i-1)$th order, with a known probability density function $f(AT)$,

expected value ET, and variance VT. Like the density function of demand, $f(AT)$ is also affected by advertising, marketing, and promotion strategies.

6. Once committed to a chosen rate of factor inputs, the firm accepts all orders received throughout the planning period TM, even though it may not be able to finish production (or possibly begin production) on all such orders in the period.
7. At the beginning of planning period TM management must make two different types of decisions: (a) those pertaining to levels of expenditure for advertising and marketing and (b) those pertaining to factor input allocations for the k production processes. Recall that the former completely determine $f(d)$, $E(D)$, and Var (D) over TM, while the latter likewise govern $f_j(q)$, $E(Q_j)$, and Var (Q_j) $(j = 1, 2, \ldots, k)$.

We now turn to the formulation of a mathematical model describing our dynamic multiprocess firm. Let

(14-1) AT_i = time interval between the arrival of the ith order and the $(i - 1)$th order, where an order is defined as the demand by a customer for the firm to produce one unit of final output and $i = 1, \ldots, m$.

(14-2) ST_{ij} = process time for the ith order in the jth process, where $i = 1, \ldots, m$ and $j = 1, \ldots, k$.

(14-3) WT_{ij} = amount of time which the ith order spends waiting to enter the jth process, where $i = 1, \ldots, m$ and $j = 1, \ldots, k$.

(14-4) DT_{ij} = amount of time which the jth process remains idle while waiting for the ith order to arrive, where $i = 1, \ldots, m$ and $j = 1, \ldots, k$.

(14-5) $T_{ij} = WT_{ij} + ST_{ij}$, $i = 1, \ldots, m; j = 1, \ldots, k$,
= the total time which the ith order spends at the jth process.

When the first order arrives at the firm, that is, when $i = 1$, the following equations are assumed to describe the multiprocess system.

(14-6) $$AT_1 = 0$$

(14-7) $$DT_{11} = 0, \quad DT_{12} = ST_{11}, \ldots, DT_{1k} = \sum_{j=1}^{k-1} ST_{1j}$$

(14-8) $$WT_{11} = 0, \quad WT_{12} = 0, \ldots, WT_{1k} = 0$$

(14-9) $$T_{11} = ST_{11}, \quad T_{12} = ST_{12}, \ldots, T_{1k} = ST_{1k}$$

For subsequent arrivals, that is, when $i = 2, 3, \ldots, m$, these equations must be modified accordingly. The T-equations become

$$
\begin{aligned}
T_{i1} &= WT_{i1} + ST_{i1} \qquad i = 2, \ldots, m \\
T_{i2} &= WT_{i2} + ST_{i2} \qquad i = 2, \ldots, m \\
&\vdots \\
T_{ik} &= WT_{ik} + ST_{ik} \qquad i = 2, \ldots, m
\end{aligned}
\tag{14-10}
$$

Whether waiting time or idle time occurs at a particular process depends on the sign of the following differences, where $i = 2, \ldots, m$:

$$
\begin{aligned}
DIF_1 &= T_{i-1,1} - AT_i \\
DIF_2 &= (T_{i-1,1} + T_{i-1,2}) - (AT_i + WT_{i1} + ST_{i1}) \\
&\vdots \\
DIF_k &= (T_{i-1,1} + T_{i-1,2} + \cdots + T_{i-1,k}) \\
&\qquad - (AT_i + WT_{i1} + ST_{i1} + \cdots + WT_{i,k-1} + ST_{i,k-1})
\end{aligned}
\tag{14-11}
$$

If DIF_j is positive for the jth process, then idle time will be zero, and waiting time can be calculated by

$$WT_{ij} = DIF_j \qquad i = 2, \ldots, m; j = 1, \ldots, k \tag{14-12}$$

If DIF_j is negative for a particular process, then waiting time will be zero, and idle time will be equal to

$$DT_{ij} = -DIF_j \qquad i = 2, \ldots, m; j = 1, \ldots, k \tag{14-13}$$

If DIF_j is equal to zero for a particular process, then both waiting time and idle time will be equal to zero for that process.

Furthermore, AT_i is assumed to be a random variable with probability density function $f(AT)$, expected value ET, and variance VT. And for each process ST_{ij} is assumed to be a random variable with probability density function $f_j(ST_j)$, expected value ET_j, and variance VT_j.

Having set forth the model, let us now endow the firm with more specific characteristics. The length of the firm's planning horizon is three months ($TM = 90$ days) and is assumed to have been determined by the environment of the firm rather than on the basis of statistical considerations. That is, the firm's decision makers are interested in making plans for the next 90 days—no more, no less.

The *response variable* or dependent variable in our simulation is profit. The *factors* in the experiment are (1) expenditures for productive inputs (labor, raw materials, equipment, etc.) and (2) expenditures for advertising, marketing, and promotion. As previously defined in the description of the model, both of these factors are *quantitative*. That is, in theory there exists a functional relationship between the numerical values of the levels of (1) expenditures for productive inputs and (2) expenditures for advertising, marketing, and promotion and the profitability of the firm. Although the firm's decision makers may choose from among an infinite number of levels for each factor, in practice, owing to indivisibilities, institutional rigidities, incomplete information, and other reasons, the decision makers may restrict their factor-level decision to a finite number of levels. In our example model, we assume that the firm has simplified its factor-level decision to the point where it is considering only five different operating plans, each featuring (1) a particular advertising and marketing strategy, (2) a particular allocation of inputs to the various stages of production, which we limit to four in number ($0 < k \leq 4$), and (3) a total cost, C. (We have already elaborated on points (1) and (2) in the preceding section; total costs appear in Table 14-1.) In other words, the firm's controllable quantitative factors have in effect been reduced to five levels of a single qualitative factor, i.e., five operating plans or decision rules.

As a further simplification, we specify $f(d)$ and the $f_j(q)$ to be Poisson distributions (arising from Poisson processes) for all five operating plans. This means that each operating plan consists of the specification (Table 14-1) of a total expenditure C and a set of values for the parameters $E(D)$, $E(Q_1)$, $E(Q_2)$, $E(Q_3)$, and $E(Q_4)$. For simulation purposes, it is convenient to take advantage of the well-known relationship between the *exponential* and *Poisson* distributions. It can be shown that if (1) the total number of events occurring during any given time interval is independent of the number of events that have already occurred prior to the beginning of the interval and (2) the probability of an event occurring in the interval t to $t + \Delta t$ is approximately $\lambda \, \Delta t$ for all values of t (where λ is a constant), then (1) the density function of the interval t between the occurrence of consecutive events is given by the negative exponential distribution,

$$f(t) = \lambda e^{-\lambda t} \tag{14-14}$$

and the probability of x events occurring during time t is

$$f(x) = e^{-\lambda t} \frac{(\lambda t)^x}{x!} \quad \text{for all } x \text{ and } t \tag{14-15}$$

TABLE **14-1**

Theoretical values for expected demand and expected production rates (in units per day) and total cost (in dollars) for a computer model of the firm.

Plans	Expected demand rate, $E(D)$	Expected production rates: Process 1 $E(Q_1)$	Process 2 $E(Q_2)$	Process 3 $E(Q_3)$	Process 4 $E(Q_4)$	Total cost, C
I	3.00	3.33	3.75	4.00	3.50	$ 800
II	3.00	3.50	3.33	6.00	3.50	$ 800
III	3.00	5.00	4.25	6.00	5.00	$1,250
IV	3.75	5.00	4.25	6.00	5.00	$1,550
V	3.75	5.00	—	4.50	4.50	$1,720

For the language of our model, $f(d)$ and $f_j(q)$ are Poisson with parameters $E(D)$, $E(Q_1)$, $E(Q_2)$, $E(Q_3)$, and $E(Q_4)$ respectively. The time interval between orders AT and the process times ST_j have negative exponential distributions with parameters

(14-16) $$EAT = 1/E(D)$$

(14-17) $$EST_j = 1/E(Q_j) \qquad j = 1, 2, 3, 4$$

The computer simulation experiment which we conducted with this model consisted of 5 runs, one for each operating plan. The parameters used—demand rate (in units per day), production rates (in units per day), and total cost—are tabulated in Table 14-1. Note that plan V consists of 3 processes rather than 4. A price P of $15 per unit of finished product is assumed to prevail throughout the experiment.

THE COMPUTER PROGRAM

Figure 14-2 contains a computer flow chart of the logic of our model of the firm. This flow chart will generate n replications of a given plan for our model. Each replication is run for TM units of time. The output of each replication is total profit:

(14-18) $$\text{Profit} = P \cdot Q - C$$

where P is price, Q is the number of units of product completed during time period TM, and C is total cost. The flow chart (and computer program) assumes the availability of a computer subroutine for generating negative exponential variates with a given expected value.

In block 1 of Figure 14-2 the parameters K (total number of processes) and N (the number of replications of the simulation run) are read into the computer as input data. Next the values of P, C, TM, EAT, and EST_j ($j = 1, \ldots, k$) are read into the memory of the computer. These are the parameters for a given plan. Note that EST_j is expressed as $EST(J)$ in the flow chart so as to conform with the FORTRAN computer programming language. Blocks 3 and 4 are initialization procedures in which L (an index for counting the number of replications) and Q (the number of units of output) are set equal to zero. In block 5, process times are generated by the negative exponential subroutine. Next we compute idle time, waiting time, and total time for each process for the initial order according to (14-7), (14-8), and (14-9) respectively.

This program makes use of a simulated clock. The clock is set equal to idle time plus process time for process K in block 7. At the end of the planning horizon TM, the clock will have a value which is at least as great as TM. The arrival of a second order is indicated in block 8 by the generation of an arrival time AT, i.e., the time which has elapsed between the arrival of order 1 and the arrival of order 2. Since a new order has been received, K additional process times must be generated in block 9. Total completed output is incremented by 1 in block 10.

B and D are set equal to $T(1)$ and AT, respectively, in blocks 11 and 12. Blocks 13 through 21 are repeated K times, i.e., once for each of the K production processes. In block 14 the appropriate difference indicated by equation system (14-11) is obtained. If $WT(J)$ is positive, idle time will be equal to zero and waiting time will be equal to $WT(J)$. If $WT(J)$ is equal to zero, then both waiting time and idle time are equal to zero. If $WT(J)$ is negative, waiting time will be equal to zero and idle time will be equal to $-WT(J)$. In block 19, $T(J)$ is calculated according to (14-10) for the jth process. B and D are recalculated in blocks 20 and 21 in accordance with (14-11). Clock time is updated in block 22.

If clock time is less than TM, then we return to block 8 and generate another inter-order time and a set of K process times. However, if clock time is greater than or equal to TM, then we have completed one replication of the first simulation run. Total profit for that replication is calculated according to (14-18) and printed on the output report. If the number of completed replications, L, is less than N, the number of replications required for the run, then L is increased by 1 and a new replication is begun in block 4. If the number of replications which have been completed is greater than or equal to N, then the run is terminated and a card is read in block 2 which contains the parameters for the next run.

The FORTRAN computer program corresponding to the flow chart in Figure 14-2 is displayed in Figure 14-3. Since there is almost a one to one correspondence between the statements of the FORTRAN program and the blocks in the flow chart, it will not be necessary to repeat the explanation of the logic of the program. However, a brief digression will be included to explain the FORTRAN subroutine for generating exponential variables.

A random variable, X, is said to have an exponential distribution if its density function is defined as

(14-19) $$f(x) = \alpha e^{-\alpha x}$$

for $\alpha > 0$ and $x \geq 0$.

The cumulative distribution function of X is

(14-20) $$F(x) = \int_0^x \alpha e^{-\alpha t}\, dt = 1 - e^{-\alpha x}$$

and the expected value and variance of X are given by the following formulas:

(14-21) $$EX = \int_0^\infty x\alpha e^{-\alpha x}\, dx = \frac{1}{\alpha}$$

(14-22) $$VX = \int_0^\infty \left(x - \frac{1}{\alpha}\right)^2 \alpha e^{-\alpha x}\, dx = \frac{1}{\alpha^2} = (EX)^2$$

Since the exponential distribution has only one parameter α it is possible to express α as

(14-23) $$\alpha = \frac{1}{EX}$$

FIGURE **14-2**

A flow chart for a computer model of the firm

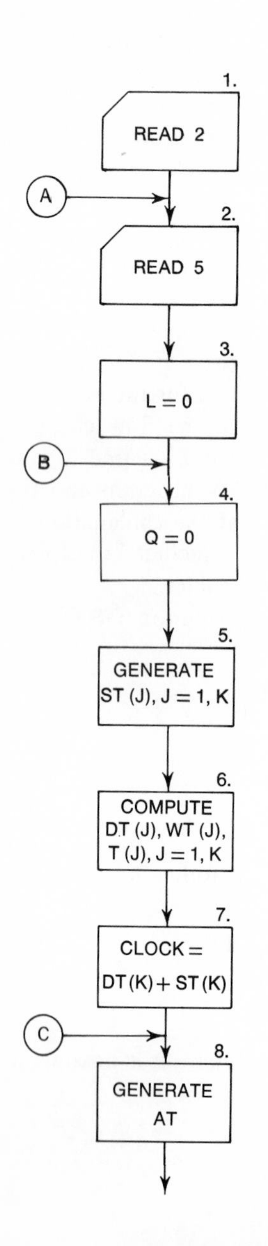

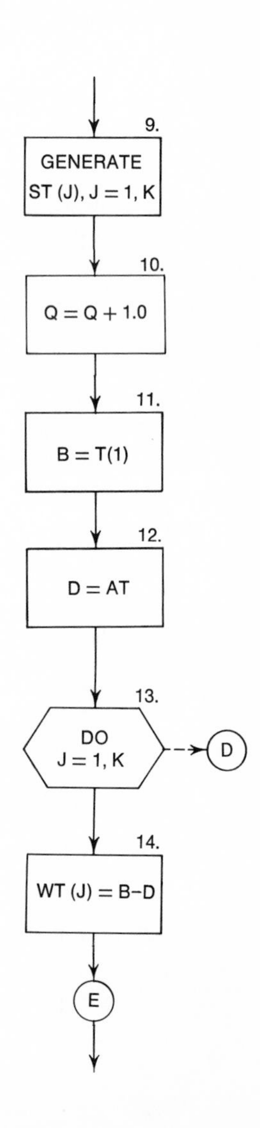

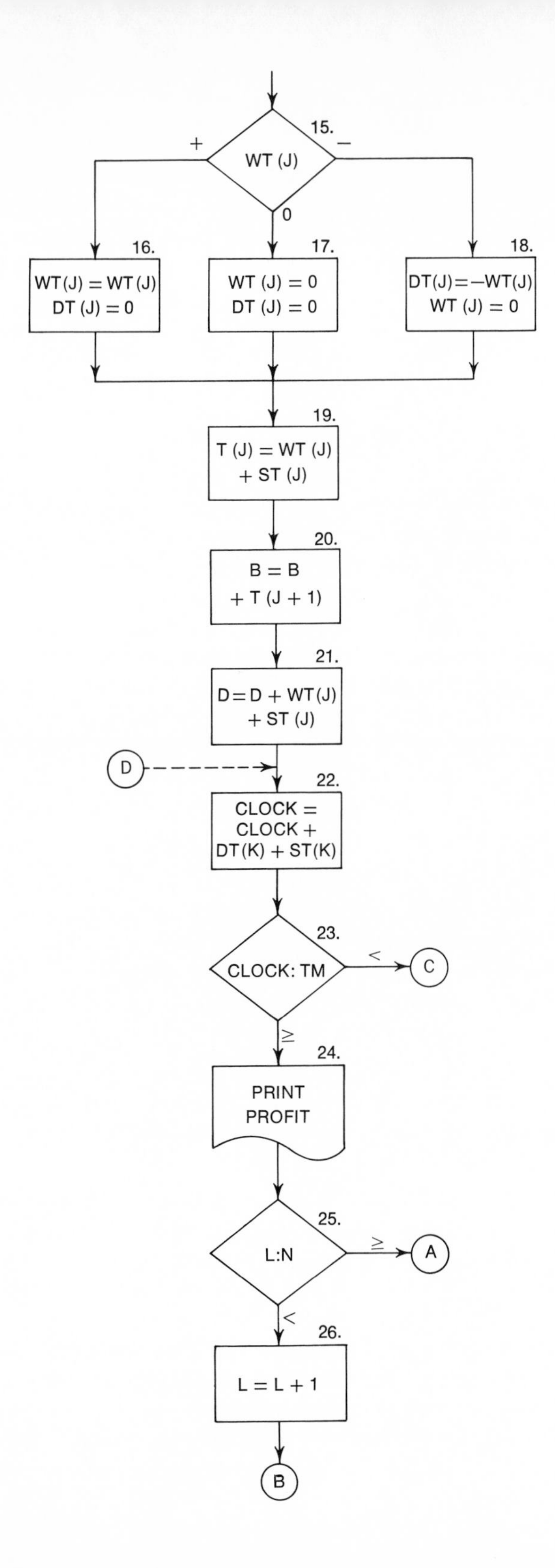
15.
WT (J)
+
−
0
16.
WT(J) = WT(J)
DT (J) = 0
17.
WT (J) = 0
DT (J) = 0
18.
DT(J)=−WT(J)
WT (J) = 0
19.
T (J) = WT (J)
+ ST (J)
20.
B = B
+ T (J + 1)
21.
D = D + WT(J)
+ ST (J)
D
22.
CLOCK =
CLOCK +
DT(K) + ST(K)
23.
CLOCK: TM
<
C
≥
24.
PRINT
PROFIT
25.
L:N
≥
A
<
26.
L = L + 1
B

The generation of exponential random variables can be accomplished in a number of different ways. But since $F(x)$ exists in explicit form, the inverse transformation technique provides a straightforward method. Because of the symmetry of the uniform distribution, $F(x)$ and $1 - F(x)$ are interchangeable. Therefore,

$$r = e^{-\alpha x} \tag{14-24}$$

and consequently,

$$x = -\left(\frac{1}{\alpha}\right) \log_e r = -EX \log_e r \tag{14-25}$$

Thus for each value of the pseudo-random number r a unique value of x is determined, which will take only non-negative values (since $\log_e r \leq 0$ for $0 \leq r \leq 1$), and will follow the exponential density function (14-19) with expected value EX. Although this technique seems very simple, the reader is reminded that the computation of the natural logarithm on digital computers includes a power series expansion (or some equivalent approximation technique) for each uniform variable generated.

Two FORTRAN instructions are required to generate an exponential variable.

(14-26) R = RAND(R)

(14-27) X = −EX*LØGF(R)

where RAND is a subroutine for generating uniformly distributed variables on the (0, 1) interval and LØGF is a subroutine for taking the natural logarithm of a number. Both of these subroutines are available on nearly all of the digital computers which are in use today. The subroutine for generating exponential variables appears in statements 9 and 10, 19 and 20, and 22 and 23. These FORTRAN statements correspond to blocks 5, 8, and 9 respectively of Figure 14-2.

VALIDATION

In the preceding chapter we suggested that in order to validate a computer model we must compare simulated data (data generated by the computer) with actual and historical data. Since our example is a purely hypothetical model, this type of validation is clearly impossible. However, another alternative is available to us.

The steady-state properties of a single-channel, multistation queueing model with Poisson arrivals and service rates are available and can be used to check on the validity of the results of our simulation experiment. Normally, we would not perform a simulation experiment when an analytical solution exists for the problem to be solved. However, in the case of an expository treatment of

```
 1  READ 2, K, N
 2  FØRMAT (2I2)
 3  DIMENSIØN EST(K), ST(K), T(K), WT(K), DT(K)
 4  READ 5, P, C, TM, EAT, (EST(J), J=1, K)
 5  FØRMAT (10F10.2)
 6  L=1
 7  Q=0
 8  DØ 10 J=1, K
 9  R=RAND(R)
10  ST(J)=-EST(J)*LØGF(R)
11  K1=K-1
12  DT(1)=0.
13  DØ 14 J=1, K1
14  DT(J+1)=DT(J)+ST(J)
15  DØ 17 J=1, K
16  WT(J)=0.
17  T(J)=ST(J)
18  CLØCK=DT(K)+ST(K)
19  R=RAND(R)
20  AT=-EAT*LOGF(R)
21  DØ 23 J=1, K
22  R=RAND(R)
23  ST(J)=-EST(J)*LØGF(R)
24  Q=Q+1.0
25  B=T(1)
26  D=AT
27  DØ 37 J=1, K
28  WT(J)=B-D
29  IF(WT(J))30, 30, 33
30  DT(J)=-WT(J)
31  WT(J)=0.
32  GØ TØ 34
33  DT(J)=0.
34  T(J)=WT(J)+ST(J)
35  B=B+T(J+1)
36  D=D+WT(J)+ST(J)
37  CØNTINUE
38  CLØCK=CLØCK+DT(K)+ST(K)
39  IF(CLØCK-TM) 19, 40, 40
40  PRØFIT=P*Q-C
41  PRINT 42, PRØFIT
42  FØRMAT (F10.2)
43  IF(L-N) 44, 4, 4
44  L=L+1
45  GØ TØ 7
46  END
```

FIGURE **14-3**
A computer program for a computer model of the firm

simulation, an analytical solution provides a means of validating the results of the experiment. Our model can accommodate without complication any type of probability distribution or empirical distribution for both $f(d)$ and any number of $f_j(d)$, thus extending the reach of investigation into the realm where analytical solutions or approximations are too difficult to obtain.

Approximate expected total profit π may be calculated analytically by the following formula for the case of Poisson demand and Poisson production processes [30,44]:

$$\pi = (\text{Expected total revenue}) - (\text{Expected total cost}) \tag{14-28}$$

$$= P\left[E(D)\cdot TM - \sum_{j=1}^{k} \frac{E(D)/E(Q_j)}{1 - E(D)/E(Q_j)}\right] - C$$

where

$$E(D)\cdot TM = \text{expected number of orders which enter the system or expected total demand during the planning period} \tag{14-29}$$

$$\sum_{j=1}^{k} \frac{E(D)/E(Q_j)}{1 - E(D)/E(Q_j)} = \text{expected number of units remaining in the system either being processed or waiting to be processed at the end of the planning period} \tag{14-30}$$

$$E(D)\cdot TM - \sum_{j=1}^{k} \frac{E(D)/E(Q_j)}{1 - E(D)/E(Q_j)} = \text{expected number of completed orders or expected sales measured in units during the planning period} \tag{14-31}$$

P, TM, K, and C have already been defined. This formula for expected profit assumes $E(D)/E(Q_j) < 1$, and is merely an approximation, since it assumes that the system has reached a steady state within 90 days.

Table 14-2 contains a comparison of the theoretical values of π for each of the five plans with the sample means for each plan generated by the simulation

TABLE **14-2**

Comparison of approximate expected profit with simulation results for five alternative plans for a computer model of the firm.

Plans	Approximate expected profit, π	Sample mean of profit, $\bar{X}$	Sample standard deviation of profit, s
I	$2,918.64	$2,976.40	$175.83
II	$2,918.64	$2,992.30	$202.20
III	$2,704.00	$2,675.20	$250.51
IV	$3,285.00	$3,265.30	$221.81
V	$3,147.50	$3,131.90	$277.04

experiment. The theoretical values were calculated from (14-28) and the data in Table 14-1. More will be said about this table later, but for the moment it will suffice to say that the sample means of profit for each of the five plans are very close to their corresponding theoretical values, and thus tend to confirm the validity of the results of our simulation experiment.

THE EXPERIMENT [39]

The *initial conditions* for our experiment were identical for all replications of each simulation run. The system was assumed to be "empty" at the beginning of each replication for all 5 simulation runs. [See (14-6) through (14-9).] Activity was simulated for a period of 90 days and total profit was calculated for the period. The simulation was repeated 50 times using the given parameters for Plan I. (Repetition was accomplished by altering the starting value of the pseudorandom number generator.) In a similar manner, 90-day runs, each repeated 50 times, were made for strategies II through V. For each sample of 50 observations, the sample mean and standard deviation were calculated and tabulated in Table 14-2.

We now turn our attention to the rationale underlying the sample sizes chosen for this experiment as well as an analysis of some of the effects which these sample sizes have had on the experimental results.

The problem of sample size with computer simulation experiments is indeed complex and has been treated by a number of researchers including Burdick and Naylor [6], Fishman and Kiviat [19], Gafarian and Ancker [20], and Geisler [21]. With computer simulation, sample size may be increased in two different ways: (1) the total length of the simulation run may be increased from, say, one month of simulated time to two months of simulated time; (2) runs of a given length may be replicated by using different sets of pseudorandom numbers.

First consider the length of the simulation run. The length of the firm's planning horizon, 90 days, is assumed to be given. The choice of a suitable planning horizon is assumed to have been made by the firm's policy makers prior to and independent of the decision to use simulation as a mode of analysis. In other words, the length of the simulation run was not determined on the basis of statistical considerations.

Second, we consider the number of replications for each of our five simulation runs. We elected to use the same number of replications for each of the five simulation runs because inequality of variances over the five operating plans has little effect on inferences about population means in the analysis of variance when the sample size is the same for all five operating plans [46, p. 345].

It is well known that the optimal sample size in analysis of variance depends on the answers to the following three questions: (1) How large a shift in means do you wish to detect? (2) How much variability is present in the population?

(3) What size risks are you willing to take? Power-function charts for the specification of sample size in analysis of variance are available for determining n, the number of replications per plan for: (1) a given number of plans m; (2) a given population variance σ^2 for each plan; (3) a given level of significance α; and (4) a given power P to detect (5) a specified difference $\pi_j - \pi$ between the jth population mean and the grand mean.

Although it may be possible to specify a difference $\pi_j - \pi$ which we wish to detect for each plan, a level of significance and a power for our experiment, meaningful estimates of the unknown parameter σ^2 are not so easy to obtain. Estimates of σ^2 must be based on past experimentation, a pilot study, or familiarity with the system being simulated. Matters are further complicated by the fact that there is reason to believe that the variance is not exactly the same for all five plans in our experiment. In order to obtain some idea of what n should be, we assume that

$$m = 5$$

$$\sigma = 225$$

$$\alpha = 0.05$$

$$P = 0.90$$

$$\begin{aligned} \pi_j - \pi &= 100 \qquad j = 1, 2 \\ &= 0 \qquad j = 3 \\ &= -100 \qquad j = 4, 5 \end{aligned}$$

Using the power-function charts described in [51, p. 104], we obtain a sample size of $n = 20$ for each plan. For $\sigma = 350$, and everything else held constant, we would obtain $n = 50$. To be safe, we have set the sample size at 50 replications per plan.

In the remainder of this chapter we shall apply the F-test, multiple comparisons, and multiple rankings to the data generated by the aforementioned experiment. Before turning to these specific data analysis techniques we should inquire about the accuracy of the sample means which appear in Table 14-2. This question can be answered in part by constructing 99% (or any other appropriate level) confidence intervals using the formula:

$$\pi = \bar{X} \pm \frac{zs}{\sqrt{n}} \qquad \text{(14-32)}$$

where $\bar{X}$ is the sample mean, s is the sample standard deviation, $n = 50$ is the sample size, z is the percentile of the normal distribution which leaves 0.5% probability in each tail, and π is the true profit. (This formula is only an approximation since s is used for σ.) Constructing 99% confidence intervals for each of the five plans we obtain:

Plan I	$2{,}912 < \pi_1 < 3{,}040$
Plan II	$2{,}918 < \pi_2 < 3{,}065$
Plan III	$2{,}584 < \pi_3 < 2{,}766$
Plan IV	$3{,}185 < \pi_4 < 3{,}345$
Plan V	$3{,}031 < \pi_5 < 3{,}233$

The approximate (steady-state) true profits π_j are, in fact, contained in these confidence intervals. We notice, however, in plans I and II that the steady-state π_j come close to missing the confidence interval. This is because these two plans involve the most congested queues (which take longest to reach the steady state), and therefore have their true π_j approximated most poorly. A longer planning horizon (greater than 90 days) would have brought us closer to the steady state and doubtless improved the accuracy of the approximate true profit in Table 14-2.

DATA ANALYSIS

The analysis of variance is a collection of techniques which are appropriate when the factors affecting the response are qualitative. We shall illustrate three different forms of the analysis of variance: the F-test [46], the multiple comparisons of Tukey [49] and Dunnett [15], and the multiple-ranking procedure of Bechhofer, Dunnett, and Sobel [4].

All of these procedures were developed on three assumptions: (1) independence of the statistical errors, (2) equality of variance, and (3) normality. The first assumption is satisfied by virtue of the independence of the pseudorandom numbers. We know that the second and third assumptions are not exactly satisfied by our queueing model. The means of the five plans are slightly different (Table 14-2). The variances are doubtless different too, although the sample standard deviations in Table 14-2 indicate that the differences are slight. Profit fluctuates according to the number of orders arriving in 90 days, less the number of orders remaining in the system. Both of these numbers are approximately normally distributed (Poisson variates with large means are very nearly normal), so that we can expect the total profit to be approximately normal too. This expectation was borne out by sample histograms and data analysis.

However, all is not lost as a result of the departure from assumptions (2) and (3) of the analysis of variance. Certain procedures such as the F-test are known to be robust—that is, quite insensitive to departures from assumptions [46, pp. 331–368]. For example, Scheffé argues that "inequality of variances in the cells of a layout has little effect on inferences about means if the cell numbers are equal, serious effects with unequal cell numbers" [46, p. 345]. It is for this reason that we have chosen equal sample sizes for each of our five simulation runs. With regard to nonnormality, Scheffé concludes in Chapter 10 that "the effect of violation of the normality assumption is slight on inferences about means but dangerous on inferences about variances." Unfortunately, the robustness properties of multiple comparisons and multiple ranking procedures are not as well known as those of the simple F-test. We can safely hope that our departures from the assumptions of a common variance and normality are small enough not to seriously matter.

F-test

We may wish to test the null hypothesis, H_0, that the expected profits for each of the five operating plans are equal; in symbols:

$$H_0: \pi_1 = \pi_2 = \cdots = \pi_5$$

By employing the F-statistic, the decision rule for accepting or rejecting H_0 becomes

$$\begin{array}{lll} \text{If} & F \geq F_{\alpha,m-1,m(n-1)} & \text{reject } H_0 \\ & \text{Otherwise} & \text{accept } H_0 \end{array}$$

where F is the appropriate percentile of the F distribution, α is the significance level, $m = 5$ is the number of operating plans, and $n = 50$ is the number of replications per operating plan. If H_0 is accepted, we tentatively conclude that the sample differences between plans are attributable to random fluctuations rather than to actual differences in population values (expected profits). On the other hand, if H_0 is rejected then further analysis, such as multiple comparisons and multiple rankings, is recommended.

TABLE **14-3**

Formulas for one-way analysis of variance.

Source of variation	Sum of squares	Degrees of freedom	Mean square
Between plans	$SS_{\text{plans}} = n \sum_{j=1}^{m} (\bar{X}_{.j} - \bar{X}_{..})^2$	$m - 1$	$MS_p = SS_{\text{plans}}/m - 1$
Error	$SS_{\text{error}} = \sum_{i=1}^{n} \sum_{j=1}^{m} (X_{ij} - \bar{X}_{.j})^2$	$m(n - 1)$	$MS_e = SS_{\text{error}}/m(n - 1)$
Total	$SS_{\text{total}} = \sum_{i=1}^{n} \sum_{j=1}^{m} (X_{ij} - \bar{X}_{..})^2$	$nm - 1$	

Since the pseudorandom numbers generated for the jth operating plan are independent of those for the other four plans, our experiment is analyzed as a single-factor experimental design. Let X_{ij} denote the total profit for the ith replication of plan j. $\bar{X}_{.j}$ is the average profit for plan j over all 50 replications. $\bar{X}_{..}$ is the grand average for all 5 plans over all 50 replications.

Table 14-3 contains a summary of the formulas necessary to compute the statistics used in the analysis of a single-factor experiment.

The F statistic is then computed by the formula:

$$F = \frac{MS_p}{MS_e}$$

By substituting the results of our experiment for the quantities in Table 14-3, we obtain Table 14-4. From the data in Table 14-4, we see that $F = 46.6$, easily exceeding the critical value $F_{0.05,4,245} = 2.21$. In this case F is even much greater than the critical value for $\alpha = 0.001$. Hence, the data generated by the simulation experiment do not support the null hypothesis that the expected profits are equal for each of the five strategies. One may check the decision to reject H_0 against Table 14-2, which shows that the approximate expected profits do indeed vary from plan to plan.

Multiple comparisons

Typically, economic policy makers are interested not only in whether alternatives differ but also in *how* they differ. Multiple-comparison and multiple-ranking procedures often become tools relevant to meeting the latter query, for they have been designed specifically to attack questions of how means of many populations differ.

In contrast with the analysis of variance, multiple-comparison methods emphasize the use of confidence intervals rather than the testing of hypotheses. Because our concern in this chapter has centered upon differences in population means, it may be tempting at this point to construct a number of, say 95%, confidence intervals for $\pi_j - \pi_J$

$$(\bar{X}_j - \bar{X}_J) \pm t \cdot \sqrt{2MS_e/n} \qquad j, J = 1, 2, \ldots, m \tag{14-33}$$

TABLE **14-4**

Statistics for one-way analysis of variance.

Source of variation	Sum of squares	Degrees of freedom	Mean square
Between plans	9,677,758	4	2,419,440
Error	12,715,825	245	51,901
Total	22,393,583	249	

by employing the familiar Student's-t statistic. But a problem arises. The intervals developed in this manner are not all *simultaneously* true at the 95% level; indeed, the confidence level for the aggregate of intervals sinks considerably.

What is needed, therefore, is a way of constructing a *set* of confidence intervals which will all simultaneously be true with probability 95%. The May, 1965, issue of *Technometrics* [11,12,22,24] contains a comprehensive review of alternative methods which have been proposed for solving this problem. For illustrative purposes, we shall discuss two of these methods and relate each of them to our simulation experiment: (1) Tukey's method [46,49,51], and (2) Dunnett's method [15]. The general form of these methods can be found in the appropriate references. In this chapter we shall give the specific form for *one-factor* experiments, although they are equally valid for many-factor experiments.

Tukey's method [46,49,51] will yield simultaneous confidence intervals (of the type previously described) for the differences between *all* pairs. With 95% probability, *all* of the following confidence intervals for $\pi_j - \pi_J$ are true:

$$(\bar{X}_{.j} - \bar{X}_{.J}) \pm q_{m,v}\sqrt{MS_e/n} \qquad j, J = 1, 2, 3, \ldots, m \tag{14-34}$$

where $q_{m,v}$ is tabulated under the title "Distribution of the Studentized Range Statistic" [51], m is the number of sample means, and v is the number of degrees of freedom for MS_e, $m(n - 1)$ in the case of one-factor experiments. For the actual data generated by our single-factor computer simulation experiment the formula for 95% confidence intervals is given by

$$\begin{aligned}(\bar{X}_{.j} - \bar{X}_{.J}) \pm q_{5,245}\sqrt{MS_e/n} &= (\bar{X}_{.j} - \bar{X}_{.J}) \pm 3.86\sqrt{(51{,}901)/50} \\ &= (\bar{X}_{.j} - \bar{X}_{.J}) \pm 124 \\ & \qquad\qquad j, J = 1, 2, 3, 4, 5\end{aligned} \tag{14-35}$$

Table 14-5 contains a tabulation of the differences between sample means for all 10 pairs of differences in our experiment. An asterisk (*) indicates that a particular difference exceeds the confidence allowance 124, thus making the difference "statistically significant," if this form of inference is desired. At the same time, and still covered by 95% certainty, we can make more subtle comparisons, technically called linear contrasts. For example, "Does the difference

TABLE **14-5**

Differences of sample means ($\bar{X}_{.j} - \bar{X}_{.J}$).

j \ J	2	3	4	5
1	−15.9	301.2*	−288.9*	−155.5*
2	—	317.1*	−273.0*	−139.6*
3	—	—	−590.1*	−456.7*
4	—	—	—	−133.4*

$(\pi_1 - \pi_2)$ exceed the difference $(\pi_2 - \pi_3)$ and by how much?" "Do the first three means exceed the last two means on the average, and by how much?" If general linear contrasts are of more interest to the experimenter than the paired comparisons, then Scheffé's method [46] is usually preferred.

Dunnett's [15] method of multiple comparisons compares one specific mean, called the control mean, with all others. In simulations of business and economic systems the control mean is usually the mean associated with the present operating plan, decision rule, or managerial strategy. Dunnett's multiple comparison procedure is summarized as follows: with 95% probability, all of the following confidence intervals for $\pi_j - \pi_c$ are true

$$(\bar{X}_{.j} - \bar{X}_{.c}) \pm d\sqrt{2MS_e/n} \qquad j = 2, \ldots, m \tag{14-36}$$

where π_c = the control population mean

$\bar{X}_{.c}$ = the control sample mean

d = the percentile of Dunnett's t statistic [15,51] with degrees of freedom equal to $m(n - 1)$ for one-factor experiments

In our simulation experiment we assume that plan I is the control plan and compare it with all the other plans. The formula for 95% confidence intervals is given by

$$(\bar{X}_{.j} - \bar{X}_{.c}) \pm 2.16\sqrt{[(2)(51{,}901)]/50} = (\bar{X}_{.j} - \bar{X}_{.c}) \pm 98.4 \qquad j = 2, 3, 4, 5 \tag{14-37}$$

Table 14-6 contains a tabulation of the differences between sample means for comparisons between the control mean (plan I) and the means for plans II through V. Again an asterisk (*) indicates that a particular difference exceeds the confidence allowance 98.4 thus making the difference "statistically significant" if this form of inference is of interest.

Multiple rankings

Frequently, the objective of computer simulation experiments with economic systems is to find the "best," "second best," "third best," etc. plan (or others unlisted). Although multiple comparison methods of estimating the sizes of differences between plans (as measured by population means) are often used as a way of attempting, indirectly, to achieve goals of this type, multiple-ranking methods represent a more direct approach to a solution of the ranking problem.

The best estimate of the rank of a set of operating plans is simply the ranking of the sample means associated with the given plans. Because of random

TABLE **14-6**

Differences of sample means $(\bar{X}_{.j} - \bar{X}_{.c})$

j	2	3	4	5
$(\bar{X}_{.j} - \bar{X}_{.c})$	15.9	−301.2*	288.9*	155.5*

error, however, sample rankings may yield incorrect results. With what probability can we say that a ranking of sample means represents the true ranking of the population means? It is basically this question which multiple ranking procedures attempt to answer.

Bechhofer [1] has developed a procedure for selecting a single population and guaranteeing with probability P that the selected population is the "best" provided some other condition on the parameters is satisfied. Like the F-test and multiple comparisons, Bechhofer's procedure assumes normality and statistical independence. However, it also assumes *known variances* which may be equal or unequal. Unfortunately, this procedure is not applicable to our experiment, since σ^2 is unknown.

The paper by Bechhofer, Dunnett, and Sobel [4] is of particular interest, since it describes a two-sample multiple-decision procedure for ranking the means of normal populations with a common *unknown variance*. Similar problems with various specific probability distributions have been treated by Gupta [23,24], Gupta and Sobel [25,27,28], and Seal [47]. The article by Gupta [24] contains a comprehensive review of multiple ranking procedures.

We now turn to a more detailed description of Bechhofer, Dunnett, and Sobel's two-sample multiple-decision procedure for ranking means of normal populations with a common unknown variance [4] and the application of this procedure to our experiment. Using the notation of our experiment, we assume that for a given population (plan) j, X_{ij} is a normally and independently distributed random variable with expected value π_j and common variance $\sigma_j^2 = \sigma^2 (j = 1, 2, \ldots, m)$. We further assume that σ^2 and the π_j are unknown. Denote the ranked π_j by

$$\pi_{[1]} \leq \pi_{[2]} \leq \cdots \leq \pi_{[m]} \tag{14-38}$$

and the differences between the ranked means by

$$\delta_{ij} = \pi_{[i]} - \pi_{[j]} \qquad (i, j = 1, 2, \ldots, m) \tag{14-39}$$

We do not know which population is associated with $\pi_{[j]}$.

Assume that the experimental goal calls for the selection of the population having the largest expected value. (This is by no means the only goal which may be chosen.) Assume also that the experimenter specifies a parameter δ^* which is the smallest value of $\delta_{m,m-1}$ that he is willing to accept. In addition, the experimenter specifies the smallest acceptable value P for the probability of achieving his given goal when $\delta_{m,m-1} \geq \delta^*$.

Bechhofer, Dunnett, and Sobel's two-sample procedure consists of the following five steps:

1. Take a first sample of N_1 observations from each of the m populations.
2. Calculate the mean-square error, MS_e, which is an unbiased estimate of σ^2 having $v = m(n - 1)$ degrees of freedom for $n = N_1$.
3. Take a second sample of $N_2 - N_1$ observations from each of the m populations, $N_2 = \max \{N_1, [2MS_e(h/\delta^*)^2]\}$, where the brackets [ ]

denote the smallest integer equal to or greater than the rational number contained within the brackets, and h is obtained from Table 3 of Dunnett and Sobel [16] for given values of v and P. If $2\, MS_e(h/\delta^*)^2 \leq N_1$, then no second sample is necessary and, therefore, $N_2 = N_1$.

4. For each population calculate the overall sample mean $\bar{X}_j$, where

$$\bar{X}_j = 1/N_2 \sum_{i=1}^{N_2} X_{ij} \qquad (j = 1, 2, \ldots, m) \tag{14-40}$$

5. Denote the ranked values of $\bar{X}_j$ by

$$\bar{X}_{[1]} < \bar{X}_{[2]} < \cdots < \bar{X}_{[m]} \tag{14-41}$$

Rank the populations according to the ranking of the observed $\bar{X}_j$ and select the population which gives rise to $\bar{X}_{[m]}$ as the population having the largest population mean.

For our experiment, suppose that we want to select the plan having the largest expected profit and to guarantee that the probability of correctly choosing that population will be at least 0.90 when the difference between the plan with the highest expected profit and the plan with the second highest expected profit is \$100. In other words, we are assuming that $P = 0.90$ and $\delta^* = 100$. We then let $N_1 = n = 50$ and calculate $MS_e = 51{,}901$. For $P = 0.90$ and $v = m(n - 1) = 245$ we obtain $h = 1.58$ from Table 3 of [16]. Next we determine

$$\begin{aligned} \max\{N_1, [2MS_e(h/\delta^*)^2]\} &= \max\{50, [2(51{,}901)(1.58/100)^2]\} \\ &= \max\{50, 26\} = 50 \end{aligned}$$

Since $26 < 50$ no second sample is required and $N_2 = N_1 = n = 50$. Sample means for $n = 50$ were previously calculated in Table 14-2. On the basis of the ranking of the sample means we would select operating plan IV as the plan with the highest expected profit. If in fact the best operating plan has an expected profit that is \$100 larger than the next best, we have at least a probability of 90% of correctly choosing it despite the random statistical fluctuations of sampling. Similar probabilistic statements can be made with this procedure concerning (1) the "best two" plans, (2) the "best three" plans, (3) the "best," "second best," "third best," etc., plans.

With the aid of a simple example we have attempted to demonstrate the use of three alternative forms of the analysis of variance to analyze data generated by computer simulation experiments with economic systems—F-test, multiple comparisons, and multiple rankings. The differences in these three types of analysis of variance lie not so much in the assumptions underlying their use, but rather in the types of experimental objectives with which they are most compatible. If one's experimental objective is to test the hypothesis that there is no difference between two or more plans or policies, then the F-test is an appropriate analytical tool. If one's objective is to obtain estimates of the sizes of these differences, then multiple comparisons are more appropriate. But if the object is to find with a specified degree of certainty the best plan, second-best plan, etc., then multiple ranking procedures represent the more direct approach. The reader is cautioned, however, to avoid the indiscriminate use of these techniques without due regard for the assumptions on which they are based. This is particularly true of the latter two techniques.

Finally, we note that although we have limited our analysis to a single-factor experiment, all of the techniques described in this chapter can be extended to experiments with many factors.

BIBLIOGRAPHY

[1] BECHHOFER, R. E. "A Single Sample Multiple Procedure for Ranking Means of Normal Populations with Known Variances," *Annals of Mathematical Statistics*, **XXV** (1954), 16–39.

[2] BECHHOFER, ROBERT E. "A Sequential Multiple Decision Procedure for Selecting the Best One of Several Normal Populations with a Common Unknown Variance, and Its Use with Various Experimental Designs," *Biometrics*, **XIV** (1958), 408–429.

[3] BECHHOFER, ROBERT E., and SAUL BLUMENTHAL. "A Sequential Multiple-Decision Procedure for Selecting the Best One of Several Normal Populations with a Common Unknown Variance, II: Monte Carlo Sampling Results and New Computing Formulae," *Biometrics*, **XVIII** (March, 1962), 52–67.

[4] BECHHOFER, ROBERT E., C. W. DUNNETT, and M. SOBEL. "A Two-Sample Multiple Decision Procedure for Ranking Means of Normal Populations with a Common Unknown Variance," *Biometrika*, **XLI** (1954), 170–176.

[5] BECHHOFER, ROBERT E., and MILTON SOBEL. "A Single-Sample Multiple Decision Procedure for Ranking Variances of Normal Populations," *Annals of Mathematical Statistics*, **XXV** (1954), 273–289.

[6] BURDICK, DONALD S., and THOMAS H. NAYLOR. "Design of Computer Simulation Experiments for Industrial Systems," *Communications of the ACM*, **IX** (May, 1966), 329–339.

[7] CHU, KONG, and THOMAS H. NAYLOR. "A Dynamic Model of the Firm," *Management Science*, **XI** (May, 1965), 736–750.

[8] CLARK, C. E. "Importance Sampling in Monte Carlo Analyses," *Operations Research*, **IX** (1961), 603–620.

[9] CONWAY, R. W. "Some Tactical Problems in Digital Simulation," *Management Science*, **X** (October, 1963), 47–61.

[10] CONWAY, R. W., B. M. JOHNSON, and W. L. MAXWELL. "Some Problems of Digital Machine Simulation," *Management Science*, **VI** (October, 1959), 92–110.

[11] COX, D. R. "A Remark on Multiple Comparisons," *Technometrics*, **VII** (May, 1965), 223–224.

[12] DUNCAN, DAVID B. "A Bayesian Approach to Multiple Comparisons," *Technometrics*, **VII** (May, 1965), 171–122.

[13] DUNCAN, DAVID B. "A Significance Test for Differences Between Ranked Treatments in an Analysis of Variance," *Virginia Journal of Science*, **N.S. II** (1951), 171–189.

[14] DUNCAN, DAVID B. "On the Properties of the Multiple Comparisons Test," *Virginia Journal of Science*, N.S. **III** (1952), 49–67.

[15] DUNNETT, C. W. "A Multiple Comparison Procedure for Comparing Several Treatments with a Control," *Journal of the American Statistical Association*, **L** (1955), 1096–1121.

[16] DUNNETT, C. W., and M. SOBEL. "A Bivariate Generalization of Student's T-Distribution with Tables for Certain Special Cases," *Biometrika*, **XLI** (1954), 153.

[17] EHRENFIELD, S., and S. BEN-TUVIA. "The Efficiency of Statistical Simulation Procedures," *Technometrics*, **IX** (May, 1962), 257–275.

[18] FISHMAN, GEORGE S. "Problems in the Statistical Analysis of Simulation Experiments: The Comparison of Means and the Length of Sample Records," *Communications of the ACM*, **X** (February, 1967), 94–99.

[19] FISHMAN, GEORGE S., and PHILIP J. KIVIAT. "The Analysis of Simulation-Generated Time Series," *Management Science*, **XIII** (March, 1967), 525–557.

[20] GAFARIAN, A. V., and C. J. ANCKER. "Mean Value Estimation from Digital Computer Simulation," *Operations Research*, **XIV** (January–February, 1966), 25–440.

[21] GEISLER, MURRAY A. "The Sizes of Simulation Samples Required to Compute Certain Inventory Characteristics with Stated Precision and Confidence," *Management Science*, **X** (January, 1964), 261–286.

[22] GOODMAN, LEO A. "On Simultaneous Confidence Intervals for Multinomial Proportions," *Technometrics*, **VII** (May, 1965), 247–254.

[23] GUPTA, S. S. "On a Decision Rule for a Problem in Ranking Means," Mimeograph Series No. 150, Institute of Statistics, University of North Carolina, Chapel Hill, N.C., 1956.

[24] GUPTA, S. S. "On Some Multiple Decision (Selection and Ranking) Rules," *Technometrics*, **VII** (May, 1965), 225–246.

[25] GUPTA, S. S., and M. SOBEL. "On a Statistic Which Arises in Selection and Ranking Problems," *Annals of Mathematical Statistics*, **XXVIII** (1957), 957–967.

[26] GUPTA, S. S., and M. SOBEL. "On Selecting a Subset Which Contains All Populations Better than a Standard," *Annals of Mathematical Statistics*, **XXIX** (1958), 235–244.

[27] GUPTA, S. S., and M. SOBEL. "On Selecting a Subset Containing the Population with the Smallest Variance," *Biometrika*, **XLIX** (1962a), 495–507.

[28] GUPTA, S. S., and M. SOBEL. "On the Smallest of Several Correlated F Statistics," *Biometrika*, **XLIX** (1962), 509–523.

[29] HAMMERSLEY, J. M., and D. C. HANDSCOMB. *Monte Carlo Methods*. New York: John Wiley & Sons, 1964.

[30] JACKSON, R. R. P. "Queueing Systems with Phase Type Service," *Operational Research Quarterly*, **V** (1954).

[31] KAHN, HERMAN. "Use of Different Monte Carlo Sampling Techniques," The RAND Corporation, P-766, November 30, 1955.

[32] KAHN, HERMAN, and IRWIN MANN. "Monte Carlo," The RAND Corporation, P-1165, July 30, 1957.

[33] KAHN, H., and I. MANN. "Techniques of Systems Analysis," The RAND Corporation, RM-1829-1, June, 1957.

[34] LEHMANN, E. L. "A Theory of Some Multiple Decision Problems," *Annals of Mathematical Statistics*, **XXVIII** (1957), 1–25.

[35] LEHMANN, E. L. "Some Model I Problems of Selection," *Annals of Mathematical Statistics*, **XXXII** (1961), 990–1012.

[36] MORSE, PHILLIP M. *Queues, Inventories, and Maintenance*. New York: John Wiley & Sons, 1958.

[37] MOSTELLER, FREDERICK. "A K-Sample Slippage Test for an Extreme Population," *Annals of Mathematical Statistics*, **XIX** (1948), 58–65.

[38] NAYLOR, THOMAS H., JOSEPH L. BALINTFY, DONALD S. BURDICK, and KONG CHU. *Computer Simulation Techniques*. New York: John Wiley & Sons, 1966.

[39] NAYLOR, THOMAS H., KENNETH WERTZ, and THOMAS H. WONNACOTT. "Methods for Analyzing Data from Computer Simulation Experiments," *Communications of the ACM* (November, 1967), 703–710.

[40] NAYLOR, THOMAS H., KENNETH WERTZ, and THOMAS H. WONNACOTT. "Some Methods for Evaluating the Effects of Economic Policies Using Simulation Experiments," *Review of the International Statistical Institute*, **XXXVI** (February, 1968), 184–200.

[41] PAULSON, EDWARD. "A Multiple Decision Procedure for Certain Problems in the Analysis of Variance," *Annals of Mathematical Statistics*, **X** (1949), 95–98.

[42] PAULSON, EDWARD. "On the Comparison of Several Experimental Categories with a Control," *Annals of Mathematical Statistics*, **XXIII** (1952), 239–246.

[43] PAULSON, EDWARD. "An Optimum Solution to the *k*-Sample Slippage Problem for the Normal Distribution," *Annals of Mathematical Statistics*, **XXIII** (1952), 610–616.

[44] SAATY, THOMAS L. *Elements of Queueing Theory*. New York: McGraw-Hill Book Co., 1961.

[45] SCHEFFÉ, HENRY. "A Method for Judging All Contrasts in the Analysis of Variance," *Biometrika*, **XL** (1953), 87–104.

[46] SCHEFFÉ, HENRY. *The Analysis of Variance*. New York: John Wiley & Sons, 1959.

[47] SEAL, K. C. "On a Class of Decision Procedures for Ranking Means of Normal Populations," *Annals of Mathematical Statistics*, **XXVI** (1955), 387–398.

[48] SIEGEL, SIDNEY. *Nonparametric Statistics*. New York: McGraw-Hill Book Co., 1956.

[49] TUKEY, J. W. *The Problem of Multiple Comparisons*, Mimeographed manuscript, Princeton University, 1953.

[50] WALSH, JOHN E. *Handbook of Nonparametric Statistics*, Vols. I and II. Princeton, N. J.: D. Van Nostrand Co., 1962 and 1965.

[51] WINER, B. J. *Statistical Principles in Experimental Design*. New York: McGraw-Hill Book Co., 1962.

PART 6

Investment models of the firm

15

Investment models of the firm: certainty

INTRODUCTION

In this chapter and the next we shall consider the decisions which firms must make in the determination of the optimal quantities of *durable* factors of production, e.g., plant and equipment. In this chapter we will take the values of all relevant variables to be known with perfect certainty. In Chapter 16 we will relax this rather strong assumption.

Since durable plant and equipment is used as an input in the production process, we should consider why this problem was not treated in Chapter 3, where the theory of production was discussed. A major reason is tradition. The theory of investment of the firm has always been associated with the theory of production, but it is also closely related to the theory of capital. Thus concepts arising in both topics need to be developed in a treatment of the theory of investment. For this reason, it is convenient to treat investment separately. For an attempt to integrate durable inputs into the theory of production, see the excellent book by Smith [48].

In order better to understand the problem of treating durable factors within the framework of production theory, consider the optimality conditions for the multiproduct, multifactor firm as described in Chapter 5. That analysis provides that some factors—call them plant and equipment—remain fixed over the period for which decisions on nondurable inputs and outputs are made. In principle it would appear possible that this framework could accommodate durable inputs as variable factors of production. The only basic requirement would be that the length of the period be set at the life of the durable factor. With this additional requirement, the valuation of a proposal to invest in durable goods could proceed on the basis of the optimality conditions. One drawback of this approach is its inability to consider the interest factor. That is, since there is only a single period involved, there can be no time distinction attached to the receipt of revenues or expenditures within the period. The time factor is generally considered insignificant in the case of short periods of time, say one year or less, and can be safely ignored. But for longer periods of time we cannot ignore interest.

In the next section we shall digress somewhat from the main theme of this chapter in order to give a brief sketch of capital theory. As a transitional step from capital theory to modern investment theory of the firm, we shall present the well-known point-input–point-output model of the firm. The following section will be concerned with an evaluation of investment criteria employed by firms in making investment or capital-budgeting decisions. To conclude the chapter, we shall present a mathematical programming model of investment, as developed by Weingartner [59].

CAPITAL THEORY

According to Samuelson, "Capital theory is one of the most difficult parts of economic theory" [45, p. 570]. Since we fully agree, we wish to emphasize that this brief section is provided only for completeness, and to provide references for the reader who would prefer a more thorough treatment.

"Capital theory first arose as an offshoot of the theory of pricing and distribution, in the course of discussion of the determination of interest rates and their functions" [4, p. 407]. The first great name in capital theory is Eugene von Böhm-Bawerk, and his importance stems from the publication of the *Positive Theory of Capital* in 1889 [11].

Böhm-Bawerk is perhaps best known for his three reasons, or causes, for interest. The first cause is that many people expect to be better provided for in the future than they are in the present; hence, they place a higher value on present goods than on future goods. The second cause is that people systematically underestimate future wants for a number of reasons (errors in forecasting, defects of will, uncertainty of life, etc.). Böhm-Bawerk's third cause is that more lengthy methods of production are more fruitful than shorter methods; hence command over present consumption goods provides for subsistence during the present period while more lengthy production methods are initiated. These causes will be related more explicitly to the rate of interest shortly.

A second, equally great name in capital theory is Irving Fisher, whose *The Rate of Interest* was published in 1907. (Fisher revised this book in 1930 [21].) In a recent monograph on capital theory (1965), Dewey praised Fisher as being the "last economist who offered a treatment of capital theory that was at once comprehensive, rigorous, and readable. Fisher's most remarkable achievement, *The Rate of Interest*, . . . is the oldest treatise on active service in American economics" [18, p. 11]. Unfortunately, our discussion of Fisher's contribution must be limited to a brief graphical exposition of his theory of the rate of interest.

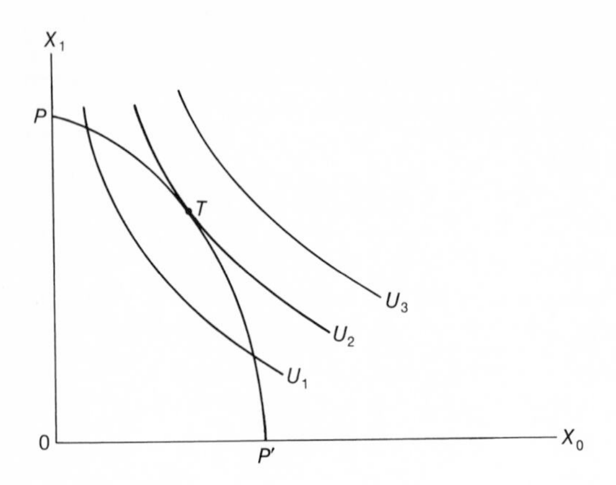

FIGURE **15-1**

Fisher showed that the rate of interest is determined by the interaction of two factors: (1) the opportunity to invest, and (2) the impatience to spend (often called "time preference"). The first factor is a basic technical fact, corresponding to Böhm-Bawerk's third cause. As Samuelson puts it: "There exist roundabout processes, which take time to get started, that are more productive than direct processes. After allowing for all depreciation requirements, capital has a net productivity (or real interest yield) that can be expressed in the form of a percentage per annum. . . ." [45, p. 572]. The second factor refers to Böhm-Bawerk's second cause: people systematically value present consumption over future consumption.

In Figure 15-1 we show these two factors, and how they interact to determine the interest rate. For simplicity, we consider only two time periods and a single good, X. The quantity of X for consumption in period 1 is denoted by X_1 and is plotted on the vertical axis; similarly, X_0 denotes the quantity of X for current consumption. The curve, PP', is the *product-transformation curve* which shows the technical possibilities available to a typical consumer.

As we saw in Chapter 3, the slope of the PP' curve has an important interpretation. For example, we start at P' where the consumer is consuming maximum X_0 with no provision of X for the future. At this point, the opportunity to invest is relatively the greatest: the consumer would obtain the highest possible return (in terms of X_1) for a sacrifice of one unit of X_0. But, as the consumer moves up along the PP' curve, the opportunity to invest becomes less and less attractive, reflecting the principle of diminishing returns to investment.

Similarly, we can interpret the consumer's indifference curves. In Figure 15-1 we show three indifference curves, where U_3 represents a higher level of utility than U_2, and U_2 represents a higher level of utility than U_1. Again, the slope of the curves is the important point. For example, as we move up along any particular indifference curve, we observe that the consumer must be compensated by progressively greater increments of X_1 for successive unit sacrifices of X_0. Logically, then, the consumer will reach an equilibrium position as determined by these two factors. And, as in earlier marginal analyses, the equilibrium is at the tangency point T which corresponds to the highest level of utility attainable under the product-transformation curve constraint.

It is meaningful to write out the algebraic condition of equilibrium. At the tangency point, the slopes of the two curves are equal to each other and, according to the Fisherian analysis, are equal to $1 + r$, where r is the *rate of interest*. That is,

$$\frac{dX_1}{dX_0} = \frac{MU_0}{MU_1} = 1 + r \tag{15-1}$$

The reader should consider the interpretation of each term carefully. The first term is likely to be greater than 1 because roundabout methods of production are usually more productive than direct methods. Thus sacrificing 1 unit of X_0 (current X) should permit the production of *greater* than 1 unit of X_1 (future X). For example, if a sacrifice of 1 unit of X today permits the attainment of 1.3 units of X tomorrow, the net productivity of the sacrifice is 0.30, or 30 percent.

The second term, the ratio of the marginal utility of X_0 to the marginal utility of X_1, is also likely to be greater than 1 because people generally prefer present consumption to future consumption. Thus the consumption of an additional unit of X in the present period yields a greater increment to utility than would be forthcoming from the consumption of that unit of X in period 1. And, this ratio is also equal to $1 + r$ in equilibrium. Observe that for r to be negative (zero), MU_1 would have to be greater than (equal to) MU_0.

Although we cannot pursue traditional capital theory any further here, the interested reader is urged to examine some of the following books, in addition to those previously mentioned: Wicksell [60], Hicks [28], Keynes [30], Solow [52], and Knight [31]. Also, for a treatment of modern investment theory stemming directly from the Fisherian theory of interest, see the article by Jack Hirshleifer [29]. Before turning to the point-input–point-output model of the firm, we should review the mathematics of compound interest.

MATHEMATICS OF INTEREST

We assume that the rate of interest r is determined in a perfectly competitive capital market (this assumption permits us to take r as fixed). If we place P dollars in the bank today at interest, at the end of the year it will be worth $P(1 + r)$ dollars. Hence, the main theme of this discussion is immediately apparent: dollars at different points in time are as different as apples and oranges, and they can only be compared after they have been reduced to a common denominator, that is, reduced to dollars at one point in time.

Using subscripts to indicate the year number, we can write the equation of exchange between P_0 dollars today and P_1 dollars at the end of year 1 as

$$P_1 = P_0(1 + r) \tag{15-2}$$

The logic is simple. No one would be indifferent between a dollar at time 0 and a dollar at time 1 because he could place a dollar today at interest and it would be worth *more* than a dollar at the end of the year. Equation (15-2) gives the value that current dollars will attain at the end of the year. But it is a simple matter to reverse the question and deduce the value of dollars receivable at time 1 as expressed in current dollars. This is known as *discounting* and the procedure determines the *present value* of the dollars. Solving equation (15-2) for P_0 is all that is required.

$$P_0 = P_1/(1 + r) \tag{15-3}$$

Thus, equation (15-3) discounts P_1 dollars (to be received in one year) to their present value, or P_0. For example, \$106 to be received in one year would be worth only \$100 today, if the rate of interest is 6 percent per annum.

The extension of the above analysis to the more general case of the receipt or loan of dollars annually over a number of years is straightforward. First, however, the reader should recognize that if interest is compounded annually, then

$$P_n = P_0(1 + r)^n \tag{15-4}$$

where n is any year. At the end of year 2, $P_2 = P_0(1 + r)^2$.

The more relevant question for the theory of investment concerns the present value of a series of varying yearly receipts of dollars. This present value PV is obtained exactly as we obtained equation (15-3). Hence, letting P_i represent the dollars to be received at the end of year i, we get

$$PV = \sum_{i=0}^{n} P_i/(1 + r)^i \tag{15-5}$$

In theoretical work, it is convenient to assume that interest is compounded *continuously* rather than *annually*. In general, if interest is compounded f times a year, we have

$$P_n = P_0(1 + r/f)^{fn} \tag{15-6}$$

Equation (15-6) can be rewritten as

$$P_n = P_0[(1 + r/f)^{f/r}]^{rn} \tag{15-7}$$

The term in the brackets approaches the number 2.7183..., or e, as the frequency of compounding, f, grows very large. Thus for *continuous* compounding, equation (15-7) reduces to

$$P_n = P_0 e^{rn} \tag{15-8}$$

And, of course, the present value of P_n to be received at the end of year n, is P_0, or

$$P_0 = P_n e^{-rn} \tag{15-9}$$

The continuous version of (15-5)—the present value of a *stream* of dollar receipts—is given by

$$PV = \int_0^n P(t)e^{-rt}\,dt \tag{15-10}$$

One further point should be mentioned. It is not strictly correct to use an interest rate expressed in *annual* compounding terms in equation (15-10). The equivalence between the two is given by

$$r' = \log_e (1 + r) \tag{15-11}$$

where r' is the value of the interest rate which should be substituted in (15-10) for an interest rate, r, expressed in annual compounding terms.

A POINT-INPUT–POINT-OUTPUT MODEL

The point-input–point-output model refers to "the situation in which labor is expended at a specific moment in time; the well-defined product of that labor is permitted to mature for some period and is then consumed at some other moment" [4, p. 419]. This model introduces *time* as an explicit factor in the production function.

First let us list the *assumptions* relevant to this model:

1. The firm possesses knowledge of the values of all relevant variables with perfect certainty.
2. A perfect capital market exists. Thus the firm can borrow or lend as much money as it needs at a fixed rate of interest.
3. The product price and the labor wage rate are determined in perfectly competitive markets and are fixed insofar as the firm is concerned.
4. The production function is subject to diminishing returns with regard to labor and time.
5. The firm seeks to maximize the present value of profit.

The objective function of the firm is to maximize the present value of profit, PV:

$$PV = pZe^{-rT} - wL \tag{15-12}$$

where p = selling price of output
Z = number of units of output
r = fixed rate of interest
T = length of production period
w = fixed wage rate
L = number of labor units

The production function is given by

$$Z = Z(L, T) \tag{15-13}$$

The reason for applying the discounting factor e^{-rT} to the revenue term in (15-12) and not to the cost term is clear when it is recognized that output Z is sold in the future, while cost wL is incurred now. This is the meaning of point-input–point-output. Input takes place at the present time (the application of labor services), whereas the output is sold only after time has elapsed. The usual example is that of planting a tree which requires certain labor services during planting but none over the growing period. Then at the end of a certain period of time the tree is sold. The problem of the firm is to decide on the amount of labor, L, to use in planting the tree and the length of time T which the tree should be permitted to grow before harvesting.

The problem can be solved by a straightforward application of classical optimization techniques. Substituting (15-13) in (15-12), partially differentiating (15-12) with respect to L and T, and setting each partial derivative equal to zero, we obtain

$$\frac{\partial PV}{\partial L} = p\frac{\partial Z}{\partial L}e^{-rT} - w = 0 \tag{15-14}$$

$$\frac{\partial PV}{\partial T} = p\frac{\partial Z}{\partial T}e^{-rT} - rpZe^{-rT} = 0 \tag{15-15}$$

Since we assume that the production function is of the proper shape to ensure the satisfaction of second-order conditions, we need only consider (15-14) and (15-15) as the conditions which must be fulfilled for the maximization of the present value of profit.

Equation (15-14) can be written as

$$w = p\frac{\partial Z}{\partial L}e^{-rT} \tag{15-16}$$

This condition is easily interpreted. The firm should continue to hire labor until the *present value* of the marginal revenue product of labor is equated to the market-determined wage rate w.

We can write equation (15-15) as

$$r = \frac{\partial Z/\partial T}{Z} \tag{15-17}$$

This condition can also be easily interpreted. The firm should allow the tree to grow until the point where diminishing returns reduce the *percentage* marginal product of time to equality with the rate of interest (also a percentage).

This last condition can be illustrated graphically. In Figure 15-2 we plot dollars of revenue on the vertical axis, and time on the horizontal axis. The curve labeled PZ is the current value of the tree at any T (the production function multiplied by the price per unit, for a given input of labor). The curves PV_1,

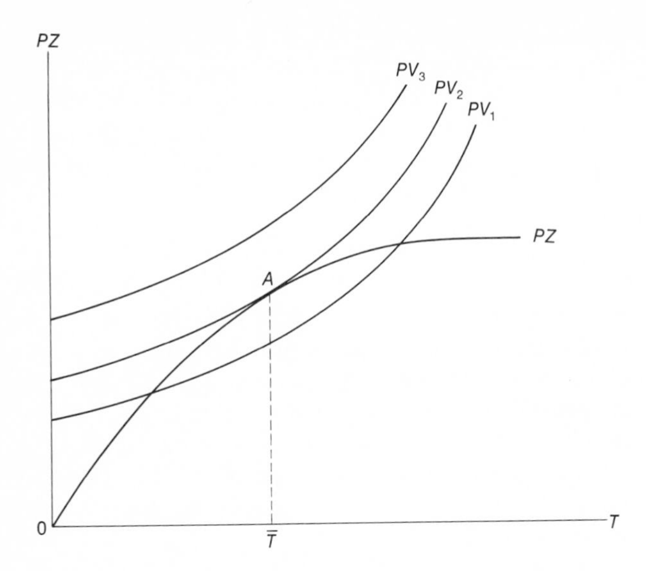

FIGURE **15-2**

PV_2, and PV_3 are isopresent value contours, with $PV_3 > PV_2 > PV_1$. Clearly, the optimal point is A, the highest present-value contour attainable when constrained by the production function. The tangency point, of course, is given algebraically by (15-17) and the optimal length of the production period is determined graphically in Figure 15-2 as $\overline{T}$.

Having introduced time into the analysis, we can now specify three types of input–output relationships that go beyond the point-input–point-output relationship. The three additional relationships are: (1) continuous-input–point-output, (2) point-input–continuous-output, and (3) continuous-input–continuous-output.

The continuous-input–point-output case involves investment in circulating capital, *viz.*, goods in process. Thus the outputs of successive moments are singly supplied by different inputs. This property makes it possible to link particular units of input with particular units of output and thereby calculate the profit for a production period unambiguously.

The point-input–continuous-output case involves investment in durable capital goods. That is, a bundle of factors or inputs produces a stream of products or outputs over time. Because of this it is not possible to associate particular units of input with particular units of products. Therefore the period profit cannot be determined unambiguously. It is this very same problem of having a whole series of outputs of different periods that are *jointly supplied* by the same inputs that has stymied the accountant's search for a depreciation method that would allocate the cost of the durable good over its useful lifetime in accordance with the rate at which the good is being consumed.[1] Accountants "have reluctantly concluded that there is no 'true' depreciation method, and that all the methods used or proposed are merely conventions, the choice between which is a matter of convenience" [35, p. 7].

EVALUATION OF INVESTMENT: THE LUTZES AND DEAN

The inability of the theory of production to go beyond the insignificant solution and the failure of capital theory to successfully treat the point-input–continuous-output case prompted the Lutzes and Dean to propose an alternative [35, p. 15]. To determine whether to accept a proposal to invest in a durable good we must compare the benefits over time with the amount that must be expended to obtain these benefits. Considering the investment selection problem in this manner eliminates the need for allocating a portion of the original investment to successive periods in the future.

> The profitability of investment in fixed equipment can be calculated only by taking into account the whole stream of revenues from the equipment, the initial costs of the equipment itself, and the whole stream of costs of the variable "inputs" that have to be combined with it. Thus when fixed equipment is used, the production function is much more complex than it was either under the assumption of "timeless" production, or under the assumption that investment took place exclusively in circulating capital [35, p. 8].

Assumptions

There are certain assumptions underlying the approach developed by the Lutzes and Dean which we should make explicit [59, p. 3]:

1. The firm possesses knowledge of the values of all relevant variables with perfect certainty.
2. A perfect capital market exists. Thus the firm can borrow or lend as much money as it needs at a fixed rate of interest.
3. The firm seeks to maximize the present value of profit.
4. All proposed investments of the firm are strictly independent.

Thus the acceptance or rejection of a particular proposal has no effect on the acceptance or rejection of any other proposal.

The approach can be expressed as a relationship.

$$I_0 \overset{>}{\underset{<}{=}} \sum_{i=0}^{n} \frac{(R_i - 0_i)}{(1 + r)^i} \tag{15-18}$$

[1] It should be noted that if the stock of durable goods is evenly staggered with respect to age, the period profit can be calculated because all costs are constant over time. However, this case is regarded as so strict that it precludes consideration of the most common investment problems of the firm.

I_0 is the dollar amount invested in period zero; R_i is the dollar revenue in the ith period and is defined as the difference between the revenue with the proposed investment and the revenue without the investment; 0_i is the dollar outlay in the ith period and is defined as the difference between the amounts that will be expended with the proposed investment and the amounts that would be expended if the investment was not undertaken; n is finite and is the economic life of the proposed investment; r is the percent cost of the investment funds (a constant with a perfect capital market).

The present-worth approach

The present worth or value of an investment proposal is defined as the sum of the discounted net returns for each future time period, where the discount rate is the cost of obtaining investment funds [50]. The relationship (15–18) implies that this sum may be equal to, less than, or greater than the amount required to produce these returns. The decision rule for a profit-maximizing firm is to accept the proposed investment if the sum of discounted net returns exceeds the amount of original investment, I_0. A proposed investment is rejected when the sum of the discounted net returns is less than the amount of the original investment. Where there is more than one investment the decision rule is to accept all proposals for which the sum of discounted net returns exceeds the amount of the original investment. If two mutually exclusive investment proposals each produce a sum of discounted net returns that exceeds I_0, the decision rule is to choose that proposal for which the difference is a maximum.

The internal rate of return

Investment valuation and selection is not restricted to the present-worth approach outlined above. Among others, the internal rate of return method deserves attention. The internal rate of return is defined as that value of r, call it r^*, which makes the sum of discounted net returns exactly equal to the amount of the original investment. Comparing the value of r^* with the cost of obtaining funds, r, leads to the following decision rule: a proposed investment is acceptable when r^* is greater than r. This formulation appears to be particularly desirable under the certainty assumption because the calculated value of r^* does not depend on the value of r, the cost of obtaining funds. Only after r^* has been calculated is there any reference to the cost of funds. The present-worth approach does not share this invariance, since the sum of the discounted net returns changes as a result of changes in the cost of obtaining funds.

It should also be recognized that the internal rate of return is essentially equivalent to Keynes' marginal efficiency of investment [30, Chapter 11]. However, Keynes was using this measure in a context not designed to evaluate a particular investment. Stemming partly from the change of context, there are three reasons why the internal rate of return is not widely accepted for use in investment valuation [34].

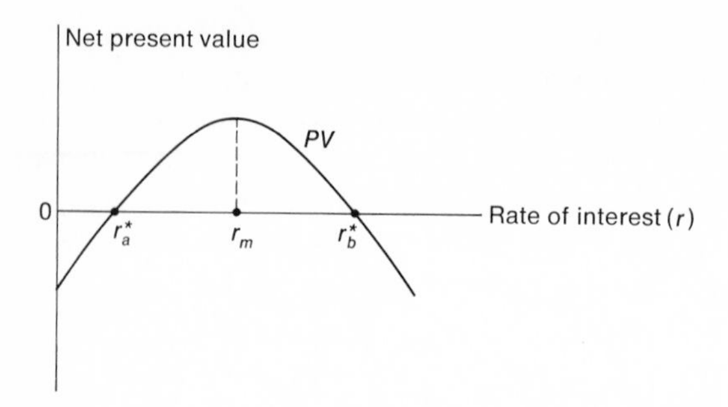

FIGURE 15-3

The first reason is that there are rather common conditions under which the internal rate of return is not unique and therefore the decision rule previously cited is ambiguous. In other words, it is possible for a particular investment proposal to yield more than one value of r that will equate the sum of discounted net returns and I_0. Supposing that one value is greater than the cost of obtaining funds while the other is less, there is no way to decide whether or not to invest in the given proposal.

To illustrate, we plot the *net* present value PV in Figure 15-3, where

$$PV = \sum_{i=0}^{n} \frac{(R_i - 0_i)}{(1 + r)^i} - I_0 \tag{15-19}$$

Where the curve PV intersects the horizontal axis, we have a value of r that meets the definition of r^*, the internal rate of return. But, in Figure 15-3, *two* values of r qualify, *viz.*, r_a^* and r_b^*. If the market rate of interest is r_m, the criterion is ambiguous.

The second reason for the rejection of the internal rate of return is that it may not provide the correct choice among mutually exclusive investments. Thus for two mutually exclusive investment proposals, x and y, proposal x may have a greater internal rate of return than proposal y. However, if decisions are made on the basis of contribution to the wealth of the firm, and if the market for funds is perfect, then it is possible for proposal y to be chosen. For example, see Figure 15-4.

The internal rate of return of proposal x, r_x^*, exceeds that of proposal y, r_y^*. But at the market rate of interest r_m, proposal y contributes a greater increment of present value to the wealth of the firm.

The third reason is essentially a point of emphasis. All discounting procedures require a reinvestment assumption. Recall that discounting a future dollar at a given rate is simply the reverse of compounding some amount less than a dollar, for the required time at a given rate. Where the discounting takes place over several time periods the assumption is that during intervening periods any funds

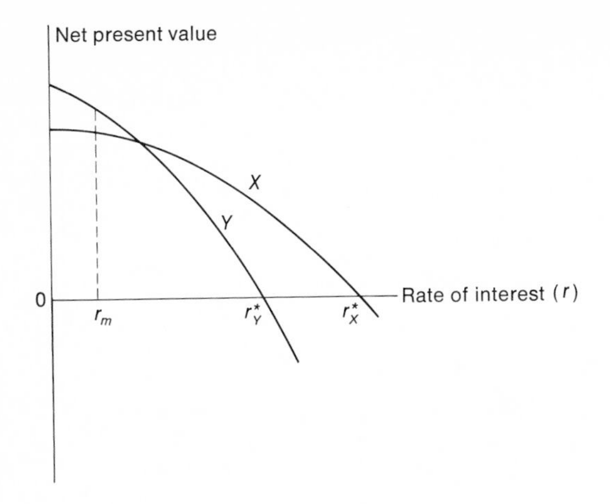

FIGURE **15-4**

made available must be invested at the discount rate. For example, if the internal rate of return for a project with a ten-year economic life is calculated at, say, 30%, then it is assumed that all funds produced during the first nine years can be continually reinvested at 30%.

While the same basic assumption is required for the present-worth approach the actual reinvestment requirements are not so stringent. Thus if the discount rate in the present-worth calculations is the market rate of interest, then reinvestment at the same rate can be expected. However, if the internal rate of return is substantially above the market rate, it seems unrealistic to assume that reinvestment can continually occur at this rate.

THE REVISIONISTS

A search of the more recent literature on investment theory reveals numerous attempts to refine and revise the original work of the Lutzes and Dean. The revisionists have generally attempted to strengthen the original work by weakening the assumptions. In this chapter we will describe the work of only one revisionist in any detail, *viz.*, Weingartner's use of mathematical programming to treat the problems of interdependence among investment proposals and limitations on investment funds [59]. However, all of Chapter 16 is devoted to the analysis of investment when the assumption of perfect certainty is relaxed.

Before turning to Weingartner's work, we should at least sketch some of the work which has been concerned with questions of the following type: (1) What is the correct discount rate to use with a present-worth approach? and (2) How is the cost of investment funds measured? Both questions are concerned with

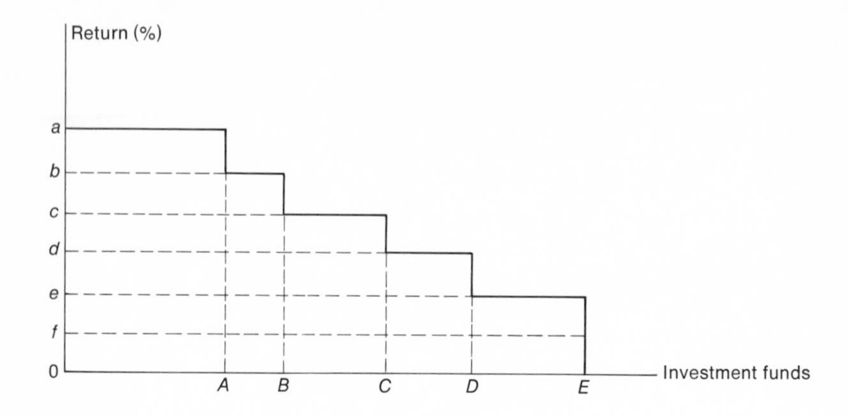

FIGURE 15-5

weakening the assumption that a perfect capital market exists. That is, as long as a firm can borrow or lend as much money as it needs at the market rate of interest, then this is the correct discount rate, and the cost of capital.

The proper discount rate

Baumol has pointed out that "the discount rate is just a measure of what we lose by receiving our money later rather than now" [4, p. 426]. Hence, with a perfect capital market, what we lose is simply the forgone market rate of interest.

> If, however, the capital market is imperfect—if the businessman can only borrow limited amounts, if the rate of interest on his loans rises the more he borrows, . . . the connection between the interest and discount rates is not so simple. But, in any event, the discount rate remains the opportunity cost of postponed receipts of money [4, p. 426].

As an example, suppose a firm were to list all possible investment projects by amount of funds required and internal rate of return.

The list could be displayed graphically as shown in Figure 15-5.

The most lucrative project has an internal rate of return of *a* percent, and requires an investment of *OA* dollars. Similarly, the second most profitable project promises a return of *b* percent, and requires *AB* dollars.

Now, *given a perfect capital market*, if the market rate of interest is *f* percent, the firm would undertake *OE* dollars worth of investment. However, suppose that the firm can borrow only *OB* dollars, even though the market rate of interest is still *f* percent. Clearly, the opportunity cost of postponed receipts of money to the firm is no longer *f* percent; rather, the opportunity cost, or discount rate, is now *c* percent. The reason is simple. If the firm had more money today it could invest it at *c* percent; hence, this is the cost of not having the money now.

The cost of capital

The second question listed above concerned the measurement of the cost of investment funds, i.e., the cost of capital. According to Baumol, the cost of capital is the "rate of yield against which prospective investment projects should be compared. That is, any investment which yields a rate of return greater than the 'cost of capital' will be beneficial to stockholders, while any project whose return is less than the cost of capital will reduce the return to stockholders" [4, p. 469]. For an excellent, though brief, survey of some of the complications which arise in attempting to measure the cost of capital, see Baumol [4, pp. 469–471]. For more detailed analyses, see [20,39,40,49].

A mathematical programming model

Weingartner significantly extended the mathematical programming approach to the theory of investment in an important book published in 1963 [59]. Weingartner examined both linear and integer programming as tools for analyzing capital budgeting problems. Here, we shall consider only the integer programming model of investment.

The Weingartner approach permits the firm to handle the evaluation of investment proposals where the proposals are interdependent. That is, the fourth assumption underlying the approach developed by the Lutzes and Dean can now be relaxed. Mathematical programming also permits the second assumption to be relaxed, that is, the assumption of a perfect capital market. Limitations on investment funds can be handled by way of the usual mathematical programming constraints.

We turn first to the relaxation of the assumption that all potential projects are independent.

> How strong this assumption is may be seen when one considers that alternative to almost every project is the possibility of its postponement for one or more periods, with concomitant changes in outlays and payoffs. These, of course, form a mutually exclusive set of alternatives since it would be deemed uneconomical, if not impossible, to carry out more than one of them. Mutual exclusion is by no means the only alternative to independence, . . . Contingent or dependent projects can arise, for instance, when acceptance of one proposal is dependent on acceptance of one or more other proposals [58, p. 491].

An example of *mutually exclusive* projects is provided by a power company which must obtain additional electrical capacity for its system. The company can invest in one of three alternatives: (1) a nuclear power plant, (2) a coal-fired power plant, or (3) a contract with a neighboring company to provide the needed power. A project to establish a center to train employees in the nuclear technology would, of course, be *contingent* upon the acceptance of the first alternative.

Integer programming constraints can easily handle the types of interdependence described above. For our example, the following constraints are adequate:

(15-20) $$X_1 + X_2 + X_3 \leq 1$$

(15-21) $$X_4 \leq X_1 \qquad \text{all } X_i \text{ are non-negative integers}$$

where X_1 = nuclear plant
X_2 = coal-fired plant
X_3 = contract for power
X_4 = nuclear training center

The interpretation is that if X_i is 0, the project is rejected; and if X_i is 1, the project is accepted. Clearly, by (15-20), only one of the three mutually exclusive projects can be accepted. And (15-21) makes it possible for the nuclear training center to be accepted *only* if the nuclear plant is accepted. Of course, the acceptance of the training center is not *required* even if the nuclear plant is chosen.

Next we consider the problem of budget constraints, namely, that the capital market is imperfect and the firm is limited to a fixed amount of investment funds. On the surface, it appears to be relatively easy to incorporate this budget limitation as another integer programming constraint. For the same example and symbols as discussed earlier,

(15-22) $$I_1X_1 + I_2X_2 + I_3X_3 \leq I_0$$

where I_i = investment funds required for project i.

I_0 = total funds available to the firm

The constraint (15-22) makes it possible to build fund limitations into the integer programming framework. However, the constraint raises an important problem which we must discuss shortly. To understand the problem though, we must turn to the formulation of the objective function.

Given the objective of maximizing the present value of profit, the objective function can be tentatively written as

(15-23) $$PV = P_1X_1 + P_2X_2 + P_3X_3 + P_4X_4$$

where P_i = present value of profit resulting from project i.

Now we must consider how the P_i are obtained. Clearly, the P_i are supposed to be obtained by discounting the stream of net profits. But what is the rate of discount? Earlier, we pointed out how the discount rate is determined when investment funds are limited. From that discussion, it should be apparent that the proper discount rate must be determined simultaneously with the optimal configuration of projects. Thus the discount rate becomes a variable itself. In other words, it is not strictly correct to consider the P_i as constants in (15-23). For an analysis of this problem, see the article by Baumol and Quandt [6].

To conclude this discussion, we will formulate a general integer programming model of investment. In this model we will ignore the problem raised above and treat the discount rate as a constant.

The firm seeks to maximize

$$PV = P_1X_1 + P_2X_2 + \cdots + P_mX_m \tag{15-24}$$

subject to

$$\begin{aligned} I_{10}X_1 + I_{20}X_2 + \cdots + I_{m0}X_m &\leq I_0 \\ I_{11}X_1 + I_{21}X_2 + \cdots + I_{m1}X_m &\leq I_1 \\ &\vdots \\ I_{1n}X_1 + I_{2n}X_2 + \cdots + I_{mn}X_m &\leq I_n \end{aligned} \tag{15-25}$$

and

$$X_1, \ldots, X_m \geq 0 \qquad \text{and all integers} \tag{15-26}$$

where

X_i = units of project i undertaken
P_i = present value of profit resulting from project i
I_t = total funds available to firm in period t
I_{it} = investment funds required for project i in period t

Thus we have added one further dimension to the problem by the constraints (15-25). Now the firm can consider the problem of investment in all n time periods simultaneously. Of course it would be a simple matter to add constraints where groups of projects are mutually exclusive, and constraints where projects are contingent upon the acceptance of others. That is, constraints similar to (15-20) and (15-21) could be added as required.

We should not fail to mention one of the most important advantages of the mathematical programming approach. This advantage is that programming permits the firm to consider *all* projects in *all* combinations systematically. Hence the firm is not left to a random process of evaluating projects singly and hoping that good judgment will lead it to the optimal combination.

SUMMARY

In this chapter we have treated investment models of the firm under the assumption that perfect certainty prevails. Clearly this assumption is unrealistic. However, it can be argued that investment theory is by no means simple even where all variables are taken as given. Therefore it seems only prudent to try to understand the simplest models first before compounding the difficulty (as we shall do in the next chapter when we introduce uncertainty into the investment decision).

A brief survey of traditional capital theory was given at the beginning of the chapter in order to provide a foundation for the modern theory of investment of the firm. Then the investment criteria developed by the Lutzes and Dean were presented. Finally, while maintaining the assumption of perfect certainty, some of the other assumptions underlying the Lutzes and Dean approach were relaxed and the effects on the investment criteria were noted.

BIBLIOGRAPHY

[1] ALCHIAN, ARMEN. "The Rate of Interest, Fisher's Rate of Return over Costs, and Keynes' Internal Rate of Return," *American Economic Review*, **XLV** (December, 1955), 938–943.

[2] ARROW, K. J. "Optimal Capital Policy, the Cost of Capital, and Myopic Decision Rules," *Annals of Institute of Statistical Mathematics*, **XVI** (1964), 21–30.

[3] BARGES, A. *The Effect of Capital Structure on the Cost of Capital*. Englewood Cliffs, N. J.: Prentice-Hall, 1963.

[4] BAUMOL, WILLIAM J. *Economic Theory and Operations Analysis*. Englewood Cliffs, N. J.: Prentice-Hall, Inc., 1965.

[5] BAUMOL, W. J. "On Dividend Policy and Market Imperfection," *Journal of Business*, **XXXVI** (January, 1963), 112–115

[6] BAUMOL, W. J., and R. E. QUANDT. "Mathematical Programming and the Discount Rate under Capital Rationing," *Economic Journal*, **LXXV** (June, 1965), 317–329.

[7] BERANEK, W. "Review of Barges," *Journal of Finance*, **XIX** (September, 1964), 562–564.

[8] BIERMAN, HAROLD, and SEYMOUR SMIDT. *The Capital Budgeting Decision*. New York: The Macmillan Co., 1960.

[9] BLAUG, M. *Economic Theory in Retrospect*. Homewood, Ill.: Richard D. Irwin, Inc., 1968.

[10] BODENHORN, D. "On the Problem of Capital Budgeting," *Journal of Finance*, **XIV** (December, 1959), 473–492.

[11] BÖHM-BAWERK, EUGENE VON. *Positive Theory of Capital*. Wagner'schen Verlag, Innsbruck, 1889 [English translation: Libertarian Press, South Holland, Illinois, 1959].

[12] CHING, PAO L., and JOHN P. SHELTON. "A Contribution to the Theory of Capital Budgeting," *Journal of Finance*, **XVIII** (December, 1963), 623–636.

[13] CHARNES, A., W. W. COOPER, and M. H. MILLER. "Application of Linear Programming to Financial Budgeting and the Costing of Funds," *Journal of Business*, **XXXII** (January, 1959), 20–46.

[14] CLOWER, R. W. "An Investigation into the Dynamics of Investment," *American Economic Review*, **XLIV** (March, 1954), 64–81.

[15] DEAN, JOEL. *Capital Budgeting*. New York: Columbia University Press, 1951.

[16] DEAN, J. *Managerial Economics*. Englewood Cliffs, N. J.: Prentice-Hall, Inc., 1951.

[17] DEAN, J. "Measuring the Productivity of Capital," *Harvard Business Review*, **XXXII** (January–February, 1954), 120–130.

[18] DEWEY, DONALD. *Modern Capital Theory*. New York: Columbia University Press, 1965.

[19] DORFMAN, R., P. A. SAMUELSON, and R. SOLOW. *Linear Programming and Economic Analysis*. New York: McGraw-Hill Book Co., 1958.

[20] DURAND, DAVID. "The Cost of Capital in an Imperfect Market: A Reply to Modigliani and Miller," *American Economic Review*, **XLIX** (September, 1959), 639–654.

[21] FISHER, IRVING. *The Theory of Interest*. New York: The Macmillan Co., 1930.

[22] GORDON, M. J. "Security and a Financial Theory of Investment," *Quarterly Journal of Economics*, **LXXIV** (August, 1960), 472–492.

[23] GORDON, M. J., and ELI SHAPIRO. "Capital Equipment Analysis: The Required Rate of Profit," *Management Science*, **III** (October, 1956), 102–110.

[24] GORDON, MYRON J. "The Payoff Period and the Rate of Profit," *Journal of Business*, **XXVIII** (October, 1955), 253–261.

[25] GRANT, E. L. *Principles of Engineering Economy* (3rd ed.). New York: The Ronald Press, 1950.

[26] HAAVELMO, TRYGVE. *A Study in the Theory of Investment*. Chicago: The University of Chicago Press, 1960.

[27] HAYEK, FRIEDRICH A. *The Pure Theory of Capital*. London: Macmillan & Co., 1941.

[28] HICKS, JOHN R. *Value and Capital*. Oxford: Clarendon Press, 1939.

[29] HIRSHLEIFER, JACK. "On the Theory of Optimal Investment Decision," *Journal of Political Economy*, **LXVI** (August, 1958), 329–352.

[30] KEYNES, J. M. *The General Theory of Employment, Interest, and Money*. New York: Harcourt, Brace & World, Inc., 1936. [Also available in paperback as KEYNES, J. M. *The General Theory of Employment, Interest, and Money*. New York: Harcourt, Brace & World, Inc. 1965.]

[31] KNIGHT, FRANK. *Ethics of Competition*. New York: Harper, 1935.

[32] KNIGHT, F. H. "The Quantity of Capital and the Rate of Interest," *Journal of Political Economy*, **XLIV** (August, 1936), 433–463.

[33] LINTNER, J. "Dividends, Earnings, Leverage, Stock Prices and the Supply of Capital to Corporations," *Review of Economics and Statistics*, **XLIV** (August, 1962), 242–269.

[34] LORIE, JAMES H., and LEONARD J. SAVAGE. "Three Problems in Rationing Capital," *Journal of Business*, **XXVIII** (October, 1955), 299–339.

[35] LUTZ, FRIEDRICH, and VERA LUTZ. *The Theory of Investment of the Firm*. Princeton: Princeton University Press, 1951.

[36] LUTZ, FRIEDRICH. "The Essentials of Capital Theory," in F. Lutz and D. C. Hague (Eds.), *The Theory of Capital*. London: Macmillan & Co., Ltd., 1961.

[37] MARTIN, A. D. "Mathematical Programming of Portfolio Selection," *Management Science*, **I** (January, 1955), 152–166.

[38] MASSE, PIERRE. *Optimal Investment Decisions*. Englewood Cliffs, N. J.: Prentice-Hall, Inc., 1962.

[39] MODIGLIANI, FRANCO, and MERTON H. MILLER. "The Cost of Capital, Corporation Finance and the Theory of Investment," *American Economic Review*, **XLVIII** (June, 1958), 261–297.

[40] MILLER, M. H., and F. MODIGLIANI. "Dividend Policy, Growth, and the Valuation of Shares," *Journal of Business*, **XXXIV** (October, 1961).

[41] PORTERFIELD, J. *Investment Decisions and Capital Costs*. Englewood Cliffs, N. J.: Prentice-Hall, 1965.

[42] PREINREICH, GABRIEL A. D. "The Economic Life of Industrial Equipment," *Econometrica*, **VIII** (January, 1940), 12–44.

[43] ROBERTS, H. V. "Current Problems in the Economics of Capital Budgeting," *Journal of Business*, **XXX** (January, 1957), 12–16.

[44] ROBICHEK, A., and S. MYERS. *Optimal Financing Decisions*. Englewood Cliffs, N. J.: Prentice-Hall, 1965.

[45] SAMUELSON, PAUL A. *Economics, An Introductory Analysis* (7th ed.). New York: McGraw-Hill Book Co., 1967.

[46] SMITH, VERNON L. "Problems in Production-Investment Planning over Time," *International Economic Review*, **I** (September, 1960), 198–216.

[47] SMITH, V. L. "The Theory of Investment and Production," *Quarterly Journal of Economics*, **LXXIII** (February, 1959), 61–87.

[48] SMITH, VERNON L. *Investment and Production*. Cambridge, Mass.: Harvard University Press, 1961.

[49] SOLOMON, EZRA. "Measuring a Company's Cost of Capital," *Journal of Business*, **XXVIII** (October, 1955), 240–252.

[50] SOLOMON, E. "The Arithmetic of Capital Budgeting Decisions," *Journal of Business*, **XXIX** (April, 1956), 124–129.

[51] SOLOMON, E. (Ed.). *The Management of Corporate Capital*. Glencoe, Ill.: The Free Press, 1959.

[52] SOLOW, ROBERT M. *Capital Theory and the Rate of Return*. Amsterdam: North-Holland, 1963.

[53] TEICHROEW, D., A. A. ROBICHEK, and M. MONTALBANO. "Mathematical Analysis of Rates of Return under Certainty," *Management Science*, **II** (1964), 395–403.

[54] TEICHROEW, D., A. A. ROBICHEK, and M. MONTALBANO. "An Analysis of Criteria for Investment and Financing Decisions under Certainty," *Management Science*, **XII** (1965), 151–179.

[55] TERBORGH, GEORGE. *Business Investment Policy*. Washington: Machinery and Allied Products Institute, 1958.

[56] TERBORGH, G. *Dynamic Equipment Policy*. Washington, Machinery and Allied Products Institute, 1949.

[57] WALTER, J. "Dividend Policy: Its Influence on the Value of the Enterprise," *Journal of Finance*, **XVII** (May, 1963), 280–291.

[58] WEINGARTNER, H. MARTIN. "Capital Budgeting of Interrelated Projects: Survey and Synthesis," *Management Science*, **XII** (March, 1966), 485–516.

[59] WEINGARTNER, H. M. *Mathematical Programming and the Analysis of Capital Budgeting Problems*. Englewood Cliffs, N. J.: Prentice-Hall, Inc., 1963.

[60] WICKSELL, KNUT. *Lectures on Political Economy*, Vol. I. London: Routledge & Kegan Paul, Ltd., 1934.

16

Investment models of the firm: risk and uncertainty*

INTRODUCTION

The preceding chapter considered investment models of the firm in a world of certainty. In this chapter we will relax that rather unrealistic assumption and survey some of the more important approaches to investment under risk and uncertainty. Few readers need to be convinced of the importance of noncertainty in investment models. However, J. M. Keynes has made the point emphatically:

> The outstanding fact is the extreme precariousness of the basis of knowledge on which our estimates of prospective yield have to be made. Our knowledge of the factors which will govern the yield of an investment some years hence is usually very slight and often negligible. If we speak frankly, we have to admit that our basis of knowledge for estimating the yield ten years hence of a railway, a copper mine, a textile factory, the goodwill of a patent medicine, an Atlantic liner, a building in the City of London amounts to little and sometimes to nothing; or even five years hence [24, p. 149].

Under perfect certainty all relevant information is assumed to be known to the decision maker. This assumption is perfectly acceptable so long as we do not attempt to use the perfect-certainty model in the real world. However, the traditional approach (described in Chapter 15), has been advocated for use in real-world situations. This is quite clear in the original work by Dean [9] and the more recent work by Ezra Solomon [39]. Under such use, and with the perfect-certainty assumption, the decision maker is required to possess, or develop, single-valued estimates for the variables in the model. This requirement is quite formidable. That is, it is usually impossible for a decision maker to have the information in this form.

Hence in this chapter we shall continue to examine the work of the revisionists which we began at the end of Chapter 15—we shall relax the certainty assumption which is made in the traditional approach of the Lutzes and Dean.

* The author of this chapter is Eugene T. Byrne , Jr.

There are four main sections. The first section treats the "practical" models for handling noncertainty in investment decisions. Although these methods raise serious theoretical objections, they do have the virtue of being easy to apply, and for this reason they are popular in real-world situations. The second section presents the Shackle model, which is at the opposite end of the spectrum of operational techniques. The third section, single-project models, considers the Hillier and Hertz models. The distinguishing characteristic of these models is that each deals with developing a probability distribution of the return of single-investment proposals. The purpose is to develop more information about a particular proposal than one single-valued estimate provides. The last section, multiproject models, presents two models. The Markowitz approach to the derivation of efficient portfolios and Farrar's model of the investment decision under uncertainty will be discussed.

PRACTICAL MODELS

In this section we shall discuss three well-known methods for treating noncertainty in investment decisions: (1) the finite-planning-horizon model, (2) the risk-discounting model, and (3) sensitivity analysis.

The finite-planning-horizon model

The finite-planning-horizon method is perhaps the simplest way of treating noncertainty. The principle is to alter the length of the period over which returns are expected, depending upon the degree of noncertainty. Even though a project is expected to last 40 years, the decision maker may arbitrarily decide to consider only returns over the first 30 years. If positive returns are expected over the last 10 years, then the effect of the alteration is to reduce the attractiveness of the project by an amount equal to the present value of the omitted returns. One obvious problem is how the specific alteration is determined. What made the decision maker choose a 30-year life rather than, say, a 32-year life?

Furthermore, as Baumol has pointed out:

> A finite and arbitrary horizon, then, is not really a defensible method for dealing with imperfect foresight. It takes no account of our limited ability to predict events in the more immediate future (which is sometimes as distant as twenty-five years from the present) and forces us to ignore totally what little we can forecast about the more distant future with some degree of confidence [4].

Risk-discounting model

To evaluate the risk-discounting method for treating noncertainty, it will be useful to recall the formula for net present value given in Chapter 15, equation (15-19). Thus

$$PV = \sum_{i=0}^{n} \frac{(R_i - 0_i)}{(1 + r)^i} - I_0 \qquad (16\text{-}1)$$

The risk-discounting model would substitute g for r in (16-1), where

$$g = r + \delta \tag{16-2}$$

Baumol refers to δ as the *risk factor* [4, p. 454]. Presumably, the value of δ is directly proportional to the degree of uncertainty, or risk. For example, a very risky project might be assigned $\delta = 0.10$, whereas a less risky one might be assigned $\delta = 0.03$. Clearly, from (16-1) and (16-2), a higher risk factor corresponds to a lower net present value of the project, which is the desired direction of the adjustment. Again, however, we are confronted with the formidable theoretical problem of determining the value of δ for specific projects. Apparently it must be estimated "on the basis of some sort of judgment or intuition" [4, p. 455].

There is another special assumption involved in the use of risk discounting which should be made explicit. The assumption is that "the probability of a dollar of estimated cash actually materializing will decrease each year by a fixed percentage of the probability in the preceding year" [5, p. 54]. Bierman and Smidt have given a good example of a project where risk discounting would be inappropriate because of this special assumption:

> Suppose we consider an investment to build and equip a plant for producing a new product. In some instances the major uncertainty may be related to the cost of constructing the plant, while the demand for the resulting output may be easily predictable in advance with very little uncertainty. . . . The use of atomic energy to generate electric power is a tangible example of this situation. In such a situation the discounting of future revenues, themselves fairly certain, seems a poor way of allowing for the uncertainty about how much the fixed plant will cost [5, p. 54].

Sensitivity analysis

This technique is quite simple to perform, and sometimes provides meaningful information about a project. Basically, sensitivity analysis "involves revising uncertain estimates of prospective cash flows and investigating the sensitivity of the measure of merit of the investment to such revisions in the estimates" [21, p. 444].

An example should be instructive. Consider a firm that manufactures parts for existing types of lawn mowers. Let us assume that an innovation in lawn mowers is expected in the future which will seriously reduce the demand for the parts. However, the date of the innovation is uncertain, and the firm is now trying to evaluate the profitability of an addition to its manufacturing capacity. In the profitability calculations the firm has used the year 1975 as its best estimate of the date the innovation will be introduced. The firm could use sensitivity analysis to study the effect of an earlier or later date on profitability. Thus it might calculate that an introduction date of 1973 would make the addition unprofitable, a date of 1974 would make it marginally profitable, and a date of 1975 would be quite profitable. On the other hand, the firm might discover that the profitability of the addition is relatively insensitive to dates within two years of 1975.

The major advantage of sensitivity analysis is its simplicity. However, it is also subject to some rather serious shortcomings.

> . . . Sensitivity analysis is quite limited in the amount of information it can provide. For example, it is difficult to draw precise conclusions about the possible effects of combinations of errors in the estimates, even though this is the typical situation of concern. For statistical reasons, it would usually be misleading to consider the case where all the estimates are too optimistic or where all are too pessimistic. In short, sensitivity analysis is useful but its conclusions tend to suffer from a lack of conciseness, precision, and comprehensiveness [21, p. 444].

THE SHACKLE MODEL

Shackle has presented an analysis of the problem of decision making under uncertainty that should be discussed [36]. Shackle's approach is generally regarded as an exposition of the psychological factors involved in decision making under uncertainty and is currently incapable of being used as a decision-making device in real-world situations. For these reasons, only the rudiments of Shackle's approach will be presented.

Shackle suggests that people are motivated to act based on the feelings they experience when they contemplate future events, thoughts of which give them pleasure or distress. The future events which people contemplate are referred to as hypotheses. For the particular problem of business investment the hypotheses, denoted by X, are the sum of discounted values of revenues and outlays minus the purchase price. For every given set of actions or strategies there is a calculated value of X. For every hypothesis there is a numerical measure called *potential surprise*. Potential surprise is a number that measures the degree to which a particular hypothesis or outcome is possible. If all evidence leads to the absence of disbelief in a particular outcome, then the actual occurrence is not surprising. This particular outcome would be assigned zero potential surprise. If a particular hypothesis is regarded with total disbelief then its occurrence would offer the greatest surprise. This hypothesis would be assigned maximum potential surprise. There will, of course, be hypotheses or outcomes for which the degree of potential surprise is neither zero nor the absolute maximum. Allowing X to be continuously variable, Shackle presents a diagram (Figure 16-1) relating degrees of potential surprise for values of outcome X for a single investment.

Next Shackle develops the notion of the stimulus function. First, a decision maker regards an outcome with given X as less interesting or stimulating if it has some potential surprise than if it has zero potential surprise. Shackle further states that ". . . the degree of stimulus is a monotonic increasing function of numerical face value X, and a monotonic decreasing function of potential surprise . . ." [36, p. 44]. In accordance with these suggestions a set of stimulus functions $\phi = \phi(X, Y)$ can be drawn (Figure 16-2).

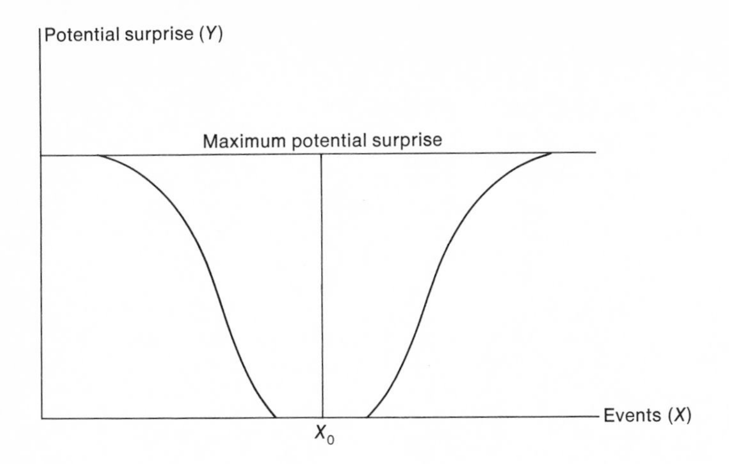

FIGURE **16-1**

Degrees of potential surprise

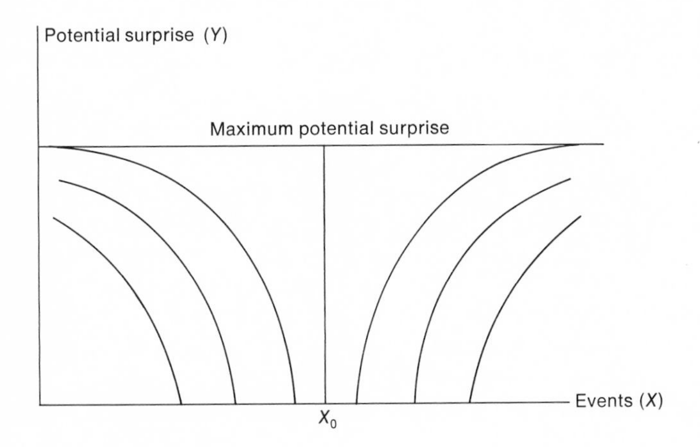

FIGURE **16-2**

Stimulus curves

Each curve to the right and left of X_0 gives an equal amount of stimulus. Curves further to the right or left have greater stimulus. Superimposing the curve for degrees of potential surprise on the latest diagram gives two determinate hypotheses, or values of X, which create maximum stimulation (Figure 16-3). One value of X will be positive and one will be negative. These occur at the points of tangency. The values of X labeled h_p and g_p in Figure 16-3 are called

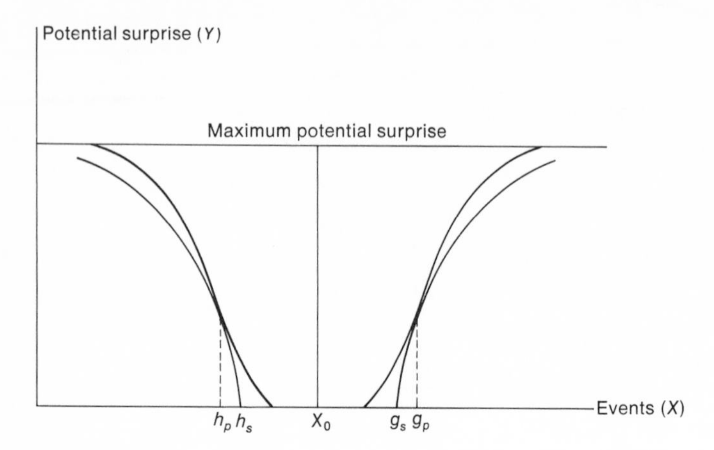

FIGURE 16-3

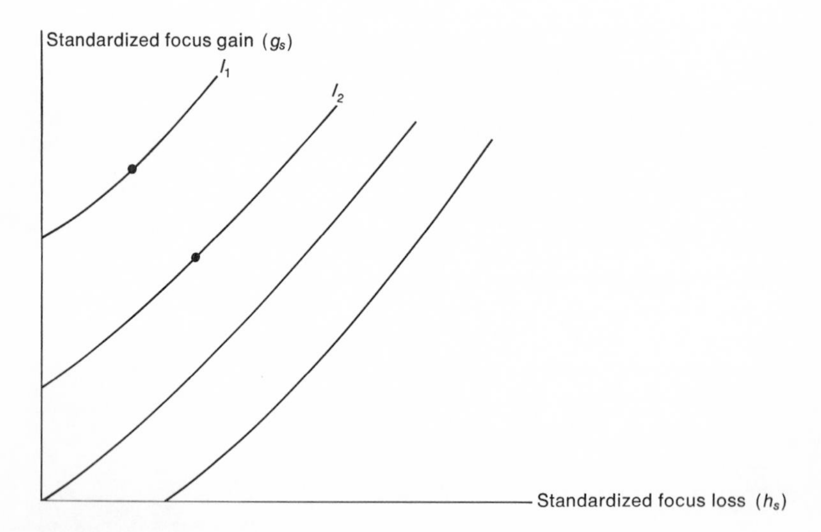

FIGURE 16-4
Gambler's indifference map

primary focus loss and *primary focus gain* respectively. Since such values would be incomparable between different investments, they are "standardized" by choosing those values of X which have zero potential surprise and the same degree of stimulation. Thus h_s is called the *standardized focus loss*, and g_s the *standardized focus gain*. It is now possible to compare different investments, for which there are values of X representing the standardized focus gains and losses.

At this point Shackle introduces the notion of a *gambler's indifference map* (Figure 16-4). The horizontal axis represents values of standardized focus loss, while the vertical axis represents standardized focus gains. Then for every investment there is a single point in this plane. The gambler's indifference curve slopes upward to the right with the slope increasing as standardized focus loss increases, indicating that these losses have increasing marginal disutility. A single curve gives the values of loss and gain to which the decision maker is indifferent, and curves higher above the horizontal axis yield preferred combinations of loss and gain.

To illustrate choice, consider two investments I_1 and I_2 as represented by the points shown on the loss-gain coordinates with a given system of gambler indifference curves. Figure 16-4 shows that I_1 is preferred to I_2.

Despite the interesting insights we can gain into the mental processes involved in decision making under uncertainty, it is clear that the required functions are not available for real-world situations.

SINGLE-PROJECT MODELS

The Hillier model

Hillier presented an approach for specifying more explicit information about the riskiness of single projects in a well-known article [21]. Here we shall present his derivation of the probability distribution of the present value of a proposed investment.

Hillier states that his approach is really a tool "for more clearly exhibiting the risk involved and should complement, rather than supersede, most current procedures for evaluating investments" [21, p. 445]. That is, it is not unusual for a firm to make *single-valued* estimates of all of the variables relevant to the evaluation of a particular proposal. Since individuals who make the estimates generally base them on subjective probabilities (however ill-defined they may be), by reporting only single-valued estimates some information is lost. In essence Hillier argues that a probability distribution of the present value of a project can and should be derived from the subjective probability distributions of the relevant variables.

Consider a simple example. Suppose our lawn-mower parts firm is comparing two mutually exclusive proposals: (1) an addition to its present capacity, and (2) partially withdrawing from the industry to enter the automobile-parts industry. It has calculated that the present values of (1) and (2) are each one million dollars. That is, *a priori* the firm would be indifferent between the two projects. It is likely, however, that the firm would not regard the present values of the two as equally likely. Hillier's approach is precisely this: to supply *explicit* information as to the likeliness of the two proposals, by way of probability distributions of present values.

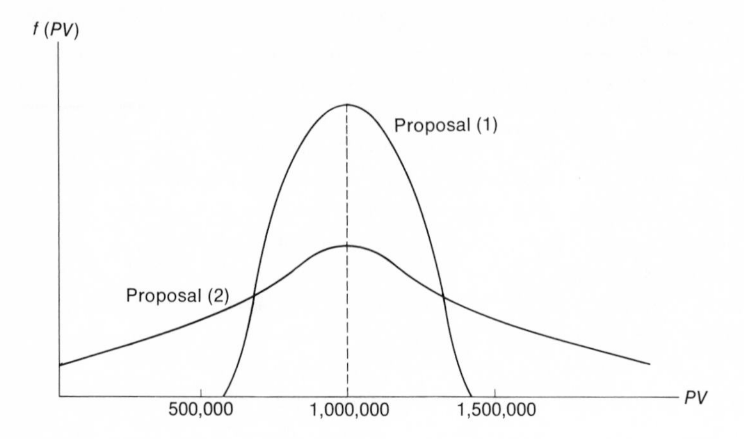

FIGURE **16-5**

Figure 16-5 represents one possible way of depicting this additional information. Thus the probability density function of proposal (1) compared with that of proposal (2) makes it clear that the *PV* of (1) is more likely to be near one million dollars than is the *PV* of (2). However, the larger variance or riskiness of (2) is also associated with a better chance of a much higher present value (and also a better chance of a much lower present value!). Hillier's approach, therefore, provides more information, but it does not offer a way of choosing between the two—except, possibly, by enabling "the executive to quickly apply, in an intuitive and implicit sense, the theoretical procedure of evaluating expected utility" [21, p. 445].

Now we shall describe the simplest Hillier model. Assume that the investment will result in net cash flows, X_i, over the next n years, and that the X_i are mutually independent. Furthermore, assume that the X_i are normally distributed random variables with known mean, μ_i, and known standard deviation, σ_i. Let the initial outlay (I_0 in equation 16-1) be included in X_0, and we get the usual formula for present value, PV:

$$PV = \sum_{i=0}^{n} \frac{X_i}{(1 + r)^i} \tag{16-3}$$

The reader should observe that PV is now a random variable. The expected value of PV, or μ, is

$$\mu = \sum_{i=0}^{n} \frac{\mu_i}{(1 + r)^i} \tag{16-4}$$

Also, given our assumption, a standard theorem in mathematical statistics leads to the following formula for the variance of PV, σ^2:

$$\sigma^2 = \sum_{i=0}^{n} \frac{\sigma_i^2}{(1 + r)^{2i}} \tag{16-5}$$

Since the distribution of PV is also normal, equations (16-4) and (16-5) completely define the probability density function of the proposed investment.

The simple model above is obviously not very realistic. Hillier does relax some of the assumptions in his article, e.g., the assumption of mutual independence of the X_i; however, we cannot pursue these extensions here. It should be noted, though, that the mathematics quickly becomes complex as assumptions are relaxed.

The Hertz model

In a 1964 article [18], Hertz developed an approach to risk analysis in investment decisions which is quite similar to the Hillier model. However, where Hillier's approach was analytical, Hertz introduced computer simulation techniques. As discussed in Chapter 13, computer simulation techniques permit us to solve problems that are too complex to solve analytically. In this sense, the Hertz model is an extension of the Hillier model.

We shall use an example of a manufacturing firm to illustrate the Hertz model. Thus we seek to determine the present-value distribution of the firm's proposal to build a new plant.

First we must select those variables which are important to the present-value calculation. Let us choose only three for simplicity: (1) operating costs OC, (2) share of the market SM, and (3) market size MS. Next we must obtain estimates of these three variables. These estimates are listed in Table 16-1.

It will be useful to think of the following general function:

$$PV = f(OC, SM, MS, \ldots) \tag{16-6}$$

That is, the present value of the proposal, PV, is a function of the three variables listed in Table 16-1. The dots indicate that there are many other variables which we have ignored here. Of course, we should only be interested in the *crucial*

TABLE **16-1**

	Expected value	Standard deviation
Operating costs, OC	\$ 110,000	\$ 11,000
Share of the market, SM	10%	2%
Market size, MS	\$2,750,000	\$250,000

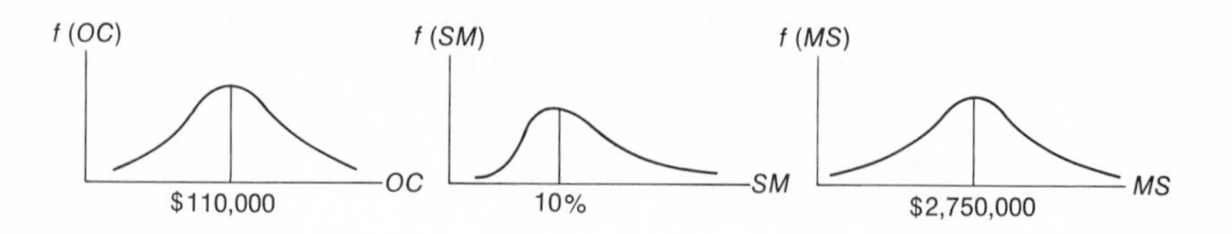

FIGURE **16-6**

variables anyway, namely, those variables to which *PV* is sensitive and about which much uncertainty exists.

We should point out again that a normal investment evaluation procedure is to simply substitute the values in the expected value column of Table 16-1 in equation (16-6). However, in doing this, the information in the standard-deviation column would be ignored. As to the source of the standard-deviation estimates, we shall only state that they are subjectively arrived at by the individual making the expected value estimate. Of course there are other ways of indicating the uncertainty of the estimates, e.g., by selecting values above and below which the individual expects the actual value to occur with, say, only a 25% chance. Thus the actual manner in which the individual makes known his subjective evaluation of uncertainty is a matter of detail and not substance. The main requirement is to obtain enough information to construct probability distributions of the crucial variables.

In Figure 16-6 we construct the probability density functions of the three variables in Table 16-1.

The probability functions can, of course, take any shape, and are by no means restricted to symmetrical ones. For the moment we shall make the assumption that the three random variables are mutually independent. Later we will relax this assumption.

We can now complete the description of the Hertz model by relying on the discussion of computer simulation techniques given in Chapter 13. That is, by using the computer to generate artificial random variables from the three distributions, we can generate a probability density function of the present value by simulation. Thus the computer generates a random variable from each distribution in Figure 16-6. These three values are substituted in equation (16-6), and the present value is computed, and stored. Then three more random variables are generated, and *PV* is computed and stored again. Repeating this process a thousand times would provide us with enough observations on *PV* to construct the desired distribution. That is, the end result would be a distribution of *PV* such as is shown in Figure 16-7.

It is important to note that the *PV* equation (16-6) is likely to be nonlinear in the variables *OC*, *SM*, and *MS*. Thus the mean of the *PV* distribution in

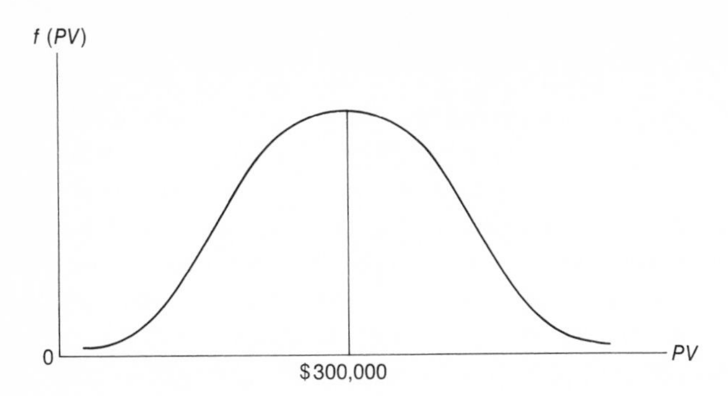

FIGURE **16-7**

Figure 16-7, *viz.*, $300,000, is unlikely to be the same value of PV that would be obtained by simply substituting the expected values from Table 16-1 in equation (16-6).

Hertz used an internal rate of return criterion in his model rather than the present-value criterion which we have used. However, in reporting the results of his example, he observed a rather large difference between the rate calculated with expected values only and the rate determined via simulation.

> . . . Management had been informed, on the basis of the "one best estimate" approach, that the expected return was 25.2% before taxes. When we ran the new set of data through the computer program, however, we got an expected return of only 14.6% before taxes. This surprising difference not only is due to the fact that under the new approach we use a range of values; it also reflects the fact that we have weighted each value in the range by the chances of its occurrence [18, p. 183].

Finally, the Hertz model is capable of handling *dependency* among the random variables. For example, it is reasonable to view our variables OC and SM as being interdependent. That is, it could be argued that the lower the firm's operating costs OC, the higher will be its share of the market SM.

The method for handling this dependence of SM on OC is straightforward. The firm would develop a *number* of probability distributions of SM, each corresponding to a different *range* of values of OC. As an example, say only two distributions of SM are constructed, one with an expected value of 8% and the other 12%. Now, the computer generates a random variable from the OC distribution *first*. If it happens to fall in the *lower half* of the range of OC values, the computer then generates a random variable from the SM distribution with *the 12%* expected value. The rest of the procedure is the same as was described earlier.

MULTIPROJECT MODELS

The Markowitz approach

The Markowitz approach represents an advance over the traditional model because it focuses on the portfolio aspect of investment decisions [28]. In effect, Markowitz emphasized and gave substance to the fact that individuals tend to regard an investment as part of a group of investments. An individual will select an investment only insofar as it can make a positive contribution to a number of decision criteria that are defined in terms of the group of investments.

Basically Markowitz employed the concept of covariance between the securities in a portfolio to prove that the variance of a portfolio could be less than the variance of any of the securities contained in the portfolio. This can be seen by considering the following analysis. The return from investing in a set of securities whose returns are random variables R_i, $i = 1, \ldots, n$ is

$$R = \sum_{i=1}^{n} X_i R_i \tag{16-7}$$

where X_i is the percentage of money assets invested in the ith security. Taking the expected value of (16-7) gives $E(R)$ as the expected return from the portfolio. That is,

$$E(R) = \sum_{i=1}^{n} X_i \mu_i \tag{16-8}$$

where μ_i is the expected value of R_i, or the expected return of the ith security. To derive the variance of the portfolio, we write

$$R - \sum_{i=1}^{n} X_i \mu_i = \sum_{i=1}^{n} X_i (R_i - \mu_i)$$

and

$$\left[R - \sum_{i=1}^{n} X_i \mu_i\right]^2 = \sum_{i=1}^{n} [X_i (R_i - \mu_i)]^2 + 2 \sum_{j=1}^{n} \sum_{i>j}^{n} X_i X_j (R_i - \mu_i)(R_j - \mu_j)$$

Taking the expected value and noting that

$$\sigma_{ij} = E[R_i - E(R_i)][R_j - E(R_j)]$$

is the covariance between two securities, we obtain the variance of the portfolio:

$$\sigma_R^2 = \sum_{i=1}^{n} X_i \sigma_i^2 + 2 \sum_{j=1}^{n} \sum_{i>j}^{n} X_i X_j \sigma_{ij} \tag{16-9}$$

Examination of this expression reveals that the variance of a portfolio, σ_R^2, can

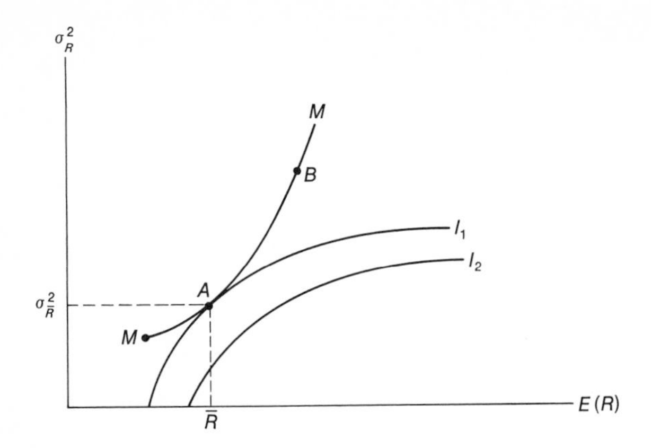

FIGURE **16-8**

be less than the smallest variance of the individual securities if there are sufficient negative covariances. A negative covariance between two securities can be interpreted as meaning that when the return from one security is above its average value, the return from the other is below its average value.

Based on these considerations, and with the aid of quadratic programming, Markowitz developed a boundary line composed of portfolios. The portfolios on this boundary are efficient in the sense that for any given efficient portfolio there can be no other portfolio with greater return for the same variance or lesser variance for the same return. This boundary line is shown in Figure 16-8 as the curve *MM*.

To understand the Markowitz boundary *MM*, the reader should recognize that any point on the curve, say point *A*, represents a particular portfolio. Thus *A* might represent a portfolio consisting of 10% of security 1, 18% of security 2, and 72% of security 3. No other percentage of the three securities would yield a portfolio with the same return, $\bar{R}$, but with a lower variance than $\sigma_{\bar{R}}{}^2$. Nor would any other percentages yield the same variance but with a greater return than $\bar{R}$. However, it *is* possible to obtain a greater return if we are willing to accept the associated higher σ_R^2. Point *B* illustrates such a portfolio.

Unfortunately Markowitz does not specify how the decision maker should choose between portfolios on the boundary. This is considered to be a function of the individual's attitude toward risk. The theoretical solution is to assume that the utility indifference curves are known; hence, for the indifference curves shown (I_2 represents a higher level of utility than I_1), *A* would be the optimal portfolio.

> One interesting result of the Markowitz analysis is that it will usually lead to the choice of a diversified portfolio of investments rather than one *best* (highest present value) investment. By not putting all of our nest eggs into one investment, we are, in effect, hedging against the possibility that one of the projects will turn out very badly [4, p. 458].

The Farrar model

We shall present only a sketch of the Farrar model. For a complete exposition, the reader is referred to the book by Farrar [12].

The model relies on two main assumptions [12, p. 19]:

1. The investor possesses a utility of money function which is positively sloped and concave.
2. The investor's strategy is to maximize expected utility.

If R_1, the investor's net worth, is a random variable and μ is the expected value of R_1, then it can be shown that the investor's expected utility function can be written [12, p. 20] as

$$E[U(R_1)] = \mu - A\sigma^2 \tag{16-10}$$

where

$$A = -\frac{U''(\mu)}{2}$$

$$\sigma^2 = \text{variance of } R_1$$

Since $U''(\mu)$ is the second derivative of utility with respect to R_1, evaluated at $R_1 = \mu$, it is necessarily negative by the first assumption. Hence A, the coefficient of risk aversion, is positive. Clearly, for other assumed shapes of the utility function, A could be positive, thereby yielding a function with a preference for risk.

Now if the investor considers a portfolio rather than a single project, the new expected utility function becomes [12, p. 22]

$$E[U(R)] = \sum_{i=1}^{n} X_i\mu_i - A\sum_{j=1}^{n}\sum_{i>j}^{n} X_iX_j\sigma_{ij} \tag{16-11}$$

where R, the portfolio, is a weighted sum of securities, R_i, $i = 1, 2, \ldots, n$. The symbols are the same as defined in the Markowitz model.

The Farrar model can now be formulated as a quadratic programming problem. (See Chapter 9 for a discussion of this tool.)

The objective function is equation (16-11). The investor seeks to find those values of the X_i (the percentages of the securities in the portfolio) for which his expected utility is maximized. The constraint is simply

$$\sum_{i=1}^{n} X_i = 1 \tag{16-12}$$

Thus the sum of the percentages must equal one. And the usual non-negativity condition is

$$X_i \geq 0 \qquad i = 1, 2, \ldots, n \tag{16-13}$$

The obvious limitation of this model for real-world application is the difficulty of determining the parameter, A, the coefficient of risk aversion. "Knowing that it is a constant multiple ($= -\frac{1}{2}$) of a hypothetical utility of money function's curvature is of little help to the decision maker" [12, p. 33].

CONCLUSION

In this chapter we have discussed only a few of the existing models of investment under risk and uncertainty. Hopefully, however, we have selected the more important ones, and have conveyed to the reader that much research is needed in this area. The rather low level of sophistication of the *workable* models (finite horizon, risk discounting, and sensitivity analysis) should attest to this latter statement.

We conclude with a pertinent quotation from Dorfman:

> In this long discussion of decision-making under uncertainty we have been compelled to point out flaws and shortcomings in every solution that has been proposed. One would hope that this will not always be the case, and that some day satisfactory solutions will be found to this pervasive and fundamental problem. At present, however, the problem of uncertainty is clouded by uncertainty [26, p. 158].

BIBLIOGRAPHY

[1] ADELSON, R. M. "Criteria for Capital Investment: An Approach Through Decision Theory," *Operational Research Quarterly*, **XVI** (March, 1965), 19–50.

[2] ANSOFF, H. I. "A Model for Diversification," *Management Science*, **IV** (July, 1958), 392–414.

[3] ARCHER, STEPHEN H., and CHARLES A. D'AMBROSIO. *The Theory of Business Finance: A Book of Readings*. New York: The Macmillan Co., 1967.

[4] BAUMOL, WILLIAM J. *Economic Theory and Operations Analysis*. Englewood Cliffs, N. J.: Prentice-Hall, Inc., 1965.

[5] BIERMAN, HAROLD, and SEYMOUR SMIDT. *The Capital Budgeting Decision*. New York: Macmillan, 1966.

[6] BYRNE, EUGENE T. *Theory of Investment of the Firm Under Uncertainty*. Unpublished Ph.D. Dissertation, Tulane University, New Orleans, Louisiana, May, 1967.

[7] COHEN, K., and F. HAMMER. *Analytical Methods in Banking*. Homewood, Ill.: Richard D. Irwin, Inc., 1966.

[8] CORD, J. "A Method for Allocating Funds to Investment Projects When Returns are Subject to Uncertainty," *Management Science*, **X** (January, 1964), 335–341.

[9] DEAN, JOEL. *Capital Budgeting*. New York: Columbia University Press, 1951.

[10] DURAND, DAVID. "The Cost of Capital, Corporation Finance, and the Theory of Investment Comment," *American Economic Review*, **XLIX** (September, 1959), 639–654.

[11] DYCKMAN, T. R. "Allocating Funds to Investment Projects When Returns are Subject to Uncertainty—A Comment," *Management Science*, **XI** (November, 1964), 348–350.

[12] FARRAR, D. E. *The Investment Decision Under Uncertainty*. Englewood Cliffs, N. J.: Prentice-Hall, Inc., 1962.

[13] FELLER, WILLIAM. *An Introduction to Probability Theory and Its Applications*, Vol. I (2nd ed.). New York: John Wiley & Sons, 1957.

[14] FELLNER, WILLIAM. *Probability and Profit*. Homewood, Ill.: Richard D. Irwin, Inc., 1965.

[15] FISHER, IRVING. *The Theory of Interest*. New York: The Macmillan Co., 1930.

[16] GRAYSON, C. JACKSON. *Decisions Under Uncertainty*. Cambridge: Harvard University Press, 1960.

[17] GREEN, P. E. "Risk Attitudes and Chemical Investment Decisions," *Chemical Engineering Progress*, **LIX** (January, 1963), 35–40.

[18] HERTZ, DAVID B. "Risk Analysis in Capital Investment," *Harvard Business Review*, **XLII** (January–February, 1964), 95–106.

[19] HESPOS, RICHARD F., and PAUL A. STRASSMAN. "Stochastic Decision Trees for the Analysis of Investment Decisions," *Management Science*, **XI** (August, 1965), 244–259.

[20] HESS, S. W., and H. A. QUIGLEY. "Analysis of Risk in Investments Using Monte Carlo Techniques," *Chemical Engineering Progress*, Symposium Series, **XLII** (1963), 55–63.

[21] HILLIER, F. "Derivation of Probabilistic Information for the Evaluation of Risky Investments," *Management Science*, **IX** (April, 1963), 443–457.

[22] HIRSHLEIFER, JACK. "Risk, the Discount Rate, and Investment Decisions," *American Economic Review*, **LI** (May, 1961), 112–120.

[23] HIRSHLEIFER, J. "Efficient Allocation of Capital in an Uncertain World," *American Economic Review*, **LIV** (May, 1964), 77–85.

[24] KEYNES, J. M. *The General Theory of Employment, Interest, and Money*. New York: Harcourt, Brace & World, Inc., 1936.

[25] LINTNER, JOHN. "The Valuation of Risk Assets and the Selection of Risky Investments in Stock Portfolios and Capital Budgets," *Review of Economics and Statistics*, **XLVII** (February, 1965), 13–37.

[26] MAASS, ARTHUR *et al. Design of Water-Resource Systems*. Cambridge, Mass.: Harvard University Press, 1962.

[27] MARKOWITZ, H. "Portfolio Selection," *Journal of Finance*, **VII** (March, 1952), 77–91.

[28] MARKOWITZ, H. *Portfolio Selection* (Cowles Foundation Monograph No. 16). New York: John Wiley & Sons, 1959.

[29] MASSE, PIERRE. *Optimal Investment Decisions*. Englewood Cliffs, N. J.: Prentice-Hall, Inc., 1962.

[30] MAGEE, JOHN F. "How to Use Decision Trees in Capital Investment," *Harvard Business Review*, **XLII** (September–October, 1964), 79–95.

[31] MODIGLIANI, FRANCO, and MERTON H. MILLER. "The Cost of Capital, Corporation Finance, and the Theory of Investment," *American Economic Review*, **XLVIII** (June, 1958), 261–297.

[32] MORRIS, WILLIAM T. "Diversification," *Management Science*, **IV** (July, 1958), 382–391.

[33] NÄSLUND, BERTIL. "A Model of Capital Budgeting Under Risk," *The Journal of Business*, **XXXIX** (April, 1966), 257–271.

[34] NAYLOR, THOMAS H., J. L. BALINTFY, D. S. BURDICK, and K. CHU. *Computer Simulation Techniques*. New York: John Wiley & Sons, 1966.

[35] PAINE, NEIL R. "Uncertainty and Capital Budgeting," *The Accounting Review*, **XXXIX** (April, 1969), 330–332.

[36] SHACKLE, G. L. S. *Expectations in Economics*. Cambridge: Cambridge University Press, 1952.

[37] SHARPE, WILLIAM F. "A Simplified Model of Portfolio Selection," *Management Science*, **IX** (January, 1963), 277–293.

[38] SHARPE, W. F. "Capital Asset Prices: A Theory of Market Equilibrium," *Journal of Finance*, **XIX** (September, 1964), 425–442.

[39] SOLOMON, EZRA. *The Theory of Financial Management*. New York: Columbia University Press, 1963.

[40] SOLOW, ROBERT M. *Capital Theory and the Rate of Return*. Amsterdam: North-Holland, 1963.

[41] WEINGARTNER, H. MARTIN. "Capital Budgeting of Interrelated Projects: Survey and Synthesis," *Management Science*, **XXII** (March, 1966), 485–516.

[42] WEINGARTNER, H. M. *Mathematical Programming and the Analysis of Capital Budgeting Problems*. Englewood Cliffs, N. J.: Prentice-Hall, Inc., 1963.

PART 7

Other models of the firm

17

Game theoretic models of the firm

INTRODUCTION

Game theory is a mathematical approach to conflict of interest. Since conflict of interest is typical in economics (union-management wage negotiations, oligopoly, etc.), it is understandable why this recent development in mathematics was greeted with such enthusiasm. Some economists believed that at last a tool for resolving oligopolistic indeterminancy was at hand.

Shubik has argued the case for game theory in economics as follows:

> The basic feature of the theory is to show that in economics one is not confronted with maximum problems but with a conceptually different and, *a fortiori*, more difficult situation. This stems from the fact that the outcome of the behavior of firms and individuals does not depend on their own actions alone, nor on those combined with chance, but also on the actions of others who sometimes oppose, sometimes fortify, those of the former. Stating it differently: firms and individuals are not in control of all variables on which the result or "payoff" depends. This is most clearly seen when there are only a few in a market, as in an oligopoly. In such a case no maximum problem exists; indeed the notion of a maximum has no meaning. It is necessary to erect a new conceptual and, by necessity, mathematical edifice. This is precisely what has been accomplished by the theory of games [20, p. viii].

The classic volume on game theory, *Theory of Games and Economic Behavior* by von Neumann and Morgenstern, was first published in 1944 [24]. In his well-known review article of that book, Hurwicz gave an excellent description of the gap in economic theory which the authors hoped to fill:

> There is no adequate solution of the problem of defining "rational economic behavior" on the part of an individual when the very rationality of his actions depends on the probable behavior of other individuals: in the case of oligopoly, other sellers. Cournot and many after him have attempted to sidetrack the difficulty by assuming that every individual has a definite idea as to what others will do under given conditions. . . . Thus, the individual's "rational behavior"

> is determinate *if* the pattern of behavior of "others" can be assumed *a priori* known. But the behavior of "others" cannot be known *a priori* if the "others," too, are to behave rationally! Thus a logical *impasse* is reached [13, p. 910].

In this chapter, we hope to provide the reader with an elementary knowledge of the mathematics of game theory. For two of the best expository volumes on this topic, see the books by Luce and Raiffa [14] and McKinsey [16]. We will survey some of the applications of game theory in economic models. The reader should then be able to assess for himself the place of game theory in economic theory.

The plan of this chapter is as follows. In the next section we introduce briefly the fundamental definitions and classify the various types of games. Following that, a two-person, constant-sum, strictly determined game is solved. The specific game is a model of duopoly in which the two firms are assumed to maximize their share of the market. The section that follows then considers a mixed-strategy model of a union-management wage negotiation. Basically, the extension beyond the duopoly model is that the game is nonstrictly determined (i.e., an equilibrium is not as easily found as in the duopoly model, but *can* be found by introducing probabilistic decision making). We also demonstrate the relation between game theory and linear programming in this section. The final section is concerned with two-person, nonconstant-sum games. Although game theory "is in a far less satisfactory state outside the area of the two-person, constant-sum game" [3, p. 542], the economic theory of duopoly abounds with alternative solutions. We shall compare several of these solutions (e.g., Cournot, Stackelberg, and the von Neumann-Morgenstern solutions).

FUNDAMENTALS OF GAME THEORY

A *game* is simply a competitive situation in which two or more participants, the *players*, are involved. Each player is assumed to have a known *payoff function*, which depends upon the *strategy* selected by that player and the strategies selected by the other players. A strategy is simply one of a number of courses of action available to each player.

One way of classifying games is by the number of players. Thus we may have *two-person*, *three-person*, or *n-person* games. In this chapter, we shall restrict ourselves to two-person games. As Baumol has stated [3]: "n-person games have so far proved rather intractable to analysis. . . . Certainly there is nothing in n-person theory resembling the well-rounded analysis of the two-person case." For an excellent discussion of n-person games, the reader should consult Baumol [3, pp. 544–549].

Games can also be classified as either *constant-sum* or *nonconstant-sum* games. A *constant-sum* game is one in which the payoffs of all players add up to a fixed constant *for all possible outcomes*.[1] We can easily demonstrate this type of

[1] A special case of the constant-sum game is the *zero-sum* game. That is, the fixed constant is zero.

game with a *payoff matrix*. A payoff matrix is merely a table depicting the payoffs to the players for all possible combinations of strategies of the players. Table 17-1 shows the payoff matrices, one for each of the two players, A and B. Each player is assumed to have two strategies available.

These payoff matrices define a *two-person, constant-sum* game. The constant-sum in this game is 100. That is, the total payoff is 100: what A gains is at the expense of B, and vice versa. For example, if A plays his strategy 1 and B plays his strategy 2, the payoff to A is 40 and the payoff to B is 60, a total of 100. There is no advantage to be gained by *cooperation*, and the players are said to have directly conflicting interests, or to be in *pure opposition*.

In contrast, *cooperation* may be advantageous in *nonconstant-sum* games. A classic illustration is the "Prisoner's Dilemma." Here the strategies of the two players are simply (1) to confess or (2) not to confess. Under separate interrogation, each player faces the payoff matrices in Table 17-2.

The numbers in the matrices are intended as indices of the severity of punishment. Thus if both choose to confess, each will receive a payoff of -25, or a

TABLE **17-1**

Player A's payoff matrix

Strategies of A	Strategies of B: 1	2
1	30	40
2	50	20

Player B's payoff matrix

Strategies of A	Strategies of B: 1	2
1	70	60
2	50	80

TABLE **17-2**

Player A's payoff matrix

Strategies of A	Strategies of B: Confess	Not confess
Confess	-25	0
Not confess	-100	-5

Player B's payoff matrix

Strategies of A	Strategies of B: Confess	Not confess
Confess	-25	-100
Not confess	0	-5

total payoff of −50. But if both select the strategy of no confession, the total payoff is higher than before, or −10. This then is a *nonconstant-sum* game.

It is interesting to observe why cooperation might be beneficial in this example. Consider player *A*'s payoff matrix. If he were kept apart from *B* and thereby forced to select his strategy independently, he would probably elect to confess. In any event, this strategy could be argued to be the rational one: if *A* confesses, his payoff is more favorable than if he did not confess regardless of *B*'s *play*.[2] Thus −25 is preferable to −100 (if *B* confesses), and 0 is preferable to −5 (if *B* does not confess). Based on an identical argument, *B* should also choose to confess. But *if both confess*, each receives a payoff of −25, which is *worse* than the cooperative play of no confession by either. If they could so cooperate, each would receive a payoff of only −5. Of course, the "dilemma" is that if, say, *A* could convince *B* that *B* should not confess (on this mutually beneficial cooperative argument), then *A* would be better off still by "cheating" *B* and confessing! And presumably *B* recognizes such a possibility, and its disastrous results (and vice versa).

Two further categories of *two-person, constant-sum* games are *strictly determined* games and *mixed-strategy* games. Rather than defining these here, we shall devote the next section to a strictly determined game, and the following to a mixed-strategy game.

A TWO-PERSON, CONSTANT-SUM, STRICTLY DETERMINED MODEL OF DUOPOLY

We assume that two firms, *A* and *B*, have a pure duopoly. In addition, each firm is concerned only with its share of the total market. Since total share of the market will always be 100, no matter how divided by *A* and *B*, we can consider the duopoly as a two-person, constant-sum game.

We require the further rather strong assumptions that each firm has available to it only two alternative courses of action, or strategies, and that each knows, in advance, the complete payoff matrix. Of course, the firm could possess many more strategies without posing any real analytical problems; we limit the number of strategies to two each for convenience only.[3]

The payoff matrix for firm *A* is given in Table 17-3. There is no necessity for constructing *B*'s payoff matrix, since this is a constant-sum game: *B*'s payoff is always 100 less *A*'s payoff.

Before analyzing *A*'s strategies more closely, we must make one further stipulation. While each player, or firm, is assumed to have full knowledge of the payoff matrix, he cannot have any information as to the particular strategy that his opponent plans to adopt. The value of this type of information to a player is obvious.

[2] *A*'s strategy, to confess, is said to *dominate* his other strategy, not to confess.

[3] The possibility of *infinite strategy* games, of course, does raise some new analytical problems. Here, we consider only *finite strategy* games.

Now if firm *A*'s management has a propensity for gambling, *A* might select strategy 2. *A*'s greatest possible market share would result if *B* played its strategy 1, i.e., a share of 60. But, if *B* played its other strategy, *A*'s share would be the lowest possible, or 20. Hence a more conservative management of *A* might opt for strategy 1. Clearly, we must specify some behavioral assumption about the two firms to obtain a "solution." Here, we shall follow the usual game-theory assumption that the firms are conservative, and, in fact, always "expect the worst." This permits us to obtain the so-called *maximin* (and *minimax*) solution.

According to this behavioral assumption, *A* expects *B* to play the strategy which harms *A* the most. Thus if *A* were to play strategy 1, *A* would expect *B* to play its strategy 2. The result would be that *A*'s share would be 40, the *minimum* value in row 1. Similarly, *A* would expect *B* to play strategy 2 if *A* played its strategy 2, resulting in a share of 20. Again, *A*'s expected payoff is the *minimum* of row 2. Now, *A*'s decision has been reduced to choosing between strategy 1 with an *expected* share of 40, and strategy 2 with an *expected* share of 20. Clearly *A* would choose the strategy associated with the higher expected share, i.e., strategy 1. In other words, *A maximizes* over the row *minima*; hence, the origin of the term *maximin* strategy.

We have argued that *A* will play his maximin strategy, or *A*'s strategy 1. The next step is to determine *B*'s play. Since *B* operates under the same behavioral assumption as *A*, *B* "expects the worst" for each possible play. Hence, *B* would expect a payoff of 60 *to A* if *B* were to play its strategy 1. Since this is a constant-sum game, the higher is *A*'s payoff, the lower is *B*'s. So *B* seeks a low payoff in Table 17-3. Similarly, *B*'s expected payoff to its strategy 2 would be 40 *to A*. Thus *B*'s *expected* payoffs (as defined by *A*'s share of the market) are the column *maxima*. *B* would then elect to play the strategy corresponding to the *minimum* of the column *maxima* (its *minimax* strategy). This strategy is obviously *B*'s strategy 2.

Finally we have a solution. *A* will play its strategy 1, *B* will play its strategy 2, and *A*'s share of the market will be 40 (making *B*'s share 60). This solution is circled in Table 17-3. Since the expectation of each player was realized and no

TABLE **17-3**

Payoff matrix of firm *A* (Showing *A*'s share of the market)

		B's strategies 1	*B*'s strategies 2	Row minima
A's strategies	1	50	(40)	40 (maximin)
	2	60	20	20
Column maxima		60	40 (minimax)	

advantage would accrue to either player by changing its play, we have an equilibrium. Whenever such an equilibrium exists, the game is said to be *strictly determined* and possesses a *saddle point*. The payoff, 40, corresponding to the saddle point, is called the *value* of the game.

A MIXED-STRATEGY MODEL OF BARGAINING

Not all two-person, constant-sum games are strictly determined. To see this, consider *A*'s payoff matrix in Table 17-1. *A*'s maximin strategy would be strategy 1, and *A* would expect a payoff of 30. *B*'s minimax strategy would be strategy 2, and *B* would expect the payoff to be 40. Clearly the players' expectations do not coincide. The result of this play would be a payoff to *A* of 40. Of course, *A* would be quite pleased and would have no desire to change his play. But *B* would be better off to change to his strategy 1, *given that A is playing A's strategy 1*. The reader should understand that if *B* were to change, then *A* would wish to change, then *B* again, and so forth. There is no equilibrium or saddle point. That is, there is no combination of strategies such that both players would be content to play those strategies indefinitely.

One approach to this problem has been the introduction of *mixed strategies*. The mixed strategy permits a player more flexibility. He is no longer restricted to a choice between two *pure strategies*. That is, *A* is not limited to either strategy 1 or strategy 2. He is permitted to choose some probability combination of the two. For example, he could choose to play strategy 1 with a probability of $\frac{1}{3}$ and strategy 2 with a probability of $\frac{2}{3}$.

The importance of the introduction of mixed strategies is that a saddle point, or equilibrium solution, is attainable *even for games which are not strictly determined*. This result was first proved by von Neumann, and is called the fundamental theorem of two-person, zero-sum game theory.

For variety, and to illustrate a mixed-strategy saddle point, we shall present a labor-management bargaining model.[4]

The management of the Key Largo Shipyard will soon be negotiating a new contract with the union that represents the company's employees. The one issue involved at this time is the wage rate. As has been the case for the past twenty years, both the company and the union have agreed to submit their dispute to an arbitration board.

The tripartite arbitration board consists of three members, a company representative, a union representative, and an impartial member who acts as chairman. In most cases the final decision is usually made by the chairman, since the union representative seldom feels compelled to vote with management and vice versa.

[4] This model is based upon "The Key Largo Shipyard Case," a problem which appears in Thomas H. Naylor and Eugene T. Byrne, *Linear Programming*. Belmont, Calif.: Wadsworth Publishing Company, 1963.

The selection of a management representative is of utmost importance, since his actions may well influence the final outcome of the dispute, even though the chairman is actually impartial. The chairman's decision may well be influenced by the choices made by both the union and management as to their respective representatives. For example, if management selects as its representative an individual who is a radical company man, and the union chooses an individual who is either unbiased or does not express his favoritism toward the union vocally, the chairman may have a negative reaction against the company and favor the union in his final decision.

Management is considering four different types of individuals to represent the company on the arbitration board. These individuals are indicated below by the symbols M_1, M_2, M_3, and M_4.

Management representative	Characteristics
M_1	An unbiased individual.
M_2	An individual whose voting record in arbitration cases indicates a slight bias in favor of management, but who on occasions has voted against management.
M_3	A company man who utilizes a "soft-sell" approach.
M_4	An outspoken company man.

The union has a similar set of individuals whom it is considering to represent it in the dispute. The individuals are indicated below by U_1, U_2, U_3, and U_4.

Union representative	Characteristics
U_1	An unbiased individual.
U_2	An individual whose voting record in arbitration cases indicates a slight bias in favor of the union, but who on occasions has voted against the union.
U_3	A union man who utilizes a "soft-sell" approach.
U_4	An outspoken union man.

Past experience in arbitration cases has indicated that the average hourly wage increase (in cents per hour) associated with the type of representative that management employs at the bargaining table is completely dependent on the type of representative that the union chooses. And likewise, the average hourly wage increase (in cents per hour) associated with the type of representative that the union employs is dependent on the type of representative that management chooses.

It should be emphasized that neither the union nor management knows the other's final strategy decision until the arbitration hearing actually begins. Neither party can alter its choice of a representative once the representative's name has been submitted to the chairman of the arbitration board.

Twenty years of arbitration experience indicates that Table 17-4 is an *approximate* indication of the expected average wage increases (in cents per hour) associated with the different possible combinations of union and management representatives chosen to serve on the arbitration board. Although the average wage increases in this table are not an exact representation of the wage increases associated with the different union-management strategies utilized over the past twenty years, management does feel that it will prove to be a useful guide in selecting the type of individual to represent the company in future wage negotiations. Furthermore, both the union and the management know the approximate wage increases associated with each union-management strategy combination.

Although management would like to select the strategy that will minimize the average hourly wage increase during the forthcoming contract period, it is more concerned with selecting a set of strategies that will enable it to minimize the increase in wage rates over an extended period of time. Management finds that its optimum strategy is one in which it does not choose the same particular (pure) strategy each year. Instead it selects strategies randomly according to some predetermined optimal probability distribution imposed over its pure strategies (M_1, M_2, M_3, and M_4). In other words, this is a two-person, zero-sum, *non-strictly determined* game. Mixed strategies permit the establishment of a saddle point.

The union must also determine a mixed strategy that will maximize wage increases over an extended period of time.

Before determining the solution we need to specify that all of the behavorial assumptions described in the preceding section pertaining to firms A and B also apply here. It is further assumed that this is a zero-sum game: management's gain is labor's loss, and vice versa.

The concept of *dominated strategies* will permit us to reduce the computational problem considerably. Management need never play its strategies M_1 and M_4. It can *always* do at least as well by playing M_2 and M_3 (M_2 dominates M_1 and M_3 dominates M_4). Similarly, U_2 dominates U_1 and U_4. Hence, we can simply eliminate these dominated strategies, and the payoff matrix is reduced to the one shown in Table 17-5.

TABLE **17-4**

Payoff matrix of union (wage rate increases in cents per hour)

		Management strategies			
		M_1	M_2	M_3	M_4
Union strategies	U_1	15	5	10	10
	U_2	45	40	20	25
	U_3	20	10	30	30
	U_4	25	20	15	20

First, we should check to see if this is a strictly determined game. The union's maximin strategy is U_2, management's minimax strategy is M_3, and these two strategies do *not* determine a saddle point. That is, the union expects a wage rate increase of 20, management expects an increase of 30, and the actual increase would be 20. Since *both* players' expectations would not be realized, this is not a strictly determined game.

Now, let the players employ mixed strategies. The union's task becomes that of determining the optimal probabilities with which to play the two pure strategies. If P is the probability, or relative frequency, for U_2, then $1 - P$ is the probability for U_3. Similarly, let Q be management's probability for M_2 and $1 - Q$ for M_3.

Consider the union's problem first. If management plays its pure strategy, M_2, the *expected* payoff of the union, E_2 (the subscript 2 is a reminder that management is employing its pure strategy M_2), is

$$E_2 = P(40) + (1 - P)(10) \tag{17-1}$$

That is, the union should gain a payoff of 40 (determined by U_2 and M_2) with a probability of P and a payoff of 10 (determined by U_3 and M_2) with a probability of $1 - P$. Hence the expected value, or payoff, is simply the weighted average of the possible outcomes, where the weights are the probabilities of the outcomes actually occurring.

In analogous fashion, if management plays its pure strategy M_3, the *expected* payoff of the union is

$$E_3 = P(20) + (1 - P)30 \tag{17-2}$$

The expected payoffs to the union, equations (17-1) and (17-2), are functions of a single variable, P. We can plot these two equations as in Figure 17-1.

We need only consider the interval on the horizontal axis from 0 to 1 (P is a probability and thus $0 \leq P \leq 1$). Now the E_2 line gives the expected payoff to the union (when management plays its pure strategy M_2) as a function of P. For example, if $P = 0$ (which means the union will *never* play U_2), then the union plays U_3 as a pure strategy and its payoff is, of course, 10. The E_3 line

TABLE **17-5**

Payoff matrix of union
(wage rate increases in cents per hour)

		Management strategies	
		M_2	M_3
Union strategies	U_2	40	20
	U_3	10	30

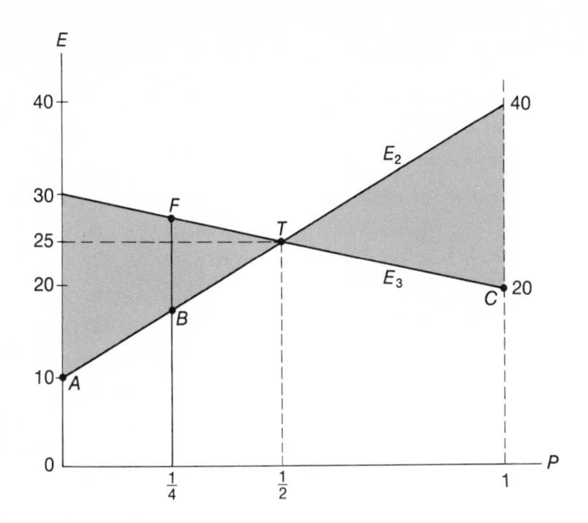

FIGURE **17-1**

Expected payoff to union

has the same interpretation, except that it corresponds to a management choice of M_3 as a pure strategy.

The shaded area, determined by E_2 and E_3, corresponds to all possible expected payoffs to the union for various mixed strategies of management. For example, let the union select $P = \frac{1}{4}$. Then, point B represents the union's expected payoff for the management pure strategy M_2, and point F represents the union's expected payoff for the management pure strategy M_3. And, the intermediate points on the line segment BF correspond to convex combinations, or mixtures, of management's two pure strategies.

The union, in pursuing the maximin principle, first determines the set of all *minimum* expected payoffs (this principle states that the union "expects the worst" for every possible P). From Figure 17-1 this set is the set of all points on the lower boundary of the shaded area, or the kinked line ATC. Next, the union chooses the P corresponding to the maximum of the minimum expected payoffs. Point T is the maximin expected payoff, and the associated $P = \frac{1}{2}$. Observe that P can be obtained algebraically by solving (17-1) and (17-2) simultaneously.

We have determined the union's maximin strategy. The union should play strategy U_2 with a probability of $P = \frac{1}{2}$, and strategy U_3 with a probability of $1 - P = \frac{1}{2}$. Its expected payoff is $\frac{1}{2}(40) + \frac{1}{2}(10) = 25$. Next, to see if a saddle point, or equilibrium, exists, we must determine management's minimax probabilities and see if its expected payoff is equal to the union's expected payoff. This, of course, is what von Neumann's fundamental theorem asserts.

We can determine the two expected payoff functions for management, E_2' and E_3', exactly as we did for the union. The subscripts 2 and 3 indicate that the

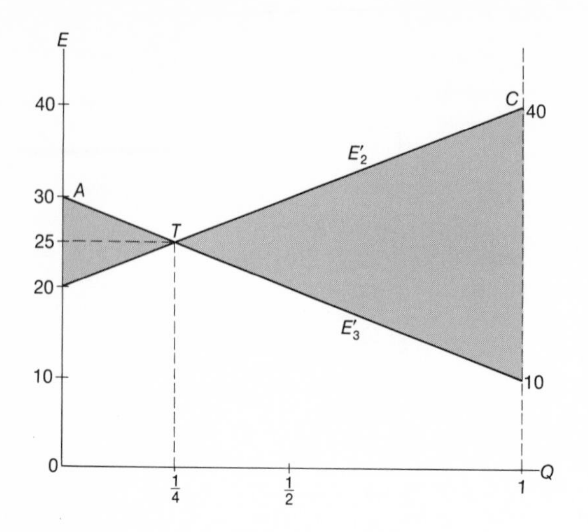

FIGURE 17-2
Expected payoffs to management

union plays its pure strategies, U_2 and U_3, respectively. As defined previously, Q is the probability management associates with its strategy M_2, and $1 - Q$ the probability it associates with M_3. Thus

(17-3) $$E_2' = Q(40) + (1 - Q)20$$

(17-4) $$E_3' = Q(10) + (1 - Q)30$$

These two functions of Q are plotted in Figure 17-2.

The shaded area again represents all possible expected payoffs. Remember that the expected payoffs are in terms of wage rate increases. Hence, *management* is interested in *lower* wage rate increases. The minimax principle states that management first determines the set of all *maximum* expected payoffs (this is management's version of "expecting the worst"). In Figure 17-2 this set is the set of all points on the upper boundary of the shaded area, or the kinked line *ATC*. Management then chooses the Q corresponding to the minimum of the maximum expected payoffs. Since point T is the minimum expected payoff, the minimax strategy dictates that management set $Q = \frac{1}{4}$.

Management then plays M_2 with a probability of $Q = \frac{1}{4}$, and M_3 with a probability of $1 - Q = \frac{3}{4}$. Its expected payoff is $\frac{1}{4}(40) + \frac{3}{4}(20) = 25$, or *the same payoff that the union expects*. Hence, there is a saddle point to the game when mixed strategies are permitted.

USE OF LINEAR PROGRAMMING TO SOLVE MIXED-STRATEGY GAMES

We were able to solve the above game graphically because there were but two strategies. But if the original payoff matrix, Table 17-4, had not contained any dominated strategies, we could not have reduced it to a two-by-two matrix amenable to graphical solution. Linear programming is an appropriate solution technique in such cases. In this section we shall set up the original game for solution by linear programming as if there were no dominating strategies. This arrangement should also provide the reader with some insight into the underlying mathematical relationship between game theory and linear programming.

First, we shall set up the union's linear programming problem.

(17-5) maximize E

subject to

$$
\begin{aligned}
15P_1 + 45P_2 + 20P_3 + 25P_4 &\geq E \\
5P_1 + 40P_2 + 10P_3 + 20P_4 &\geq E \\
10P_1 + 20P_2 + 30P_3 + 15P_4 &\geq E \qquad (17\text{-}6) \\
10P_1 + 25P_2 + 30P_3 + 20P_4 &\geq E \\
P_1 + P_2 + P_3 + P_4 &= 1
\end{aligned}
$$

and

(17-7) $P_1, P_2, P_3, P_4, E \geq 0$

where

P_i = probability of employing U_i

E = lower limit of expected payoff

The first four constraints of (17-6) state that all expected payoffs (one for each pure management strategy) must be greater than or equal to some unknown limiting payoff E. The last constraint states that the sum of the probabilities must equal 1. Now since the union follows the maximin principle, the objective function (17-5) simply says that the union must find those P_i and E for which the lower limit of the expected payoffs E is a maximum. Thus, the union expects the worst for every possible play of management, and then selects the "best of the worst."

We now formulate the management's problem:

(17-8) minimize H

subject to

$$
\begin{aligned}
15Q_1 + 5Q_2 + 10Q_3 + 10Q_4 &\leq H \\
45Q_1 + 40Q_2 + 20Q_3 + 25Q_4 &\leq H \\
20Q_1 + 10Q_2 + 30Q_3 + 30Q_4 &\leq H \qquad (17\text{-}9) \\
25Q_1 + 20Q_2 + 15Q_3 + 20Q_4 &\leq H \\
Q_1 + Q_2 + Q_3 + Q_4 &= 1
\end{aligned}
$$

and

(17-10) $Q_1, Q_2, Q_3, Q_4, H \geq 0$

where

$$Q_i = \text{probability of employing } M_i$$

$$H = \text{upper limit of expected payoffs}$$

Briefly, management seeks to find those Q_i and H for which the minimum upper limit H of all expected payoffs is determined.

Of course we could apply the simplex algorithm (as described in Chapter 7) to each problem. If we did, we would obtain the following results:

$$E = 25 \qquad P_1 = 0 \qquad Q_1 = 0$$

$$H = 25 \qquad P_2 = \tfrac{1}{2} \qquad Q_2 = \tfrac{1}{4}$$

$$P_3 = \tfrac{1}{2} \qquad Q_3 = \tfrac{3}{4}$$

$$P_4 = 0 \qquad Q_4 = 0$$

Thus the value of the game is 25, and the union's maximin strategy yields the same expected payoff as management's minimax strategy.

There is a further observation we should make. Recalling the duality theorem from Chapter 7, we should have anticipated that E would equal H. Upon closer inspection, we note that management's linear programming problem is nothing more than the *dual* of the union's problem.[5] The duality theorem states that the values of the objective functions of the primal and the dual are equal!

[5] There are some minor modifications to the above two formulations which need to be made for exact conformity with the primal-dual relation described in Chapter 7. To illustrate, we rewrite the primal problem denoting the objective function as π:

$$\text{maximize} \qquad \pi = OP_1 + OP_2 + OP_3 + OP_4 + 1E$$

subject to

$$\begin{aligned} -15P_1 - 45P_2 - 20P_3 - 25P_4 + 1E &\leq 0 \\ -\ 5P_1 - 40P_2 - 10P_3 - 20P_4 + 1E &\leq 0 \\ -10P_1 - 20P_2 - 30P_3 - 15P_4 + 1E &\leq 0 \\ -10P_1 - 25P_2 - 30P_3 - 20P_4 + 1E &\leq 0 \\ 1P_1 + 1P_2 + 1P_3 + 1P_4 + 0E &\leq 1 \end{aligned}$$

and

$$P_1, P_2, P_3, P_4, E \geq 0$$

Notice that the direction of the inequalities has been changed by multiplying through by -1. This was done simply to conform to the usual convention for a maximum problem. Also, we have written the last constraint as a "less than or equal to" inequality rather than as an equality. This is permissible since the union will never "waste" any of the opportunity to play. That is, the sum of the probabilities will necessarily equal one at a π maximum. We might also mention that where the payoff matrix contains negative entries, a transformation is required in order to make it legitimate to impose non-negativity conditions on E and H. An excellent discussion of these topics is contained in Chiang, Chapter 20 [7].

DUOPOLY: A TWO-PERSON, NONCONSTANT-SUM GAME

In this section we shall again be concerned with a market composed of two firms—a duopolistic market. However, as a step toward greater realism, we shall consider models in which the behavior of the firms can influence the total payoff. Previously, by focusing on market share as the only objective of a firm, we could view duopoly as a constant-sum game. Clearly the total market would be 100%, no matter whether combined profits were one million dollars or one hundred dollars. However, it is rather unbelievable to expect a firm to be indifferent between two situations, each corresponding to a 50% market share, yet where profit in the first situation is twice as great as in the second.

To illustrate a two-person, nonconstant-sum game we shall formulate a simple numerical model of duopoly. Assume that two firms sell a single homogeneous product at the same market price P. To avoid needless complication, the cost of the product is taken to be zero. Let Z_1 and Z_2 denote the output of firms 1 and 2 respectively, where

(17-11) $$Z = Z_1 + Z_2$$

is the total output of the two firms. The market-demand function is given by

(17-12) $$P = 12 - Z = 12 - Z_1 - Z_2$$

Total profit, π_1, of firm 1 is

(17-13) $$\pi_1 = (12 - Z_1 - Z_2)Z_1$$

and total profit of firm 2 is

(17-14) $$\pi_2 = (12 - Z_1 - Z_2)Z_2$$

Each firm is assumed to maximize its profit function. The problem, of course, is that the profit of firm 1 depends *not only* upon its *own* quantity decision, but *also upon the quantity decision of firm 2*, and vice versa. Furthermore, it is clear that the *sum* of π_1 and π_2 will vary depending upon the values of Z_1 and Z_2. Consequently, we are confronted with a two-person, nonconstant-sum game.

We met this problem before in the discussion of duopoly and oligopoly in Chapter 5. There the point was made that there can be *many* possible solutions, or equilibria, depending upon the nature of the further assumptions which must be attributed to the firms. Thus if we follow the Cournot model, the further assumptions (or conjectural variations) are that firm 1 regards Z_2 as a constant and firm 2 views Z_1 as a constant. Each firm believes that it can vary its own output freely, and that no matter what value of output it selects, the other firm will not alter its output. This behavior is quite strange, but has the virtue of permitting us to determine a solution, or equilibrium pair of output values.

The Cournot model provides us with one solution to a two-person, nonconstant-sum game. The particular solution can be found by differentiating π_1 partially with respect to Z_1, differentiating π_2 partially with respect to Z_2,

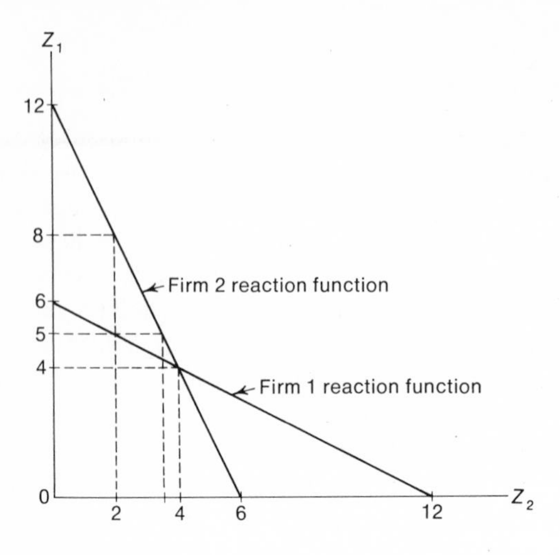

FIGURE **17-3**

setting each partial derivative equal to zero, and solving the two resulting equations simultaneously for Z_1 and Z_2. Of course, second-order conditions should be checked to ensure that we have a maximum rather than a minimum profit.

(17-15) $$\frac{\partial \pi_1}{\partial Z_1} = 12 - 2Z_1 - Z_2 = 0$$

(17-16) $$\frac{\partial \pi_2}{\partial Z_2} = 12 - 2Z_2 - Z_1 = 0$$

Solving (17-15) and (17-16) simultaneously yields

$$Z_1 = 4, \qquad Z_2 = 4$$

Graphically, we can obtain the solution by plotting the reaction functions of the firms. The reaction functions can be found by solving (17-15) for Z_1 and (17-16) for Z_2:

(17-17) $$Z_1 = 6 - 0.5Z_2$$

(17-18) $$Z_2 = 6 - 0.5Z_1$$

Thus, for example, firm 1's reaction function, (17-17), gives the value of its profit-maximizing output, Z_1, as a function of the output of firm 2. Figure 17-3 shows both reaction functions, and their intersection corresponds to the Cournot equilibrium. It is an equilibrium, because if both firms were producing 4 units neither would have reason to change its output. The reader should convince himself that if firm 1 were producing, say, 8 units, then firm 2 would no longer want to produce 4 units, and by (17-18) would choose $Z_2 = 2$. But if

$Z_2 = 2$, then firm 1 would change from $Z_1 = 8$ to $Z_1 = 5$. Now, however, firm 2 is unhappy with $Z_2 = 2$, and changes to a higher output, etc. Such a sequence leads to the only pair of outputs consistent with the two reaction functions, $Z_1 = 4$, $Z_2 = 4$. It also illustrates the fundamental error of the Cournot model: even though each firm observes that the other firm unfailingly changes its output in response to its own output change, it nonetheless continues to believe that, next time, the other firm will not so respond.[6]

Before presenting the von Neumann and Morgenstern solution, we shall consider a second possible solution. Then, we shall compare all three graphically. Our second case is the Stackelberg model. Of course it too requires that we impute further behavioral assumptions to the two firms.

The Stackelberg model (refer to Chapter 5 for a more general discussion) assumes that firm 1 is a "follower" and firm 2 is a "leader." Being a follower, firm 1 is thus assumed to behave exactly as it did in the Cournot model. Consequently, firm 1 will act in accordance with its reaction function

$$Z_1 = 6 - 0.5Z_2 \tag{17-19}$$

Firm 2, in contrast, is assumed to *recognize* that firm 1 behaves so naïvely. Firm 2 realizes that firm 1 will set its output strictly on the basis of (17-19). In other words, the leader can take Z_1 to be a function of its own output, Z_2. Hence firm 2 will again maximize its profit function, (17-14), but now it considers the Z_1 in its profit function to be a function of Z_2 rather than a constant. Its profit function is obtained by eliminating Z_1 in (17-14) by (17-19):

$$\pi_2 = [12 - (6 - 0.5Z_2) - Z_2]Z_2 \tag{17-20}$$

The Stackelberg solution is obtained by differentiating (17-20) with respect to Z_2, equating the derivative to zero, and solving for the profit-maximizing value of Z_2. Again, second-order conditions need checking.

$$\frac{d\pi_2}{dZ_2} = 6 - Z_2 = 0 \tag{17-21}$$

and

$$Z_2 = 6$$

By firm 1's reaction function (17-19), the equilibrium value of Z_1 is

$$Z_1 = 6 - 0.5(6) = 3$$

Thus Stackelberg equilibrium is defined by $Z_1 = 3$ and $Z_2 = 6$. Figure 17-4 contrasts these two equilibria. The Cournot solution is denoted by C and the Stackelberg by S.

We have now described two of many possible solutions to a nonconstant-sum game. As a last example, we present the von Neumann–Morgenstern solution to the *cooperative* version of a two-person, nonconstant-sum game [14,

[6] Though using slightly different assumptions, the Cournot solution is a special case of a Nash noncooperative equilibrium point [20, p. 65].

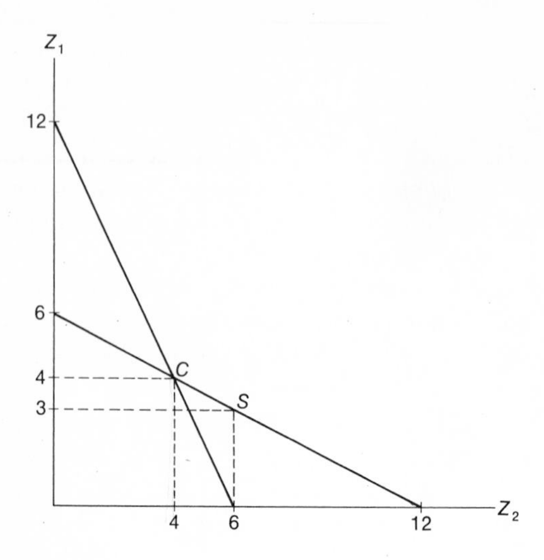

FIGURE 17-4

p. 118]. The further assumption here is that the two firms will cooperate in such a manner as to jointly maximize profits.

Jointly maximizing profits amounts to choosing the same total output that would be selected by a pure monopolist. If π is total profit and Z is total output

$$\pi = (12 - Z)Z \tag{17-22}$$

To maximize π, differentiate π with respect to Z, set the derivative equal to zero, and solve for Z:

$$\frac{d\pi}{dZ} = 12 - 2Z = 0 \tag{17-23}$$

and

$$Z = 6$$

Or, for π to be a maximum

$$Z_1 + Z_2 = 6 \tag{17-24}$$

defines the locus of all possible pairs of Z_1 and Z_2. In general, it is not possible to determine the share of each firm in total profit. Since the firms are identical, it might be reasonable to take each firm's share as one-half. Thus the von Neumann-Morgenstern solution could be represented as

$$Z_1 = 3, \quad Z_2 = 3$$

Graphically, we label this solution as *NM* in Figure 17-5. Of course, in general, any point on the dashed line connecting $Z_1 = 6$ with $Z_2 = 6$ could also be considered as a von Neumann-Morgenstern solution. For comparison, the Cournot (C), and Stackleberg (S) solutions are also shown.

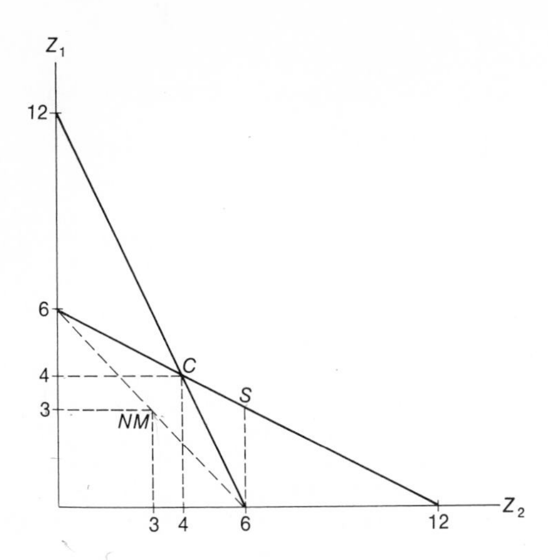

FIGURE **17-5**

The von Neumann-Morgenstern solution is also the solution which Chamberlin holds will be automatically established by the mere fact of "mutual dependence recognized" [6]. For a disagreement with Chamberlin, as well as a stimulating tour through a number of "warfare" solutions to duopoly, the reader is referred to Bishop's article [4].

Table 17-6, the payoff matrix for this two-person, nonconstant-sum game, indicates three possible solutions. The entries in solution cells are placed in parentheses with the identification symbol appearing immediately above. Many other solutions could be determined *by imputing appropriate behavioral assumptions to the two firms*. For a more extensive comparison of duopoly solutions, see

TABLE **17-6**

Payoff matrix (payoff to firm 1 given first in each cell)

		Z_2: 0	3	4	6
	0	0, 0	0, 27	0, 32	0, 36
	3	27, 0	*NM* (18, 18)	15, 20	*S* (9, 18)
Z_1	4	32, 0	20, 15	*C* (12, 12)	8, 12
	6	36, 0	18, 9	12, 8	0, 0

[15]. Hopefully, however, the reader has gained some appreciation of the difficulties which arise once we leave the simpler world of two-person, *constant*-sum games.

CONCLUSION

To conclude this introduction to game theory, we quote a few remarks from the excellent book by Dorfman, Samuelson, and Solow:

> The theory of games has had a profound impact on statistics and on military science; in economics it is still merely a promising and suggestive approach.
>
> What . . . has game theory to contribute to economics? Oddly enough, since game theory is an attempt to determine optimal strategies explicitly, the contribution seems to be qualitative rather than quantitative. The conceptual framework developed in game theory provides a useful set of constructs for the qualitative discussion of problems of opposing interests in economics. . . . Game theory provides solutions to simple conflict situations and valuable hints for understanding more complicated ones. This is as much help as an economist can expect from a new branch of mathematics [10, p. 445].

Hurwicz's assessment of game theory, made in 1945 only one year after the publication of the *Theory of Games*, appears to be as appropriate today as it was then:

> The potentialities of von Neumann's and Morgenstern's new approach seem tremendous and may, one hopes, lead to revamping, and enriching in realism, a good deal of economic theory. But to a large extent they are only potentialities: results are still largely a matter of future developments [13].

BIBLIOGRAPHY

[1] ALLEN, R. G. D. *Mathematical Economics.* New York: Macmillan & Co., 1960.

[2] BALIGH, HELMY H., and LEON E. RICHARTZ. "Variable-Sum Game Models of Marketing Problems," *Journal of Marketing Research,* **IV** (May, 1967), 173–183.

[3] BAUMOL, WILLIAM J. *Economic Theory and Operations Analysis.* Englewood Cliffs, N. J.: Prentice-Hall, Inc., 1965.

[4] BISHOP, ROBERT L. "Duopoly: Collusion or Warfare?" *American Economic Review,* L (1960), 933–961.

[5] BLACKWELL, D., and M. GIRSHICK. *Theory of Games and Statistical Decisions.* New York: John Wiley & Sons, 1954.

[6] CHAMBERLIN, E. H. *The Theory of Monopolistic Competition.* Cambridge: Harvard University Press, 1933.

[7] CHIANG, ALPHA C. *Fundamental Methods of Mathematical Economics.* New York: McGraw-Hill Book Co., 1967.

[8] COURNOT, AUGUSTIN (trans. by N. T. Bacon). *Récherches sur les Principes Mathematiques de la Théorie des Richesses.* New York: Macmillan & Co., 1897.

[9] DANTZIG, GEORGE B. *Linear Programming and Extensions.* Princeton: Princeton University Press, 1963.

[10] DORFMAN, R., P. A. SAMUELSON, and R. M. SOLOW. *Linear Programming and Economic Analysis.* New York: McGraw-Hill Book Co., 1958.

[11] FELLNER, WILLIAM. *Competition Among the Few: Oligopoly and Similar Market Structures.* New York: Alfred A. Knopf, 1949.

[12] GALE, DAVID. *The Theory of Linear Economic Models.* New York: McGraw Hill Book Co., 1960.

[13] HURWICZ, LEONID. "The Theory of Economic Behavior," *American Economic Review,* **XXXV** (1945), 909–925.

[14] LUCE, R. D., and H. RAIFFA. *Games and Decisions.* New York: John Wiley & Sons, 1957.

[15] MAYBERRY, J. P., J. E. NASH, and MARTIN SHUBIK. "A Comparison of Treatments of a Duopoly Situation," *Econometrica,* **XXI** (1953), 141–154.

[16] MCKINSEY, J. C. C. *Introduction to the Theory of Games.* New York: McGraw-Hill Book Co., 1952.

[17] NAYLOR, THOMAS H., and EUGENE T. BYRNE. *Linear Programming.* Belmont, Calif.: Wadsworth Publishing Co., 1963.

[18] NASH, J. F. "Non-Cooperative Games," *Annals of Mathematics,* **LIV** (September, 1951), 286–295.

[19] NASH, J. F. "The Bargaining Problem," *Econometrica,* **XVIII** (April, 1950), 155–162.

[20] SHUBIK, MARTIN. *Strategy and Market Structure.* New York: John Wiley & Sons, 1959.

[21] SHUBIK, M. *Game Theory and Related Approaches to Social Behavior.* New York: John Wiley & Sons, 1964.

[22] STACKELBERG, H. V. "Grundlagen einer reiner Kostentheorie," *Zeitschrift für National-Oekonomie* (May, 1932).

[23] STACKELBERG, H. V. (trans. by Alan T. Peacock). *The Theory of the Market Economy.* New York: Oxford University Press, 1952.

[24] VON NEUMANN, J., and O. MORGENSTERN. *Theory of Games and Economic Behavior* (2nd ed.). Princeton, N. J.: Princeton University Press, 1947.

[25] WILLIAMS, J. D. *The Complete Strategyst.* New York: McGraw-Hill Book Co., 1954.

18

Behavioral models of the firm

CONVENTIONAL WISDOM REVISITED

In Chapter 1 we stated that the theories of the firm developed in this book would consist of four basic elements: (1) goals, (2) production transformation process, (3) information, and (4) decisions. The models described thus far have varied considerably with regard to assumptions made about (1) the firm's production transformation process and (2) the information available to the firm's decision makers regarding product demand, factor supply, and production technology. The assumptions about the firm's production process have ranged from the highly inflexible marginal analysis assumptions of Chapters 3, 4, and 5 to the somewhat more viable assumptions outlined in the mathematical programming models found in Chapters 6–10. With regard to the information available to the firm's decision makers about factor supply, product demand, and production technology, we have moved from the assumption of complete certainty in Chapters 2–12 to the assumption of risk and uncertainty in Chapters 12–17.

Throughout this book two of the elements of our economic theory of the firm have remained relatively fixed. First, in each of the models described thus far we have focused on a single objective for the firm's decision makers, and, for the most part, this objective has been profit maximization. Second, we have restricted ourselves to only two different types of decisions on the part of the firm's managers—input decisions and output decisions. In short, we have used a highly aggregative theory to treat a rather specific set of decisions and have devoted little or no attention to the actual process by which firms reach decisions [33, p. 16].

In reflecting on the models we have investigated thus far, the number of questions about the behavior of firms and their managers which remain unanswered is indeed striking. Among the unanswered yet important questions that remain are:

1. How does the allocation of resources within the firm's budget relate to the organizational goals?
2. How do objectives change over time?
3. What happens to information as it flows through the organization?
4. Are there biases in the information?
5. How do these biases affect the decisions that are finally made?
6. What is the relationship between decisions made by management and the final form of the decision as it is implemented by the organization? [24, p. 330]

In order to answer these questions and others, Cyert and March [33] have proposed an approach to the theory of the firm which "takes as its focus the economic decisions with which economic theory has traditionally dealt and as its research commitment the emphasis on organizational process" [32, p. 62].

A FRAMEWORK FOR BEHAVIORAL THEORIES OF THE FIRM

In attempting to integrate organization theory into the economic theory of the firm, Cyert and March have developed a new approach to the theory of the firm which they call *A Behavioral Theory of the Firm* [33]. Although organization theory means different things to different people, Cyert and March utilize only those aspects of organization theory "that emphasize the empirical study of behavior in organizations" [33, p. 18]. They focus on three major branches of organization theory:

1. *Sociological*—which concentrates on the phenomena of bureacracy.
2. *Social psychological*—which is concerned with the experimental determination of some small set of independent variables on the efficiency of an organization.
3. *Administrative*—which centers on the problems of the executive in dealing with an organization and on classic administrative axioms [33, p. 17].

In summary, Cyert and March make the following three points about organization theory and its relationship to the traditional theory of the firm.

1. The theory focuses on a set of problems that are different from those of the economic theory of the firm. Its problems are not specifically economic; virtually nothing is said about how output levels are set, advertising expenditures determined, and so forth.
2. Although it places considerable emphasis on the study of "process"—the study of what goes on in an organization—only the third branch of the theory focuses primarily upon organizational decision-making processes.
3. Unlike the theory of the firm, there is no consideration of "aggregation." Indeed, there is nothing to aggregate [33, p. 18].

Cyert and March's behavioral theory of the firm centers on the organizational decision-making process of the firm, with special emphasis given to decisions such as price, output, and resource allocation. Their theory consists of four subtheories:

1. *A theory of organizational goals* to consider how goals arise in an organization, how they change over time, and how the organization attends to them.
2. *A theory of organizational expectations* to treat the questions of how and when an organization searches for information or new alternatives and how information is processed through the organization.
3. *A theory of organizational choice* to treat the process by which the alternatives available to the organization are ordered and the decisions made among them.
4. *A theory of organizational control* to explain the differences between managerial choice in a firm and the decisions actually implemented [33, p. 21].

In their theory of organizational goals, Cyert and March treat the firm as a coalition of individuals, some of whom are members of subcoalitions. Not unlike game theory, this theory of organizational goals assumes that conflicts may arise among coalition members. Cyert and March argue that, "the goals of a business firm are a series of more or less independent constraints imposed on the organization through a process of bargaining among potential coalition members and elaborated over time in response to short-run pressures" [33, p. 43]. These goals are assumed to be inconsistent, dynamic, and multiple rather than single. As indicated in Chapter 1, Cyert and March have identified five major goals of the firm: production, inventory, sales, market share, and profit. Finally, organizational goals are assumed to be attainable or satisficing rather than maximizing and they shift with changes in aspiration levels [46, p. 253].

Cyert and March have pointed out that "just as a theory of the firm requires certain assumptions about organizational goals, it also requires certain assumptions about expectations" [33, p. 44]. McGuire has succinctly summarized Cyert and March's theory of expectations:

> Decisions made within organizations depend upon the expectations formed within the organization and upon the information possessed by it. Cyert and March specify a hierarchy of search activities by the firm. Search activity will tend to be standardized at some level. If this sort of routinized activity fails to produce solutions that satisfy organizational constraints and obtain coalition support, the search will proceed at a higher, more intensive level. There is no effort, however, to secure perfect information. Decisions are based on a relatively small number of alternatives and the firm ordinarily looks only at a few anticipated consequences of their decisions. The firm also includes in its expectations such factors as bias and the aspirations of organizational subunits. As a result, its expectations may be unreliable, although often bias is recognized and corrected prior to decision [46, p. 253].

Cyert and March's theory of organizational choice and control is based on the following assumptions:

1. *Multiple, changing, acceptable-level goals.* The criterion of choice is that the alternative selected meet all of the demand (goals) of the coalition.
2. *An approximate sequential consideration of alternatives.* The first satisfactory alternative evoked is accepted. Where an existing policy satisfies the goals, there is little search for alternatives. When failure occurs, search is intensified.
3. *The organization seeks to avoid uncertainty* by following regular procedures and a policy of reacting to feedback rather than forecasting the environment.
4. *The organization uses standard operating procedures* and rules of thumb to make and implement choices. In the short run these procedures dominate the decisions made [33, p. 113].

Cyert and March have applied their behavioral theory of the firm to the development of a duopoly model, an oligopoly model, and a model of a department store. These models (as well as other behavioral models) are described in the next sections of this chapter. The reader is encouraged to investigate in detail the book by Cyert and March [33] as well as Chapters 16 and 17 of the book by Cohen and Cyert [24]. In addition, the reader may find Chapters 8, 9, and 10 of McGuire's book [46] to be quite enlightening and stimulating. Finally, the bibliography at the end of this chapter contains a list of some of the more important papers and books on organization theory and behavioral theories of the firm.

TWO SPECIAL CASES OF THE NEOCLASSICAL MODEL

As early as 1943 the profit-maximization assumption of the neoclassical model of the firm was being subjected to criticism by economists including Scitovsky.

> Doubts have been raised by several writers whether maximizing his profits is always the entrepreneur's best policy. But such doubts were few and have died away without reverberation; mainly, I think, because it has never been made clear what exactly profit maximization implies; and perhaps also because we have a vested interest in maintaining this assumption—it makes economic analysis so much simpler. . . . The assumption that the entrepreneur maximizes his profit is based on observation and implies a special hypothesis concerning the businessman's psychology. It is, therefore, an empirical law, which need not apply to every businessman, and may conceivably be untrue even about the representative entrepreneur. Its justification lies in its usefulness, which should be enhanced by a better understanding of its exact meaning and limitations [61].

Papandreou [57] proposed the use of a general preference function to replace the unnecessarily restrictive assumption of profit maximization. Other economists

[11] have suggested that the firm's decision makers maximize some type of utility function rather than profits.

In this section we consider two special cases of the neoclassical model, each of which is characterized by an alternative behavioral assumption to profit maximization. Baumol's [9] sales-maximization model and Williamson's [72] utility-maximization model are based primarily on the neoclassical assumptions but relax the rigid assumption of profit maximization and may, in a sense, be considered as behavioral models of the firm. Baumol's model assumes that the firm maximizes total revenue subject to a minimum profit constraint. Williamson's model assumes that the firm's decision makers maximize their utility function, which depends on the size of the firm's staff, managerial emoluments, and discretionary profits.

A sales-maximization model [9,10]

Baumol has suggested that firms maximize total revenue subject to a minimum profit constraint rather than maximizing total profit as is usually assumed to be the case [9]. In defense of his revenue-maximization hypothesis, Baumol has stated,

> Surely it is common experience that, when one asks an executive, "How's business?" he will answer that his sales have been increasing (or decreasing), and talk about his profit only as an afterthought, if at all. . . . Almost every time I have come across a case of conflict between profits and sales the businessmen with whom I worked left little doubt as to where their hearts lay . . . a program which explicitly proposes any cut in sales volume, whatever the profit considerations, is likely to meet a cold reception [10, pp. 47–48].

Baumol argues that the sales-maximization goal may be explained, in part, by the desire of management to maintain the competitive position of their firm in the market and by the possibility that management's salaries may be more closely related to the size of the firm than to the profitability of the firm. He explains the firm's minimum profit constraint by referring to the capital market from which the firm obtains its external financing.

> The firm which hopes to have more securities to sell in the future, and wishes to pay what it may consider proper regard to the interests of its current stockholders, must take [profitability] into consideration. Its minimum earnings must supply funds sufficient to pay dividends and to reinvest in such amounts that the combination of dividend receipts and stock price rises can remunerate stockholders adequately. If this is so, each company's minimum rate of profits is set competitively in terms of the current market value of its securities [10, pp. 50–51].

Consider a perfectly competitive, multiproduct, multifactor firm with total revenue and total cost given by

$$TR = \sum_{k=1}^{p} P_k Z_k \tag{18-1}$$

and

(18-2) $$TC = \sum_{i=1}^{m} C_i X_i$$

respectively. The problem of the firm is to maximize total revenue TR subject to the profit constraint

(18-3) $$\pi = TR - TC = \pi_0$$

and the constraint imposed by the firm's production function,

(18-4) $$Q(Z_1, \ldots, Z_p, X_1, \ldots, X_m) = 0$$

We can formulate the Lagrangian function

(18-5) $$L = TR + \lambda Q + \mu(\pi_0 - TR + TC)$$

where λ and μ are Lagrangian multipliers and π_0 is a constant. The first-order conditions for constrained revenue maximization are

(18-6) $$L_k = P_k + \lambda Q_k - \mu P_k = 0 \qquad (k = 1, \ldots, p)$$

(18-7) $$L_i = \lambda Q_i + \mu C_i = 0 \qquad (i = 1, \ldots, m)$$

(18-8) $$L_\lambda = Q = 0$$

(18-9) $$L_\mu = \pi_0 - TR + TC = 0$$

The first-order optimality conditions for the *profit-maximizing* model of the perfectly competitive, multiproduct, multifactor firm can be expressed in the form of the following three decision rules.

Rule 1 The price ratio of any two products must equal the rate of product transformation between the two products.

Rule 2 The price ratio of any two factors must equal the rate of technical substitution between the two factors.

Rule 3 The price ratio of any factor-product combination must be equal to the marginal product for the particular factor-product combination.

Using equations (18-6) and (18-7), it is easy to demonstrate that rules 1 and 2 are also applicable to our constrained revenue-optimization model. However, there is no analog to rule 3 for the revenue-maximization model.

We can show that if we select any two products a and b and a single factor c, then by simple algebraic manipulation of (18-6) and (18-7) the following relationship will hold for the revenue-maximizing model,

(18-10) $$\frac{P_a(\partial Z_a/\partial X_c)}{P_a(\partial Z_a/\partial X_c) - C_c} = \frac{P_b(\partial Z_b/\partial X_c)}{P_b(\partial Z_b/\partial X_c) - C_c}$$

or

(18-11) $$\frac{VMP_a}{M\pi_a} = \frac{VMP_b}{M\pi_b}$$

That is, any variable factor c should be allocated between two products a and b in such a manner that the ratio of the value of the marginal product of a, VMP_a, to the marginal profit of a, $M\pi_a$, equals the ratio of the value of the marginal product of b, VMP_b, to the marginal profit of b, $M\pi_b$. This is analogous to the rule for the profit-maximizing firm which states that any variable factor c should be allocated between products a and b in such a manner that the marginal profit of factor c in the production of a equals the marginal profit of the factor c in the production of b,

$$M\pi_a = M\pi_b \tag{18-12}$$

A utility-maximization model [71,72]

As an alternative to profit maximization and sales maximization, Williamson has suggested that what managers maximize is their own utility. Although Williamson has developed several different utility-maximization models of the firm, we shall consider only one of them. The special case which we shall analyze is one in which management's utility is a function of (1) staff, (2) emoluments, and (3) discretionary profits.

Regarding the importance of *staff* to management Williamson asserts that

> Expansion of staff is an activity that offers positive rewards, the benefits of which can be enjoyed quite generally. Indeed, since promotional opportunities within a fixed-size firm are limited, while increased jurisdiction has the same general effect as promotion but simultaneously produces the chance of advance for all, the incentive to expand staff may be difficult to resist. Not only is it an indirect means to the attainment of salary, but it is a source of security, power, status, prestige, and professional achievement as well [71].

Williamson defines *emoluments* as that fraction of managerial salaries and perquisites that are discretionary.

> . . . Emoluments represent rewards which, if removed, would not cause the managers to seek other employment. They are economic rents and have associated with them zero productivities. Thus they are not a return to entrepreneurial capacity but rather result from the strategic advantage that the management possesses in the distribution of the returns to monopoly power. Being a source of material satisfaction and an indirect source of status and prestige, they are desirable as a means for satisfying goals in each of these respects [71].

Williamson argues that the existence of a satisfactory level of profit is "necessary to assure the interference-free operation of the firm" [71].

> Precisely what this level will be involves a complicated interaction of the relative performance of rivals, the historical performance of the firm, and special current conditions that affect the firm's performance. Management, however, will find it desirable to earn profits that exceed the acceptable level. For one thing, managers derive satisfaction from self-fulfillment and organizational achievement, and profits are one measure of this success. In addition, profits are a source of discretion (indeed, we define "discretionary profits" as the difference between actual

profits and minimum profits demanded). Discretionary profits represent a source of funds whose allocation may be importantly determined by managerial, in addition to economic, considerations. As with expansion of staff, the expansion of physical plant and equipment provides general opportunities for managerial satisfaction for much the same reasons [71].

Williamson's model consists of the following variables:

Z = output
S = staff (in money terms) or (approximately) general administrative and selling expense
ϵ = the condition of the environment (a demand-shift parameter)
$TR = P \cdot Z$ = total revenue
P = price
$TC = TC(Z)$ = production cost
M = managerial emoluments
$\pi = R - C - S$ = actual profits
$\pi_R = \pi - M$ = reported profits
π_0 = minimum (after tax) profits demanded
T = taxes, where t = tax rate and $\overline{T}$ = lump-sum tax
$\pi_R - \pi_0 - T$ = discretionary profits
U = the utility function

The following assumptions are stated explicitly:

$$\frac{\partial^2 TR}{\partial Z\, \partial S} \geq 0 \tag{18-13}$$

$$\frac{\partial P}{\partial Z} < 0 \tag{18-14}$$

$$\frac{\partial P}{\partial S} \geq 0 \tag{18-15}$$

$$\frac{\partial P}{\partial \epsilon} > 0 \tag{18-16}$$

The objective of the firm is to maximize:

$$U = U(S, M, \pi_R - \pi_0 - T) \tag{18-17}$$

subject to the constraint that reported profits are at least as great as some minimum level π_0 plus taxes:

$$\pi_R \geq \pi_0 + T \tag{18-18}$$

Since the constraint is of the same form as the last term in the objective function, and assuming that second-order conditions are satisfied, the constraint becomes redundant and the problem becomes one of straightforward maximization. By substitution, (18-17) may be rewritten as

$$U = U[S, M, (1 - t)(R - C - S - M) - \pi_0] \quad (18\text{-}19)$$

The first-order conditions for utility maximization are given by

$$\frac{\partial TR}{\partial Z} = \frac{\partial TC}{\partial Z} \quad (18\text{-}20)$$

$$\frac{\partial TR}{\partial S} = \frac{-U_1 + (1 - t)U_3}{(1 - t)U_3} \quad (18\text{-}21)$$

$$U_2 = (1 - t)U_3 \quad (18\text{-}22)$$

where

$$U_1 = \frac{\partial U}{\partial S} \quad (18\text{-}23)$$

$$U_2 = \frac{\partial U}{\partial M} \quad (18\text{-}24)$$

$$U_3 = \frac{\partial U}{\partial(\pi_R - \pi_0 - T)} \quad (18\text{-}25)$$

Equation (18-20) indicates that the firm will produce at that level of output at which marginal revenue equals marginal cost. According to (18-21), staff will be employed at a level where the marginal-value product of staff is less than its marginal cost. This can be seen by rewriting (18-21) as

$$\frac{\partial TR}{\partial S} = 1 - \frac{1}{(1 - t)}\frac{U_1}{U_3} \quad (18\text{-}26)$$

where U_1/U_3 is the marginal rate of substitution between profits and staff. "In the profit-maximizing organization, staff has no value other than that associated with its productivity, so that this exchange rate is zero, and the equality of marginal costs and value products obtains" [71]. Equation (18-22) implies that the firm will absorb some fraction (which depends on the tax rate) of actual profits as emoluments.

BEHAVIORAL MODELS OF THE FIRM

In this section we shall briefly summarize the behavioral models of the firm which have been contributed to the literature by Balderston and Hoggatt [4,5], Bonini [13], Cyert and March [33], and Cohen and Cyert [24].

Balderston and Hoggatt [4,5]

The joint work of Balderston and Hoggatt [4,5] is a simulation study of the United States' West Coast lumber industry and attempts "to show how limits on market information, decentralization of market decisions, and institutional alignments affect and are affected by economic forces" [5, p. 183]. This study grew out of the initial investigations by Balderston of the communication networks in intermediate markets of the West Coast lumber industry and Hoggatt's [40,41] doctoral dissertation "Simulation of the Firm," which employed simulation techniques to analyze several problems in traditional microeconomic theory.

Three sets of participants were involved in this industry model—manufacturers, wholesalers, and retailers. The FORTRAN computer program for this model utilized six different classes of variables (of which there were 16,000) and functional relationships: economic, physical commodity flow, accounting and cash flow, decision, information, and institutional. Manufacturers are assumed to sell to wholesalers who resell to retailers who in turn sell to final consumers according to explicit decision rules concerning price and output. However, physical shipments go from the manufacturer directly to the retailer (bypassing the wholesaler) and from the retailer to the final consumers. Complete accounting records (balance sheet, cash flow, net revenue, etc.) are maintained for each firm in the industry. Manufacturers and retailers obtain information from wholesalers in the form of "messages" concerning possible transactions. Messages are a prerequisite for a transaction to occur and must be paid for by the manufacturers and the retailers. They are analogous to long-distance telephone calls and telegraph messages between manufacturers and wholesalers, and retailers and wholesalers concerning prices and commodity supplies. Decision making is autonomous and completely decentralized among firms following a set of institutional decision rules for all transactions.

> The principal value of this study lies not in its empirical accuracy in describing the behavior of the West Coast lumber industry but rather in the information it yields concerning the effects of changes in two key experimental parameters: "(1) the unit cost of sending a message . . . and (2) the choice of a method for setting the preference ordering by each firm on its potential partners in transactions" [5, p. 187]. This type of information could not have been otherwise obtained, if at all, without copious and laborious computations. Although this study provides a valuable linkage between economics, sociology, and marketing, it possesses four features that are of primary interest to economists in particular.
>
> (1) It represents a multi-stage rather than a single-stage market; (2) the firms constituting the market face uncertainty and operate with limited information; (3) transactions occur by means of sequences of steps that are reminiscent of the Walrasian "tatonnements" though not identical with them; and (4) the system is dynamic in the strict, technical sense that its path develops, period by period, as a consequence of the interactions that occur [4, p. 16].

Recently this model has been extended by Preston and Collins [59] to include a final-demand stage in the marketing process. A number of parameters and decision rules have been modified in the revision of the model, so as "to eliminate certain features of particular relevance to the study of the West Coast lumber industry and to replace these features with others of greater conceptual simplicity and more general theoretical interest" [59, p. 5]. One unique feature of this study is the use of response surface techniques to analyze the output data of the simulations.

Bonini

Another interesting behavioral model was developed by Bonini for his doctoral dissertation entitled "Simulation of Information and Decision Systems in the Firm" [13]. This model of a hypothetical business firm represents a synthesis of some of the important theories from a number of disciplines, among which are economics, accounting, organization theory, and behavioral science. The Bonini model consists of a series of difference equations which are used to

> ... specify in quantitative terms the behavior of individuals or groups within the organization as a function of the behavior of other individuals and of the information available, both past and present. The sum of these behavior parts for individuals represents the total model [13, p. 11].

The essential elements of the Bonini hypothetical business organization include: decision centers, information centers, decision rules, information links, information systems, and decision systems. The purpose of the model was to study the effects of three types of changes on the behavior of the firm—changes in the external environment, changes in the information system, and changes in the decision system. This analysis was accomplished by a factorial experimental design in which the main effects and the various interactions of eight specific changes in the model on prices, inventory levels, costs, sales, profits, and organizational pressure were estimated. In addition, the factorial experimental design yielded estimates of the effects on the behavior of the firm of differences in the initial starting conditions of the firm. The eight types of alterations that were made on the model and whose effects on firm behavior were analyzed included:

> 1. Low versus high variability in the external environment of the firm. More specifically, we are interested in the effect of small versus large standard deviations in the probability distributions for sales and production costs.
> 2. Two different market trends for the firm; one a slow (2 percent per year) growth upon which is imposed a three-year cycle; the other a fast (10 percent per year) but irregular growth.
> 3. A "loose" versus "tight" industrial engineering department in the matter of changing standards.
> 4. An organization that is contagious to pressure as opposed to one that is not.
> 5. An organization in which the individuals are sensitive to pressure as opposed to one in which they are not.
> 6. An average cost method of inventory valuation versus a LIFO method.
> 7. Knowledge on the part of the sales force about the inventory position of the company versus the absence of such knowledge.
> 8. The reliance primarily upon present versus past information for control within the firm [13, pp. 86–87].

Bonini then tested null hypotheses according to which these changes taken both one at a time and two at a time had no significant effect on the behavior of the firm as measured by changes in prices, inventory levels, costs, sales, profits, and organizational pressure.

Cyert and March

In their book [33] Cyert and March describe three complex behavioral models of the firm and industry—a duopoly model, an oligopoly model, and a model of a department store. Each of these models is a computer simulation model.

Duopoly The duopoly model is one of the most interesting recent extensions of classical oligopoly theory from the standpoint of the degree of detail incorporated into the assumptions underlying the model. Their model is considered by some economists as an indication of the direction that research on the theory of oligopoly will take in the future. The assumptions of the Cyert, Feigenbaum, and March model are summarized as follows:

> In rough outline, each firm is assumed to: (1) forecast the reactions of its competitor, (2) revise its estimate of the demand curve, (3) revise its estimate of its own cost curve, (4) specify its profit goal (on the basis of its profit achievement in the past), (5) evaluate the alternatives available to it. If no alternatives which meet its goal are available, the firm (6) searches for opportunities for cost reduction, (7) re-examines its estimates of demand, and (8) lowers its profit goal to a more modest level. Finally, the firm (9) sets its output for the coming period [22, p. 926].

In contrasting behavioral duopoly models with classical duopoly models, Cyert, Feigenbaum, and March have stated that

> (1) The models are built on a description of the decision-making process. . . . (2) The models depend on a theory of search as well as a theory of choice. They specify under what conditions search will be intensified. . . . They also specify the direction in which search will be undertaken. . . . (3) The models describe organizations in which objectives change over time as a result of experience. . . . (4) Similarly, the models describe organizations that adjust forecasts on the basis of experience. Organizational learning occurs. . . . (5) The models introduce organizational biases in making estimates. . . . (6) The models all introduce features of organizational slack [30, pp. 93–94], [22, p. 926].

Oligopoly The oligopoly model is essentially an extension of the duopoly model and represents an attempt to describe and analyze a general behavioral theory of price and output determination for an oligopoly.

> The model portrays the process of decision making in terms, consistent with a behavioral theory of the firm. The firm uses multiple, changing, aspiration-level goals; it solves problems in each of its decision areas more or less independently; it searches for solutions in a manner learned from experience; it adjusts its decision rules on the basis of feedback on experience. Decisions on price, output, and sales strategy are made on the basis of profit, inventory, production-smoothing, sales, market share, and competitive position goals [33, p. 182].

One unique feature of this model is the use of multiple regression analysis "to determine the extent to which behavior in the model is sensitive to variations in various internal parameters" [33, p. 173].

Department Store The department-store model was used by Cyert and March to illustrate the applicability of their general behavioral theory of the firm to a particular type of firm, namely a large retail department store. The modeled firm is a part of an oligopoly which consists of three large downtown department stores. Although each of the firms in the market operates one or more suburban stores, attention is focused on the downtown market, where each firm makes most of its sales. The firm in question has several merchandizing groups, each of which has several departments. The department store has over 100 departments.

The model assumes that price and output decisions are made independently of each other. For the most part, price and output decisions are made on the basis of different goals and different stimuli. Each department in the firm is assumed to pursue two general goals:

> (1) *A sales objective;* the department expects (and is expected by the firm) to achieve an annual sales objective; (2) *a mark-up objective*; the department attempts to realize a specified average mark-up on the goods sold [33, p. 129].

Decisions are made in response to actual problems and perceived potential problems with respect to one or the other of the aforementioned goals.

A flow chart of the decision-making process of a department with respect to the sales goal is outlined in Figure 18-1.

> The organization forms sales "estimates" that are consistent with its sales goal and develops a routine ordering plan for advance orders. These orders are designed to avoid overcommitment, pending feedback on sales. As feedback on sales is provided, results are checked against the sales objective. If the objective is being achieved, reorders are made according to standard rules. This is the usual route of decisions. . . .
>
> Suppose, however, that the sales goal is not being achieved. Under such circumstances a series of steps is taken. First, the department attempts to change its environment by negotiating revised agreements with either its suppliers or other parts of its own firm or both. Within the firm, it seeks a change in the promotional budget that will provide greater promotional resources for the goods sold by the department. Outside the firm, the department seeks price concessions from manufacturers that will permit a reduction in retail price. If either of these attempts to relax external constraints is successful, reorders are made according to appropriately revised rules.
>
> Second, the department considers a routine mark-down to stimulate sales generally and to make room for new items in the inventory. . . . The department ordinarily has a pool of stock available for mark-downs and expects to have to reduce the mark-up in this way on some of the goods sold. It will attempt to stimulate all sales by taking some of these anticipated mark-downs. Once again, if the tactic is successful in stimulating sales, reorders are made according to slightly revised rules.
>
> Third, the department searches for new items that can be sold at relatively low prices (but with standard mark-up). Most commonly such items are found

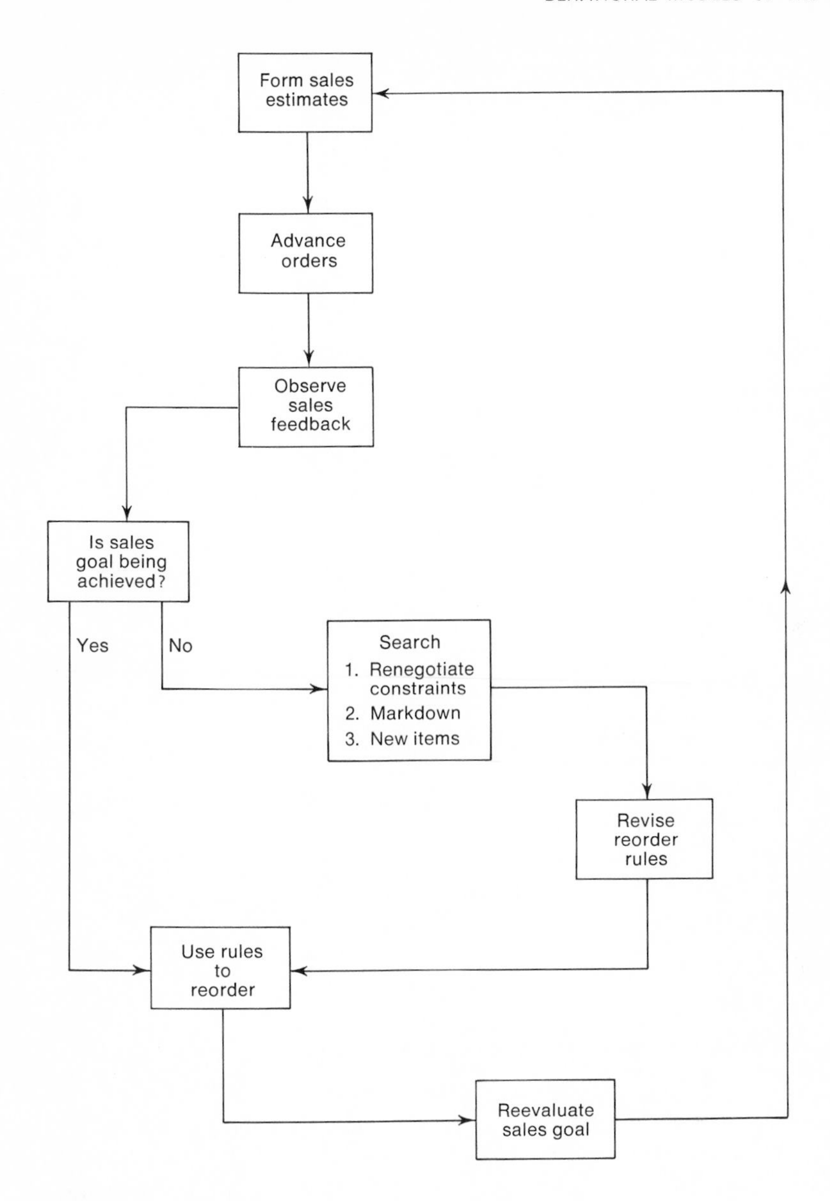

FIGURE **18-1**

General form of reaction to sales-goal indicators

when domestic supplies are eliminating lines or are in financial trouble. A second major source is in foreign markets.

In general, the department continues to search for solutions to its sales problems until it finds them. If the search procedures are successful, all goes well. In the long run, however, it may find a solution in another way. The feedback on sales not only triggers action, but also leads to the re-evaluation of the sales goal.

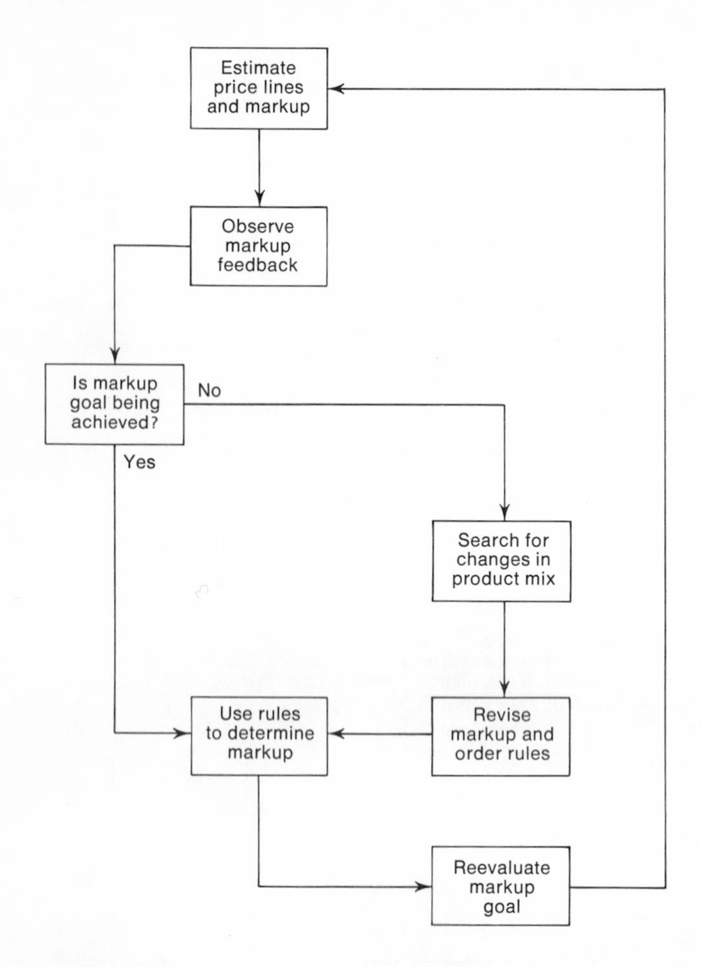

FIGURE **18-2**

General form of reaction to markup goal indicators

In the face of persistent failure to achieve the sales goal, the goal adjusts downward. With persistent success it adjusts upward [33, pp. 129–131].

The flow chart in Figure 18-2 describes the departmental decision process with respect to the markup goal.

On the basis of the mark-up goal (and standard industry practice), price lines and planned mark-up are established. Feedback on realized mark-up is received. If it is consistent with the goal, no action is taken and standard decision rules are maintained.

If the mark-up goal is not being achieved, the department searches for ways in which it can raise mark-up. Basically, the search focuses on procedures for altering the product mix of the department by increasing the proportion of high mark-up items sold. For example, the department searches for items that are

> exclusive, for items that can be obtained from regular supplies below standard cost, and for items from abroad. Where some of the search efforts led to price reduction (and maintenance of mark-up) when stimulated by failure on the sales goal, here they lead to maintenance of price and increase in mark-up. At the same time, the organization directs its major promotional efforts toward items on which high mark-ups can be realized. In some instances, the department has a reservoir of solutions to mark-up problems (e.g., pressure selling of high mark-up items). Such solutions are generally reserved for problem solving and are not viewed as appropriate long-run solutions. Finally, as in the case of the sales goal, the mark-up goal adjusts to experience gradually [33, p. 131].

Following this general description of their department-store model, Cyert and March then developed a detailed model of the major price and output decisions for the modeled firm and compared the results of computer simulation experiments with the model with actual results from the organization being investigated.

Cohen and Cyert [24]

Another behavioral model (which is also a computer model) has been proposed by Cohen and Cyert [24]. Their model describes the behavior of a monopolist in the absence of a well-defined objective function which it is trying to maximize.

> This model assumes behavior by the firm which is characterized by an aspiration level mechanism defining when satisfactory performance has been attained and by the existence of organizational slack which allows members of the firm to absorb part of the profits as costs.
>
> The model embodies a single type of dynamic behavior: it is a sequence of one-period decisions in which the environment at the start of each period is affected by the firm's past behavior. The internal climate of the firm and its mechanism for making decisions are also affected by past behavior. The firm makes its decisions on a one-period basis, however, ignoring any implications for the future which may be implicit in its present behavior.
>
> The demand function facing the monopolist is the same each period, except for the addition of a random term which varies over time. The firm's aspiration level equals its profits last period. Over time the firm tries to increase its profits. If it succeeds, organizational slack increases and it becomes less precise in determining output. Thus in good times there is less pressure on the managers of the firm, and they have more freedom to pursue their own aims independent of the firm's profit goal. During any period that the firm fails to increase its profits, the reverse effect occurs. Organizational slack decreases and the managers become more attentive to business and set the firm's output more precisely [24, pp. 363–364].

REFLECTIONS ON BEHAVIORAL MODELS OF THE FIRM

In December 1960 *The American Economic Review* published a symposium on simulation consisting of papers by Orcutt, Shubik, and Clarkson and Simon. The central theme of the latter two papers was that with the advent of computer simulation techniques, economists could look forward to some major innovations in the theory of the firm resulting from the use of simulation to develop more realistic, less aggregative, dynamic models of the firm. Shubik concluded his article with the following optimistic forecast:

> . . . simulation studies promise to provide the way to add the richness (in terms of explicit consideration of information costs, marketing variables, organizational structure and so forth) needed to obtain adequate theories of the firm, pricing and market structure. The promise is two-fold. The new methodology is beginning to offer the opportunity both to construct more complex theories and to validate them [62, pp. 917–918].

The predictions of Clarkson and Simon were even more glowing than those of Shubik concerning the future impact of simulation on the development of behavioral models. They asserted that

> . . . one advantage of simulation models lies in the complexity they permit. Another advantage of simulation derives from our new-found ability to construct directly computer programs describing human problem-solving and decision-making processes without first going through the intermediate step of constructing mathematical models. We can look forward to theories that will handle the qualitative aspects of human decision-making as readily as the quantitative. . . . These theories incorporate adaptive and learning behavior and include one or more aspects of heuristic reasoning. Since expectations play a central role in economic theory, and since all evidence suggests that expectations are formed by a process of pattern recognition, this process, incorporated in heuristic programs, will be the object of much research.
>
> Finally, simulation appears to offer a new approach to the aggregation problem. . . . One of its attractions lies in the new opportunities it affords for direct confrontation of the theory with concrete behavior. It does not restrict us to viewing the economic system through the wrong end of a telescope—limiting ourselves to census data and similar kinds of statistics. It permits us to see whether the decision-making processes we observe in the executive and the individual business firm correspond to the postulates about process that we incorporate in our models, and—if we are even moderately successful in finding satisfactory aggregation techniques—to work back and forth in our theory testing between microobservations and aggregative data [22, pp. 930–931].

Similar prognoses were made by Cohen and Cyert [23] in February of 1961 in their article in *The Quarterly Journal of Economics.*

Surprisingly enough, very few innovations in the theory of the firm have appeared in the published literature since 1960. Although Cyert and March's book was not published until 1963, most of the results which appeared in the book had been previously published in the form of journal articles and were well known in 1960. In fact, their work was cited by Shubik [62], Clarkson and Simon [22], and Cohen and Cyert [24]. Since 1960 (and particularly since 1963) the number of articles published in the leading economic journals on behavioral or computer models of the firm has indeed been small. Given these developments, it is quite natural to ask why the theory of the firm has not been significantly modified beyond the initial perturbations injected by the work of Cyert and March. Why have computer simulation techniques had so little influence on the theory of the firm? Is this pattern likely to continue in the future?

Although we do not claim to have answers to all of these questions, we can perhaps shed some light on a number of problems which have tended to impede the development of behavioral models of the firm.

First there is the problem of adequate data. If there is one common underlying characteristic of all of the behavioral models described thus far, it is the fact that they all have a strong empirical base. But if we are to construct an empirical model based on the behavior of one or more actual firms we must have adequate data. Typically, data of the type required to build a highly disaggregative computer model of the firm are simply not available to professional economists. In part, this problem is due to the fact that business firms are simply not willing to make their data available to "outsiders." This is likely to be particularly true of firms in a highly competitive industry. While it is true that a number of large corporations such as Xerox, Sun Oil, Minneapolis-Honeywell, Standard Oil of New Jersey, and others have constructed large-scale corporate models, these firms do not generally make available to outsiders detailed information about their models including data, behavioral assumptions, or output results. Although there is a strong possibility that some of these models contain interesting extensions of the theory of the firm, thus far the results of these simulation studies remain virtually unknown to academic economists.

Second, behavioral models require a detailed knowledge of the decision processes actually followed by firms. In order to obtain knowledge of this type, the economist must not only possess empirical data about the decision processes of actual firms, but he must have a thorough grasp of the contributions to decision theory, theory of group behavior, etc., of a number of behavioral-science disciplines including psychology, sociology, political science, business administration, and economics. Unless he has both empirical data and a sound theoretical base on which to build, he is likely to encounter difficulty in constructing realistic behavioral models. Although economists have shown an increasing willingness to participate in interdisciplinary studies in recent years, there is still some degree of reluctance on their part to engage in such projects. This type of behavior is found in an extreme form among those economists who find it necessary to construct narrow definitions as to what constitutes "economics." As long as this type of economic provincialism continues to exist, it will serve as a constraint on the future development of behavioral and computer models of the firm.

Third, in a computer simulation experiment with a behavioral model of the firm, as in any experiment, careful thought should be given to the problem of experimental design. Although a number of researchers have considered the need to utilize experimental design techniques in computer simulation experiments, and have noted the extensive literature on the subject of experimental design,[1] economists have had little or nothing to say about the problem of designing simulation experiments with models of the firm. For this reason, the results of many of the existing simulation experiments with models of the firm have proven to be inconclusive and difficult to interpret. Clearly there is a need to devote more careful attention in the future to problems of experimental design and data analysis in conducting simulation experiments with computer models of the firm. Unless this is done, we should completely avoid making generalizations on the basis of poorly designed simulation experiments with models of the firm. Unfortunately this rule has been violated all too many times in the past and is perhaps a major source of the skepticism of some economists about the usefulness of computer models of the firm.

Fourth, it may be that in some cases computer models have been applied to cases where traditional methods would have been more appropriate. For example, Machlup has argued that the simple marginal formula based on profit maximization is suitable where

> (1) *large groups* of firms are involved and nothing has to be predicted about particular firms, (2) the effects of a *specified change* in conditions upon prices, inputs, and outputs are to be explained or predicted rather than the values of the magnitudes before or after the change, and nothing has to be said about the "total situation" or general developments, and (3) only *qualitative answers*, that is, answers about directions of change, are sought rather than precise numerical results [48, p. 31].

It goes without saying that we should avoid applying a particular type of model or analytical technique to a situation in which the facts are in direct conflict with the assumptions underlying the particular model or technique. In the case of behavioral models of the firm, we should never use numerical or simulation techniques when analytical techniques exist for analyzing the properties of the model.

BIBLIOGRAPHY

[1] ALT, R. M. "The Internal Organization of the Firm and Price Formation," *Quarterly Journal of Economics*, **LXIII** (1949), 92–110.

[2] ANDREWS, P. W. S. *On Competition in Economic Theory*. New York: St. Martin's Press, 1964.

[3] ARGYRIS, C. *Understanding Organizational Behavior*. Homewood, Ill.: Dorsey Press, 1960.

[4] BALDERSTON, F. E., and AUSTIN C. HOGGATT. *Simulation of Market Processes*. Berkeley: Institute of Business and Economic Research, 1962.

[5] BALDERSTON, F. E., and A. C. HOGGATT. "Simulation Models: Analytic Variety and the Problem of Model Reduction," in A. C. Hoggatt and F. E. Balderston (Eds.), *Symposium on Simulation Models*. Cincinnati: South-Western Publishing Company, 1963.

[1] See Naylor, Burdick, and Sasser [54], "Computer Simulation Experiments with Economic Systems: The Problem of Experimental Design," and Chapters 13 and 14 of this book.

[6] BALDWIN, WILLIAM L. "The Motives of Managers, Environmental Restraints, and the Theory of Managerial Enterprise," *Quarterly Journal of Economics*, **LXXVIII** (May, 1964), 238–256.

[7] BALIGH, HELMY H., and LEON E. RICHARTZ. *Vertical Market Structures.* Boston: Allyn & Bacon, 1967.

[8] BARNARD, C. I. *The Functions of the Executive.* New York: Cambridge University Press, 1962.

[9] BAUMOL, WILLIAM J. *Business Behavior, Value and Growth.* New York: Macmillan, 1959.

[10] BAUMOL, W. J. *Economic Theory and Operations Analysis.* Englewood Cliffs, N. J.: Prentice-Hall, 1965.

[11] BECKER, GARY S. "Irrational Behavior and Economic Theory," *Journal of Political Economy*, **LXX** (February, 1962), 1–13.

[12] BLAU, P. *Dynamics of Bureaucracy.* Chicago: University of Chicago Press, 1955.

[13] BONINI, CHARLES P. *Simulation of Information and Decision Systems in the Firm.* Englewood Cliffs, N. J.: Prentice-Hall, 1963.

[14] BOULDING, KENNETH E. *A Reconstruction of Economics.* New York: John Wiley & Sons, 1950.

[15] BOULDING, K. E. "Implications for General Economics of More Realistic Theories of the Firm," *American Economic Review*, **XLII** (May, 1952), 35–44.

[16] BOULDING, K. E. "The Present Position of the Theory of the Firm," in K. E. Boulding and W. Allen Spivey (Eds.), *Linear Programming and the Theory of the Firm.* New York: Macmillan, 1960.

[17] BOULDING, K. E., and W. A. SPIVEY (Eds.). *Linear Programming and the Theory of the Firm.* New York: Macmillan, 1960.

[18] CHAMBERLIN, NEIL W. *A General Theory of Economic Process.* New York: Harper & Row, 1955.

[19] CHAMBERLIN, N. W. *The Firm: Micro Economic Planning and Action.* New York: McGraw-Hill Book Co., 1962.

[20] CHARNES, A., and W. W. COOPER. "The Theory of Search: Optimum Distribution of Search Effort," *Management Science*, **V** (1958), 450–458.

[21] CLARKSON, G. P. E. *The Theory of Consumer Demand: A Critical Appraisal.* Englewood Cliffs, N. J.: Prentice-Hall, Inc., 1963.

[22] CLARKSON, G. P. E., and H. A. SIMON. "Simulation of Individual and Group Behavior," *American Economic Review*, **L** (December, 1960), 920–932.

[23] COHEN, KALMAN J., and RICHARD M. CYERT. "Computer Models in Dynamic Economics," *Quarterly Journal of Economics*, **LXXV** (February, 1961), 112–127.

[24] COHEN, KALMAN J., and RICHARD M. CYERT. *Theory of the Firm: Resource Allocation in a Market Economy.* Englewood Cliffs, N. J.: Prentice-Hall, Inc., 1965.

[25] COLE, A. H. *Business Enterprise in its Social Setting.* Cambridge: Harvard University Press, 1959.

[26] *Contributions to Scientific Research in Management.* The Proceedings of the Scientific Program following the Dedication of the Western Data Processing Center, Graduate School of Business Administration, University of California, Los Angeles, 1959.

[27] COOPER, W. W. "Theory of the Firm: Some Suggestions for Revision," *American Economic Review*, **XXXIX** (December, 1949).

[28] COOPER, W. W. "A Proposal for Extending the Theory of the Firm," *Quarterly Journal of Economics*, **LXV** (1951), 87–109.

[29] CYERT, R. M., E. A. FEIGENBAUM, and J. G. MARCH. "Models in a Behavioral Theory of the Firm," *Behavioral Science*, **IV** (April, 1959), 81–95.

[30] CYERT, R. M., and J. G. MARCH. "Organizational Structure and Pricing Behavior in an Oligopolistic Market," *American Economic Review*, **XLV** (March, 1955), 129–139.

[31] CYERT, RICHARD M., and JAMES G. MARCH. "Organizational Factors in the Theory of Oligopoly," *Quarterly Journal of Economics*, **LXX** (1956), 44–46.

[32] CYERT, R. M., and J. G. MARCH. "Research on a Behavioral Theory of the Firm," *Contributions to Scientific Research in Management*. The Proceedings of the Scientific Program following the Dedication of the Western Data Processing Center, Graduate School of Business Administration, University of California, Los Angeles, January 29–30, 1959.

[33] CYERT, R. M., and J. G. MARCH. *A Behavioral Theory of the Firm*. Englewood Cliffs, N. J.: Prentice-Hall, Inc., 1963.

[34] DAHL, R. A., and C. E. LINDBLOM. *Politics, Economics, and Welfare*. New York: Harper, 1953.

[35] ETZIONI, A. *Complex Organizations*. New York: Holt, Rinehart & Winston, 1961.

[36] FELLNER, WILLIAM. *Competition Among the Few: Oligopoly and Similar Market Structures*. New York: Alfred A. Knopf, 1949.

[37] GORDON, R. A. *Business Leadership in the Large Corporation*. Berkeley: University of California Press, 1961.

[38] GOULDNER, A. W. *Patterns of Industrial Bureaucracy*. Glencoe, Ill.: Free Press, 1954.

[39] HAIRE, M. *Modern Organization Theory*. New York: John Wiley & Sons, 1959.

[40] HOGGATT, AUSTIN C. "An Experimental Business Game," *Behavioral Science*, **IV** (1959), 192–203.

[41] HOGGATT, A. C. "A Simulation Study of an Economic Model," *Contributions to Scientific Research in Management*. The Proceedings of the Scientific Program following the Dedication of the Western Data Processing Center, Graduate School of Business Administration, U.C.L.A., January 29–30, 1959.

[42] HOROWITZ, IRA. "The Advance of the Theory of the Firm: One Step Forward, One Step Back," *Quarterly Review of Economics and Business*, **VII** (Summer, 1967), 53–63.

[43] KATONA, G. *Psychological Analysis of Economic Behavior*. New York: McGraw-Hill Book Co., 1961.

[44] LEIBENSTEIN, H. *Economic Theory and Organizational Analysis*. New York: Harper, 1960.

[45] LIKERT, R. *New Patterns of Management*. New York: McGraw-Hill Book Co., 1961.

[46] MCGUIRE, JOSEPH W. *Theories of Business Behavior*. Englewood Cliffs, N. J.: Prentice-Hall, Inc., 1964.

[47] MCGUIRE, J. M., JOHN S. Y. CHIU, and ALVAR O. ELBING. "Executive Incomes, Sales and Profits," *American Economic Review*, **LII** (September, 1902), 753–761.

[48] MACHLUP, FRITZ. "Theories of the Firm: Marginalist, Behavioral, Managerial," *American Economic Review*, **LVII** (March, 1967), 1–33.

[49] MARCH, JAMES G. "The Business Firm as a Political Coalition," *Journal of Politics* (October, 1962), 662–678.

[50] MARCH, J. G. *Handbook of Organizations*. Chicago: Rand McNally, 1965.

[51] MARCH, J. G., and H. A. SIMON. *Organizations*. New York: John Wiley & Sons, 1958.

[52] MARGOLIS, JULIUS. "The Analysis of the Firm: Rationalism, Conventionalism, and Behaviorism," *Journal of Business*, **XXXI** (July, 1958), 187–199.

[53] MESSINGER, S. L. "Organizational Transformation: A Case Study of a Declining Social Movement," *American Sociological Review*, **XX** (1955), 3–10.

[54] NAYLOR, THOMAS H., DONALD S. BURDICK, and W. EARL SASSER. "Computer Simulation Experiments with Economic Systems: The Problem of Experimental Design," *Journal of the American Statistical Association*, **LXII** (December, 1967), 1315–1337.

[55] NEWELL, A., J. C. SHAW, and H. A. SIMON. "Elements of a Theory of Human Problem Solving," *Psychological Review*, **LXV** (1958), 151–166.

[56] OSWALD, KNAUTH. *Business Practices, Trade Position, and Competition*. New York: Columbia University, 1956.

[57] PAPANDREOU, ANDREAS G. "Some Basic Problems in the Theory of the Firm," in Bernard F. Haley (Ed.), *A Survey of Contemporary Economics*. Homewood, Ill.: Richard D. Irwin, Inc., 1952.

[58] PENROSE, EDITH T. "Biological Analogies in the Theory of the Firm," *American Economic Review*, **XLII** (December, 1952), 809–816.

[59] PRESTON, LEE E., and N. R. COLLINS. *Studies in a Simulated Market*. Research Program in Marketing, Graduate School of Business Administration, University of California, Berkeley, 1966.

[60] REDER, M. W. "A Reconsideration of Marginal Productivity," *Journal of Political Economy*, **LV** (1947), 450–458.

[61] SCITOVSKY, T. "A Note on Profit Maximization and its Implications," *Review of Economic Studies*, **XI** (1943), 57–60.

[62] SHUBIK, MARTIN. "Simulation of the Firm and Industry," *American Economic Review*, **L** (December, 1960), 908–919.

[63] SIMON, H. A. "A Behavioral Model of Rational Choice," *Quarterly Journal of Economics*, **LXIX** (February, 1955), 99–118.

[64] SIMON, H. A. *Models of Man*. New York: John Wiley & Sons, 1967.

[65] SIMON, H. A. "Theories of Decision-Making in Economics and Behavioral Science," *American Economic Review*, **XLIX** (June, 1959), 253–283.

[66] SIMON, H. A. *Administrative Behavior*. New York: Macmillan Co., 1961.

[67] SIMON, H. A., "New Developments in the Theory of the Firm," *American Economic Review*, **III** (May, 1962), 1–15.

[68] SIMON, H. A., D. W. SMITHBURG, and V. A. THOMPSON. *Public Administration*. New York: Alfred A. Knopf, 1950.

[69] THOMPSON, JAMES D. *Organizations in Action.* New York: McGraw-Hill Book Co., 1967.

[70] THOMPSON, J. D., and W. J. MCEWEN. "Organizational Goals and Environment: Goal-Setting as an Interactive Process," *American Sociological Review*, **XXIII** (1958), 23–31.

[71] WILLIAMSON, OLIVER E. "Managerial Discretion and Business Behavior," *American Economic Review*, **LIII** (December, 1963), 1032–1057.

[72] WILLIAMSON, O. E. *The Economics of Discretionary Behavior: Managerial Objectives in a Theory of the Firm.* Englewood Cliffs, N. J.: Prentice-Hall, Inc., 1964.

[73] WINTER, SIDNEY G. "Economic Natural Selection and the Theory of the Firm." *Yale Economic Essays* (Spring, 1964), 225–272.

Indexes

Author index

Subject index

A 9
B 0
C 1
D 2
E 3
F 4
G 5
H 6
I 7
J 8